Human Interests

Human Interests

or Ethics for Physicalists

Joseph Mendola

OXFORD

UNIVERSITY PRESS

OXFORD
UNIVERSITY PRESS

Great Clarendon Street, Oxford, OX2 6DP,
United Kingdom

Oxford University Press is a department of the University of Oxford.
It furthers the University's objective of excellence in research, scholarship,
and education by publishing worldwide. Oxford is a registered trade mark of
Oxford University Press in the UK and in certain other countries

First Edition published in 2014

Impression: 1

Published in the United States of America by Oxford University Press
198 Madison Avenue, New York, NY 10016, United States of America

British Library Cataloguing in Publication Data
Data available

Library of Congress Control Number: 2014934430

ISBN 978-0-19-968282-9

As printed and bound by
CPI Group (UK) Ltd, Croydon, CR0 4YY

For my colleagues at UNL—
Ed Becker,
Aaron Bronfman,
Al Casullo,
John Gibbons,
Reina Hayaki,
David Henderson,
Harry Ide,
Jennifer McKitrick,
Colin McLear,
Mark van Roojen
—and my colleague at Royal Coffee—
Tom Carson

Acknowledgements

I am grateful for very helpful comments on an early version from Lily Griffin, John Gibbons, Jennifer McKitrick, Steve Swartzer, and several anonymous referees, on Chapter 3 from the Florida State Philosophy Department, on Chapters 4 and 5 from Mark van Roojen, on Chapter 6 from the Dalhousie Philosophy Department, on Chapter 7 from David Sobel, and on Chapters 8 and 9 from Aaron Bronfman. Thanks to Eleanor Collins, Rosie Chambers, Joy Mellor, Peter Momtchiloff, and Jo North for editorial help. And special thanks to Tom Carson for very helpful comments on the whole, four times!

Modified versions of four papers are incorporated. Thanks for permissions to The University of Illinois Press for "The Indeterminacy of Options," *American Philosophical Quarterly* 24, 1987, 125–36, to The University of Chicago Press for "Gauthier's *Morals by Agreement* and Two Kinds of Rationality," *Ethics* 97, 1987, 765–74, and to Wiley for "Review Essay on Fred Feldman, *Pleasure and the Good Life*," *Philosophy and Phenomenological Research* 74, 2007, 220–32, and "Real Desires and Well-Being," *Philosophical Issues* 19, 2009, 148–65.

Contents

1. Introduction   1

   1.1 Physics and Ethics   1

   1.2 Outline   6

Part I. Alternatives

2. The Indeterminacy of Options   13

   2.1 Introduction   13

   2.2 Outline of the Argument   14

   2.3 Step One   16

   2.4 Background for Step Two   19

   2.5 Step Two   23

   2.6 Attempts to Evade the Argument   33

   2.7 Option Indeterminacy is Moderate   35

3. The Conditional Analysis and Modal Stability   40

   3.1   The Conditional Analysis: First Pass   42

   3.2   Chisholm and Lehrer   43

   3.3   Other Counterexamples   46

   3.4   Strawson   49

   3.5   Frankfurt's Case   52

   3.6   Libertarian Objections   58

   3.7   Trying   60

      3.7.1 Temporality and trying   62

      3.7.2 Content diversity of trying   63

         3.7.2.1 Bodily action   64

         3.7.2.2 Mental action   66

      3.7.3 Accepting reasons   68

   3.8   Subjunctive Conditionals   72

   3.9   Alternatives   74

   3.10 Flukes   77

   3.11 Group Acts   80

   3.12 Summary of Part I   85

Part II. Moral Theory

4. Meaning and Morality   89

   4.1   Terminology   89
   4.2   Evaluation and Normativity   90
   4.3   Physics and Full Normativity   95
   4.4   Quasi-Normativity   99
   4.5   DC1-NORMS   100
   4.6   DC2-BASIS   102
   4.7   DC3-METHODS   105
   4.8   Quasi-Normativity and the Constraints   107
   4.9   Contrasting Proposals   109
  4.10   Non-Cognitivism   111
  4.11   What "Ought" Means   116
  4.12   "Good"   117

5. The Road to Desire   119

   5.1 Ecumenism   119
   5.2 Crude Sensory Hedonism   122
   5.3 Refined Sensory Hedonism   130
   5.4 Attitudinal Hedonism   132
   5.5 Mixed Forms   138
   5.6 Concessions to Objectivism   139
   5.7 Robust Objectivism   142
   5.8 Species and the Good   147
   5.9 Normative Conclusion   159

6. Desire and the Good   160

   6.1 Problems of Informed Desire   160
   6.2 Sophisticated Simple Desire   165
   6.3 The Nature of Desire I   166
   6.4 The Nature of Desire II   172
   6.5 Intrinsic Versus Instrumental Desires   177
   6.6 Desire Intensities   182
   6.7 Where We Are   185

7. Very Simple Desire   186

   7.1 Basic Preferences   186
   7.2 Consensus Congruence   191
   7.3 Momentary Individual Good   194
   7.4 Interpersonal Good   198
   7.5 Summary of My View   201

7.6 Special Objections   201
7.7 Standard Objections   205
7.8 Animals, Babies, and Groups   215

8. The Leximin Desire Principle   219
    8.1 Introduction   220
    8.2 The Leximin Core   222
    8.3 Cardinal Complications   230
    8.4 Egalitarian Middle Ground   234
    8.5 Objections   237
    8.6 Moments or Lives?   240
    8.7 Time   247
    8.8 Population   251

9. MAC2   256
    9.1 Core Argument   256
    9.2 Structural Objections   259
    9.3 Other Objections   268
    9.4 Intricate Objections   275
    9.5 Conclusion   279

10. From the Good   281
    10.1   Reason and Sentiment   281
    10.2   Against Prudence   284
    10.3   Consequentialism   287
    10.4   Desert and Outcomes   294
    10.5   Hobbes and Gauthier   302
    10.6   Harsanyi and Rawls   309
    10.7   Scanlon   312
    10.8   Kant and Golden Rules   317
    10.9   Golden Rule Consent   321
    10.10 Hare   324
    10.11 Conclusion   331

Part III. Applications

11. Individual Obligations   335
    11.1 Summary of Parts I and II   335
    11.2 Deontic Restrictions   336
    11.3 Analytical Worries   339
    11.4 The Duties   347
    11.5 Special Obligations   356

12. What Morality Demands   361

    12.1 Duties and Demandingness   361
    12.2 The Virtues   362
    12.3 The Responsibility System   370
    12.4 Austerity   380
    12.5 Conclusion   392

Bibliography   393
Index   409

1

Introduction

On the third planet of a mediocre star, chattering apes scribble moral judgments regarding the rightness and wrongness of actions, the goodness and badness of circumstances, the virtue and viciousness of characters, and the justice and injustice of social arrangements. But it is a vast, godless, and physical world. Microphysical entities constitute everything, and much more than these monkeys.

So there is a question whether our moral judgments are true. There is more than one reason for worry. For one thing, even highly reflective and well-informed hominid philosophers do not agree about the moral facts, so not all can be correct. Some are *consequentialists*, and say that the rightness of acts depends on the goodness of consequences. Others are *contractarians*, and hold that right acts are rooted in proper reciprocity, in something like a mutual contract or agreement, whatever the consequences. Some are *deontologists*, and think that certain types of acts, for instance lies or murders, are wrong regardless of consequences or contracts. But our central worry here is different. It is that none of our various, mutually contradictory moral theories and judgments are true, that all of us moralizing, squabbling apes are in error.

This book develops an ethical theory in the consequentialist tradition, but which also incorporates contractarian and deontological elements. It reconciles some of our apparent disagreements. But, more important, we can reasonably hope that it is true in reality. We begin with that point.

1.1 Physics and Ethics

No moral claim is true if its truth requires more of the world than physical reality can deliver. And many revered philosophical ethicists held that true ethical claims require a great deal. Immanuel Kant thought it a necessary condition for the propriety of moral judgments that people make radically free choices of their characters from outside of time.[1] Henry Sidgwick, G. E. Moore, and W. D. Ross thought the truth of moral judgments requires non-natural properties, not constituted by the physical.[2]

---

[1] Kant (1996a: 5: 97–8); Kant (1998: 6: 24–6).
[2] Moore (1903: 1–36); Sidgwick (1907: 31–5); Ross (1930). Sidgwick held that the notion of right is simple and relevant to self-evident truths, but did not explicitly claim that simple rightness is instantiated in mind-independent reality, and allowed that a simple notion might have complicated psychical antecedents.

Plato insisted on the central importance of the transcendental Form of the Good, and Aristotle on physically irreducible *tele*.[3] Ockham and Scotus thought moral truth requires divine commands.

Perhaps these philosophers were right about the very metaphysical conditions that legitimate ethics requires. But they were surely wrong about what conditions in fact obtain. Human action is embedded in a physical world. Either the past causally determines the present, or if it doesn't that is only because microphysical entities are governed by probabilistic laws that leave no more intuitive space for counter-causal human freedom. There is no god. And the truth of physicalism assures there are no non-natural properties, Forms of the Good, or irreducible *tele*.

Or so I will presume here. I will presume that physicalism is true: Everything that exists is constituted by the microphysical, by atoms in the void, or more exactly by quarks, leptons, and force-carrying particles with their characteristic physical properties in curved spacetime.[4]

And so the grand ethical systems, with their robust metaphysical supports and specific and controversial normative advice about how to live, are idols of philosophical theater, ruins. We must be more modest in our theoretical aspirations.

Some claim that, in our barren world, ethics is bankrupt and everything is permitted. Some even hold that there is no human action under such conditions, that action must be radically free in a way inconsistent with physicalism and a plausible understanding of physical law.[5] But I am somewhat more optimistic. It seems to me that recognizable actions result from what we try to do, even though physicalism is true. And I also think that a suitably modest form of moral and political evaluation of such actions and other human alternatives is legitimate even in reality.

But, on the other hand, physicalism puts real constraints on proper normative claims. Some ethicists are quite unconcerned about the independent plausibility of the conditions required for the truth of their moral claims. They find themselves after normative reflection strongly inclined to make certain ethical claims, and that seems to them enough. Or at least it seems enough when their normative intuitions cohere in some reflective equilibrium. But it is not enough.[6] Specialization in even philosophy has now reached the unfortunate point that *normative ethics*, concerned with

---

[3] *Physics* II 8, 198b35–199a8, *On the Parts of Animals*, and *Politics* I 2, 1253a8, and I 8, 1256b20, suggest non-physical truth conditions for claims "if X had not benefited Y, then Y wouldn't have had X," which Irwin (1988: 525 n25) holds central to Aristotle's teleology. In other words, Aristotle thought that current structure fixes function, and current physical structure does not plausibly fix function.

[4] For greater precision, see Mendola (1997: 369–446).

[5] Kim (1998: 29–120) suggests that such conditions are inconsistent with any causal effects of action, since action that supervenes on the microphysical is epiphenomenal. And maybe action requires effects, so again there is no action.

[6] Nevertheless, constructivist versions of reflective equilibrium have some affinities with Part II's metaethical proposal. The central example is Rawls (1971).

what acts are right and what outcomes good, and *metaethics*, concerned with what makes moral claims true, are somewhat distinct disciplines. But it is a central point of this book that this is a mistake. We cannot hope to understand what, if anything, makes ethical claims true, without understanding which ethical claims it is whose truth we must deliver. And we cannot hope to understand what ethical claims are plausible without understanding what their truth requires of the world and whether the world can supply it. Ethicists must provide objective vindication of their normative intuitions, in the manner attempted by the grand traditional ethical systems. By this I mean that ethicists must provide a plausible explanation of how their moral claims are true,[7] and how competitor claims that suitably cohere for others are not.

And in a physical world, this isn't easy. Some ethicists who rest content with their intuitions about normative matters think that they, unlike those who disagree with them, have access to non-natural truth. But physicalism is not consistent with non-natural normative properties. So more work is required, of a kind I will better describe, and try to do, in Part II. But this is not to say that normative intuition doesn't matter. I think that if we cannot deliver the truth of the most deeply held consensus moral beliefs, for instance that murder of the innocent is wrong, then philosophical ethics is bankrupt. Indeed, I even think that if non-natural rightness did exist but happened to be attached to intuitively heinous murder, then ethics would also be bankrupt. This is a constraint of the meaning of "right" and "wrong" in ethical contexts.[8] We can't be radically mistaken in all our moral judgments and yet there be a moral truth. But we must also respect physical reality and the need to provide some genuine rationale for our moral beliefs; we must deliver the truth of those beliefs. That too is a constraint of the meaning of "right" and "wrong" in ethical contexts. The claim that murder is generally the right thing to do couldn't be true,[9] but the claim that murder is wrong could fail to be true. If we are strongly attached to the claim that murder is wrong, but its truth requires the existence of non-natural properties that we otherwise have no reason to believe in, then ethics is also bankrupt. Our strong normative confidence is not in itself sufficient evidence for belief in such an extravagance. It may seem that we wouldn't be confident of the truth of normative claims unless reality delivers their truth. But if we don't understand what in an otherwise plausible world could make such claims true, then we should not be sure that our normative confidence reflects anything beyond social indoctrination or evolutionary pressure.

We must seek some explanation of how the central and most crucial ethical and social-political judgments really are true in our physical world. But though ethicists must deliver the most central and obvious ethical truths, this is not to say that a moral

---

[7] Or at least very truth-like. This qualification is required by complications explored by Mendola (2008: Chapter 4), and because you may object that what I deliver is insufficient for truth.

[8] Part II discusses complications regarding the relevant consensus.

[9] What if we all wanted to be murdered? Chapter 7 discusses wildly hypothetical desires.

theory is false just because it fails to deliver the relatively idiosyncratic and less than central normative intuitions of some of us, for instance the intuition that there is no demanding duty of charity to others, at least when such an intuition is not supported by a suitable objective vindication. Reality may provide some normative surprise to some of us.

And reality may also provide surprises for those without idiosyncratic moral intuitions. That is partly because of a second set of important consequences of physicalism. Physicalism not only forbids some familiar normative resources, for instance non-natural properties. It also undercuts some intuitive non-normative claims that ethicists have deployed to help explain normative truths. For instance, consequentialists root normative evaluation of someone's action in non-normative facts about the range of options in action open to that person. Given those options, and some suitable normative means to assess the value of the options, they conclude that, excepting ties, one option is best. But we will see that one implication of physicalism is that in some situations options are not fully determinate, that there is no fact of the matter whether an agent has a particular option or lacks it, that the claim that the agent has that option is indeterminate in truth, neither determinately true nor determinately false. This is not merely epistemic or *ex ante* indeterminacy; it is full-blown metaphysical indeterminacy, indeterminacy when all the facts are known. And this may in turn generate normative indeterminacy, for instance regarding what available option is best.

There are a variety of forms of relevant metaphysical indeterminacy that we will trace. Certain claims are what I will call *virulently* indeterminate in truth, by which I mean so wildly indeterminate as to be unsuited to the roles they are slotted to play in ethical theory.[10] But there are also some still useful claims that have a kind of limited and *moderate* indeterminacy, which creates unexpected difficulties with which ethicists must deal, but does not make such claims wholly without proper ethical relevance, does not wholly disqualify them for their roles.

Many resources deployed in crucial roles by contemporary ethicists—including the desires people would have if they were fully informed, and their greatest individual self-interest figured over their lives—are not sufficiently determinate to play a serious foundational role in ethics. They are virulently indeterminate, too indeterminate to play their roles. I will argue here, often on the basis of such virulent indeterminacies, that various familiar attempts by ethicists to deal honestly with physicalism and yet deliver central normative claims, for instance by appeal to natural kinds or individual rationality or certain motivational conceptions of ethical reasons, do not succeed.

---

[10] A resource might be sufficiently determinate to play one role in ethical theory but not another. I will call a resource "virulently indeterminate" when it is too indeterminate for the particular role under consideration.

The relations of physicalism to ethics are complex. Some of the problems we will discuss for moral theories do not depend on physicalism. And sometimes even when physicalism is relevant, the problem isn't just physicalism by itself. Physicalism by itself for instance does not *imply* that all these virulent indeterminacies exist. It is rather that given an otherwise plausible conception of the world, physicalism removes any remaining hope of determinacy. Perhaps there is some possible world where physicalism is true but there isn't a particular such indeterminacy, but there is indeterminacy in physical reality.[11] But despite these complications, the key point will be that in physical reality there are many problems for extant ethical theories.

Still, I think there is a way out of our predicament. There are abstract principles of equal treatment that are an essential part of ethical and social-political discourse in its central guise as justificatory reason-giving—in its guise as giving reasons for or against things—and that help link our normative claims to reality in an acceptable way. These claims are reflected in certain familiar consequentialist, contractarian, and other rationales for ethical claims, differing rationales that in our world can be reconciled. And our desires provide some physical grounds for value. The nature of this theoretical mechanism, why it is consistent with physical reality, and how it is more than a mere reflective equilibrium of my intuitions, is a complicated story for Part II, but 1.2 will outline the theory. While ethicists must deliver the truth of the most central normative claims, they can do so, not by plausible appeal to straightforwardly normative properties like non-natural goodness, but still in a somewhat complex manner crucially involving (i) a quasi-normative constraint absolutely essential to ethical evaluation and all other sorts of justificatory reason-giving, namely equal treatment of like cases, (ii) various physically acceptable rationales familiar from the history of ethics, and (iii) physical conditions that provide some at least weak, other-things-equal grounds for favoring one outcome over another, namely our desires.

Of course, all this will require considerable explaining. But I will make a positive normative proposal to accompany my negative arguments against familiar competitors. Still, while in my negative arguments I ask ethicists to be more self-critical about the resources they deploy, and while I attempt to develop a positive theory that does not deploy similarly questionable resources, and while I think it works, I do not claim to know with any great certainty that my positive theory is true. For one thing, as you will see, I allow myself some optimism about the consequences and identity of various group acts, about the existence of a certain consensus of our preferences, and about the merely moderate indeterminacy of certain ethically relevant

---

[11] I also appeal to lack of reality when I dismiss the relevance of wildly hypothetical counterexamples. But this merely marks the limits of my aspiration. I will not attempt to deliver an account of ethical truth for circumstances wildly different than our own, though I would be delighted if someone more ambitious succeeded.

phenomena. This optimism reflects our best evidence, I think, and I will argue that my proposals do not in fact face virulent indeterminacies. But our evidence isn't good enough for certainty on these matters. And indeed for all I know there may be alternative constructions, focused on different constraints found within the complex normative traditions that we inherit, that can do the job at least as well. But, as we proceed, I will present my reasons for doubting it.

So I'm not certain that the way out I develop here is really available, although we can reasonably hope that it is. The theory developed here is my best shot for a physical world. We will see that it is better, given constraints set by reality, than familiar forms of utilitarianism, contractarianism, and deontology. Nevertheless, I hope that someone else will do it still better. But we cannot do it better by appeals to normative intuition unsupported by a plausible story about what makes those intuitions true, or by deploying notions that do not make properly determinate sense when applied in cold reality.

1.2   Outline

This book has three parts. The first two are theoretical. They sketch positive conceptions of the two main resources required by legitimate moral evaluation—modest conceptions suited to our physical world—and argue that competitors are not viable in reality. The third part consists of crucial applications of this theory.

Normative evaluation requires things to be evaluated. Part I is an account of two sorts of alternatives that are legitimate objects of normative evaluation even in our world.

Chapter 3 develops an account of individual alternatives in action that is rooted in the traditional conditional analysis of ability of Hobbes, Locke, and Hume. It defends a version of that hoary conception against recent skepticism. While the details require explanation, I will claim that a human conscious agent at a time has an option in action if and only if it is true that (i) there is something such that if they were to try to do it at that time, then they would succeed in taking that option, (ii) that thing is coherently conceivable by humans, (iii) the antecedent of the conditional in (i) does not entail its consequent, and (iv) that antecedent does not involve trying to try. We will see that our options incorporate objective *ex ante* probabilities but no lucky flukes. Chapter 3 also develops a related conception of social alternatives, and especially of group acts. These collective acts of many individuals are very important in the moral theory to be developed here.

This conception of our options rests crucially, as we will see, on three things that are key resources throughout the book: trying, accepting reasons, and subjunctive conditional truths, that is to say truths that certain things would be true if certain other things were true. All of these key resources are, I think, required for even the most modest sorts of ethical evaluation. But they are a somewhat uneasy fit with the physical facts. They are not inconsistent with those facts, but the truth of physicalism sometimes leaves the truth of claims involving these phenomena at least moderately indeterminate.

For instance, because of the nature of physical reality, many subjunctive conditional claims that are relevant to normative disputes, many relevant claims that if something were the case then something else would be true, are indeterminate in truth value. Chapter 2 will more specifically argue, on this basis, that there is a moderate indeterminacy of options and alternatives in individual action. While you do what you do, while you have some determinate options underwritten by the conditional analysis of ability, and while relevant indeterminacies are not so virulent as to make the notion of your options useless for ethics, still there is sometimes no fact of the matter whether you might have done something that you didn't do. We often do not face a completely determinate set of options for individual choice. For related reasons, our social options are also moderately indeterminate. But this is just one set of cases. The indeterminate truth of certain subjunctive conditionals will also have many other important implications throughout the book. In Part II, virulent indeterminacies wreak havoc with familiar moral theories.

Nevertheless, Part II develops a positive moral theory that allows at least somewhat determinate normative evaluations of our somewhat indeterminate individual and social options, even in cold reality. Chapters 4 and 5 develop a metaethical view—in particular a view about the meaning of key moral terms—that supports this theory and underwrites my arguments for it. It is a moral theory in which impartial concern plays a crucial role. But Chapter 7 develops another crucial element of this theory, which it will be useful to sketch first.

That is an account of individual good or well-being rooted in actual preference satisfaction, where preferences are themselves rooted in facts involving trying and subjunctive conditionals. There are some indeterminacies about what our preferences are, but not virulent and unworkable ones, merely moderate and bearable ones. The dominant contemporary accounts of individual well-being are, to the contrary, *informed* desire-based accounts, which deploy, instead of crude actual preferences like my proposal, fancier and more specific sorts of desire, and subjunctive conditional claims about the idealized desires that we would have if suitably rational or fully informed. But in Chapter 6, I argue that these sorts of refinements are not properly viable in our physical world. They depend on claims that are *virulently* indeterminate in truth. In Chapter 5, I dismiss other competing accounts of individual good largely on the basis of physicalism, although we will also see that the true desire-based account can provide a relevant confluence with those familiar competitors. It can deliver their most intuitive and characteristic values: pleasure, health, and knowledge. Still, the only viable basis in reality for normative evaluation is actual preference. Human interests are the root of human good. This conception of individual good is less robust than traditional forms. By that I mean it does not aspire to controversial and specific advice regarding how to live when only one's own interests are at stake, and it involves some indeterminacy. But it is a minimal workable basis for moral evaluation.

But there is also the other key element of my normative proposal. Even if we understand individual good, we don't yet understand all moral truth. So Chapters 8 and 9 develop a two-part mechanism to bridge the basic individual good discussed in Chapter 7, on one hand, and normative claims about individual actions and social alternatives, on the other.[12] This mechanism is rooted in two sorts of impartial concern, for the subjects and objects of moral action, for moral *agents* and moral *patients*.

Chapter 8 argues that outcomes—overall states of the world—are to be assessed by the Leximin Desire Principle, or LDP. This holds, in the basic case, that one alternative outcome is better than another if it is better from the perspective of the worst-off human atomic agent, where atomic agents are time-slices of people, people in brief periods of their lives. It holds that the worst-off such agent is defined by a kind of consensus among the preferences of normal adult human atomic agents, though this consensus is sometimes moderately indeterminate. In case of ties, we move on to consideration of the second worst-off, and so on. But that is only the basic case; there are also important qualifications of this "lexical maximin" structure that are incorporated into LDP. For instance, when there is a consensus of preference among all affected human agents that delivers cardinal comparisons of the well-being of those agents, assessments of options that involve simply a difference within that "pocket of cardinality"[13] are properly governed by the maximization of the total of that value, though considerations of equality become important again once that value is maximized. A second cluster of qualifications involves a lesser weight for the interests of non-human agents that have a good, in particular the interests of certain sorts of group agents and of animals beyond us snow monkeys.

Chapter 9 argues that the proper way in which the value of outcomes determines right action involves a new form of consequentialism, in fact a particular variant called "MAC2" of a new class of theories I call "multiple-act consequentialism."[14] Consequentialism in general bases positive normative judgments on good consequences. Multiple-act consequentialism governs group actions and agents, which exist when several distinct agents literally try together to do something. MAC2 in particular has five central tenets, though we will consider further complications in Chapter 9: (1) Direct consequentialist evaluation of the options of group agents is

---

[12] Mendola (2006) develops a simpler form of this two-part mechanism conjoined with a type of hedonism that is not viable in physical reality. In other words, it develops a somewhat contrasting normative theory appropriate to a world involving irreducible phenomenal properties of the sort deployed to help constitute human agency in Mendola (1997: Part Two). Part II of this book instead develops a normative theory appropriate to a physical world of the sort deployed to constitute human agency in Mendola (2008).

[13] This phrase is from Griffin (1986).

[14] Mendola (2006: Part One) develops another version of multiple-act consequentialism.

appropriate. For instance, when a particular set of options for a particular group agent includes a best option, it is most choiceworthy.[15] (2) Sometimes we should follow our roles in a group act even at the cost of the overall good we could achieve by defection from those roles. In particular, one should only defect from a group act with good consequences if one can achieve better consequences by the defecting act alone than the entire group act achieves. This is the principle of Very Little Defection, or VLD. (3) When different beneficent group acts of which one is part specify roles that conflict, one should follow the role in the group act with more valuable consequences. This is the principle of Defect to the Dominant, or DD. (4) One should join whatever group acts it is consequentially best to join, given the constraints set by VLD and DD. (5) Defection is required from group acts with harmful consequences, and more important when those consequences are more harmful.

While this two-part mechanism involves various indeterminacies, I argue that they are not virulent ones. Chapter 10 critically considers various more familiar and apparently alternative mechanisms for moving from individual good to overall normative evaluation—various forms of traditional utilitarianism, contractarianism, and golden rule constructions—and argues that the workable forms of these apparent alternatives in fact converge on my two-part proposal in our physical world. Sometimes the problems of unworkable forms are virulent indeterminacies. My negative arguments here and throughout Part II will reveal that many traditional resources deployed by ethical theories—including a robust distinction between intrinsic and instrumental desires, robust facts about the comparison and summation of desire-satisfactions, robust facts about what we would want if fully informed, robust facts about what is in our individual self-interest, and robust facts about what is due to one's action—are not available in reality.

Part III applies the theoretical conception developed in the two preceding parts, and also answers the most pressing objections to that conception. It argues that, despite the indeterminacy of alternatives of Part I and the relative modesty of the normative proposal of Part II, the most crucial commonsense moral judgments about our individual ethical obligations are correct. It hence answers standard objections to consequentialism, in particular those of deontologists, who focus on intuitive ethical duties rather than good consequences.

Chapter 11 develops an account of our general deontological obligations not to lie, murder, injure, or steal. It also accounts for our special deontological obligations to those close to us or to whom we owe gratitude or reparation.

Chapter 12 replies to the traditional objection that consequentialism is too demanding. It does this in part by developing a conception of individual virtue

---

[15] Because of the indeterminacy of options, there may not be a determinately best option. But group acts function in the true moral theory in a way that blunts the significance of this. And of course there may be ties.

that is a recognizable refinement of traditional conceptions, and in part by showing how MAC2 and LDP largely underwrite—though also suggest refinements of—our intuitive practices of assigning risks, benefits, and harms. It also explores some relevant practical implications of our strict duty to refrain from participation in harmful group acts, including group acts that devastate our natural environment and impoverish other people.

PART I
Alternatives

2

The Indeterminacy of Options

There is no practical point in evaluation of acts as right or wrong, of characters as good or bad, or of social arrangements as just or unjust, unless there are alternatives available to our actual acts, characters, and social arrangements. The nature of these alternatives, and hence of the objects of practically-relevant normative evaluation, is our central concern in this part. We will focus principally on the objects of one traditional type of ethical assessment—the actions of individuals—and briefly on a closely related set of social-political alternatives.

This chapter argues that there are sometimes unexpected indeterminacies regarding whether or not someone has an option in action, because of the indeterminate truth of certain conditional claims in our physical world. It further isolates a larger class of conditional claims, which I call "Failed Type Three" cases, whose indeterminate truth is a very significant fact for ethics, and a crucial premise in negative arguments against familiar moral theories throughout Part II. Chapter 3 argues that, despite these indeterminacies, there is a correct positive conception of our alternatives in individual action, reflected in the traditional conditional analysis of ability, which it defends against considerable recent skepticism. Indeed, these indeterminacies will help us to see that the correct conception of our options incorporates objective *ex ante* probabilities, but not flukes of luck, which is also a crucial premise of Part II. Ethicists now largely ignore these issues, but that, we will see, is a mistake.

2.1 Introduction

There are actions: Caesar crossed the Rubicon. We may envy his decisiveness, for there are things we can do that we don't. Caesar himself could have stopped at the edge of the chilly Rubicon and hopped around on one foot. At each waking moment in our lives, there is a repertoire of alternative actions open to us, a range of things we can do, including some acts we will perform and many we won't. Call these our "options." Caesar's options, as he neared the Rubicon, included both acts cited.

Some question the platitude that there are actions.[1] Some reject the common notion that there are things we can do that we don't.[2] But I will stand with common

---

[1] Mendola (1997) discusses skepticism about psychological states necessary for action.
[2] Hard determinists believe that the past determines the present and that this is inconsistent with free will.

sense on these points.[3] There is a related platitude, though, that I will question. That is the notion that our options are determinate, that there is at each moment in our lives some specific repertoire of alternatives in action open to us.

This chapter argues that our options are somewhat indeterminate, that there is no fact of the matter about whether or not we can do certain things. This is a metaphysical indeterminacy, not merely an epistemic one. Options are indeterminate even when all the facts are known.

A number of assumptions made in this argument will require scrutiny. But they do have cogency, and are underwritten by physicalism. Many of us do buy these assumptions, and it is important to see that if we do buy all of them then we must conclude that options are indeterminate in fact.

I think that this indeterminacy is merely moderate, in a way I will explain. But it is still normatively significant. For instance, if the options open to agents aren't very determinate, then some sorts of common ethical assessments may be impossible. The best thing we can do in a situation depends on what our options are. If Cleopatra's options were not determinate when Antony lost in Greece, there may not have been a best act for her in that situation.[4] If consequentialism is true, and hence the rightness of an act depends upon the value of its consequences and the values of the consequences of its alternatives, there may not have been a fact about whether Cleopatra's flight to Egypt when Antony lost was right. And even opponents of consequentialism ordinarily maintain that alternatives sometimes matter. Even if consequentialism isn't true, still the nature of an agent's options is ethically significant. If options are indeterminate, important elements of commonsense ethics are at risk.

On the other hand, in Chapter 3 we will see that the indeterminacy of options also has some helpful implications for ethics. It helps pick out the correct conception of our options from among normatively significant competitors. And this chapter's arguments will in fact reveal that a very large class of conditional claims—not merely those relevant to options—are indeterminate in truth, which will be very significant during our attempt in Part II to locate the correct moral theory. However, focus for the moment neither on generalizations nor on normative advantages and disadvantages, but on the specific facts of indeterminacy in front of us.

2.2 Outline of the Argument

The argument for option indeterminacy has two steps. Each is a familiar point with philosophical champions. But we haven't realized how disturbing their conjunction is. Here is an outline:

---

[3] Mendola (2008) develops a physicalist account of mental states and actions, further refined here. Chapter 3 explains how there are things we merely *can* do.

[4] "May not have been" rather than "was not" because all problematic options may be worse than some unproblematic one.

Step One: *There will be determinate options for an agent in a situation only if certain subjunctive conditionals ("counterfactuals" for short) have determinate truth values.*[5] Paradigmatic subjunctive conditionals are claims like "If X had been true, then Y would have been true."

Step Two: *But the subjunctive conditionals in question do not have determinate truth values.*

Before I make the argument, though, I need to specify more exactly the thesis for which I will argue, at least in my first sally. It is this: *The options of agents are indeterminate, in the sense that, for some agent in some situation at some time, there is some alternative such that there is no fact of the matter whether or not the agent has it.*

You will notice that this is a *very* weak indeterminacy thesis. It says only that in *some* situation there is *some* indeterminate option. I believe that the considerations to be noted do suggest that *all* agents in *all* situations have *many* indeterminate options, and will later make the obvious generalization. But at first we are concerned only with a very weak indeterminacy.

You will also notice that the thesis mentions alternatives rather than actions. This will allow us to avoid, at least for a time, controversies that would obscure the particular indeterminacy I want to underline. By "alternatives of an agent in a situation at a time" I mean mutually exclusive things the agent could do at that time, different options the agent could take at that time, a time which I presume to be quite brief. To say they are "mutually exclusive" is just to say that the agent can't do two or more of them together in that short period.

Why bother with this notion of alternatives? Why not talk about actions?

(1) Because there is a controversy about *act*-individuation that is, for our immediate purposes, irrelevant. Antony moved his arm, and so signaled to the legions, alerted Cleopatra of his intentions, and began the battle. Were all of these one action under different descriptions, or several different actions related in an intimate way, or various small actions that are parts of one larger action?[6] We will return to this issue in Chapter 3, but in any case, they *weren't* different alternatives. Antony did his part in all these things at once, just by moving his arm. The indeterminacy I wish to underscore is an indeterminacy regarding alternatives, not sensitive to these controversies about act-individuation.

(2) The situation in which Antony moved his arm helped fix either the other three actions he performed, or the other three true descriptions of the one action he performed, or the various parts of the large action that he performed. But some think that the situation, the context, of Antony's action is relevant in other ways to its

---

[5] On the distinction between subjunctive conditionals and indicative conditionals, see E. Adams (1970). For complexities see Bennett (2003: 1–15).

[6] A. Goldman (1970, 1971) is fine-grained. Davidson (1980a) and Anscombe (2000) are coarse-grained. Beardsley (1975), Thomson (1977), and Ginet (1990) favor part–whole views.

ethical assessment. For instance, a utilitarian may believe that the act was best only if, given Antony's circumstances, it led to greatest happiness. I am not certain if all ethically relevant context is part of the context that helped fix what actions he performed, but it did help fix what his alternatives were. It may be that alternatives include more context than actions. I discuss alternatives rather than actions because our target indeterminacy sometimes infects that extra context as well, if there is any.

(3) Alternatives are mutually exclusive while actions may not be. For instance, some acts are conjunctions of other acts. Cleopatra might have stood up, or said the equivalent of "Damn," or said that and stood up. Furthermore, alternatives exhaust our possibilities, while actions in any usual sense may not. Cleopatra might have sat there doing nothing. That was an alternative, even if not in any ordinary sense an action. There are disputes concerning how alternatives of agents are constructed from their possible actions.[7] I discuss alternatives rather than actions because to become enmeshed in these disputes would be to risk losing focus on the indeterminacy I want to reveal.

(4) Some actions, say pursuit of the title "Caesar," take a long time. Such long-scale actions may be *temporal* conjunctions of actions that are more quickly completed, for instance getting Antony thrown out of the triumvirate. This may be the source of some ambiguity in the notion of what we can do. Does what we can do include acts that would take a very long time and require long commitment, or only acts that can be completed before a change of mind could ensue?[8] We will return to this topic, but such an ambiguity is also not at issue here. We will discuss *alternatives at a time*, rather than actions, so we can avoid more controversies that would obscure the particular indeterminacy I wish to suggest.[9]

2.3 Step One

Now Step One of the argument: *There will be determinate options for an agent in a situation only if certain counterfactuals have determinate truth values.* Why is this? Because options are alternatives an agent *has*, and it has them if and only if it *can* take them. But "can" is closely tied to counterfactuals.

A number of authors have remarked that there are many different senses in which it is true to say that we can do something.[10] But we are concerned here with a particular sense of "can," that relevant to our options. This is called "the 'can' of being able." And there is an old chestnut that attempts to link this sense of "can" to conditionals: the conditional analysis of ability.[11] This has been subject to much

---

[7] Bergstrom (1966, 1976).   [8] Feldman (1975); H. Goldman (1978).

[9] I assume that the agent's contribution to current alternatives is complete in the current time, but allow that later conditions help constitute alternatives. Because what one can do over a longer period will depend on what one can do in various particular times, this indeterminacy will infect the longer acts also. In general, if there's an indeterminacy of alternatives, then there's an indeterminacy of actions, however these disputes turn out.

[10] Austin (1961); D. Locke (1976).   [11] Moore (1912: 40–78); Nowell-Smith (1960).

criticism, and we will return to that criticism in Chapter 3. But Step One of our argument doesn't require a counterfactual *analysis* of ability. It only requires that there be a link between the determinacy of abilities and the truth values of counterfactuals. And an initial consideration of the conditional analysis will help us to see why Step One is appropriate, and why the most telling criticisms of the analysis are not problems for Step One.

J. L. Austin, in his classic paper "Ifs and Cans," criticized early conditional analyses. But he suggested one that had, he said, some plausibility. That, to paraphrase, was this: "Person *P* can do *y* at time *t*" means that if *P* tries to do *y* at *t*, then he or she will do *y*.

But even this formulation seems subject to counterexample, as Austin himself and Roderick Chisholm were first to point out.[12] When Austin suggested the analysis, he rejected it in this way:

> Consider the case where I miss a very short putt and kick myself because I could have holed it. It is not that I should have holed it if I had tried: I did try, and missed. It is not that I should have holed it if conditions had been different: that might of course be so, but I am talking about conditions as they precisely were, and asserting that I could have holed it. There is the rub.[13]

Sometimes there are things we can do, but won't do if we try to do them. Sometimes we can tell jokes without being self-conscious, but won't if we try. Sometimes we can hole putts, but only if we try to do something else, say put pressure on our thumbs and swing freely. Examples like these suggested to Chisholm an emendation to the analysis: "Person *P* can do *y* at *t*" means that there is something such that if *P* tries to do it at *t*, then *P* will do *y* at *t*.[14] If Austin had tried to concentrate on the hole, he would have holed the putt; otherwise he couldn't have made it. But there may also be a second criticism lurking in Austin's remark. Maybe there are cases where I can do something but there is nothing that I might try to do such that, if I try to do that, I will *certainly* succeed in doing that first thing. Maybe if I try to do *x*, I might and then I might not succeed, but still I *can* do *x*. Maybe "can do" requires only that it be more probable, if I try to do something, that I will succeed.[15] Or maybe it doesn't even require that. But for our purposes we needn't worry the point. We're talking about alternatives, not actions. So if there's slack in the world of this sort, we can say there's corresponding slack in our alternatives. There's something such that if we tried to do it, we'd certainly succeed in taking our alternative, but our alternative merely incorporates various chances of various outcomes.

Unfortunately, when Chisholm proposed his emendation, he also suggested a form for counterexamples that may seem impossible to evade.[16] There seem to be cases in which (i) if you try to do something, you will succeed, but (ii) you can't do it. These

---

[12] Austin (1961); Chisholm (1964).   [13] Austin (1961: 166 fn).   [14] Chisholm (1964).
[15] Consider Stalnaker versus Lewis on "might"-conditionals in Harper, Stalnaker, and Pearce (1981).
[16] Chisholm (1964).

are cases in which you cannot try to do something, but if you (*per impossibile*) did, then you would succeed.

Keith Lehrer provided cases. Caesar is offered a bowl of red candy balls. He doesn't take any because of a pathological aversion to red candy balls, which remind him of innocent blood he has shed. If he tried to take some, he would, but he is utterly unable to bring himself to try. He *can't* take any, though the conditional analysis says he can.[17]

There may seem to be only one way to avoid such counterexamples: "P can do y at t" requires that there be something such that (i) P can try to do it at t and (ii) if P tries to do it at t, then P will do y at t. But notice "can" inside clause (i). The threat of a vicious circle, an infinite regress, or a special notion of being able to try may be sufficient to undercut the conditional analysis.

Chapter 3 returns to these issues. But remember that for the moment we don't need an *analysis*. We only need the right sort of link between counterfactual conditionals and "can." And we have such a link here, even if we lack an analysis. You can't get out of my argument for indeterminacy just by denying the conditional analysis of ability on these classic grounds. That's why I'm holding off my stronger positive claim about that analysis for a while.

Consider T: P can do y at t if and only if there is something such that (i) P can try it at t and (ii) if P tries to do it at t, then P will do y at t. Does it make sense to say that you can try to do something *and* that if you do try you will succeed, but that you can't (in the sense of "being able") do it? Might it be that you can (in that sense) do something, but that it won't happen whatever you try to do of the things you can try to do?[18]

Well, there is our recent worry about mere probability rather than certainty, which leads us to prefer talk of alternatives to talk of what is done. Also, perhaps you would prefer to speak of willing or volition rather than trying. Although those seem to me terms of art and "trying" more ordinary, and although we will return to this issue, for now it doesn't matter. You can make that substitution in what follows in this chapter, to what I take to be no effect. But these are details. Whatever the fate of the counterfactual analysis of ability, we can properly conclude that there's a link between the determinacy of the truth values of certain counterfactuals and the determinacy of options. We can make Step One. We need merely to notice two things:

(1) There are analogues of T which govern *alternatives* rather than actions. Consider T_2: P has alternative y at t if and only if there is something such that (i) P can try to do it at t and (ii) if P tries to do it at t, then P will take alternative y at t.[19]

---

[17] Lehrer (1968).

[18] I assume that the relatively brief times that t ranges over are longer than moments and begin with the trying. This may generate further indeterminacy, to which we return.

[19] Deploying *alternatives* in (i) and in the antecedent of (ii) might lead to difficulties given Chisholm's counterexamples to Austin's analysis. But what you try to do are actions, not alternatives. And taking an alternative does not generally entail trying to take it under its full description as an alternative.

(2) The conditional on the right side of T_2 is a subjunctive conditional.[20] I am calling these "counterfactuals" for short.

We first want "weak indeterminacy": *For some agent in some situation at some time, there is some alternative such that there is no fact of the matter whether or not the agent has it.* We will have it from T_2 if, for some agent P in some situation and at some time t, there is some alternative a with the following feature: There is nothing b that P can try to do such that "if P tried at t to do b, P would take a" is determinately true, but there is something c that P can try to do such that "if P had tried at t to do c, P would take a" is not determinately false. A proposition is not determinately false if it is either determinately true or possesses an indeterminate or vague truth value.[21] In other words, nothing tried would determinately provide the option, but something tried would not determinately exclude it.

Step One is now complete. The determinacy of the repertoire of agents' options depends upon the determinacy of the truth values of counterfactuals.

2.4 Background for Step Two

Now we turn to Step Two, which is rooted in physicalism. But before I take Step Two in 2.5, before I argue that sometimes the requisite counterfactuals do not have determinate truth values, some background is in order.

First, there are different accounts of the truth or propriety of counterfactuals:

(1) There are the classic "suppositional" views of Nelson Goodman, Chisholm, and John Mackie. These may, like Chisholm's and Goodman's, hold that the counterfactual "If P, then Q" means that there are some propositions that are true, "cotenable" with P, and such that their conjunction with P entails Q.[22] Or they may, like Mackie's, hold that counterfactuals are not higher-order statements *about* such entailments, but rather themselves telescoped forms of such arguments.[23]

(2) There are possible worlds similarity analyses, like those of Robert Stalnaker and David Lewis.[24] Lewis' holds that a counterfactual is true if and only if there is some possible world, some way the universe might have been, in which the antecedent and consequent are true and that is more similar to the actual world than is any possible world in which the antecedent is true and the consequent false.[25]

---

[20] Lehrer and Taylor (1968); Lehrer (1975); Tomberlin (1979); Walton (1980) discuss the link between subjunctive conditionals and action.

[21] Some hold that all vagueness is merely epistemic, that there is no indeterminacy of fact, that there is a specific boundary to a cloud whether or not we can know what it is. But I am arguing that our world does not supply determinate truth values for certain counterfactuals, and that this particular vagueness of truth values implies a particular kind of indeterminacy of fact.

[22] Chisholm (1946); Goodman (1947). Talk of meaning is the idiom of their time. At evident risk of circularity, R is said to be "cotenable" with P iff it is not the case that R would not be true if P were true.

[23] Mackie (1973: 64–119).   [24] D. Lewis (1973b); Stalnaker (1975).

[25] Counterfactuals with impossible antecedents are supposed vacuously true.

(3) There are event analyses, such as William Lycan's. He holds that a counterfactual is true just in case the consequent is true in any relevant possible event or situation in which the antecedent is true.[26] Events or situations are characteristically smaller than worlds.

(4) There are accounts of the propriety of indicative conditionals, conditionals like "If Caesar didn't burn this smoldering bridge, then someone else did," that might be stretched through idealization or regimentation to also cover subjunctive conditionals, like "If Caesar hadn't burned the bridge, it would still have stood here." For instance, Peter Gärdenfors has suggested that we can modify the Ramsey test for conditionals (according to which one should accept the conditional "If A, then B" in a state of belief K if and only if the minimal change of K needed to accept A also requires accepting B) so that it can also plausibly cover even subjunctive conditionals the denial of whose consequents is very firmly entrenched in our belief.[27] And there are also "probabilistic" accounts like that of Ernest Adams.[28] These hold that the propriety of a conditional is a function of the conditional probability of the consequent given the antecedent.

The determinacy problem I will outline below would be a problem on any of these accounts, and I will explain why in a moment.[29] But it will make matters clearer if I concentrate on Lewis' analysis, which has the virtues of familiarity and vividness despite its profligate ontological commitments, which are hard but not impossible to square with the physicalist conception of the world that we presume.[30] For our immediate purposes, this ontological complication will be irrelevant, and I am about to note grounds for the relevant generalization to other sorts of accounts.

The main point I wish to make is, in a general way, familiar: The truth values of some counterfactuals are vague or indeterminate. Consider "If Caesar and Cleopatra had been compatriots, then they would have both been Roman" and "If Caesar and Cleopatra had been compatriots, then they would have both been Egyptian."[31]

The vagueness of some counterfactuals is not in dispute. Lewis' analysis of counterfactuals rests on the comparative similarity of possible worlds. Here's Lewis on the vagueness of that relation:

---

[26] Lycan (2001).   [27] Gärdenfors (1988: 166).   [28] E. Adams (1975).

[29] Perhaps the fourth class of accounts seems to generate merely epistemic and not metaphysical indeterminacies. But they are epistemic accounts of the truth; there are supposed to be no relevant facts to know beyond those that they deliver.

[30] Merely possible worlds might be, as David Lewis thought, large concrete physical particulars like that we inhabit, but without spatio-temporal relations to here. This is consistent with physicalism, although implausible. Or they might be constituted by recombinations of actual physical entities, as suggested by Armstrong (1989). Or, as I think, different types of modal claims might have different truth grounds, rooted ultimately in basic physical modal facts. But I hope to be excused from that long story here.

[31] Quine (1960: 222).

[C]omparative similarity … is vague—very vague, in a well understood way. Therefore it is just the sort of primitive that we must use to give a correct analysis of something that is itself undeniably vague.

Overall similarity consists of innumerable similarities and differences in innumerable respects of comparison, balanced against each other according to the relative importances we attach to those respects of comparison. Insofar as these relative importances differ from one person to another, or differ from one occasion to another, so far is comparative similarity indeterminate.… [T]he limited vagueness of similarity accounts nicely for the limited vagueness of counterfactuals. It accounts for the fact that some sensitive counterfactuals are so vague as to be unsuitable for use in serious discourse; that others have definite truth values only when context serves to narrow their range of vagueness; and that many more have quite definite truth values.[32]

Lewis later reiterated such points. He claimed that some counterfactuals suffer truth-value gaps.[33] He held that vagueness is endemic to his account and to counterfactuals, but that in many cases the context in which counterfactuals are used will serve to disambiguate them sufficiently to allow them truth values.[34]

Vagueness of truth is not really in dispute. All that is at issue are particular cases. I will argue in the next section that many counterfactuals of the form "If person P had tried to do y at t, then P would have taken alternative z" are vague in this way, given the truth of physicalism. But let me be very clear. There are constraints of reality beyond physicalism that are relevant to these cases in ways I will explain. Still, the key point is that physicalism also matters. In fact, Alvin Plantinga cited an ancestor of this chapter as part of an argument for the existence of God, since he supposes that the vagueness of truth of our target conditionals might be removed in the mind of God.[35] And the right sort of dualist substance might also help. However, we presume physicalism and no God. We face relevant vagueness.

Nevertheless, ability ascriptions are crucial to our ethical discourse, and since the propriety of ability ascriptions depends upon the determinacy of the truth values of counterfactuals of this sort, these are hardly conditionals that are "unsuitable for use in serious discourse." They can't be relegated wholesale to the dustbin of truth-value gaps without a serious adjustment in our way of thinking. However, often the context in which they are used does not serve in reality to narrow their range of vagueness enough to give them determinate truth values.

On Lewis' account, the vagueness of counterfactuals is due to the vagueness of the comparative similarity of possible worlds. And this relation is vague in the case of the counterfactuals relevant to ability ascriptions, even given their context of use. It is indeterminate how "the innumerable similarities and differences in innumerable respects of comparison" are to be weighted to fix overall comparative similarity in these cases. That is centrally so because it is indeterminate which features of the

---

[32] D. Lewis (1973b: 91–4).   [33] D. Lewis (1981).
[34] D. Lewis (1979).   [35] Plantinga (2007).

actual world are important bases of comparison, which must be comparatively well approximated or duplicated in comparatively similar possible worlds.[36] We will see why in detail in a moment.

But, of course, there are other accounts of conditionals than Lewis'. Still, they can't help. Vagueness is the issue, and while vagueness enters the different sorts of analyses in various ways, it is always there. On Lewis' account, the truth vagueness of counterfactuals is primarily due to that of comparative similarity, resting on the vagueness of the relative importance of respects of comparison. But the suppositional accounts were notoriously subject to vagueness regarding which propositions were properly to be held cotenable with the antecedent. Event accounts like Lycan's must specify which events are "relevant" to the evaluation of counterfactuals, and this involves vagueness in another way. Gärdenfors must somehow modify the relevant belief sets to plausibly apply his test to most counterfactuals, and that is the location of vagueness in his proposal. Probabilistic accounts would locate the vagueness in a different place, partly because they may assign not truth but probability to conditionals, but mostly because the probabilities themselves are vague in a way I will shortly explain. But, at least for the counterfactuals I discuss, the problem would be roughly the same on all these accounts.

I will call the features of the actual world that must be, according to Lewis, preserved or closely approximated in the most relevantly similar worlds for purposes of evaluating the truth of particular counterfactuals, the "background conditions" for the counterfactuals. The notion of background conditions can help make the connection between Lewis' account and the other sorts of accounts more explicit. In Lewis' terminology, comparative similarity in the cases that I will treat is seriously vague because the relative importance of respects of comparison is vague or indeterminate. In other words, the background conditions of the counterfactuals, conditions true in the actual world that must be preserved or closely approximated in the most relevantly similar worlds, are vague or indeterminate. But the relevant background conditions also fix the properly cotenable premises of the suppositional accounts. They either are the cotenable premises, or the cotenable premises are close approximations of them. They are also the conditions that specify what events are relevant according to event accounts. Background conditions also fix the conditions that cannot be properly modified in a Gärdenfors-style belief set. Probabilistic accounts rest on the determinacy of probabilities, but these, at least in the classic view of the objective probabilities[37] relevant to the options we are attempting to ascertain,

---

[36] On Lewis' account, but not on cotenability accounts, there need not be any very specific proposition true in the actual world that is also true in the comparatively similar possible worlds relevant to evaluating a counterfactual. There must merely be worlds in which the consequent and antecedent are both true and that are more similar to actuality than others are, perhaps because they closely *approximate* every specific feature of the actual world while getting none exactly right.

[37] At least of objective probabilities that are, like those here, not those of irreducibly probabilistic microphysical laws or propensities.

depend on the determinacy of an appropriate reference class, a space of relevant instances across which the probabilities are defined.[38] The specification of this space of instances depends on the specification of the relevant background conditions.

So the differences among the various competitor accounts of counterfactuals don't matter from our perspective. Our problem remains. It is that some counterfactuals relevant to ability ascriptions do not, even in context, have sufficiently determinate background conditions. Indeed, there are also other problems with these counterfactuals. The next section develops all these problems.

2.5 Step Two

This section argues that many counterfactuals of the form "If person P tried to do y at t, then P would take alternative z" are indeterminate in truth value, even in context. So many that for at least one agent in some situation at some time, there is at least one option that is indeterminate, because the conditions for option indeterminacy noted earlier are met. So this will be Step Two of our larger argument. If it succeeds, then some option is indeterminate. And indeed we will have grounds for thinking that many are.

It will serve to highlight the indeterminacy under consideration if I make two simplifying assumptions in the spirit of our physicalist presumptions. One of them may be false and those presumptions yet true, but we will see later that relaxing that assumption in the relevant way doesn't make any difference. Making both assumptions will allow me to construct a simple model that dramatically points up the problem, which we then can see extends to more and perhaps more realistic situations.

Along with Lewis' analysis of counterfactuals, assume:

(A) *Microphysical Supervenience*: All the possible worlds relevant to determining the truth of the counterfactuals under consideration are worlds in which microphysical supervenience holds. For microphysical supervenience to hold of a world is for it to be the case that, once the microphysical facts of the world are fixed, all the facts of that world (except those that depend on other worlds) are fixed.[39]

Also assume:

(B) *Determinism*: The prevailing laws of nature in the actual world are such that there do not exist any two possible worlds that are exactly alike up to some time, that differ thereafter, and in which those laws are never violated.[40]

---

[38] On interpretations of probability, see Fine (2007). On the ubiquity of the problem of the reference class, see Hájek (2007). See also Levi (1977); Kyburg (1977).

[39] Kim (1979, 1984).   [40] D. Lewis (1973a: 559).

Remember that "background conditions" are features of the actual world that are important bases of comparison between worlds, which must be duplicated or approximated in relevantly similar possible worlds. When assessing a counterfactual, there are three things that might help fix the relevant background conditions. They are (1) the state of the actual world, (2) the counterfactual itself, and (3) its context of use. Since we are assuming microphysical supervenience, the state of the actual world is fixed by the microphysical state of that world. The contribution of the counterfactual itself should be taken to include the meaning of the antecedent and consequent and, perhaps, implicit meaning conventions governing the specification of background conditions for that counterfactual.[41] Given these resources, what sorts of true counterfactuals might there be on Lewis' model?[42]

Type One: First, there are those to whose truth the state of the actual world and the context of utterance are irrelevant. These include counterfactuals in which the antecedent entails the consequent, in the suitably loose sense, like "If Caesar had been a bachelor, he'd have been unmarried." But most of the counterfactuals relevant to ability ascription aren't of this kind.

Type Two: There might be counterfactuals in which (i) the meanings of the antecedent and consequent, and (ii) the microphysical facts of the world, fix the truth of the counterfactual, without regard to an implicit convention about the relevance of certain background conditions and without regard to the context of utterance. Here are two sub-types:

(a) There might be counterfactuals whose truth or falsity is built right into the microphysical facts. Some think that there are irreducible causal powers in the world, and that these are the basic microphysical properties, like charge or quark-color.[43] This is consistent with our physicalist presumptions. And those who believe in causal powers may believe that certain microphysical entities irreducibly have dispositional powers to do y, powers only released under circumstances c. If these circumstances are counterfactual, then the existence of such a disposition is in some cases—in particular when the realization of the disposition is not masked in some way—immediately equivalent to the truth of a counterfactual "If c, then y." But whether such irreducible powers are intelligible or not, still the psychological counterfactuals relevant to ability ascriptions aren't in reality of this irreducible microphysical sort.

(b) There might be counterfactuals that are such that (i) the microphysical facts of the actual world that make the antecedent false and (ii) those that fix the background conditions (on any appropriately admissible conception of those background conditions given all the microphysical facts and the meanings of the antecedent and consequent) are easily and clearly partitionable from each other. To save words,

---

[41] D. Lewis (1973b: 93).   [42] Excepting those with impossible antecedents.
[43] Harre and Madden (1975); Shoemaker (1984). Shoemaker's basic properties are second-order powers, powers to produce powers.

I will call these candidate background conditions, on any appropriate conception, "admissible" background conditions.

Perhaps there are possible worlds that are *very* similar to the actual one, in which the antecedent is true and *nothing* else (at least at that time) is different from the way it actually is.[44] With such counterfactuals, there's no indeterminacy of background conditions. The background conditions are everything in the actual world (at least at the time) but what makes the antecedent false. Even these counterfactuals may suffer some indeterminacy, if there is some range of different ways the antecedent could be true. Some of those ways with the background conditions may serve to make the consequent true, while others make it false. But except for these "precision problems," such counterfactuals have determinate truth values. When thinking of counterfactuals, we may think of possible worlds as rather too Tractarian,[45] as easily decomposable into independent facts all on a metaphysical par. So we may think there are many more counterfactuals of this sort than there really are. But microphysical supervenience ensures that not all facts are on par. There is a basic set of facts, the microphysical facts, which may be more or less independent of each other. But other facts are fixed by these. Two of those dependent facts may be fixed by some of the same basic facts. Those two are not easily disentwined from the basic facts and from each other. And this may cause problems, when one of the dependent facts is relevant to the falsehood of the antecedent of a counterfactual, and the other is an admissible background condition. I need to explain this point, but I will do this by reference to our last and most important class of cases.

Type Three: Many counterfactuals are such that (i) the microphysical facts, and (ii) the meanings of the antecedent and consequent of the counterfactual, are not sufficient to determine the background conditions relevant to the counterfactual's truth or falsity. For a counterfactual of this sort (iii) an implicit meaning convention specifying the relevant background conditions for that conditional, or (iv) its context of utterance, may have to do a good deal of work if the counterfactual is to be determinately true or false.

In Type Three cases implicit meaning conventions or contexts of utterance serve to delimit admissible background conditions. Lewis discusses one case in which he thinks at least implicit meaning conventions succeed in doing the job:

There might be a man who was inclined to deny that if he had stepped out of his window he would have fallen to the ground; to deny this not—as we might expect—because he had eccentric factual opinions, but rather because he attached eccentric relative importances to respects of comparison of worlds and therefore favored a system of spheres [of similarity of worlds] unlike that others would favor. He is not entitled to give in to his inclination to deny this, at least not without giving warning of his eccentric notions. If he denies it without warning he lies; if he denies it with warning, he temporarily changes the conventional meaning of his words.[46]

---

[44] If Determinism is true, then the past must vary, and the future may as well.
[45] Wittgenstein (1961).   [46] D. Lewis (1973b: 93).

Notice, on Lewis' view, how little we have to say to this crackpot. He isn't making a factual error about the world. There aren't *facts* that determine what should be considered important. He just attaches relative importances to things in a way that violates our implicit meaning conventions. But the main point is that not all relevant disputes about the relative importance of respects of comparison, about the propriety of background conditions, are resolved by meaning conventions and contexts of utterance. Some counterfactuals are in trouble; they are indeterminate in truth. I will call them Failed Type Three cases.

Many counterfactuals are of this sort, are such that (i) the actual microphysical facts that make their antecedent false, and (ii) features of the world that are admissible background conditions of the counterfactual, are not easily disentwined and separated, even given a fixed context of utterance and meaning conventions. Consider "If the Egyptian economic situation had been better in the time of Caesar and Cleopatra, there would have been less political instability." Some of the admissible background conditions of this, and some of the conditions that made the antecedent false, are quite general and fairly abstract. They are a long way from the microphysical details and fixed by many and overlapping microphysical details. The features of the world relevant to determining the truth of this counterfactual seem to be that it is a place where this or that more or less general psychological or economic theory is true, and where certain general economic and social conditions obtained in Egypt at the time of Caesar and Cleopatra. A dispute about the truth of this counterfactual would be a dispute about such theories and general conditions. If there were a dispute between such general theories that was not adjudicated by the microphysical facts, meaning conventions, and the context of utterance, perhaps because such theories differed solely on what general facts were important, our counterfactual might have an indeterminate truth value. And in reality, it seems to me, many such disputes are of this sort.[47]

There might seem to be a way around this problem, whenever it occurs. Perhaps a relatively small group of people may agree on some conventional model of what is important, and so the context of a conditional utterance within that group helps specify a determinate truth value for that conditional. But it will not be a context or truth value that can be carried outside of the group to those with other conceptions. And it would be of no help in resolving many real normative disputes. This is a way of saying that any relevant context of utterance for many normatively relevant conditionals cannot be taken to simply include a specification of the relevant background conditions. There are relevant disputes within the relevant context.

Unfortunately, not all counterfactuals that cannot be sufficiently disambiguated by implicit meaning conventions in their relevant context of utterance are unsuited for serious discourse in any suitably dismissive sense. There are many homey and not

---

[47] Perhaps you don't share my view of these cases. But I will soon be giving an argument that there is analogous indeterminacy in the cases that matter to us.

easily abandoned counterfactuals that have the following feature: Given even (i) their most relevant context of utterance and (ii) meaning conventions and (iii) the actual microphysical facts, they have indeterminate truth values. They do so because (i) there are different selections of features of the actual world that are admissible sets of candidate background conditions given the world and the meaning conventions and the context, and these different sets of conditions are such that (ii) some of them with the antecedent would guarantee the truth of the consequent, and (iii) some would guarantee its falsity. Another important problem is that the same intuitive background conditions might be admissibly realized in actual microphysical facts in a variety of relevant ways. But it will save words if we also call that a difference in admissible background conditions.

Some such set of admissible background conditions might be more precise than some others—that is it might be all true and entail what truth the others have—but not all such sets will be comparable in this way. If two sets of putatively relevant background conditions are each all true, and one isn't more precise than the other, and if meaning conventions and the context of utterance don't tell between them, both are admissible. If they don't fix the same truth value for a counterfactual, that counterfactual has an indeterminate truth value.

When assessing counterfactuals, we often agree about what background conditions are relevant. Sometimes when we initially disagree we can come to agree that there is a more fully specified set of background conditions, taking all the controversial features into account, that can serve for evaluation. But there are no grounds whatever for hope that this will always be the case, even when we know all the physical facts. Even if we agreed to always consider as part of the relevant background conditions anything that anyone considered important, we'd face a problem. If A and B are different admissible candidates for background conditions of a counterfactual, it need not be the case that there is a possible world in which A and B and the antecedent all obtain (or the antecedent obtains and approximations to A and B obtain).

Consider a case. Cleopatra argued with Antony about a counterfactual that can be translated as: "If she had gone closer to the water, she would have picked him a lotus blossom." She thought that the relevant background conditions for assessing the counterfactual were that there were lotus blossoms by the water in plain view, and that she brought him flowers when she had a chance. He said that she wouldn't have brought him one, because she was always distracted when rushed, had been rushed when she'd neglected to walk down by the water, and tended to forget him when distracted, though it is true that she never forgot *that other guy*. Assume that all of these things were true. It may be that there was nothing in the world or the context of utterance or in meaning conventions to decide the case between them. They may just have attached importance to different things. And so, depending on the details, this may be a Failed Type Three case.

Not all such disputes are plausibly adjudicated by meaning conventions and the context of utterance. Such a dispute would often survive agreement about those things. And not all such disputes are plausibly adjudicated by the truth, by some complete account of the facts of psychology and situation that makes it clear whether she'd have picked the blossom if she'd gone to the water. A complete account of the facts would note that she *didn't* go to the water. We need to leave some of the facts out of any story we construct that gets her to the water. Antony and Cleopatra may just disagree about what facts are important and must be kept, or at least approximated, when evaluating the conditional in question. Truth may not adjudicate between them. There is the further problem that there might be different microphysical ways to realize even those parts of an abstract story they agree on, and those differences are conceivably relevant to the truth of the consequent, although probably Antony and Cleopatra didn't argue about micro-particles.

Disputes about counterfactuals like these are often disputes about the appropriateness of relatively abstract theories about the world, of psychology or economics or a person's character. Sometimes such competing theories may be equally true or approximately true, while they emphasize different features of the world as important. They may suggest the construction of different abstract models of the world. In doing so, they may suggest different truth conditions and truth values for counterfactuals. Unless we can find some non-controversial way to rank models all of which are more or less equally true, we will need to relativize the truth of certain counterfactuals not only to a context of utterance but to a specification of a general theory or model or a set of background conditions. In the absence of such a relativization or such a ranking of models, many counterfactuals will have indeterminate truth values.[48] And there is also the other type of problem mentioned earlier. We might have to further relativize the assessment of at least some counterfactuals to certain ways of microphysically realizing claims within even a specific model.

The punch line of this discussion is that crucial counterfactuals relevant to ability ascriptions are sometimes of this indeterminate sort. Consider "If Cleopatra had tried to put the asp down, she would have taken an alternative in which she would have lived at least a few more years," said in reference to the time when Cleopatra raised the asp to her breast to commit suicide.[49] Remember that we are assuming microphysical supervenience, so Cleopatra's trying to put the asp down would have been something, had it happened, that supervened on microphysical states of the world. Does this counterfactual have a determinate truth value?

---

[48] There may be relevant general conventions. Some have thought that *backtracking* counterfactuals, whose consequents include crucial conditions that temporally precede the crucial conditions encompassed by their antecedents, are generally second-class, or at least irrelevant to ability ascriptions. See Heller (1985).

[49] A more realistic alternative would involve a certain probability that she would live a few more years, a complication I ignore. And much of what we think about Cleopatra may be propaganda due to Octavian. See Tyldesley (2008).

There are three possible sorts of indeterminacy here, though I will insist for the moment only on the third. The first is what I called earlier a "precision problem." There might have been different ways Cleopatra could have tried to put the asp down that would have had different effects on her longevity. She might have flung it across the room or nervously dropped it on her bare feet. We will return to relevant precision problems later. I think they are important, but for the moment I won't rest my argument on them.

A second problem might make an ability ascription indeterminate even if the counterfactual in question were determinately true or false. It might not be determinate whether Cleopatra could have *tried* to put the asp down. Whether she could have tried might seem to depend on what model of her situation and psychology is appropriate, on what is *important*, and not just on the microphysical facts. We will return to this point in Chapter 3. In the end, I think this worry can be gotten around, though many will disagree.

My focus here will be on a third problem. Consider our sketch of the types of true counterfactuals. There's no entailment between the antecedent of this counterfactual and its consequent, and it isn't irreducibly written into the microstructure of the world. It isn't Type One, or Type Two-a. Could it be Type Two-b? Is it plausibly a counterfactual in which the falsehood of the antecedent and any admissible background conditions are easily localizable and separable? That seems very unlikely, for more than one reason. Our counterfactual seems to be Type Three. And our third problem is that it seems to be, indeed for more than one reason, a Failed Type Three case.

(1) Various features of Cleopatra's psychology are, intuitively, relevant background conditions. For instance, even if she had tried to put the asp down she might not have successfully done so had she been the sort that panics or freezes or passes out. And certainly features of her psychology are relevant to whether or not she would have lived a few more years if she had gotten rid of the asp. These features of her psychology are not likely to be easily localizable and separable from whatever makes the antecedent of the counterfactual false. She tried in fact to bring the asp to her breast. That was a feature of her psychology. So were all the other psychological states that supported her choice, say her pride. We don't even need to insist on some general holism of the mental to realize that the microphysical facts that underlie these psychological features are not easily disentwined.[50] To make a "single" change in her psychology, we'd need to do more than adjust one neuron and leave the rest alone, at least in a case like this one. There isn't plausibly a single neuron whose alternative states constitute alternative states of trying. We'd have to decide what more or less general psychological story about her was most appropriate, then see how on that

---

[50] Mental holism is associated with Davidson (1980c). But functionalists also believe in it. And Mendola (2008) involves a measure of holism.

model things would be if the antecedent were true but all the other important psychological background conditions were unchanged. Such psychological stories about individuals are notoriously controversial, and judgments about relative importance would sometimes keep them so even if all the microphysical facts were revealed. There is no reason to expect that the components of such stories will map cleanly onto different highly localized neural states. So our only remaining hope is that this is a successful Type Three case, in which meaning conventions and context of utterances do the work. But it is implausible that they can do the heavy lifting, at least in most cases like this. There is no evidence for special meaning conventions that will remove these particular indeterminacies, and claims about our alternatives play an important role in ethical evaluations that must remain stable across many possible contexts of discussion. Even a god who knew all the microphysical facts, and relevant facts about meaning and contexts of utterance, would not be able to resolve disputes about such a counterfactual. We can properly conclude that the microphysical facts and the meaning of our counterfactual in its relevant contexts of utterance are not sufficient to determine our counterfactual's truth. It is a Failed Type Three case. And indeed in the particular case we are considering there is an extra reason to think that there is unfortunate entwining. The psychological facts that we need to vary and to preserve are both motivational. We need to consider how Cleopatra's other motivational properties would affect her success in getting the asp out of range even at the same time we are varying those motivational properties that constitute her not trying to rid herself of the asp. Her neural states that make for both kinds of motivational properties are quite plausibly closely intertwined.

(2) There is also a second reason to think that this cannot be a Type Two-b case, and is indeed a Failed Type Three case. It involves relevant features of the world beyond Cleopatra's immediate psychology. First of all, remember that we are assuming that Determinism is true. We cannot change one feature of Cleopatra's psychology without changing the prior history of the world, or admitting miracles or even perhaps inconsistencies into the world. So to evaluate our counterfactual we have to consider, as comparatively similar, (i) worlds where the past history of the world is different (perhaps infinitesimally so), and/or (ii) worlds in which Determinism is more or less relaxed. But (i) some features of the past of the actual world, and (ii) the fact that Determinism is at least more or less true, would have to be preserved in relevantly similar worlds. Here again we might have irresolvable disputes about exactly which worlds are more relevantly similar, and these disputes might affect the truth of the counterfactual. For instance, some might think that some of the features of Cleopatra's psychology or the microphysical facts that got her to the state she was in might be very relevant to the assessment of our counterfactual. Others might disagree. And there is no reason to think that meaning conventions or contexts of utterance can resolve such disputes. So once again we seem to be confronted with a Failed Type Three case.

I should admit that I myself think that another possible aspect of this second reason for worry can be gotten around. I think that the microphysical basis of Cleopatra's most central psychological states needn't include the past, and so we can consider what would be true if we varied relatively current conditions that constitute those states, irrespective of their history.[51] This might be true of the most basic sorts of trying and also other relevant psychological background conditions. But, to the contrary, most are externalists in philosophy of mind who think that past conditions crucially constitute even our current psychological states, and so they should not agree with my optimism on this point. And even I admit that there are some intuitively relevant claims about what her current psychological conditions are and alternative tryings might be that aren't quite central and basic in these ways and hence to which history is relevant.

And there is also a third aspect of this second reason. Given Determinism, the general conditions out in the world that lead to the truth of one alternative rather than another on the basis of what Cleopatra tries to do are entwined with those that must be varied if she succeeds in getting rid of the asp. And here even a radical internalist like me has to admit that a disagreement about which of these general conditions are most important might well be beyond adjudication by the microphysical facts, meaning conventions, and contexts of utterance. It might turn on different preferences among equally true models, or different judgments about the importance of certain facts.

Despite all this, it is also true and relevant to our second reason that Chapter 3 will endorse Lewis' suggestion that, when Determinism is true, the evaluation of counterfactuals relevant to alternatives will often involve the hypothetical consideration of small and localized miracles, local violation of generally deterministic laws. This would eliminate some indeterminacies of the sort under consideration. But you may reasonably disagree. And even this suggestion leaves room for indeterminacy regarding the exact nature of the small miracle. And this in fact introduces another key issue about such a counterfactual: The background conditions might be properly realized in different microphysical ways that are themselves differentially relevant to the truth of its consequent. This is a new kind of precision problem.

In fact, this third aspect of our second reason doesn't even really require the truth of Determinism. Even if Determinism were false, there might still be a problem about the determinacy of the background conditions. For instance, there might remain relevant disputes about our target counterfactual even if all could agree that Cleopatra could have gotten rid of the asp. Consider the form such a dispute would take. One side might tell a geo-political story based on a certain model of public and general psychological workings applied to that situation, leading to her execution

---

[51] Mendola (2008) argues that the past is irrelevant to our basic psychological states.

within a month. Another might tell another story leading to her alliance with Octavian. The model each party assumes might equally fit the actual microphysical history of the world and its (deterministic or indeterministic) microphysical laws, and involve (if necessary) even the same general sorts of microphysical miracles. The parties might disagree simply about the facts that are important. In other words, neither party might accept that (i) the actual microphysical history of the world, plus (ii) some momentary cross-section of the universe[52] involving some physically localizable deviation from reality (in turn perhaps requiring a small miracle given the past and its laws), plus (iii) the actual laws of nature hereafter, constitutes the hypothetical situation most relevant to the evaluation of such a counterfactual. The differing geo-political and general psychological theories that both parties favor might be too far away from the microphysical details to allow this fussy pattern of analysis to be determinative.[53] Alternatively, *which* physically localizable deviations or stable background conditions are properly deployed in such a fussy analysis might be in legitimate dispute.[54]

So here we are: Our case isn't plausibly a Type One or Type Two case. And it would seem that meaning conventions and contexts of utterance are also insufficient to resolve it. We are faced with a Failed Type Three case. Indeed, there may well be additional grounds for indeterminacy in our case, due to precision problems, and Chapter 3 will show that the facts of trying are often indeterminate in a way that will underscore this.

We have focused on a single example. Still the case is not relevantly unusual. Counterfactuals of the form "If person P tried to do y at t, then P would taken alternative a" seem often to be like this. Their truth depends not solely on meaning conventions and context of utterance and the microphysical facts, but on what model of the facts is relevant, on what features of the world are important. They are often Failed Type Three cases. They may also involve precision problems. Lacking a relativization to a certain set of background conditions, many of these counter-factuals are indeterminate in truth value. Certainly enough are indeterminate that there is no fact of the matter about whether or not Cleopatra had the option of living at least a few more years. Step Two is complete, and weak indeterminacy is established.

But the considerations that show Cleopatra's options to be indeterminate are not peculiar to her case. A further generalization is obviously appropriate. Many options are indeterminate, although in 2.7 we will need to talk about what that means.

---

[52]   Special Relativity, which denies absolute simultaneity, makes this problematic.

[53]   Perhaps this dispute ought to be not about the truth of a counterfactual but about the conditional probability of a consequent given an antecedent. But models and background conditions are important in that case as well, fixing the reference class that defines the relevant probabilities.

[54]   Hence these problems are ultimately precision problems.

2.6 Attempts to Evade the Argument

We have assumed an over-simplification. Determinism may be false for quantum mechanical reasons, and even Special Relativity makes its characterization difficult.[55] But we have already seen that Determinism isn't always the problem. And for the falsehood of Determinism to make any relevant difference, Determinism would have to be false in particular ways. It would have to be the case that tryings and their relevant background conditions were easily separable and isolable. For instance, it might help if tryings were weird dualist events, if they were not subject to causal influences and were able to immediately influence other events only at specifically localizable points, say pineal glands. But we physicalists can expect no help on this front.[56] It is too much to expect help on this front even if we relaxed our physicalism in the most plausible ways, like dualists about qualia, or even robust substance dualists who yet acknowledge some significant psychological role for our brain states or plausible forms of holism about the psychological.[57]

The facts eventually fix how the world turns out given what we do try. But they do not always or even mostly determine uniquely how things would be if we were to try otherwise. This predicament may suggest various responses, but there is no easy way out.

If there were truths about which higher-order psychological typologies were correct even though micro-concrete details did not adjudicate between them, then there might be a way out. But physicalism conflicts with the Platonisms and unusual and very implausible forms of dualism that could help enough in this way. Nor is there some privileged language of God at just the right level of abstraction.

Some might try to abandon the commonsense tie between counterfactuals and ability, or at least try to fix abilities on other grounds and then let the abilities suggest what background conditions are relevant. Some might hold that an agent's options are those the agent actually considers. Some might claim they are those the agent would consider under idealized epistemic conditions. And some might ascribe an ability to an agent when other agents of the same kind have done the thing in question or when the agent has done it in relevantly similar circumstances. But these alternatives are unhelpful. The first possibility is far from the commonsense conception, and would allow ignorance to be much more of an excuse than we consider it to be. The second itself depends on a suspiciously ambiguous counterfactual. The third suffers from

---

[55] On the orthodox interpretation of quantum mechanics, particles outside of measurement evolve in a deterministic way governed by the Schrödinger equation, but upon measurement evolve in a probabilistic way. For relativistic difficulties in characterizing determinism, see Earman (1986).

[56] The quantum mechanical collapse of particles in the brain governed by physically specified probabilities would not constitute a will that is metaphysically free in the ways that traditional libertarians about free will require.

[57] There are action theorists who are dualists of approximately the right sort. Still, there are reasons to think that indeterminacy of options would obtain even if these forms of libertarianism were correct. See R. Adams (1977).

indeterminacies as virulent as those that affect counterfactuals, since it depends on similarity relations.

Some may hold that to say that one has an alternative is just to say that one is appropriately praised or blamed for taking or avoiding it. They take the *moral* sense of "can" as primary, and think we should decide ability ascriptions on moral grounds. We will return to problems for such proposals in Chapter 3. But at least consequentialists can take this route only if there are determinate alternatives in praise or blame, for individuals or for societies, which have determinate consequences. And this determinacy is thrown into doubt by considerations quite like those we have noted. Counterfactuals expressing the consequences of alternative practices of praise are very likely subject to truth vagueness.

Some might propose new conventions to fix the truth of ability ascriptions by refining relevant background conditions, or alternatively insist on the relevance of very narrow contexts of utterance, which include presumptions about any relevant background conditions. But not any conventions would do. Ability ascriptions play a crucial role in ethics, and ethics is committed to the *justification* of claims, and not just within the very narrow contexts and shared presumptions of a few like-minded friends on a given afternoon. Relevant new conventions would have to be justifiable, not arbitrary. And the determinacy of even our options in conventions is in doubt, at least in regard to their consequences, so it is difficult to provide the requisite justification of a particular set of new conventions, and even some old ones.

So we have a few bad choices. I prefer to say that ability ascriptions sometimes have indeterminate, vague truth values. But some might prefer to say that such ability ascriptions are appropriate only when relativized to certain arbitrary sets of models or admissible background conditions and not when relativized to others. This terminological maneuver won't resolve any more normative controversies, unless perhaps two individuals arbitrarily agree on some relativization, and it fits uncomfortably with the plausible hope that some ability ascriptions, those that aren't vague, are not so relative. But it is consistent with my claims of non-relativized indeterminacy. Others might prefer to say that the problematic ascriptions are *neither* true nor false, that they be consigned to the garbage heap of truth-value gaps. I prefer vagueness or relativity because they seem less desperate. We shouldn't suggest that problematic ability ascriptions are so hopelessly vague as to be beyond repair. We know a way to make the vagueness disappear, through relativization, though it is bad enough.

There is, at least sometimes, indeed at least often, no unqualified fact of the matter about some of our options. There are just facts about what our options are relative to a specification of a set of arbitrarily specified background conditions. Plausibly, some options are determinate. And one option may be the best of a specific set of options determined by some specific background conditions. But there may be no unqualifiedly best alternative open to an agent, and hence perhaps no unqualifiedly right act. We can disagree about the options for an agent, and the facts not adjudicate between us. There is determinacy of some options. But in many cases our options are indeterminate.

2.7 Option Indeterminacy is Moderate

How common and threatening is the indeterminacy of options? There might be mere *minor* indeterminacy, by which I mean that relatively few options are indeterminate, or options are only indeterminate when described in a fussy, over-precise way. For instance, it can be determinate that you would have thrown a ball if you had tried, while it is not determinate that you would have thrown it at some very specific speed. Such minor indeterminacy would leave more than enough determinacy for any practical ethics. Aristotle told us long ago not to look for more precision than a subject matter admits. On the other extreme, there might be *virulent* indeterminacy of options, by which I mean that there is such widespread indeterminacy that serious use of the notion of options in ethical theory is impossible. For instance, it might be that no option characterized in a commonsense way is ever determinately available to anyone.

But the truth is in-between. The indeterminacy of options creates more indeterminacy of resulting ethical fact than we want or expect, enough to surprise even Aristotle, enough to cause some problems for ethical theory, but not so much that ethics cannot properly deploy the notion of options, say in consequential assessment. This is what I call *moderate* indeterminacy.

There are three clusters of general reasons, which apply to all sorts of commonsense options, not just when they are fussily described, to think that the indeterminacy of options is more than minor. The first cluster involves problems with the notion of trying that we have yet to confront. Chapter 3 will try to get clearer about trying, and we will see that it involves relevant ambiguity. The truth of subjunctive conditionals with antecedents that invoke trying often turns on what counts as important in a way that is not resolved by facts and meaning conventions and contexts of utterance governing "trying," and this is partly because of some ambiguity in what would count as trying. This generates one form of what I earlier called a "precision problem." There are indeterminacies about whether under certain conditions you would have counted as having tried to do something, say if you had made a weak gesture in the right direction. And there are sometimes different possible modes of trying to do something, which would have different relevant results.[58] This is a more straightforward form of precision problem.

Two other clusters of general reasons to think that option indeterminacy is more than minor involve, respectively, (i) the psychological conditions that intervene between trying and immediate actions like limb movements, and (ii) the external conditions that intervene between immediate actions and other actions (or conditions relevant to true descriptions of these actions, including even consequences) that

---

[58] Also, present meaning conventions governing "trying" may shift in ways that the facts do not adjudicate. Trying may not be a natural kind. And meaning conventions governing other words that are recognizably sufficient to serve in the antecedents of subjunctive conditionals determining recognizable options may not be the same as those governing "trying," nor undercut by the facts. Consider terms of art like "volition" and "willing," or other natural languages.

one hence performs (or brings forth), which I will much too roughly call "social-political conditions."[59] We considered these two sorts of factors already during our discussion of Cleopatra and her asp, factors which suggested there a Failed Type Three case. But such factors bear on many commonsense options, so I should now make my earlier points in a more suitably general way.

An optimist may claim that when the final true psychological and social-political theories come along, and they are properly fitted onto the microphysical facts, then all disputes about options that don't depend on difficulties about what counts as trying will be resolved by the true descriptions of individual psychologies and social-political conditions in the language of those new theories. These will specify appropriate and determinate background conditions for all relevant conditionals. We will have conditionals with properly determinate background conditions.

But it is whistling in the dark to presume that there can be such theories of the requisite abstraction, with a vocabulary that captures all the conditions that could be reasonably maintained as governing all options whatever anyone tries try to do, that captures all admissible background conditions. And we have little reason to presume that everyone would accept the vocabulary in which such a very general theory is stated. They may insist on an old-style vocabulary of vice and hope that doesn't fit the new-fangled social-psychological theory much better than it fits physics or neurobiology, or they may insist on a more detailed theory that suits some people in some conditions better and in more detail but other people in other conditions not so well. No falsehood need be involved if they cling to their old vocabulary, or their more detailed theory. Since physicalism is true, there isn't some irreducible, Platonic truth of one abstract psychological or geo-political theory rather than another. There are merely the messy physical facts that make one such theory true to a degree of approximation and another also, so that there may be no truth of the matter between them. Our actual social and psychological theories are not created with an eye to smooth reduction into physical neurophysiology, let alone into physics, and any theory that is may not have an obvious advantage in truth over those that are not, which may be more fruitful or explanatory or interesting for the likes of us. Individuals can differ without falsehood about what is fruitful or explanatory or interesting. Social and psychological theories are often in fact implicitly stories about the importance of certain background conditions, and many such stories are no more true than many others.[60] Our optimist may hope that all psychological theories and

---

[59] Someone's persisting psychological conditions may affect the long-term consequences of their immediate actions. That should be considered relevantly external.

[60] Perhaps it seems that relevant truths of psychology or sociology are a priori, a commitment of action talk, and that this resolves all these indeterminacies. That is implausible, but anyway the vocabulary of such conceptual truths would have no greater objective validity than possible alternatives in our physical world. And even if we the actual (and all the relevantly rational and hypothetical) can agree about some suitably abstract social and psychological theory, still there would be relevant disputes that fall within its abstract range.

all sociological theories can be ordered by regards to their accuracy to physical reality, and that the more accurate theory is always appropriately dominant. But we cannot presume that all the physical facts outside the space of one's trying are to be preserved when conditionals relevant to one's alternative options are assessed, even if somehow all that physical detail is relevant to the true social and psychological theory. That is because the conditions required for various sorts of trying on one hand, and admissible background social-political and psychological conditions that would realistically bridge various sorts of trying and alternatives on the other, are often entwined in our world. We already saw this in detail during our discussion of Cleopatra, but let me give some other examples.

Begin with the psychological cluster of reasons to think that indeterminacy is more than minor. We don't think that everything your body was up to in a certain circumstance is something you could do, often because of features of your psychology. Chapter 3 will dismiss some of these problems. It will discount some alleged differences in our ability to try to do certain things due to our contrary past psychological conditioning and training, though even juries are very subject to worry about these issues, and you may reasonably disagree with my optimism about this point. But there are other similar cases that can't be dismissed. Some involve things that we can only achieve under some circumstances, not unlike Cleopatra's flinging of the asp. My French is barely good enough to order in Parisian restaurants without comical incident if I am not too nervous and suitably acclimated and motivated, but you shouldn't count on my ability to dredge up the right French expression in this cold moment to save your life. Maybe I'd get it, and maybe I wouldn't, and maybe there is no fact whether I would. We'd have to see how it would turn out if I tried. If such a situation is counterfactual, if I don't try, then there may be no fixed fact about whether I could have come up with the right phrase and sufficiently well-formed pronunciation. Nor need there even be a very determinate probability about that. Or consider another case: When Caesar doesn't reach for the red candy balls, and doesn't even try, there may be no fixed fact about whether he would have succeeded in controlling his hands sufficiently had he tried.

Now consider the social-political cluster. One problematic set of cases involve actions that have large effects on the world. Caesar crossed the Rubicon. There is unlikely to be any very robustly determinate fact about what would have happened had he not, for instance determining whether or not Hitler would have invaded England or even probabilities of that occurrence. Consider a physicist god, who knows all the truth of the microphysical history of the world and tries to square claims in human language with that truth. It is not determinately true that the proper thing for that god to do when considering the truth or falsity of the claim that "Rome would have been dominant longer had Caesar not crossed the Rubicon" would be to partition the world at that moment in December by the river into (i) Julius' trying to act one way or the other, and (ii) everything else, and (iii) then run a simulation of the whole microphysical complex forward in time with various options in that trying slot. The language of these grand historical claims doesn't fit in the right way onto particular microphysical facts. And Determinism (or whatever true analogue of Determinism obtains) may require that the past history of the world be of necessity changed in some of those alternatives in a way that undermines general background conditions that someone could plausibly hold relevant to the fate of Rome. Even if we are tempted to appeal to small miracles in such cases, which may be on the wrong scale to be relevant, such miracles might require violation of quite salient historical or psychological generalities, and there would often be in such cases no fact of the matter regarding which alternative small miracle was most relevant.

The three clusters of general worries now under consideration are widely applicable even to options that are not fussily described. A large number of commonsense claims about our options do not have determinate truth values in our physical world. I think that all agents in all situations have many indeterminate options.

Still, many of our commonsense claims about options remain determinately true, because they are not undercut by the three clusters. This is why there is only moderate and not virulent indeterminacy of options. The ambiguities of trying and of proper psychological and social-political background conditions are not so great as to plausibly undercut the determinacy of some commonsense options.

Let me give some examples of plausibly determinate options. Here I stand, and I don't raise a finger to save you as you slowly roll towards the edge of a nearby cliff. It is a determinate fact that I cannot flap my arms and fly down to save you now. I have no feathers on my arms. It is also a determinate fact that even in my creaky middle age I'm still up to getting to you before you roll over. There are physical facts about human bodies that help give particular people particular options in particular circumstances. Not everyone has the same alternatives, if only because one is poised on one foot or the other, and one is a body builder and the other is on crutches. And these are facts about what these individual people can and cannot do that are robust and ethically relevant.

Still, we cannot stay on the surface of the body in this way to determine alternatives. We must go inside to psychological details and outside into the world, and in these ways this tidy and optimistic picture breaks down, and our second and third clusters of worries come into play. But not all options that turn even on psychological or social-political background conditions are indeterminate. Consider a few more cases.

You coolly put a gun to the head of a rival and pull the trigger. You have no pathologies of the sort with which most jurors might sympathize. You have no mad obsession that in any intuitive way forces this act. I think that it is determinately true that you could have done otherwise. There are no admissible psychological background conditions for the relevant conditional that undercut its truth. Perhaps someone might object on grounds of hard determinism to this claim, but Chapter 3 will answer that worry.

I make omelets for dinner. I think it is determinately true that, even with my limited culinary skills, I could have made fried eggs instead. The conditions involved in my making the omelets include enough truths that are consistent with my trying to make fried eggs and that assure I would make the fried eggs if I tried.

You once chose to try to be a philosopher, and not a lawyer. I think you could have been a lawyer. On the other hand, I don't think that there are very determinate facts, nor even probabilities, about how your life would have gone had you been a lawyer. To see what I mean, consider one last case:

In adolescent turmoil, you wanted badly to ask someone (to whom you were reasonably well-suited and at a time that might have mattered) out to the Winter Dance. But you didn't, because you got too nervous. You could have persisted and tried, perhaps; let me grant that there are determinate facts about that. I don't think there are always determinate facts in realistic cases of this sort about whether you could have successfully managed to execute that intention given your emotional turmoil; perhaps there are not even facts about whether you could have coherently asked, but waive that point also. I am yet more skeptical that there are determinate facts about whether you could have gotten the date. But the main contrast to note is this: I am quite confident that there aren't very determinate facts about how things would have gone in your life if you had, nor even reasonably determinate probabilities about that. The hypothetical physical facts that would be involved in a very different life for you stemming from that choice point are quite different (at least in regards to your life) from physical reality, and not closely specified by most intuitively admissible sets of social-political and psychological background conditions for the counterfactual. And there are different and conflicting sets of intuitively admissible psychological and social-political background conditions in such a case. You could have asked, but there are no very determinate facts about what would have resulted.

Options are moderately indeterminate. But this chapter also has a more general conclusion. We have discovered grounds to worry that there are many Type Three counterfactuals that are indeterminate in truth. We will see repeatedly in what follows that this is a very significant fact for moral theory.

3

The Conditional Analysis and Modal Stability

This chapter propounds a positive account of our options, despite their moderate indeterminacy. It defends a form of the conditional analysis of ability that I will call "CA." A rough statement of CA is reminiscent of Chapter 2's negative argument: *Agent P has alternative y at t if and only if there is something such that if P were to try to do it at t, then P would take alternative y at t.* But we will need to add several refinements as we proceed.

A plausible moral theory must evaluate alternatives in action, and this will be my account of those alternatives. But the details and implications of the analysis are also an important source of the viability of the moral theory developed in Part II. That theory is a form of *consequentialism.* Its assessment of some act of Caesar depends on the value of that act's consequences, and more specifically on the value of its consequences relative to the value of the consequences of other options open to Caesar. Indeed, the theory is a form of *objective* consequentialism: What matters normatively in the most basic sense is not Caesar's conception of his options, nor even his justified conception of his options, but rather the facts about them. We have already worried that it might be indeterminate which of Caesar's options is best, and we will return to that particular worry in its relevant guise later on. But the details and implications of CA matter because there are two other pressing normative problems for objective consequentialism, especially if physicalism is true, which they allow us to outflank.

First, there is a traditional worry that physicalism implies that we have no options beyond those we actually take. Caesar ordered a rash and ill-considered military maneuver, motivated only by vanity and cruelty. But everything is constituted by the microphysical. If the laws of microphysics are deterministic, then microphysical conditions prior to Caesar's birth plus the laws of nature together implied that he would give that order. And surely even Caesar was not responsible for, could not change, the laws of nature and what happened prior to his birth. So the worry is that really he had no other option, that he could not have done otherwise, and hence objective consequentialism cannot prescribe an alternative. Even if the laws of microphysics are not deterministic, because there are irreducible quantum mechanical transition probabilities, still Caesar couldn't control random transitions of particles in his brain. They were not up to him in the way that alternative options intuitively must be, it may seem.

But this chapter develops a conception of our options that is consistent with physicalism, and yet evades this classic difficulty, that allows that we can do otherwise. It is not a fundamentally new idea. Something resembling CA was favored by Hobbes, Locke, and Hume, as an analysis of free will that is consistent with determinism, and as the basis of moral assessment and responsibility. So the main positive motivation for such a view is familiar: One's options are up to one in a sense that seems intuitively captured by CA, even in its unrefined version. Even if physical law fixes that you would not try to do something, it can still be true that if you had tried to do it, you would have succeeded. But such a traditional view, such a familiar response, is now quite unpopular. My first task here will be to defend the conditional analysis against many standing objections, which will also serve to introduce necessary refinements. We will also need to examine in some detail the plausibility of the resources that CA requires.

This discussion will also point us towards the solution of a second pressing problem for objective consequentialism. Objective consequentialism assesses acts by regards to the value of their consequences. But the value of the consequences of an action can turn on lucky flukes, or unlucky ones. Caesar ordered his brutal, wild military maneuver. But through dumb luck it was militarily successful, and through still more dumb luck had hugely beneficial consequences throughout the future history of the world. Objective consequentialism may seem to require a positive moral evaluation of his rash cruelty. And that may seem a significant objection to objective consequentialism. This problem is further inflamed by physicalism. As the microphysical world rolls forward, the tiny unknown details of microphysics plus deterministic laws, or alternatively the flukes of quantum mechanical probabilistic transitions, may lead to good effects in a way that is wildly accidental and hence intuitively irrelevant to any positive moral assessment of what Caesar did.

We need a way around this problem also. And so the second normatively significant task of this chapter will be to show that the correct conception of our objective options involves objective *ex ante* probabilities but not flukes, in other words that this apparent problem for objective consequentialism depends on a false conception of what our options are. The moderate indeterminacy of options discerned in the last chapter will in this instance surprise us with a helpful implication. It will take some time to properly explain this point, but the short version is that this indeterminacy implies that lucky flukes consequent on Caesar's action should not be understood to be incorporated in his options, to be parts of the normatively relevant consequences of his action, because flukes are not modally stable. By this I mean that if another option had been taken, it is not determinately true that these flukes would have been consequent on his action. This conception of modally stable options is a crucial premise supporting the moral theory of Part II.

All this will require considerable discussion. Along the way, we will also develop certain positive resources—including conceptions of the variety of trying, of accepted reasons, and of group acts—that are crucial positive elements of Part II's moral theory.

As in the last chapter, I will be asking ethicists here to stretch to consider issues that they do not customarily consider. Just as some normative ethicists have no concern for metaethics, so too many ethicists have no concern for action theory, and hence for the nature of those crucial objects of moral assessment. But if I'm right, this is a mistake.

3.1 The Conditional Analysis: First Pass

We begin with a rough initial statement of the particular form of the conditional analysis of ability that I am calling "CA": *Agent P has alternative y at t if and only if there is something such that if P were to try to do it at t, then P would take alternative y at t*. Our hope is that true counterfactual claims like "If Caesar had tried to run at *t*, then Caesar would have run at *t*" specify alternative options for Caesar even if determinism is true.

Our central concern until 3.6 will be standard objections to the conditional analysis, which will require some refinement of CA. This discussion will put us in position to see in 3.6 that determinism presents no real difficulty for the existence of alternative options in action. We will then turn to an exploration of the resources that CA requires, which will allow us to see in 3.10 that flukes are not parts of our relevant options. We start with some relatively minor objections to CA:

Objection One: The conditional analysis of ability deploys counterfactual claims that Chapter 2 showed to be indeterminate in truth.

Reply: While this chapter will characterize options by subjunctive conditionals involving trying, Chapter 2 was less ambitious, and argued for the moderate indeterminacy of options on the grounds that the truth of such conditionals is merely *necessary* for the existence of options. And I put things in this order partly to squelch the possible illusion that one can avoid the indeterminacy of options merely by denying the now unpopular conditional analysis. While CA ensures that there is moderate indeterminacy of individual options, we have already seen that this would be true even if CA were false. So indeterminacy constitutes no special objection to CA, although I have promised to return to its interaction with the moral theory of Part II.

Objection Two is that there are highly contrasting accounts of ability. But this objection can be defused by close attention to the sense of "ability" at issue for us, the sense relevant, for instance, to consequentialist assessment. What one is able to do in this sense shifts as one's opportunities shift. But there is *another* sort of intuitive ability that is exhausted by individual know-how or skill, and contrasted with the opportunities required for the expression of that skill,[1] exhausted by individual capacity contrasted with conditions that mask its expression.[2] Ability in our sense can shift relatively quickly, while that other sort of ability involves a relatively stable state of individuals.[3] So that other sort of ability is not directly relevant to our concerns, not grounds for genuine objection to CA.

3.2 Chisholm and Lehrer

Objection Three is more significant. It is the cluster of traditional counterexamples to the conditional analysis introduced in Chapter 2. Remember Chisholm's general worry.[4] There are alleged to be cases in which (i) if you try to do something, you will succeed, but (ii) you can't do it. These are cases in which you cannot try to do something, but if you (*per impossibile*) did, then you would succeed. Recall Lehrer's example: Caesar is offered a bowl of red candy balls. He doesn't take any because of a pathological aversion to red candy balls, which remind him of innocent blood he has shed. If he tried to take some, he would, but he is unable to bring himself to try. He can't take any, though CA says he can.[5]

I will take a hard line against these cases. Those impressed by Chisholm's worry think it obvious that there are relevant things we cannot try to do. But it is not obvious at all. It is false at least in this classic type of case. Indeed, it is not unreasonable to claim that there is nothing at this moment that is both such that (i) if you tried to do it then you would succeed in doing it (or indeed succeed in doing anything that adds an option to your repertoire),[6] but which (ii) you cannot try to do. But we will come back to very general claims like that in a little bit, and when we do, we will see that there are some recherché exceptions. Still, they do not affect what should be said about the classic cases.

The key point is this: The case of Caesar and the candy is under-described in a way that makes it sound plausible when in fact it isn't.[7] There are three plausible scenarios that can be confused with the in itself implausible Caesar scenario, as well as other realistic scenarios that involve indeterminacies among these three sorts of plausible possibilities.

First, and most likely, Caesar *can* try to take the balls, and if he did try, he would succeed, though perhaps some would excuse him, since it would be unpleasant. The fact that he can try would be evident were he given enough motive to grab the candy, by news that he needs to grab the candy to save his empire from destruction or get a date with Cleopatra. Merely trying is too easy for Caesar to plausibly claim that he can't try in such a case. Trying is cheap. He doesn't even have to try hard.

---

[1] Vihvelin (2000: 141–3).   [2] M. Smith (2003).   [3] Mele (2003a: 450).
[4] Chisholm (1964).   [5] Lehrer (1968).
[6] There is an intentional route to doing nothing.
[7] We return to the relevant kind of plausibility.

There is also a second realistic scenario involving Caesar. Perhaps he is so moved by the resemblance to innocent blood that he cannot keep his hands from shaking, cannot get them to move towards the candy no matter how hard he tries. Perhaps he just can't take the candy. But still he can try.

Third, perhaps it is remotely plausible that there are some such cases in which Caesar is so pathological that he is literally incapable of even trying to grab the candy. But to that degree he is not at that time an agent. Let me come back to this possibility after we consider a second type of counterexample also due to Lehrer, which will put this response in the proper light:

Cleopatra is fast asleep, or in a coma. If she tried to get up, then she would succeed, partly because, on that counterfactual assumption, she would not be asleep or in a coma. But she isn't able to get up. It is true that if she tried, then she would succeed. But she doesn't have that option.

But, I reply, she is not at that moment an agent. She is not acting in any way. CA requires no emendation when applied to agents.[8] The restriction to agents should be no surprise. It might be true that if a rock were to try to speak about quantum mechanics, then it would, since even such an attempt would require fancy linguistic mediation. And the P and t in my original formulation of CA were in fact an agent and a time at which the agent is an agent. So no emendation is required. Still, you may find this reply problematic. Perhaps dreamers act within sleep. I myself doubt this, and also think that if they try in the relevant dream sense, they will not get up in fact. But you may disagree, or think that it sometimes makes literal sense to say that someone in a coma was trying to become conscious. So to evade these worries, we can restrict CA to *conscious* agents. This, our first emendation of CA, will more obviously suffice as a reply to Lehrer's second type of counterexample.

Come back now to Caesar in our third realistic scenario. Caesar sees the candy, and the resemblance to blood throws him into madness. He sits there completely stunned. He is incapable of even trying to grab the candy. Perhaps he isn't conscious, but even if he is conscious, he is not at that moment an agent, and hence not a conscious agent. He is only incapable of trying to grab the candy in the same degenerate sense that he is incapable of trying to do anything.

So that is my general reply to these classic cases: Trying is so easy that at any moment when you try anything, or at least at any moment you are a conscious agent, you are also capable of trying just about anything else, and surely anything that would generate a new option by the mechanism of CA. As I said, we will soon return to some rare exceptions to this unrestricted claim, but they do not affect the classic counterexamples.[9]

---

[8] In a weak sense all entities with psychological states are agents, and in a weaker sense an entity that is at any time an agent in any stricter sense counts also as an agent at other times. Section 3.7 explicates the sense relevant here.

[9] But see Sripada (2010).

Other classic counterexamples to the conditional analysis involve addiction.[10] You are addicted to heroin and in horrible withdrawal, and there it is in front of you. Certainly physical anguish is a powerful motive to reach out. Perhaps if you try not to reach out, then you will be swept along by your anguish anyway. You aren't able to not take the heroin, though you can try not to. Of course, you may not try to resist, and we may excuse you, in part because failure is so predictable. At a higher-order, you may love your love for the heroin, or you may hate it but find the pain overwhelming, or higher-order reflection may have nothing to do with it. But still you can try not to reach out, or you are not at that moment an agent.

This hard line with the classic cases does not imply that the agent is appropriately blamed in such scenarios. It may be that when philosophers are reluctant to grant that people can even try to do certain things and hence reluctant to grant the plausibility of the venerable conditional analysis, they are forgetting this fact. We will return to other cases that suggest this diagnosis in 3.4.

There are natural worries about the form of my replies here: Chisholm had his general formula for counterexamples, and Lehrer might *stipulate* that his own understanding of his cases is the true one. But, I reply, that has no bearing on the real alternatives of real agents, in this or indeed any reasonably similar possible world. It is too unrealistic to be relevant to the project of this book. Perhaps in wildly unfamiliar sorts of possible worlds, there are conditions that allow for actions and alternatives that have a morally relevant nature radically unlike our own. But that doesn't concern us here. There are no *plausible* scenarios—no suitably realistic scenarios—that can underwrite the classic counterexamples to the conditional analysis.

Still, you may object to my restriction of our consideration to plausible scenarios, or wonder what it means. For instance, physicalism is itself not inconsistent with some of these wild scenarios, and while it is highly unlikely that I will win a million dollars in a lottery, and hence that is in some sense implausible and unrealistic, it is also something that a practical ethics should be prepared to deal with. I grant this. But here in reality people have won millions of dollars in lotteries, and there is some small but real chance that I will win the next time I play. There are real choices available to real agents that constitute the reception of such windfalls as real and relevant possibilities for normative evaluation. My talk of Cleopatra and Caesar has been of course mostly fanciful, but the relevantly realistic choice situations we have considered involving them have been open to real humans in real history. Such choices are within the range of human options even in reality. But those are the only sorts of hypothetical possibilities in play in this book. For instance, as will be relevant in Chapter 7, I am not attempting to develop an ethical theory that would succeed if

---

[10] Such cases may be mythological.

human preferences were significantly and generally different than they are in fact.[11] I applaud attempts by ethical theorists to develop something more modally robust. But I think it cannot be done with only realistic physical resources.

3.3 Other Counterexamples

Objection Four: While the classic concrete counterexamples to the conditional analysis do not succeed, perhaps there are other realistic concrete counterexamples that do succeed, including some that flesh out Chisholm's abstract formula in a physically plausible way.

First Case: There are deviant causal chains. Caesar is paralyzed from the waist down, but Cleopatra will move his legs if he tries to square the circle.[12] He lacks the intuitive ability to move his legs, and yet by CA he has an alternative that involves moving his legs. The antecedent and consequent of the relevant conditional seem not properly connected.

But, I reply, the sense of ability in question for us is that relevant to consequential *alternatives*. And what other people like Cleopatra will do is relevant to Caesar's options of this sort, even if he has diminished moral responsibility for features of those alternatives that depend in this way on the actions of others.[13] Even such deviant causal chains are relevant to alternatives. And notice also that there is some action of Caesar's that corresponds to this alternative, if only just his moving his stylus around in the manner of George Berkeley when *he* was trying to square the circle, indeed if only just Caesar's trying to square the circle itself.

CA quantifies specifically over possible actions, things one might try to do. And that itself may be grounds for worry. While I hope to be excused here from serious treatment of the grounds of modal truth,[14] and a substitutional reading of the quantifiers in question is possible,[15] still it may seem that there are possible or even impossible tryings that will generate options according to CA that do not exist in the relevant sense. So we need to focus more closely on that key point, and hence on Chisholm's worry in yet another way.

Hence our Second Case: You can try to square the circle, just like Berkeley. Perhaps you can even try to square the circle thinking it to be impossible, by taking your best bad shot at that outcome. But can you try to do that *knowing* it to be impossible? Reply: I don't know, because I don't know what knowledge requires. But unless such an attempt involves trying to do something else that you can do, and will characteristically think you can do, for instance moving your pencil around in a certain way,

---

[11] Although we must allow for the variation that different social arrangements and choices from among real options would create.

[12] Thanks to Al Mele.   [13] We return to this in Chapter 12.

[14] But see Chapter 2, n30, or Mendola (1997: Part One) and (2008: Chapter 10).

[15] On a substitutional reading, a some-quantification is true only if some instance of it is true.

that problematic possibility does not generate any new option. So it isn't relevant to CA.

Still, it may seem that some conceivable tryings would suffice to give real agents options that they do not have. And so it may seem that Chisholm's general recipe for a counterexample to CA is telling, even if we haven't yet found the right concrete counterexample to exploit it. Perhaps a case in which the antecedent is too close to the consequent will serve:

Third Case: Imagine that an infant cannot count to 10. They can't intuitively try to count to 10 either. And so perhaps it is true that if they were to so try, then they would so count, while it is not true that they have that alternative.[16] So perhaps this is a counterexample to CA.

Reply: This is the toughest case we face, and requires extended discussion. There are a variety of different more specific cases that share this general description, which I will call "baby counting cases." I need to distinguish them, since I will reply to different specific cases in different ways.

First, it might be that some very young infants are not literally agents, and don't really try to do anything. But then my reply regarding Cleopatra in a coma is available.

Second, there are cases in which at least a young child can try to count to 10 and fail, say by skipping a number. But that would provide no counterexample to CA.

Third, sometimes trying to X may entail doing X. Perhaps trying to think of something entails thinking of it, in the sense that in every possible situation where anyone tries to think of something they hence do. And perhaps a baby counting case could meet that entailment condition, say if a purely mental action of counting is in question.[17] If the baby tried to count in that way, then that would entail that it succeeded, just because such an attempt would itself require quite a bit of mental activity.

This case is a real problem, and requires a second emendation to CA: *One has no alternative involving X*[18] *when the only true conditionals with antecedents specifying a trying and consequents involving taking that alternative are (in the language of Chapter 2) Type One conditionals, which have antecedents that entail their consequents, in the somewhat loose sense that in all possible worlds in which their antecedent is true their consequent is also true.* If someone is to have a genuine alternative, that requires some space between the antecedent and consequent of the relevant conditionals. In some baby counting cases, there isn't the necessary space, and this emendation to CA is required to avoid them.

---

[16] Thanks to Randy Clark.

[17] I presume that the baby counting is not a merely mental action, but rather counting out loud. Section 3.7 considers the entailment worry for mental actions.

[18] Alternatives might involve the mere chance of X. So take this to mean there is no alternative that involves the certainty of X.

There is also a fourth class of baby counting cases that are subtly distinct from the third type, and require a more complicated response. But they require background, which itself involves other problematic cases.

First piece of background: There are wild scenarios in which it is true that if one tried to X then one would take alternative X, and in which there is a suitable space between antecedent and consequent, but yet in which intuitively one can't take alternative X. For instance, perhaps there are things that only Martians and not humans can try to do, and so for us to even try to do such things would require Martian mental capacities that we lack, capacities that would in turn give us implausible alternatives. So here is need for another qualification. Elsewhere I have developed an account of the range of contents available to human thought.[19] *The third emendation of CA is that the antecedents of the conditionals that specify options for humans involve tryings with only humanly conceivable contents.*

Second piece of background: Perhaps it seems that some adult humans cannot try to do some things that other adult humans can do, say because they are color blind. And perhaps it seems that if someone who is radically red–green color blind could try to sort socks into red and green, then they would have to be able to do that thing that they cannot in fact do, even though such an attempt would not entail that they would succeed. So this may seem to be a counterexample that evades my emendations. Reply: They can retain their actual colorblindness and yet take their best bad shot at that outcome, their Hail Mary pass, which will in all likelihood fail. And that is all the trying CA requires.

Our fourth type of baby counting case resembles these background cases, but cannot be evaded by any of the fixes I have suggested so far. Perhaps a human baby has the ability to successfully execute certain attempts that only other humans can make, enough capacity to count to 10 given an attempt to so count, but not the ability to try to do such a thing, to make the attempt. So perhaps while the baby's trying to count to 10 would not entail that they succeed, it would entail the possession of whatever extra capacities they would need to succeed (given other capacities that they have in fact). This then would be a case where CA even when amended says that the baby has an alternative that they intuitively lack.

My reply is that such a complex set of conditions is unrealistic. I have already granted that unrealistic counterexamples to CA, such as Lehrer's specific understanding of Caesar-type cases, may be available, but claimed they are irrelevant. Here is another instance of that sort. But the reason for the unreality of this case is different:

Very young infants may not be properly subject to description by our ordinary language of action and intention, and indeed it may be a matter of degree whether such language is appropriate to even slightly older children, but the main basis of my

---

[19] Mendola (1997: Part One). If what humans try to do is so constrained, that does not imply that human alternatives are similarly constrained. Our actions may have consequences we cannot understand.

reply, the main reason for the unreality of this case, is that even human toddlers are normed against ordinary adult humans in the following way: Normal adult humans have a range of capacities to try to do various things, and such abilities to try are extended somewhat by courtesy, though partly on the basis of real physical similarity, to at least most other conscious humans, including normal toddlers when the toddlers are old enough for optimistic but still realistic attempts at teaching them the acts in question. Normal toddlers can be properly said to try to count to 10, though they lack the capacities to pull it off or even to explicitly conceive of such a thing. The capacity to try to count is hence easier for a young child to have than the capacity to succeed in counting if it did try; it requires less physical similarity to normal adult humans. This is why this otherwise problematic fourth variant of the baby counting case is not available in reality. What of an extreme case where it is absurd to try to teach a very young toddler to count? Then, if it is case where the child can be truly said to try to do anything and hence to be an agent, whatever problem is present is a problem with the teacher and not the child, so that whatever rudimentary response to such training the child exhibits counts in them as trying. Such an attempt is almost entirely parasitic in its content on what the over-ambitious teacher is attempting to do.

That's the general idea of my reply, but its full explanation requires mechanism that I have not yet developed and defended. I don't expect you to believe me yet. To see properly what is wrong with the fourth type of baby counting case, to understand fully why it is unrealistic, requires close attention to the varieties of trying. So we will need to return to this issue in the context of our discussion of those positive resources of CA in 3.7. But before I discharge that promissory note, we will first consider other objections.

3.4 Strawson

Objection Five: Much recent work on options is located in the literature on action and free will, and much contemporary discussion of free will rests on the notion of what we can appropriately hold people morally responsible for, in a sense descended from Peter Strawson's "Freedom and Resentment."[20] In this sense, someone is morally responsible for something or did it freely only if it is appropriate to adopt "reactive attitudes" towards that individual for that outcome or act, attitudes like blame, gratitude, resentment, and moral indignation. And it may be inappropriate on various grounds to blame someone for things they did but yet had an alternative to avoid in my sense. Having an alternative in my sense to what one does is not sufficient for moral responsibility for what one does, nor perhaps for having relevant

---

[20] P. Strawson (1962); Fischer (1986); Wallace (1994); Fischer and Ravizza (1998); Kane (2002).

freedom or morally relevant options. And so CA may seem objectionable. It may seem to grant us too many options.

There are various specific grounds for this worry. First, we might not be inclined to blame someone for doing something very bad if we think that the fact that they tried to do that bad thing is easily predictable on the basis of horrendous treatment by their parents when they were very young. That history may seem an excuse that would make such negative moral sentiments inappropriate, even though it is true that if they had tried to do otherwise, which would have been surprising given their unfortunate history, then they would have done otherwise. They shouldn't be blamed, and lacked intuitive freedom, even though they had an alternative in my sense.[21]

Second, consider the excuses that Aristotle suggests in the *Nicomachean Ethics*.[22] One can do something in ignorance, back over a child's toy inadvertently. One was able not to back over the toy in my sense, but perhaps one shouldn't be blamed for ignorantly doing so. Ignorance of certain sorts mitigates blameworthiness, but it doesn't eliminate the fact that there are alternatives in my sense.[23] And consider his discussion of threats: "Suppose, for instance, a tyrant tells you to do something shameful, when he has control over your parents and children, and if you do it, they will live, but if not, they will die."[24] Presume that you do it. Aristotle seems right. You shouldn't be blamed. Maybe your judgment is so obviously appropriate under the circumstances that moral praise is in order. But even if the shameful act is wrong, we will not and should not blame you for doing it. And yet you had an alternative in my sense.

Reply: I have no complaint about these various sorts of mercy, only about their relevance to our topic. The crucial point is that the notion of responsibility that is most relevant for us, on which ethicists and indeed action theorists should focus *first*, is not the notion of something for which reactive attitudes are appropriate. It rather reflects a basic metaphysical sense of what one is free or able to do, which can help ground normative claims about the propriety of punishment or reactive attitudes, but which isn't itself a richly normative notion like that of the grounds for appropriate moral responsibility in the Strawsonian sense. I make no claim that having

---

[21] Some think that less horrible histories are relevant excuses, that it is necessary for moral responsibility that autonomy isn't undercut by advertising or indoctrination. See Mele (1995: 144–76). But I am skeptical.

[22] Aristotle, *Nicomachean Ethics* III 1, 1109b30–1111b5.

[23] Ignorance may seem to affect what one is able to do in my sense. See Howard-Snyder (1997 and 1999) and Carlson (1999). I might not know what buttons to push to turn on the machine. And in some sense I am capable right now of typing the magic English words that will one day convince all the rational to be good, though any attempt in my current ignorance would be a wild stab that will not succeed, and that could only succeed by dumb luck. There is some temptation to say I cannot type the magic words, even if I try. But on the other hand I just might, through dumb luck. And if I do it, then I surely could have done it. And there is a set of finger movements I could try to make, a sequence of keys I could intentionally depress, that would deliver the magic words. On balance, such cases suggest merely that there is another kind of ignorance that is an excuse, not that I literally am incapable in any relevant sense of typing the magic words. Similar things seem true of the mysterious machine.

[24] Aristotle, *Nicomachean Ethics* III 1, 1110a6–9, in Irwin and Fine (1995: 376–7).

an alternative in my sense to what one does is a *sufficient* condition for moral responsibility.

Indeed, the very fact that being abused by your parents may be an excuse for killing them suggests that there must be two senses of what someone is responsible for at issue; the very notion of an excused action requires that. Caesarion is, we might say, metaphysically responsible for some death; it is a murder. Yet he should not be blamed for it, not held in that sense morally responsible, because he has an excuse due to his horrendous upbringing. Our reactive attitudes are not a sure guide to what someone is responsible for in this metaphysical sense, which I will call "agency responsibility." This notion is closely related to alternative options. P assumes at t agency responsibility for something x that occurs within the alternative they take at t if and only if there is also some other alternative for P at t that does not contain x.[25]

Agency responsibility is not mere causal responsibility. I may be causally responsible for someone's death if while asleep I accidentally roll out of a window and crush them, or if someone picks me up while I am sleeping and throws me out the window to similar effect.[26] Yet I lack agency responsibility for the death. It doesn't result from action on my part. But, on the other hand, agency responsibility certainly incorporates more than merely things one does intentionally. Sometimes when I *do* something *un*intentionally, some of the features of the alternative that I take are unknown to me in a way that makes those features of the action unintentional. And indeed alternatives may include consequences that don't count as part of actions at all. And maybe even some things that I know I'm doing, for instance tapping my foot nervously in a certain way, are unintentional despite the fact that I know about them and they are in some sense up to me and hence voluntary. I could try not to tap, and if I did I would succeed. But despite all this, probably it is true that only by doing something intentionally (at least intentionally refraining from other intentional action) that I *do* anything even unintentionally, or take any alternative.

There are various reasons why we should begin with a modest metaphysical notion like agency responsibility, and then work by qualification towards a rich Strawsonian notion of what we are morally responsible for. First, Strawsonian moral responsibility is too normatively rich for some normative jobs. One is consequential assessment. Second, there may be arguments that show that attitudes of blame or other familiar reactive attitudes are *always* inappropriate, which yet leave room for moral assessment. Strawson himself suggested that reactive attitudes will disappear if we take a suitably objective view of things.[27] One hopes that he didn't think that all ethical judgment should also then disappear, after suitably objective contemplation of Nero and Caligula. Third, since it is a goal of ethical theory to provide a rationale for our normative judgments, even our judgments about appropriate sorts of blame and

---

[25] Ordinarily x will occur after t.
[26] If my going asleep was an action, these claims require a certain way of individuating alternatives.
[27] P. Strawson (1962).

praise, it is important that the legitimacy of many such judgments plausibly rests on non-normative facts that include facts about alternatives and agency responsibility. If actions for which individuals are morally responsible are those for which they are appropriately blamed, that suggests that there is a range of options in blame that people have, and it also seems futile to blame people in general for kinds of acts to which they generally have no alternatives. But the fourth and main reason it is important to begin with agency responsibility is the existence of excuses. Properly excused action, properly blameless wrong action, is yet characteristically voluntary, and even intentional. One characteristically could have done otherwise. It just muddies the waters to claim that I cannot refrain from a shameful act motivated by fear or loathing in the same basic metaphysical sense that I cannot fly around the moon by flapping my arms.

3.5 Frankfurt's Case

Objection Six is a famous counterexample due to Harry Frankfurt. The conditional analysis of ability is neglected in most contemporary discussions of alternatives largely because of this case. This literature presumes that any relevant freedom of choice is a metaphysical condition that is at least *necessary* for moral responsibility. And Frankfurt's case it taken to show that things like agency responsibility, and the conditions articulated by CA that it reflects, are not even strictly necessary for moral responsibility.

My reply to this objection will be to develop a way in which moral responsibility does depend on agency responsibility, and hence on CA. This will undercut the significance of Frankfurt's case. I think it is important to kill this case, which has led us to ignore the conditional analysis of ability and hence into normatively significant error.

But it will further our discussion of the case to begin with some background. Note that there are two immediate though somewhat finicky reasons to worry, even independent of Frankfurt's case, that agency responsibility is not strictly necessary for moral responsibility. First, although the point is debatable and we will return to it, the tryings deployed by CA at least sometimes suffice in themselves for intentional action. This is enough to show that agency responsibility is not strictly necessary for moral responsibility, since trying is independent of agency responsibility, and one may be morally responsible for trying something.

Second, there can be a difference between your actual options and your conception of your options, and the second rather than the first seems in some ways more important to moral responsibility. You may think that you have an alternative that you lack, or lack an alternative that you think you have. You may think that various conditional claims like those deployed in CA are true, when in fact they are not true. There is agency responsibility, and there is also an agent's conception of their options, which underlies what we might call "self-apparent agency responsibility."

You have self-apparent agency responsibility for something that you know that you do at t if and only if you think at t that you have some other alternative at t that does not contain that thing. Given this distinction between agency responsibility and self-apparent agency responsibility, it is not unreasonable to object that we have been focusing on the wrong member of the pair as a plausible necessary condition for moral responsibility and intentional action. Mark Antony may think that there is a way out of some moral quandary when there isn't. And if out of temptation he takes what he assumes to be an avoidably awful option, when in fact, contrary to what he thinks, there is no better alternative available, then he may well have moral responsibility for the awful outcome nonetheless, and pursue it intentionally, even though he has no agency responsibility for that outcome. So there is moral responsibility without agency responsibility. But Antony does have self-apparent agency responsibility for the awful outcome.[28]

Still, neither of these two finicky reasons—that trying alone can suffice for intentional action and that self-apparent agency responsibility is what is truly necessary for moral responsibility and intentional action—is enough to show that agency responsibility is not crucial to moral responsibility. If sometimes one can try to X even if one has no agency responsibility for X, that doesn't show that one can try to X when one lacks agency responsibility for everything. And there is a sense in which the notion of self-apparent agency responsibility is crucially dependent on the notion of agency responsibility. So if moral responsibility requires intentional action and it in turn requires self-apparent agency responsibility, then there is also a sense in which agency responsibility is basic to moral responsibility, even though agency responsibility is not strictly necessary for moral responsibility.

But that was just a warm-up. It is in fact the viability of another sort of convoluted dependence of moral responsibility on agency responsibility that I will defend here, a dependence that is more suited to consequentialist ethicists like me who don't worry too much about intentions or people's ignorance about their options, although it will still suffice to undercut the significance of our two initial finicky worries.[29] This relatively convoluted dependence will be my response to Frankfurt's case. Because of Frankfurt's case, it has come to seem sometimes appropriate to blame someone in the Strawsonian sense for something that they do even when they lack an alternative to doing that thing. So having an alternative in my sense seems unnecessary for moral responsibility or relevant freedom. And so the conditional analysis of ability has fallen out of consideration. It is only the last point, as we will see, that is a mistake, in a way that the convoluted dependence in question will help reveal.

---

[28] While objective consequentialists insist on Antony's basic responsibility for actual outcomes, regardless of how he conceives his options, still agency responsibility for x is not necessary for intentionally or voluntarily doing x. Yet it may still seem plausible that self-apparent agency responsibility is necessary for those things, and hence for moral responsibility.

[29] Because it allows for trying to do x when one has no alternative to x, and because it is a way in which moral responsibility depends on agency responsibility even though we can be mistaken about our options.

But enough background. Consider Frankfurt's case:[30] Black wants Jones to do something. And Black is resolved to do nothing unless it becomes clear that Jones will not do that thing of his own volition. Still, if that becomes clear, then Black is prepared to assure that Jones will do that thing, by suitable manipulation of Jones' brain. Jones does it of his own volition, and hence is intuitively responsible, but he could not have done otherwise. In his presentation of the case, Frankfurt mentions other forms of possible manipulation besides brain manipulation: terrible threats, hypnosis, and potions. But I will focus on the brain manipulation variant, as has become standard in the literature based on the case, because, as we saw in 3.4, threats don't intuitively remove alternatives, and because hypnosis and potions undercut intuitive agency.

I am going to resist the widespread judgment that Frankfurt's case is important. I am going to question the deep significance of that case for the issues that centrally concern us, issues that should also concern the literatures on free will. And the first part of my strategy to that end will be to note that Frankfurt's case is an unacknowledged modification of an earlier and somewhat different case due to John Locke. Locke, you will recall, favored the conditional analysis, which is one reason it is instructive to begin with his case:

[S]uppose a Man be carried, whilst fast asleep, into a Room, where is a Person he longs to see and speak with; and be there locked fast in, beyond his Power to get out: he awakes, and is glad to find himself in so desirable Company, which he stays willingly in, *i.e.* preferrs his stay to going away. I ask, Is not this stay voluntary? I think, no Body will doubt it: and yet being locked fast in, 'tis evident he is not at liberty not to stay, he has not freedom to be gone.[31]

Locke favors something like CA, and he plausibly does not take his case to show that the ability to do what you will is not constitutive of ability, freedom, or liberty, but rather that the notion of what is voluntary, which is also plausibly relevant to moral assessment, is somewhat distinct. As he immediately concludes from his case, with original italics: "*Liberty is not an* Idea *belonging to Volition*, or preferring; but to the Person having the Power of doing, or forbearing to do, according as the Mind shall chuse or direct."[32] The man stays in the room of his own volition, though he had no ability or liberty to leave.[33]

Locke, to my mind, is almost exactly right about his case. We should not think that ability is all that is relevant to proper reactive assessment, to praise or blame. Perhaps we may properly honor the man in Locke's case for liking such desirable company and for not even trying to leave, even though he had no ability to leave.

But still, this reaction may seem to miss the relevant point. It may reasonably be insisted that even Locke's case shows that agency responsibility is not a necessary

---

[30] Frankfurt (1969).   [31] J. Locke, II, XXI, 10 (1975: 238).   [32] J. Locke (1975: 238).
[33] Gideon Yaffe suggests that in II, XXI, 11, Locke presents a case even more similar to Frankfurt's in some ways: a paralyzed person who prefers to sit still. But that presumably involves self-knowledge of the paralysis, which is one disanalogy.

condition for moral responsibility. The man does not have an alternative in which he leaves the room, but, it may seem, he is morally responsible for staying in the room, since he stays of his own volition.

This also seems correct. But I have already admitted that agency responsibility is not necessary for moral responsibility in the Strawsonian sense. And notice that Locke's case apparently encompasses both the finicky considerations that I cited as grounds for this conclusion. Locke's man apparently does not realize that he is locked in, and he intentionally remains. Frankfurt's case invokes these same general considerations also.

Yet the key point about Locke's case is this: All it can be plausibly thought to show is that agency responsibility for a particular outcome is not a necessary condition for moral responsibility for that particular outcome. Locke's man has lots of options in my sense, and indeed some things that are up to him would have revealed a thwarted attempt to leave, and it may be that it is just because he fails to make that attempt that we hold him morally responsible for staying. He had some alternatives in my sense to just sitting there, and hence agency responsibility for sitting there. And so agency responsibility in general might still be a necessary condition for moral responsibility in general. Moral responsibility for X might still require agency responsibility for *something*, even if we restrict ourselves to consideration of an agent at a single time.

Though this involves some extension of Locke's case, perhaps it will be claimed that the man wouldn't have even tried to leave had he known that the doors were locked. But still, even under that presumption, there are lots of things he could do at will in the room, things that turn on his variously trying. Certainly he could express remorse about being locked in the room. And so his general possession of agency responsibility seems still to be a necessary condition for moral responsibility of the specific sort in question.

However, perhaps Frankfurt's derivative though less realistic case can show something more. It *is* less realistic, at least in the brain-manipulation version that has, on the good grounds already noted, become dominant in the literature. Brain manipulation of this sort, apparently involving the manipulation of neurons into states constituting intentions, is mere science fiction, even if it is consistent with physicalism. We have no good reason to presume that there ever will be any real social or individual options that will include this technology, especially because anything we can do now with electrodes in the brain undercuts agency even more intuitively than hypnosis. Nevertheless, let me be concessive, and grant the relevance of Frankfurt's unrealistic case. Let me waive the significance of its unreality. Still, we have already seen that even one of the originators of the conditional analysis himself suggests that moral responsibility for X does not always requires agency responsibility for X. What more might Frankfurt's more unrealistic case show? What is the point of the extra unreality?

Perhaps we are to see that moral responsibility and agency responsibility are more divorced in Frankfurt's case than in Locke's, because there is nothing that Jones could actually try to do that would reveal that he decided against doing what Black will force him to do.[34] But there is more than a little tension in this description of the case.[35] And notice that even if we grant such a description, agency responsibility in general might still be a necessary condition for moral responsibility in general. Moral responsibility for anything might still require agency responsibility for something, even at the time in question.

So we must further augment Frankfurt's already unrealistic case for it to reveal something relevantly more than Locke's. Black leaves Jones free in certain ways. We must presume that all the things Jones does are bound around by mechanisms of the sort that Black is contemplating, at least if we are to use such an augmented case as grounds for thinking that agency responsibility in general is not a necessary condition for moral responsibility in general.[36]

But now there is a problem. We should hesitate to make grand conclusions on the basis of such a wild case. It is far from clear that Jones bound around by the awful mechanism in the augmented Frankfurt case is an agent at all at that time. The notion of an agent that can do nothing but what it actually does is not obviously a coherent notion. Even if we grant that the fanciful technology Frankfurt requires will someday become available in our physical world, this particular application of that technology might simply eliminate the agency of one person from the world.

I think that Frankfurt's unrealistic case and even this extreme augmentation do no relevant extra work. I think that even Locke showed us that moral responsibility for X does not require agency responsibility for X. And I think we have no real reason from Frankfurt to doubt that agency responsibility in general is a necessary condition for moral responsibility in general, no reason to doubt that moral responsibility for X requires agency responsibility for something, and so no reason to abandon the conditional analysis. The extremely augmented case is too wild. Still, there is another more certain but more convoluted dependence of moral responsibility on agency responsibility that I will defend with greater assurance, which is related to other grounds for worries about the significance of Frankfurt's case, at least to the degree that it is augmented into an attempted advance on Locke's.

Something doesn't have to be a strictly necessary condition for something else to be very central to that second thing. John Mackie introduced "inus conditions," insufficient but necessary parts of unnecessary but sufficient conditions.[37] Let me vary the figure. An "inqcus" (pronounced INKUS) condition for something B is an Insufficient but Necessary part of the strictly Unnecessary but still Quite Common condition in our world that is Sufficient for B.

---

[34] This feature of Frankfurt's case is shared by Locke's paralytic case.

[35] On this tension and other problems with Frankfurt's case, see Fischer (1994: 131–59, 2002); Widerker (1995); Kane (1996); McKenna (1997); Mele and Robb (1998); Otsuka (1998); Pereboom (2000).

[36] Mele (1995: 141).   [37] Mackie (1965).

Now for some claims: I am confident that agency responsibility in general is at least an inqcus condition for moral responsibility in general. I am also reasonably certain that it is more than that, what we might call a universal inqcus condition: Everyone in the actual world who is morally responsible for something at some time has agency responsibility for something at that time. Indeed, I think that moral responsibility crucially depends on agency responsibility in a way I will shortly explain, which is the basis for my first two claims. Because of this, I even think that agency responsibility is a universal inqcus condition for moral responsibility in every possible world, or at least in every possible world that is remotely similar to reality. And so the conditional analysis of ability, on which agency responsibility rests, is still relevant and important.

But, it may be rejoined, if Frankfurt has succeeded in constructing a case that at least when augmented reveals that agency responsibility for someone at a time is not strictly necessary for their moral responsibility at that time, then there might be a merely possible world in which all or most cases of moral responsibility were like that too. There might be a possible world in which agency responsibility is quite uncommon and very far from a universal inqcus condition for moral responsibility. And while very wild possibilities are not relevant to my attempt in this book to build an ethics suitable for our actual physical world, perhaps someday the technology to create such conditions will even become available in our physical world, and then it will be at least within our social options to bind everyone around with these terrible mechanisms.

But, I reply, if the kind of scenario present in the already augmented Frankfurt case were globalized, so that all or even most of our actions were always bound round by machines playing the role of Black and his instruments in Frankfurt's case, that would undercut the point and intuitive probity of attitudes of blame and moral responsibility in such a world, and even any intuitive sense that there is agency in such world. This reveals the central way in which moral responsibility for action depends on agency responsibility, and hence on the conditional analysis. There would be no practical point, and hence no legitimate ethical point, to claims of moral responsibility in a world without very common agency responsibility. There would indeed not be agency or action, at least of any familiar sort, in such a world. It is on such grounds that I also think that even Frankfurt's original case can at best be an isolated case, which counts as a case of moral responsibility because it is similar to the dominant cases of moral responsibility, in which agency responsibility is more closely involved. In fact, I think that even cases like Locke's can't be too common. And I doubt on these grounds that even the first augmented Frankfurt case, involving a single person at a time, is coherent.

But of course one is able to do what one does. And maybe we could see our way to ascriptions of agency even in a world where Frankfurt-style conditions were globalized, although I don't see the point. And if Frankfurt wants to hold individuals sometimes morally responsible for what they do in such a world, even though no one could ever do otherwise than they do, even though it would have no practical significance at all beyond the punishment and blame he would thus inflict, my objections to that are mostly practical and moral rather than metaphysical. But it is important also to remember this: There are those in our tradition who think that it is appropriate for all of us to be held morally responsible by God because of inherited original sin for what Adam and Eve did. I also have practical and moral objections to that claim. But if such claims are admissible in philosophy, which they seem to be, then it cannot be uncontroversial that *any* metaphysical condition of free will of the agent, even of the reasonable sort now under consideration,[38] is strictly necessary for moral responsibility.

Frankfurt's case is too unrealistic and quirky to bear the weight that it is granted in recent discussions of free will. And its more realistic classical ancestor—Locke's case—is obviously irrelevant to the more radical conclusions drawn on its basis. And anyway Frankfurt's case merely reveals that some would be inclined to hold those without agency responsibility morally responsible, which because of our dark theological history we've known for a long time. Still, while Frankfurt's case does not suffice to show that CA does not provide the proper basis for consequentialist and related sorts of ethical assessment, a consideration of the case has helped us understand why and in what way CA provides the proper ultimate basis for such assessment, despite the fact that having an alternative in my sense is not strictly necessary for moral responsibility.

3.6 Libertarian Objections

Objection Seven: Libertarian conceptions of free will specify that some radical metaphysical freedom from causal determination by the past is a necessary condition for genuine agency.[39] But the truth of the conditional claims invoked by CA does not require this fancy libertarian freedom. So it may seem that CA does not require fancy enough conditions for genuine options, for genuine agency responsibility.

Reply: While physicalism does not entail the truth of determinism, the kinds of indeterminism suggested by our physics are no more hospitable to libertarian conceptions of free will than is determinism.[40] And by defending CA, I have also defended a natural compatibilism of even determinism and free will, like that embraced by the classical proponents of the conditional analysis. I have undercut the standard grounds for libertarianism. Let me explain this point.

---

[38] Some Kantians claim that we each make a noumenal choice of the entire history of the world from outside of time, including what our ancestors did, and that we all make relevantly similar depraved choices. But we are ignoring such fantasies, and such a condition could not be an uncontroversial necessary condition for moral responsibility.

[39] Clark (2003).   [40] See Chapter 2.

One classical argument against the compatibility of free will and determinism is this:

(P1) If determinism is true, then all our actions are causally determined by events prior to our births.

(P2) If an action A is causally determined by events prior to its agent's birth, then the agent could not have acted otherwise.

Hence if determinism is true, the agent of A could not have acted otherwise.

But CA reveals why P2 is false. Determinism is consistent with the conditions required for the truth of the relevant subjunctive conditionals. And so determinism is consistent with the conditions required for agency responsibility and the possession of options. It is consistent with the conditions required for it to be true that the agent of the act could have acted otherwise in the relevant sense, although we did see in Chapter 2 that determinism may generate some indeterminacy regarding our options, and hence about what we have agency responsibility for.

Intuitive worries about the compatibility of free will and determinism are in contemporary discussions often funneled through the more specific Consequence Argument of David Wiggins, Peter van Inwagen, and Carl Ginet, which is descended from an argument of Diodorus.[41] So let's consider that specific form of libertarian motivation also.

Let L be the conjunction of the laws of nature. Let P be some proposition that describes some past state of the world. And let A be some true proposition stating that you perform some act that is determined by the laws of nature and the truth of P. Then the argument goes like this:

(P1) Necessarily, if P and L, then A.
(P2) You have no choice about P.
(P3) You have no choice about L.
Hence you have no choice about A.

Why does this argument fail? For this reason: Even its partisan Peter van Inwagen admits that the general inference rules that would underwrite this argument are subject to a counterexample due to Thomas McKay and David Johnson:[42] Consider a coin not tossed yesterday. It seems that you have no choice about the fact that the coin did not land heads yesterday, nor about the fact that the coin did not land tails yesterday, which I will call the two facts. Even if you had tossed the coin, you would not have had those particular choices. But you had a choice about whether the proposition is true that the coin did not land heads yesterday and the coin did not land tails yesterday, because after all you could have tossed the coin. But that proposition follows from the conjunction of the two facts. Still, van Inwagen claims

---

[41] van Inwagen (1983: 93–104); Ginet (1990: 90–123). Harry Ide reports this misconstrues Diodorus.
[42] van Inwagen (2002: 160–1).

that we have no reason to doubt the use of these inference rules in the Consequence Argument in particular. However, if CA is correct, we do have such a reason. If CA is correct, the truth of all the premises of the Consequence Argument is consistent with the falsehood of its conclusion. You may have options to do A or to refrain even when you have no options to avoid the P or L that necessitate A. The principles of inference in question are illegitimate in the application that matters.

Libertarianism is not properly motivated. But another way to put this point is that even determinism does not undercut the existence of alternative options. By defending CA, we have answered the first objection to objective consequentialism with which this chapter began.

3.7 Trying

We turn now from an organizing focus on objections to CA to a focus on the positive resources it requires. There are three: subjunctive conditionals, trying, and alternatives. These resources have features that will matter to us in other ways throughout the book. And our discussion of these resources will allow us, in 3.10, to answer the second objection to objective consequentialism that we face. Unfortunately, this discussion will also uncover some new difficulties for CA to which we must attend.

Begin with trying. Trying matters in more than one way to the moral theory of Part II. Trying is the basis of the type of good isolated by that theory, and also of the group acts it crucially deploys. And it is immediately crucial to us not only because of its presence in the antecedents of our target counterfactuals, but also in a second way. To evade Lehrer's counterexamples, I tied the existence of options to prior facts about the existence of agents,[43] and that involves another role for trying. Roughly speaking, agents are all and only those things that try. Let me first explain this point and add necessary qualifications:

Sometimes we say "the car is trying to start." But we don't literally mean it. When we literally mean there is trying, we imply there is an agent. And at nearly every moment you are awake, you try to do something, if only think about something. Still, there may be exceptions. You lie passively in the sun, not thinking of anything in an actively directed way. Your mind drifts. But even then you have a special and immediate capacity to try things, a latency of active trying I will call "idling." So there are agents when and only when there are either active tryings or idlings. And probably our folk word "trying" is broad enough to apply even to idling in some cases: In ordinary English, you might complain, if interrupted while daydreaming, that you were trying to rest, that you were trying not to do anything. You were resting voluntarily, even if you lacked the active intention to rest. In that case, you try without actively trying. Perhaps, it may be objected, such a treatment also applies

---

[43] Indeed to *conscious* agents, though without certainty the extra constraint is necessary. That notion would take us far afield, but for possible links with trying, see O'Shaughnessy (2000).

when I have claimed that at least conscious agency is absent, and so if it proves anything, it proves too much. Perhaps Cleopatra will complain, when somebody makes a noise and wakes her up, that she was trying to sleep. But, I reply, she doesn't literally mean, in ordinary cases, that she was, at the moment she was sleeping, trying to sleep. She means rather that as she went to sleep, she had a plan to sleep for a while, that she fell asleep intentionally or at least voluntarily. There are also other relevant complications: You nervously tap your foot. You could stop yourself from tapping. You are voluntarily tapping, and might be held morally responsible for it. But you aren't intentionally tapping your foot. Then it seems you aren't trying to tap your foot. So sometimes something active and indeed voluntary happens even when you are idling and also not trying.[44] Analogously, sometimes when you are awake but doing nothing, it doesn't seem true to say that you were trying to do nothing. Indeed, there are three cases: Sometimes you are actively trying to lie still. Sometimes your resting seems intentional, and then you are trying to rest even when you are merely idling. But in some cases it seems merely voluntary. While sometimes you do nothing on purpose, sometimes you just do nothing. Your mind drifts in all these cases, but it drifts on a shorter tether when you rest intentionally, and on a very short leash when you actively try to rest. So, to sum up, I don't claim that idling can always be said to involve the presence of trying, and certainly not active trying. But even in cases of idling that involve no trying at all, there is a certain pregnant absence of active trying. Agency involves either trying or idling. In light of these complications, it is worth saying that I don't think that idling without trying, or even without active trying, introduces antecedents for true conditionals defining new options, options otherwise unavailable.[45] You can actively try to rest or do nothing, even if sometimes you do those things without trying. In general, when you can try to do something, you can actively try to do it. So we can concentrate here on active trying, even if the antecedents of counterfactuals defining options are not restricted to active trying.

We have seen now that trying plays two important immediate roles for us, in constituting agency and in the counterfactuals specifying options. So CA requires that trying be a very common state. But there is a traditional objection to any such view. Wittgenstein claimed that "When I raise my arm, I do not usually *try* to raise it."[46] Perhaps it only makes sense to say that I try to raise my arm when I fail, or at least when it is difficult.

But still, Brian O'Shaughnessy and Jennifer Hornsby plausibly answered that even when an agent easily succeeds, an onlooker can have a doubt about that success that makes speech of the agent's trying appropriate.[47] The onlooker can know that the agent tried without knowing that the agent succeeded. And Paul Grice convinced

---

[44] On the other hand, perhaps such cases sometimes involve the Ginet-like volitions we soon discuss.
[45] This presumes that alternatives are not individuated by descriptions like "without trying."
[46] Wittgenstein (1968: 161).   [47] O'Shaughnessy (1974); Hornsby (1980).

most of us that it sometimes doesn't make sense to say what is true, in particular when it isn't sufficiently informative and hence can be misleading, like the claim that someone tried when they actually succeeded.[48] And Severin Schroeder plausibly suggests that when someone succeeds it does generally at least make sense to say that it was because they tried hard.[49] So my reply to the traditional objection is merely that O'Shaughnessy, Hornsby, and Grice won this dispute.

Nevertheless, there is an important way in which my proposal is more in the spirit of Wittgenstein than of Hornsby and O'Shaughnessy, and hence has some of the argumentative advantages of ecumenism. Those who defend the omnipresence of trying characteristically treat trying as a single more or less natural mental state. This is a strong and doubtful claim. But I have already noted that at least two different states can count as trying to do some things, active trying and some sorts of idling, and there are also many other sorts of relevant diversity. Also, in some physical conditions it is a rather soft fact, only marginally determinate, that one is trying to do certain things. I don't think that trying is even approximately a natural kind.

To properly understand the trying that is the first key resource of CA, and which is also a crucial resource for Part II, we will need to attend to its full diversity. And there are three important forms of diversity that we need to discuss. First, there is temporal diversity. Consideration of this will help us discern a key analytical focus for CA. Second, there are diversities of content, including those relevant to the difference between bodily and mental acts. These will require further emendation of CA. Third, there is diversity between the kinds of trying available to squirrels and humans. Consideration of this will introduce the notion of accepting a reason, which will play crucial roles in Part II.

3.7.1 Temporality and trying

The first sort of diversity of trying (beyond that involved in idling) concerns time. Is trying something that can be done in a reasonably brief moment, or does it take a while to try to do certain things?

Both, I think. CA specifies a particular time for a trying and an alternative, but it doesn't specify that these times are moment-like. There plausibly are active tryings that I will call "immediate tryings," which can be undertaken in something like the briefest period in which it is possible for an individual to actively try to do anything. And they can be deployed in a set of conditionals defining a similarly immediate set of options. But sometimes when we say someone is trying to do certain things, it is on the basis of an overall judgment rooted at least partly in the presence (or presumed presence) of a series of such immediate tryings, or executive dispositions to a series of immediate tryings. In such a case, there is in fact a particular temporal sequence of sets of immediate options that will unfold for the agent over time and specify an ever

---

[48] Grice (1989).
[49] S. Schroeder (2001). His claim that someone may try hard without trying seems less plausible.

narrowing set of routes into the future of the world, but we might consider counterfactual temporal chains of such immediate options, spreading out within each possible immediate option that might be taken.

These complexities may introduce what Chapter 2 called a precision problem, and hence generate some indeterminacy in our options. That is partly because executive dispositions at a time that underwrite these various routes may be somewhat indeterminate. But it is also partly because it may be unclear what temporal scale is properly in question, by which I mean that perhaps immediate tryings and options don't always have the kind of basic metaphysical role just suggested. And even when they do, new indeterminacies may be introduced just because of the indeterminacy of iterated conditional claims that would be relevant to various counterfactual temporal chains of immediate options.

Despite these complexities, I will focus on immediate tryings, and hence chains of them and executive dispositions for such chains, as at least one kind of proper analytical basis for understanding our options. Consider this, if you wish, a refinement of CA, although I won't build it explicitly into that analysis.

3.7.2 Content diversity of trying

Another important type of diversity of trying is diversity in its content. There are many relevant complexities. (a) For instance, while the immediate options of an agent are its options at a quite specific time; they need not be options that involve alternatives that can be achieved at that time,[50] nor need it be the case that what one is trying to do at a specific moment is something that can be achieved in that moment. (b) And if trying is at least characteristically present when we intentionally do things, it is natural to conclude that when we are intentionally doing X under a specific description then we are also trying do that thing under that same description. When you intentionally hole the putt, it is natural to conclude that you tried to hole the putt. But we know from our discussion of Austin's example in Chapter 2 that we need sometimes to aim less directly at what we want to achieve. Maybe we can hole a putt only if we concentrate on something else. (c) And indeed, as we will shortly see, there is another sort of content that it is plausible that the most analytically central tryings have.

I will focus here specifically on two important kinds of content complexity, involved respectively in bodily action and mental action. This will allow us to understand point (c), which is exploited in Part II, and will also introduce the need for further refinement of CA.

---

[50] In Chapter 2, I suggested that the alternatives include only activity by the agent at the time in question, so as to focus on a particular sort of indeterminacy, but allowed that later external conditions might constrain alternatives. These could include future immediate tryings.

3.7.2.1 BODILY ACTION

Many things that we intentionally do involve things out in the world that we can get at only through bodily activity. For world-directed action, a certain sort of body activity seems fundamental in at least one sense.

Octavian wants to get the chicken in the refrigerator. That is all he is explicitly thinking about doing as he goes to the kitchen. But there are a variety of ways he could try to get into the refrigerator. He might go through the door with his ax, or open the door with one limb or another. And each of those ways of performing the worldly action that he is focused on will involve a different sequence of body movements. Perhaps if he fails in his attempt to get the chicken, either because it is not in the refrigerator or because he can't get the door open, it will only be if he succeeds in some other action, say pulling at the door. And so perhaps his trying to get the chicken is in that case his pulling at the door.[51] Maybe his pulling the door is in turn his clasping his hand and pulling with his arm.[52] But even if it isn't, it depends on that bodily activity. If we focus on actions that involve body movements like these, it is quite natural to presume that they all involve certain specific intentions to move one's body or limbs or fingers or eyes or tongue in one way or another and with different degrees of force.

Carl Ginet is one proponent of the view that things like tryings are generally present in bodily activity, but he calls them "volitions," and thinks that they have contents like these.[53] I myself think that, when you are trying to do something out in the world, you are characteristically also engaging in a series of Ginet-style tryings, and that a focus on such fundamental sorts of trying has the same sort of analytical virtue as a focus on temporally immediate tryings. To everything that you can try to do at a moment out in the world there corresponds at least one complex type of fundamental trying of this sort. I will presume that we should consider such contents the contents of the most analytically central immediate tryings in most ordinary cases of bodily activity.

They are intuitive tryings, at least in common cases and presuming commonsense understandings of their contents. It makes sense to say in English that Octavian is trying to pull the door open with his arm and even to close his hand around the handle when he is explicitly focused only on the chicken in the refrigerator. Still, we may not be very aware of how we are moving our bodies to achieve our goals in these ways. We speak by moving our tongues, but it isn't plausible to claim that most of us have very explicit intentions to move our tongues in necessary ways as we speak. The tryings in question would sometimes plausibly need to be unconscious.

---

[51] Jones (1983).

[52] We will return to act-individuation. It is to avoid these issues for now that I discuss bodily activity rather than bodily action.

[53] Ginet (1990: 23–44).

People differ in their bodily capacities. And some may object to CA on the grounds that these fundamental bodily tryings depend on our bodily capacities, and even on the existence of analogous options, rather than the contrary order of explanation that CA presumes. My response is that, while our bodies differ in capacities, we can all *try* to move them in more or less the same ways. And so if we are paralyzed or have lost a leg, we will fail in ways captured by CA. Our capacity for Ginet-style volitions is not dependent on our bodily capacities, or rather, to put it more exactly, adult humans do not differ in what roughly Ginet-style volitions they are capable of. Let me explain this point.

I do admit that there are concrete limits to the Ginet-style volitions of which *humans* are capable, because of our general physical nature as a species. I think that at least hypothetical animals have a capacity for such volitions that we lack. A creature who could turn color directly and at will (and not merely by holding its breath) or move things telepathically would have very different sorts of action capacities and Ginet-style volitions than we do. We are stuck with a capacity for such volitions that only have a certain type of content, that involve moving limbs or body parts in various ways and with various force through three spatial dimensions and one temporal dimension. I develop a rough account of what I call normal human motor intentions and their contents elsewhere, and argue that the contents of quite alien motor intentions are not coherently conceivable by human beings, so this constraint is in fact folded into our earlier emendation of CA to involve merely humanly conceivable tryings.[54] But I think that even these capacities allow us to *try* to fly around the moon by flapping wings on our backs. I just did it, though I didn't get very far.

Still, I should also admit that it may be that some human beings are sufficiently abnormal that they lack the capacity to actually form some motor intentions that other humans can form. And so my response requires another point, and a consequent distinction between two forms of trying, relevant to different cases of bodily activity.

I claim that all adult humans who are currently agents have the ability to *try* to move in the same fundamental physical ways, even if in fact not all of them can succeed in doing so because of various forms of physical disability. It makes sense to say of someone who has a lost a limb or suffered some neurological movement disorder, or even who has never had such a limb,[55] that they can try to move the limb in some way through space and with some force, even if they lack a capacity for exactly the same sort of very detailed unconscious motor intentions that would be present in such a case in someone who can actually move the relevant limb. This is

---

[54] Mendola (1997: 143–65, 280–3, 320–1); Mendola (2008: 269–72).
[55] This is a more questionable case. But an experimenter may be investigating neural precursors to motor activity in someone who never had a limb, and make the request that they try to move the missing limb, to observe the resulting neural activity.

like what I suggested earlier in the case of the color blind person trying to sort socks, and especially like what I said about one of our baby counting cases. All adult human action is normed in this way against the usual human abilities. Normal adult human capacities to try are extended almost by courtesy to all adult human agents.[56] Well, it isn't just courtesy. All adult human agents have enough and the right sort of physical similarity or relation to normal adult humans to make this ascription appropriate. But this involves another diversity of trying. The relevantly abnormal can try to perform some bodily activity X without a very detailed motor intention of some sort even if such an intention is present when the normal try to do X. Perhaps what counts as trying to X in the abnormal is not even sufficient to count as trying to X in the normal.[57]

There is no bodily activity performed by adult normal humans that other adult humans capable of action cannot at least try to perform in one of these ways.[58] And through bodily activity of some sort we can always take our best Hail Mary shot at whatever worldly action some human might attempt. So the fact that we can share something at least analogous to Ginet-style volitions ramifies in a way that helps to defend CA against Chisholm-style counterexamples. Strictly Ginet-style volitions allow a plausible analytical refinement of CA in normal adult humans, and something looser but analogous is also available in other cases.

3.7.2.2 MENTAL ACTION

But there are also mental actions, and they introduce new diversities of content in trying that introduce new complexities, and indeed require further emendation of CA.[59] Some intuitively mental actions, for instance thinking in words, seem to

---

[56] This is a point about ordinary language, accessible from our armchairs, not an a priori point about our neural capacities.

[57] Internal differences among the normal and abnormal constitute all the differences relevant here, so this is not a new argument for externalism in philosophy of mind. Even if the explanation why our English phrase "trying to move his left arm" applies to someone who has no left arm depends on the states of normal humans, still merely internal physical conditions of the man without the arm are sufficient for that phrase to be appropriately applied to him. He would still meet those conditions if there were no one else in the world, though in that case it is unlikely that there would be such a phrase. And any internal physical duplicate of that individual who was a member of another species or none at all would yet properly be ascribed human bodily trying simply because of his physical similarity to us. Perhaps this implies that other species could properly ascribe tryings to us that we cannot coherently conceive, so there is more than one sense in which this book is focused on merely human interests.

[58] Perhaps it seems that gymnasts can attempt bodily movements that the normal can't, a certain twirl. But I can as easily try to do such things as to flap my wings. Perhaps the worry rather is about the precision of spatio-temporal movements that gymnasts can intend. But our general capacity for spatial thought allows us to zoom even our tryings, but not necessarily our motor intentions, into fine levels of imaginative detail.

[59] There are disagreements about the frequency of mental actions. G. Strawson (2003) argues that they are infrequent. Peacocke (2007) suggests that they are very frequent. I will focus on a set of cases on which most agree, and which are only slightly beyond what Strawson would accept.

involve a kind of activity that is a shadow of bodily activity. We speak to ourselves in our mind's throat and hear that speech in the mind's ear.[60] That involves an analogous shadow of Ginet-style volition. But other mental actions seem different, and apparently involve different sorts of fundamental activity and also merely mental Ginet-style volitions:

You can listen in an actively concentrated way to a concert,[61] or do a complicated math sum in your head,[62] or make an active decision or form an intention in cases in which considerations pro and con seem evenly balanced.[63] You can try to do these complex things, and you may fail. And there are also more fundamental forms of mental activity involved in these complex mental actions, which involve what seem to be mental analogues of Ginet-style volitions.

At least sometimes, these fundamental forms of mental activity are mental actions in their own right, and for at least some of these fundamental mental actions it isn't very plausible to say you might fail to do them if you tried. For instance, you can suppose one thing or another. You can attend to some current sensation. You can imagine a giraffe and then in imagination spin the giraffe around.[64]

In these cases, unlike Ginet-style volitions focused on bodily activity, there seems to be no space between trying and succeeding.[65] And so we are threatened with the need for Type One conditionals of the sort we earlier ruled out in order to avoid counterexamples to CA. So CA faces a new problem. A related complication suggests a second problem. Trying itself seems not only sometimes a bodily action like pulling at the refrigerator door, but sometimes a mental action, as Ginet believes volition generally is. And so we face Ryle's familiar worry:[66] If all intentional acting involves trying, and trying is at least sometimes an intentional action, then such trying requires trying to try, and that may require trying to try to try, and so forth in a vicious infinite regress. An initial reply to this second problem is that for at least some tryings that are mental actions, we are prepared to say that acting in that way and trying to act in that way are in fact the same thing. That would undercut the regress. Trying to try would be no more than merely trying, in such cases. But then once again we seem to need the forbidden Type One conditionals. Our first problem gets worse.

Focus first on the second problem, on trying to try. We can add a fourth emendation to CA that evades this problem, mandating that *the conditionals relevant to CA not include those whose antecedents involve trying to try to do something.* Sometimes active trying is just pulling at the refrigerator door, but such an action is

---

[60] Sidgwick (1907: 73) suggests that bodily activity helps control feelings.
[61] Crowther (2009).   [62] Buckareff (2005).   [63] Sidgwick (1907: 73–5).
[64] There are individual differences among adult humans involving the capacity for quasi-visual mental imagery. We will return to such issues.
[65] O'Shaughnessy substantially agrees with this.
[66] Ryle (1949).

available to the analysis when you merely try to pull at the door, so ruling out trying to try in the relevant antecedents in such cases loses CA no alternatives. This fix helps us avoid Ryle's regress when some trying is a purely mental action that has no other relevant characterization than as a trying. And it fits with comfortable English. But still we need some explanation of how our capacity for fundamental mental actions of trying is delimited if not by our inability to perform such tryings when we try to. And still we face the collapse of trying and acting in the case of fundamental mental actions, which seems to require forbidden Type One conditionals.

Fortunately, we already have the resources to deal with these remaining worries. The only cases of mental acts in which it is plausible to say that trying to act and acting are the same seem to be in one sense fundamental mental acts. (While some fundamental mental acts seem to be conjunctions of other cases where collapse seems plausible, still then there is a collapse between an analogously conjunctive trying and the larger act in question.) And the tryings and fundamental mental acts in question only seem to collapse under ideal conditions, by which I mean normal conditions in normal adult members of the species. Under less than ideal conditions, humans can try and fail to perform even fundamental mental actions characteristic of humans. Perhaps the color blind cannot form some mental image of a sort that you can, but they can at least try. Those with various cognitive problems may be unable to concentrate on a sensation, or rotate a mental image of a giraffe. Because of the diversity of states that count as trying to perform a certain mental action, and because abnormal cases are normed against ideal cases, in the ideal case we get a collapse between tryings and fundamental mental actions, indeed a collapse that helps to specify the class of analytically fundamental mental actions and tryings, and in the abnormal case we do not have a collapse. And so no forbidden Type One conditionals are in question. While in normal cases an individual's state of trying is no different from their state of succeeding when a fundamental mental action is performed, still the antecedent of the relevant conditional can be true and yet its consequent false, in an abnormal case.

With this mechanism in place, we are finally in position to rely securely on my reply in 3.3 to the final baby counting case, even in an especially troubling variant in which a mental action of counting is in question. The baby is able in the relevant sense to try when it yet lacks the capacity to succeed, because it tries in a different way than normal adults.

3.7.3 Accepting reasons

There is a third diversity of trying that we need to consider. It involves accepting reasons. This notion will also play other crucial roles in Part II.

While squirrels lack moral responsibility, it is plausible to say that a squirrel has alternatives in my sense. It can try to do one thing or another, climb this tree or that. And yet humans seem capable of a fancier sort of trying than squirrels.

It is customary to claim that when a normal adult human performs an intentional action, they ordinarily do it for a reason.[67] They can report that they are doing such a thing because the action serves a goal they have, or because it is part of a larger action that they are performing, and this often helps reveal what features of the action are intentional. The person can provide a rationalization of their action in something like one of these senses, an answer to a certain sort of "why question" about the action, which also provides a plausible answer to the question of what they are trying to do.

It is also true that, as Anscombe said, "a possible answer to the question is ... 'I just thought I would' or 'It was an impulse' or 'For no particular reason' or 'It was an idle action—I was just doodling'."[68] But even then there is something like the negative relation to reasons that idling has to active trying.

Normal human adults take their "rationalizing reasons" of this general sort to be reasons.[69] They act on them, and they are reasons that they recognize, whether or not they are illusory or mistaken or irrational. They help constitute what a normal adult human is trying to do in a sense of trying richer than any available to a squirrel.

But there are distinctions we must beware. It is not only that such reasons may not in fact *be* justifying reasons, reasons positively relevant to ethical or rational justification, but that they need not be *taken* to be so.[70] Someone out of irrationality of familiar sorts can recognize that there are even all-told justifying reasons for action that they do not take to be reasons in the sense on which we are focused, that they do not act on nor are even inclined to act on.[71] And people can act on various reasons that they do not take to be justifying reasons. Consider Michael Smith's development of Ayer's case, a kleptomaniac who intentionally steals but doesn't take that to be at all justified.[72] Consider Frankfurt's addict who hates his addiction and yet acts consciously on the basis of his hated desires.[73] Sometimes but only sometimes rationalizing reasons for an agent's action are taken by the agent to be truly justifying reasons of one sort or the other. But there is always what I will call *weak* acceptance of the rationalizing reasons.[74] This notion of weak acceptance of a reason is very like Allan Gibbard's notion of linguistically inflected acceptance of a norm, but it doesn't involve his stipulation that the norms you accept are reflectively endorsed, that you would express them in sincere, spontaneous normative discussion.[75]

---

[67] Anscombe (2000), though with qualifications to be noted; Davidson (1980b) is less qualified.
[68] Anscombe (2000: 25).   [69] Setiya (2003) stresses this sense of "take."
[70] But see Buss (1999b), which criticizes a distinction in Railton (2003d) between High Brow and Low Brow accounts of action that is closely analogous to my suggestion.
[71] Stocker (1979).   [72] M. Smith (1994: 133).   [73] Frankfurt (1971).
[74] I think that you may believe that reasons are justifying reasons without having a tendency to act on them, but I also think that is unusual.
[75] Gibbard (1990: Chapter 4). See Mendola (2006: 53–4 and Chapter 4) for discussion of the contrast between Gibbard's notion and the particular kind of weak acceptance that I will shortly call "moderate acceptance."

Another relevant complexity is that people recognize reasons in different rationalizing roles and with different weights. This is certainly true of reasons that agents take to be justifying reasons; they cede them not only different weights but also other complex interacting roles in generating overall judgments of normative propriety. Some reasons may completely overbalance others; some may undercut others. But merely rationalizing reasons also have different weights and analogous sorts of roles that play into the generation of intentional action and intention and trying in complex ways. For instance, Frances Kamm has provided cases in which reasons without which one would not perform an action do *not* help constitute what one is intentionally doing in doing that, but merely defeat reasons that would otherwise count decisively against doing that thing. You may give a party for the fun that will result, although you hate messes, only because you know that your friends will feel guilty enough to help you clean up, while it can't be said that that is part of your goal or intention in giving the party.[76] And Joshua Knobe claims that we sometimes judge that recognized side effects of actions that someone isn't specifically aiming at are intentional when they are bad, though not intentional when they are good,[77] and that when you take a Hail Mary shot at something and are successful that achievement counts as intentional when the outcome is significantly good or bad, but not when it is morally neutral.[78] These particular cases involve generally recognized rather than unrecognized but objective goods and bads; they involve things thought by the actor to be good and bad, and so something richer than mere weak acceptance seems in question. But they do reflect complexities in moving from judgments about someone's reasons to judgments about what they are intentionally doing.

Despite these complexities, there is certainly some connection between the rationalizing reasons accepted by someone and their intentions and tryings and intentional actions. However, whether someone acts on the basis of certain reasons isn't always merely a matter of what we might call this "structure" of the rationalizing reasons themselves, for instance not merely a matter of their rationalizing weight, but is rather sometimes in part a matter of decision, or of differential motivation of other sorts, say different emotional backgrounds in which certain sorts of reasons are more apt to be acted on. But sometimes when someone acts it does seem merely to be a matter of such structure.

To save words, when I hereafter say that people weakly accept various reasons, I will take that to include not only a specification of what rationalizing reasons they accept but in what sorts of rationalizing roles they accept them, so that when the very same reasons count as rationalizing considerations to two people yet they sometimes may not in my richer sense accept the same reasons. However, I will not take this acceptance to be a matter of the extra motivational conditions like emotion or decision

---

[76] Kamm (2007: 95).   [77] Knobe (2003a).

[78] Knobe (2003b and 2006). I think that when we achieve the goal of a Hail Mary pass it is often intentional when it is part of a plan even when the goal is morally neutral.

that I have just noted, so that people may weakly accept the same reasons in my sense and yet be in different motivational states. I do not claim that these distinctions are very clean. But this is the most useful way to set up terminology for later.

Whatever the complications, the reasons for which someone does something are at least customarily among the reasons they weakly accept. And the reasons for which someone does something, and hence reasons they weakly accept, characteristically have something to do with its being one particular intentional action rather than another. And they characteristically help determine what the person is trying to do, at least in one sense. This I will call trying in a reason-inflected way.

On the other hand, even if someone weakly accepts reasons that lead them in this fashion in one direction, so that we are inclined to say that they are trying to do something in that direction, they may also have more animal motives not unlike that of the squirrel, which push in another direction. And I think that sometimes when humans try, they try merely in more or less the same manner as a squirrel. Consider a baby, or an angry adult breaking something.

It seems to me that in normal human adults this squirrel-like trying will only lead to action when they fail to try hard to do otherwise in the other, reason-inflected way. They at least negatively assent in that reason-inflected way, we might say, in a way that is analogous to idling. Even if reason-acceptance is offline, it could be put back online in an immediately effective way. But, nevertheless, since squirrels can try in one sense, there are at least two different sorts of trying of which humans are capable, which may tend in different directions. And perhaps I can't always succeed in what I in the reason-inflected way try to do if my animal desires pull too hard in a different direction. Still, this discussion suggests one kind of dominance in humans of reason-inflected trying. Negative reason-inflected assent is perhaps always required for animal trying to succeed in us, but animal trying only occasionally undercuts reason-inflected trying in this way. And if there is some conflict between reason-inflected and animal trying relevant to the judgment of what a human agent is overall trying to do, the reason-inflected sort is characteristically dominant. The human is trying to act in accord with the reasons it weakly accepts, but fails because of contrary squirrel-like trying. And humans seem almost always to be doing something in the fancier and dominant sense. Nevertheless, despite this dominance, these two sorts of trying can at least sometimes generate indeterminacies regarding what someone is trying to do, when the two sorts pull forcefully in different directions. And they can sometimes provide two distinct ways one might try to do one thing.

There are other varieties of the acceptance of reasons. It is clear that among the reasons that persons accept, they accept some to be justifying reasons, to be genuinely normative, unlike the reasons underlying the action of Smith's kleptomaniac. This is what I will call strong acceptance,[79] which will matter to us and which we will further

---

[79] This is not quite implied by the mere belief that reasons are justifying.

discuss in Chapter 4. Perhaps it introduces yet a third differential form of trying along the general axis now under consideration, and even suggests further indeterminacies of overall trying.

We have seen that there are luxuriant varieties of trying, even sometimes different ways in which one can try to do the same thing. Some of these types of trying are themselves somewhat soft; it may be not highly determinate whether someone is trying in these ways. And since the different varieties of trying may pull against each other and require balancing in any overall judgment about what a person is trying to do, this softness is increased.

Still, we can at least reasonably hope that there are moderately determinate facts about what people try to do, and what they would be trying to do under various alternative physical conditions. This is partly because of the refinements involving analytically fundamental forms of trying that we have discerned, partly because the differences between bodily and mental fundamental trying characteristically involve distinct acts, and partly because of the limited dominance in humans of reason-inflected trying. This apparently allows enough determinacy for CA.

This complicated account of trying also provides a crucial analytical resource for the desire-based account of the good developed in Part II, in which trying plays a central role. And the acceptance of reasons underlying some human trying will matter to us later in more than one other way. It is important to the metaethical theory of Part II, and also crucial to group acts, which are another element of the moral theory I will propose.

3.8 Subjunctive Conditionals

The second resource required by CA is a collection of true and false subjunctive conditionals linking trying with alternatives. In Chapter 2, we saw that they are moderately indeterminate in truth. But now I can add some details.

The determinate truth of a subjunctive conditional is threatened when the conditions that must be varied from reality to allow its antecedent to be true are closely entwined with admissible background conditions. And trying is not a highly localized phenomenon in the relevant sense. The conditions that make it true that one tries to do something are entwined with psychological conditions that are admissible background conditions for assessing what one would do if one tried to do various things. And we have seen here that there are precision problems involving trying, as well as some indeterminacy about whether someone in fact tries one thing or another in various physical situations.

But there is some mitigation of the indeterminacy that looms by the internalism about mental states that I argue for elsewhere.[80] Past conditions and conditions

---

[80] Mendola (2008).

external to the skin are not constitutive parts of the most central psychological states, and at least reasonably determinate analytically fundamental immediate tryings seem among the states that meet this internalist constraint, along with dispositions to unfold a series of immediate tryings that are relevant to what one is at the moment in the midst of trying to do in a longer-range sense. And while internal psychological conditions relevant to what one would do if one variously tried may be dangerously entwined with conditions that help fix what one in fact tries to do even in this basic sense, still alternatives also involve external and hence relatively distinct background conditions as well. In fact, alternatives include external context relevant to conse-quentialist normative assessment even if that context is not relevant to what *actions* are performed. So at least some degree of disentwining is possible for the conditionals in question, especially for normal adults, though this does not eliminate the indeter-minacies we discussed in Chapter 2. Our discussion in this chapter does not suggest that options are more than moderately indeterminate.

Our consideration of counterfactuals has been hedged in talk of background conditions so we can avoid the debate among accounts that variously deploy possible worlds, cotenability, events, probabilities, and factors relevant to indicative condi-tionals. But there is some more to say about the analysis suggested by our particular conditionals.

We are focused on an objective conception of options; it isn't someone's own conception of their options, nor that of observers, that matters. So accounts modeled on indicative conditionals, which are highly susceptible to differences in individual belief, seem irrelevant. And we hope for a tighter than merely probable link between trying and alternatives (although the alternatives themselves may incorporate prob-abilities), so accounts based on conditional probabilities also seem irrelevant.

Concentrate, then, on event accounts, possible world accounts, and cotenability accounts. The deepest difference between possible world and cotenability analyses is structural. Possible world accounts potentially allow for tradeoffs among different background conditions in assessing the similarity between worlds relevant to the truth of counterfactuals, while cotenability accounts involve a propositional form that constrains background conditions and that doesn't naturally allow for trading off. Event accounts are like possible worlds accounts in this respect,[81] but one relevant difference is that most events are spatio-temporally smaller than the whole world.[82]

Because of the soft facts about trying and other precision problems, and because at least some of the relevant background conditions of our target conditionals are not easily disentwined from those that help constitute relevant tryings, possible world and event accounts are better suited to our needs than cotenability accounts. Tradeoffs are

---

[81] But Lycan's event analysis takes what is for our purposes an unfortunately subjectivist form.
[82] Event accounts also potentially ignore internal spatio-temporal details, though that isn't a feature that is useful to us.

important. Yet because of the somewhat localized nature—consistent with the strictures of internalism—of analytically fundamental immediate tryings, we can hope that a relatively localized event account can provide greater specificity, or at least more economical specificity, than a possible world account, in fixing what one might call the narrow options available to an agent, what the agent would do relatively quickly within or at skin's end if the agent immediately tried thus and so, at least in normal cases.

Still, much more context is relevant to which alternative each narrow option would be. In many cases, we can focus merely on extra current conditions that can causally affect outcomes that also can be causally affected by what narrow option is adopted, and so by exploiting prior relatively localized event analyses of narrow options, we can perhaps achieve a reasonably clean sense of different analytically primary alternatives had by an agent, rooted in a somewhat more expansive event account. With further luck, internally determinate dispositions to other immediate tryings, often conditional on what immediate trying has already occurred, and some more background context, can help provide a more extensive analytical basis for determining options at a time. Under these happy conditions, a somewhat expansive event account of our target conditionals is possible. We can focus on a relatively localized region of actuality, and consider only possible events that vary from it in controlled ways.[83]

But past occurrences are sometimes intuitively relevant background conditions even when they do not causally affect the present, although at least in general the conditionals relevant to options are not back-tracking conditionals. So we are pushed back towards possible worlds accounts. We noted in Chapter 2 that when past conditions and general determinism are relevant background conditions, it is ordinarily appropriate to deploy a small local miracle, without widespread violation of natural laws and historical facts that are relevant background conditions,[84] though possible variety in this may itself be a source of further indeterminacy.

3.9 Alternatives

Alternatives are the third positive requirement of CA. They were introduced in Chapter 2 as mutually exclusive options at a time. But now it is possible to say more about the alternative actions that are open to agents.

First, some hold that trying is an action,[85] and some deny it. But we have already seen that at least some tryings are actions. Second, some think that all tryings are complete internal to skin's end, or are even purely mental acts that involve nothing

---

[83] We cannot hope, with Lycan, that in *all* relevant possible events in which the antecedent of one of our conditionals is true the consequent is also true; rather, similarity between relatively localized possible situations will play a role in determining the truth of the conditional in the Lewisian manner.

[84] D. Lewis (1979); Vihvelin (2000). But see Bennett (1984).

[85] Hornsby (1980); Jones (1983).

like contraction of muscles or movement of limbs.[86] We have seen that neither of those claims is true of all things we legitimately call trying, but there are at least in many cases analytically fundamental immediate tryings (and chains of and executive dispositions for such tryings) that are complete within skin's end. And, to put our two points together, it is not unreasonable to consider these actions. More exactly, we can presume that there is at least one internally determinate action being performed at any point in which any alternative is being taken by an agent, except when the individual does nothing either bodily or mentally and doesn't even do nothing by actively trying to do nothing. And it is always open to an agent to do nothing on purpose as well. So what I have called analytically fundamental immediate tryings are one type of analytically primary action, at least in normal cases.

Still, we should not presume without further ado that these primary actions exhaust all our actions, let alone our alternatives, nor even that temporal chains of such primary actions constitute all our actions, even if we restrict ourselves to normal cases. So consider the related issue of act-individuation.

Recall from Chapter 2 that some hold the *coarse-grained view*, that merely one action occurs when any alternative is taken.[87] Some, like Hornsby, identify these lonely actions with tryings. Others favor a *fine-grained view*. They identify a single alternative with a very wide range of acts, each specified by a different property that is instantiated in the world because that alternative is taken, and where some of these acts are done by doing others, and all are ultimately done by performing an (in one sense) "basic action" by which all the others are performed. But we have reason to adopt instead the *moderate view*, that only some of these properties help constitute distinct actions, all done by doing the basic action by which they all are done:

(1) Assume there is an analytically fundamental immediate trying, internally determinate. It is constituted by either a fundamental mental act of the sort recently described, identical to a fundamental mental trying, or by a Ginet-style volition focused on body activity, but in either case it is what I have called a primary action. It might be a basic action in the appropriate sense, by which all the other consequent actions are done.[88] In particular, assume you form some simple Ginet-style volition, which we will presume is an act, and you smile. Perhaps your smiling is a distinct act that you do by forming the Ginet-style volition. Still, even though you smile cheer-fully, there isn't plausibly an act of cheerfully smiling that is distinct from your act of smiling, so a very fine-grained view of act-individuation is too profligate. And some consequences of an action are not a part of the action itself, or indeed of any action

---

[86] Hornsby (1980); Pietroski (2000).

[87] Or hold that if there are difficulties in this sort of identification it is only because a specific alternative may require a cluster of different movements that are distinct acts, or because an alternative is merely one way to perform an intuitive act.

[88] Sometimes temporal chains of analytically fundamental immediate tryings and executive dispositions to such will be important to what you are in the midst of doing. But I will suppress that complication for the moment, along with babies, reason-inflection, and the abnormal.

hence performed. If by smiling you do something that affects what is happening in the Andromeda galaxy in millions of years, that is not plausibly relevant to the identity of your action, at least in normal cases.

(2) But, on the other hand, sometimes there clearly are acts other than the analytically fundamental immediate trying, the relevantly basic action, that helps constitute an alternative, and so the coarse-grained view is too stingy. Your smiling and your Ginet-style volition may perhaps be distinct acts, but such a difference is more obvious when there are significant temporal differences between relatively basic actions and other actions hence performed.[89] You pull the trigger and throw the gun immediately away, though Caesar will only die of his wounds tomorrow. Your actions of shooting and killing Caesar require different amounts of time to unfold. Your shooting Caesar is only a spatio-temporal component of the longer act of killing him. It is sometimes objected to this that you don't have to do anything more to kill Caesar than shoot him.[90] But sometimes in such cases you do have to do something more to kill him, or at least refrain from doing something more, just because of the time delay. If you shot him, but then changed your mind and skillfully treated his wound, then you wouldn't have killed him. Something went on later than the shooting that is distinct and for which you are responsible. And we should also accept that in some cases you do something A by doing something B while you do not do B by doing A.[91] But, to revert to our first point, not all cases are like this. It cannot plausibly be said that your smiling is a spatio-temporal component of your smiling cheerfully. And in fact, if anything, you intuitively should be said to smile by smiling cheerfully. And Andromeda is just too far out of our current human range.

So here's where we are: Though alternatives at least normally involve a basic action that is internally determinate, many involve (a moderate number of) other actions partly constituted by external or other internal conditions, actions that are performed in that context by performing that internal basic action. And of course alternatives can include consequences even beyond actions. They reach out into the world.

One important normatively issue about the nature of alternatives is how far out into the world they go, and how determinate they are when they do so.

We are focused on objective conceptions of options.[92] But, as we will shortly see, this will characteristically involve objective risks. Alternatives don't ordinarily go far enough out into the world on the correct conception to specify certain outcomes in all future detail. But there are different objective conceptions of options even of this sort, because there are different objective conceptions of risks. So indeterminacy looms.

Recall that my argument for the indeterminacy of options rested on the indeterminacy of background conditions. And analogous background conditions play a crucial role in determining objective probabilities as well. Perhaps some objective

---

[89] L. Davis (1970); Thomson (1971).   [90] Davidson (1980b: 59).
[91] A. Goldman (1970).   [92] Zimmerman (2008) has a contrary focus.

probabilities are written into the microphysical laws that govern the world, but in most cases this is not highly relevant to the risks involved in our alternatives. Rather, it is orthodox to define these objective probabilities as relative frequencies in a reference class of relevant possible alternatives.[93] For instance, a fair coin has a 50 percent chance of landing heads if and only if in half of the relevant alternatives it lands heads, even if we presume that determinism is true and so in another sense there is always certainty about the outcome of a specific flip. But possible alternatives are relevant only when relevant background conditions that govern our coin's actual situation are maintained. So considerations of the same sort that underlie the indeterminacy of options also suggest a similar indeterminacy of risks. And certainly conditional probabilities are subject to like difficulties.

So there are no facts of the matter between some suitably objective conceptions of risks. That is one of kind of indeterminacy of alternatives with which we must live, when risky alternatives are involved.

But there is sometimes mitigation of the normative effects of this indeterminacy by this fact: An option specified by one particular conception of our objective risks, involving certain background conditions, should be evaluated relative to other options specified by the same conception, by the same background conditions. And, in happy cases, all of the best options—in each of the different sets of alternatives that are internally related by a shared conception of relevant risks—are what we might call "analogous options," constituted by the same basic action (say one Ginet-style volition) in all of these option sets.

Surely, however, these optimistic conditions are not always available. There will then be indeterminacy about which option is best because of indeterminacies regarding true objective risks. We will need to examine this matter closely later, when we consider the best options that are most relevant to the true moral theory, to be sure that virulent indeterminacy does not ensue. But the short answer is that it doesn't. Still, there are other virulent indeterminacies very close by, to which we now turn.

3.10 Flukes

We are now in position to understand why objective options do not include flukes, and hence why the second worry about objective consequentialism with which we began this chapter can be evaded. They rather include objective risks of the type we just discussed, in particular *ex ante* objective probabilities, which are fixed at the time when the options are all available. While the indeterminacy of options presents various practical ethical difficulties, there is one way in which embedding more familiar normative worries into consideration of the indeterminacy of options can defuse one standing normative dispute. And it is a dispute that matters to us.

---

[93] See for instance Kyburg (1974). See Hájek (2007) on the ubiquity of the problem of the reference class.

Focus on the controversy between those who think that in consequentialist assessment we should focus on objective risks and those who think we should focus on how things will in fact turn out. And consider a variant of a class of examples introduced by Frank Jackson, which brings out one aspect of this dispute:[94]

Mark Antony suffers from a hideous disease, and Cleopatra can treat it with two different potions, A or B. Her accurate and objective evidence is that A will either kill him or cure him completely, but that B will cure him partially. So presume that the relevant *ex ante* objective probabilities are that there is an 80 percent chance that A will kill and a 20 percent chance that it will cure. It isn't merely that Cleopatra doesn't know the precise nature of potion A or the details of Antony's disease, but that the potion is in itself a risky potion. These are objective probabilities. Presume that Cleopatra, always the wild gambler, gives A to Antony. But her luck holds and it cures him completely.

We are focused on a dispute between two sorts of objective conceptions of options, not on a contrast between subjective and objective conceptions. There are complicated disputes about how moral assessment should rest on consequential assessment. But ask this simple question to bring out the contrast we need: Which was the objectively best option for Cleopatra when she faced her choice? Some will say that the relevantly best option was potion B, and some will say A.

What do I say? The first thing I say is that, on the surface, there is an indeterminacy of options here. There are two conceptions of one alternative, and the differences are practically crucial, so it even seems to be virulent indeterminacy, an indeterminacy that makes the notion of a best option in these instances not up to its normative job. But dig a little deeper.

Some may claim of this case that relevant background conditions involve what will turn up, and others may claim that prospective objective probabilities are all that is relevant. So this would be a standard case of indeterminacy if no truth adjudicated between those two views. But notice that one conception of the options seems to include more facts. So it may seem that there is no indeterminacy at all, because there is a way to order the two candidate conceptions of the alternatives so that the conception that takes into account what will in fact turn up is just more accurate. That is because in the situation in which in fact Cleopatra pours A into Antony's goblet, it is stipulated that it doesn't kill him.

But there is a very important set of complications we need to notice at exactly this point. It cannot be presumed as a relevant background condition that governs *all* the alternatives that Cleopatra pours A and it doesn't kill, because that would give us no coherent alternatives to A. And while if we insist on the *subjunctive* background condition that A *wouldn't* have killed Antony whatever option Cleopatra takes, then it is clear that A is the best option, still the probity of that condition isn't assured as a

---

[94] Jackson (1991). For structurally similar "Mine Shaft" cases, see Regan (1980: 265 n1) and Parfit (2011a: 159–60).

more accurate picture of actuality, given the case as I stated it. If we presume counterfactually that Cleopatra pours B, there may be no fact of the matter whether A would have killed or not. There are just the relevant objective *ex ante* probabilities.

Perhaps the best way to put it is that the initial case as I gave it was under-described. It bifurcates into two more specific cases. In one, despite the *ex ante* objective probabilities I specified, there are facts that assure that A will cure whatever is done. But then that is not a fully coherent case, or at least not the best description of it, since the relevant *ex ante* objective probabilities should reflect that fact about A. They should swell to include that determinate constraint on the future. In the other specific case, the objective probabilities I gave were right, and the fact that A cured turned merely on the soft contingencies of what turned up in later reality, on a lucky fluke. It is the second version of the case that is interesting. It introduces a new sort of indeterminacy of options.

There is what happens as the world rolls. A is poured and cures. But there is no fact, from as it were the perspective of all the options, about what would have happened if A had been poured. There is no relevant subjunctive background condition. If B had been poured, then it wouldn't have been determinate that A would have cured. There would have just been the objective probabilities noted.

In general, we can expect that there are objective *ex ante* probabilities inside of alternatives. And whatever alternative is taken, the world will roll and incorporate flukes. But there will be no coherent set of options that includes all the flukes within all the alternatives fully rolled out, since they aren't reflected in the *ex ante* objective probabilities.

In the cases at hand, we have two normative choices. We can compare the alternative actually taken in all its fluky detail with other alternatives specified merely by *ex ante* objective probabilities. Or we can compare all the options merely by reference to *ex ante* objective probabilities.

If we do the first, we are comparing apples with an orange. But the crucial point is that, when the actual outcome is better, still it won't generally be true that it would have been better even if another alternative had been taken. There is no modally stable fact, true whichever alternative we take, about which is best. This is a new kind of indeterminacy of options, which because it undercuts normative comparisons it will turn out in Part II we often need to make, is even virulent indeterminacy.

To avoid it, we are forced to the second normative choice. We must compare all alternatives by *ex ante* objective probabilities, and ignore lucky flukes. Only then will there be modally stable facts, true on all options, about which is best. That is hence the conception of alternatives I will henceforth deploy. *Ex ante* objective probabilities matter, and we should ignore lucky flukes, including the flukes of military success and good consequences that flowed by accident from Caesar's vain cruel act. And we hence evade the second problem for objective consequentialism with which this chapter began. That problem was that objective consequentialism appeared to rest normative assessment in some cases on fluky consequences, and hence delivered the wrong normative assessment. But the problem assumes the wrong conception of alternatives.

This mechanism will not serve to remove all possible objections to objective consequentialism, of course. Jackson-style cases, and structurally similar cases due to Regan and Parfit, present other difficulties, to which we will return briefly in Chapter 12. And of course we must see that *ex ante* objective probabilities don't themselves introduce virulent indeterminacies. But this conception of options does evade the second problem with which we began.

Not all flukes are lucky. Some are disasters. But we should ignore them all. What's a fluke? Well, the important ones we must beware are elements of an actualized alternative that would overturn the normative verdict rooted in the *ex ante* objective probabilities.[95] But the simple thing to say is that a fluke is something not specified by the relevant *ex ante* objective probabilities.

There is a possible objection. I granted earlier that you sometimes do something intentionally by taking your best Hail Mary shot at it. So if options are restricted to *ex ante* probabilities, the options we actually take will not include all our intentional actions. But, I reply, while if you take option A in fact, you may succeed in a Hail Mary shot, it isn't generally true that if you had taken alternative option B then it still would be determinately true that you would have succeeded had you taken A. But there will be some small objective chance that you would have. So the action in question isn't strictly banished from your alternatives, though its normative weight is, as it should be, discounted. And notice that our moderate conception of act-individuation implies that it is modally stable that in each option there is *some* specific action done, regardless of how things turn out.

3.11 Group Acts

Here's where we have come: *A human conscious agent at a time has an option in action if and only if it is true that (i) there is something such that if they were to try to do it at that time, then they would succeed in taking that alternative, (ii) that thing is coherently conceivable by humans, (iii) the antecedent of the conditional in (i) does not entail its consequent, and (iv) the antecedent does not involve trying to try.* And we have seen that there is a moderate indeterminacy of our alternatives, which incorporate *ex ante* objective probabilities but not flukes.

Two immediate generalizations of this conception provide other crucial resources for the moral theory of Part II. The first involves group acts.

Caesar's attempt to conquer Gaul took more than a moment. It involved a kind of cooperative activity with himself over time, involving different days of his life, whatever his momentary temptations. He was trying to do that for a long time.

---

[95] Although options root normative properties, it is only *ex ante* options that do so, so this introduces no circularities.

And it also sometimes makes sense to say that a group of distinct individuals try together to do something, to lift a wagon that no one can lift on their own.

There are acts, even in our physical world, and they occur when trying occurs.[96] We may say that it's trying to snow, but we don't literally mean it. When there is literal trying, then there is action. But there are a variety of different levels at which it makes literal sense to say that things try. There are agents of various types. Cleopatra in a moment can try one thing or another, but Cleopatra over time may try something more complicated. And it also makes literal sense to say that certain groups of individuals—say an army or a pair of friends—try to do certain things.[97] Indeed, individual acts that take time to execute are group actions of shorter selves, coordinating together on a long range plan. So there are group acts of two sorts, involving many distinct individuals working together, or a single individual working in such a way that requires temporally-extended cooperation among different periods of their life.

Group acts are a crucial resource for the moral theory of Part II. And at the risk of greater controversy, I can be more specific. Elsewhere, I develop a particular account of group action applicable to humans.[98] I argue that group action involving human agents exists when there is (i) common action by a number of these agents rooted in (ii) common true belief that there is a shared goal and (iii) acceptance by all the members of the group that there is a reason to continue to coordinate activity, either until the goal is adequately accomplished, or indefinitely if it is not the sort of goal that can be finitely and definitely accomplished, a reason whose acceptance we can expect to occasion criticism and the acceptance of criticism for failure to continue coordination until the point (if any) at which the goal is accomplished or mutually abandoned.

This conception of group action is related to the notion of accepted reasons, but there are some terminological complexities that complicate the link: I am not certain if (iii) requires reasons that are taken to be more normatively rich than merely rationalizing reasons or less normatively rich than reasons taken to be full-blown justifying reasons, but I believe so. I think the reasons we need now are in-between. We might call the reasons involved in group action "group rationalizing reasons" and the intermediate kind of acceptance of reasons involved "moderate acceptance." I recently dubbed the acceptance of mere rationalizing reasons "weak acceptance," partly so I can hereafter call moderate acceptance just "acceptance" for short. It is possible that group rationalizing reasons generally have less motivational efficacy than those reasons we take to be rationalizing reasons, because we are not always active in a group project that we are yet suitably inside, but I will ignore this complexity.

---

[96] With qualifications specified earlier.
[97] For extended defense, see Mendola (2006: Chapter 2).
[98] Mendola (2006: Chapter 2).

We can further refine and compress my analysis of group action by deploying the notion of moderate acceptance of a group rationalizing reason. As I just said, not every member of a group needs to be intuitively active for the group to try, but there will characteristically be shared acceptance of group rationalizing reasons specifying what constitutes *defecting* inaction. Furthermore, what makes something a shared goal in the relevant sense is the shared acceptance of it as a positive group rationalizing reason for common action. And, as I suggested earlier, it is probably only when accepted reasons have enough motivational efficacy to cause action, or at least to constitute permission of squirrel-like activity, that there is trying in normal humans.[99] So the central notion in my proposal is moderate acceptance, which I will hereafter call "acceptance" for short, of a group rationalizing reason.

All the group actions in which you of the moment take part overlap in you of the moment; you accept reasons that make you part of a variety of group agents. For instance, it is in your continued acceptance of reasons that your temporally extended individual agency is rooted, but your current acceptance may also help constitute your membership in an army with a shared goal. This overlap will be very important to us in Part II. If I'm right, it is the key to defending the legitimacy of consequentialism.

But let me be clear about the immediate point. I do not think that acceptance of reasons is strictly necessary for trying or action or even group action. There can be, I've granted, mere weak acceptance of the reasons that constitute individual trying at a moment, and not the lightly moralized moderate acceptance on which we are now focused. And in any case I do not think that hungry sharks, who accept no reasons at all, do not act. If a shark is chasing you around, that is enough for us to properly say that the shark is trying to get you. There are even forms of intuitive group action that do not involve reasons, which dogs and fish exhibit as they hunt or swarm. Still, our central concern here is *human* action. Normal humans are capable of accepting reasons. Their agency is dominantly constituted by the capacity for at least weak acceptance of reasons,[100] and much of the acceptance relevant to their intentional action seems also to be moderate, and hence at least potentially capable of supporting continuing action over time. There are forms of intuitive group action that do not involve accepted reasons, which dogs and fish exhibit. But for animals like humans who accept reasons, that "higher" capacity is where genuine group trying is dominantly rooted. Perhaps a crowd of humans is governed to act by their shared dog-like emotions, or by accidental confluence of their merely weakly accepted reasons. Perhaps a single human can be in the grip of a dog-like emotion over time, or weak and not

---

[99] Though the immediate relevance of this point is complicated by the fact that we are not always active in support of a group project that we are inside, and by the possibility that only weak and not moderate acceptance is required of reasons relevant to individuals trying at single moments.

[100] Humans can try in a squirrel-like way, but for us reason-inflected trying is dominant in ways discussed earlier.

moderate acceptance at a moment. But this will constitute group action, even in the case of the continuing action of a single human individual over time, only when there is moderate acceptance of reasons that at least permit that group behavior.

So there is human action and group action of the specific sort indicated, even in our physical world. And we have seen that a particular variant of the conditional analysis of ability is correct. CA in particular involves individual agents at times, but we noted that the times can be somewhat extended, and a generalization to cover many individuals forming one group agent is trivial.[101] And so there are, despite the indeterminacies noted in Chapter 2, a certain range of options had by various sorts of agents, which include momentary agents, long-acting individuals, and intuitive group agents involving many individuals. All that is rooted in the phenomenon of literal trying, and ultimately in the conditions required for the acceptance of reasons that such trying characteristically involves in humans.[102] And all these options involve *ex ante* objective probabilities, but no flukes.

Let me note a related complexity about group acts that matters later. Some group agents are constituted by acceptance of reasons in a way that makes the existence of the agent itself independent of the specific group project in which it engages. There are two levels of accepted reasons in such a case, a first level whose acceptance constitutes the existence of the group agent, and a second level whose acceptance gives that group agent a particular project. An army might be like this. But on the other hand, there are also "one-off" group agents, constituted as group agents solely by the single projects in which they engage. Perhaps the cooperative practice of refraining from heinous lies is a group agent of this sort. And that complexity generates this question: In what sense can one-off group agents have alternatives? In the sense that all the individuals[103] who make up the group could adopt a different group project. So there are really two sorts of group agents that have alternatives: those who are group agents that are not merely one-off, and those made up of individuals who constitute a particular one-off group act and might constitute another.

That completes our first useful generalization, but there is also a second one. Group acts are very significant in the moral theory of Part II, and they are one sort of social alternative. But we will see in Part III that social alternatives of all sorts are highly relevant in another way to individual morality, and group acts cannot plausibly constitute all social alternatives. There are intuitive groups that are relevant to social and political evaluation that are not group agents. The citizens of Rome or

---

[101] Group agents consisting of distinct individuals need not be conscious, although the group consists of conscious beings.

[102] If humans at a moment accept reasons relevant to trying in a way that isn't sufficiently normatively robust to constitute moderate acceptance, then this claim must be qualified.

[103] More exactly, all the individual agents at times who make up the group. Another complication is that they might constitute another one-off group agent, or another group agent that also has a specific group project.

residents of some small town may not be literally trying to do anything together. Since social alternatives in general are relevant to moral theory in ways we will later discuss, we need something more general.

But it is very close at hand. Since accepted reasons are the root of human group action, that suggests a generalization to cover the proper objects of social-political evaluation for humans even when group acts are not involved. While there are social arrangements for certain human groups—and hence social options for those groups—that are not group acts, yet they can be characterized as involving alternative patterns of reason acceptance.[104]

Perhaps a group shares accepted reasons that don't help constitute group agency, that don't meet the conditions for group action that I recently articulated. For instance, the accepted reasons may not specify a shared goal. In other words, perhaps there is moderate acceptance of reasons other than group rationalizing reasons. There can also be acceptance of reasons by members of a group that are not generally shared within the group; the pattern of accepted reasons in question need not be a pattern of *shared* reasons. Different individuals may have different roles in the group that require that they accept different reasons. It may not make sense in all cases to call these "group rationalizing" reasons, but we can presume, I think, that they involve the same sorts of criticism of violators, that they involve the moderate attitude we are now calling acceptance of reasons for short, although what counts as a violation may be different for different people.

Many groups of competent adult humans who don't in fact act as groups can potentially try as groups, and would do so if they accepted the right reasons. We can cooperate on a plan with those now on the other side of the earth, or those long dead. I think we can even cooperate on an accidentally shared plan with those with whom we share no history, but in any case all humans share a history. And all sorts of alternative forms of reason acceptance, even those that do not constitute literal group trying and action, seem appropriate objects of social and political evaluation, simply because they are always one kind of alternative to group action. If how a group tries is rooted in reason acceptance, and alternative forms of reason acceptance would constitute alternative group attempts, then yet other alternative forms of reason acceptance seem also to be appropriate social options, appropriate additional alternatives for normative evaluation in social-political philosophy.

There is space between weak acceptance of reasons and trying on the basis of those reasons, sometimes between trying and acting, and often between acting and doing various things that are consequences of that action. Likewise, it isn't exactly true that a group accepting reasons in itself constitutes group action, and it is clear that intuitive social alternatives include consequences of group acts that are outside the

---

[104] Mendola (1988).

group acts. So, strictly speaking, alternative forms of reason acceptance *ground* different social alternatives without fully *constituting* the different alternatives. They are analogous to basic acts. What's more, a group of individuals, or different groups, might accept the same reasons with different degrees of motivational commitment, and that may be normatively important. As a consequentialist, I presume that if there is a set of basic social alternatives for some group fixed by different sets of accepted reasons, then each corresponds to a particular social alternative that includes both the context and the consequences of acceptance of those reasons, both the background facts about prior motivational commitments and the relevant causal effects of their acceptance on the world, including future motivational commitments.

There is no doubt that there are indeterminacies of our social alternatives. Some social alternatives are group actions, and this suggests by quick extension of the arguments of Chapter 2 at least moderate indeterminacies. But even when group actions are not at issue there are analogous indeterminacies, because social alternatives include consequences of various forms of reason acceptance, and so are defined by conditionals similar to those we considered in Chapter 2. For familiar reasons, social alternatives also involve *ex ante* objective probabilities, but no flukes.

3.12 Summary of Part I

Here's the minimum you need to take away, what you will need to accept on faith if you've skimmed or skipped:

Chapter 2 argued that there is a moderate but not virulent indeterminacy of options, because of precision problems involving antecedents and because of the indeterminate truth of Failed Type Three counterfactuals. A Failed Type Three counterfactual is such that (i) the actual microphysical facts that make its antecedent false, and (ii) features of the world that are admissible background conditions of the counterfactual, cannot be adequately disentwined and specified, even given a fixed context of utterance and meaning conventions. We will see in Part II that failures of Type Three counterfactuals undercut much contemporary moral theory.

This chapter explored varieties of trying that will matter to the moral theory of Part II, because the facts of individual good deployed by that theory rest on facts about trying. We considered the acceptance of reasons, which will also be an important resource. We noted that there are group acts, involving either continuing activity within one individual's life or distinct individuals cooperating together. These group acts are also a very central element of the moral theory of Part II. We considered a generalization of the notion of a group act that provides a more suitably general conception of social arrangements.

This chapter also argued that a human conscious agent at a time has an option in action if and only if it is true that (i) there is something such that if they were to try to do it at that time, then they would succeed in taking that alternative, (ii) that thing is coherently conceivable by humans, (iii) the antecedent of the conditional in (i) does not entail its consequent, and (iv) the antecedent does not involve trying to try. We noted generalizations of this conception that specify social options. And we saw that our moderately indeterminate individual and social alternatives incorporate *ex ante* objective probabilities but not flukes.

PART II
Moral Theory

4

Meaning and Morality

The merely physical world constrains any moral truths. Still, there is a true moral theory applicable to our alternatives, which I will call "Material Morality" or "MM." It is itself rooted in agency, and involves two main components: a desire-based conception of individual good, and a certain egalitarian mechanism for moving from individual good to the evaluation of individual actions and social arrangements.

This part has seven chapters. Chapters 5 through 7 develop the correct desire-based conception of individual good, and argue that apparent competitors are either not viable in physical reality or equivalent to my proposal. Chapters 8 through 10 sketch the proper egalitarian mechanism for deploying individual good in moral evaluation, and contrast it with other, more familiar ways to pass from individual good to overall normative judgment. Some of these apparent alternatives are not viable in reality, but the others support MM.

There are yet other moral theories that do not rest on individual good at all. But they either invoke non-natural properties of rightness that are no more realistic than the dragons of medieval romance, or they begin with individual motivation and work outwards to ethical truths, and so are implicitly encompassed by our discussion.

This chapter concerns the meaning of certain moral terms. This account will underlie and organize, but also be developed through, my specific arguments regarding particular ethical theories in the rest of this part.

4.1 Terminology

It will be useful to begin with terminological clarifications.

First, some ethicists distinguish between the "moral" and the "ethical," and say that ethical evaluation is a broad sort of practical evaluation retained by those who reject morality in some narrow sense. But I will not make this distinction. I will use these terms interchangeably.

Second, it is customary to distinguish, in Bernard Williams' terminology, between "thin" moral concepts, including concepts of the right and good, and "thick" moral concepts, for instance concepts of courage and kindness.[1] Thin concepts are general-

---

[1] Williams (1985: 140–52).

purpose evaluative notions, and useful in overall moral judgments. Thick notions like courage are properly applicable only to a fairly limited and specific range of non-normative circumstances, for instance only those that someone might plausibly count as brave. There is an analogous distinction between thin and thick moral terms.

Here I will focus on two thin concepts, the concept of what ought to be done and the concept of what is good. I will also speak of what should be done, which I take to be equivalent to what ought to be done, and also equivalent to what is obligatory, required, or right. What ought not to be done is wrong. And I will also presume that one wrong act, say a murder, can be worse than another, say a lie, and that there are permissible acts that are neither wrong nor obligatory. This involves some regimentation of ordinary English, but not an excessive amount.

A third terminological point governs our discussion of moral *reasons*. Some think that reasons have to do in particular with what is right and ought to be done, and not with what is good. But my treatment of accepting a reason in Part I implies that both the right and the good can constitute reasons.

Fourth, our principal concern is to develop a *moral* theory, providing ethical evaluations of actual individual options in action. But we are also tangentially concerned with the evaluation of social-political alternatives. Still, we can focus on moral theory, because the theory we hence develop will also be applicable to the evaluation of social-political alternatives, and because the two sorts of evaluation are less distinct than it may seem. This helps explain the name of my theory: Material Morality.

4.2 Evaluation and Normativity

Consider the words "ought" and "good," as used in moral contexts. There can be individual differences in what is thought through the mediation of the same word.[2] But focus on the public meaning of such words, since it is in the realm of public meaning where most agreement, disagreement, and argument on ethical matters is found. While for some individuals there is a deep entwining of moral thought with, for instance, very specific religious belief, it is fortunate that shared ethical words allow the deeply religious to argue about morality with atheists and various other sorts of theists, without merely talking past them. The thin moral word "right" can be shared by those with significantly different moral views, and allow them to disagree about the acts to which it properly applies.

I will presume that we must take moral agreement, disagreement, and argument seriously, if we are to understand the meaning of moral terms. Various forms of relativism about the truth of ethical claims, specifying that moral truth is relative at a

---

[2] Mendola (2008).

deep level to varying individual or community beliefs, so that lying is wrong for Arthur just in case he believes it is or lives in fastidious Camelot, miss real disagreements about moral truth between those with different beliefs. When Arthur says that lying is always wrong and Lancelot says it often is not, they disagree in a way that would not occur if moral belief were sufficient for moral truth. And there can be real moral disagreements about lying between those who live in different societies with relevantly different norms about lying. Furthermore, moral arguments deploy evidence and logical consistency in a way that naturally suggests that they are arguments about truth in a fairly full-blooded sense, that they are about the way things are (or even must be) in fact. So it is natural to conclude that moral sentences express propositions and have genuine truth-conditions, that moral terms have what I will call "descriptive meaning," and of a specifically objective sort. To claim that something ought to be done is to claim that something specific is true of the world, something independent of varying individual or community beliefs.

Still, we noted in Chapter 1 that some of the most revered ethicists held that such moral truth requires physically irreducible *tele*, Forms of the Good, non-natural properties, divine commands, or noumenal choices of individual character from outside of time. So in physical reality there is a serious question whether there are any moral truths. It needs to be explained both why these various forms of extravagant metaphysics have seemed necessary, and how there can be ethical truth in their absence.

What are the descriptive meanings of "ought" and "good," as they are used in moral contexts? The short, rough answer is that they are governed by three descriptive constraints, which I will call "DC1-NORMS," "DC2-BASIS," and "DC3-METHODS." These descriptive constraints play an important argumentative role here.

The characteristic forms of moral agreement, disagreement, and argument are the key to understanding these three constraints, and hence the descriptive meanings of our thin moral terms. But we have a distance to travel before I can explain these constraints and their significance. We have to see both why traditional ethicists deployed absurd metaphysics, and how we can hope to do without it. Begin with this point:

Ethical discourse is a kind of evaluative discourse; it involves the giving of general reasons for evaluations. I don't intend to provide a full characterization of evaluations, but moral, epistemic, and aesthetic evaluations are paradigmatic. They rank; they separate the sheep from the goats. And they all involve the giving of general reasons for or against. Much human action involves accepted reasons, as we saw in the last part, but accepting reasons as genuinely moral reasons is a more complicated and richer phenomenon. Accepting reasons as genuinely moral reasons is an example of a specific kind of acceptance characteristic of evaluative discourse. This itself is a special form of what I earlier called "strong acceptance." Perhaps one strongly accepts highly selfish reasons, in dark but rational calculations focused on one's own interest or the current time in particular. But strong acceptance of the special kind characteristic of evaluative discourse would rule this out. It involves only general reasons.

Let me explain. Evaluative discourse, of which ethics is an example, has four key features:[3]

First, it requires like evaluation of like cases. For instance, it is not appropriate to judge one act morally right and another descriptively identical act not to be right, since the same reasons apply in both cases.

Second, even non-naturalists about moral properties characteristically accept the richer condition that it is inappropriate to judge one act right and another that is identical in "natural" properties—that is in non-normative properties—not to be right.[4] They accept the so-called "supervenience" of the normative or evaluative on the non-normative, on the natural. It would be absurd to claim that two otherwise identical acts were such that one was wrong and the other right.

Third, the natural properties in question must be general, which is to say that they cannot incorporate haecceities—which are properties of being identical to particular individuals—and also cannot incorporate analogous particularities of time or place. It would be absurd to claim that two otherwise identical acts done by people who differed merely in an haecceity were such that one was wrong and the other right. This third condition distinguishes the strong acceptance characteristic of what I am calling 'evaluations' from other forms of strong acceptance involved in highly selfish calculations, say reasonings rooted ultimately in claims that something is mine or me. My terminology is somewhat artificial at this point, but it marks a useful divide. And nothing important will turn on this terminological stipulation, because I will later explain why moral reasons are not brutely particular in the way this third condition forbids.

Of course, few if any acts are identical in general natural properties. And while we can reasonably hope[5] that individuals who make particular moral claims often have natural descriptive criteria at least implicitly in mind, as grounds for making their moral claims, and that the criteria have generalizing bite, still individuals' grounds for judgment are often idiosyncratic, and hence unable to provide a descriptive meaning for moral terms that can be shared with others, or with themselves at later times when they've changed their views. And very few individuals have a complete general theory of the natural conditions that make things right even implicitly in mind each time they make a judgment that a particular act is right. What's more, not all such criteria which individuals have in mind as the basis of particular moral judgments are legitimate. That's a fourth key point about evaluative discourse, which also points towards another characteristic feature of all strong acceptance of reasons, along with the first two key points I've mentioned.

---

[3] We return to differentia of *moral* strong acceptance.
[4] This characterization of "natural" is suitable to non-naturalists, but Chapter 5 will refine it.
[5] Hare (1952: 111–26) and (1963: 7–29).

Because ethics is a species of evaluative discourse, when someone cites some natural criteria as grounds for a thin moral judgment, it is appropriate to demand a justification for the use of those criteria in that judgment, to ask why that makes something right. This is not a merely epistemic request, as might be made for someone's evidence for any claim. Rather it is specifically due to the nature of ethical discourse as a species of evaluative discourse. Natural grounds for an ethical evaluation must themselves be appropriate to that form of evaluation. And of course a similar question can be raised later about any second set of natural explanatory criteria cited as grounds for appropriateness of the first set of criteria. And so on.

We are forced to natural criteria as grounds for ethical evaluations. But none may seem enough. In some cases of evaluative discourse, for instance epistemology, perhaps certain natural grounds do sometimes seem enough, although this too is controversial. But ethics has seemed an especially difficult case at this point. In ethics, many have felt that we face a kind of vicious infinite regress here. Call it a "justificatory regress."

It is precisely at this juncture that the extravagant metaphysics of traditional ethics has seemed necessary. One way to think of a justificatory regress in the case of ethical notions is this way: G. E. Moore's famous open question argument suggested that no account of an ethical property given in purely naturalistic, non-normative terms will ever be adequate.[6] The open question argument, applied by Moore specifically to "good" but of obvious generality, is the argument that, given any proposed natural property P which is claimed to be the property good, one can see that the question "Is P P?" is closed in a sense in which the question "Is P good?" is open, so that the properties are, it is alleged, in fact distinct.[7] If someone proposes that pleasure is the good, still that question seems much more open than the question of whether pleasure is pleasure. But if pleasure were the good, there would be no difference between the two questions.

There are telling objections to the open question argument, to which we will return, but such an argument has seemed convincing to many philosophers. It is in many ways central to the history of metaethics, and keeps returning in different forms. Whatever its detailed fate, it captures a recurring worry, that the natural is not enough for the moral. However, even Moore thought there was at least one way out of his problem, and there is also at least one analogous way out of our type of justificatory regress.

There might be Moorean non-natural good: a simple property of goodness, not constituted by natural properties. It would be what I will call a "fully normative" property. It would constitute entities that possess it to be morally good in the most normatively robust sense possible. Its presence would decisively and immediately end

---

[6] Moore (1903: 10–21). Harry Ide reports Alexander of Aphrodisias gave the open question argument.
[7] Moore (1903: 15–16).

any justificatory regress for evaluations involving "good." No more explanation would be required.

Because of complexities in the meaning of the word "good," due partly to differences among the good of individuals and of overall outcomes, intrinsic goods and instrumental goods, and virtues that are themselves goods, I will focus in this chapter on what is "right" or "ought to be done," and leave most of the generalization regarding "good" to you. And I will presume that these particular evaluative terms are to be applied to actions, or more exactly to the taking of alternatives as characterized in Chapter 3. So it is only a quite specific class of thin moral terms on which we will focus immediately, different from the one on which Moore focused. But Ross applied a Moore-like argument to "right,"[8] and Sidgwick also thought right was a specific non-natural property.[9] Non-natural rightness should also supervene, as non-naturalists characteristically think and is indeed characteristic of evaluations generally, on specific natural properties, so that those properties can specify the correct natural criteria for rightness. But reference to such a non-natural property might provide the descriptive meaning shared by all individuals who argue about the concrete nature of what ought to be done. And its presence could terminate a justificatory regress.

This property, because of its particular relation to actions, would deliver a particular kind of full normativity, which we might call "to-be-doneness." It is important to notice that to-be-doneness would be a very strange thing.[10] You may reasonably worry that fully normative properties like non-natural goodness or rightness make no coherent sense. However, I am a little more optimistic.

I will argue in Chapter 5 that fully normative properties do make coherent sense, although most obviously in the case of the good and not the right, and not in the exact form traditional non-naturalism like Moore's requires. I will exhibit a *natural* property that yet would be irreducibly and fully normative.[11] This property seems to be present in our experience of certain crudely physical pleasures and pains. I think it has a kind of semantic centrality: If it existed, it would be the best candidate to be goodness of the most basic sort. And our experience of such a property indeed plays a central role in the meaning of all our moral terms, since it provides us with our only completely coherent and comprehensible example of a fully normative property. It is in this sense the paradigmatic normative property.

But the problem is that there are no such properties in physical reality. Our experience is in that respect misleading, as we will see in Chapter 5. So our question will become whether we can get close enough to such a fully normative property in physical reality for moral claims to be true, in other words whether something real can break a justificatory regress in the ethical case.

---

[8] Ross (1930).   [9] Chapter 1 n2.   [10] Mackie (1977: 38–41).
[11] This requires an improved characterization of "natural" property.

I think it can. Though there is in reality neither ethical rightness nor goodness of the central and paradigmatic sorts, and indeed the first may not be wholly coherently conceivable, there are properties close enough to count as rightness and goodness in a somewhat secondary and dependent sense, because of their adequate similarity to fully normative rightness and goodness. What these available properties are is only fully explained by the rest of the book. But I will say that ethical properties of this secondary sort, which are adequately similar to the paradigmatic sorts of normative property, have "quasi-normativity." And the descriptive constraints DC1 through DC3 will help explain what this is, especially for the case of the right.

4.3 Physics and Full Normativity

But before we discuss the descriptive constraints, let me better explain why the fully normative is absent from physical reality.

We presume physicalism, that everything is constituted by quarks, leptons, and force-carrying particles in curved spacetime. The basic properties and relations found in physical reality are, we can reasonably presume, spatio-temporal and causal relations, and also characteristic Galilean physical properties on the rough order of charge and mass, which are themselves broadly causal properties.[12] None of these basic physical properties and relations is itself fully normative, in the robust way that non-natural good or the natural normative property I discuss in Chapter 5 would be.

But of course there are horses and swords in physical reality, even though being a horse is not a basic physical property. Horses and swords are constituted by microphysical particles, and their characteristic properties in reality are also fixed once all the basic physical properties and relations of all microphysical particles are fixed. The horses and swords and their properties *supervene* on the microphysical, but in particular they so supervene because they are *constituted* by the microphysical.

Perhaps it might be thought that a physical structure of some complex sort might constitute in this way a fully normative property. But it can't. This fact depends on the correct understanding of constitution, as well as the highly robust thing I mean by full normativity. Remember that a fully normative property of to-be-doneness halts justificatory regresses and Moorean open questions decisively and immediately, with no more explanation required. And there is no reason to hope that such a thing can be constituted by the physical, partly because of the correct understanding of constitution: If A constitutes B, then A entails B in a certain sense. If there is nothing to being Y but being X, then being X necessitates being Y, and there is no plausible explanation of this necessitation unless being X is itself sufficient for being Y. There is nothing to being Y but being X, at least in the case in question.[13]

---

[12] For complications, see Mendola (1997).
[13] Something else might constitute being Y in another instance. Y is multiply realizable.

This view of constitution is controversial, but along with others I argue for it elsewhere,[14] and it is not highly controversial in the particular application in front of us, as indeed is revealed by the historical popularity of Moore's open question argument.[15] Many find it hard to see how a fully normative property, in the very robust sense in question, could be nothing but a complex physical structure. No physical configuration in itself plausibly constitutes to-be-doneness.

I mean by the fully normative something *very* robust and problematic. Those who hold that moral properties like rightness are constituted by the physical do not characteristically hold that even moral properties are fully normative in this sense. For instance, David Brink has developed what is in effect an alternative account of the lesser thing I call quasi-normativity.[16] Considerable explanation must be given before it can plausibly seem to close justificatory regresses.

Nevertheless, we should pause to consider objections to the conception of constitution I presume, and to its bearing on the presence of the robustly non-natural in a physical world.

The first objection is that, while I construe non-natural properties to involve extravagant metaphysics, there are more deflationary understandings. For instance, Russ Shafer-Landau characterizes ethical properties as non-natural when they do not figure in a science, and suggests that they are no more ontologically problematic than geological or biological properties.[17] An alternative deflationary understanding is that while a moral *concept* involves some crucial "non-natural" semantic component lacking in a natural concept, for instance something that prescribes action, yet both concepts might refer to exactly the same thing in the world, say the same natural universal, while yet strict property identity is absent, because it requires that there be no semantic difference of that non-natural sort, as well as reference to the same universal.

But, I reply, the differences here are merely terminological. I am taking non-natural properties to involve non-natural metaphysics, as Moore did. If moral properties exist but are no more ontologically problematic than geological or biological properties, or simply fail to figure in a science, or require of the world no more than natural universals, then non-naturalism in my robust sense is false. And the quasi-normative properties that I endorse might be non-natural in one of these deflationary senses.

But consider a second objection. It is that even geological and biological properties involve special robust metaphysics, yet metaphysics which is plausibly consistent with physicalism, and so robustly non-natural ethical properties might also be

---

[14] Horgan (1984); Kim (1993: 68–71 and 149–55); Chalmers (1996); Mendola (1997); Jackson (1998). Mendola (2008) specifies a qualification for experience of phenomenal properties. Chalmers (2010: 541–68) articulates a close alternative, and Chalmers (2010: 305–36) criticizes qualifications for phenomenal experience.

[15] I will articulate reservations about Moore's argument, but they do not affect this point.

[16] Brink (1989: 37–80).   [17] Shafer-Landau (2003: 55–79 and 63–4).

consistent with physicalism. Focus on the application of such a view to the moral case: Take whatever structure of non-moral natural properties constitutes some heinous murder. Indeed, take all the natural structures that constitute wrong acts in all possible worlds. Disjoin all of them. That is a disjunctive natural property that is necessarily co-extensive with being wrong.[18] On my view, there might well be such a disjunctive property. But that vast disjunction is not plausibly a fully normative property. Its complicated disjunctive physical details don't plausibly constitute not-to-be-doneness of the strange sort in question for us, which is not a merely disjunct-ive property and requires no further explanation to close justificatory regresses. Still, the current objection is that being wrong may be a distinct but necessarily co-extensive and yet suitably physical property, which yet is fully normative not-to-be-doneness. The same conception may be supposed applicable to geographical and biological properties.

I reply that there are no necessarily co-extensive properties of this sort.[19] There is nothing more to the metaphysics of geology and biology out there in the world than the metaphysics of physics. Some alleged examples of necessarily co-extensive prop-erties involve numbers, but numbers are not natural entities like acts. So consider instead the predicates "being a closed figure with three sides" and "being a closed figure with three angles." Those predicates may seem to ascribe distinct properties. But in fact they do not, since they each ascribe the property of being a figure with a certain shape. To see this, consider the predicate "is a triangle." As Bart Streumer says, if "the predicates 'is a closed figure that has three sides' and 'is a closed figure that has three angles' ascribe two different properties, there would be no reason why the predicate 'is a triangle' would not ascribe a third property."[20] But these predicates do not plausibly ascribe three different properties. If you think they do, then "suppose that we started to call one half of a side a 'half-side' and one half of an angle a 'half-angle'. These figures would also satisfy the predicate 'is a closed figure that has six half-sides and six half-angles'."[21] And surely that is not a distinct property. In other words, it is only plausible to hold that these various properties are distinct on the grounds that they are characterized by different terms with different meanings in different combinations. But the metaphysics of the world itself, which is our concern here, is not answerable in that way to our words and meanings. These various predicates are all made true of triangles by the same properties in the world. Of course, there are differences between angles and sides. But there are also differences between sides and half-sides, between angles and half-angles. So this objection fails. There are no necessarily co-extensive properties of the correct sort.

---

[18] I assume that non-natural properties must supervene on natural properties.

[19] There are determinate and determinable properties. But there is no physical determinable property, no physical natural kind, corresponding to that vast and idiosyncratic physical disjunction. And a physical determinable property would not be a fully normative property.

[20] Streumer (2008: 542).   [21] Streumer (2008: 543).

Objection Three is that nevertheless we can get the fully normative from the physical, that fully normative rightness and wrongness are no more physically problematic than geological or biological properties. Perhaps rightness is a large disjunctive property, or even a physical determinable property.[22] But, I reply, this again is just a terminological difference. Later we will see how Moore's open question argument in fact fails, and how our moral terms do refer to physically acceptable properties of the same rough sort as those discussed in biology and geology. But such properties will not be fully normative in the specially robust sense I have introduced. They will not immediately and decisively end justificatory regresses in the way Moorean non-natural properties would. Considerable explanation will be required to show how they provide a suitable termination for such a regress, and hence how they deliver what I am calling quasi-normativity.

Fourth objection: Derek Parfit suggests that we be "Non-Metaphysical Non-Naturalist Normative Cognitivists."[23] He says there "are some claims that are irreducibly normative . . . and are in the strongest sense true. But these claims have no ontological implications."[24] So perhaps robust normative truths are consistent with physicalism after all. The motivations for such a view are clear; it has all the benefits of ordinary non-naturalism and none of the extravagant metaphysical cost.

But, I reply, Parfit's proposal doesn't work. We need some account of the distinct meaning or content of distinct normative claims that allows that they are true in the strongest sense and yet have no ontological implications, and Parfit does not provide one. He does suggest an analogy with necessary truths of logic and mathematics.[25] This is to explain the obscure by the obscure, but he further suggests that mathematical truths are conceptual truths.[26] However, he also claims that neither mathematical, logical, nor normative claims are analytic,[27] apparently because in that case their truth would depend on contingent facts about language.[28] But conceptual truths depend in a closely analogous way on contingent truths about the concepts of cognizers, unless perhaps conceptual truths depend instead on strange Platonic relations among strange mind-independent Platonic concepts, which has very robust ontological implications.[29] And in any case, at least some intuitively distinct normative truths that are true in the strongest sense, as well as distinct logical and mathematical truths, plausibly require different truth-makers, which are somehow reflected in the different meanings of sentences that report them. These seem to be different ontological implications. Those who favor Non-Metaphysical Non-Naturalist Normative Cognitivism owe us a plausible account of why that isn't the case for normative truths,

---

[22] Red is a determinable property of which scarlet is a determinate.
[23] Parfit (2011b: 261–620).   [24] Parfit (2011b: 486).   [25] Parfit (2011b: 479–80).
[26] Parfit (2011b: 485).   [27] Parfit (2011b: 490).   [28] Parfit (2011b: 744–7).
[29] Parfit (2011b: 481–2) deploys an analogy with negative facts, and Parfit (2011b: 485–6) notes that nothing might be worse than something that is merely possible. But the normative facts we need are not merely negative or modally relational in these ways.

consistent with physicalism, and there is no antecedent reason to expect they can provide one.

In physical reality, we can't get the kind of fully robust normativity that non-natural goodness or even the natural property I will discuss in Chapter 5 would deliver. But we can get close; we can get quasi-normativity.[30] And this is enough to break justificatory regresses involving "right" and "good" in moral contexts. But to see why this is so, we need to consider what sorts of quasi-normativity there might be.

4.4 Quasi-Normativity

There are two ways to understand quasi-normativity. Perhaps it would be better to say that there are two aspects of quasi-normativity, which end up being the same, although that depends on the details of the true moral theory.

The first way to understand quasi-normativity is by appeal to Bernard Williams' distinction between internal and external reasons.[31] A good example of an *external* reason is something with non-natural rightness. Non-natural rightness authoritatively directs any agent about what is to be done, independent of any relation to the agent's actual motivational states. If one of Arthur's alternatives is non-naturally right, then he must take it, whatever he wants. Williams was, with some reason, skeptical about external reasons.[32] But perhaps what he called "internal reasons" are available in physical reality, and provide quasi-normativity.

So-called internal reasons for someone are so only because they bear some relation to that agent's actual motivations. And perhaps everyone has internal reasons to be moral, and that provides sufficient quasi-normativity. However, it is generally granted that the relation between motivations and internal reasons cannot plausibly be too simple or direct. If internal reasons include moral reasons, then evil Mordred has many internal reasons against what he is doing, despite his actual desires and evil motives. So we must complicate the relation between internal reasons and actual motives to develop a plausible account of the quasi-normativity of the moral. Still, it is customary to think that internal reasons require some rational connection with actual motives; it is customary to think there must be some rational route from actual motivations to morality if internalism about moral reasons is true, if morality is to be supported by internal reasons.[33] There are different ways this link might be attempted. One might ascribe a meaning to "rationality" whereby the possession of rationality requires by definition that one be moved by appropriate moral reasons, so

---

[30] More exactly, there are physical conditions in the world that are sufficient grounds for quasi-normativity. Talk of quasi-normativity may involve non-cognitive meaning, as explained later.

[31] Williams (1981). See also Williams (1995 and 2006).

[32] Although curiously unskeptical about one thing's being better than another. See Williams (1981: 111).

[33] For worries about this connection, see D. Sobel (2001). But see also the discussion of Railton in Chapter 6.

that there is a tautological sense in which the rational will be moved by moral reasons, and certainly we should at least be internalists in the tautological sense this would underwrite.[34] But tautologies aren't going to help us much to deliver moral facts or facts about genuine reasons. Still, over the rest of this part, we will see that there is even a non-tautological sense in which all the rational would be moved by moral reasons, that ethics rests on phenomena that are essentially tied to every human agent's motivational states and that require in substantively rational agents further motivations to be moral. There is the necessary rational route. This aspect of quasi-normativity is available in reality, although we aren't yet in position to see why and how it works. In fact, we aren't even really in position yet to understand why internal reasons of the right sort provide quasi-normativity, how they are sufficiently analogous to non-natural moral properties. For instance, it may not be clear how evaluative discourse, which forbids justifying appeal to haecceities, can be rooted in internal reasons. But we will return to the kind of internal reason in question and the way in which it supports morality in Chapter 5.

I will focus here instead on a second way of understanding quasi-normativity, which is based on a closer analogy to the external reasons that would be provided by non-natural properties of rightness or goodness. This better and more directly explains how a justificatory regress is properly blocked, and underlies the structure of my main arguments in this part.

One way to approach it is this way: We have yet to see what properly distinguishes moral evaluations, rooted in moral reasons, from other sorts of reason-based evaluations, for instance those deployed in epistemology and aesthetics. I believe that there is a complex subject matter constraint on ethics and morally relevant reasoning that does this, and also provides a descriptive meaning for some thin moral terms, especially "ought" and "right." It will play a significant role in the rest of the book,[35] and also delivers quasi-normativity. This subject matter constraint on ethics involves the three descriptive constraints noted earlier: DC1, DC2, and DC3. We are at last in position to consider these constraints.

4.5 DC1-NORMS

There is a somewhat vague consensus of ethical judgment about certain sorts of generally characterized cases, a consensus across a very wide temporal and social range that I will try to survey in Part III. We, in a very broad sense of "we," think that slanderous and harmful lies are, other things equal, morally wrong. We think that playful torture of humans is wrong. We accept moral norms that forbid these things. DC1-NORMS treats this vague consensus as a constraint on the meaning of thin moral terms.

---

[34] Though it will fail to capture reasons had by someone because they are less than fully rational.
[35] It is analogous to "the moral point of view."

Perhaps Hitler and Nietzsche and the witch Morgan le Fay disagreed with us about playful torture. But some people also think the world is flat. Some individuals may have wildly deviant moral beliefs while yet a consensus of moral belief exists, and is relevant to the conventional meaning of moral terms and the nature of specifically moral reasons. To claim that all the actions traditionally recognized as morally wrong are morally right, and that all the actions traditionally recognized as morally right are morally wrong, would be to violate the meanings of those thin moral terms. Significant deviation of judgment from the consensus that is yet less than such a full deviation may also violate the fixed meanings of those terms, although I hope for the moment to be excused from specifying the details. One might think that the constraints set by this consensus are merely characteristically implied by speech of the morally right and wrong, and that such an implication might be canceled by indication of contrary belief. But if we communicate with creatures firmly and fully outside of this range of consensus judgment, we should not translate their terms as moral terms, whatever motivation or prescription their terms express and whatever reasons they provide, and we could not learn anything about moral truth from them. So this constraint reflects a truth-condition of our moral terms. I will make concrete suggestions about the details of this consensus of judgment in Part III. But we will see that it bridges many secular and religious traditions, including Confucian, Buddhist, Islamic, African, and ancient and medieval European traditions.

DC1-NORMS is not capable of resolving moral disputes within our vague broad consensus. In that way, it allows that we can have the real disagreements about particular moral judgments that we do have. And this constraint is not so robust as to imply that any deviation of individual judgment from any single detail of the consensus will change the topic.

I admit that it is somewhat accidental that we have the consensus that we do, that Xingis Khan[36] was not ultimately more socially influential than fans of the golden rule, that the descendants of the Vikings are now inside the consensus. And such a consensus may migrate over time. But under current conditions of global communication, it is unlikely that isolated communities making radically distinct judgments will form. It is likely that something roughly like the broad consensus that we now have will survive, though with slow changes. While some ethicists consider very notional confrontations of our ethical judgments with those of very foreign and isolated communities to be revealing, such confrontations are not very realistic in our global world. Once they were, but those days are gone. There is anthropological evidence of considerable diversity of moral judgment across different traditional groups regarding cannibalism, human sacrifice, blood sports, marriage and sexual practices, infanticide, requirements of honor, and slavery.[37] But much of this

---

[36] Who said: "Happiness lies in conquering one's enemies, in driving them in front of oneself, in taking their property, in savoring their despair, in outraging their wives and daughters." Rodzinski (1979: 164–5).

[37] Prinz (2007: 187–95); Doris and Plakias (2008: 313–27). But see Moody-Adams (1997).

diversity no longer exists. And in any case there can be consensus on many ethical judgments even when there is disagreement about others.

This consensus of judgment is clearly not enough. That is not merely because of its vagueness, because it doesn't resolve any real moral arguments we have inside it, nor because certain elements of the consensus can be modified without breaking the chain. Even complete and permanent consensus in detail on all ethical judgments of this kind would not be enough. That is because ethical judgments involve a form of *evaluation*, are rooted in general reason-giving and justification. Ethical judgments express acceptance, and indeed strong acceptance, and indeed a particular kind of strong acceptance, of reasons.

Some within our rough consensus of judgment have little concern with the justification of judgments, with the giving of reasons. And there is wide variation and widespread error in the theological premises of those who are so concerned. There is greater variation in the justifications for ethical claims we deploy than in the claims we make. But almost all of us also share, I believe, some attachment to certain forms of justification that can be elaborated into a proper vindication of our consensus of particular moral judgments, and that can also serve to properly refine it. This is reflected in two more descriptive constraints on ethics and the meaning of thin ethical terms, which help provide for quasi-normativity, and which underwrite the consensus of judgment of DC1-NORMS.

4.6 DC2-BASIS

DC2-BASIS is a cluster of general subject matter restrictions on ethics, as opposed to epistemology, aesthetics, and selfish rational calculation. It has several elements.

First, the subject matter of ethics is, at least at its core, action and well-being. It is about requirements on action that have somehow to do with individual good.[38] If we find people arguing about details of proper stone arrangements when they don't care enough about the stone arrangements for that to be relevant to their well-being in itself and the stone arrangements have no even putative instrumental relations to their well-being, or if we find people discussing fine nuances of their feelings of searing shame about their birthdates, independent of any belief that they can affect their birthdates, then we can properly conclude that they are not engaged in ethical discussion.

There are nuances. Perhaps a concern with birthdates would be ethical if, in some fans of honor, claims about birthdates are entwined with paradigmatically ethical

---

[38] Scanlon (1998: 6) suggests that ethics is paradigmatically about sexual behavior, which may violate this aspect of DC2. But some traditional restrictions on sexual behavior are motivated by false understandings of genuinely ethical considerations, and we lack the consensus on these matters required by DC1. Scanlon (1998: 108–43) also dissents from the focus of ethics on well-being. We return to key aspects of this dissent.

judgments, as the judgments of a deviant subculture, or those with false beliefs about the interaction of birthdates and well-being, might be. What I claim is that, at the very least, the class of ethical judgments is *dominantly* concerned with individual well-being and action.

But it may be objected that even such a qualified element of DC2 reveals my parochial liberal bias. Jonathan Haidt holds that, beyond concerns with care, harm, fairness, loyalty, and liberty, which do play significant roles in MM that rest ultimately on DC2 (although we aren't yet in position to understand all of them), there are also other important independent bases for moral concern present in at least some of us: respect for hierarchies, supported by the characteristic emotions of respect and fear, and respect for various sorts of sanctity, supported by disgust.[39] But, I reply, I am seeking a broad consensus that includes most of the contemporary world, and that depends on no divine hierarchies or holy purities such as physicalism forbids. Fortunately, those who disagree on some things can agree on others and retain sufficient consensus to retain a common language, including the moral language governed by our three descriptive constraints, in which to discuss their differences. In addition, the desire-based account of the good incorporated within MM does afford any actual human interests in hierarchical or sanctified lives some suitable, although also suitably delimited, respect.

The next two components of DC2-BASIS are not specially characteristic of ethics. They do not help differentiate moral evaluation from epistemological or aesthetic evaluation, although one of them does help differentiate evaluation from other forms of strong acceptance. Still, they are important constraints on the meanings of thin moral terms.

The second element of DC2 is a requirement that ethics involves reason-giving. And evaluation built on reasons is committed to like treatment of like cases, of even naturally like cases. This second element of DC2 interacts with the first. Ethics is committed to suitably like treatment of both human agents, who act, and what we might call human *patients*, who have a good or well-being that can be affected by acts.[40] If someone's well-being is to be favored over another's in ethical evaluation, there must be a reason that justifies that. And if someone's action is evaluated differently than another's, there must be a reason that justifies that. Still, reasons may seem cheap. We can always find some grounds of difference between any two real cases. But ethics as I understand it is also committed to something at least a little stronger, impartiality.[41]

Impartiality is the third element of DC2-BASIS. Perhaps there is some ethical argument that should convince everyone to be selfish or to look out only for their own, but that must be a conclusion and not a premise. At the deepest level, ethical

---

[39] Haidt (2012: 93–186).   [40] We later consider animals and group acts.
[41] This is not inconsistent with the importance of special obligations, as I will shortly explain. Chapter 11 will return to them.

justification cannot appeal to reasons expressible only by indexicals like "me" or "now" or by use of proper names or definite descriptions rigged to pick out specific individuals.[42] If it is to be a demand of ethics that we all look specially after our own, there must be an argument that applies to all of us that shows this. This impartiality rules out arguments from self-interest or prudence as being of great foundational weight in ethics. The quasi-normativity of ethical reasons can't merely be that they serve one's self-interest, and it may not matter that they don't serve that interest.

I expect it to be controversial that there is this third element of DC2, which makes ethics a form of evaluation in the sense I characterized earlier. We will repeatedly return to it. It is quite possible that some ancient ethicists in the European tradition, maybe even Plato in some of his voices, were outside this aspect of what I am calling ethics and morality, which I think governs *our* use of at least the thin words "right" and "ought" in moral contexts. We will return to this point also.

The fourth key feature of DC2-BASIS is again specially characteristic of ethics, as opposed to aesthetics and epistemology. This partly involves the way it links, on one hand, the third subject matter constraint DC3-METHODS, which I am about to characterize, with, on the other hand, the intuitive consensus of judgment that constitutes DC1-NORMS. It will take a moment to explain this complex fourth feature.

I have numbered these three descriptive constraints in the order of priority I think they would have in governing change in the meaning of moral terms under extreme conditions where it suddenly became evident that not all can be met. DC1 would be mostly likely preserved, and DC3 least so, I think, in those conditions, although it is also true that DC1 could slowly change over time perhaps more radically. But it is another sort of priority or asymmetry among them that will matter most here, which is due, I claim, to the meaning of our moral terms. This complex asymmetry is the fourth key feature of DC2 that I am now explaining. It also helps explain its name.

Elements of DC2-BASIS may seem implied as a kind of generalization of elements of DC1-NORMS. It may seem that when we look at the consensus judgments, we see that they have this sort of subject matter. But the most important point about the relation of DC2 to DC1 is that DC2 has justificatory priority. That is the central asymmetry in question here. Ethics must provide arguments that start from something like the very weak and abstract premises of DC2-BASIS and reach up to support the detailed traditional judgments of DC1-NORMS, or those consensus ethical judgments have no validity. And it is also in arguments that begin from DC2 that we can hope to properly revise or refine that ethical consensus.

Even the totality of the very general DC2 may seem a long way from a decision procedure in ethics. But I believe that I succeed in arguing in an abstract way from its elements to MM in Chapters 7, 8, and 9, which in turn we will see in Part III can

---

[42] See Rawls (1971: 131) on names and rigged descriptions. This constraint is consistent with the proper internalism about reasons, as we will see in Chapter 5.

bring us all the way to DC1. I think that by the end of Chapter 9, when DC3-METHODS is not yet in play, we will already have enough for a kind of quasi-normativity that breaks the relevant justificatory regresses.

But you may not agree with my optimism on this point. And that is where DC3 comes in. DC3-METHODS more obviously provides the necessary bridge between DC2 and DC1. It helps to flesh out DC2 and so the kind of quasi-normativity I think ethicists need to deliver, and in that way more obviously serves to underwrite DC1 in the necessary way.

4.7 DC3-METHODS

What is DC3-METHODS? The tradition of ethical discussion and reasoning involves a series of traditional ways to interpret the constraints set by DC2-BASIS so that they become more concrete and can more obviously reach up to support the judgments of DC1-NORMS. These are various ways of understanding the impartiality restriction, and also of how reasons in ethics are supported by characteristic motives. There are diverse traditional mechanisms of this sort, but we inherit them all, and they are all present to one degree or another, I believe, in most of our ethical thinking, and even in the meanings of our moral terms, especially the meanings of "right" and "ought." Sidgwick would have called them "methods of ethics," although he had a different list than mine.

Begin by considering three possible methods of ethics that *won't* be useful to us: If there were non-natural facts of rightness, or other sorts of fully normative properties, that would be a legitimate way to understand impartiality. Such a truth would be truth for all; it would break a justificatory regress. And we do have some respect for truth. Full normativity would suffice for quasi-normativity. That is a constraint, in fact a central constraint, on the meaning of moral terms. But there is no non-natural rightness, nor even the close concrete surrogate with full normativity that we will discuss in Chapter 5. So other traditional mechanisms are more important in reality.

A second traditional mechanism seeks impartial grounds for morality in the impartial will or omniscience of God. Religious sentiments may seem intuitively moral motives. While I am not confident about it, and indeed am somewhat hostile to the very idea, I am prepared to grant that the relevance of this mechanism might even be a constraint on the meaning of "right" in moral contexts. But this mechanism too is not available in reality.[43] And realistic temporal rulers and social norms, prone to injustice, are inadequate substitutes.

Partly because of the long history of this traditional theological mechanism, linked with threats of divine sanctions for the immoral, ethics has also often involved arguments from prudence to morality, arguments based on long-term self-interest.

---

[43] An appeal to ideal observers, as in Firth (1952), inherits this conception in more realistic form. It has aspects we consider under the guise of informed desire accounts of well-being and utilitarianism.

They are a third traditional mechanism. Such arguments also have historical roots in very fancy conceptions of self-interest that are nonsense in reality, whereby Plato for instance claims that the just man would be well-off on the rack, fancy conceptions that are perhaps themselves a natural reaction to secularization that undercuts familiar prudential support for morality from traditional religion. But I've already noted that I will treat this third traditional mechanism as a mistake, since ethics is about impartiality, and this mechanism, at least absent divine influence or fancy forms of non-physical self-interest that do not exist, is not suitably impartial. In the absence of those fantasies, it violates the constraints set by DC2. So I think the relevance of this third mechanism, rooted in prudence, isn't itself a relevant constraint on the meaning of "right," although perhaps it is something that might have properly constrained the meaning of "right" under conditions in which robust Platonic well-being or divine insight into moral reality when allied with hellfire were available. Selfishness is one sort of paradigm immorality, and no constraint in itself on moral truth. And in any case, I will later argue that the notion of self-interest isn't sufficiently determinate without ethical shaping, and even with it, to do the kind of work that needs to be done here. There are contemporary physicalist moral realists who understand the reasonability of morality as rooted in the self-interest theory of rationality.[44] But this will be a frequent target of my negative arguments in what follows. And I am here developing an impartial understanding of the reasonability of morality, that properly respects the impartiality of DC2.[45]

So these first three traditional mechanisms are not helpful for us. It is quite possible that our widespread consensus of moral judgments reflected in DC1 would not be so widespread if these traditional methods hadn't been popular, but my hope is to provide sufficient legitimation for that consensus of judgment without appealing to these problematic aspects of tradition. Even the religious and the selfish and the fans of the non-natural also have, I believe, the sentiments and commitments on which viable methods depend.

I will henceforth focus on three viable traditional mechanisms for fleshing out impartiality, which are properly available in reality. First, there is the method developed by the utilitarian tradition, which is rooted in a characteristic moral sentiment of benevolence or sympathy, and focused on equal treatment of moral patients. Perhaps a subsidiary concern with distributive justice of one sort is also traceable to a concern with equality among moral patients. Second, there is the method developed by the contractarian tradition, which is rooted in a characteristic

---

[44] Brink (1989: 37–80).

[45] There are other possible methods of ethics. Chapter 10 returns to Sidgwick's and Parfit's alternative lists, and discusses, under the rubric of contractarianism, mechanisms that root fairness in choices rooted in self-interest under ignorance, developed by Harsanyi, Rawls, and Gibbard. Korsgaard (1996) specifies another typography of mechanisms, and Korsgaard (2009) develops the Kantian conception of morality as a law we give to ourselves, in the guise of a claim that unified action and personality require morality. But unified persons can be highly immoral, by forming a lifetime commitment to a complicated evil plan.

moral sentiment of reciprocity, and focused on equal treatment of moral agents. Third, there is a long tradition of golden rule constructions, which enlace these motives and forms of equal treatment. These three traditional methods of ethics will be the central subject of Chapter 10.

4.8 Quasi-Normativity and the Constraints

Let me summarize our discussion of the three descriptive constraints: We inherit a broad moral tradition that crucially includes a very rough consensus of judgment about cases, and a species of impartial, reason-giving evaluation focused on human action and well-being, fleshed out by three workable traditional methods of ethics: the utilitarian, the contractarian, and the golden rule methods.[46] It is important that this is an asymmetric structure. We must build up from impartiality, at least as interpreted in these three ways, to justify the judgments, and the judgments can be refined and revised in that way. We can't work backwards. We can't properly fudge the mechanisms or the general subject matter of ethics to deliver the results we want. There must be a suitable rationale for our moral judgments.

There is an obvious difficulty. There are three available methods, and they might not coincide. They each might be internally inconsistent, or support different and conflicting moral judgments. But in Chapter 10 I try to reconcile the methods. Sidgwick had a somewhat different list of methods, and Parfit has another, but we share a general project of reconciliation. In my version of reconciliation, what we need to do is to show that the three viable methods—the utilitarian, contractarian, and golden rule traditions—are, when applied in reality, reconciled in a single consistent normative theory that supports our consensus moral judgments. I will attempt to execute that project over the remainder of the book, although as I said I will also provide arguments in Chapters 7, 8, and 9 that do not depend on DC3-METHODS.

My further claim is that the three-part structure of descriptive constraints is reflected in the descriptive meaning of moral terms, especially our target thin term "ought." I have no general analysis of word meaning to propound, and couldn't propound it in a short space if I did. But what "ought" means in moral contexts is constrained by DC1, DC2, and DC3. We can share the consensus of judgments and the methods and the conception of morality as about impartial evaluation of agents and well-being, and still find plenty to argue about, while sharing ways by which to argue about it.[47]

---

[46] Scanlon (1998: 12) calls such things different "accounts of the property of moral wrongness." But I show that they aren't rivals in his sense.

[47] We can also argue about the viability or importance of the traditional methods I have ruled out, or the legitimacy of the methods I haven't.

The details are of course vague in our minds, but I think we all have tendencies to reasoning based in reciprocity and benevolence that underlie the consensus judgments that we mostly share, though many of us also have the various unworkable tendencies grafted on in complex ways, and we have many relevant individual differences. And, in any case, Hilary Putnam with help from Saul Kripke and Tyler Burge has convinced most philosophers that there is a linguistic division of labor, with experts who fix the extension of certain terms, which are used by others who only incompletely understand the extensions of the terms but use them with their full public meaning.[48] I don't have the faintest idea what a buckler is, but it is what I'm thinking about through the mediation of that word because of what the experts know. And the tradition of philosophical ethics constitutes the relevant experts in this case.[49]

So we come to the punch-line of this chapter: Quasi-normativity reflecting the three descriptive constraints, which is supported by impartial justification based in traditional moral motives, which is rooted in central ethical concerns with action and well-being, which supports a very broad consensus of judgment, and which is also reflected in the meaning of our moral terms, is, I believe, enough to break a justificatory regress involving "ought" and "right" in ethical contexts. When full normativity is unavailable, broad consensus with a consensual and impartial rationale consistent with reality, and with all of that reflected in the meanings of the relevant terms, will have to do. Wide consensus rooted in justification of this sort is the best available analogue of mind-independent, fully normative truth. But despite its focus on consensus, this proposal can explain our range of moral argument and disagreement. It leaves us room to argue, and means to argue. And it can deliver ethical truth in reality, while acknowledging the reasons that revered ethicists have been tempted by implausible metaphysics.

Still, this proposal may seem too specific to capture what is meant by "ought" or "right" in moral contexts. I don't feel the force of this objection. Discussion of meaning in philosophy is one place where we have little more than theory, I have no general theory of linguistic meaning to defend, and I am sympathetic to Nietzsche's warning that no word with a history can be defined. However, if you feel its force, there is also a more generic conception of "ethically justified action" available to characterize the descriptive meaning of "ought to be done," in which case what I have proposed here would be merely a certain understanding of what that might be relevant to our world. Let me explain this point. In Chapter 5, we will see that the notion of a fully normative property does make coherent sense, even though

---

[48] Putnam (1975). Mendola (2008: Part One) provides extended discussion. I am tempted by a metalinguistic component for the content of many of our ethical thoughts.

[49] There are religious experts, but they have false beliefs that undercut their expertise when it doesn't overlap with that of philosophers. All relevant philosophers have long been aware of all three methods I develop. Contractarianism wasn't on Sidgwick's list, but he knew Hobbes, and also golden rule arguments. And anyway relevant expertise can be distributed.

there are no such properties in our world. An alternative and more general understanding of "right" in moral contexts can appeal simply to sufficient similarity to fully normative rightness relevant to action and well-being, perhaps conjoined with something like DC1-NORMS or with an insistence that the similarity be relevant to justificatory concerns. But, as I said, my more specific main proposal does seem to me sufficiently ecumenical. Most of our contemporary arguments about ethical fact do make sense in this framework, though of course some ethicists have been wrong about the nature of reality or the quality of certain arguments.

4.9 Contrasting Proposals

Consider some popular contrasts to my metaethical proposal: There is a contemporary tradition of argument in moral philosophy by appeal to intuitions about concrete cases that may seem hard to fit inside my account. Still, as you will see in Part III, I think that many who make such arguments are surprisingly adept at discovering elements of our normative consensus that we have overlooked, and that should play a role in DC1-NORMS. Indeed, other consequentialists will likely worry that I end up ceding these intuitions too much respect. And in the absence of non-natural properties that someone might better intuit than someone else, it is not plausible to claim simply on the basis of an idiosyncratic intuition that one has thereby discovered a moral truth that is not reflected in that consensus. There is nothing in the world to make such an intuition true, as opposed to its denial, except perhaps arguments rooted in DC2 or DC3.

There is also a contemporary tradition, stemming from Rawls, of seeking a kind of reflective equilibrium between moral intuitions at different levels of generality, including levels of generality that encompass not only DC1 but DC2 and DC3.[50] However, in light of our three descriptive constraints, I presume that there is an important asymmetry built into the structure of moral reasoning, whereby the judgments of DC1-NORMS must be vindicated on the basis of DC2-BASIS fleshed out by DC3-METHODS. And this is in conflict with some contemporary appeals to reflective equilibrium, which violate that sort of asymmetry. Still, I insist that we aren't simply concerned with moral epistemology, coherentist or otherwise. We are concerned to discover what makes moral claims true. And moral truth flows up from the world through the impartiality of reason-giving, as captured by the traditional methods of ethics, to particular moral judgments. In the absence of such a rationale, any intuitive ethical judgment is false, even if there is a general consensus about it. And any revision or refinement of consensus requires a like rationale. What's more, we cannot properly fudge the rationales simply to yield the particular judgments about cases to which we are attached, no more than it is appropriate to fudge

---

[50] Rawls (1971: 20).

descriptive claims about the world—that truth tellers aren't welcomed into Valhalla, that there is no noumenal choice of one's character from outside of time—simply to deliver the particular normative judgments to which we are attached.[51] I think that would be a way of taking morality not seriously enough. To some, I will seem too demanding when I insist on this asymmetry, and rule out normative theories that cannot meet it. And of course, my attempt to provide such asymmetric arguments for MM may fail, and then I will have failed in my own terms. Still, if you think I am merely wrong about the need for asymmetric argument, you can accept all my positive arguments for MM, and simply think I haven't disposed of some alternatives, although as we will see MM is normatively ecumenical in many other ways you may welcome.

Another contemporary conception related to reflective equilibrium is Jackson and Pettit's moral functionalism.[52] This semantic proposal about the descriptive meaning of moral terms is that our folk theory of morality can be encapsulated in a Ramsey-sentence that identifies (for instance) rightness as the (with luck) physically acceptable property that meets folk morality's various demands.[53] I have no objection to this proposal as long it can be adapted to specify exactly the constraints I have already articulated, in particular the asymmetries I am insisting on.[54] But notice that the wildly disjunctive physical property of right acts that ends up meeting these constraints might not reveal very well the dependencies among our constraints that constitute it as appropriately quasi-normative.[55]

One standard criticism of moral functionalism as it has been developed by Jackson and Pettit is that moral facts, on their proposal, are supposed to turn on where we end up in folk morality after maximum debate and reflection, which seems either to involve the false claim that it is tautological that after sufficient time we will end up agreeing on the moral truth, or the false claim that if we split into different groups who can't agree then there will differing truths.[56] But in my version, we don't have to wait very long. Either I'm performing the single relevant trajectory in this book, which is certainly no tautology, or MM is false.

Another contrasting but popular view about the descriptive meaning of moral terms is that such a term refers to whatever it is that causally regulates competent speakers' use of the term, which may suggest a very different and more empirical

---

[51] I am *not* claiming that one cannot infer from normative claims to non-normative claims, from the fact that someone lied to the fact that they told an untruth. I am *not* claiming that moral properties cannot help explain non-moral facts, that Hitler's evil can't explain some of his heinous actions.

[52] Jackson and Pettit (1995); Jackson (1998: 113–62).   [53] D. Lewis (1970).

[54] Jackson (1998: 134–5) suggests that the asymmetries will fit in. It is characteristic of moral functionalism to treat morality holistically, and to consider the folk constraints on its content to be a priori. I prefer a less holistic and an explicitly semantic rather than epistemic conception of the relevant constraints. See Mendola (2008: Chapter 10). But these are not large differences.

[55] This favors understanding rightness as "the higher-order property of having a property that occupies the rightness role" from among the candidates suggested by Jackson and Pettit (1995: 28).

[56] Yablo (2000); Horgan and Timmons (2009).

methodology for ethics.[57] But we will consider this account in its most plausible application, to the notion of well-being, in Chapter 5. And we will see that when properly developed even it does not conflict with the present proposal.[58]

4.10 Non-Cognitivism

Still, my semantic proposal faces serious objection. Even if I succeed in arguing from the three descriptive constraints to MM, you may still think that it remains a Moorean open question whether what MM specifies as what ought be done is in fact what morally ought to be done, and you may object that that open question shows that I have missed something of what "ought" means. In other words, it may seem that the kind of quasi-normativity that I deliver, which ends justificatory regresses by appeal to the impartial focus of ethics on actions and well-being and to the consensus of judgment rooted in the confluence of all three workable methods of ethics, is not sufficiently analogous to full normativity. The sort of rooted consensus I can deliver may not seem sufficiently analogous to non-natural moral rightness. And you may further think that my discussion of internal reasons that accompanies this main line of our advance will also fail to close the relevant question. In fact, you may even complain that Moorean full normativity would not be enough to do that.[59] So we need now to focus on this cluster of objections, which do require some refinement of my metaethical proposal.

Begin with some terminology. "Non-cognitivists" deny that moral sentences express propositions or have genuine truth-conditions or descriptive meaning.[60] They think that moral terms in assertive sentences rather serve to *express* emotion or other motivational states (as opposed to *asserting* that there is that emotion or motivation), or alternatively serve to *prescribe* in something of the manner of commands. Lancelot may express his surprise by saying "Oh!," but he doesn't hence assert that he is surprised. He may express a belief by saying "That dragon has wings," but he doesn't hence assert that he has such a belief. And he is doing something like prescribing when he yells "Run!"

Non-cognitivism is often motivated by skepticism about genuine moral truth, and we have discovered a way to outwit that skepticism. But it also has positive motivations, related to certain understandings of Moore's open question argument:

---

[57] Boyd (1988).

[58] The suggestion of Brink (1997) that general referential intentions may focus moral terms on what is interpersonally justifiable is even closer to my proposal.

[59] van Roojen (2010) asks whether one might entertain the descriptive content of the notion of right and not realize that it engages the reasons one accepts, even when it does.

[60] Another way to characterize non-cognitivism is as the claim that moral sentences do not express beliefs. But there is a state that might legitimately be called "belief" which merely involves the assertion of moral sentences to oneself, whatever they mean. So this doesn't work.

(1) Whatever set of descriptive conditions in the world we specify as those that constitute an action as such that it ought to be done, a non-cognitivist may suggest that it is an open question whether the action ought to be done, that its being such is not entailed by its meeting those conditions.

(2) In particular, they may claim that it is an open question because of a particular fact about the meaning of "ought" revealed by such cases: There could be a society which had a term that picked out exactly such descriptive conditions of actions and yet would not properly be translated as "ought to be done," if it failed to express motivation or prescribe in the requisite way.[61]

(3) A non-cognitivist may even claim that it doesn't matter what descriptive conditions of actions anyone and everyone in that society attaches such a phrase to. As long as the phrase prescribes or expresses motivation in the requisite way, it can still be properly translated by our moral expression "ought to be done."[62]

I do not think that such open question arguments could be successful against descriptive properties that were fully normative in the sense either of Moore's non-natural good or even the fully normative natural property that we will discuss in Chapter 5. If there were fully normative properties present in the actual conditions characterized by moral sentences then all three of these claims would be false, as long as DC1-NORMS were not hence violated. But such arguments can be more plausibly deployed against my sort of quasi-normativity. I think that this cluster of non-cognitivist motivations reveals something important about the meaning of our moral terms, which requires emendation of my proposal.

Still, we need to exercise some care here. For one thing, most contemporary philosophers think that the questions "Is Hesperus identical to Phosphorus?" and even "Are physicians doctors?" can seem open in a way that "Is Hesperus identical to Hesperus?" and "Are physicians physicians?" never do, while yet Hesperus is Phosphorus and physicians are nothing other than doctors.[63] So ethicists should not deploy an open question argument without further ado. But perhaps we can augment these open question arguments with an insistence that such claims as my proposal about ought-to-be-doneness seem open even to those who fully understand the meaning of the relevant terms, unlike the claims that Hesperus is Phosphorus and that physicians are doctors.[64] So I need another reply to this objection.

The first part of my reply is to say that claim (3) is wrong. If the society in question prescribes or expresses positive emotion only about what are, by our consensus of judgment, all the intuitively heinous acts, including random and gratuitous tortures and murders for fun, then we would not take them to be talking about what is morally right. DC1-NORMS would be violated, as well as the other descriptive constraints. Of course, there may be marginal deviations from consensus, but not

---

[61] Hare (1952: 149) develops this for "good."   [62] Hare (1952: 148–9).
[63] See Mendola (2008: Part One).
[64] This proviso governed our previous discussion of the open question argument.

whole-scale inversion of this sort. There is also a second problem with claim (3). Notice that even if there were a non-natural irreducible property of *wrongness* of actions picked out by a term, and meeting the constraints for moral wrong set by DC1, claim (3) requires that it be translated as "ought to be done" as long as the term prescribes or expresses positive emotion. That is absurd, and while of course it isn't absurd to deny that there is non-natural rightness and wrongness, we are attempting to develop an admissible physicalist substitute. Perhaps it is thought that a society of people who positively emote about or prescribe merely heinous acts yet have a *moral* disagreement with us that my proposal cannot capture. But the primary form of moral disagreement we have with such wildly hypothetical people is that, if they follow their prescriptions, we think they are heinously immoral, and that is something my proposal can capture, although those people don't much think about morality at all. If they think they do, then they are confused.

But the second part of my reply is more concessive, and requires an amendment to my proposal. Claim (2) and even claim (1) are plausible in a physical world, where the only true descriptive conditions are at base physical and not fully normative conditions. These claims do suggest, I think, that there is a non-cognitive component to the meaning of moral terms. Still, we shouldn't get carried away. Claim (2) does not imply that moral terms have no descriptive meaning, only that they also have a non-cognitive content or meaning. And the non-cognitive content cannot plausibly be too robust. We can of course utter moral judgments insincerely, but we can also make moral claims honestly and sincerely and yet be subject to weakness of will and hence act in a contrary direction. We can know the right and yet do the wrong. And I think it is not implausible to claim that there are among us open amoralists, who use ordinary moral language to sincerely express truths, but then truthfully tell us they don't care.[65] I even think that there might be large groups of sincere amoralists, or even societies of sincere amoralists,[66] with whom we could communicate about morality in a fruitful way. Perhaps they have very accurate perceptions of non-natural normative properties, but whatever the fate of non-natural properties, let me tell you a secret: I've been informed by helpful angels that Kant and Sidgwick were in fact amoralists in the motivational sense, although not sincere and open ones.[67] They wrote their wonderful books about morality, but they just didn't care. Now imagine a large society like that, filled with equally able if less than morally admirable philosopher-ethicists. I think we could learn quite a bit from them about moral truth.

Still, I admit that there is a non-cognitive component of the public meaning of our moral terms, for which claims (1) and (2) reveal the need. What is it?

---

[65] Brink (1989: 46–8); Svavarsdóttir (1999: 176–83).

[66] Contrary to Dreier (1990) and Lenman (1999).

[67] It is interesting to consider what passages in their books would be dishonest if they failed to meet various motivational conditions.

Here's the short version, although it will take a moment to explain it and its relationship to similar proposals: When A asserts in a moral context "B ought to z" that conventionally imputes that A accepts corresponding reasons, but such an imputation is canceled when A merely asserts a sentence which has such a phrase in an *unasserted* context, such as "If B ought to z, then B ought to y" or "It is not the case that B ought to z" or "C believes that B ought to z,"[68] and is also canceled when A asserts something analogous to "But I don't care." To say that a proposition is conventionally imputed by some form of words is to say (i) that by convention such a proposition is expressed but not said by those words, so that, while problematic and potentially misleading, such words are not strictly false when such a proposition is false, and (ii) that such a proposition is not expressed when the imputation is canceled due to conventionally specified context.

This is not a new idea. David Copp and Stephen Barker have proposed that there is in such cases a conventional implicature, meaning by that very much what I mean by a conventional imputation.[69] In Barker's proposal, analogously to Hare's, the descriptive content of a moral term will vary across users, and maybe over time for one individual, depending on what natural criteria they favor for the term in question.[70] But in Copp's proposal, the descriptive meaning is, at the most abstract level, generally shared. The abstract descriptive meaning for *wrong* is supposed by Copp to be "some relevantly justified or authoritative moral standard or norm prohibits it,"[71] and that is quite like the summary abstract descriptive meaning I noted earlier.[72] Copp favors a "society-centered" account of authoritative norms whereby they are norms that will best meet the relevant society's needs. But we could consider DC1 through DC3 as an alternative account of justified or authoritative moral standards or norms. So I think the idea of using conventional implicature to defend the descriptive meaning of moral terms is a good one, especially in Copp's version.

But let me explain this notion, and why Copp has felt the need to move beyond it. The notion of a conventional implicature is due to Paul Grice. It is the notion of something that is by convention implied by words though not said.[73] If what is implied but not said by an utterance is false, that would not strictly speaking make the utterance false. So far, so good. I also believe that one reasonable test for this is that the implication can be canceled, and that is what Copp originally thought.[74] But there are problems with this, which explain why Copp has moved on.[75] One problem consists of Kent Bach's arguments that there is no such thing as conventional

---

[68] This phenomenon is in this way unlike emotional expression tied to racial epithets. See Hay (2013) for further disanalogies. This point also suggests that M. Schroeder (2009) does not address a crucial class of hybrid views.

[69] Barker (2000); Copp (2001, 2007: 153–202).

[70] van Roojen (2005) discusses problems this creates.   [71] Copp (2007: 182).

[72] Boisvert (2008) develops another proposal in this vicinity.   [73] Grice (1989: 24–6).

[74] Grice (1989: 41–57); Copp (2007: 171).   [75] Copp (2009).

implicature, strictly speaking.[76] Another problem is that it is more orthodox to claim that cancelability is the mark of what is called conversational implicature as opposed to conventional implicature, and indeed there is much in Grice to suggest this. Still, let me say on this third point that Grice only seems to me to suggest cancelability as a *necessary* condition of being a conversational implicature, and gives cases in which the conventional element of the meaning of a term is canceled.[77]

Despite these problems, whatever the details of Grice scholarship and the requirements of conventional implicature in any strict sense, it is clear that there is the phenomenon on which Copp originally focused. To capture it, Copp now talks of conventional *simplicature*, present when there are propositions communicated but not explicitly asserted.[78] But his account of this has fine details on which we should not become stuck. That is why I am speaking more vaguely of conventional imputation. The imputation in question is a matter of linguistic convention, and isn't strictly said, and can be canceled in the cases I have noted. That's all I mean by "conventional imputation." For instance, an amoralist can sincerely and openly say "That is the morally right thing to do, but I don't care," and so cancel the non-cognitive conventional imputation of "right." And the amoralist can also say "That is the morally right thing to do" without giving any evidence of their amorality and still say what is, while misleading and problematic, strictly true.[79]

What in particular is conventionally imputed by use of a positive moral term like "ought to be done"? We already possess a useful resource for this role, mostly cribbed from the non-cognitivist Allan Gibbard.[80] Copp himself suggests Gibbard-style expression of acceptance of allied norms as the non-cognitive component of meaning in question.[81] And we have been developing notions that are closely analogous. Consider the notion of accepting a reason, which I applied in Part I to the analysis of action and group action. This is very similar to Gibbard's notion of accepting a norm, though it doesn't imply, as his notion does, what I called in Chapter 3 "reflective endorsement." One needn't reflectively endorse all the group acts in which one yet participates. In fact, Gibbard himself more recently has stressed the similarity of accepting norms to decisions of practical reasoning,[82] which apparently do not imply reflective endorsement in this sense.[83] And individual action supported by a stable plan over time is group action in my sense. So there is considerable

---

[76] Bach (1999). But see also Potts (2007) and Copp (2009).

[77] "If we all know that Macbeth hallucinated, we can quite safely say that Macbeth saw Banquo, even though Banquo was not there to be seen, and we should not conclude from this that an implication of the existence of the object said to be seen is not part of the conventional meaning of the word *see*, nor even (as some have done) that there is one sense of the word *see* that lacks this implication." Grice (1989: 44).

[78] Copp (2009).

[79] There is a question how a society of amoralists could have a term with such a conventional imputation.

[80] Gibbard (1990: 23–82).   [81] Copp (2007: 184–5).   [82] Gibbard (2003).

[83] Bratman (2008: 95–6) and Broome (2008: 105–6) make this point as an objection to Gibbard.

confluence between my notion and Gibbard's.[84] Accepting a reason is at least characteristically linguistically mediated, by declarative sentences whose internal utterance, in the mind's throat and ear, might be considered a kind of belief. But it is principally a kind of motivational state. It involves no cognitive commitments to representing the world as involving particular normative properties in any very robust sense.[85] It is certainly consistent with physicalism.[86] We accept reasons for all sorts of things. We accept reasons which support all the group actions in which we participate, however heinous or ill-conceived they may be, indeed however morally heinous we take them to be. Certainly no robust moral facts are required to constitute the mere acceptance of reasons.

Still, we want something a little richer. Our target now is a very particular kind of acceptance of reasons, that involved in taking things to be morally right or good. We have considered two notions that are even closer to this. They are strong acceptance, and the particular form of strong acceptance which underlies all evaluative discourse. But we need just a little bit more now than either. Gibbard thinks that the acceptance of moral norms in particular involves planning for particular emotions of guilt and anger.[87] But while I am here telling you what to do and not to do, I am reluctant to tell you how to feel. And I also think that neither guilt nor anger, nor any specific emotions, are generally characteristic of moral judgment.[88] We seem too emotionally diverse for that. Many seem sincerely moved to genuine moral judgment and action by shame, pride, or cool calculation of salvation.

But we have already developed another sort of specification of the acceptance of reasons as moral. It involves belief reflecting the cognitive or descriptive component of the meaning of moral terms, captured by our three descriptive constraints. It implies that moral judgments are true or false in a robust sense, as a matter of correspondence to quasi-normative facts in the world.[89]

4.11 What "Ought" Means

So here we are: When I say in a moral context "Arthur ought to fight," I say something that has the descriptive meaning discussed earlier in the chapter, governed by DC1 through DC3. But it also conventionally imputes that I accept corresponding

---

[84] Other differences are that norms in Gibbard's sense specify conclusive deontic requirements and permissions, and that, while positive reasons for an action do weigh in favor of it, I don't accept his account of this. See Gibbard (1990: 87 and 160–4).

[85] Perhaps there is a trivial minimalist sense in which it does involve the representation of normative properties. See Gibbard (2003).

[86] Mendola (2008) explains how psychological states are consistent with physicalism.

[87] Gibbard (1990: 40–5).

[88] Although I sketch ways that the general motives of reciprocity and benevolence play another role in morality.

[89] Or at least the physical basis of quasi-normativity.

reasons,[90] while the extra conditions required for the kind of strong acceptance of the reasons characteristic of evaluative discourse to be involved are implied by the descriptive meaning. It is part of the conventional meaning of such words that they impute such acceptance, but that imputation is canceled in non-assertive contexts, and also in certain other contexts. I also believe that my sentence conventionally imputes a *prescription* of such action in all cases supported by exactly the same reasons, in the manner developed by R. M. Hare.[91]

There is a traditional objection to non-cognitivism, the so-called embedding problem. Peter Geach, building on suggestions of Frege, argued that non-cognitivism could not provide a proper account of the validity of arguments like this: "If tormenting the palfrey is bad, getting your little brother to do it is bad. Tormenting the palfrey is bad. Therefore, getting your little brother to do it is bad." Non-cognitivism can't properly help itself to the customary explanation of logical validity as truth preservation, and because the conditional first premise in this argument can be sincerely asserted by those who don't accept its antecedent, it can't plausibly account for the meaning shared by the antecedent of the first premise and the second premise.

But these are tasks that the descriptive meaning of moral terms, as long as it is shared by different speakers of a language, can handle easily. The non-cognitive conventional imputations of a moral sentence are canceled in non-assertive contexts like the antecedent of a conditional, and play no role in the validity of such an argument. So we have a viable proposal about the semantics of thin moral phrases like "ought to be done," which will be developed and refined throughout what follows.

4.12 "Good"

We have been discussing the notion of what ought to be done, and not the good. The notion of the good involves many complexities. But we will focus now specifically on the notion of intrinsic individual well-being or good, on what is good for a person independent of means–ends relations to other goods.

There are distinct traditional conceptions of this sort of good that need to be rectified and unified, though in a somewhat different manner than contractarianism, utilitarianism, and the golden rule tradition. That is our job in Chapters 5 through 7. The nature of this rectification will allow an analogous account of the complex meaning of the thin term "good," although I will leave it as an exercise for the reader.

This account might involve interesting differences. I suggested earlier that it is possible that there was a relevant change of meaning between us and ancient Greek

---

[90] What sort of correspondence is required is a complicated matter.
[91] Hare (1952 and 1963). If you claim an act is right on grounds of certain reasons, you hence prescribe that everyone so act in all other circumstances in which exactly those reasons apply.

moralists, which involves the impartiality required by DC2, which now governs the meaning of "ought" in moral contexts. Perhaps this change also involved related features of DC1 and DC3. And I admitted that it is historically contingent that we are now where we are with this. On the other hand, it is also possible that the ancient Greek ethicists were outliers, since as we will see in Part III there were widespread ancient religious traditions that shared our contemporary focus on the moral importance of impartial benevolence. But the immediately relevant possibility is that there may have been much less change in the meaning of analogues of the thin term "good" as applicable to individual well-being between us and ancient Greek moralists. Perhaps we share only some thin terms with them. But, as I said, I won't here attempt a detailed account applicable to "good."

We aren't done with metaethics. Chapter 5 will discuss the natural but irreducibly and fully normative property that has a kind of semantic centrality for all thin ethical terms even though it does not exist, as well as the aspect of quasi-normativity that involves internal reasons. And since DC2 depends on facts about individual good and well-being, our discussions of the good will help us to more fully probe even my metaethical proposal about "ought." But our principal focus hereafter will be on more specifically normative matters, on ethics rather than metaethics. And we will begin those discussions with a focus on individual good.

5

The Road to Desire

It is customary to distinguish (i) desire-based conceptions of well-being, which identify individual good with the satisfaction of desire, (ii) hedonist conceptions, which identify that good with pleasure and the absence of pain, and (iii) objective conceptions, according to which certain things are objectively good for individuals regardless of their attitudes of desire or pleasure. And there is a rationale for this division: Objective conceptions contrast naturally with conceptions that hold that well-being varies with individual psychological attitudes of desire or pleasure, and desire and pleasure also provide another natural contrast. There is also intuitive motivation for each conception, reflecting goods characteristic of each. Health and knowledge seem objectively good for Lancelot, whatever his desires and pleasures. But Guinevere's pleasure is also intuitively good for her. And what Arthur wants seems highly relevant to his individual good.

This chapter will discuss hedonism and objective conceptions. Chapters 6 and 7 consider desire-based conceptions. My positive proposal about individual good is desire-based, so this chapter is primarily negative. But the account also has ecumenical aspects I explain first.

5.1 Ecumenism

Chapter 4 argued that the correct account of individual good must suffice to terminate relevant justificatory regresses, for instance those expressed by open question arguments. It must be possible to explain why the conditions specified by an account of the good are in fact good.

Moorean non-natural goodness would be a fully normative property, capable of immediate and decisive termination of such a regress, with no further explanation required. But there is no non-natural goodness in reality. I indeed believe, as I will shortly explain, that it is not coherently conceivable.[1] Still, there is one form of hedonism that deploys a coherently conceivable *natural* property that is irreducible goodness, and hence fully normative. One key ecumenical aspect of my desire-based proposal is that this form of hedonism retains a kind of semantic centrality, even

---

[1] Mendola (1997: Part One) discusses coherent conceivability.

though the paradigmatic form of goodness that it propounds does not exist in reality. The quasi-normative goodness that does exist in reality must sufficiently resemble this unreal but still paradigmatic normative property.

In the absence of fully normative goodness in reality, we must fall back. We must seek a kind of good that is merely quasi-normative, which is sufficiently similar to fully normative good to end justificatory regresses, after some further explanation, and also to provide the relevant sort of internal reason. We will continue to focus on the aspect of quasi-normativity relevant to justificatory regresses, but along the way we will discover the elements for a proper account of internal reasons. The explanation that an account of the good provides for the termination of justificatory regresses, what I will call the "rationale" of that account, is hence central for us. It is not enough for an account to provide a list of things that are good; it must provide a sufficient explanation of why, even in our physical world, they are good.

The three traditional conceptions of the good overlap to a considerable degree. Many of their forms are to a degree extensionally equivalent: specify the same list of things as good for us. But even when they are extensionally equivalent, what will matter here is the rationale they provide for thinking such things good. For our purposes, accounts that differ in such a rationale will essentially differ, and the three traditional conceptions do so differ.

Also, the three types of accounts are not in ordinary forms *exactly* extensionally equivalent. There are goods especially characteristic of each type of account. But this is a second way in which my desire-based proposal will be ecumenical. The true desire-based account can deliver, given the facts of what we desire, the value of the putative goods that are most characteristic of both hedonism and objective conceptions: pleasure, knowledge, and health. In addition, pleasure, knowledge, and health have other subsidiary roles in my positive proposal. There is a rough commonsense consensus about individual good, reflected in DC1-NORMS, which I aim to respect.

Nevertheless, I will not be entirely ecumenical. I will argue that physicalism, in conjunction with other realistic constraints, requires a principally desire-based account. In other words, our desires provide the central operative rationale for a conception of human good. That is because physicalism in conjunction with obvious facts implies, as we will see, that the correct account of well-being must be modest rather than robust. By this I mean that it cannot provide any expert correction of someone's conception of what is good for them, because there is no genuine outside expertise on such matters. Of course, there are experts on how to get things you want. If you want money, there are financial experts. If you want a subjective feeling of happiness, there are experts on that as well. There are also experts who can help you ascertain what in fact you want. But there is no *fundamental* expertise, about what things are good for you regardless of what you actually want.

How is the absence of fundamental expertise consistent with the existence of a rough consensus of good reflected in DC1-NORMS? Because that consensus is too vague to provide useful advice to most of us about our own good, and primarily governs the good of others that properly moral action must respect. It does not overrule your own conception of what is good for you if you lie outside the consensus and only your own good is at stake in your action, although there is a complication due to a possible difference between your immediate interests and those of your future selves to which we will return.

But these are details. The key immediate point is that robust good would both refine our rough commonsense consensus about the good and provide corrective advice to individuals about their own good. And as we will see, there is no such robust good in reality.

Objective conceptions are naturally robust. They specify things that are good for you whether you want them or not. Since some people do not care most about their own pleasure,[2] so too are the most paradigmatic hedonist conceptions. Desire-based conceptions, now the most popular accounts of well-being, include both robust and modest forms. But the form I will propound in Chapter 7 is modest. And modesty is all reality allows.[3]

It may seem that even our individual conception of our own well-being is not well represented by our individual desires, as I will presume, since we can see the good and be drawn to the worse. Indeed, the very fact that our tradition incorporates hedonism and objectivism may seem to imply that any desire-based account is robustly revisionary. But the desire-based account I eventually propose will incorporate mechanisms that undercut these worries, including endorsement of the goods most characteristic of hedonism and objectivism. However, these too are details to which we will return. Focus now on the central point:

There are no fully normative properties of goodness in physical reality. But there is nevertheless one form of individual desire-based good that is quasi-normative in a sense closely analogous to that characterized for the right in Chapter 4. And it is modest enough for physical reality.

My positive story about the good awaits Chapter 7. Although we are about to consider a contrasting theory of the good that does reveal the semantically central normative property, and although the true theory of the good must deliver some specific goods more characteristic of its competitors, the rest of this chapter is

---

[2] Intrinsic and not instrumental care matters most. But see 6.5.

[3] It may seem that I propound a robust revision of moral beliefs, when I later claim that morality is demanding and traditional prudence immoral. But this develops themes implicit in traditional morality and reflected in our consensus of moral judgment, which does not consistently deny these things. And we have special reason to expect that individual intuitions rejecting such demands are distorted by self-indulgence, and hence lack authority, which is less plausible about our conception of our own good. You may also later worry that I make a robust appeal to consensus desires, when the satisfaction of all one's desires should count towards one's well-being. But consensus functions there in a different way than in DC1. I only appeal to consensus desires when there is a distributional conflict involving individuals with different desires, to allow a consensual resolution of practical conflict. One can have a desire relevant to one's own well-being and yet be outside any consensus of desire.

oriented in a largely negative way. It argues that the only forms of objectivism and hedonism that are tenable in reality are desire-based conceptions in disguise.

Part of my argument will be that robust accounts of these two sorts would require various implausibly metaphysical resources. Part will be that the best forms are not as distinct from the correct desire-based conception as it may appear; they are largely extensionally equivalent to desire-based forms, and the only viable rationale for the goods they specify is desire-based. But part of my argument will be that even thoughtful contemporary proponents of hedonist and objectivist accounts do not accept some of those views' characteristic robust normative implications, but rather embrace significant normative qualifications for whose truth there would be no plausible rationale if such an account were correct. While it is not sufficient to appeal to idiosyncratic normative intuitions to show some normative view false, it is still a problem to propound an account of well-being whose implications you yourself cannot accept.

5.2 Crude Sensory Hedonism

There are two basic forms of hedonism, which involve different accounts of pleasure and pain. Most of the few contemporary hedonists are "attitudinal hedonists," who hold that the pain and pleasure relevant to well-being involve a specific sort of psychological attitude, analogous to belief or desire. But "sensory hedonists" hold that the pains and pleasures relevant to well-being are certain kinds of feelings or sensations. And there are also mixed forms. We begin with sensory hedonism.

Sensory hedonists hold that the kind of pleasure that constitutes well-being is a mere feeling or sensation. Sensory hedonism is a robust and revisionary conception of well-being, since many of us care about much more than our own sensory pleasures and pains. We worry about the truth of our beliefs and the satisfaction of our desires, even if these things won't impinge on our conscious experience and hence our pleasure. And so the truth of sensory hedonism would require robust metaphysical resources that are not consistent with physicalism, in a way I will shortly explain.

The particular form of sensory hedonism which will be our initial focus is indeed especially robust, because it is especially crude. This crude sensory hedonism holds that the pleasure relevant to well-being is a *sensation*, a positive analogue of physical pain. Such crude physical pleasure does not stretch to incorporate, for instance, feelings of enjoyment at most achievements. But I will also shortly explain how this crude sensory hedonism provides our best shot—though still an unsuccessful one— at fully normative truths consistent with reality. I think it is indeed central to the meaning of moral terms, though in a way that doesn't ensure its truth. It deploys the only type of property with full normativity that is coherently conceivable by humans, and to which quasi-normative goodness, which is available in reality, must approximate. So despite its current unpopularity, its revisionary nature, and its falsehood, it is worth considering crude sensory hedonism closely.

Mendola (2006: Part Two) develops a metaphysics of normative properties whereby the experience of physical pain and physical pleasure—a sword in the leg, the scratch of an itch—involve at once objective, natural, and yet irreducibly and fully normative properties, in particular the felt nastiness of physical pains and the felt pleasantness of crude physical pleasures. It argues that this metaphysics of value would underwrite the truth of robust hedonist claims about individual good, claims that could refine our rough commonsense consensus about well-being and provide robust normative advice about one's own good.[4]

It becomes slightly tricky on this proposal to characterize what natural properties are, since Moore himself seems to have taken them to be non-normative properties, which would make the proposal false by definition. But felt physical painfulness and pleasantness are as concrete and paradigmatically natural as the colors we experience, indeed as the yellow that was Moore's own central example of a natural property.[5] So this is a form of naturalism about value.

According to this proposal, the painfulness of physical pains is the nastiness of such pains. To feel such a pain is to feel bad, literally. To feel crude physical pleasure is to feel at least one kind of the good. And, further, this sort of good and bad are not constituted by other sorts of natural properties; they are irreducible, irreducibly and fully normative, and yet natural. Crude sensory hedonism says that individual well-being is increased by the presence of this natural goodness and decreased by the presence of this natural badness.

Consider an analogous case, color as it appears within experience, so-called "phenomenal color." Bluish purples and some reds are quite phenomenologically similar, despite the fact that the physical bases of these colors on external objects, for instance corresponding surface spectral reflectances, and also mediating light frequencies, are as physically different as such bases and frequencies can be. And indeed many physical bases of what appear to be the same colors are very different.[6] So if phenomenal color were really out there in our world, it would plausibly be irreducible, not constituted by other properties. Its essential similarities and differences do not match those of reasonable physical candidates for its constitution. Or perhaps it would not sit irreducibly out there on apples and tables, but instead in here on sense data or dualist substance. In any such case, it would be an irreducible part of what there is.

---

[4] Though not in ways we by consensus cannot accept. Sensory hedonists include Sprigge (1985 and 2000); Goldstein (1989 and 2003); Tännsjö (2008: 20).

[5] Mendola (1997: Part One).

[6] Thanks to David Hilbert for correcting an error about purplish reds and bluish reds that I have frequently made in this context, and suggesting that I deploy metamers, which appear similar in normal light but involve very different physical bases.

A plausible physicalism has no room for anything with such irreducible phenomenal colors.[7] Still, it does have room for the *experience* of such properties, just as it has room for belief in unicorns despite the fact that there are no unicorns.[8]

Phenomenal color, if it did exist, would be a natural property. And it is a property we can coherently conceive. And it even plays, I think, a crucial semantic role in the meaning of our color terms.[9] But the key point is that phenomenal color also provides a good model for at least one kind of goodness and badness. If there were such irreducible phenomenal colors in reality, then it would also be likely that the painfulness of physical pains and the pleasantness of physical pleasures would be in the world, if only on the relevant sense data. And they would be a kind of irreducible but natural disvalue and value. Such painfulness and pleasantness, like phenomenal colors, would be natural and concrete properties, unlike G. E. Moore's irreducible non-natural good. And yet they would be normative properties. Unlike Moore's non-natural normative properties, I believe, they can be coherently conceived by human beings.[10] And unlike Moore's non-natural normative properties, as I will shortly explain, it would be possible to plausibly if degenerately explain their supervenience on natural properties, and hence why two things that have the same natural properties also have the same normative properties.

Sensory hedonism of this sort is not a new idea. P. J. E. Kail has exhibited ways in which even David Hume embraced a tradition descending from Malebranche, Locke, Hutcheson, and Berkeley that cedes to phenomenal pleasantness and painfulness a central semantic role in our notion of individual good.[11] And he has traced ways in which Hume inherits from Malebranche the conception that our commonsense judgments about both phenomenal colors and goodness involve a kind of falsifying projection of features present in our experience onto the external world. I agree with Hume about this. But let me put it in the way physicalism demands:

Even though there is no phenomenal color out there on the samite, Lancelot experiences the samite as if it were phenomenal blue. Still, it is not as if he has a dualist substance or sense data stained with phenomenal blue. Rather he merely has a state of experiencing *as of* phenomenal blue, an experience that is physically constituted by neurons firing, none of which are blue. It is the mere content of that experience that he projects onto the world, much as someone with an hallucination of unicorns projects unicorns onto the world. Likewise, when Lance has the experience of a throbbing pain in his ankle, there is no such thing literally in his mind or ankle, a detachable entity throbbing with natural badness. Rather there is an

---

[7] This depends not just on physicalism but on the actual physical similarities of light waves and spectral reflectances.

[8] Mendola (2008: Chapter 7).

[9] Mendola (2008: Chapter 7) and (1997: Parts One and Three). This role is such that most commonsense claims about color are false. For a less revisionary but related view, see Chalmers (2010: 381–454).

[10] Mendola (1997: Part One).　　[11] Kail (2007: Part III).

experience as of throbbing natural badness, the content of which he projects as being right there in his ankle.[12]

Despite its illusory nature, it is plausible that this sort of natural badness and goodness are paradigmatic forms of fully normative individual good and bad, that they are semantically central in the way that early modern philosophers generally assumed. This is the only sort of goodness and badness that obviously appears in our experience. It is the only sort of fully normative property that I think we can coherently conceive. Perhaps this explains why, despite its current unpopularity, hedonism of even a crude sort has traditionally been a serious contender. I think that quasi-normative individual good must approximate to this natural and fully normative and hence semantically central good. Indeed, I believe that another kind of projection than Hume discerned is involved in Moore's conception of non-natural goodness, while I also believe that non-natural goodness, and especially non-natural goodness that supervenes with necessity on natural properties, is in fact not coherently conceivable by human beings. It is an abstracted form of the goodness of sensory pleasure that is too abstract to be other than a determinable, yet is treated as a determinate. Plato's Form of the Good involves analogously incoherent projection.

But focus on this point: Like Moore's non-natural good, natural goodness of the sort suggested here, which we can call "hedonic value," could terminate justificatory regresses, because it is fully normative, and hence certainly delivers that aspect of quasi-normativity.

Now consider internal reasons in Bernard Williams' sense, the other aspect of quasi-normativity which we hope to deliver. The connection between sensory pains or pleasures and desire is not extremely tight: Perhaps we can coherently conceive a creature with experience of this throbbing badness and goodness, but with no motivation that tracks that experience, no motivation towards that good and away from that bad. Certainly real humans can prefer a physically painful experience that yields a long sought and important good to a bland experience without that gain. Perhaps some mild pains of exercise are even sometimes in themselves desired. While Hume thought, at least at the time of the *Treatise*, that all desires were rooted in pleasures and pains,[13] we probably shouldn't go that far. Still, it is evident that our physical pains and pleasures do, at least in the vast majority of cases, engage our motivation, if sometimes in weak and over-balanced ways. This provides the rudiments for a hedonist conception of well-being, and even a general ethics built on hedonic value, that meets the constraints of internalism about reasons. But we need some more materials to construct it.

---

[12] This implies that, like phenomenal blue, we can conceive of such throbbing badness existing unperceived. Chalmers (2010: 450–3) develops a related proposal without this implication.

[13] Hume (2000: 2.1.1.4). Kail (2007: 180). Hume did *not* think pleasures and pains were the *objects* of all desires.

Hume notoriously thought that it isn't contrary to reason to prefer the destruction of the world to the scratching of your finger, or your acknowledged lesser good to your greater good.[14] But Williams allowed that deliberation has a greater role in moving us from given motives to acts that yet still leaves us with internal reasons for those acts.[15] Consider Christine Korsgaard's discussion of one case of reason's power that even Hume accepts:

Being motivated by the consideration that an action is a means to a desirable end is something beyond merely reflecting on that fact. The motive force attached to the end must be transmitted to the means in order for this to be a consideration that sets the human body in motion.... A practically rational person is not merely capable of performing certain rational mental operations, but capable also of transmitting motive force, so to speak, along the paths laid out by those operations. Otherwise even means/end reasoning will not meet the internalism requirement. But the internalism requirement does not imply that nothing can interfere with this motivational transmission.... Rage, passion, depression, distraction, grief, physical or mental illness: all these things could cause us to act irrationally, that is, to fail to be motivationally responsive to the rational considerations available to us.[16]

Presumably those who claim that they no longer mind their own pain after taking certain drugs but yet feel the same pain are similarly irrational.[17] But once we allow that deliberation and practical reasoning can transmit motivation in this way, as Hume was apparently required by consistency to accept and Williams apparently did accept, then we are in position to argue that rational deliberation may deliver adequate internal reasons in other similar ways that Hume would not have accepted but Williams should have. Thomas Nagel has plausibly argued that the recognition that you will receive in the future a certain pain or pleasure should, if you are rational, generate a motive now to act in an appropriate way.[18] He has also plausibly argued that in the rational the recognition that someone else will receive a pain or pleasure should generate a motive to act in a suitably respectful way. In other words, the case of physical pain and pleasure provides an excellent case of in this way timeless and impersonal reasons, even if we insist on internalism about reasons. It is sometimes objected that our physical pain presents itself as specifically bad for us, as providing a reason only for the agent who feels it. But that is an implausibly fancy feature to be present in our immediate sensory experience in the ways these crudely sensory normative properties are, while the flat-out badness of pain is not.[19] Physical pain of the sort in question can be present in the experience of babies and non-human animals who lack the concept of a self.

So we can conclude that sensory hedonism provides a promising case for internal reasons supporting a utilitarianism rooted in pleasure and pain. We are rationally motivated by our own present pleasure and pain, and appropriate deliberative reason

---

[14] Hume (2000: 2.3.3.6).   [15] Williams (1981: 104–5).
[16] Korsgaard (1986: 13), omitting a paragraph break.   [17] Parfit (1984: 501).
[18] Nagel (1970 and 1986).   [19] Nagel (1986: 160–1).

may transmit that motivation when our own future or the states of others involve pleasure and pain. This is a breezy way with complex and controversial matters. But it provides a simplified model for a way in which, if a proposal about one's own individual good at a moment meets the motivational strictures of internalism, the case in which such strictures seem after all most pressing, then rational deliberation tracking the more complicated impartiality-based structure linking that good with ethical truth developed in Chapters 8 and 9 might also be said to assure internal reasons for ethical judgments. At least if sensory hedonism were deployed in such a structure, the strictures of internalism could be, I believe, met.[20]

Despite all this good news, the form of hedonism under consideration may seem to face a familiar objection.[21] Since it is a form of naturalism, since it identifies at least one sort of goodness with a natural property, it may seem subject to Moore's open question argument. It may hence seem unable to close justificatory regresses.

One possible reply to this worry is that, as in the case of "right," we can presume that "good" has non-cognitive meaning in moral contexts, which might make such a question seem open even if the descriptive meaning of good corresponded exactly to my hedonist proposal, and even if we fully understood all the terms involved. Of course, that exact descriptive meaning is unlikely, since there are instrumental goods and goods of other various sorts. But still hedonic good might satisfy the relevant component of the descriptive meaning of "good" even though such a question remains in one sense semantically open, because of non-cognitive meaning.[22]

But it may seem that this first reply doesn't get at the guts of the objection. So let me also provide a second reply, which will take longer to state. It involves examination of Moore's own discussion of such a proposal.

Moore agrees that there is an irreducibly normative property, in fact irreducible goodness. And the open question argument in its original formulation is directed by Moore against reductive, indeed definitional, accounts of good in terms of collections of non-normative natural properties, while my hedonist proposal is not a naturalist account of that sort. In fact, the only relevant difference between this hedonist proposal and Moore's is that I claim that the irreducible good in question is a *natural* property. Moore's argument against *this* sort of proposal, his argument that irreducible goodness is not natural, occurs about 25 pages beyond the famous central statement of the open question argument. It is worth examining closely:

I do not deny that good is a property of certain natural objects: certain of them, I think, *are* good; and yet I have said that 'good' itself is not a natural property. Well, my test ... concerns their existence in time. Can we imagine 'good' as existing *by itself* in time, and not merely as a property of some natural object? For myself, I cannot so imagine it, whereas with the greater

---

[20] This resembles Darwall (1983) but involves another type of impartiality.
[21] Mason (2007).
[22] I implied earlier that there might also be differences in descriptive meaning without differences in properties.

number of properties of objects—those which I call the natural properties—their existence does seem to me to be independent of the existence of those objects. They are, in fact, rather parts of which the object is made up than mere predicates which attach to it. If they were all taken away, no object would be left, not even a bare substance: for they are in themselves substantial and give to the object all the substance it has. But this is not so with good. If indeed good were a feeling, as some would have us believe, then it would exist in time. But that is why to call it so is to commit the naturalistic fallacy. It will always remain pertinent to ask, whether the feeling itself is good; and if so, then good cannot itself be identical with any feeling.[23]

There is a good deal of questionable metaphysics deployed in this passage.[24] Nothing in the real world is outside of time. But let's give Moore all the metaphysics he wants. He takes (phenomenal) yellow to be a paradigm irreducible natural property.[25] Perhaps with a good deal of charity we can understand him to claim that concrete objects are merely bundles of core natural properties like yellow, and that such a core natural property is independent of the thing that has it.[26] We also can see from the passage that he thinks that good is different, and hence outside of time even though the objects that have it are in time, whereas according to my hedonist proposal it is like irreducible yellow in all relevant respects, and certainly in time. But even with all this charity to Moore it is hard to see how he gets to his conclusion that there is something wrong with a suggestion like my hedonism. There is really no reason to believe that the distinctions he draws in this paragraph between goodness and natural core properties are relevant to any "naturalist fallacy" committed by those who would identify pleasantness of a certain sort with value of a certain sort, or to an open question. After all, Moore's earlier discussion of open questions and related naturalist fallacies concerned only reductive naturalist definitions of normative properties. But to be fully charitable we should consider possibilities for extension of his earlier arguments on the basis of elements in this passage:

(1) Crude physical painfulness can seem both temporal and spatial. You have that pain which now seems to be in your leg and that crude pleasure now on your arm when you scratch. Perhaps the pain is really only in your mind, and hence outside of space, but it is certainly not outside of time. But, in any case, being inside or outside of time seems totally irrelevant to the issue that concerns us, even if makes sense to speak of a property had by objects in time as outside of time. But maybe this wasn't Moore's key point, as the passage on its surface suggests, but rather an oblique way of alluding to a different point: (2) We have two words, 'pleasant' and 'good'. But presumably that alone can't be sufficient to generate a genuinely open question if Moore's test is to have any validity. Remember physicians and doctors.

---

[23] Moore (1903: 41).

[24] Moore (1968: 581–2) repudiates the argument. Sturgeon (2003) discusses Moore's later views.

[25] Moore (1903: 7).

[26] Moore believed in universals. But a trope theory would also be consistent with this claim, despite the failure to understand Stout exhibited by Moore (1923). The charges of two electrons would be different tropes.

(3) There are other sorts of goodness than the kind that my hedonist proposal suggests can be found irreducibly in experience, for instance instrumental goodness, so irreducible natural goodness is a determinate of the determinable good, as one particular shade of yellow is a determinate of the determinable yellow. And Moore's irreducible goodness is perhaps more abstract than my sort, the relevant determinable and not the determinate, even though Moore must admit that the instrumental value of means to the end of irreducible good is also goodness of a kind. But remember that yellow, clearly a determinable, is Moore's own example of a *natural* irreducible property. So that can't be the point of the passage either. (4) Perhaps it is the independence of the object from its goodness that is the key point. But if an object were genuinely independent of its non-natural good, then non-naturalists like Moore would have to say that two naturally identical acts or objects could differ in goodness or rightness, which they very much don't want to say.

Let me belabor this key point a little. Moorean non-naturalism cannot plausibly explain the supervenience of the good on the natural. The most characteristic form of Moorean non-naturalism about the good, the form that we should expect if non-naturalism were true, would allow that natural duplicates could differ in normative status. This is because non-naturalism cannot plausibly explain the supervenience of genuinely independent non-natural properties on the natural. But a form of non-naturalism that denies the supervenience of the normative on the natural is too bizarre to take seriously, which is presumably why non-naturalists flee this natural implication of their view by positing *sui generis* a priori and necessary connections between distinct properties to assure supervenience. Non-natural properties are suspect enough, but this resource is physically unavailable as well. Recall that we saw in Chapter 4 that ordinary property constitution, say of geological properties by physical properties, is a very different sort of case. So it is in fact an advantage of my proposal over traditional non-naturalism that normative properties would be degenerately preserved across natural duplicates.

In any case, whatever point Moore was trying to make in this obscure and tendentious passage, it deploys much questionable metaphysics in no convincing way. There is nothing in Moore to provide a telling objection to my variant of sensory hedonism.

Nevertheless, even though I think this form sensory hedonism might evade Moore's open question and close justificatory regresses, even though I think it deploys the only type of fully normative property coherently conceivable by humans, even though I think it provides a semantically central element of our notion of individual good and normative properties in general, and even though I think it would provide suitable internal reasons, I also think it is false. Nothing in the world really has such natural normative properties, because physicalism is true. There is the experience of natural goodness and badness, but no natural goodness and badness in reality. Physicalism rules out the one sort of irreducible but natural and fully normative property that there might otherwise have been in the world, which might have served to overturn or significantly revise our commonsense intuitions about well-being in a controversial but suitably well-founded way, which might have provided robust individual advice.[27]

It might seem that the truth of a normative doctrine like sensory hedonism could not turn on the dispute between dualism, idealism, and some sorts of naïve realism on the one hand, and physicalism on the other. But sensory hedonism of my crude physical sort is quite robust. It tells people that some of the things they do care about they shouldn't, and that some of the things they don't care about they should, even when only their own well-being is in question. And its authority to do that turns squarely on its being correct about what fully normative properties exist, on whether or not the experience of physical pain involves a perceptual relationship to one sort of badness. It doesn't. The experience of natural goodness no more requires natural goodness as part of the world than the hallucination of unicorns requires unicorns in the world. And so the world has no fully normative badness or goodness in it. And that is normatively relevant, just like the absence in reality of the Form of the Good.

So much for my version of sensory hedonism, which I am calling "crude sensory hedonism" because of its focus on crudely physical pains and pleasures. It deploys the only type of coherently conceivable fully normative property, which is indeed semantically central. But it involves an illusion of our experience. Physical reality rules it out. A very robust normative proposal of this sort requires a robust metaphysical rationale, to close justificatory regresses on which there is otherwise great stress, and in reality that is lacking in this case.

We saw in Chapter 4 that Moore's non-natural goodness was inconsistent with physicalism, and now we have given up on my close naturalist alternative. But my crude sensory hedonism is in a tradition that spans variation, and includes alternative conceptions with a broader, and hence less crude and robustly revisionary, focus. We should also consider these views.

5.3 Refined Sensory Hedonism

It is not plausible to claim that all the things we call pains and pleasures involve the crudely sensory nastiness and goodness I have suggested. But C. I. Lewis held that there is a more general sort of

value-quality found in the directly experienced. One who says at the concert, 'This is good', or who makes a similar remark at table, is presumably reporting a directly experienced character of the sensuously given as such.... Directly experienced goodness or badness, like seen redness

---

[27] If the revision were too great, we would be catapulted out of the range set by DC1. But Mendola (2006) argues that sensory hedonism would not require a very significant revision of common sense.

or felt hardness, may become...the matter of a...report which intends nothing more than this apparent quality of what appears.[28]

Roger Crisp also suggests that well-being is a broader phenomenal state than crude physical pleasure.[29] Specifically, he roots good in enjoyment conceived as a feeling:

[E]njoyment is a single 'feeling tone' common to all enjoyable experiences.... That is, there is something that it is *like* to be experiencing enjoyment, in the same way that there is something that it is like to be having an experience of colour. Likewise, there is something that it is like to be experiencing a particular kind of enjoyment (bodily enjoyment, perhaps, or the enjoyment of reading a novel), in the same way that there is something that it is like to be having an experience of a particular colour. Enjoyment, then, is best understood using the determinable–determinate distinction.... Enjoyable experiences do differ from one another... [b]ut there is a certain common quality—feeling good.[30]

My first objection to these broader forms of sensory hedonism is that, I blush to confess, the only sort of hedonic value that I can introspect is the cruder physical sort. Lewis and Crisp are right that there are other states we call sensory pleasures, but I can't introspect the broad phenomenal pleasure they proclaim.

But a second and more telling difficulty is that even such broad sensory hedonisms are robust, though not quite so robust as my cruder form. We care about other things. They hence also require metaphysical buttressing, by robust fully normative facts that do not exist.[31] It is still not possible, in the absence of fully normative properties, to adequately close relevant justificatory regresses. Sensory hedonism, even in these more sophisticated forms, is not viable in physical reality.

Despite the fact that sensory hedonism is false in reality, we will eventually see that sensory pleasures and pains are given real weight by the true account of individual good. Sensory pains and pleasures in general, not just crude physical pleasures and pains, have a real weight in that account. One way to think of quasi-normative goods is as goods that can provide the kinds of internal reasons to the rational that 5.2 argued crude sensory pains and pleasures provide. And probably all sensory pleasures and pains provide these also. But the primary way in which we will fall back from fully normative to quasi-normative individual good is from fully normative

---

[28] C. I. Lewis (1946: 374). Lewis' Chapter XIII discusses phenomenal value-qualities, which contrast in other ways with those of Mendola (2006). Lewis thinks it is untypical for value-qualities to vary independently of other properties presented in immediate experience, doesn't cleanly distinguish them from motivational states, and doesn't think they are always comparable.

[29] Crisp does not presume the physical irreducibility of phenomenal experience.

[30] Crisp (2006: 108–9).

[31] Crisp is epistemically modest about hedonism, but the ethical truths in question apparently require irreducible normative properties. There is an analogue position that deploys a more generic natural normative property than my hedonic value. But all these views are inconsistent with physicalism. Another difficulty for Crisp is that some experiences we call "enjoyment" do not share even a determinable phenomenal property. "A person absorbed in a...dangerous canoeing maneuver may be enjoying it, but is hardly pleased about anything at the time" (Gosling (1969: 135)). Rather we call that enjoyment because such things leave us refreshed and pleased with life (Gosling (1969: 137)).

properties to desire—to what we care about—and especially to generally shared desire, as a basis for termination of justificatory regresses. So it will become quite relevant that we do in fact generally care about our own sensory pleasures and pains, crude and refined, quite a bit.[32]

5.4 Attitudinal Hedonism

Most living hedonists deny that the pain and pleasure relevant to well-being are particular or even relatively general phenomenal sensations. They are rather attitudinal hedonists. The attitudinal hedonist focuses on a special sort of psychological attitude, perhaps enjoyment of something, conceived not as a sensation or feeling but as a specific psychological relation to that thing. This relation is supposed to contribute a recognizably hedonist element whatever objects it is focused on.

Attitudinal hedonism has the advantage over sensory hedonism that some intuitive pleasures and pains do not seem to have any characteristic phenomenology, and yet seem important to well-being. But an immediate worry is whether such an attitude can be properly distinguished from desire. Otherwise, such accounts will collapse into desire-based accounts. One way to understand this problem is to trace it in Fred Feldman's proposal, which is the best developed contemporary attitudinal hedonism.[33] That account also suffers from a second problem, which we will encounter more than once and so is worth developing: It deploys qualifications on the characteristic normative implications of hedonism that are difficult to square with any plausible rationale for its truth.

Feldman explores varieties of attitudinal hedonism that arise as modifications of a basic attitudinal conception, which he calls "Intrinsic Attitudinal Hedonism" or "IAH." It has three tenets:

(i) Every episode of intrinsic attitudinal pleasure is intrinsically good; every episode of intrinsic attitudinal pain is intrinsically bad.

(ii) The intrinsic value of an episode of intrinsic attitudinal pleasure is equal to the amount of pleasure contained in that episode [where the amount of that pleasure is the product of its duration and its average intensity]; the intrinsic value of an episode of intrinsic attitudinal pain is equal to—(the amount of pain contained in that episode).

(iii) The intrinsic value of a life is entirely determined by the intrinsic values of the episodes of intrinsic attitudinal pleasure and pain contained in the life, in

---

[32] The false but natural human conception of the world, rooted in our mostly shared experience just as false commonsense conceptions of things' colors are rooted, is an alternative form of consensus. It includes natural good and bad. The aspect of quasi-normativity provided by internal reasons does not require the veridicality of such value experiences. But, unlike a consensus of desires, this consensus involves cognitive error, and so seems irrelevant to justificatory regresses.

[33] Feldman (2004).

such a way that one life is intrinsically better than another if and only if the net amount of intrinsic attitudinal pleasure in the one is greater than the net amount of that sort of pleasure in the other.[34]

The most central elements of this characterization are the notions of attitudinal pleasure and pain. Focus on attitudinal pleasure.

I wish Feldman had said more about this. His key characterizations are each disjunctive, and the various characterizations are different, which makes it hard to see exactly what he intends. He first says that attitudinal pleasure is enjoying, taking pleasure in, or delighting in something.[35] Then when officially characterizing attitudinal pleasure,[36] he talks also of being pleased about something and being glad that it is happening. And sometimes even mere liking seems enough.[37]

These various states are diverse. Lancelot can be glad or pleased that something is happening, say something which is what he wants all things considered, perhaps some important but mildly painful confrontation for which he's had to wait too long, but without enjoying that thing at all. And Guinevere can take mild pleasure in something or even enjoy it without being delighted by it. And it is hard to be confident that there aren't other states that Feldman doesn't mention but that belong on any complete disjunctive list. We can reasonably wonder if attitudinal pleasure is supposed to be a mental state whose type boundaries are fixed by natural kinds, which our folk vocabulary more or less captures in the way Feldman attempts, although later in this chapter we will see reasons to doubt the normative relevance of natural kinds. Or perhaps rather such pleasure is supposed to be exactly captured by a disjunction across just exactly the finely nuanced phrases of English he deploys, plus perhaps a few more. This might not correspond to any easily surveyed disjunction expressible through the fine nuances of Old English or Mandarin, and so also might be of limited normative significance.

Because of worries like these, it is perhaps most charitable to focus on what seem to be the most inclusive attitudes on Feldman's lists, say the kinds of being glad or pleased that don't require much personal joy. But then we are faced with the worry that Feldman's attitudinal hedonism is too broad to count as genuine hedonism. Then we need to be concerned about the difference between attitudinal hedonism and desire-based theories. We seem to have a form of hedonism that collapses into a desire-based account.[38]

Feldman spends time on the distinction between desire or preference on one side and enjoyment on the other. He says that the distinction is a matter of empirical psychology. But he quotes no studies, and instead makes the distinction in this armchair way:

---

[34] Feldman (2004: 66), with my insertion in brackets.   [35] Feldman (2004: 189–97).
[36] Feldman (2004: 56).   [37] Feldman (2004: 151).   [38] Chapter 6 characterizes desire.

A person may enjoy something he never desired, and a person may desire a thing he never enjoys. Think of a person who never had champagne—indeed has no concept of champagne. All he wants is beer. Yet if we switch drinks on him, and give him an unexpected glass of champagne, he might enjoy it. Even as he drinks, it might be wrong to say that he desires to be drinking champagne, or to be drinking 'this stuff'. He might be savoring the taste, and enjoying the drinking so much, that he doesn't even think about the further question whether he wants to be drinking this tasty drink.[39]

But this case is problematic. Even if someone doesn't want to do something before they do that unexpectedly enjoyable thing, that doesn't serve to show that they don't want to do it as they are doing it and enjoying it. Perhaps there is a difference between wanting to do something and wanting to continue to do it, but it would seem that the second is a species of the first. And of course plausible desire-based theories of one's good are not going to deploy just unusually explicit wants, which require that one actually formulate the question of whether one wants something to have that want. So we have reason to worry that whenever someone has attitudinal pleasure towards something, still they also want it or prefer it in some way that is quite friendly to desire-based theories.

Still, there is the other direction of possible difference between attitudinal pleasure and a want or preference. Perhaps attitudinal hedonism is properly conceived as a specific subset of desire-based theories. Perhaps enjoying something is one form of wanting it. And Feldman has another case that suggests a distinction of that sort: "[A] person might have lost the capacity to enjoy certain things. Perhaps someone has taken a drug that makes it impossible for her to enjoy beer. When she drinks beer, it tastes like a urine sample. But the old desires still linger. She may still want a beer. When she gets it, she does not enjoy it."[40] But this case is problematic too. The fact that you want something before you taste it does not imply that you will want it while you taste it. Of course, it is likely that there are some states we prefer but do not enjoy, and that is the point that Feldman is trying to make. And yet enjoyment is not the only attitude Feldman mentions as sufficient for attitudinal pleasure. There are states of being glad or pleased that something is the case, which explicitly count as attitudinal pleasures, but which don't require any sort of robust enjoyment.

Perhaps I am not being sufficiently charitable. Perhaps there is a relevant nuance which separates merely wanting something that happens and being pleased or glad about it. Or perhaps Feldman should forget about being pleased and stick with the more restrictive notion of enjoyment. But then his form of hedonism would be normatively robust and controversial in a way that he is at pains to avoid and that would require a stronger supporting rationale than any he provides. And indeed it would be a form of sensory hedonism, of Crisp's broad sort. If we decidedly prefer things that we don't enjoy or aren't pleased about in a restrictive way, then it seems

---

[39] Feldman (2004: 70).   [40] Feldman (2004: 70).

presumptuous for ethicists to tell us that our desire is mistaken even when no others' interests are in question, unless there are robust metaphysical resources available to vindicate this robust advice.[41]

We have seen that Feldman's characterization of IAH is questionably broad. It is so broad that it isn't distinct from a desire-based theory, at least if it manages to be distinct from sensory hedonism. This is the characteristic difficulty of attitudinal hedonism. But there is also a second difficulty for Feldman's hedonism. It is perhaps less characteristic of its class, but we will encounter this problem more than once, and so it is also instructive.

IAH does not exhaust even attitudinal hedonism according to Feldman. It is rather the basic form from which others arise by suitable modifications. Consider some modifications that Feldman proposes as properly hedonist: (1) To approximate Mill's view that not merely the quantity but the quality of pleasure matters to well-being, Feldman suggests that there might be *altitudes* that belong to kinds of pleasures, corresponding to Mill's differences in quality between the pleasures of pushpin and poetry. Poetic pleasures might have greater altitude and hence contribute greater value.[42] (2) Some ethicists discount pleasures due to ignorance. And Feldman's Truth-Adjusted IAH holds that the intrinsic value of an episode of intrinsic attitudinal pleasure is equal to the truth-adjusted amount of pleasure contained in that episode,[43] where the truth-adjusted amount of pleasure is the product of the amount of pleasure with 1 when the relevant propositional object is true, and with some positive number less than 1 when it is false.[44] (3) Feldman also suggests that it might be that

the value of a pleasure is enhanced when it is pleasure taken in a pleasure-worthy object, such as something good, or beautiful. The value of a pleasure is mitigated when it is pleasure taken in a pleasure-unworthy object, such as something evil, or ugly. The disvalue of a pain is mitigated . . . when it is pain taken in an object worthy of pain, such as something evil, or ugly. The [negative] value of a pain is enhanced . . . when it is pain taken in an object unworthy of this attitude, such as something good or beautiful.[45]

There is some tension in a form of hedonism that holds that there can be goods and evils somewhat independent of pleasure in these ways. Feldman's alleged hedonism has specific variants that he himself says are close to the paradigmatically non-hedonist,

---

[41] Feldman holds that the attitude of pleasure can have positive arithmetical intensities, which might provide differences between enjoyment and being pleased, or differences between Feldman's hedonism and a desire-based theory. Still, if such intensities can pass towards 0, even a nuanced difference between wanting something and being pleased about it may be insufficient to distinguish between Feldman's hedonism and a preference-based account. Wants which aren't enjoyments may be those with intensity approaching 0. Or wants and preferences may come in similar degrees. So this may exacerbate our worries rather than allay them.

[42] Feldman (2004: 75).   [43] Feldman (2004: 112).
[44] Feldman suggests 0.1.   [45] Feldman (2004: 120).

objective conceptions of Moore and Darwall.[46] If Feldman's hedonism evades our earlier worry that is not distinct from either sensory hedonism or a desire-based view, it is perhaps only because it swells to encompass objectivism as well.[47]

There's of course little in a name, and I too am straining towards ecumenism. But focus on this case: W. D. Ross urged against hedonism that two worlds that contain equal amounts of pleasure and pain could yet differ in value depending on the distribution of that pleasure and pain among the just and unjust, the deserving and the undeserving. At the extreme, it may be a good thing if the guilty suffer. Or it may simply be that the pleasure of the undeserving should be discounted relative to the same pleasure of the deserving. This suggests that we should focus not merely on the ways in which certain objects of attitudinal pleasure and pain are appropriate, but on the ways in which certain subjects deserve pleasures and pains. In reply to Ross' objection, Feldman observes that the worry doesn't undercut a hedonist conception of the *well-being* of the vicious, who do seem better off the more unjust pleasures they enjoy. It rather seems to cut against the contribution of the well-being of the vicious to the overall good of the world. It may be better for the vicious if they enjoy life, but worse for the world. That seems like an appropriately hedonist reply, and of course well-being is our immediate interest here. Still, there is a subject-centered variant of Desert-Adjusted IAH that might stretch to provide an evaluation of worlds, which Feldman has elaborated in other work, and to which we will return in Chapter 10. So perhaps the pleasure of the undeserving and vicious are supposed to receive a discount when we are assessing the value of wholes. Feldman's version of hedonism deploys, at least potentially, a very robust conception of desert, both regarding not only objects of pleasure but subjects of pleasure. I have qualms about these resources to which we will return, but let's assume for the moment that such notions make sense in our world, and don't themselves depend on the notion of which consequences are best. Still, there is a problem: Some of the uses which Feldman contemplates for the notion of deserving subjects and objects merely modify the weights of pleasures in contributing to the good of a life or a world, or merely modify the weights of pains in contributing to the bad. But he floats other possibilities, which involve what he calls *transvaluation*, in which pain of the right sort is a good thing and pleasure of the wrong sort is a bad thing.[48]

If there are robust facts about desert, then it is reasonably natural to conclude, with Kant, that it is a good thing when the evil suffer, that it is not merely that the

---

[46] Feldman (2004: 142–59).

[47] Truth-Adjusted IAH is not a form of pluralism. The truth of beliefs is not an independent source of value. It merely modulates the worth of pleasure. Pleasure does not merely modify the worth of truth, because truths involving no pleasure generate no value according to Truth-Adjusted IAH. Nevertheless, this is uncomfortably close to objectivism.

[48] Feldman (2004: 142–59, 183, 185, 189–97).

joy of the evil should be discounted but that the world is better if they feel more pain. But such claims are in very serious tension with the paradigmatic hedonist beliefs that pain is always in itself a bad thing, and pleasure in itself always a good. I think that a view that accepts transvaluation is hedonism in name only. Still, there's no use in quibbling about a term. And the well-being of the evil may be pleasure even if that well-being contributes no value to the world. Nevertheless, the real problem, my real reason for this tour of objectivist elements in Feldman's hedonism, is as follows.

What is essential to hedonism, at least for our purposes, is the rationale it can provide, the explanation it can give that is sufficient to break justificatory regresses and reveal why what it favors in fact is good. Sensory hedonism can provide such a story, but that story is false. Attitudinal hedonists could perhaps legitimately appeal to non-natural goodness if it were attached to just their list of concrete goods, but that is a fantasy. It is conceivable that they might appeal instead to their privileged attitude, much as a desire-based account appeals to desire, as revealing obvious interests of those who have it. But we haven't been able to locate such a specific attitude that is suitably different from desire and from the sensory pleasure characteristic of sensory hedonism.

Feldman himself makes no attempt to provide any particular positive rationale for his proposal. He rather adopts an historically prominent theory and defends it against intuitive objections by piecemeal modification, and follows now common practice in divorcing his discussion of normative issues from metaethics. He makes his axiological proposals without providing any story about how they are true in our world, or could be true in any world. In fact, he doesn't even insist that they are true as opposed to merely things he is emoting in favor of.[49] These two limitations are related, since a general positive rationale for Feldman's hedonism should be a story about why it in particular is true.

But despite the familiarity of such a methodology, it is not adequate for our purposes. Piecemeal alterations on the basis of intuitive objections to hedonism cannot obviously be given a rationale consistent with any plausible rationale for hedonism. Any plausible grounds for thinking that hedonism is true may well be inconsistent with the conditions that are required for the truth of some of the modifications. All the objectivist elements in Feldman threaten this problem. But, at least in the absence of Moorean non-natural good distributed in exactly the right way, transvaluation is a clear and dramatic example of this sort. We have yet to explore objectivist conceptions and their characteristic rationales, but we should not antecedently expect that, if such rationales succeed, they would vindicate a form of hedonism.

---

[49] Feldman (2004: 206).

5.5 Mixed Forms

Sensory hedonism is too robust for physical reality. Non-natural good distributed in just the right way might provide a rationale for attitudinal hedonism, but it does not exist. There is no evident attitude which attitudinal hedonism can deploy as a rationale that yet leaves it properly distinct from a desire-based or sensory hedonist account. In Feldman's version it even incorporates objectivist elements. And when we examine the most plausible grounds of truth for objectivism, we will not discover a rationale for the most characteristically hedonist element of Feldman's view, the central role it cedes IAH.

Still, there are also explicitly mixed forms of hedonism to consider. Perhaps some of these even suggest better forms of attitudinal hedonism. For instance, Sidgwick suggested that pleasure be defined "as a feeling which, when experienced by intelligent beings, is at least implicitly apprehended as desirable, or—in cases of comparison—preferable."[50] In Sidgwick, this talk of desirability imports something very fancy: Something is desirable for someone when it is what they would practically desire if their desires were in harmony with reason, their own existence alone considered.[51] And this is apparently presumed to require the non-natural. Still, something analogous might be provided by what I will call in Chapter 6 an informed desire account, but restricted in its objects to experienced feelings.

In general, those we might call "semi-sensory" hedonists propose that the satisfaction of desires focused on sensory or feeling experiences in particular constitute relevant well-being. Alternative "semi-attitudinal" hedonists propose that attitudinal pleasure is desire accompanied by some distinctive sort of pleasant phenomenology.

But both of these possibilities threaten collapse into alternatives. Begin with semi-sensory hedonism. It is not obvious why, if some phenomenal states are constituted as better for us than others by virtue of our preferences, that other objects of preference cannot also be so constituted. The basic rationale available for such a conception seems to be desire, that we care. But since we care about other things than our immediate experiences, such a restriction in what can count towards genuine well-being requires a further robust rationale that seems unavailable in our physical world. Still, it is possible that some motivation for this restriction comes from difficulties internal to desire-based accounts, involving cases in which your desires are satisfied but you fail to recognize this, or in which you desire things that don't intuitively affect your own self-interest, to which we will return during our discussion of desire-based accounts. However, this in turn suggests that this form of hedonism is in fact a kind of desire-based account, in only slight disguise. But by its severe restriction of relevant objects of desire to immediate experiences, such an account also has some affinities with questionably robust sensory hedonism. It requires

---

[50] Sidgwick (1907: 112). See also 131.   [51] Sidgwick (1907: 112).

robust normativity not available in our world, at least if the difficulties of desire-based accounts don't force it on us in some other way.

Consider then the second possibility: semi-attitudinal hedonism. One natural way to firmly distinguish attitudinal pleasure from mere wants is by appeal to a necessary feeling component, for instance a kind of sensory pleasure upon believed satisfaction,[52] or a dreamy mood of reverie when the possibility of satisfaction is considered. But this makes such accounts robust, since we care about things in ways not reflected in specific ways like these in our phenomenology.[53] And so such accounts also require robust metaphysical buttressing not available in reality, in the same manner as sensory hedonism. Again, however, there is the possibility that the difficulties of desire-based accounts force such a revisionary restriction, for instance if we must distinguish self-regarding and other-regarding desires as a plausible basis for well-being and this is the best way to do it.

Both mixed forms of hedonism are variant desire-based accounts, for our purposes. Their plausible rationales are desire-based, although the qualifications they incorporate may be due to the problems of simpler desire-based accounts. Both require unlikely robust metaphysics to support their robust advice, unless that advice is somehow required by the problems of more modest desire-based accounts.

So we can conclude our discussion of hedonism: The good of pleasure and evil of pain will be delivered by the correct desire-based account, since we care quite a bit about them, perhaps even when they are merely attitudinal. In addition, sensory pleasure and pain play a central semantic role, and pleasures of all sorts are plausibly internal reasons. But hedonism is false. Characteristic and hence robust forms of hedonism require metaphysical buttressing not available in reality. But to see this fully we will also have to consider objectivism, which is incorporated in some forms of attitudinal hedonism, and the possible problems of desire-based accounts, which may push us back towards hedonism.

5.6 Concessions to Objectivism

Objective conceptions of well-being hold that certain things are good for individuals regardless of their subjective attitudes of pleasure, pain, or desire. Perhaps there is a set of basic human needs—say health and true belief—that define well-being. Indeed, health and true belief (or knowledge) seem to be the most characteristic objectivist goods. Or perhaps there is a list of objective goods that includes more than these mere needs. Parfit contemplates a list, reflecting suggestions of Moore and Ross, that "might include moral goodness, rational activity, the development of one's abilities,

---

[52] Such a route conflicts with Feldman (2004: 79–80), which characterizes sensory pleasures in terms of attitudinal pleasure.

[53] If, implausibly, there is a phenomenology characteristic of all desires, it could not restrict desires in the way such accounts require.

having children and being a good parent, knowledge, and the awareness of true beauty. The bad things might include being betrayed, manipulated, slandered, deceived, being deprived of liberty or dignity, and enjoying either sadistic pleasure, or aesthetic pleasure in what is in fact ugly."[54] Or perhaps there is an objective form of human flourishing of another traditional sort, that specifies a true hierarchy of human lives, so that the contemplative or the amorous or the jousting life is best.[55]

Like hedonism, objectivism is embedded deeply in moral tradition, and I will begin by being concessive about the most characteristic objectivist goods. Plato's *Philebus* is an historically significant and convincing defense of the intuitive value of knowledge over pleasure.[56] And Judith Thomson suggests that we

[c]onsider a master chess player who spends his time studying chess, gets no exercise, and smokes heavily because he finds that smoking helps him to concentrate. These are things he wants to do... [b]ut... we cannot at all plausibly say that doing them is good for him. What works against the idea that what is good for a person is what conduces to the satisfaction of his wants is the idea that what is good for a person is what conduces to his health.[57]

I accept the intuitive force of these motivations for objectivism. In fact, I believe that the value of health and true belief are reflected in our consensus normative judgments, in DC1-NORMS.

Still, Chapter 7 will show that my desire-based proposal cedes significant weight to the value of health and true belief, along with pleasure, because they are the objects of relevant desires that people generally have. What's more, this provides these goods with a desire-based rationale. This is enough to support the commonsense consensus about their value reflected in DC1.

And their significance is also provided for, or at least allowed for, in other ways by my account. It cedes them some weight irrespective of the nature of our desires. Begin with true belief.

There is well-being, and there are the ideals or virtues required by morality of our preferences and actions. I am trying to explain these things. But like most ethicists, even most hedonist utilitarians, I also think that truth is an important cognitive ideal, a virtue of beliefs. But it is not practically relevant whether we count that as part of human well-being or as a specifically moral ideal. Of course, if we don't, then there is the practical question of how to balance true belief and individual well-being, or cognitively ideal action towards true belief and morally ideal action. But those practical difficulties are not eliminated by folding everything into some overarching notion of high-toned individual well-being that includes true beliefs. Then the difficulties simply become difficulties in determining how various balances of these components of flourishing affect individual well-being, or how various components of well-being affect appropriate action, what sorts of tradeoffs are appropriate. I don't

---

[54] Parfit (1984: 499).   [55] Aristotle, *Nicomachean Ethics*.
[56] Plato (1997).   [57] Thomson (2001: 54–5), with a paragraph break suppressed.

know how to resolve these tradeoffs, when my moral theory MM doesn't already resolve them, so I want to avoid them if I can. Perhaps it seems that objective accounts provide some helpful resources to deal with these questions,[58] but that will turn on details, and it is in questions of this sort where questionably robust metaphysics, which might provide robust advice about individual good, seems most necessary. There are also difficult questions about the relative weight of the cognitive virtues besides truth that make up knowledge, and their specific relations to truth, and the relative cognitive weight of various sorts of knowledge, to which some epistemologists and ethicists have attended,[59] and which I also don't know how to answer. But I can say this in general: I do not presume to favor individual well-being rooted in desire-satisfaction, nor even to favor moral action, over knowledge or truth or the pursuit of knowledge or truth. It is simply not my topic.

I myself think in particular that truth is the proper discipline of belief,[60] and that other cognitive virtues must somehow rest on it. It seems to me in the nature of what a belief is to be a mental state that in some way, by evolution or design or our individual endeavor or even merely by our shared consensus of description, aims at truth. All agents, at least as I understand them, have beliefs with such an immanent goal. That even provides for the existence of some analogue of internal reasons in such a case; agents, who have beliefs, in some sense aim at truth. In fact, I even think that truth is the ultimate root of the alternative type of discipline we are discussing in this book. As we will see, the basic motivational states are preferences. So if there were fully normative value in the world, then the proper discipline of preference would be in accord with the truth of relative value. A true preference of A to B requires that A be better than B, and that is the ideal discipline for preference. Unfortunately, the proper discipline of desire or preference in our physical world cannot be provided by any facts of fully normative value, merely by what MM can deliver on the ultimate basis of desire-based good.[61] We are stuck with a kind of consensus of desire, as we will see, and a moral theory that respects also the consensus of commonsense judgment reflected in DC1. We are stuck with merely quasi-normative truth. But these two distinct forms of discipline, of belief and of desire, provide what might easily be called a single kind of high-toned well-being, if that is all that is required to satisfy objectivists. Yet this conception is consistent with and indeed largely depends on my desire-based conception of individual good.

---

[58] Hurka (1993: 84–97) develops one relevant objectivist framework.

[59] Ross (1930: 134–41); Hurka (1993: 99–120).

[60] But see Mendola (2008: Chapter 4) and Gibbons (2013).

[61] The discipline of preference is not rational self-interest because, as we will see, genuine rational discipline is third-personal like truth; it reaches all the way to benevolence. Prudent self-interest is an arbitrarily truncated form of that. Why isn't the discipline of preference by LDP enough? Perhaps it is, but we also act, and discipline of action requires the full apparatus of MM. It may be objected that truth of beliefs should enter into the kinds of well-being deployed by MM as the basis of consequentialist assessment. But that requires a way to balance that truth and other sorts of well-being in overall outcomes, which I lack.

How about health? Health has two special roles in my proposal, beyond its role as the object of important desires. First, health of a relatively minimal sort, at least in living things, is a necessary precondition for preference and most action, though not of course for the success of action in the future. In other words, it is a prerequisite of my entire normative apparatus. As Thomson says, "health does of course have its special pleasures, but what seems fundamental to its value to us is that it is a prerequisite for our being able to do much of what most people most deeply want to do."[62] I agree. Second, intuitive conflicts of health and desire often involve cases in which one's future health would be undercut by satisfaction of current desires, and as we will see in the following chapters, the proper desire-based account of individual well-being cedes distributional significance to the fate of one's future selves. But note that neither of these roles for health requires any very robust and specific form of it. It doesn't strictly require Lancelot's beauty or his athletic capacities.

Beyond their reflection in our desires, and the special roles of health and true belief in my proposal, there is yet a third way in which characteristic objectivist goods are incorporated in MM, though only implicitly. Once one cares about chess or jousting, it is plausible that objectivist considerations about those activities provide further structure for one's proper desires. But we won't for the most part be treating matters here at the level of detail where that complication matters.

So I grant that the true desire-based account must deliver the most intuitively pressing objectivist goods, although with a physically respectable desire-based rationale. And on the basis of the mechanisms I have just sketched, it can.

5.7 Robust Objectivism

But enough concessions. For our purposes there are two things that are most distinctive of objectivism. First, any characteristic rationales that it can provide for goods. Second, what specific goods it can add beyond what the proper desire-based conception can deliver—what greater weight or specificity of objectivist ideals, or what additional objectivist ideals. These features are linked. As might be expected, when objectivist proposals move beyond what we generally care about, they require robust metaphysical buttressing, by fully normative facts about what is good for us. As also might be expected, that buttressing is not available in physical reality. But we have a way to go to understand these general charges properly.

We need to consider various possible grounds for fully and robustly normative conceptions of objectivist good. There is a rough historical consensus about our individual goods and needs, perhaps even some consensus at least about the weight of such goods beyond what is directly reflected in our desires. This consensus is incorporated in DC1-NORMS. But I do not believe it goes beyond the intuitive

---

[62] Thomson (2001: 55).

cream I have already skimmed for my desire-based account. The conventional nature of this consensus means it isn't sufficient in itself for full normativity, and it is vague partly because it spans a considerable temporal and social range. It cannot support a normatively robust objectivist conception.

There is a related subtlety, however, that might seem helpful for objectivists. Perhaps some sort of relativity to local social convention could resolve some indeterminacy in the good. Perhaps in Arthurian England and Republican Rome there were relatively local traditions that refined any vague trans-historical consensus on human good. Too deep a relativism would undercut what seems the essential possibility of reflective modification and justification of local ethical norms, but perhaps, as McDowell and Hursthouse have suggested, distinct traditions allow internal criticism that legitimates reflective modification and justification from within.[63] But the problem with this idea is that unless revision beginning within each local tradition would end up in the long run in the same robust place, which is only remotely plausible if metaphysical factors support and control the convergence, even this degree of relativism would not deliver the specificity required to go beyond our vague trans-historical consensus on the good, at least when we are faced with normative questions that bridge traditions. It will legitimately cut no ice with the ancient Romans what the medieval European tradition would say even when fully reflective. And of course within any given local tradition we can expect a more specific consensus of desires also, which as we will see is relevant to the proper desire-based conception.

So objectivists seem stuck with robust metaphysics, providing something at least very similar to full normativity, if they want to give robust advice. We must consider various robustly metaphysical possibilities.

First, those who favor lists of objective goods or needs—including Moore and Ross—characteristically also believe that there are non-natural but fully normative properties, which are not constituted by the physical. If goodness is an irreducible non-natural property attached to certain things in the world, then those things are good, whatever our consensus or desires. But such a metaphysical extravaganza is not consistent with physical reality.

On the other hand, perhaps there is some sort of unified and robust objective teleology in something resembling Aristotle's sense. Perhaps there is some sort of single proper end or function of all humans whatever our differing mundane desires. Perhaps if we move beyond lists of distinct objective goods to such a unitary rationale for a particular robust objective conception of well-being, that rationale will be consistent with physicalism.

Chapter 1 said that Aristotle's own view is not consistent with physicalism.[64] If the function of humans is activity expressing reason in Aristotle's sense, then that is

---

[63] McDowell (1998); Hursthouse (1999: 164–9). Hursthouse is less confident that our tradition can withstand these tests.

[64] See Chapter 1 n3.

surprising and informative.[65] It provides robust advice on how to live. But in our physical world, there is no true hierarchy of Aristotelian souls—living, animated, and rational—that are both ends and material causes of our particular sort of living activity. Instead, we are messy concrete beings that approximate various sorts of idealized structures of functioning that someone might dream up, which specify different forms of flourishing. Irreducible Aristotelian souls are not a plausible resource. And even if we did have an irreducible striving towards a specific sort of future inside us, which aims to blow up our rubber flesh into a specific human form, it is hard to see why it would provide any very specific normative guidance on what our good is. No more perhaps than some parasite—say a hideous dragon escaped from the film *Alien*—lurking inside us. No more than some innate tendency towards our own death.

But perhaps I am not being sufficiently charitable regarding what Aristotle meant. And many are now *neo*-Aristotelians, who think that at least reformulations of his key claims are consistent with physical reality. So we will consider several such attempts.

First, Kripke and Putnam have led analytic philosophers into tolerance of essential properties, properties that things not only have in actuality but also have, so to speak, in all possible worlds in which they exist.[66] For instance, it is now widely thought that it is an essential property of water that it be H-O-H, and indeed that that is the individual essence of water, which is to say that it is not only an essential property of water but a property had only by water in any possible world. Essential properties in the contemporary sense are not completely unlike Aristotelian kind essences, which are supposed to specify proper forms of flourishing for members of species, so maybe they can underwrite robust objectivism.[67] But there is an immediate difficulty. Essential properties in the contemporary sense are had by individuals in every possible world in which they exist. An individual cannot exist and lack its essential properties, and hence the absence of such properties cannot count normatively against the value or flourishing of something that exists. However, Thomas Hurka counters this worry by deploying essential properties that come in degrees. More of the general kind of property that is essential is better. One worry is that this is quite unlike Kripke and Putnam's examples. And it isn't obvious why it provides a suitable rationale for a robustly revisionary account of one's good. But I think the real issue is what grounds the truth of all these essentialist claims.

Kripkean essences, so-called "de re" necessities, must either be rooted in our conventions, say our linguistic conventions about what counts as a proper referent

---

[65] Aristotle, *Nicomachean Ethics* I 7, 1098a.

[66] Putnam (1975); Kripke (1980).

[67] Hurka (1993) does not claim that all Kripkean essential properties of humans are central to well-being, only those (16–17) conditioned on their being living beings.

of our term "water" or how to think about identities, or not.[68] If so, then we are faced with the problem with conventions as a root for robust objectivist conceptions I've already noted. If not, then the essences in question are genuinely objective essences, which seem to require metaphysical resources that are inconsistent with physicalism. There is H-O-H in our physical world. But nothing obvious out there in physical reality beyond our linguistic conventions and contingent forms of thought constitutes the property of being H-O-H in some objective way as the essence of water, as opposed say to a specification of the particular kind of water that there happens to be around here. It may seem that what Kripke needs is very thin. If we grant that an expression like a name or natural kind term is rigid, so that it picks out the same thing in every possible world in which the thing exists, all he needs is some way to draw a line that tells us whether something exists in this possible situation or another. But the question is what grounds these facts, facts that names or natural kind terms are rigid and about that line. The fact that there is only H-O-H in all the ponds and lakes doing its watery thing is not enough to assure these facts of language or thought or metaphysics. The relevant facts of language and thought seem too conventional and contingent to ground ethical truth. And relevant facts of metaphysics would be too robustly metaphysical.

Still, perhaps other proposals about the truth grounds of robust objectivism may provide a way to underwrite Kripkean essences that can properly refine our conventional understanding of well-being. We might look to history to specify robust objective human well-being. Appeal to the intentions of God is inconsistent with the godless physicalism we presume. But Darwinian adaptive functions may seem capable of normative work. If some organ evolved to do something particular, say if it spread throughout an ancestral population because of selective advantages due the fact that it did that thing, and also didn't disappear over the interim separating the ancestral population and us for the same reason, then that particular thing may be its function.

But there are debilitating difficulties for any attempt to deploy an evolutionary *telos* of this sort to underwrite a robust objective conception of our well-being. It is far from clear how specific a function even all the truth about our evolutionary history can constitute. Should we focus on the original development of sexual reproduction, or the development of the apparently intensified human interest in sex, when specifying the function of sex for us, which may respectively suggest that it is for avoiding parasitical infection in descendants or for some locally important form of social bonding? And even a very specific evolutionary function does not automatically tell us anything that is relevant to normative ethics, as even the most notorious socio-biologists and evolutionary psychologists are quick to admit. Ear-piercing and circumcision are not immoral or harmful simply because they violate

---

[68] Sidelle (1989) develops conventionalism about *de re* necessities.

the evolutionary *telos* of some of our skin.[69] Just because some psychological feature evolved to help kill those who insult us, it doesn't follow that we shouldn't try to avoid consequent murderous behavior. And sometimes genes evolve that harm the creatures that carry them; that is the dark side of the mechanisms of kin selection that underwrite our somewhat benevolent nature. Sometimes our genes are that monster from *Alien*. Evolutionary functions do not specify individual well-being.

Third try: Richard Boyd favors the semantic proposal that our moral terms refer to whatever causally regulates their use by competent speakers, a view to which I promised to return. And he suggests in particular that individual well-being is a homeostatic cluster property.[70] Many properties, including health and animal kinds, are alleged to be homeostatic cluster properties, which crucially means that there

is a family F of properties which are 'contingently clustered' in nature in the sense that they co-occur in an important number of cases.... Either the presence of some of the properties in F tends (under appropriate conditions) to favor the presence of others, or there are underlying mechanisms or processes which tend to maintain the presence of the properties.... [And the] clustering of the properties in F is causally important.[71]

What about good in particular?

There are a number of important human goods, things which satisfy important needs. Some of these needs are physical or medical [and hence presumably involve health]. Others are psychological and social; these (probably) include the need for love and friendship, the need to engage in cooperative efforts, the need to exercise control over one's own life, the need for intellectual and artistic appreciation and expression, the need for physical recreation, etc.... Under a wide variety of (actual and possible) circumstances these human goods (or rather instances of the satisfaction of them) are homeostatically clustered.[72]

This specific list has the same vague plausibility as our consensus about the good. It is not obviously robust. But Boyd suggests that it is an empirical question what the exact form of the homeostatic cluster that constitutes our good is, indeed whether there is a single such cluster corresponding to our term "good."[73] This sort of appeal to natural kinds to resolve normative disputes is oddly characteristic of recent discussions in ethics; perhaps it seems that natural kinds are an appropriately physical successor to Aristotelian *tele*.

But, I complain, there is absolutely no reason to believe that the choice between two normative refinements of our vague commonsense consensus about individual good should turn on which provides a homeostatic cluster, or indeed any other sort

---

[69] But we shortly return to cases analogous to these.
[70] Boyd (1988: 204 n2) propounds this model for individual good.
[71] Boyd (1988: 197–8).
[72] Boyd (1988: 203), with my insertion in brackets. But n6 makes a qualification. And this is Boyd's characterization of overall and not individual good.
[73] Boyd (1988: 217–18 and 224–5) specifies qualifications.

of natural kind. Even if we grant, as seems highly doubtful, that the dominant reference of our term "good" is the cluster or natural kind we mostly dub with that word or that mostly controls our usage, that does not suffice to adequately resolve genuinely normative disputes about how to live, disputes beyond resolution by our vague consensus on the good. If it turns out that most of intuitive human well-being is part of some natural kind but that intellectual life is not, that does nothing to undercut a conception of well-being in which intellectual life is important.[74]

Still, Mark van Roojen has developed Boyd's proposal in a way that skirts this objection.[75] Enlarging on a suggestion of Boyd, he proposes that an ethical term will refer to a property in the world only when we have socially coordinated epistemic access to that property that assures that over time our beliefs about it will become approximately true,[76] and he further proposes that the properties in the world relevant to ethical terms are specifically ethical kinds.[77] Notice however that the theory I am developing in this part, conjoined with the epistemology I am following, will, as long as the rest of my arguments stand, deliver the correct ethical properties in this sense. But my moral theory MM is a desire-based account. And so this route does not provide a rationale for robust objectivist good.

The best hope for robust objectivism in our physical world seems to be a fourth kind of neo-Aristotelian account, in which the more or less natural kinds *species* play a central role that is different from the most crucial role of homeostatic clusters in Boyd and also different from the role of species essences in Hurka. These accounts proclaim that the physical health characteristic of a member of a living species is a good model for objective good in general, whether or not health or other objective goods are themselves natural kinds or essential.[78] Such accounts are our next topic.

5.8 Species and the Good

I will call this fourth sort of neo-Aristotelian objectivism "NA" for short. Its recent champions include Philippa Foot, Michael Thompson, Rosalyn Hursthouse, and Richard Kraut, who develop suggestions of Elizabeth Anscombe and Peter Geach.[79] Living things belong to species, and species seem to have characteristic natures, which specify a form of flourishing for members of that species. Tigers characteristically have four legs, and hunt and breed in a characteristic way, even if some individual tigers fail to do so. They have eyes to see, even if some individual tigers are blind. This species form specifies a sort of well-being characteristic of tigers, which some individual tigers lack. And claims about species form don't seem to

---

[74] Horgan and Timmons (1991) make a related objection. But see Geirsson (2003).

[75] van Roojen (2006).   [76] van Roojen (2006: 176).   [77] van Roojen (2006: 180–1).

[78] These accounts vary. Kraut, for instance, more specifically suggests that we look at the developmental tendencies of species members, which they may not all fully realize, as the key to properties like plant health. But for our purposes these subtle differences aren't crucial.

[79] Anscombe (1981); Foot (2001); Kraut (2007); Thompson (2008).

require any implausible metaphysical resources or even any specific evolutionary history. A blind, three-legged tiger who can't hunt and breed is intuitively less well-off than a more representative member of the species. In this way, a fig tree may need more water, or an oak tree deeper roots.

There is something attractive in this idea. But it faces three serious problems. First, species in our evolutionary world are not fixed and independent natural kinds of the sort that Aristotle presumed.[80] Evolutionary history includes gradual transform-ations between kinds. And there are large elements of accident, indeterminacy, and convention in what is taken to count as a species. And indeed no actual biological classifications correspond well to some intuitive classifications of individuals into living kinds, for instance as lilies.[81] Second, it isn't obvious that species are the proper point in the hierarchy of biological classifications to which proper flourishing should attach, or why it should attach there. Here's an example of these two problems: There are no doubt determinate historical facts about whether certain of my ancestors bred with Neanderthals over the hill in the next village. But there may not be determinate and convention-independent biological facts about whether that involved cross-species breeding, and hence whether objective flourishing for Neanderthals and hominids like us can be distinct according to NA. Nor is it plausible that that matters normatively.

But I will focus most on a third problem for NA, which will take a moment to explain. NA is largely extensionally equivalent to the desire-based account of the good that I will eventually propound, which also provides a physically workable desire-based rationale for the significance of most of the goods NA favors. But when NA points beyond this, towards a more robust account of the good, it does not provide advice that plausibly trumps an individual's contrary preference regarding their own good, at least in the absence of very implausible metaphysics. Indeed, one way to put it is that any characteristic rationale that NA can provide for an account of the good (even if, as I doubt, it can provide such a rationale consistent with physicalism) has implications that even contemporary proponents of such accounts cannot accept. This suggests that we have genuine intuitive consensus that such a view is not correct, that it violates DC1-NORMS. And even if we lacked such a consensus, it would still be problematic for NA theorists to propound a view whose characteristic implications they cannot believe. It is striking that proponents of NA strive mightily to avoid certain characteristic implications of their own views, by introducing qualifications that are in real tension with the form of objectivism that they propound, and with any rationale it might have. This third problem for NA is analogous to one of Feldman's problems.

---

[80] Dupré (1993: 17–59); Coyne and Orr (2004); Mendola (2008: 88–94); Zimmer (2008). This is not general skepticism about natural kinds. The worry is about species.
[81] Dupré (1993: 28–9).

To understand these three general difficulties properly, we will need to look at specific normative details of NA proposals, and consider a range of cases. They involve a corresponding range of difficulties, including these three central ones, but also others as well.

First case: Some of the neo-Aristotelians under consideration are associated not merely with an objective conception of individual well-being, but with virtue ethics, with the twin ideas that the central root of morality is individual virtue (as opposed to duty or the maximization of impersonal value) and that virtue is required by individual well-being. The virtuous are supposed in the relevant sense better off. So individual good on these conceptions is rather high-toned. This is often admitted by such authors to be the most controversial and doubtful element of their proposal, and indeed it is pretty implausible to claim that the virtuous person would be well-off on the rack. That is just the sort of revisionary claim most in need of extravagant and unrealistic metaphysical buttressing. It seems impossible to get it out of any realistic conception of our species. But perhaps it is plausible, as for instance Hursthouse merely claims, that the moral virtues are the best bet in ordinary circumstances for the kinds of character traits that will maximize one's well-being.[82] Still, that concession to reality suggests that there are two discernible sorts of well-being, that which in some circumstances, say in the presence of oppressively evil institutions, only the vicious can possess, and another sort that adds to that sleekness of coat and fullness of belly the high-toned moral virtues. And notice that any plausible account of morality, including MM, allows a two-level ideal of this sort: There is the lower well-being of individuals, the sleek coat and the full belly, which may be unavailable to the moral in a suitably corrupt world. And then there is the higher kind of what we can stretch to call well-being, which requires of an individual proper morality. As I noted earlier for similar cases, there is nothing normative or practical at stake in whether that second level is called a component of individual well-being or good.

Still, perhaps there are other sorts of characteristic objectivist goods that NA can plausibly deliver, beyond the pleasure, true belief, and minimal health that the true desire-based account will itself underwrite and which are good by wide consensus, and beyond moral ideals that the true moral theory must somehow supply. However, the deepest problem is that what NA seems most obviously to add are forms of roughly Aristotelian well-being that fans of NA are not quick to embrace. To the contrary. This is the third serious problem for NA. But begin with our other worries:

It isn't clear *why* the species types that underlie NA are supposed to be merely living species types. NA's general rationale seems to push on towards the existence of flourishing in many other cases, as I will shortly explain. In fact, it isn't even clear that plant species are really plausibly symmetrical with animal species in this role. Is a tree deformed into some unnatural shape by horticultural extravagance intuitively

---

[82] She only thinks this can be seen from within a tradition that largely accepts these virtues.

stunted in the same way as a similarly deformed animal, that is to say in a way relevant to its individual well-being? I am tempted to argue on this basis that when desire is absent we have a clear consensus that something does not have a good of the sorts neo-Aristotelians embrace. But a more important point is that if humans and rhododendrons are to be said to have a specific good of this sort, then all sorts of things other than living individuals seem to have such an objective good as well, rooted in their natural type, even if that type is not a living species. Consider the state of a particular organ in an animal, or a cancer, or a particular cell, or even a rampaging tornado. Perhaps it will be said that we should discount the well-being of the tornado as we discount the well-being of a murderer, in determining the value of an overall outcome. But it is not intuitively plausible to discount the well-being of even the murderer *completely* in our deliberations about what to do with him, and the tornado has no plausible claim on us at all. Perhaps it will be said that the tornado has a good even if it is not morally relevant, and that I am confusing evaluative notions of the good with normative claims about what is right and wrong. But our aim here is to discover a kind of morally relevant well-being, useful to ethics, which a tornado lacks. Perhaps it will be said that the difference is that a tornado is not alive. But what is the NA rationale for a focus on living things in particular?[83] It can't be the fact that only living things have irreducible Aristotelian souls, since NA eschews such nonsense, as well as any appeal to evolutionary history. And in any case, an organ, a cancer, and a cell are all alive, and often have evolutionary histories, and characteristic life spans. And as we noted before, there is a great deal of arbitrariness in what is taken to count as a species. All of the things on my list seem to have a state of ideal flourishing of the same rough sort as species health, but we have a firm normative consensus that there is absolutely no moral constraint against interfering with the natural unfolding of a tornado, or (if you prefer only living cases) against interfering with the unfolding of a cancer, or against replacing your heart with a healthier one, or against sacrificing one of your cells to your happiness. These things do not possess a normatively relevant good or well-being. And so, unlike hedonist and desire-based conceptions, NA conceptions do not provide a plausible account of the proper objects of moral concern. They provide no legitimate rationale for a focus on the well-being of individual animals in species as opposed to cancers and organs and cells. Indeed, even things beyond natural phenomena like tornados have a discernible *telos* of roughly this sort. When your local virtuoso orchestra is playing middle Schoenberg very well, it is flourishing in a similar sense even if all the players and the audience are miserable about it. Perhaps these various ideal states of various entities should have a role in disciplining human action beyond truth and morality, though not I think in any way that trumps truth or morality, and perhaps they have it within the bounds of a

---

[83] Hurka (1993: 16–17) notes the traditional significance of a "good life" in the objectivist tradition, and the fact that we don't customarily speak of the good of a rock or chemical, as grounds. But we seek a rationale for these features of tradition.

desire-based account, since if you want good Schoenberg there are objectivist constraints on that. Still, it is hard to believe that *all* such forms of flourishing really
matter normatively in any way. And it is hard to see why some might plausibly
matter more than others except because we care more about some of them, the
suitably ideal orchestral performance more than the ideal tornado or flourishing cell,
or because we have desires whose satisfaction indirectly involves them, or because
they have desires themselves.

The proper root of even this sort of discipline of action seems to be desire. Fans of
NA owe us some story that distinguishes the states of whole living organisms, typed as
members of species in particular, from other similar things, in a way that provides a
genuinely normative rationale for their characteristic claims, and without recourse to
implausible metaphysics. Without such a story, without a restriction to species with a
proper rationale, NA would be too wildly implausible to take seriously. And in physical
reality there is no reason to expect that it can be provided. Of course, if an NA theorist
depends solely on our intuitive judgments about particular goods to vindicate a
particular form of their view, without providing any asymmetric rationale for it, they
are in accord with much contemporary methodology; they may feel free simply to
stipulate a focus on species. But Chapter 4 explained why I am demanding more. And it
is especially necessary for normatively robust and revisionary forms of objectivism.

A closely related point, that will bring us back to the third and most serious general
worry about NA, is that some friends of NA themselves have a somewhat ambivalent
attraction to the relevance of biological species. We will soon see that Hursthouse
suggests that some of the relevant types are subspecies, say breeds of dogs, and not
species. This should give us pause. Imagine a Nazi who insists on the normative
salience of breeds of humans. But I think the main point here is that even if that
qualification involves merely a few odd exceptions, the neo-Aristotelians often seem
more focused on species in principle than in fact. They characteristically deploy a
traditional abstract hierarchical conception of humans inherited from Aristotle, in
which little details of species life are ignored. It seems an account appropriate to all
rational animals. Indeed, if we discover rational Martians, who eat and reproduce as
squirrels but who like us are rational, I think that many NA theorists would not
attempt to specify genuinely distinct forms of well-being for such rational social
animals, involving detailed differences not simply due to differences in what they
prefer. They would follow Aristotle in their respect for common intuition, and if the
Martians characteristically raise their children in somewhat different ways from us, it
is far from intuitively obvious that that is normatively required of all of them when it
doesn't serve their desire-based interests. If humans don't characteristically read and
write or fly from place to place, it is hard to see why that means they shouldn't.
Species is intuitively irrelevant in many cases to well-being.

It is quite understandable that neo-Aristotelians wouldn't rush to embrace such
characteristic implications of a focus on species. They are unintuitive and implausible.
Human life admits of obvious variation. It would be implausible to claim that one of the

many forms of life that we live is closer to our true nature. And it would be normatively unattractive even if it were possible for us now to believe that. But this is reason to doubt that NA accounts are an improvement on desire-based accounts of the good. Proponents of NA in fact seem to prefer a very abstract normatively relevant type that would be shared by humans and our hypothetical Martians, whatever their lip-service to species. Perhaps it involves merely the possession of beliefs capable of truth, minimal health, and desires (and consequent action) capable of satisfaction and normative discipline in the way I have already embraced, and hence implies nothing contrary to the properly concessive desire-based account of the good.

I've been complaining that NA theorists are themselves ambivalent about the significance of animal species, even though such a commitment is characteristic of their view, albeit in many ways it is implausible and not properly motivated. But there are more concrete and specific examples of our third general problem with NA, that it has intuitively implausible implications that are not sufficiently well motivated to overrule individual desire, including many which its followers can't accept.

Consider this case: It is quite characteristic of NA to focus on the health of a plant as a crucial model for human good. And that suggests that our own closely analogous physical health, or even mental health, is something that should matter to our well-being, even if, like a plant, we don't care about it, even if it isn't instrumentally relevant or necessary to what we care about, and even if it isn't related to what we will care about in the future. It would be characteristic of NA to suggest that health matters more than a desire-based account can explain, or that a more specific form of health than our desires can specify properly refines or revises our rough normative consensus about the good. But the problem with this is that it is not intuitively plausible to claim that health that is not directly or even indirectly relevant to what an individual cares about is more important to their well-being than things about which they do care. If we are going to presume to give robust and corrective normative advice to someone *about their own good*, then we should have a better rationale for that advice than similarity to forms of species-specific health that they do care about. I think that we even have normative consensus that it is false that those who after careful deliberation choose something else they want for themselves, say a personal achievement of some kind, at the cost of some specific and robust NA ideal of physical health, some aspect of optional animal vigor or strength, are hence acting contrary to their own well-being, especially if we presume that later in life they have no regrets. We do think that people who regret the loss of their health to some youthful folly are sometimes worse off than they might have been, but the characteristic implication of NA accounts is that health has significance even when it is not relevant to what we want, to what we care about, in any way at all, at any time. The characteristic implication of NA accounts is that such a sacrifice of one's own health is wrong even if until death one is very glad one made it. It seems to me that we have a consensus that this is not correct. And it would require a much stronger rationale than NA can realistically provide to overturn our consensus on this point.

But, even if I am wrong about this fact of consensus, it is quite striking that, if we look closely, we can see prominent proponents of NA themselves in determined flight from characteristic normative suggestions of their proposals very close to this point.[84] While there are natural concrete normative suggestions of NA regarding the typical species life of humans that differ from what the true desire-based account will deliver, even the fans of NA seem anxious to avoid at least many of them. Let's look closely at the details of these cases.

Consider Hursthouse's account of individual good for humans. It is developed out of her prior accounts of well-being in plants and other animals.

An individual plant is a good...specimen of its species (or sub-species)...according as (i) its parts and (ii) its operations...are good or not...in the light of two ends; they are good according to whether they are contributing, in the way characteristic of such a member of such a species, to (1) individual survival through the characteristic life span of such a member of such a species and (2) to continuance of the species.[85]

But humans aren't plants, but rather social animals. A good

social animal (of one of the more sophisticated species) is one that is well fitted or endowed with respect to (i) its parts, (ii) its operations, (iii) its actions, and (iv) its desires and emotions; whether it is thus well fitted or endowed is determined by whether these four aspects well serve (1) its individual survival, (2) the continuance of the species, (3) its characteristic freedom from pain and characteristic enjoyment, and (4) the good functioning of its social group—in the ways characteristic of the species.[86]

And she thinks further "ascent up the ladder" is required to bring us to humans. Our "rationality makes for one obvious addition.... [I]t is quite certain that it is primarily our acting from reason, well or ill, rather than those occasional actions we do 'from inclination', that make us good or bad human beings in the ethical sense. So that would be a further aspect to be added."[87]

Such a hierarchical conception of species and faculties makes more sense in an Aristotelian world of irreducible *tele* than in evolutionary reality. But focus for the moment on the core elements preserved throughout all levels of this species hierarchy, and hence what seem to be the paradigmatic forms of flourishing according to Hursthouse. The general form of her account certainly suggests that we should find healthy life in that core. But Hursthouse does not conclusively say so. She says instead that the "evaluation of someone as a good, physically healthy, specimen of humanity is, for us (as it was not, perhaps, for the ancient Greeks) quite distinct from those evaluations we call 'ethical',"[88] and she nowhere makes it clear that she thinks that health is a part of human well-being regardless of individual preference. But focus on

---

[84] Anscombe, with her old time religion, was an exception.   [85] Hursthouse (1999: 198).
[86] Hursthouse (1999: 202).   [87] Hursthouse (1999: 207).   [88] Hursthouse (1999: 207).

a somewhat related case, about which she says more. Notice the stress in Hurst-house's account on reproduction and child-rearing characteristic of a species.

It is natural to worry that this means that her account implies that humans who do not reproduce and raise children do not have full human well-being, whether they care or not. And hence the exclusively homosexual, the celibate, those who always use birth-control, and probably adoptive parents, would lack well-being and perhaps even moral virtue. Indeed, this is perhaps a characteristic suggestion of NA. But Hursthouse will have none of it, though what she says in an attempt to block the implication does not seem relevant. She attempts to argue that any proper neo-Aristotelian condemnation of homosexual activity would only focus on the vice of licentiousness. She says:

It must be recalled again that what is at issue is not a particular form of sexual activity or orientation, but character traits, and by long-standing tradition we have words for the sort of character who pursues sexual gratification as an end in itself, regardless of other consider-ations, who chafes at all abstinence, whose enjoyment is unaffected by the wishes of his partner, and the sort of character who, while not insensible to sexual pleasure, pursues it and enjoys it in a much more restricted and discriminated way. The former is licentious, the later temperate (with respect to sex).[89]

And she claims that "any further step towards the conclusion that practising homo-sexuals were, in respect of their homosexuality, ethically bad or defective human beings would require a substantial premise" linking homosexuality and licentious-ness.[90] But our tradition also has other words for character traits more directly linked to even quite temperate homosexual activity, used more commonly than the fusty old words "temperate" and "licentious," and that can be linked directly to her general account of flourishing in an oppressive and immoral way, a way she herself appar-ently finds unacceptable.

Hursthouse also claims that celibacy is not problematic according to her account on similarly unconvincing grounds.[91] And this sort of difficulty is not specific to her. Consider Foot on both reproduction and life:

Lack of a capacity to reproduce is a defect in a human being. But choice of childlessness and even celibacy is not thereby shown to be a defective choice, because human good is not the same as plant or animal good. The bearing and rearing of children is not an ultimate good in human life, because other elements of good such as the demands of work to be done may give a man or women reason to renounce family life.... Moreover, the good of survival itself is something more complex for human beings than for animals. ... The human desire to live is, of course, instinctual, but it often has to do with a desperate hope that something may yet turn out well in the future. And it seems that the preciousness of the unique memories that each person has is part of what he or she may cling to even in the most terrible of circumstances.[92]

---

[89] Hursthouse (1999: 214–15).   [90] Hursthouse (1999: 215).
[91] Hursthouse (1999: 215).   [92] Foot (2001: 42).

Once again, this is a neo-Aristotelian in flight from the characteristic normative suggestions of her own view, and towards the intuitive safety of deference to individual preference, and hence towards a desire-based account of individual good. Or consider what Kraut says about another case: "If . . . one finds that one's sexual organs impede one's affective and social powers, one would be justified in altering them."[93] It seems to me that in the most obvious and intuitive cases, what would legitimate altering one's sexual organs would be a firm and stable preference. But Kraut struggles unconvincingly to find a different and neo-Aristotelian rationale. He says that in "doing so, one transforms part of one's body (and impedes the powers one could exercise through their use) in order to enjoy the exercise of affective and social powers that one correctly judges to be central components of well-being."[94] But there is no plausible NA rationale for this particular hierarchy of powers.

I have no complaints about where these enlightened neo-Aristotelians want to end up, although I'm not inclined to condemn the licentious. But I question the plausibility of their mechanisms for getting where they want to go. And I am complaining about the coherence of any possible rationale of NA with these qualifications, about the fact that NA theorists hence shun what seem to be characteristic ways in which NA extends beyond the correct desire-based account.

But consider other sorts of case, which may seem more friendly for NA. I've already indicated that the correct desire-based account will allow a serious role for familiar cognitive virtues related to truth. But Hurka explores various possible parallels in practical rationality of his objectivist account of epistemic virtues, in the process recommending long-range and complex intentions of a sort that are natural to humans.[95] There are intuitive problems with this: Those with complex cognitive capacities will naturally form complex desires and intentions, but if they don't, it seems not the same sort of intuitively objective failure that an analogous cognitive failure would be. Perhaps it is a gift to be simple in desire and intention. But my main point about this proposal is analogous to what I said about truth. MM requires a rather complex form of practical rationality of all moral agents, rooted ultimately in desire-satisfaction but involving complicated consequentialist mechanisms. MM requires, at least in our circumstances, that we all form complex and long-range intentions if we are to be morally ideal, if we are to effectively pursue consequentialist good. And long-range intentions are directly provided with considerable normative weight by MM in their guise as the basis of group acts performed by continuing selves, as we will eventually see. So objectivist goods of this sort are also incorporated in my proposal, in a way that also has the intuitive advantage of not endorsing the value of complex *evil* intentions.[96] In more recent work, Hurka has proposed that individual virtue crucially involves a relatively specific set of attitudes towards the good, that there is a kind of second-order good that rests on loving

---

[93] Kraut (2007: 147 n11).   [94] Kraut (2007: 147 n11).   [95] Hurka (1993: 120–8).
[96] Brink (1989: 232) suggests a diminished value for cruel projects.

independently specified first-order goods.[97] Christine Swanton and Robert Adams have made analogous objectivist proposals.[98] But Part III will apply MM to deliver a plausible consequentialist account of familiar virtues like benevolence which is similar to Hurka's proposal, though again not as a part of well-being. So the correct desire-based account can deliver these objectivist goods in an intuitive way.

There are other characteristic human powers that might seem to provide other candidate objective goods that desire-based accounts cannot properly deliver. For instance, in Kraut's account "a flourishing human being is one who possesses, develops, and enjoys the exercise of cognitive, affective, sensory, and social powers (no less than physical powers)."[99] Focus now on sensory, affective, and social powers.

What does Kraut conclude on the basis of the importance of our sensory powers? "Consider someone who is born with irreversible blindness and who never develops a desire or a plan to see."[100] Kraut thinks that such a person is objectively worse off than the sighted even if they care not a jot. This case is hard to assess, because the blind face all sorts of practical difficulties in our sighted world, and because people customarily care about seeing, and about the truths and beauties it can reveal. But if we consider a blind person who doesn't care at all, and for whom blindness is not an instrumental difficulty, perhaps in a world where sight can gain them nothing, Kraut's case does not seem to me intuitively obvious. And it seems even less obvious in juxtaposition with the color blind.[101] Those who can't make some visual discriminations that the normal can make may find themselves in situations in which that is consequentially relevant to the satisfaction of their desires. But there are some people called "color blind" who can make certain color discriminations in certain circumstances that the normal *cannot* make.[102] Since they are outnumbered their differences may also work to their disadvantage; the differences may be consequentially harmful to the satisfaction of their desires. But their deviation from species typicality in color experience is not itself a defect in their well-being of any plausible sort.

Let me put it this way: Qualitatively identical concrete individuals who happen to be members of different species don't seem to differ in any intuitive sort of well-being.[103] And that is what NA implies. It doesn't seem to plausibly count against one's well-being that one belongs to a species that has a specific capacity when one lacks it and doesn't care and that lack doesn't interfere in any way with what one cares about.

True belief does matter, and meets one type of internalist constraint on reasons since all agents have beliefs that aim at truth. And perhaps blindness or color blindness cut one off from some truths. But a very restrictive and specific conception

---

[97] Hurka (2001).   [98] Swanton (2003); R. Adams (2006).   [99] Kraut (2007: 137).
[100] Kraut (2007: 144).   [101] Mendola (2008: Chapter 5) discusses color blindness.
[102] Kaiser and Boynton (1996: 444).
[103] If we include what makes for the satisfaction of desires and the truth of beliefs in the conditions that are qualitatively identical.

of cognitive virtue beyond anything delivered by our desires is not our business here, and it is unlikely that color blindness and even blindness implies any very weighty cognitive failure. Still, perhaps it seems that humans with severe mental incapacity can be happy with their lot and yet not flourish as a human should. I think that this is a good intuitive case for NA, even given what I've already said about true belief, and we will return to it in the guise of a standard objection to desire-based accounts of the good in Chapter 7. So here I am merely issuing a promissory note. But notice how offensive it is to treat color blindness or blindness as relevantly analogous. And NA lumps them together.

There are other forms of what Kraut calls sensory unflourishing: physical pain, nausea, bone-chilling cold. But he himself says that these "sensory experiences... would not be bad for us to feel were they not things we dislike."[104]

Perhaps then we should look to the affective powers for characteristic normative advantages of NA. There are positive emotions like joy, and negative emotions like fear. We clearly like joy, but we may not like fear. And yet we may want overall to be someone who feels fear when it is appropriate. So far the desire-based theorist can agree. And indeed Kraut himself says that "Pains can be welcomed, or tolerated, as ingredients of a complex experience. Something similar is true of emotions. The sorrow one feels, no less than physical pain, can be tolerated or even welcomed."[105] So what emotions is it supposed that we should or should not feel irrespective of our desires, irrespective of what we tolerate or welcome? "Consider... someone whose sense of humor goes badly awry because of an injury, and who laughs uncontrollably and incessantly—with a genuine feeling of amusement—at what no one else finds funny. Or think of someone who feels a rush of passionate love for every human being he encounters."[106] To my mind, such idiosyncrasies may be fine for their bearer if their bearer doesn't care. But Kraut has a more univocal ideal of humanity. Still, what is his rationale for that? "It is implausible to say that these conditions are good even to some degree, since we would do everything in our power to avoid them."[107] But, I reply, we wouldn't do everything in our power to avoid them if we didn't care about them, and so once again desire seems the root of value in these cases.

Perhaps there are other neo-Aristotelian routes to the significance of normal human affects than those that Kraut explores. For instance, perhaps the particular human virtues of temperance, courage, and so on, are required by our own emotional nature as a species. Still, we don't have a highly specific emotional nature as a species, but lots of individual differences. And it isn't at all plausible that someone who is abnormally cheery and optimistic for a human would be hence not flourishing. And I have already mentioned that there are various indirect ways that my desire-based account can also deliver traditional virtues of character, to which we will return in Part III. But let's try once more from another direction: There are human emotions

---

[104] Kraut (2007: 151).   [105] Kraut (2007: 155).
[106] Kraut (2007: 156).   [107] Kraut (2007: 156).

that are somewhat less socially conditioned and hence less optional than romantic love or humor, and perhaps they have appropriate causes across our species that help specify some ideal of human well-being. But the problem is that jealousy and envy seem to be relevantly natural human emotions with natural causes, and they are not plausible components of human well-being.

What about social flourishing? Brink suggests that objectivism should require personal and social relationships that involve mutuality of concern.[108] Kraut suggests that those who live in isolation and don't feel lonely, those who are indifferent to human love, are not flourishing even if they don't care:[109]

Such a person is indifferent to receiving human warmth, and so we should say the same thing about him that we would say about someone who is indifferent to the pleasures of physical warmth or to any other sensual pleasure. If one is unable to taste food with pleasure, or reacts to all food with indifference, that is a loss. If one does not enjoy the warmth of the sun or a fire, that is a loss. But it is no less a loss to be indifferent to receiving the affection of others. That is one way of being a chilly person, a person who does not participate in the pleasures of human interaction.[110]

I think it would be very hard to get anything like this out of our species form that the consensus of our desires does not already deliver. But notice how very robust and directive some of these claims are. It is an objective failure *in your own well-being* to be emotionally chilly, not to enjoy the warmth of a fire, or to avoid relationships founded in mutual concern, independently of whether you care, and even independently of whether that is consequentially relevant to other desires you possess. There are intuitions of this sort, but they do not seem to be part of a consensus, and so they require a strong rationale to constitute proper advice to contrary individuals, a stronger rationale than species typicality can plausibly provide, even if they really do reflect conditions typical of our species. Stravinsky, Flaubert, and Gauguin were rather chilly people. So too was Newton. Do we really think they didn't flourish because of that? Emotional and sensory life of this sort is where we should most expect and tolerate a range of human diversity. People as individuals and as members of different cultures range widely in their emotional lives and in their tastes. It is presumptuous for ethicists to specify a single ideal of proper emotionality and taste for all humans. It is also striking that Kraut allows that we might properly change our sexual organs on the basis of other considerations, while he holds that we cannot properly become chilly on the same sorts of grounds. But our characteristic species life more obviously includes standard sexual organs than a certain warm emotionality and a taste for the fireplace.

---

[108] Brink (1989: 231–6). Brink's focus on coherence and not species as grounds for normative claims makes him doubtfully an NA theorist, but for Aristotelian aspects, see 233 n10 and n11.
[109] Kraut (2007: 162–3).   [110] Kraut (2007: 162).

5.9 Normative Conclusion

An appeal to intuitions that are not generally shared is not enough to show a normative view to be true or false, and an especially strong rationale is required if there is to be legitimate correction of someone's own inclinations regarding their own good. But objectivism, like hedonism, is only able to provide such a rationale in conditions that are inconsistent with reality, which for instance include Aristotelian *tele*.

Objectivists, like hedonists, are right about the most characteristic goods they cite: minimal health, true belief, and even some complex intentions. But I've promised that the correct desire-based account can deliver these goods, along with pleasure, or at least allow for them. Though I'm not planning to say much more about true belief and complex intentions, I've issued promissory notes to deliver various goods that are characteristic of hedonism and objectivism, and if I can't deliver, then I grant that my moral theory MM is false.[111]

Still, we have seen in this chapter that all viable accounts of well-being in our physical world are desire-based conceptions, though sometimes in disguise. The proper rationale for the significance of all the ethically relevant goods that we have discussed is provided by the fact that we care about them, or things that require them. And such a rationale is, at least for our purposes, the essence of a desire-based account. The characteristic rationales of hedonism and objectivism, that could suffice to close justificatory regresses, are not available in physical reality. The robust and revisionary elements of such accounts cannot be properly supported.

Nevertheless, it may seem that desire-based accounts provide the wrong order of explanation in some cases in which they are extensionally equivalent to hedonism or objectivism, that the satisfaction of desires is perhaps only good when the desires are focused on objects that are pleasant or have some other sort of objective value. And it may seem that by putting together elements from various types of accounts, and not under the dominance of one type as I will attempt, we can do better than by sticking to one type. For instance, Parfit suggests that "what is good or bad for someone is to have knowledge, to be engaged in rational activity, to experience mutual love, and to be aware of beauty, while strongly wanting just those things."[112] But the normative effect of such proposals, beyond cases we've already considered, is only to put certain constraints on the objects of desires that count towards well-being, to insist that the satisfaction of other desires is no real good. And we will return to such proposals in Chapter 7, in the guise of objections to simpler forms of desire-based account. In our physical world, like it or not, there are no viable alternatives to desire-based accounts, which must provide the central rationale for the correct conception of individual good.

---

[111] And Chapter 7 must reply to the objection from severe mental incapacity.
[112] Parfit (1984: 502).

6

Desire and the Good

We have been pushed towards a desire-based conception of the good, if standard objections to such an account can be answered. And Arthur's desires do provide an obvious rationale for a modest conception of his good based on the satisfaction of those desires. It is not necessary for such a view to deploy implausible metaphysics to buttress controversial normative advice like that of robust hedonism and objectivism. But there is relevant variety among desire-based accounts, and the now dominant forms harbor suspect metaphysical commitments of their own.

What I will call "simple desire-based accounts" of individual good or well-being identify an individual's good with the satisfaction of their actual desires. Such accounts are historically important,[1] and I will defend one version. But they face familiar objections, rooted in intuitive consensus. There are incorrect desires, whose satisfaction does not contribute to well-being: Guinevere wants to quaff a brew that, unbeknownst to her, is poisoned. There are also desires we ought to have that we lack: Arthur should want to run, but doesn't, because he fails to see what's lurking.

The standard response to these objections involves modification of simple desire-based accounts into "informed desire accounts," in which only the satisfaction of idealized desires that are corrected by full information or reflection constitutes well-being.[2] If Guinevere knew of the poison in the cup, then her desire to drink would disappear. If Arthur knew what lurks, then he would want to run. But informed desire accounts, though now dominant, are not viable in reality. Our next job is to see why.

6.1 Problems of Informed Desire

There are a variety of serious difficulties for informed desire accounts, despite their popularity.

---

[1] Hobbes (1955: Part 1, Chapter 6); Perry (1967); Spinoza (1994: Part Three, Proposition 9). Thomas (2008) provides historical context.

[2] Barry (1965: Chapters 10 and 11); Griffin (1986); D. Lewis (1989); Carson (2000); Railton (2003a, 2003c). Brandt (1979) and M. Smith (1994) focus on rationality, but mechanisms for moving from individual good can be applied to move from prudential rationality to normative judgment, so this difference matters little.

One's properly corrected desires may be one's actual desires that would survive a hypothetical confrontation with all relevant information. Alternatively, since perhaps no actual desires would survive that confrontation and new ones would be created, one's corrected desires may be the desires one would have if one underwent that hypothetical confrontation. But both routes are highly problematic. It is far from obvious that getting something I don't want and don't appreciate though which I would want if I were properly molded by full information increases my actual well-being.[3] Imagine that I get some fine claret when what I really like is cheap beer. And, on the other hand, my actual desires that would survive full information may not be sufficiently systematic or wide-ranging for their satisfaction to intuitively constitute my well-being. Maybe only my desires to scratch and eat would survive that confrontation.

In response to these worries, informed desire accounts deploy fancy resources. Griffin suggests that very high-order desires, preferences among alternative plans of life, are those whose confrontation with full information is most relevant to well-being, and that they underwrite a complex balancing of other actual and informed desires, and hence evade the worry about claret for the beer-lover.[4] But it is not realistic to claim that we all have desires of that abstract sort, nor is there any particular reason to believe that we would have them in light of full information. So perhaps instead with Railton we should claim that "an individual's good consists in what he would want himself to want, or to pursue, were he to contemplate his present situation from a standpoint fully and vividly informed about himself and his circumstances, and entirely free of cognitive error and lapses of instrumental rationality,"[5] or perhaps with Carson we should focus on the "choice that my ideally rational self would make for my actual (non-ideal) self."[6] But these ideal states of wanting oneself to want in non-ideal circumstances, or of making choices for one's non-ideal self, are also fancy, albeit ideal and hypothetical, mental states. It is not obvious that they are realistic mental states for many of us. And we have no good reason to believe such an ideal self would have very probative preferences about what would hence be the totally unrealistic situation in which they were not ideal. This is because it is easy to have all sorts of self-flattering preferences about what to do should you get into situations that you know you won't ever inhabit. Perhaps we can evade this worry by requiring significant sincerity, claiming that one can't when ideal sincerely prefer to do something should one be non-ideal unless one would actually do it if one were non-ideal.[7] But that fix would undercut the effect of an appeal to an ideal state that is the central feature of an informed desire account. I believe it is unlikely that the proper sort of sincerity and idealization can be made to work together in a consistent way, and so I think that these worries are sufficient to defeat informed desire accounts. But I will focus here on more standard problems for such accounts, worries about the notion of full information.

---

[3] Griffin (1986: 11).   [4] Griffin (1986: 11–12).   [5] Railton (2003a: 54).
[6] Carson (2000: 26).   [7] See 10.9.

There are two clusters of problems of even this sort. First, Gibbard, Velleman, Loeb, and Rosati have suggested that full enough information, say a vivid awareness of all the suffering in the world, might make our desires more incorrect. It might make us hard-hearted or depressed or deeply scarred.[8] And a vivid awareness of the facts about digestion or disease might make us unable to eat with others, or want to wash our hands 60 times a day.[9] Of course, someone who washes their hands 60 times a day and is unable to eat with others seems mad. And some informed desire accounts require, with Michael Smith, that we consider what we would want if we were unhindered by compulsions, addictions, and emotional distress like depression. But what counts as a compulsion or addiction rather than a strong and proper desire may be normatively controversial in a way that the physical facts do not resolve. Consider a forceful romantic attachment. And what's worse, depression in any suitably independent clinical sense seems in fact correlated with greater realism; the depressed are more responsive to the facts than those who are not.[10] It is perhaps not unreasonable to conclude from this set of worries that properly full information is simply that which corrects desires to truth. But then informed desire accounts could not properly provide a reductive account of the good. So informed desire accounts seem to require instead a very optimistic conception of the facts of human motivation, in which the possession of fuller information is correlated with greater emotional health, at least in those who lack a specific set of obvious emotional disabilities not enmeshed with the possession of information. I believe that such accounts are wrong to presume all this. But here I will focus most centrally on a second cluster of worries about the notion of full information:

Real human beings cannot in fact get all possible information, or even all information that might affect their desires, into cognition all at once, and any idealization of humans involving omniscience is too vast to generate any real understanding of what is good for them in their guise as mere limited humans.[11] But, on the other hand, different selections of the possibly relevant facts would move our desires in different ways. What's more, the order of presentation of such information would affect what desires we end up with,[12] as would the mode of presentation of that information to us.[13] And there are no plausible prior and independent facts about the proper selection, or mode or order of presentation, of information. This suggests significant indeterminacy about what it is to be properly informed.

There are different mechanisms that have been proposed to deal with these difficulties, but they involve more fancy commitments. Once again, Griffin suggests that a psychologically complex hierarchical structure of desires helps:

---

[8] Velleman (1988); Loeb (1995); Rosati (1995).   [9] Gibbard (1990: 18–22).
[10] Alloy and Abramson (1979); Dobson and Franche (1989).
[11] D. Sobel (1994) argues no account of full information allows all required comparisons among lives.
[12] Rosati (1995: 309).   [13] Velleman (1988).

We have local desires (say, for a drink) but also higher-order desires (say, to distance oneself from consumers' material desires) and global desires (say, to live one's life autonomously). The structure of desires provides the criterion for 'informed' desire; information is what advances plans of life; information is full when more, even when there is more, will not advance them further. So there is only one way to avoid all the faults that matter ... namely, by understanding completely what makes life go well.[14]

This requires complex psychological facts about which I have already expressed skepticism. And in any case, it is hard to get much guidance out of any realistic general plan of life on what specifically to do in most circumstances, unless it happens to include the goal of having a lot of local desire-satisfaction, which would defeat the mechanism proposed for skirting indeterminacy, because uninformed local desires might be incorrect.

Carson suggests instead a response modeled on Crispin Wright's notion of super-assertibility. "It is correct for S to prefer X to not-X ... if and only if, (1) there is at least one empirically possible cognitive/informational perspective (P1) from which S would prefer X to not-X and (2) there is no other empirically possible perspective (P2) which is as good as or better than P1 (for deciding between X and not-X) such that S would not prefer X to not-X from P2."[15] But the second of these two conditions is quite robust, and depends on a notion of the relative quality of cognitive/informational perspectives that is of doubtful determinacy. And so this account also suggests indeterminacy about the correctness of preferences.

Railton appeals instead to the truth of a robust psychological theory:[16]

[T]here is a reduction basis for [someone's] idealized hypothetical desires. So when we ask how his desires would change upon the impact of further information, we appeal to this basis. We, in effect, hold this basis as nearly constant as possible when asking what someone like *him* would come to desire—or, more precisely, would come to want that he pursue were he to assume the place of his original self.[17]

Though on one pessimistic (but it seems to me quite plausible) scenario, it might be that

owing to the psychological properties of actual people, it is impossible to bring them to a state of full and vivid information, yet we may see them as possessing properties in virtue of which they would be disposed to respond in certain ways to ever more complex and vivid information (supposing a capacity to absorb it), and different kinds of people, to respond differently.[18]

Notice how very much is presumed here. There must be in reality a "reduction basis," a physical basis for true claims about an individual's idealized hypothetical desires,

---

[14] Griffin (1986: 13).   [15] Carson (2000: 232).   [16] Railton (2003a: 57–62).
[17] Railton (2003a: 60).   [18] Railton (2003a: 62).

that includes at least some of their actual desires, or individual differences in desire drop out as insignificant to the good. And the properties by which someone is disposed to respond to complex information are obviously closely enlaced with whatever it is that grounds the facts about what information they can in fact absorb. So here we have two instances of the kinds of conditions that suggest the indeterminate truth of subjunctive conditional claims like "If I were fully informed, I would want X." The background conditions that must be preserved to assess the counterfactual are plausibly entwined with the conditions that must be varied counterfactually. And the kind of psychological theory of human types that allows individually tailored projections for wildly hypothetical conditions is just the sort about whose sufficiently determinate truth we should have greatest doubt given our messy neurophysiology. And indeed such a conditional seems considerably worse than those we considered in Chapter 2, because if omniscience is impossible for a human, it has an impossible antecedent.[19]

Any of these three attempts to patch up informed desire accounts suggest very significant indeterminacies of individual good. This is not a surprise. After Chapter 2, we should expect the indeterminate truth of subjunctive conditionals like "If I were fully informed, I would want X." In fact, it appears that such conditionals are too indeterminate in truth in our physical world to deliver what is required for such robust accounts of individual good, accounts that might otherwise properly correct ignorant individual desire. The conditionals are virulently indeterminate, unsuited to their work.

There are only moderate indeterminacies in our options: *those* indeterminacies do not make the notion of alternative actions completely unworkable. Why is the notion of the wants one would have if fully informed more virulently indeterminate? First, because the notion of trying found in the antecedent of the conditionals relevant to options is somewhat soft and indeterminate in application in our physical world, but not as soft and indeterminate, in ways we have just traced, as the notion of full information. There are precision problems involving trying, but they are not as serious as those involving full information. Second, some of the individual differences in our options turn on conditions that are not closely enmeshed with the conditions that make it true that we in fact try one thing rather than another. Some are external conditions out in the world, and the bodily differences between a young gymnast and someone forced to use a cane also introduce quite determinate individual differences in options. And so indeterminacy only affects some of the conditionals relevant to fixing our options, and hence some of our options. But none of the conditionals relevant to informed desires are shielded from indeterminacy in these ways.

---

[19] Carson (2000: 229).

6.2 Sophisticated Simple Desire

Informed desire accounts of individual well-being are unworkable in reality. And so are hedonism and objectivism. Are we stuck then with no workable account of individual well-being?

Not necessarily. There are other attempts to meet standard objections to simple desire-based accounts, which deploy, instead of hypothetical conditions of full information, actual psychological conditions of a robustly specific sort. Unfortunately, even these routes in their current formulations, which I will call "sophisticated simple desire-based accounts," are too fancy to be viable in reality. We will need to develop something cruder and more realistic. But first we must understand these other routes and their difficulties.

Donald Hubin holds that many intuitively incorrect desires are not incorrect *intrinsic* desires, but rather incorrect *instrumental* desires, rooted in false beliefs about what would satisfy intrinsic desires.[20] Guinevere wants intrinsically not to be poisoned, but doesn't realize that this requires avoiding a certain cup. Chris Heathwood suggests instead that the satisfaction of intuitively incorrect desires often leads to less overall desire-satisfaction for the individual in question, so that on balance it would not be recommended by simple desire-based accounts.[21] The satisfaction of Mordred's wish to kill his father would lead to a life with less desire-satisfaction overall. So perhaps simple desire-based accounts are workable after all, as long as there are robust facts about what we intrinsically as opposed to instrumentally desire, or about overall desire-satisfaction.

But I think we need to consider closely the plausibility of these familiar but still rather fancy conditions. Since similar resources are deployed even by standard informed desire accounts, informed desire theorists should take no comfort from any problems we will uncover. In fact, we need also to closely consider questionable fanciness sometimes harbored by the very notion of desire itself. It should go without saying that the truth of a desire-based theory of individual good depends on the nature of desire. But while traditional desire-based theorists like Hobbes and Perry had much to say on that topic, it has received little attention from contemporary desire-based theorists, because of philosophers' over-specialization. When we do properly attend to the facts of desire, we will see that there are other questionable resources that extant desire-based accounts of both simple and informed sorts sometimes harbor, because without comment they deploy fancy notions of desire itself.

Still, if we closely attend to the need to avoid robust advice about an individual's own good without adequate rationale, I think we can isolate a physically realistic and normatively relevant kind of desire, a very inclusive type of desire that is available in reality. Because it is a kind of desire, it can provide internal reasons, by which I mean

[20] Hubin (1996).   [21] Heathwood (2005).

that it can play the same sort of basic role in properly impartial practical reasoning that we discerned for hedonic value in Chapter 5. Because the sort of individual good such desires underwrite is modest, and because as we will eventually see it is rooted in consensus when distributions are in question and also includes the goods most characteristic of hedonism and objectivism, that good can end justificatory regresses. On the other hand, the robust facts about what we intrinsically as opposed to instrumentally desire and about overall desire-satisfaction required by sophisticated simple desire-based accounts cannot be saved.

6.3 The Nature of Desire I

Our first skeptical inquiry will attempt to isolate a normatively relevant kind of desire that is not too fancy for reality. Our discussion will be organized by a hierarchy of questions. First is a general question about the term and hence the entities on which to focus. Some recognizably desire-based theorists focus, like Carson, on preferences, others like Railton on wants, and only some like Griffin on desires. Is desire or rather some alternative state like wanting the central sort of motivational state that ought to be deployed in a desire-based account of well-being?

The word that is dominantly used in contemporary discussions is "desire." But it is highly ambiguous, partly because of its ubiquity in current philosophy despite the different theoretical commitments of different philosophers. Still, for this very reason, "desire" is a useful initial focus for us. Its ambiguity means that we can avoid the begging of questions, the smuggling in of inappropriately robust advice about individual good by the term with which we begin. But because philosophers have so many different theoretical conceptions of desire, we come quickly to our second general question: What is the proper and normatively relevant conception of desire, which should be deployed in the correct desire-based account of individual well-being?

There are many possibilities. One relatively modest conception of desire suggests that someone's desires are fixed by their choices under actual and hypothetical circumstances, and hence by what we might stretch to call their preferences, at least if those preferences satisfy certain principles of coherence. We will end up with something like this. But many philosophers distinguish between desires and other motivational factors that influence choice. They have what I will call robust conceptions of desire, which may harbor implausible commitments, or be the basis of robust normative advice. For instance, some propose with Kant that behavior is the effect not just of desire but of distinct motivational structures like reason. Others like Mill contrast habit and desire,[22] or emotion and desire,[23] or character and desire. There is not a single robust conception of desire, but many different ones. None has

---

[22] Mill (1972: 36–8).   [23] Nussbaum (2001); Prinz (2004).

an obviously greater semantic centrality.[24] Some think that natural kinds can help resolve disputes among various conceptions of desire, so that the development of neuroscience is relevant to our concerns.[25] But we know from Chapter 5 that natural kinds cannot help. We seek a kind of desire whose satisfaction is relevant to individual good. And while there may be various natural kinds discovered by motivational psychology or neurophysiology that are relevant to what we do, and maybe even a single dominant natural kind that corresponds to most of our uses of "desire," the boundaries of such natural kinds are normatively irrelevant. If it turns out that some of things we want have a very different neurophysiological basis than most of the things we want, that does nothing to support the claim that their satisfaction is less normatively significant.

Despite these difficulties, if we are guided by our own central normative role for desire, we can make some progress on at least some of the issues in question. Let me focus on three more specific questions about the normatively relevant conception of desire:

First, what is the basic structure of such desire? Perhaps it involves choice among alternative possible options, as a focus on preferences might suggest. But to focus on wants or dislikes in the guise of attraction and repulsion is naturally to focus instead on movement towards and away from actual things. Here we should be as inclusive as possible on normative grounds. We don't have any reason to think that literal attraction, what we literally tend to move towards, is more central to our well-being than what we prefer in a more abstract sense. So it is a relative advantage of the preference model that it can be stretched to cover the want/dislike model, while the contrary is not the case. Guinevere prefers what she wants to what she dislikes, but she also has preferences among the things she wants, and that balance various things she wants and dislikes. And not all her preferences involve already existing things that she shuns or runs after.

A second specific question is whether desires are to be distinguished for our purposes from other motivational states like habit, emotion, character, and reason? For instance, many have noted that there is a distinction between a broad sense of desire or want, in which when Lancelot does his irksome duty he can be said to be doing what he wants to do, and a narrow sense in which it can be said that in acting out of duty he is doing exactly what he doesn't want to do, indeed fighting his desires. Habits, emotions, character, and even reason can all play a role in helping to constitute what we desire in a broad sense.

Our question is whether broad desires or desires in some more narrow and exclusive sense are relevant to well-being. One way to approach the question is to consider standard typographies of broad desires. Wayne Davis distinguishes volitive desires—which include wants, wishes, and things one would like, which can be

---

[24] A difficulty reinforced by our lack of consensus whether desires can be unconscious.
[25] T. Schroeder (2004).

influenced by value judgments or entailed by intentions to do something, and which are good indicators of action—from appetitive desires, which include appetites, hungers, cravings, yearnings, longings, and urges, and which are good indicators of individual pleasure.[26] Lancelot has a volitive desire to do his duty but not an appetitive desire. But this distinction merely suggests another opportunity to be ecumenical on normative grounds. Desires of even the broadest sorts, both volitive and appetitive desires, seem by intuitive consensus relevant to well-being. For instance, both pleasures and more reflective goals are reflected in the consensus about well-being informing DC1-NORMS. And, even more to the point, various individuals take their broadest sorts of desires to be relevant to their own good, and there seems little rationale in physical reality to support the claim that they are wrong. Satisfaction of volitive desires, say in a case involving a carefully formed intention to achieve an important goal, seems sometimes crucial to one's well-being. We cannot construct any broadly intuitive well-being out of the satisfaction of our mere urges and appetites. But yet it doesn't seem appropriate to dismiss urges as always irrelevant either, even when we haven't yet endorsed them in some reflective way.

Still, that breadth generates a corresponding worry, because it seems intuitively contrary to Lancelot's interest to do his irksome duty. And the fact that appetitive desires are a better indicator of individual pleasure than volitive desires may reinforce this worry. Nevertheless, it is still clear that some of the things that many of us take to be in our intuitive self-interest, even in the moment, are not encompassed by our appetites and urges. We may relevantly want to be healthy or successful in some way, without having an appetite or urge to be healthy or successful. So we will need to answer the worry presented by Lancelot's duty on other grounds than by appeal to Davis' distinction. Chapter 7 returns to it.

G. F. Schueler suggests a still larger range of types of what might be called desires, and a more complicated classificatory scheme.[27] Perhaps this suggests other ways to refine our conception of the desires relevant to well-being. Schueler plausibly contrasts classes of which typical cases include (i) hunger, thirst, and the desire to eliminate bodily wastes, (ii) cravings for chocolate and tobacco, (iii) urges to see a Cary Grant movie or to go horseback riding, (iv) desires to visit one's sister and her family next summer, (v) wants implied by hopes that someone else has a pleasant trip, (vi) a want implied by an intention to do something that you only have because you are threatened with harm if you don't do it, (vii) and a desire to get coffee down from the shelf that you only have because you have decided to get some coffee and that is the only way you can see to get it. Schueler's cases certainly remind us of the variety of desire. But the desires in his first four classes all seem intuitively relevant to individual well-being. At the very least, many of us take them as relevant to our own

---

[26] W. Davis (1986).   [27] Schueler (1995: 9–41).

well-being, and it would require a robust rationale to properly convince us that we are wrong. And we have already seen in our discussion of Lancelot's duty that other-regarding wants like (v) are problematic cases for desire-based accounts, to which we need to return. And the satisfaction of mere instrumental desires like (vi) and (vii) is not customarily treated as directly constitutive of well-being by desire-based accounts, although we will return to that issue in 6.5. So even Schueler's more complicated set of contrasts does not provide us with a useful means of further specifying the desires relevant to well-being.

So far our consideration of the normatively relevant conception of desire has only given us a sense of its wide ecumenical range. But perhaps we can gain more illumination from a third specific question: What is the essential nature of (normatively relevant) desire? And we might distinguish a variety of sub-questions about that, which will structure our remaining discussion of desire.

First, is desire a sophisticated state that depends on the possession of language or involves, as Scanlon suggests, "a tendency to see something as a reason"?[28] Or do relatively simple animals like sharks have desires?

Here also a broad tent seems in order. There are quite simple desires that are intuitively relevant to the well-being of sharks. And similarly crude desires are intuitively relevant to the well-being of even normal adult humans, by general consensus and in the eyes of those very individuals themselves, at least when the acceptance of reasons by such people permits their animal desires motivational significance, in the way Chapter 3 specified. Consider Davis' appetitive desires and Schueler's first class of cases. And so normatively relevant desires do not need to be sophisticated, do not require the possession of language or an actual positive tendency to see things as reasons. But of course "higher" and less crude sorts of desires seem normatively relevant to well-being also.

But perhaps this is too quick a way with Scanlon's suggestion that desires involve tendencies to see things as reasons.[29] It may correctly characterize "higher" human desires for anything we have seen. And Scanlon is a source of current skepticism about the motivational significance of desire. And his suggestion may allow some indirect way of isolating normatively relevant desires. So consider the details:

Scanlon thinks that judgments about reasons, rather than desires, are central to human motivation. He claims that a "rational person who judges there to be compelling reason to do A normally forms the intention to do A, and this judgment is sufficient explanation of that intention and of the agent's acting on it. . . . There is no need to invoke an additional form of motivation beyond the judgment and the reasons it recognizes."[30] There is no need for desire as an independent motivational state. Still, there are a variety of senses in which desires can be said to be constituted out of our recognition of reasons according to Scanlon. (i) He admits a broad sense in

---

[28] Scanlon (1998: 39).   [29] Scanlon (1998: 17–77).   [30] Scanlon (1998: 33–4).

which one might be said to have a desire to do almost whatever moves one.[31] (ii) And he also claims that there is a narrower and more specific notion of desire that might also be underwritten by his proposal: "A person has a desire in the directed-attention sense that P if the thought of P keeps occurring to him or her in a favorable light, that is to say, if the person's attention is directed insistently toward considerations that present themselves as counting in favor of P."[32] (iii) Scanlon even admits that there are urges that involve no recognition of reasons, though he claims they are not desires in any very strict sense. Consider

Warren Quinn's example of a man who feels an urge to turn on every radio he sees. It is not that he sees anything *good* about radios' being turned on; he does not want to hear music or news or even just to avoid silence; he simply is moved to turn on any radio that he sees to be off.... [T]he idea of such a ... state fails to capture something essential ... : desiring something involves having a tendency to see something good or desirable about it.[33]

There are related cases that are difficult for Scanlon. An unreflective desire for coffee ice cream might seem required to rationalize eating that ice cream, but Scanlon argues that such a desire involves "three elements which might serve as reasons: enjoying something or finding it pleasant, having a desire for it in the directed-attention sense, and having given it the status of a consideration to be taken into account in future deliberation (or having the intention to pursue it)."[34] And the first and third elements of that might also be themselves considered desires.[35]

So, in sum, Scanlon does provide us with a new typography of motivations. Can we do anything with it? It may be that Scanlon believes his reason-based account requires the postulation of something non-natural,[36] but the analysis' central requirement is the existence of judgments about reasons and not the existence of reasons, as we can judge that there are wizards when there are no wizards, and indeed my notion of an accepted reason is very like it. So I have no quarrel with Scanlon's distinctions among kinds of motivational states. He accepts the notion of almost as wide and ecumenical a sense of desire as we have. But perhaps his account will be thought to refine the kinds of desires relevant to well-being. Perhaps the satisfaction of Quinn-like urges that involve no recognized reasons should not count towards well-being. But, to the contrary, it seems quite intuitive to claim that unsatisfied urges of that sort can undercut one's well-being. That is what many of us believe in our own case. While Scanlon can no doubt discover related judgments about reasons in such cases that are in accord with that intuition,[37] still this cannot be a normatively distinctive suggestion of his proposal. But perhaps instead desires in the directed-attention sense are most relevant to well-being. However, no more than Schueler's urges do these exhaust the sorts of desires whose satisfaction is taken by individuals

---

[31] Scanlon (1998: 37).   [32] Scanlon (1998: 39).   [33] Quinn (1993); Scanlon (1998: 38).
[34] Scanlon (1998: 47).   [35] Scanlon (1998: 37–8 and 45–7).   [36] Scanlon (1998: 55–64).
[37] Tenenbaum (2007: 38). But cravings one prefers to extinguish involve a form of balancing that might qualify other desires, and my desire-based account discounts idiosyncratic desires.

as normatively relevant to their well-being. That is also true of the first and third type of desire Scanlon associates with coffee ice cream. Scanlon's interesting proposals about desire provide us neither assistance nor trouble.

Perhaps it is worth attending to other fancy accounts of desire that explicitly insist on objective good as a strict constitutive condition for desire, which is beyond anything Scanlon claims. Metaphysically robust accounts of this sort, that imply that desires involve the veridical recognition of non-natural properties, might serve to refine our sense of normatively relevant desires. But such accounts are not consistent with physicalism. Still, perhaps there are other more plausible accounts of normatively relevant desires that deploy things like real needs (as opposed to mere tendencies to see things as needs), and which hence might be applicable to sharks as well as humans. Our second sub-question about the essence of desires is whether they involve fancy resources like these.

Dennis Stampe proposed, to a first approximation, that "To desire that p is to be disposed to act in ways that would tend to result in the obtaining of a state of affairs (i.e., that in which p), which disposition tends, under certain conditions, to be caused by a state of affairs such that it would be good were that desire to be satisfied—that is, *good were it to be the case that p.*"[38] But that is only a first approximation of his account. First, a belief that something is good might be similarly caused and have such results, and an intention might also be so caused and have such results. So Stampe postulates a faculty of appetite that is "activated, ideally, only by such a state of affairs, i.e., one such that it would be good were something or other to be the case."[39] And this mechanism is supposed not to be the (proximal) cause of such beliefs or intentions, while desires are supposed to be essentially so proximally caused. Second, we might be uneasy about the deployment of what is good in this analysis, and Stampe suggests that we might become easier by substituting the notion of a need. "It would seem relatively unobjectionable to use the concept of need in pursuit of a naturalistic understanding of desire."[40] Stampe has also proposed an analysis of the needs, and hence at least in part an analysis of the good, of living things.[41]

But the problem is that while such an objectivist proposal about well-being could perhaps serve to refine the types of desires relevant to individual good, it is clear that this fancy feature of Stampe's analysis of desire makes it unsuited for our particular task, which is the development of a desire-based theory of the good. Stampe pursued a different order of explanation than we are attempting. And in Chapter 5 we saw that robust objectivist proposals are unworkable in reality. Once again, we have discovered no useful illumination about desire-based good from the consideration of a fancy account of desire.[42] So we should turn to our third and final sub-question,

---

[38] Stampe (1986: 159).   [39] Stampe (1986: 166).
[40] Stampe (1986: 167).   [41] Stampe (1988).
[42] Tenenbaum (2007: 21–51) is another account of this sort. Page 29 says that in the absence of desire-independent good "every desire of the agent involves an illusion." But see qualifications for animals and children on 240–50.

regarding what less fancy resources might be relevant to the essence of normatively relevant desire.

6.4 The Nature of Desire II

In his treatment of the nature of desire,[43] Timothy Schroeder distinguishes between (i) the dominant motivational conception of desire, which claims that to desire that P is to be disposed to bring it about that P (championed by Robert Stalnaker and Michael Smith),[44] (ii) the hedonic conception of desire, which claims that to desire that P is rooted in taking pleasure in P (championed by Galen Strawson),[45] and (iii) accounts like Fred Dretske's in which the role of desire-satisfaction in reinforcing behavior is most crucial to desire.[46]

On this issue, the short answer is that I will be standard, and on normative grounds. Whatever its relation to pleasure or behavior-reinforcement, it seems to be the motivational role of desire that is our ordinary grounds for granting it normative significance, which provides a desire-based account its rationale. If pleasure is the proper grounds for well-being, then hedonism and not a desire-based account is correct. And no one suggests that whatever conditions are required for behaviorist forms of learning are the central components of human well-being. But this quick summary ignores important complexities that we need to consider.

Begin with the standard motivational conception of desire. Anscombe suggested that "The primitive sign of wanting is *trying to get.*"[47] Smith holds that "a desire that p ... dispos[es] ... the subject in that state to bring it about that p."[48] Stalnaker suggests that "to desire that *P* is to be disposed to act in ways that would tend to bring it about that *P* in a world in which one's beliefs, whatever they are, were true."[49] Given the relatively broad conception of desire that we are developing, it is natural to begin with the presumption that something like this capture its essence.

But this conception is subject to a number of objections. First, it may be objected that a variety of mental states, including intentions, tryings, habits, and normative beliefs meet such characterizations, but yet are neither desires nor imply the existence of desires. These other "pro-attitudes" may suggest that this general motivational characterization of desires is not adequate. But remember, we *want* a very broad notion of desire, which can stretch to encompass all pro-attitudes.

Other objections claim that dispositions to act are not necessary for desire, in two different ways. First, some desires have contents that make them difficult cases for the motivational conception. Consider Schroeder on desires about relatively necessary truths:

---

[43] T. Schroeder (2004).   [44] Stalnaker (1984); M. Smith (1994).   [45] G. Strawson (1994).
[46] Dretske (1988).   [47] Anscombe (2000: 68).   [48] M. Smith (1994: 115).
[49] Stalnaker (1984: 15).

In addition to contemporary mathematicians and logicians wanting that the logical facts be this way or that, there are people who desire, say, that there be superconductors that are ductile and that conduct at over 40° Celsius, or that superstring theory be a close approximation to a correct theory of the constitution of the universe.... Still, there is nothing an agent can do to change whether or not a certain material can, in principle, be constructed, or whether an existing physical theory is, in fact, correct, and few are deluded otherwise.[50]

Other difficult cases involve the past. "I might desire that I had never been born, or that my parents had never met, or that, right now, life exist elsewhere in the universe.... Because of necessary facts about causation, these are also desires for ends I can do nothing to bring about."[51]

Still, these are somewhat unusual and cognitively sophisticated desires. It is plausible that such desires are parasitic on the existence of desires of a more straightforward motivational sort. And it would certainly not be surprising if a motivational account of such desires would involve somewhat unusual and sophisticated dispositions. Indeed, Schroeder himself suggests several:[52] You might be disposed to bring something about if only it were possible to bring it about, and this fix might handle your desires for life elsewhere in the universe or about the past, though perhaps to treat desires regarding genuinely necessary truths in this way would require the deployment of possibilities (in fact impossibilities) too wild to seriously contemplate. Still, you might also be so disposed that if you were to *believe* that doing some particular thing would be an effective means for bringing about what you desire, then you would do that. This might handle all these cases.

Schroeder has another counterexample: "Suppose I desire that a committee make up its mind in my favor without my intervention. This is a state of affairs I might want very much, yet because of the very nature of desire it makes no sense to try to act so as to satisfy it."[53] But many real people often do things it makes no sense to try to do in something like the same way. And there are other dispositions that might be characteristic of this desire, say dispositions to sigh and complain in various ways, which are in other normal cases linked to dispositions to avoid the thing sighed or complained about. It certainly isn't obvious that in the absence of all these sorts of dispositions it is plausible to say that such a desire is present. And we have no good initial reason to believe that all desires are realized in exactly the same way. It would be something of a surprise, for instance, if intuitively intrinsic and instrumental desires were realized in the same way. And it is antecedently plausible that it would require a complex structure of more basic desires to constitute any realistic desire for a committee to do something without one's own intervention. It might for instance involve somewhat conflicting desires.

But perhaps a second type of argument for the possibility of desire without motivation is more effective. Galen Strawson has argued that a hedonic conception

---

[50] T. Schroeder (2004: 16).   [51] T. Schroeder (2004: 16).
[52] T. Schroeder (2004: 17).   [53] T. Schroeder (2004: 17).

of desire is to be preferred to a motivational conception, by deploying an imaginary case involving the Weather Watchers.

The Weather Watchers are a race of sentient, intelligent creatures. They are distributed about the surface of their planet, rooted to the ground, profoundly interested in the local weather. They have sensations, thoughts, emotions, beliefs, desires. They possess a conception of an objective, spatial world. But they are constitutionally incapable of any sort of behavior, as this is ordinarily understood. . . . They are not even disposed to behave in any way.[54]

Strawson even presumes that the Weather Watchers perform no mental actions, such as intentionally concentrating. Rather a Weather Watcher has "many mental-activity dispositions: emotional-reaction dispositions, desire-formation dispositions, train-of-thought dispositions, automatic sensory-experience-interpretation dispositions. Its thought tends to run in certain ways; it tends to welcome and regret certain things."[55] There are various issues about the coherence of this, and I commend Strawson's discussion to your attention. But the key point for us involves the alleged desires of the Weather Watchers. "The Weather Watchers are uncomplicated beings who are invariably pleased when their desires are fulfilled, and disappointed when they are not."[56] And Strawson thinks this pleasure is enough for desire. The

primary linkage of the notion of a desire to a notion other than itself is not to the notion of action or behavior but rather to the notion of being pleased or happy or contented should something come about (or at least to the notion of ceasing to be unhappy or discontented should it come about) and to the distinct but correlative notion of being unhappy or discontented or disappointed should it not come about.[57]

In other words, this is an argument for a hedonic conception of desire, according to which it is essential to desire that it engage positive or negative affect. This case still leaves the possibility that either motivation or affect are sufficient for desire. But the argument for a hedonic conception might be completed by another of Strawson's imaginative cases, the Aldebaranians, who have the motivational characteristics allegedly typical of desires, but who are not capable of "any affect states at all."[58] While Strawson is somewhat tentative in his claims about the Aldebaranians, he does say in response to their case that his "sense is that the link to the notion of affective dispositions is internal to and fundamentally constitutive of the notion of desire in a way that the link to the notion of behavioral dispositions is not."[59]

I claim that our response to Strawson's ingenious cases should be this: Affective states often involve desires in the broad motivational sense, but it is reasonable to claim that pleasures and pains of certain sorts are independent of the existence of desire. And I admit that we can stretch to see desires in the Weather Watchers. But I also think that we can stretch to see desires in the Aldebaranians. And it is also

---

[54] G. Strawson (1994: 251).   [55] G. Strawson (1994: 258).
[56] G. Strawson (1994: 280).   [57] G. Strawson (1994: 280).
[58] G. Strawson (1994: 281).   [59] G. Strawson (1994: 282).

relevant that both sorts of creatures are rather dramatically unlike us, since the Weather Watchers are incapable of action at all, and the Aldebaranians of all affect. So while it is not a strictly essential property of desire that it involve a tendency to behavior, it isn't strictly essential that it involve affect either. And, in any case, these are not central and realistic sorts of cases. In creatures capable of affect and behavior, like humans, the tendencies to behavior suggested by motivational accounts still are strictly required for there to be desire. And because there are actual desires in real people for abstract goals that don't involve the tendencies to being pleased and happy that hedonic conceptions of desire require, still the tendencies to affect are not strictly required for desire even in real people who are capable of affect.

One possible normative advantage of hedonic accounts of desire is that they clearly explain why the satisfaction of one's desires matters to one's well-being. But we are done with hedonism as a theory of well-being; its characteristic forms are too normatively robust for reality. And the satisfaction of even abstract and non-hedonic desires is sometimes intuitively relevant to well-being. However, we will return in Chapter 7 to standard objections to desire-based accounts that may motivate such a hedonic restriction on normatively relevant desires. And what is immediately relevant is that the very fact that hedonic resources might conceivably help distinguish desires relevant to one's own well-being from others that are not suggests that such resources are not essential to desire.

There are a variety of alternative conceptions of desire in the rough neighborhood of hedonic conceptions. Consider views that desires have a characteristic phenomenology, say that one desires something if and only if one experiences desiring it. But of course broad desires do not have a characteristic phenomenology. One might alternatively claim that one desires something just in case one believes one desires it. But it is quite intuitive at least in our post-Freudian world to think that one can be quite mistaken in thinking that one desires something, say something that it would be flattering to desire, if one's actions dominantly suggest otherwise.

Our basically motivational conception of desire has survived confrontation with hedonic conceptions. But there is also a third non-fancy account of the essence of desire, which focuses on the role of the satisfaction of desire in reinforcing behavior. Fred Dretske suggests this:

Rewards tend to encourage reproduction of rewarded events *only when* the organism is in a certain internal condition. Feeding a *hungry* rat when it performs satisfactorily is one thing; feeding a rat that has just eaten is quite another. Food tends to increase the probability of movements' being caused by internal indicators only when the rat is hungry, and the hungrier the better.... The effectiveness of R (food, say) as a reinforcer, its effectiveness in modifying behavior, depends on the organism's occupying state D. Without D, the occurrence of R does not tend to increase the probability of those behaviors that result in R.... Such states function as *motivational* states. They are what I will call *pure* desires, and they are desires *for* whatever condition or outcome they make the organism receptive to.... Other desires—what I shall call (cognitively) *derived* desires—are generated by beliefs about what will secure the objects of *pure* (and other derived) desires.[60]

Schroeder has elaborated such a proposal into a more ecumenical and neurophysiologically based account in which the role of desire in reinforcement is central, and explains its hedonic and motivational roles.[61]

It seems reasonable to claim that such a role in learning is characteristic of at least many desires. Perhaps we can even imagine creatures analogous to the Weather Watchers and Aldebaranians, who have mental states that generate no behaviors and involve no affect but that perform this role in learning, and I think at a far stretch we might cede them desires. But we can also and I think more easily stretch to see desires in the Aldebaranians and the Weather Watchers, and could do so even if the Aldebaranians and Weather Watchers never learned in the behaviorist manner under consideration. And it is still relevant that all these creatures are considerably unlike us. In creatures capable of affect and behavior and learning of these various sorts, for instance humans and indeed all real animals, the tendencies to behavior suggested by motivational accounts still seem strictly required for desire. But perhaps it will be claimed that, unlike affect, reinforcement is plausibly a role of all our actual desires, so that both motivation and reinforcement are equally essential to human desires. However, the satisfaction of some actual desires does not serve to reward us in ways that reinforce our behavior. Sometimes we are punished for doing what we desire to do. This is sometimes out of ignorance of what we are doing in what context, and sometimes because our desires change and we no longer want what we wanted when we actually get it, but it is also sometimes because we seek punishment. Perhaps these seem to be cases in which well-being comes apart from desire, and they reflect objections to desire-based accounts to which we will return. But even when the object of a desire successfully serves as a reward, that is generally because we are motivated to get it, and so the learning account of desires still seems generally upside down.

Motivation has priority. It is what is central and essential to human desire, and that of all known animals. And remember that our focus is on a normatively relevant conception of desire. There is no evident rationale to think that the desires whose satisfaction would reinforce are those that are centrally relevant to well-being.[62] Schroeder's version of this type of proposal is largely motivated by an attempt to discover a central neurophysiological basis of desire. Somewhat more exactly, his view is that "of the three faces of desire, it is desire's neglected face, reward, which causally guides the other two faces. The neural basis of reward is the normal cause of pleasure and an important cause of motivation, while pleasure and motivation have much less influence upon one another and neither exerts a dominating influence

---

[60] Dretske (1988: 110–11).   [61] T. Schroeder (2004).

[62] None beyond reasons to think desires whose satisfaction is pleasant are centrally relevant to well-being, not a plausible constraint on normatively relevant desire.

upon the reward structure."[63] But we have already decided that the boundaries of natural kinds are irrelevant to what counts as a normatively relevant desire.

We have surveyed extant accounts of the nature of desire. We have concluded that, at least for our normative purposes, a broad preference-based and motivational conception of desire is best.[64] Chapter 7 argues that such a conception is not too fancy for reality. But first we have two additional skeptical inquiries to undertake.

6.5 Intrinsic Versus Instrumental Desires

Hubin's defense of simple desire-based accounts rests heavily on a distinction between intrinsic and instrumental desires. And it is customary for all desire-based accounts to claim that it is only the satisfaction of intrinsic desires that counts towards well-being, since otherwise there is the possibility of double-counting of satisfactions towards well-being. After long experience, philosophers may think that they understand this distinction between intrinsic and instrumental desires. But I don't think we do. I think that there is not in reality as clean and clear a distinction as Hubin's proposal and many informed desire accounts require.[65] I think that it is often indeterminate whether something is intrinsically or instrumentally desired.

Davis suggests that a "desire is extrinsic if its object is desired as a means to something else that is desired, intrinsic if the object is desired as an end in itself."[66] Even this roughly standard way of marking the distinction seems to allow, as Davis himself suggests, that a desire can be both extrinsic and intrinsic. And this would imply that the distinction cannot plausibly deliver the quite restricted class of intrinsic desires required by Hubin's defense. But the real question is what this familiar but rather theoretical vocabulary means.

It might be claimed that it is internal to the content of each desire whether something is wanted as a means or as an end. But at least in the vast preponderance of cases this is not true in any way that I can introspect. Perhaps the presence of explicit causal reasoning in current thought, or analogous reasoning that some means raises the probability of some end, seems crucial.[67] But such conscious reasoning is not that common, certainly not so common as to allow us to sort desires without remainder into the instrumental and the intrinsic in any intuitive way. Such a sorting would leave too many desires intrinsic to capture the intuitive notion and for Hubin to work his defense, which requires that many intuitively incorrect desires be merely

---

[63] T. Schroeder (2004: 37). But 131–4 seem in tension with the localization of reward this presumes.

[64] What about mixed accounts? We've seen reasons to doubt that either hedonic or learning conditions are necessary for normatively relevant desires in humans. But my proposal does stretch to ascribe desires to the Weather Watchers and even those capable only of Dretske-style learning, so it is mixed in one sense.

[65] Chan (2004) suggests there are no extrinsic desires.

[66] W. Davis (1986: 69).

[67] But Harman (2000: 128–9) notes extrinsic desires that are not instrumental, for instance desires for things because they are signs of something else.

instrumental. Perhaps there is rather supposed to commonly be explicit unconscious reasoning of that sort, or alternatively unconscious contents that make desires explicitly instrumental. But such reasoning and thoughts seem too specific and sophisticated to be antecedently plausible explicit unconscious states. And we have no positive grounds to believe in them.[68]

Another cluster of attempts to make the distinction deploy normative resources. Perhaps some things in the world are intrinsically good and some are merely good as means to those desire-independent intrinsic goods. But a desire-based account of the good cannot deploy such objective goods. And what is of interest to us is a psychological distinction between kinds of desires, and two people might have a desire for an objective intrinsic good, which in one is an intrinsic desire and in the other an instrumental desire. Perhaps it might be claimed that such a difference in desires is constituted by a difference in beliefs about objective goods. But many of us don't believe in objective goods. And one can think that something is an objective intrinsic good and yet desire it instrumentally, or at least believe that something is merely an objective instrumental good and yet desire it intrinsically.

Perhaps then it is something about the history or the causation of a desire that constitutes it as intrinsic or instrumental. Perhaps if a desire is caused by another desire, say partly on the basis of the recognition of an instrumental relationship between their satisfactions, this constitutes the first desire as merely instrumental. But yet it is intuitive to think that through an educational history we can come to value things intrinsically that we once only valued because they were explicit means to our ends. They may persist even though the original desire on which they were based has disappeared.

Perhaps then we should deploy some conditional test. Perhaps I approve of X intrinsically if and only if it is true both that I approve of X and that I would approve of X if I were to disregard all of its consequences upon other objects of my attitudes.[69] But the kind of counterfactual embedded in this claim often lacks a determinate truth value, namely when the physical conditions that make it true that I approve of something and that I regard its consequences are closely entwined. The factors that make it true that I approve of it are not cleanly isolable and separable from my consideration of those consequences, and hence there are not sufficiently determinate facts about what background conditions must be preserved and which conditions should be allowed to vary when assessing the truth of the conditional in question, as we discussed in Chapter 2. And there is also a second problem. Even intuitively instrumental desires can have enough inertia to meet this weak test for

---

[68]   But see McDaniel and Bradley (2008: 288), which is focused on extrinsic desires generally rather than specifically instrumental desires. However, it depends on a controversial account of the content of conditional desires, an extension of that model to other desires motivated solely by the wish to have a unitary account, and a questionable claim that instrumental desires must be so because of their contents. And it has unintuitive implications regarding the satisfaction of instrumental desires.

[69]   This is modeled on Stevenson (1944: 177).

intrinsic approval. What intuitively made such a desire instrumental may be past or lost to conscious view, and of course there may not be very determinate facts about whether *unconsciously* one is now regarding or disregarding the consequences of something. Other counterfactual tests are possible. Perhaps the distinction depends on how the agent would respond if they deliberated about the question of whether they wanted X for itself or for what it could help bring about. But we have no reason to think that people have such a high level of authority about the intrinsic and instrumental nature of their desires, and such a counterfactual test also invites our standing worries about indeterminacy.

Hubin himself says that the distinction "depends on conceiving of motivation as having a roughly hierarchical structure: some motivation is dependent, in familiar ways, on other motivation together with beliefs about the world. Ultimately, though, we find motivation that is not grounded in other motivation in this way. This motivation is intrinsic motivation."[70] In a note, he elaborates, and cites the points about history that I just made:

> The notion of *dependency* here—of some motivations being based on other, more basic motivation—is to be interpreted structurally, rather than causally. To cast the point in terms of 'desire' it is, of course, possible to come to desire something intrinsically because one sees that having such an intrinsic desire is instrumentally valuable—that is, satisfies some other desire.

And in the note he refers to another discussion in which he says that he considers

> a basic desire to be one that is not motivated by some other desire (together with beliefs).... It is worth noting that the distinction between a basic and a derivative (motivated) desire is not a causal or historical one.... Rather, what matters is some current relation between this desire and the agent's other desires. I won't say more about this distinction; I shall suppose that it is clear enough for our purposes.[71]

But I don't believe the distinction is clear enough.

Perhaps Hubin thinks that the distinction involves claims about the deep hidden mechanisms of our psychologies, claims which we have little reason to believe true of our messy brains. More charitably, perhaps the dependency claims in question are claims about the truth of counterfactual conditionals that depend on current conditions only, but that are somewhat different from those we just considered. Perhaps if I were not now to desire X, then I would not now desire Y, so Y is not now intrinsically desired. But such claims can be true of both X and Y. Perhaps then we are to think that if only one of these conditionals is true, then there is the proper dependency of one of the desires on the other. But if the current conditions that make it true that we desire things are enmeshed at all closely in our brains, which seems a likely bet, then such conditionals will often not have determinate truth values.

---

[70] Hubin (1996: 44).   [71] Hubin (1991: 23).

Perhaps in light of these difficulties some will favor more theoretical accounts of the distinction.[72] For instance, some may think that intrinsic desires are a specific natural kind. But we have seen that natural kinds are normatively irrelevant, and there is little reason to believe that an intrinsic desire to prove incompleteness and the intrinsic desire of someone who is parched for a drink share the same natural basis.

There are revisionary accounts of the distinction that have been suggested by those who favor particular accounts of the essential nature of desires. Dretske suggests that his distinction between pure desires, which are receptivities to rewards, and cognitively derived desires, generated by beliefs about what will serve to satisfy pure desires, can be identified with the distinction between intrinsic and instrumental desires.[73] Schroeder proposes another revisionary account, in which intrinsic desires must have a certain stability. One implication of this that he embraces is that in humans generally "it must turn out that the desire to eat at a particular time, or to drink water, and so on, is not an intrinsic desire but an instrumental one.... The underlying intrinsic desire ... is an intrinsic desire for something like constant blood sugar."[74] But the intuitive distinction between instrumental and intrinsic desires is at least sufficiently clear so that we can see that these revisionary proposals do not adequately capture it.

Still, the intuitive distinction is not clear enough so that we can retreat to a case-based analysis. The various non-revisionary theoretical models of the distinction just discussed do reveal various elements of our ordinary notion of the distinction, elements that can be in some tension with each other when applied to cases in which they pull in different directions. And even intuitions about single cases can reveal problems with the standard distinction.

Korsgaard has drawn our attention to one relevant set of cases, which also reveal further problems with counterfactual tests for instrumentality.[75] One can want something X conditionally upon some other thing Y, without that constituting one's desire for X as instrumental. Consider your desire for very fancy cookware that you would not like if you didn't think it could actually be used for cooking, but which you don't really need or intend to use for cooking.[76] Such desires are not instrumental, though they meet familiar counterfactual tests for that condition. And it is also over-simple to say they are intrinsic. Kolnai drew attention to other intuitive cases that reveal that the standard distinction is oversimplified:[77] Aristotle himself discusses a physician, an orator, and a statesman considering the best constitution of a city-state, as examples of means–ends reasoning.[78] And as Kolnai noted,

---

[72] Carson suggests that all desires are global in content, so that ordinary propositional attitude reports significantly misrepresent that content. But this implies an even greater indeterminacy of the intrinsic/instrumental distinction than I propose.
[73] Dretske (1988: 148).   [74] T. Schroeder (2004: 152).   [75] Korsgaard (1983).
[76] I presume you aren't worried simply about the exchange value of the cookware.
[77] Kolnai (1977).   [78] Aristotle, Nicomachean Ethics III 3, 1112b.

Whereas to cure and to persuade can at first sight easily be conceived of as pre-established ends requiring only the appropriate means to be attained, a 'good constitution' has no definite meaning by virtue of which to function as a logical premiss; before the question of means can be gone into, it requires a definition or, rather, a determination of its content. Conservative liberals, radical democrats, communist totalitarians and fascist totalitarians ... certainly do not aim at bringing about the selfsame 'good constitution' by different means: what they differ about is the *conception* of a 'good constitution'.[79]

There can be intuitive hierarchies of desire in such cases that are not hierarchies of intuitive means and ends. He also suggested that we can gain "possession ... of ... a possible 'means' which starts us wondering whether we shall or shall not avail ourself of it, or to what use we might best put it. ... [W]e look around for 'ends' to be served by the 'means' at our disposal."[80] In this case, the more or less intuitively intrinsic desire is the dependent one, and this is contrary to several of the models for capturing the distinction that we just discussed.

One last theory: Michael Smith suggests that instrumental desires are "just the complex state of having ... non-instrumental desires and means-ends beliefs standing in a suitable relation."[81] And his grounds for this are that "instrumental desires disappear immediately an agent loses either the relevant non-instrumental desire or means–ends belief."[82] But we have already discussed problem cases for tests like this, in which other than instrumental desires are conditional on means–end belief, and in which an intuitively instrumental desire would persist even if the relevant non-instrumental desire disappeared.

I think that the right positive account of the distinction between intrinsic and instrumental desires (and in fact of related distinctions suggested by Korsgaard's and Kolnai's cases) is quite complex. It involves a comparison of the content of various preferences, supplemented by various other factors including immediate histories of explicit causal reasoning, whatever reasoning occurs to Aristotle's statesman, and various counterfactual dependencies. And the key points are that these factors do not always pull together in one direction, that when they pull in different directions they do not balance in any very determinate way, and that some of the factors, for instance the counterfactual tests, involve indeterminacies of their own. This account will deliver a rough intuitive distinction between instrumental and intrinsic desires that is applicable to some clear cases, when all the factors pull together and are suitably determinate. But since there are so many relevant factors that often pull in different directions, and since some of the factors themselves involve indeterminacies, this model will not deliver enough determinacy about that distinction in enough cases for Hubin to work his defense of simple desire-based accounts of the good, which requires that many intuitively incorrect desires turn out to be merely instrumental

---

[79] Kolnai (1977: 44).   [80] Kolnai (1977: 51).
[81] M. Smith (2004: 96).   [82] M. Smith (2004: 96).

desires. Nor indeed will it deliver enough for many traditional informed desire accounts of the good, which focus on the satisfaction of intrinsic desires.

In reality, the distinction between intrinsic and instrumental desires is virulently indeterminate. It isn't up to its customary normative jobs. Philosophers have been bewitched by their own terminology.

6.6 Desire Intensities

One more skeptical inquiry remains. Heathwood's alternative defense of simple desire-based accounts rests on a notion of the summed satisfaction of desires that involves many commitments, some of which are not realistic. Consider the rich resources that Heathwood deploys, along with a distinction between "basic" and instrumental desires:

(i) Every basic desire satisfaction is intrinsically good for its subject; every basic desire frustration is intrinsically bad for its subject.

(ii) The intrinsic value for its subject of a basic desire satisfaction = the intensity of the desire satisfied; the intrinsic value for its subject of a basic desire frustration = −(the intensity of the desire frustrated).

(iii) The intrinsic value of a life (or segment of a life) for the one who lives it (in other words, the total amount of welfare in the life (or life-segment)) = the sum of the intrinsic values of all the basic desire satisfactions and frustrations contained therein.[83]

Heathwood also requires "*concurrence*," a condition whereby a desire and its relevant satisfaction must be simultaneous.[84] That claim is implausible, since some of our deep desires can be satisfied only after our death, and it would require robustly supported normative advice to properly tell someone that something they care about deeply does not in fact matter to their well-being. But focus on three other worries about this proposal.

First, this mechanism depends on counting basic desires. But it is implausible that the satisfaction of two desires with the same content in someone who has two counts more for well-being than the satisfaction of just one such desire in someone who has just one. And indeed it is far from obvious that there are facts about how to count desires, even basic desires.[85]

But a second set of worries is more important. What are these intensities of desires, that we can add and subtract? They cannot be determined normatively, by the proper weighting of the satisfaction of the desires in well-being, or the account is circular and uninformative. But there are obvious questions about their psychological reality. There is much talk by desire-based theorists about the intensity of desires, but there is

---

[83] Heathwood (2005: 489).   [84] Heathwood (2005: 490).

[85] Perhaps it seems we count desires by their contents. But Arthur can have desires with somewhat distinct contents focused on the same object.

surprising little talk about what those intensities are. And it isn't obvious that there is one univocal kind of psychological intensity that is normatively relevant.

Perhaps we should focus on the natural suggestion of a motivational model of desire. Perhaps the strengths of our desires at some time are determined by the facts about what we do, or at least try to do at that moment. But this may just mean that there are facts about what desires win in actual fact, which provides little basis of comparison of the various desires that don't win. And it wouldn't yield a basis for comparison of desire intensities over time for a single individual, which can intuitively change, or across different individuals. But perhaps the proper understanding of the motivational model implies that the intensity weights of various desires are involved in some specific mechanism of summative balancing that leads to one action rather than another. But we should not be confident that such a summative balancing occurs, on some internal scale. And it is not even clear what such a claim plausibly means. If there are natural kinds that reveal physically relevant intensities that do so sum, say numbers of neuron firings per minute, there is no reason to believe that that would be normatively relevant in the way desire intensities are meant to be. Perhaps then we should consider a third motivational model of intensities. Perhaps what constitutes the intensity of a desire are counterfactual facts about how it would lead to action at some moment if other various actual desires were absent, or hypothetical desires present.[86] But, since the physical bases of different desires in a given human are plausibly interlaced, not easily localizable and separable, these counterfactuals are likely to be indeterminate in truth. In fact, these are among the very cases of indeterminacy that we discussed in Chapter 2.

It is perhaps unsurprising that alternative conceptions of desire naturally suggest alternative accounts of intensity or strength. Hedonic conceptions of desire suggest that intensities of accompanying pleasure and pain are relevant. But not all desires are accompanied with pleasures and pains, and there are a variety of different ways in which pleasure and pain might be deployed to constitute a kind of roughly intuitive intensity. Perhaps what matters most is how much pleasure you get if a desire is satisfied, or rather how much pain you feel if it is not. Schroeder suggests another alternative account of satisfaction, rooted in his conception of desires as essentially involving reward: If

to desire is to constitute a state of affairs as a reward or punishment, then a strong desire is one that constitutes a state of affairs as a substantial reward or punishment, whereas a weak desire would constitute the same state of affairs as minimal reward or punishment.... The strength of a desire will...come to the relative power of the desire to change neural connections (all else being equal), and so modify its owner's mind.[87]

I think that the truth is that the first and third motivational models I recently suggested, as well as the reward model and both hedonic models, yield roughly

---

[86] Mele (2003b: 173).   [87] T. Schroeder (2004: 138–9).

intuitive notions of the intensity of a desire, which sometimes pull in different directions when applied to particular cases and balance in no very definite way, and sometimes involve indeterminacies themselves. And so there is no reason to believe that there is one univocal and determinate sort of intensity that can play the necessary role in desire-based theories that require it. Once again, we have been bewitched by a word. Intensities of desires are virulently indeterminate. They are not sufficiently determinate to play their usual roles in ethical theory. In fact, it isn't obvious that all the various factors involved even when there are facts about intensities are normatively relevant, and I will later argue in effect that some are not.

Notice also that even if there were determinate intensities, that does not imply that they would have all the mathematical features that are often assumed. There are various conditions of coherence on preferences over risky options, for instance, that would yield satisfactions that we can add and subtract at least for given individuals, for instance those proposed by von Neumann and Morgenstern to define utilities.[88] But notice that these involve relatively global conditions of individual satisfaction, and not the intensity of specific desires. And they involve obvious idealizations away from the preferences of actual human beings, in a way that is not obviously normatively probative. It isn't really a commitment of any suitably normative rationality that you be prepared to accept even a very tiny risk of global annihilation to almost certainly gain a dollar, and that is among the conditions that von Neumann and Morgenstern require.

There is a third natural worry about Heathwood's proposal, due to its focus on summation over life. We care about the narrative trajectory of our lives in a way that puts pressure on the normative propriety of such a procedure.[89] It isn't just sums of well-being that matter, but how well-being is distributed in life. Because of objections like this, as well as for reasons we noted earlier, some desire-based accounts deploy top-down rather than bottom-up conceptions of summary satisfaction. Griffin and Carson suggest that we focus on the satisfaction of very higher-order or global desires for a life of a certain sort, which can incorporate a certain sort of balancing of overall desire-satisfactions within that life.[90] Perhaps this would also help with our worries about desire intensities. But we already noted several serious worries about this type of proposal, and there also newly relevant ones. We should doubt the psychological reality of such global desires in many of us.[91] And realistic global desires often involve a large degree of vagueness, so that they cannot yield any determinate way to balance the satisfaction of local and specific desires in ordinary cases. Since Griffin and Carson are informed-desire theorists, they may think that we would all have suitably determinate global preferences if fully informed, including those that require a pleasant life to which the satisfaction of local desires is quite important, or they may think that such global desires are always present in us in some unconscious way that

---

[88] von Neumann and Morgenstern (1944). [89] Velleman (1991).
[90] Griffin (1986); Carson (2000: 73–4). [91] But see n72.

might be elicited if were asked to specify a preference between two highly articulated lives. But I see no grounds to believe either of those things. And such an indirect appeal to local desires would reintroduce the very worries about intensities that this appeal to global desires is in part meant to avoid. And notice that at different times in our lives we might have, even if fully informed, different and conflicting global desires for a pattern of life. Carson thinks that under such conditions we should sum the satisfaction of those global desires, by appeal both to the intensity of our conflicting preferences at various times and to their number.[92] But this procedure is subject to the very worries about intensity now in play.

We should conclude, in part because of the first and third class of worries that I have noted, but largely because of the second involving the nature of intensities, that there are virulent indeterminacies regarding the summation of desire-satisfactions deployed by Heathwood, and indeed by many informed desire accounts. Desire intensities are not up to their customary role in ethical theory.

6.7 Where We Are

Reality lacks the highly determinate facts about desire intensities and the sharp distinction between instrumental and intrinsic desires on which sophisticated simple desire-based accounts of well-being depend. And we have also seen that informed desire accounts are no more workable in reality than the characteristic forms of hedonism and objectivism. But we have isolated a broad preference-based and motivational conception of desire that is normatively relevant. So we have one last hope.

---

[92] Carson (2000: 86).

7

Very Simple Desire

My positive proposal about individual well-being is an *unsophisticated* simple desire-based account, rooted in the broad motivational and preference-based conception of desire of Chapter 6. It involves two components: real preferences over hypothetical options, and consensus among those preferences. While it deploys more realistic resources than Heathwood's or Hubin's *sophisticated* simple desire-based proposals, it can evade objections to simple desire-based accounts by attention to the spirit though not the letter of their responses. Begin with its first component.

7.1 Basic Preferences

My simple desire-based proposal will be that your good at some time is determined by what might be called your all-in desire at that time. But the immediate point on which to focus is that your all-in desire is fixed by facts about what you actually prefer at that time among merely hypothetical options. I will call these "basic preferences." Basic preferences are the first component of my proposal.

Your basic preferences at this time are fixed by what alternatives you would choose to take if you thought yourself presented with each of the possible combinations of alternatives in action that you might think yourself to face, where that in turn depends on what you would try to do in each such believed circumstance. There is one basic preference for each combination of alternatives that you might take yourself to face.

Whereas informed desire accounts rest on the single set of desires you would have if you considered at once all relevant truths, my proposal rests on what you would choose to do in a wide range of different possible circumstances, if you considered, not all at once, but rather one by one, each of the possible sets of alternatives you could think yourself to have. You will recall from Part I that alternatives are mutually exclusive, and that your alternatives at a moment are exhaustive of your options. But you could believe yourself to have very different sets of alternatives than in fact you have.[1] That is the key to my suggestion. I propose not that we consider a wildly hypothetical state in which some human becomes godlike in omniscience, but rather

[1] Such belief might require different perceptual experience.

merely a very large number of more realistic hypothetical states in which they think they have different options. Rather than throwing all reality into the brain to fix the proper evaluation of real options, as in informed desire accounts, lots of different more realistic but still hypothetical alternative sets of beliefs about options are sequentially thrown in.

It may seem that sometimes, for instance when weak willed, you don't try to do what you most prefer. But after Chapter 6 we should be skeptical that there are genuine facts about what you prefer in *that* fancy sense, which can be cleanly disentangled from other factors that determine what you try to do, and we should also be skeptical about its special normative significance. In general, the mechanics of what would lead you from a consideration of certain options to what you would try to do are irrelevant according to my proposal. So there is for instance no relevant difference between unconscious and conscious desires, between those that one articulates as reasons and does not, between those that rest on emotion and on cool assessment.

So we begin with facts, for each individual at each time, about first preferences among various sets of options, in other words with basic preferences. There is one basic preference for each set of options the individual could believe they have.[2] We still have a long way to go to determine individual good at a time, let alone any sort of individual good that might be compared among different individuals.

But before we move on, you may wonder why basic preferences, which rest on the truth of conditional claims, are more determinate than properly informed desires. The answer is that they have been crafted to be, in several ways.

First, the counterfactuals deployed by informed desire accounts involve much more wildly hypothetical antecedents, and indeed antecedents that might be realized in a variety of ways involving for instance different orders and modes of presentation of information. It might seem that different ways of presenting even realistic options to us might affect our basic preferences regarding them. But that would generate distinct basic preferences in my sense, as long as the modes of presentation are cognitive. If they must be rectified, they are only rectified by the second component of my proposal. It might also seem that I need to deploy basic preferences across huge sets of options that we cannot realistically entertain. But the only sets of options relevant are those that we can realistically entertain, with our human cognitive limitations intact.

Second, the entertaining of relatively realistic sets of options that I propose does not generally involve inhumanly intense contemplation of huge ugly facts about the totality of misery in the world that might drive us mad. While there are some possible

---

[2] In normal human adults, conceived options are roughly captured by the content theory of Mendola (1997: Part One), with relevant contents characteristically centered on the agent or its location at a time. But the contents must be limited in realistic ways, and might also be chancy. Another complication is that someone may be indifferent among best options, so that choice among them is arbitrary.

and even real options that include huge ugly facts, it is still reasonably determinate what you prefer among such options that you entertain in any realistic way, at the level of human abstraction and partial ignorance at which you can in fact confront huge ugly facts.

Third, I presume that there is a specific limitation on the truth grounds of the counterfactuals that aids their determinacy. Elsewhere I've argued for an internalism about thought and perception that is consistent with physicalism; your thoughts and perceptions generally, and hence the kinds of thoughts that your desires and preferences are, are constituted by your contemporaneous internal conditions only.[3] This helps disentwine conditions relevant to the assessment of the conditionals in question from features of the outside world, and hence to disentangle them from the background conditions relevant to the existence of our most determinate actual alternatives. It means that we can hold an individual's actual options fixed while at the same time it is more or less determinately true what his or her basic preferences over the full range of hypothetical sets of options would be. Conditions outside Arthur's body are a large part of what gives him his alternatives, but conditions inside are those that can be varied to allow him to choose otherwise and also to believe otherwise regarding his options.[4] And those two different sorts of psychological conditions—conative and cognitive—can also be plausibly disentangled, so that the conditionals that fix his basic preferences are not virulently indeterminate. To understand this point, focus on the consequents of the relevant conditionals:

The consequents involve choosing an alternative, taking (or so you believe) that alternative.[5] And we know from Chapter 3 that this will involve trying in a particular way, except in a few cases in which there is voluntary inaction. Hence the viability of my proposal requires that the internal physical basis of thinking that one has various options does not much overlap with the internal basis that helps fix that one would try thus and so if one had various beliefs about one's options. Otherwise we cannot adequately disentangle the conditions in the world that make the antecedents of our key conditionals false from background conditions that are highly relevant to the truth of those conditionals. But notice that this does not require that whatever general neurophysiological conditions are required to have any beliefs and any desires be separate, so that one could have beliefs without desires or desires without beliefs. It merely requires that the specific conditions that, in the context of one's general neurophysiology and other physical states, give one particular preferences

---

[3] Mendola (2008).

[4] Sometimes options depend on psychological capacities. But recall from Chapter 2 that those are often indeterminate. Perhaps options constrain some psychological states, since whatever differences make some gymnasts and others tottery are largely internal, and differences in motor abilities can affect the contents of causal thoughts. But the general causal abilities that allow ordinary causal thoughts do not differentiate gymnasts and tottery seniors.

[5] You may not take the alternative that, in the appropriately minimal sense, you think you are. We are considering different possible beliefs about what your options are even though your actual alternatives remain fixed. What you try to do depends more on belief than the truth of belief.

with particular contents, are distinct from the specific conditions that give one particular beliefs with particular contents. What we must preserve invariant across the relevant hypothetical cognitive states is the core of one's motivation. And that seems at least antecedently possible. Remember also from Chapter 3 that, at least in humans, trying characteristically involves the acceptance of reasons, so it would aid relevant disentwining if beliefs that there were options of the relevant sort weren't partly constituted by the acceptance of reasons constituting trying. That might seem to require a normatively colorless presentation of the options,[6] and it might be objected that our acceptance of some reasons is clearly relevant to what we in fact want and try but also to the nature of our options as we conceive them. But the kind of acceptance characteristic of trying is plausibly distinct from that preserved with relevantly general normative belief. After all, in different options one is trying different things. So it is plausible to think both that the physical bases of desire and of belief are at least largely distinct in the necessary ways, and that the beliefs and motivations of the particular sorts we need to disentwine are a rather specially distinct sort in any case. And so it would appear that there are not virulent indeterminacies regarding the conditionals in question, and indeed fairly determinate facts about basic preferences. I might be wrong about this, but there is room for reasonable hope.

One might wonder how these claims fit with my arguments in Chapter 2. There I argued that counterfactuals like "If Cleopatra had tried to get rid of the asp, then she would have lived on for years" are frequently indeterminate in truth because of the enlacing of different psychological conditions that must be varied and that must be held constant for proper assessment of the conditionals. But those cases differ from the cases now under consideration: The antecedent of a conditional relevant to options in the ways discussed in Chapter 2 involves trying, and what you are in fact trying to do generally involves not merely your motivations but your understanding of your options. Because trying is in the *antecedent* of such a conditional and not in its consequent, it must be disentangled from other relevant psychological conditions if we are to assess the conditional, while it is especially hard to so disentwine trying. But trying is only in the *consequent* of conditionals relevant to basic preferences, and so doesn't have to be generally disentangled to allow assessment of those conditionals.[7] And while one of Cleopatra's claims in Chapter 2, that if she had gone to the water then she would have picked Antony a flower, is more similar to the conditionals relevant to basic preferences and yet indeterminate, notice that it is a prediction of fact about what her preferences would have been had she been in a different factual situation, and not a statement of fact about her current preferences. Antony would

---

[6] This is assured by the content theory of Mendola (1997) if we eschew linguistically mediated normative contents, except for the positive and negative hedonic tone of Chapter 5, whose conception does not imply the acceptance of reasons.

[7] Trying isn't explicitly present in the consequents of the conditionals whereby I initially characterized basic preferences, which mention rather choosing an alternative. But this rests on trying.

not complain to her about what he admits she now prefers, faced with him and his complaint. But he thinks she is mistaken in her assessment of what she would have wanted had she gone to the water earlier on. Generally, one will not have highly privileged access to what one prefers in my sense, since, for instance, when one imagines what one would do if presented with some opportunity for heroism, one's conception may be more a pleasant daydream than access to the dark reality of one's current dispositions.

Nevertheless, we saw in the last part that trying involves indeterminacy in various ways that may still seem troubling now. There are precision problems involving trying to X, just because a range of consequentially different things might count as trying to X. But all we need now is one trying that corresponds to the preferred option from any given set, assuming that one can always try actively to "do nothing." And since the notion of basic preferences is a somewhat artificial notion, it is appropriate for me to regiment things a bit to get such a specific trying: Alternatives are mutually exclusive, and so the sorts of refined tryings in question can be what I will call "global" tryings, that exhaust what one can try to do at once, rather than distinct tryings to do one thing with one hand and something else with another. Even the notion of what one globally tries to do might be relevantly indeterminate, if there are various consequentially distinct ways that one can globally try to do something X that generate distinct options, so we should further focus on the most finely characterized global tryings. And we already have mechanisms to do that. Chapter 3 distinguished immediate tryings, tryings to do things more or less in the moment, from temporally extended tryings, and also suggested that counterfactual chains of immediate tryings might be a relevant analytical basis for claims about temporally extended tryings. It also distinguished a set of analytically fundamental tryings, of both mental and physical sorts, in normal human adults, which we could now conjoin into finely characterized global basic tryings. In sum, immediate finely characterized global basic tryings, and counterfactual temporal chains of such tryings rooted in current dispositions, can constitute the tryings and hence choosings centrally relevant to our basic preferences, at least in normal cases. Such a specific analytical focus for the notion of basic preferences helps avoid some indeterminacies due to the ambiguity of "trying."[8] It also helps disentangle the relevant forms of trying from the acceptance of reasons involved in general normative beliefs.

---

[8] There is a cost. This makes it impossible to read the intuitive content of a basic preference off the content of the associated trying, independent of the set of believed alternatives in which it would take place. And ordinary descriptions of alternatives do not include much implicit knowledge of what such tryings would cause. But this does avoid analytical difficulties whenever finely shaded alternatives involve the same intuitive trying. And the intuitive content of the basic preference can be read off the alternative that would hence be taken (or rather would be thought to be taken) from among the relevant set of conceived alternatives, even if the relevant conceptions of the alternatives are not captured by ordinary descriptions. Your choice is of a particular alternative (from among others) that is psychologically tied to a particular trying, even if that is not explicit in the trying's content. Some understanding of some options is plausibly unconscious.

7.2 Consensus Congruence

Basic preferences are the root of individual good. But there is also another component of my proposal, a mechanism that will allow us to move from facts about the basic preferences of individuals at times to facts about well-being to be deployed as the basis of moral judgments. That mechanism crucially involves consensus of preference.

It may be immediately objected that consensus of preference is irrelevant to individual well-being, that whether other people share Arthur's preferences is irrelevant to whether the satisfaction of those preferences is good for him. But in fact my proposal deploys consensus in a more complicated way than this worry presumes. It specifies different sorts of good or well-being as relevant to different sorts of circumstances, different sorts of good rooted in different ranges of consensus. When it is only the satisfaction of Arthur's desires that is affected by a choice, only the consensus of his own preferences matters.

This point requires some explaining, and there are also other complexities of my account relevant to this objection. The consensus mechanism I will deploy has a rather specific nature, and it can be applied in more than one way. Begin with the second point.

In the next two sections, I develop my consensus mechanism in two steps. First, I develop a notion of somewhat solipsistic individual good, from the perspective of a moment of a person's life, rooted in a consensus of their basic preferences. Second, I move directly from that solipsistic momentary individual good, via a second consensus, to a notion of momentary good for an individual suitable for comparisons deployed in the overall evaluation of states of affairs including many human individuals or one human individual with changing desires.

There are alternative possible mechanisms of this general type, which for instance involve an intermediate step determining well-being for a single individual over time before we assess distribution between lives. And there are further complexities relevant even to the specific variant I develop. As I've already said, I think that different ranges of consensus are relevant to different moral issues. And there may be agents who aren't human. In the end, my normative theory will incorporate such complications. But focusing initially on the basic two-step mechanism should suffice to make the necessary complications clear when their time comes.

Still, before we consider these two steps, it is important to note three general points about preference consensus in my sense.

First, a shared preference is the most basic consensus of preference. In one simple case, Lancelot and Guinevere have a consensus of preference when both prefer a life of luxurious romance to being executed. Notice that preferences are sometimes focused on oneself at a time. Lancelot and Guinevere are dead, and are quite different people, but you can share the preference in question with both, though you care not a jot about their medieval adventures. Notice also that shared preferences in this sense can generate conflict: Lancelot and Arthur may both want something only one of them can have.

Second, there can be an intuitive consensus of preference among a large group of people when a few lack the preference. And here I have a problem: If I cite a percentage, you may complain that it is arbitrary and discriminates against the idiosyncratic, and if I don't, you may complain that I am being vague. But what I think is this:

In reality, there is some range of indeterminacy about what people's preferences are. So there is some indeterminacy of fact regarding whether they share some preferences. In addition, among any large group even with exactly determinate preferences, there is a cluster of different sorts of intuitive consensus of preference that might be specified, that involve variously all the shared preferences of a certain specific 85 percent of the population or another 85 percent, of a certain 99 percent or another, and so on, or alternatively that involve any specific preference shared by any 85 percent, or 99 percent of the population, and so on. What's more, as I already noted, there are various sorts of consensus-based good relevant to various distributions and evaluations. In particular, all those who are affected by such a choice, by which I mean who are such that there is some *ex ante* objective probability within the relevant alternatives that the satisfaction of their basic preferences would be affected, have a specific preference-based good relevant to that choice, to which the variant desires of people not affected by that choice are irrelevant. And that point bears on our current concerns because, given the indeterminacy of options, it will often be to some degree indeterminate which individuals will or might be affected by a choice. All of these factors generate a considerable normative complexity and also some normative indeterminacy regarding relevant consensus of preference, as well as real epistemic problems.

What I will do in light of these complexities and indeterminacies of fact is this: Heeding Aristotle's admonition not to look for greater precision than a subject matter admits,[9] I am prepared to take 99 percent consensus, figured in any of the ways noted above, as my working model, as in my view sufficient consensus for ethics, although the particular group of individuals among whom the 99 percent is sought will vary depending on which individuals are affected by a choice. It is 99 percent of those affected that counts. This is the sort of consensus I will aim to reveal in my subsequent discussions, while admitting that greater and lesser degrees of consensus may be normatively relevant and also hoping for more than 99 percent consensus, and while admitting there will be considerable indeterminacy of fact regarding what this 99 percent consensus is. I believe that these details about percentage don't matter much, because the notion of individual good that we will need in the most important applications in the following chapters, in which very

---

[9] Aristotle, *Nicomachean Ethics* I.3.

many people are involved, is vague, and as far as I can see identical whatever percentage between 60 percent and 99.99 percent we specify, and however we figure it. Another important point is that it is plausible that all humans share some basic preferences involving pleasure and general desire-satisfaction that provide even an individual's highly idiosyncratic preferences, at least when they are strong, considerable indirect normative weight on my view, even when they lie outside of some relevant 99 percent. I will explain this in detail later. In fact, my fear is that our later discussion of idiosyncratic desires like apotemnophilia may lead you to worry that the mechanisms I deploy provide idiosyncratic desires *too much* significance. Much of this turns on details to come, but perhaps the best quick way to put it is that the normative apparatus that we will be constructing over the next several chapters is not highly sensitive to fine details of individual good, so this issue doesn't introduce virulent indeterminacies.

There is a third general point about preference consensus to notice, before we move on to the first step of our mechanism. In theory, there might have been no consensus of preference whatever. A consensus of preference depends on the facts of what we actually prefer. Ethics and social-political philosophy must consider alternatives to what actually happens, but only alternatives that are available to us in reality, in the ways I described in Part I. I am not hoping for a consensus of preference among wildly hypothetical people, but among real people as they are, and also among real people as they might be (or possible people there might be) within the range of our real alternatives. I wish that I could deliver a plausible ethical truth applicable to wildly counterfactual circumstances, but that is beyond my ambition. I believe that, under the constraint of physicalism, it cannot be done.

The thrust of our actual desire provides a rationale for desire-based good, and meets the strictures of internalism about reasons in a way that can underwrite that aspect of quasi-normativity. But in the absence of fully normative properties, there are no genuinely true desires. There is, however, a close analogue of the truth of desires: consensus of actual preference among those affected. It isn't ideal as a way to end relevant justificatory regresses; an ideal termination would require full normativity, and unanimity would be better than 99 percent consensus. But I think it is (approximately) the best we can do in reality, even though it rests on the contingent facts of what we desire.

It will be useful to have a phrase to distinguish the sort of consensus I will seek from others in the vicinity, for instance from a consensus of normative judgments. And of course we will need to remember that those with shared desires in my sense may not have a consensus on how the world should be, on who should win some conflict. So I will call the very particular type of consensus of preference in which we are interested "consensus congruence."

7.3 Momentary Individual Good

Turn now to the first step of our two-step mechanism, from basic preferences to solipsistic momentary individual good. This is good from the perspective of a particular time in an individual's life, that needn't necessarily be comparable to the good of other people or even of other times in that individual's life.

Desire-based accounts hold that the satisfaction of desire is good, but what is it to satisfy a preference? Preference intuitively delivers an ordering of options, a gradation in that sense from worst to better. So it would seem that some sort of ordinal momentary individual good can be determined by the individual's preferences at that moment. But we are now short of even that modest goal, which is why the first step of our mechanism is required.

The basic normative fact with which we begin is a function from all relevantly possible sets of options to the best option of each set according to the basic preferences of the individual at the moment. And so we must generalize in some way from all the huge number of best options within distinct sets of conceived alternatives, from all those basic preferences, to a conception of the good for the individual that is based in the moment in which those preferences occur. It might most accurately be called a conception of the good for that individual as seen from that moment.

This is one form of consensus congruence, among basic preferences. But how do we generalize in the relevant way?

With luck, there won't often be a difference in Arthur's preference at a given moment between options A and B depending on whether or not he thinks option C is also present. And so we can roughly order all the options in a given set of options, by considering which of those options he would prefer if various subsets of those options were conceived by him to exhaust his options, and can coherently summarize his consensus preferences across different sets of options drawn from just those alternatives. If the alternatives are merely chocolate ice cream, strawberry, and vanilla, and he prefers vanilla, we can hope that he would generally prefer vanilla in any single comparison with strawberry or with chocolate, and that he would generally prefer vanilla to chocolate and strawberry even when we add in other flavor choices. With luck, there also won't often be a difference in what ice cream Arthur prefers given any fixed background he believes present for that choice.

But this sort of easy generalization will not always be possible. Someone may well prefer chocolate to strawberry in the presence of vanilla as an option but not in the presence of coffee ice cream as an option. And sometimes the fact that option C is present might give us information about the relative desirability of A and B; it might be relevant that in choosing between fish and steak there are also frogs' legs on the menu, which may indicate that the restaurant does fish well. And real options include a lot more than a single food, and involve another sort of context effect. You may prefer vanilla ice cream over chocolate in all sets of options except when it will follow a shot of bourbon, and that context effect is plausibly relevant to your well-being in situations that make ice cream with bourbon an option. So we must in fact look for relatively global patterns of consensus congruence that include all relevant context effects. One might worry that because of some context effects it isn't strictly true that if in 99 percent of all basic preferences one prefers vanilla to chocolate it is better for one. It might be worse after bourbon even if that case is very rare among one's conceivable alternatives, and one may in fact drink bourbon a lot. But notice that we can also plausibly presume that in almost all cases in which one might have vanilla after bourbon or else chocolate after bourbon one prefers the second; such context effects are more likely to be stable across basic preferences than are odd glitches that should be ignored.

It might be objected to this last point that we can determine more accurately our preference among certain specific goods if we completely ignore the environment that we take them to share, and of course such highly restricted toy option sets may be very revealing of preferences. But still there appear to be ways humans can conceive such backgrounds as stable without disrupting choice. It may also be objected that there is more than one way, say consciously and unconsciously, for an individual to cognitively entertain some set of univocally conceived options. But if this generates differences in preference it seems to me they must play a role in forming the relevant consensus.

There are many complexities. But in reality there seem to be sufficient forms of relevant consensus congruence among any actual individual's basic preferences at a moment to characterize a somewhat vague but coherent ordinal good for that individual from the perspective of that moment. There are stable and sufficiently congruent preferences across various sets of more inclusive options that differ only in what ice cream is eaten, so that vanilla really is better for the individual at that moment than chocolate, whatever else is going on. And there are other patterns of consensus that reveal it is better for the individual in question to have ice cream than to be tortured. We can look inside the various alternatives that are preferred within various different sets of options, and discover general features that are preferred by that individual at that time, at least to a normatively relevant degree of consensus, to other general features, when other things are equal.

If such a consensus of one's basic preferences is absent to some degree, then there is some indeterminacy regarding one's good from the perspective of that time. If one's basic preferences are completely incoherent in these ways, then I doubt it makes sense to say that one has any genuine good rooted in that time.

Perhaps coherence of the relevant sort, and hence individual desire and a good, requires a certain sort of optional discipline or training for humans. And perhaps madness or illness or drugs sometimes destroy coherence. But it seems to me that even all of the badly trained, mad, ill, and drugged but conscious, still retain some basic preferences that are suitably coherent. For instance, they may at least prefer, when other things are equal, pleasure to excruciating pain. And this affords them at least a limited good from the perspective of the moment.

Other complications remain: Real alternatives involve risks and probabilities of various outcomes, not the certain choice of particular outcomes. But we still have basic preferences across hypothetical toy options that are not chancy, which reveal the facts deployed in the preceding paragraphs. And patterns of preference among risky options may reveal further forms of consensus that we can mine for further determinacy of the good. We cannot reasonably hope for all the determinate and fixed attitudes towards risk exploited by von Neumann and Morgenstern, but perhaps some further determinacy of individual good at a moment is also available in this way, especially relevant to risks.

Another set of complications involve cases in which one has preferences about one's own motivational states. While the factors that make for Arthur's weakness of will and also his higher-order preferences about how he wishes to be are all relevant motivational factors that help determine what Arthur would try to do in the face of certain ranges of believed options, still he might even in single moment have a higher-order preference not to be a person who is so weak-willed in the face of temptation as in fact he is at that moment. What determines his good if he is presented with such a temptation? Too much dissonance between what he would actually try to do and his higher-order preferences about what to choose may undercut the determinacy of his individual good at the moment, but in most realistic cases Arthur's weak will is instead analogous to the context effect of bourbon on ice cream. This treatment implies that taking the temptation is better for him than not, fallen as he is, while the most intuitively relevant pattern of preference may seem to exclude that unfortunate effect of his weak will. Still, if he would really try to change his personality and avoid the temptation rather than take the temptation if he were presented with *those* two options, then at least that change in his personality would be better for him than taking the temptation. And, most important, many of the intuitive normative problems about falling to temptation are due to its effects on one's future, which we are not yet in position to understand how my proposal will handle, but to which we will return. Arthur will often agree that the temptation is better for him *temporarily*.

One might object that there is an infinity of sets of different alternative options, so that 99 percent consensus congruence makes no sense. But basic preferences rest on humanly realistic conceptions of options. Each real human is capable of a differential response to only a finite number of different sets of conceived options. It is not just that each set must be finitely presented to them, but that there are finite numbers of different sets that can be differentially presented to them. So it makes sense to talk about a 99 percent consensus of preference.

Another objection may be that I complained when Railton deployed a robust individual motivational core that was supposed to be preserved even in the situation in which one was suitably idealized by the possession of full information and hence had properly informed desires, while now I am presuming an analogous motivational core preserved across ranges of hypothetically entertained options. But remember that on my proposal we do not need to consider a wildly hypothetical state in which some human becomes godlike in omniscience, but rather merely a very large number of more realistic hypothetical states in which they think they have different sorts of options. And we do not need to distinguish a motivational core preserved across ideal and non-ideal selves who differ in other desires, but rather motivation in general that is preserved while beliefs about options differ. These two points aid considerably in disentwining the background conditions of the relevant conditionals.

While there are many complexities, perhaps the main point to stress is that I do not expect this first step of our mechanism to yield a highly specific conception of individual good from the perspective of a moment. I believe only that this first step will yield enough determinacy for us to execute the second, in which various individual and even momentary peculiarities of desire will be smoothed away. It is not plausible to expect that very fine details of contrast effects or glitches will be preserved in a consensus congruence spanning any wide range of humans, or even one individual over time. Rather, we can hope only for an interpersonal or inter-temporal consensus in which, say, torture that yields nothing else of personal interest to someone is worse for them than tasty treats of any flavor. I hope for little more determinacy than that in the end, which is I believe all that we need to vindicate common moral judgments. That considerably reduces the strain on the first step of our consensus mechanism. The first step involves significant indeterminacy, but because there is not a heavy demand on the determinacy of that step, it isn't relevantly *virulent* indeterminacy. There is all the determinacy we need.

Given this rough conception, we still have the problem of applying it to reality, of determining the objective satisfaction of preferences. That depends on the contents of preferences and of consensus built on those preferences, and the match of those contents to reality. In the simple case, Arthur will have a sufficient understanding of chocolate and vanilla ice cream that it is obvious when he gets in reality which he prefers. And while there are significant complexities introduced by this issue,[10] they

---

[10] In a simple case, someone's internally determinate conception of their possible sets of options would include one set that matched their various real alternatives one to one, so they have one conceived option in such a set for each real option, and such that each conceived option matched its real corresponding option to a larger degree than it matched any other real option, though overlooking details. Their basic preference among that set of conceived options specifies a best real option for them. But even then it would be important that differing features of real options they cannot stretch to comprehend don't matter very much, which requires appeal tor consensus congruence. But there are more complex cases: An agent has options that it cannot understand, or someone can conceive only five options when there are thousands, or an agent conceives of two options both which constitute the same real option. It is even remotely conceivable that an agent understands none of its options even partially, although it is also plausible that when you do anything you also do something intentionally, and that you cannot do anything intentionally unless you know you are doing something. These aren't idle possibilities. Mendola (2008) discusses views whereby vagaries of social usage of which one is unaware suffice to make one's preferences obtain or not. Mendola (2006) considers whether the truth of some metaphysical hypothesis one doesn't believe, say

are somewhat eased by the fact that the consensus of basic preferences will deliver such a vague and marginally determinate good.

7.4 Interpersonal Good

That was the first step of our mechanism for moving from basic preferences to a kind of good for individuals useful to ethics. But there is also a second. Consider individuals at moments who have the basic sort of good from the perspective of a moment that we discerned in the last section. In particular, consider all such individuals at moments the satisfaction of whose good from the perspective of a moment is affected by some specific normatively relevant choice.

Depending on the choice, this might involve a number of distinct individuals, or all humanity, or just one continuing individual with changing desires, and the second component of our mechanism will yield a different sort of good for each case, a good which can differ when different individuals at moments are affected.[11] But consider first one simple case.

There is one form of normatively relevant good that bridges all individuals in moments, or more exactly all normal adult human individuals from the perspective of moments, a kind that we can compare across all such individuals and also across the moments of anyone's life. This depends in particular on consensus congruence among the different individual goods from the perspective of moments of all actual humans, or rather of all non-infant and non-decrepit actual humans. This will allow us to make some assessments of the relative overall value of states of affairs including many such individuals, or including a single individual with changing desires, given mechanisms I will develop later.

This is the particular instance of consensus good that will be most frequently relevant in our later discussions. But I stress that there are also often richer forms of consensus available that deliver more robust sorts of goods that are relevant to distributions among more restricted groups of individuals at moments of their lives, for instance those which make up but one individual life. Nevertheless, I do not claim that there are very determinate facts about comparisons of individual well-being between different lives or even within lives over time that can be delivered by the apparatus of our second step, in any of its applications. Still, I do believe that this second type of consensus will eventually allow us to answer the most crucial distributional questions, the questions that must be answered if ethics and social-political philosophy are to be viable.

Berkeley's idealism, may be relevant to the satisfaction of preferences incorporating the presumption of another metaphysics. Mendola (1997) considers the possibility that the world is unlike any humanly conceivable situation, on all our options.

[11] I hence agree with Scanlon (1998: 108–43) that there is no univocal well-being relevant to ethics.

Focus on our initial, simple, and yet probably most important case, the consensus good suitable for comparisons among all adult non-decrepit humans. What is crucial is that there be a useful consensus among all our actual individual goods from the perspective of moments, themselves rooted in our actual basic preferences. And I think we can see that there is, once we remember that consensus congruence doesn't require unanimity, and that it is not what you claim you prefer (or even think you would prefer) but what you would actually attempt to do if you believed that you were presented with various options that matters. I think almost all of us almost always prefer to be minimally well-off rather than very poor, to be contented rather than tortured, to be well-fed rather than starving, to be healthy rather than sick, at least when little else can be gained, in our opinion, by sickness, starvation, being tortured, or being poor. Religious ascetics and those who scorn wealth from political principle characteristically think some other good will come of their denial.

Perhaps you want details. I think the relevant consensus is reflected in Martha Nussbaum's attempt at a cross-cultural agreement on worthwhile human capacities: bodily health, bodily integrity, capabilities for properly human uses of senses and imagination and thought, capacities for emotional attachment, being able to form a conception of the good, dignified affiliation, being able to live with concerns for and in relation to animals and plants and the world of nature, play, control over one's environment both political and material.[12] These capabilities and at least some form of their realization are things that by general consensus we want, though there is considerable disagreement among us about what these very general categories more specifically involve (for instance, some relate to nature only to play by killing bugs) or how to balance them for the best life. We prefer some of each to none, and more of each to less, other things equal. I also think this consensus is reflected in Ed Diener and Martin Seligman's review of empirical work on subjective feelings of well-being. They conclude that a partial formula for well-being is to live in a democratic and stable society that provides material resources to meet needs, to have supportive friends and family, to have rewarding and engaging work and an adequate income, to be reasonably healthy and have treatment available in case of mental problems, to have important goals related to one's values, and to have a philosophy or religion that provides guidance, purpose, and meaning to one's life.[13] Of course worthwhile capacities and subjective feelings of well-being don't exhaust the good in my sense, but these lists reveal relevant consensus. I also think that three things that should be explicitly added to any list of goods rooted in consensus preference are true beliefs, pleasure, and the absence of pain. Nussbaum and Diener and Seligman have already explicitly noted the good of minimal health.

Perhaps some of our busybody philosophies and religions, of the sort mentioned by Diener and Seligman, suggest that some of our desires are not most relevant to our

---

[12] Nussbaum (2000: 78–81).   [13] Diener and Seligman (2004).

own well-being, and we will need to return to that point. But while we clearly have preferences for things intuitively outside our lives, and those preferences characteristically reflect some of our values and philosophical and religious ideals, we have virulent differences in those values and ideals when they are stated in any remotely concrete way. Only stated in the vaguest way are they part of any consensus of preference among humans. But serious real consensus exists about central features of our own lives. My belief is that it is enough to deliver all that ethics and social-political philosophy requires of generally comparable individual good. If there is less consensus than I hope, then there is greater indeterminacy of the good of that sort. But in any case it seems to be less than the virulent indeterminacy implied by informed desire accounts.

It may be objected that such a shared ordering of options as I am suggesting does not really provide interpersonally comparable value, because even if two individuals agree on a preference ordering, still one might have more intense desires than the other. One of the two might want all of the alternatives more than the other does. But we saw in the Chapter 6 that there are virulent indeterminacies regarding desire strengths. All the factors that plausibly could be thought to root stronger desires and that are not reflected in basic preferences, for instance the number of neuron firings involved in a preference, or the intensity of hedonic satisfaction that occasions an achieved preference, or the amount of behaviorist learning it generates, are properly seen, I claim, merely as individual differences that attend rather than constitute differences in preferences. They are, on my proposal, without direct normative significance to the satisfaction of the preference they attend, although of course you may want hedonic satisfaction or behaviorist learning itself, and so they may be a good for you because of other preferences. When we all order alternatives in the same ways, then that delivers the only interpersonal comparability of goods that there is. Various other vectors of alleged desire strength are irrelevant. They are just differences in the mechanics that attend shared and normatively relevant preferences. Why is this treatment appropriate? Because it isn't plausible that different numbers of neuron firings or strength of behaviorist learning effects are directly normatively relevant to the distribution of goods. And while it may seem more intuitive to claim that hedonic satisfaction levels are relevant to well-being, even beyond their reflection in preferences, remember that we are done with robust hedonism, and in any case consensual preferences for more pleasure are very relevant according to my proposal. There are other mechanisms relevant to desire intensity. Perhaps consensus among one's own basic preferences can approximate the conditions required by von Neumann and Morgenstern and in that way fix desire strengths. But any relevant consensus of that sort involving different individuals or even the same individual at different times will be shared among them and so is respected by my proposal. Still, it might be objected, if desire intensities are available in this way then the degree of one's desires for certain things should be taken into account in distributions even if we don't desire the same things to the same degrees; everyone should get more of what they desire more even if we all want different things most. I will return to worries like this in a moment, but in intuitive cases of this sort the intensity of what we desire is reflected in a shared pattern of preference in another way. It involves a shared preference for subjective happiness or pleasure and the absence of nagging frustration.

Beyond consensus congruence among all normal adult humans, it is also plausible, as I've said, that there are sometimes more robust patterns of consensus among a more limited selection of solipsistic individual goods from the perspective of moments. Whenever there is such a more robust consensus congruence among all individuals affected by a choice, say when only one person is involved and over the stretch of time in question their preferences do not change, or when a small group of people is involved and all share fairly specific preferences, then that is normatively relevant. The second component of our apparatus yields a characteristically more robust sort of relevant good when applied to such cases. In particular, when only the satisfaction of your preferences is affected by some choice, it is properly governed only by the consensus of your own preferences.

7.5 Summary of My View

Here is a brief summary of my unsophisticated simple desire-based account of well-being:

(1) X's basic preferences at a time are fixed by what alternatives X would choose to take at that time if X thought herself presented with each of the possible combinations of alternatives in action that X might think herself to face.

(2) X's individual good from the perspective of that moment rests on the satisfaction of the consensus congruence of X's basic preferences at that time.

(3) The well-being relevant to a particular choice is determined by the consensus congruence of all individual goods from the perspective of moments that are affected by that choice.

7.6 Special Objections

We turn now to a consideration of pressing objections. We begin with some that are specific to the unusual details of my particular desire-based account.

Objection One is that while simple desire-based accounts customarily conceive individual good as the satisfaction of all desires, my form focuses on the satisfaction of consensus desires. And the satisfaction of even one's idiosyncratic desires seems important to one's well-being.

There are two replies. First, when only the satisfaction of one's individual desires is in question, and they are temporally stable, my proposal grants to that stronger and more local consensus full normative weight. It is only when situations involve the distribution of well-being among distinct individuals who do not share that consensus, or among analogous distinct periods of one life, that that more robust local consensus is discounted. When only Guinevere's well-being is at issue, her own desires are all that count. Still, it may seem that facts about whether other people are affected by something cannot determine whether it is relevant to Guinevere's self-interest at all; it may seem that her well-being cannot be affected simply because her desires cease to be widely shared through changes in other people. But my point is that there are different sorts of individual good and well-being, and so different sorts of self-interest, that are relevant to different cases, especially when different sorts of distributional conflicts are present. And my point is that the moral evaluation of overall outcomes, which is not yet to say all ethical judgment, is not properly held hostage to the satisfaction of idiosyncratic desires when that has a cost to those who do not share them. The kind of well-being that we pursue here is that relevant to overall evaluation of outcomes which will ultimately form the basis of consequentialist moral assessment, and there are different sorts of well-being of even this general type relevant to different cases, when different individuals are affected. We should not expect a single specific conception of individual well-being that can be ripped out of my overall normative proposal and placed within moral theories with a very different structure.

My second reply to the objection that idiosyncratic desires are too much discounted by my proposal depends on the fact that there are somewhat indirect ways of sharing preferences. For one thing, real people share a considerable concern with happiness, enjoyment, pleasure, and satisfaction with their lives, with subjective feelings of well-being. And so even when a non-consensus desire for a particular good is discounted, any significant subjective dissatisfaction that would be occasioned by the lack of that good still provides significant indirect weight to that desire according to my proposal. If Lancelot is miserable because his idiosyncratic desire for a certain sort of tournament is discounted in some social arrangement that affects other people who lack that desire, still his misery itself is not discounted. In addition, even when we do not share finely characterized preferences, we may share more generally characterized preferences. If we each care greatly about building a monument to our own idiosyncratic god,[14] we may share a more general preference for the production of religious statuary. Depending on its content and our beliefs, say about which god is best, this may of course generate a practical conflict, but it is nonetheless relevant to consensus congruence. Any pattern of similarity among the content of preferences, ultimately among basic preferences, may constitute an appropriate consensus.[15]

---

[14] Scanlon (1975: 659).
[15] Relevant consensus among two preferences is the most specific such consensus that exists. Mendola (1997) specifies relevant similarities between contents.

Despite these replies, or because of them, it may seem that my proposal does not provide sufficient protection for unusual individual desires against contrary oppressive desires of the majority. But we will return to such cases in the next section, since they trouble all simple desire-based accounts, and since their proper treatment requires more background.

Its focus on consensus congruence allows my desire-based account of the good to meet the internalist constraint which is one aspect of quasi-normativity. We can expect that all inside such a consensus spanning some language community with a word for individual well-being share relevant preferences, and preferences are motivational. But this in turn suggests Objection Two: The 1 percent in the community who may be outside of the consensus do not meet that internalist constraint, yet share the language.

There are two replies: First, a plausible internalist meaning constraint need not be so strict as to require motivation in those outside of the relevant consensus. Just as an amoralist may not be motivated by moral considerations even though such motivation is characteristic of moral claims and yet still share our language, so too the internalist constraint in question may be characteristic of morality even though some fail to meet it. Second, while real individuals lack some preferences that are characteristic of the general human consensus, no real individuals lack some of them, for instance a concern with subjective well-being, other things equal. And so all real individuals fall inside any relevant internalist constraint on moral language involving well-being to at least some degree, when it is underwritten by the preference-based goods they do share with the wide consensus. There are also other sorts of moral language that plausibly involve internalist meaning constraints, for instance those which claim that some act is right or wrong. But the moral mechanisms that we will develop in the following chapters as relevant to such judgments are so insensitive to fine details of individual well-being, that it is likely that even a concern with mere subjective satisfaction can underwrite the most characteristic demands of morality via those mechanisms.[16]

There is another aspect of quasi-normativity besides internal reasons. Objection Three is that justificatory regresses will not be closed in the eyes of those outside a consensus of preference. But the significance of this worry is mitigated by the fact that there can be indirect forms of consensus, focused say on subjective satisfaction. And just as the meaning of "right" in moral contexts is constrained by the consensus of normative judgment reflected in DC1-NORMS, so too the meaning of "good" in such contexts is constrained in an analogous way reflected in the proposal I am now suggesting. This is relevant both to linguistically mediated justificatory regresses and to arguments based on individual good that I make in the following chapters. But my main reply is that in the real world we can do no better than what I have proposed

---

[16] Mendola (2006) shows this for crude sensory pleasures and pains.

here. We are working over the abyss. The conception of individual good I am attempting to deliver is modest and does not propound controversial normative advice to some individual about the value of their life when only their own good is in question, except to point out the relevance of consensus among their own changing desires. It is rooted in the consensus preferences of all those affected when distributions are in question. And in a reality shorn of robust objective and hedonist good, that is the best we can hope for as a way of assessing the value of overall outcomes in which one individual's well-being conflicts with another's. What's more, this proposal does in fact deliver the goods most characteristic of hedonism and objectivism. It does the best job that can be done of ending relevant justificatory regresses that is available in a reality without robust normative facts, when only quasi-normativity is available.

Objection Four is a worry about the interaction of the two elements of my proposal, its focus on basic preferences of individuals at times and on consensus congruence. Individual preferences may fluctuate over time because of emotional variation. When Lancelot is angry he may much prefer revenge at some cost to his future well-being, but when he is calm he may not. And it may seem that the emotional and temporally idiosyncratic preferences he has when angry or depressed should not block any consensus of preference that governs his well-being in the calm portions of his life.

I have four replies.[17] When the distribution of well-being only within a calm period of one's life is in question, then the more robust consensus within that period should govern that distribution. That removes some of the problematic cases. Second, different people differ considerably in their dominant forms of emotionality, in something like the range traversed within ordinary individual lives over time. So any consensus that governs general distributional issues in morality will encompass such a wide range in any case. And as I've said, I think that in fact we have considerable general consensus of that sort, even if we disagree about fine details just as an angry individual might disagree with how he feels about details when he is calm. It may seem that this doesn't get at the root of the problem, which is that we need to discount the desires of the depressed or irrational more than my account allows. But my third reply is that I do discount idiosyncrasies within the range of some distributional issue. Many intuitively irrational desires are highly idiosyncratic, and hence irrelevant to consensus congruence, while on the other hand when idiosyncratic desires are not intuitively irrational it is often because they are related in the indirect ways I recently noted to generally shared desires, for instance to shared desires for happiness or enjoyment. So my proposal provides a nicely intuitive balance on this issue. My fourth reply is that some worries about anger and depression are general

---

[17] Another possible reply is to modify our consensus mechanism to deliver individual good over life directly from a consensus of all basic preferences whenever they occur in that life.

worries about all simple desire-based accounts, and not just my particular version. We turn now to this class of objections.

7.7 Standard Objections

We need to consider standard objections to all simple desire-based accounts. We will start by recalling the types of cases that began Chapter 6 and motivate informed desire accounts: Arthur may in his ignorance want to stay at his table sipping champagne even though a piano is about to fall on his head. And if Lancelot in romantic turmoil wants to jump out the window, you may sit on him (if you can), thinking he will thank you in the morning.

I believe that Hubin is right that the key to some of these problems is lack of information by the agent that yet does not undermine their possession of relevant individual preferences revealing judgments about the value of outcomes. And I believe that Heathwood is right that the key to some is the proper balancing of the satisfaction of conflicting desires. But I think they are mistaken when they deploy these abstract insights through the use of psychological resources that are too robust for reality, as we saw in Chapter 6.

Begin with Hubin's idea. The piano is about to fall, but Arthur in ignorance wants to stay at his table. He doesn't want to leave. Hubin suggests that the only desire he has to remain at the table is an instrumental desire, but we have seen that there are not adequately determinate facts about what we intrinsically and instrumentally desire. Still, my response to this case is quite similar to Hubin's: Arthur prefers options in which he successfully flees such a piano to otherwise identical options in which he sits sipping and is crushed. The consensus of his basic preferences that fixes his individual good from the perspective of the moment in question delivers the ordering of alternatives this case intuitively requires. Since it will take a moment for the piano to fall, perhaps this case also involves distribution of individual good over time, but not in a way which introduces any plausible conflicts. Even now he doesn't prefer to be crushed in 30 seconds. The consensus congruence rooting his individual good over time assures that it is determinately better to get up from an otherwise pleasant table and avoid a piano about to crush him, and this sort of congruence among all those affected is relevant. In fact, even the consensus congruence of all normal humans plausibly delivers the same result. Even the depressed who want to be crushed are considering different alternatives than Arthur is facing, given his otherwise pleasant life. But we are anyway returning to the case of the depressed.

There are other sorts of cases that informed desire accounts of well-being assimilate to the cases we have just been discussing, but that both Hubin and I think should not be assimilated. For instance, Lancelot hasn't fully confronted the suffering of others, and if he did, he would reform. But I am not attempting now to reform desires. I am attempting to root individual well-being in desires.

There are other sorts of cases somewhat like the falling piano case that seem to provide objections to simple desire-based accounts. Maybe I want that fancy buckler only because I have been influenced by advertising. My desires are not authentic. And some desires, say those of a deferential spouse, may be due to reduced circumstances and oppression, and hence seem inauthentic in another way. Some facts of these sorts might be revealed by contemplating the full set of one's basic preferences at the moment and also other factors like causal histories and counterfactual dependencies between desires. I wouldn't buy that buckler unless I thought it would cause me to have fancier friends, like those in the commercial. I would rather not buy the buckler at all than buy it after being brainwashed into it. But I think the main points are these: There is no even moderately determinate truth about what I would desire if I were suitably insulated from distorting social influences, because it is not objectively fixed in some prior way what is proper education and what is distorting influence. And we have no good reason to believe that even inauthentic desires can be properly ignored when determining well-being. Even paradigmatically high and beautiful desires may be formed under worries about the loss of parental love. Should their satisfaction be discounted when assessing individual good or the overall value of outcomes? And to discount a person's desires that they only have because they are oppressed is sometimes a way of further oppressing them.

Another objection to desire-based accounts involves desires that are more voluntary. Ronald Dworkin worries that the satisfaction of intentionally cultivated expensive tastes should not be a normative priority.[18] But, I reply, idiosyncratic preferences are not directly relevant to the consensus that governs distributions among different individuals; they are merely indirectly relevant when they engage shared goals like happiness. And there are many ways in which people can fail to effectively pursue their own good beyond the cultivation of expensive tastes. This may be normatively relevant, but it does not suggest that their good isn't good.

There is also an objection that involves desires for objects to which volition seems intuitively irrelevant. Scanlon objects that someone "might have a desire about the chemical composition of some star, about whether blue was Napoleon's favorite color, or about whether Julius Caesar was an honest man. But it would be odd to suggest that the well-being of a person who has such desires is affected by these facts themselves (as opposed to the pleasure he or she derives from certain beliefs about them)."[19] I reply that such cases are unrealistic, at least absent complicating contexts, for instance involving the truth of that person's public theoretical commitments, which would make such things intuitively relevant to their well-being. And in any case such desires are idiosyncratic, and hence discounted by my focus on consensus congruence.

---

[18] Dworkin (1981: 228–40).   [19] Scanlon (1998: 114).

Another traditional worry about desire-based accounts is that some people's choices are due to concern for others, while others are selfish.[20] It seems that we shouldn't count satisfaction of concern for others as one's own good, lest the selfish gain an unfair moral advantage. When Lancelot does his irksome duty, he may in some broad sense want to, but it doesn't seem good for him.

My reply to this important objection has three components: First, the difference between so-called self-regarding and other-regarding desires is in fact significantly indeterminate. *Some* intuitive differences between self-interested and other-regarding desires are delivered by the full set of one's basic preferences conjoined with additional factors analogous to those relevant to the distinction between instrumental and intrinsic desires. For instance, sometimes you are riveted in contemplation of the effect on your subjective happiness of the satisfaction of some desire that involves no other people at all. And sometimes you only do something because some otherwise unknown individual wants it or needs it, although you very much wouldn't want to do it otherwise and find it quite unpleasant. So there are some clear cases. But there are other cases in which various relevant factors pull in different directions. Someone may find deep emotional satisfaction in doing something that sacrifices much of their time and professional interests for their children. Tristram would rather have a fancy car only in scenarios where others are involved and will see him driving around and will like that, but it doesn't make clear sense to deny he is doing it for his own sake; his well-being no more intuitively excludes than includes a car had merely for the sake of happily impressing others through their opinion of his coolness. Arthur's no more intuitively excludes than includes the state of his beloved children, or of some large group of people to which he is deeply attached. Second, we lack consensus that a division of things into things you want for your own sake and for the sake of others always matters normatively to your individual good even in cases where it is determinate, and even if we did it would not be supported by a suitable rationale. Consider things that happen after your death to your deeply beloved children or to some central project of your life to create an institution to feed the starving. Even if you intuitively don't want such things for your own sake, since after all you will be dead and gone and your focus of concern is on others, it isn't intuitively clear that they aren't relevant to your normatively relevant good or well-being. And in fact while you are alive even your intuitive well-being may well depend on the future unknown success of your current projects to aid your children or relieve the suffering. And, above all, the basic rationale for a desire-based account is that what matters for your good or well-being is whether you care about things. Those with cramped and intuitively self-directed and narcissistic desires, or overly socially subservient desires, or expansive and benevolent social desires, have different sorts of interests, and that is all. Third, there are other elements of MM, of my overall

---

[20] Overvold (1980); T. Schwartz (1982); Parfit (1984: 493–502).

normative theory, that undercut the significance of this distinction. These include the ways to properly balance the satisfaction of different people's desires and even your own desires at different times. And consensus congruence will discount idiosyncratic preferences, including idiosyncratically self-sacrificing or self-indulgent ones. And, as I suggested earlier, there is more consensus about things that are intuitively relevant to one's own individual well-being. But perhaps the relevance of the first element of this third reply will be most evident if we turn to a related objection.

That objection is that my proposal makes self-sacrifice impossible, when clearly it is possible. But, I reply, self-sacrifice involves the sacrifice of what in my conception are the interests of your future selves, as we will see in Chapter 8.[21] And that is quite possible according to my proposal, since your future selves may have different desires, though its normative propriety will depend on features of the case in ways we are not yet in position to consider. You may give up your future happiness and overall preference satisfaction to satisfy some dominant current preference to help another, and that is sacrifice of your future self. It is true that there are other forms of intuitive self-sacrifice, in which you always prefer the sacrifice you have made. But we will return to those cases in a moment, when they can be properly juxtaposed with analogous cases involving self-punishment.

Another objection related to my treatment of the distinction between self-regarding and other-regarding desires is due to the fact that some of our desires can be satisfied only after our death, when we are in no position to know it. Even during life some of our desires may be satisfied or frustrated without our knowing it. This may in itself suggest that my desire-based proposal is objectionable. But, I reply, we lack normative consensus that what happens after someone's death or otherwise beyond their knowledge is irrelevant to their well-being, as indeed some of the cases I recently mentioned reveal. Many of us care about much more than things whose occurrence we can confirm, and it would require a robust rationale to undercut the significance in someone's life of strong preferences regarding things that happen after their death, or that happen to their children in some inaccessible new world. Such a rationale is not available in reality. Certainly many of us care about more than some hedonists claim, about more than our own phenomenal experience, and it would require a robust and hence unrealistic rationale to show us that we are wrong about that.

There are other standard objections. Philosophers have proposed people with very strange and intuitively irrational preferences, who don't care what happens on Tuesdays,[22] or want to drink saucers of mud,[23] or want to spend most of their lives counting the blades of grass in the backyard, or have the life-consuming goal of the smallest handwriting.[24] We are supposed to see that their strange desires should be discounted or ignored. But I don't care about hypothetical people. I am seeking a consensus of preference across real people only, or more exactly across people that

---

[21] Parfit (1984: 128).   [22] Parfit (1984: 123–4).
[23] Anscombe's example. The next is Rawls'.   [24] Brink (1989: 227).

exist within the range of the real alternatives sketched in Part I. And if there are any relevantly real people who count grass or drink mud, they are idiosyncratic and outside of many forms of relevant consensus congruence in that respect, though the relation of the satisfaction of their idiosyncratic desires to shared goals like happiness may make such desires indirectly relevant to their well-being in morally relevant cases. And a handwriting fixation and counting grass seem no more objectively or intuitively worse for them than some actual highly revered religious practices. And of course drinking mud and counting blades and ignoring Tuesdays may conflict with other desires they have at this time or at others.

There are other objections we need to consider, but first it will be useful to focus a little on the last point, the issue of balancing the satisfaction of conflicting desires, and hence on Heathwood's mechanism for defending simple desire-based accounts. I think that Heathwood, like Hubin, has a good general idea, but that he also develops his idea through resources that are too fancy and robust. There are no very determinate facts about the intensities of desires or the normatively relevant numbers of desires that we have at each moment, and we should not only count concurrent satisfactions of desires. Still, my proposal does first deliver individual good from the perspective of a moment, and then treats different moments of a person's life, as well as different individuals, as a proper object of distributional concern. So I can deploy Heathwood's general idea in a different and more realistic way:

Sometimes the real problem with allowing strong drunken desires for self-mutilation their head, or even drunken desires for some unpleasant tattoo, is that there will be another subject of desire tomorrow bearing one's name but with contrary preferences.[25] Our desires change over time. Tomorrow morning and every day forward you will be very sorry you cut off your ear, or had the tattoo, or gave so much money to that unhappy drunk on the neighboring bar stool. But as Heathwood suggests, this traditional objection to simple desire-based theories seems properly disposed of by a proper account of distribution. It doesn't suggest that some of your desires now don't count, but only that some of your later desires count too. And in many such cases they characteristically persist longer. One might worry that if desires change over time they cannot be part of a relevant consensus. But there can be relevant patterns of consensus among those who differ somewhat in their desires. For example, your happiness may be something that you care about tonight in the bar but also tomorrow morning, although your desires differ over time in other ways.

There are many cases to which distribution within a life is relevant. You are depressed, and see things in a dark way. But depression will likely lead you to care insufficiently about your future interests, and so depressed desires should be restrained by a proper distributional concern for the satisfaction of your future desires. But perhaps the worry is that you are so depressed that you want to kill

---

[25] Even self-sacrifice in another's interest may sometimes be inappropriate.

yourself. If we sit on you, you will thank us in the morning, but if you succeed, then you won't be around to complain or to have contrary preferences. Still, in most realistic cases, yesterday, before your depression hit, you had strong preferences that differ significantly from your current self-destructive desires. And the satisfaction of the preferences of your later selves that would be lost if you die today also counts. And of course there are botched suicide attempts, and people who wake up filled with regret at having made them. And real suicides often seriously affect other people in a way that is normatively important. These in fact do not exhaust the ways in which death is a relevant evil either intuitively or according to MM. Suicide destroying your future selves is somewhat morally analogous to killing someone else contrary to their will, or at least killing them in their sleep when they aren't in position to express a contrary preference. We will not be in position to understand MM's treatment of murder, including self-murder, until Chapter 9, and indeed in detail until Part III, so on this highly relevant point I must request your patience. But the punch-line is that MM can deliver any normative restriction on self-murder during depression that is firmly and legitimately rooted in commonsense, and a strong rationale that is not available in reality would be required for any more definitive restriction.

My reply to the worry about suicide depends on the general claim that we have obligations towards our future selves that are analogous to our obligations to others, and that may itself seem objectionable. It may for instance seem unacceptably unintuitive to claim that we have moral obligations to be health nuts so as to maximize our own future preference satisfaction. Since the proper treatment of such cases depends on many details of MM we have yet to consider, I must request your patience on this issue also, until Part III propounds a full account of the practical implications of MM, which we will see are properly intuitive. But it is also relevant that one of the most intuitive objectivist goods, which I have promised that my desire-based theory can deliver to avoid other traditional objections, is health.

My treatment of the depression case also appeals in part to the satisfaction of one's past desires, and that may suggest another objection to simple desire-based accounts. Consider Parfit's real-life case:

Between the ages of 7 and 24 what I most wanted was to be a poet. And this desire was not conditional on its own persistence. I knew that I might be tempted by other careers. I wanted to be a poet even if this is not what I later wanted. Now that I am older, I have no desire to be a poet.[26]

It may seem that the satisfaction of this past desire, and hence perhaps past desires generally, has now no relevance to well-being.[27] But, I reply, such a past desire is not directly relevant to any consensus congruence governing the well-being of Parfit's current self, and the satisfaction of his past desires to be a poet is no more weighty on

---

[26] Parfit (1984: 157).
[27] I am sympathetic with Parfit's using the case against the self-interest theory of rationality.

my proposal than the satisfaction of the desires of others that he be a poet. It is relevant to good from the perspective of his past selves that had such a desire, but that good is of limited current distributional significance.[28]

Richard Kraut has objected that we can specifically desire to harm ourselves, which seems contrary to simple desire-based accounts, and seems to support objectivism.[29] But, as Heathwood suggests, self-punishment is most obvious when we do things that we later regret, and hence distributional concerns are in play. Certainly, if we truly enjoy some alleged self-punishment, it doesn't seem to be a harm that we have suffered. Still, there are other cases, analogous to troublesome forms of self-sacrifice to which I promised to return. Perhaps someone resolutely wants to be punished at every moment of their life by serious forms of physical self-mortification that they never enjoy but always prefer, or by analogous forms of cognitive sacrifice. I think that most realistic such cases depend on false religious beliefs or false beliefs about robust forms of individual responsibility, forms that later chapters will debunk. Such desires are hence discounted by my proposal in ways we've already discussed. And any case in which the interests of others are affected in some way must properly be governed by a less idiosyncratic consensus, which underlies the intuitions supporting the case. And I do not need to deny that people sometimes sacrifice their future health or knowledge to current goals, while having false objectivist beliefs that that negatively affects their well-being, even when they will always prefer that the sacrifice was made. People can be deceived about their own good. Still, it is possible that there are some realistic and intuitively telling cases of this general sort that slip by these replies. If so, then I claim that they are analogous to the following objection:

There are those with apotemnophilia, urgent desires to have a healthy limb amputated.[30] Perhaps this seems grounds for objectivism, and an objection to all simple desire-based accounts. But while I share your distaste with such surgery, and action on such a desire might be later regretted, and the distaste of others counts for something on my proposal, still these factors do not appropriately trump strong and stable individual desire (in other words a dominating preference) when the significant interests of others are not affected, unless we have a plausible explanation of how objectivism is true in our world. We don't, and so our outside perspective on such a desire does not possess relevant normative authority.

Another factor that may seem to support objectivism over desire-based accounts is a feature of the phenomenology of desire. We seem often to want things just because they are important in some objective way.[31] But there are some kinds of objectivity of individual goods that can be delivered by my proposal, for instance those rooted in a wide consensus, and those refining the standards for things we care about, say

---

[28] Similar things are true of one's future desires that depend on value judgments that one doesn't now endorse. See Parfit (1984: 153–5) and Nagel (1970: 74).

[29] Kraut (1994).   [30] Elliott (2007); Orbach (2009).   [31] Brink (1989: 224–6).

jousting. And we have seen that there are no other sorts of objective importance to be found in reality.

Another objection that might be thought to favor objectivism is that the satisfaction of evil desires may seem irrelevant to well-being.[32] Cruel Mordred may revel in Arthur's disgrace, but satisfying that desire may seem of no positive normative significance. But, I reply, that the satisfaction of one's evil desires is relevant to one's own well-being does not imply that it is good for the world as a whole, though of course this is an issue to which we will need to return when we consider overall evaluation of outcomes in Chapter 8. And Arthur's disgrace is intuitively good *for* *Mordred*. Part of the immorality of evil is that the evil find their good in the suffering of others. Also, the most strikingly evil desires are idiosyncratic, and so discounted by my proposal anyway.

Still, consider this related case. There have been traditional communities in which 99 percent of all those affected would be deeply offended by a gay interracial couple. And so it may seem that consensus congruence requires that we discount the desires of the couple in favor of the oppressive interests of the majority. But, I reply, in reality most such oppressive desires are conditional on false religious or moral beliefs or analogous fantasies, and so are severely discounted by my proposal, just like Arthur's ignorant desire to stay at his table. Even in traditional communities far fewer than 99 percent have such preferences whose satisfaction counts in reality. Still, perhaps forgotten histories of false indoctrination sometimes affect such preferences in ways not reflected in their content. Perhaps certain things now just seem disgusting. But in reality almost all individuals share preferences involving their own sexual and social satisfactions that are stronger than aesthetic preferences for policing others' romantic lives that are not conditional on false belief. Still, it may seem that even the tiny individual satisfactions of weak aesthetic preferences of a large community of oppressors will together trump the strong preferences of some isolated individuals. But in the next chapter we will see that my proposal for assessing overall outcomes focuses primarily not on sums of well-being but on maximizing the well-being of the worst-off. And in cases such as these that provides considerable protection to minority interests.

Cases similar to apotemnophilia, though less dramatic, may suggest hedonist objections. Consider Daniel Haybron's case for the importance to well-being of a kind of happiness involving positive moods and emotions:

Claudia...has chosen a life of unhappiness...because she prefers wealth and social status to happiness, and she found lawyering to be the most efficient means to these ends. She has succeeded, amassing great hordes of money, acquiring the finest luxuries, and earning the envy of her peers. But work...is, for her, stressful and emotionally unfulfilling. As a result, she is short-tempered, stressed out, anxious, and mildly depressed. She could be happy in other

---

[32] Brink (1989: 227).

pursuits...[yet such activities would] not bring her the riches and social prominence she desires. She does not regret her choice.... [H]er choice does not depend on errors in reasoning, factual ignorance, or thoughtlessness: these are her values.[33]

But, I reply, our external qualms about Claudia's life lack weighty authority in a world without the robust metaphysics required to support hedonism.[34] If you love being a philosopher but it makes you anxious and perpetually dissatisfied with yourself, your dean or parents have no legitimate authority to pronounce that you would be better off in another field where you'd be better tempered, and no consensus makes their qualms weightier than your preference, as long as you are making no factual errors about how life would be for you in the various careers. Recall that my proposal has a different means of dealing with such factual ignorance than informed desire accounts. Perhaps such a pronouncement by others would be illegitimate interference even if it were correct, consensus congruence does cede some weight to pleasure, sometimes other people's interests are seriously affected by one's career choice, and sometimes one will change one's mind or is mistaken about what some career will yield. But still, in a case in which your interests alone are in question, and your preferences are stable, and you are making no factual errors, and your preference for pleasure and subjective happiness does not trump your preference for being a philosopher, there is no objective rationale to support the claim that you would be better off if you quit.

It may be further objected, by fans of informed desire, that if you were to vividly confront the possibility of another life, you would prefer it and hence should change careers. But there are two cases. In the first, if you were presented with such a life as an option then you would prefer it, given your preferences as they are. Then that is reflected in your basic preferences that help constitute your individual good at a moment according to my view. In the second, what would make you prefer such a life is only some sort of preference-altering brainwash, and then it is irrelevant to your good,[35] though of course there is no barrier to undergoing such a brainwash if you prefer one and no one else is affected. Perhaps you *believe* such a brainwash would be good for you, but don't prefer it. Again there are two cases: In one, the brainwash would lead you from outside to inside of some relevant consensus congruence. Then my proposal delivers an analogue of truth for that belief.[36] But in the second case the brainwash would not lead you inside. Then your belief is false, and we should ignore it.

---

[33] Haybron (2009: 180).

[34] Similar points apply to Darwall (2002: 43–5).

[35] The first case is distinguished from the second because the basic preferences of the first are characterized by the counterfactuals noted in 7.1.

[36] It is a difficult case for me when you move from a more robust, narrow consensus congruence to a broader, less robust one, and the broader one isn't required by practical circumstances. There is a conflict of two truths about well-being. But, like Scanlon, I think there are different types of well-being applicable to different cases.

Perhaps the most famous objection to simple desire-based theories is that it is better to be Socrates dissatisfied than a pig satisfied, even if Socrates at some despairing moment wants to become a pig, or a clam under the sea. Such cases are cognitive analogues of apotemnophilia, and are hence friendly to objectivists. But notice that these cases also involve distribution over time within a life. At most few actual humans consistently prefer to be a clam, a pig, or even a sleek tiger, in the relevant sense that they would choose to be one if they believed that an option.[37] Before the moment of despair, Socrates has other preferences, though of course there is also the happy pig or clam after the transformation. And, on my view, such cases must generally be governed by relevant consensus congruence. We humans certainly do not have the general consensus required to say it would be better for a human to become a pig, nor would such a consensus be plausible across most individual human's lives. Paternalism is legitimate when it involves protection of your future selves from a deviant and transient desire for species transformation, just as it would be to prevent the similar manipulation of other humans. We will also see in 7.8 that there are not cross-species comparisons possible in such cases, that there is no consensus congruence across species that generates a fact about who it is better to be, so to speak from the point of view of the universe,[38] a somewhat dissatisfied human or a happy pig, and not merely who it is better to be from the perspective of human beings, who are generally attached to their own form. So there are no grounds that can properly legitimate a transformation of any human into a pig or tiger, except for a very singular circumstance: Perhaps some particular human has stable and weighty desires to become some sort of attractive animal, say a tiger, or even an ugly frog, and the weighty interests of others, for instance their children, are not in the balance. And perhaps in some wild technological future this won't be practically irrelevant. In that case, I think it is not intuitively clear that the transformation is inappropriate. I think that the same treatment applies to people who want a lobotomy in pursuit of greater individual happiness.[39] If you have wanted that all of your life, and can foresee with certainty that you won't care after the transformation and would have always preferred it even if you hadn't had it, and it doesn't interfere with the satisfaction of weightier preferences, and no one else cares sufficiently, then go ahead and knock yourself out. Reality lacks the metaphysics required to honestly say you are mistaken.[40]

---

[37] But Tom Carson reports that 10–15 percent of his students claim they would rather be happy tigers than unhappy humans.

[38] Sidgwick (1907: xvii and 382).   [39] Carson (2000: 81–2).

[40] One might object that, even if from the human perspective it is worse to be a pig, still if there is no objective fact that that is so, then it is morally appropriate to force this transition. If it isn't determinately worse to be a pig, what's the problem? Issues of what to do in the face of normative indeterminacy are difficult, but I think that in the face of indeterminacy of this sort action is forbidden by the proper consequentialism. I also think that there are deontic practices that constitute beneficent group acts that forbid forced species transformations and lobotomies and are supported on consequentialist grounds by MM. But we aren't yet in position to discuss these points. One might also object that I granted in Chapter 5

You will notice that while I have suggested that distribution within lives and over lives matters, I haven't sketched any proposal about proper distribution, though I have dropped some broad hints. The proper treatment of distribution is a job for Chapter 8. Right now we have another task left hanging, which is also relevant to the difficulties for simple desire-based accounts that we have been just discussing.

7.8 Animals, Babies, and Groups

Trying in humans involves the acceptance of reasons,[41] and the modal beliefs about options that help fix basic preferences are also a sophisticated human capacity. But sharks have desires that involve no accepted reasons or complex modal conceptions. In general, creatures with intensional mental states, which conceive things under certain of their features rather than others (perhaps only as yellow and to be eaten and as there rather than here), are capable of differences in motor activity because of differences in intensional perception and also motivation, and so seem capable of trying and wanting of the central and motivational sort. A shark might follow Lancelot around the pool trying to eat him, or it might be sufficiently satiated to leave him alone. And so a function from possible states of perception (and not possible conceptions of options) to sharkish trying not involving reason-acceptance might fix a shark's relevant preferences in a way that would also suffice to provide the shark with a good. Were the shark hungry, then Lancelot would be, for the shark, in the category of best eaten. And it isn't obvious that the modal conceptions involved in even human consideration of options always have a sophisticated form. Perhaps ordinary perceptual belief involves a conception of seen things that one might approach in various ways and would experience in various ways if only one cared to, a kind of presentation of latent alternative practical possibilities. And just conceivably all that is present in a shark's experience as well.

Still, as suggested by 7.7, my proposal does not generally allow cross-species comparisons of well-being. I do think that at least to the limited degree that a human can conceive what it would be to become sharkish, a pig, or a clam under the sea, there may be a basis of comparison relevant to the human's well-being. We can't in such a case rely on the judgment of someone who has experienced both states,[42] but, to vary Mill's suggestion, we can somewhat rely on someone who can to a degree imagine both. We can see that for the human it is best not to become a shark or a pig or a clam. But since the shark can make no such comparisons and has

---

that there are cognitive virtues, of the sorts sacrificed in these cases, which I don't know generally how to balance with the practical virtue commanded by MM. But in these specific cases I do know how to balance them.

[41] If there were consensus across humans about accepted reasons, that might constitute an alternative consensus about the normatively relevant good, but people have more agreement about what to do than about the reasons for it.

[42] Mill (1972: 8–10), also the source of Socrates and the satisfied pig.

relevantly different desires, I don't think there is an objective fact about how to weigh these kinds of animal lives, from the point of view of the universe. No consensus congruence exists in such case, because one necessary party to any consensus isn't up to the comparisons involved in even a rudimentary or approximate way. Perhaps all shark mental states are so different in content from human mental states, given internalism about mental content, that no cross-species consensus congruence is possible at all. But I think that there is a limited cross-species consensus relevant to some mundane goods, specifying that food is better than pain, other things equal, for humans and for sharks. Perhaps there is even consensus congruence that 2X pain is twice as bad as X pain.[43] But there is no way to fix the relative weight of the good of some more shrimp for a satiated human and a satiated shark by this mechanism. Still, perhaps some other primates, dolphins, and whales, are capable of symmetrical comparison and a large degree of suitable consensus with us.

There are related cases involving only humans. Like sharks, babies and the sufficiently decrepit may be able to try without meeting the conditions required for complex modal belief or accepting reasons.[44] So I think we can stretch my conception of a good to cover their cases. But perhaps comparisons of good in such cases also sometimes become impossible or limited, in a way not unlike the case of the shark. But we share sensory capacities with even infant and most decrepit humans that we do not share with sharks, which makes meaningful comparisons more frequent. And certainly baby pain is a relevant and comparable evil.[45]

There is also another set of complications involving humans. There are group agents. The basic human agents—the atoms of preference, desire, trying, action, and individual good—are not long-lived people but brief temporal segments of people. Preferences are what give a thing at least one sort of moral status, and preferences for a human can change over time, and so a long-lived person consists of a series of things with moral status, and indeed can constitute one kind of group agent, if their temporal parts cooperate in the right way on some shared goal. But there are also group agents that consist of intuitively distinct individuals. If agents matter to ethics and to social-political philosophy as I think they do, then all agents matter. But notice that, according to the particular mechanism in question in this chapter, it isn't exactly agents that matter, things that try, but rather things with preferences, with a good.

---

[43] But how should we compare amounts of pain between big and little species?

[44] We might consider what they would try to do if they did consider such options, as a suitable trustee for their interests. But that will involve highly indeterminate counterfactuals.

[45] Why is it wrong to painlessly kill a human baby who doesn't have the cognitive capacity to prefer life to death? Because of loss of future desire satisfaction, because the baby will otherwise become someone who prefers existence to non-existence, because continued life is a necessary condition for things the baby does care about (like pleasure), because of the strong consensus preferences of others, and because of beneficent deontic practices that are weighty group acts in which we participate, to which we will return. The third, fourth, and fifth factors do not apply to the different case of abortion. Even those inside a deontic practice that forbids abortion are not inside a practice that meets necessary consequential tests to constitute it as suitably beneficent.

And at least some group agents probably try without preferences and hence without a good. What an ordinary human agent prefers is fixed by what they would try to do if they thought themselves presented with various combinations of alternatives in action. Group agents consisting of intuitively distinct individuals try, but do they meet the other conditions required for preferences and a good? Group agents can be degenerately considered to have the simple binary preference for their action over its absence, at least when there is some sufficiently determinate shared conception by the members of the group of what option that trying engages, so that the preference has sufficiently determinate intensional content, which seems to characteristically turn on what shared reasons are accepted. But that particular single preference seems insufficient basis for any realistic comparison of well-being between that group agent and humans at least in most cases; it hence seems insufficient for an individual good of any significant sort. Still, it is possible that at least some group agents involving distinct individuals meet the richer conditions required for a good that might theoretically be compared with the goods of other agents. For such group agents it will make literal sense to say that there are things they would try to do as a group if they thought themselves presented with various combinations of alternatives in action,[46] and so the group agent has a good in the sense I have articulated. This is disconcerting, but it helps defuse the oddity that the only actual group agents which play a significant role in our lives are made up of more ordinary human agents, who have intuitive human interests. And I also think that it is very unlikely that the preferences of such group agents can generate any useful consensus with those of ordinary humans. It seems likely that for most group agents that consist of intuitively distinct individuals, there are not going to be facts about preferences that are sufficiently comparable to those of ordinary individuals for it to make sense to say that there are facts about how to balance the well-being of those group agents and of ordinary humans, or of different group agents. It is similar to a distant cross-species comparison case.[47]

It is clear that the good of a group agent that consists of a series of temporal slices of a single intuitive individual should not count beyond those of these momentary agents that make it up, or otherwise there will be double-counting of the goods of that person, and indeed there will be many forms of over-counting because such group agents often have others as subcomponents. So perhaps we should also discount the goods of group agents consisting of distinct individuals as also threatening a kind of double-counting, even if we can compare the well-being of such a group and humans.

---

[46] In one-off group action there is no distinction between the group agent and its particular project. The subject of action in such a case consists of all the individuals who participate in the action. But one-off group acts provide less opportunity for preferences.

[47] If there are many sub-personal agents in each of us, as Pierre Janet imagined, then similar incomparability might occur. And if dreamers try and consider options and hence have a good, it is not obvious that they have goods highly comparable with those of the waking.

But this is not to say that the satisfaction of group goods doesn't matter in an additional way when individual good is not at issue, and it isn't even to say that the interests of groups shouldn't be the first concern of, say, groups. The same sorts of things are true of sharks. But as an individual human at a certain point in my life, I invite you as another such human to focus first on the facts about the well-being of human individuals at times, and then build outwards to a consideration of the well-being of other entities on the basis of possible comparisons, but with no double-counting even of we humans.

There are many facts of comparison of well-being relevant to distributions among humans. And, other things equal, it is good for animals to be fed something, or even for a group agent with preferences to get what it wants. But there are no very determinate comparisons of their good with our own, no comparisons which allow their good to often trump our human interests, although animal pain and suffering matters in much the way our own does.[48] So much for the point of view of the universe.

---

[48] Most animals do not have an explicit conception of their own health, but may have preferences for components of a rudimentary kind of health. Also, continued life can be a necessary condition for things they care about, like pleasure. But on the other hand a desire to mate or to take care of one's extant young does not necessitate having offspring. Still, our common treatment of animals must be revised, since non-human animals have some interests, including the avoidance of pain, that we do share. Some revision will be implied later, but I won't focus on animals. I hope that it is not true that humans are such a planetary blight that even the deontic group acts that constitute our morality are harmful once animal interests are considered.

8

The Leximin Desire Principle

The second half of my overall normative proposal MM is a two-part mechanism for moving from facts about desire-based good—in particular the desire-based good of normal adult human agents from the perspective of moments of their lives—to overall ethical evaluations. The first part of this two-part mechanism involves a qualified though still fundamentally "maximin" principle for assessing distributions of the good within outcomes, which strongly prioritizes increased well-being for the worst off in a way that was suggested for some cases by John Rawls.[1] But it focuses on distribution within lives in a way suggested by Derek Parfit and Thomas Nagel.[2] This principle is the Leximin Desire Principle, or LDP. The second part of this mechanism applies such an assessment of outcomes through one variant of a new form of consequentialism called Multiple-Act Consequentialism, or MAC. I call the complex of these two parts "LEXIMAC."

This chapter develops LDP and my initial arguments for it. Chapter 9 does this for MAC. These arguments are based on DC2-BASIS, which you will recall from Chapter 4 is a cluster of constraints on the general subject-matter of ethics. But we will also consider natural objections.

I believe that these arguments are sufficient to show that both components of LEXIMAC are true. But because of the traditional methods of ethics recognized by the descriptive constraint DC3-METHODS, these arguments may not seem sufficient. Utilitarianism, contractarianism, and the golden rule tradition may suggest several competitors. So Chapter 10 will compare LEXIMAC with these views, and argue that the alleged competitors in fact converge, in our physical world, on LEXIMAC. The traditional methods of ethics are unified and rectified by LEXIMAC, and they flesh out the relatively abstract arguments of Chapters 8 and 9.

[1] Rawls (1971) favors maximin of income prospects of representative members of basic social groups, within other constraints of justice.
[2] Nagel (1979: 124–5 n16). Parfit (1984: 332–4 and 342–5); Parfit (1986: 837–43 and 869–72). Parfit (1984: 334–42) suggests giving less *weight* to issues of distribution, compensating for this increase in their *scope*.

8.1 Introduction

DC2-BASIS specifies that ethics concerns requirements on action that have to do with individual good, that it is a species of reason-giving requiring like evaluations where like reasons apply, and that it is impartial, so that ethical justification cannot appeal at the deepest level to reasons expressible only by indexicals, proper names, or rigged definite descriptions. Our goal is to build up from DC2, through the facts of desire-based good, to a normative theory that can underwrite the consensus of normative judgments recognized by DC1-NORMS. Our discussion will aim especially to deliver the aspect of quasi-normativity that allows the suitable termination of justificatory regresses, rather than internal reasons. But by Chapter 10 we will also possess the materials for a suitable elaboration of the internalist model that was sketched for the simple case of hedonic value in Chapter 5.

Ethics involves agents in two crucial roles, not only as subjects of governance but also as objects of concern. It is not merely relevant that the actions of agents are what ethics seeks to evaluate and govern. It is also relevant that some agents have a trying- and hence action-rooted good. My primary direct arguments for the two parts of LEXIMAC rest on like and impartial treatment of agents in each of these two crucial roles. Trying is the essence of moral *agency*, in the sense that there are agents if and only if there is trying.[3] But some agents, those with good or well-being of the preference-rooted (and hence trying-rooted) sort discerned in Chapter 7, are also moral *patients*, whose well-being can suffer or be served by action. These two features of agents are relevant in different ways to the discipline for preferences and actions that we now seek. Ethical evaluation involves like and impartial treatment. But there are two kinds of suitable likeness and two kinds of interests involved in ethical evaluation. Humans are not merely moral patients, who should receive one sort of impartial treatment that we will discuss in this chapter. They are also moral agents, whose various sorts of agency deserve impartial status of a sort we will discuss in Chapter 9.

These vague claims must be fleshed out to bear any argumentative weight. I will do so to a first degree in this and the following chapter, and I think it is sufficient. But in case you think it isn't, I will do so to a second degree in Chapter 10, through an exploration of the three traditional methods of ethics.

But it is also worth noting another abstract pattern of argument that unites this chapter and the next. I will argue in three cases that what might otherwise seem an intuitive middle ground between two extremes cannot be given a suitable rationale in our physical world. Reality lacks the necessary resources.

First case: We saw in Part I that the analytical basis of all sorts of human agency, including both intuitive group agents and particular individuals, are what I will call "atomic agents," lasting but a moment. We saw in Chapter 7 that the analytical basis

---

[3] Subject to Chapter 3's qualifications involving idling.

of all sorts of relevant human moral patience and well-being are also atomic agents, since the preferences of individuals often change with time, and basic preferences at a time are the root of well-being. In particular, the brief time that an atomic agent persists is the briefest period in which coherent basic preferences can be had, which seems to me about 2 seconds. It is from the good of individuals from the perspective of such brief periods in their lives that we must construct the value of overall outcomes.

These analytical points may seem a strange aspect of my proposal, but there is precedent. Parfit and Nagel have suggested that between the maximization of one's immediate individual interests and a very general maximization of value of the sort favored by utilitarians, traditional long-range individual prudence is an unstable middle ground that cannot be properly defended.[4] I agree. Arguments that might be thought to support this familiar middle-ground conception of rationality either push on to utilitarianism or back towards maximization of the goals of a moment. The traditional philosophical presumption of the default rationality of long-term individual prudence, the traditionally unquestioned rationality of the maximization of one's own well-being summed over one's life, is a mistake. If indexical differences expressed by "I" properly made a rational difference, so too would indexical differences expressed by "I *now*." My proposal, by its focus on temporally brief atomic agents as the basic locus of well-being and also by its focus on the good of all normal human atomic agents as the proper basis of the normatively relevant goodness of outcomes, has a structure similar to that suggested by Parfit and Nagel. I think that we are pushed by proper reason-giving out of a focus on our overall individual lives in one way back to the moment as the locus of individual well-being and in another way out to the interests of all humans as the proper goal of rational pursuit. You may object. Chapter 10 will explain in detail why I think that traditional individual prudence is not rationally or normatively fundamental, but you may also object that even impartial ethics must respect the boundaries between individual lives in a deeper and more fundamental way than LDP allows. You may think that entire individual lives are the proper principal focus of ethical concern. Still, we will see that in reality this familiar idea cannot be sustained.

A second argument in this chapter shares this abstract form. During our discussion of the way distribution of well-being is relevant to the goodness of outcomes, some will be tempted by an intuitive middle way between maximizing utilitarianism— concerned to maximize the sum of well-being in the world irrespective of its distribution—and the sort of radical prioritization of the well-being of the worst off that I take from Rawls. But that middle ground is also unstable. It cannot be properly defended given resources available in reality, except in a very limited way incorporated into qualifications present inside LDP despite its basically maximin form.

---

[4] Nagel (1970); Parfit (1984: 117–217); Broome (1991).

Third case: During our discussion of Multiple-Act Consequentialism in Chapter 9, some will be tempted to defend the central importance and integrity of individual action over time, beyond an individual's action in a moment and yet short of the central importance and integrity of all group actions that I favor, where group actions include not only continuing individual actions but many more besides. However, that temptation is also towards an unstable middle ground, which cannot be suitably justified in reality.

But all this is just abstract orientation. What will matter are the details.

8.2 The Leximin Core

The first part of LEXIMAC is a principle for ranking outcomes as relatively better or worse called "LDP," for Leximin Desire Principle. It is a significantly qualified version of a lexical maximin (or "leximin") principle. Leximin principles tell us to maximize the well-being of the worst-off (at least as long as they don't hence become better off than someone else), and then, in case of ties regarding the well-being of the worst-off, tell us to so maximize the well-being of the second worst-off, and so on. This section will present my basic argument for the leximin core of LDP. 8.3 will introduce necessary complications.

LDP is centrally focused not on distributions among long-lived individuals, but rather on distributions among atomic agents, among brief periods of individual lives. While this may be a surprising feature of my proposal, it is required by the fact that the basic moral patients are atomic agents, lasting but a moment. But please abstract away from your worries about this feature of LDP until 8.6, where it will be our central focus. Consider first how we should resolve conflicts of good or well-being, whatever the basic loci of distribution should be.

If there are only two alternatives, and the second is better for every moral patient, then there is no distributional conflict to resolve. But in the real world, there are many distributional conflicts. For instance, many pairs of alternatives are such that one is better for some but worse for others. Guinevere's interests and Arthur's interests in their guise as moral patients—their individual well-being or good— may conflict, so that Lancelot cannot satisfy both of them by choosing a single alternative.

Indeed, there are two types of conflicts. Sometimes Tristram and King Mark do not agree about the desirability of two states of the world that do not specifically include them. One wants fewer churches in the world and the other wants more. On the other hand, sometimes they each share a preference centered on himself and that is what generates the conflict. They both want to be Pope, or to possess a certain portrait.

Robust forms of individual good could help resolve distributional conflicts. The things that Guinevere wants might be more objectively important than those that Arthur wants. But we saw in Chapters 5 and 6 that there is no robust good in our physical world. There is nothing but a conflict of preferences, and also some rough facts of consensus among preferences. And so our problem is to balance various competing individual interests by deploying these minimal resources.

The first step to an answer is obvious, since we seek a normative evaluation of outcomes, of states of the world, governed by impartiality. Each relevant interest, everyone's individual well-being, has equal weight. Everyone involved is an agent with a preference-based good, and like should be treated as like, and impartially.

But even at this initial point, there is a complication. Recall from Chapter 7 that we have abandoned the point of view of the universe. We are working outwards from the interests of normal adult humans. We have qualified impartiality, because there are few determinate facts about the relative weight of the interests of non-human animals when compared to human interests that are delivered by consensus congruence. So LDP starts with the interests of normal adult humans, and then works outward to incorporate a concern with animal interests when they are relevantly comparable to our own. This cross-species comparability is sufficiently limited that we might as well forget about non-human animals initially, just as we are abstracting away from concern about my focus on atomic agents.

Perhaps you worry that nonetheless LDP isn't far enough away from the point of view of the universe. Perhaps you think that we should focus first on the idiosyncratic rankings of overall outcomes from the perspective of different individuals, who for instance cede the interests of their own children greater weight. But in a sense we are already doing that, since the basic preferences of atomic agents are the root of value, and are often centered on the self. Almost everyone prefers the flourishing of their own children. And the normatively fundamental evaluation of overall outcomes that involve many individuals requires an impartial and objective evaluation of outcomes, an evaluation from the perspective of all, and hence resting on a consensus congruence of preference that spans all. Still, it will sometimes be true that a richer consensus about the good is possible among all the *affected* normal adult human atomic agents in some choice situation, as characterized in Chapter 7, than is possible among *all* normal adult human atomic agents. And that is a fact we will eventually exploit.

We are going to deploy consensus to resolve conflict. How can there be at once a conflict and a consensus of preference? When for instance there are shared preferences focused on the self, and Mark and Tristram both want to be Pope.

Even if the first step to our goal is obvious, the second step is less obvious. What specifically does giving all interests, of all (affected) normal adult human (atomic) agents in their guise as moral patients, equal or impartial treatment require?

The impartiality required by DC2-BASIS forbids the relevance of certain factors. Two things might be qualitatively identical, might share all ordinary properties, and yet differ merely in an haecceity or some other brute principle of individuality, say a location or a constituting piece of prime matter, or merely in being referred to by a given token of a proper name or a particular use of an indexical term. But treating such qualitatively identical things differently at any fundamental normative level would violate impartiality. Perhaps there is some normative argument that shows we should all favor our own in certain cases, but that must be a conclusion and not a premise. Such brute individualities are irrelevant to the fundamental normative evaluation of outcomes that we now seek. What's more, treating differently two things whose qualitative differences are ethically irrelevant would also violate impartiality. King Mark can't properly resort simply to reiterating "Because of a swirly fingerprint pattern" (of which he just happens to have the only instance) as a proper grounds for preferential treatment in fundamental ethical assessments of overall outcomes. Nor can he even properly resort in such a fundamental assessment to the claim that for all of us as individuals an indexical claim like "Because it is me" should have significant weight. But still, what are the ethically relevant differences in assessing outcomes? DC2 focuses us specifically on the well-being of the affected individuals. And there is only one kind of basic well-being in physical reality: desire-based good. So we can see what the relevant differences are in ethically fundamental assessment of outcomes, if we attend both to the nature of ethics and to reality, which together focus us on the limited range of relevant considerations.

Consider a particular choice between two alternative outcomes involving desire-based good, Situation A in which two people, Lancelot and Arthur, will be quite relatively well-off for a period and one, Guinevere, will be relatively badly off, and Situation B in which all three will be moderately well-off for that period. Assume that all three are otherwise equally well-off in their lives as a whole, that the distributional conflict is in that sense local, so we can ignore worries about whether the central focus of distribution should be periods or lives. Assume also that no one else will be affected. Any real case like this will involve a complex background of institutions and standing obligations that require complex treatment, but assume finally that factors like that are absent. Perhaps Lance and Arthur can pursue bonding in a joint quest while leaving Guinevere to stew for a while. Call this simple choice between A and B "The Dilemma." The Dilemma is one sort of distributional conflict that we must resolve.

Which outcome is better? The answer to this question comes in two steps, one required by reality, and the other required by the proper response to that reality. Begin with the reality.

There is strictly limited comparability of the well-being of different moral patients. The preference-based good of different individuals, and indeed of the same individual at different times, is properly comparable only by methods introduced in Chapter 7. We look for patterns of consensus congruence among the goods of non-decrepit adult human atomic agents, goods themselves constituted by consensus congruence among individual basic preferences of a moment. In particular, we seek the richest consensus congruence that can be found among all those affected by the choice in question.

Such a preference-based formulation naturally suggests an ordering of alternative outcomes from worse to better, allowing for ties. But consensus congruence among all affected atomic agents will not characteristically reach as far as a complete ordering of all relevant alternatives, even allowing for ties and even if there are no distributional conflicts of the sort faced by Tristram and Mark in their pursuit of the papacy. For one thing, outcomes may involve many different types of ordinally comparable goods that can't be balanced. Still, it is realistic to think that we can frequently develop at least rough ordinal comparisons of different atomic agents' overall well-being, well-being from the perspective of moments, by the mechanism of consensus congruence. We can often say which are better off than which, though not any specific amount better off. This delivers sufficient comparative information, even in our physical world, to provide a very rough and partial ordering of different possible outcomes from the perspective at once of all the individuals affected by a choice. It delivers enough for the test case I presented to make realistic sense, and also, as we will shortly see, to be resolved.

The Dilemma is not unusual in this respect. There are many cases which exhibit the same relevant pattern of comparable well-being. For instance, it is realistic to presume that our three characters also share, other things equal, the following preference ordering for outcomes centered on themselves: A period of imprisonment, torture, and humiliation is not as good as a free but relatively impoverished period with ordinary failures and pains, and that is not as good as a period with enormous success on all commonsense axes. Indeed, I think that for most of us most of the time, consensus rooted in basic preferences delivers that particular ordering of outcomes centered on ourselves, which because they are centered on ourselves can generate a distributional conflict.

It might be claimed that one of our chivalrous characters has more intense desires than the other two, so that a period of torture would be worse for that one than for the others. But after Chapters 6 and 7, we are skeptical about the reality and normative relevance of desire strengths. When all that is shared by people is a preferential ordering of outcomes, then the only type of interpersonal comparison possible specifies, for instance, that the worst of the outcomes is in the relevant sense equally worst for all. This is not a merely epistemic point, but a metaphysical one. There is nothing in reality to make it true that the worst option is worse for one of our three than for another. So it isn't. And impartiality implies in that condition that it is equally bad for all. Any proper differential treatment in such a case would require a legitimating reason, and no such reason exists.

Of course, complications are possible. Perhaps Lance prefers anything to all three of his options and Arthur prefers nothing to any of them. But when preferences are not shared they are irrelevant to interpersonal comparisons. Perhaps Arthur is more sensitive than Lance, so that his subjective feelings of well-being would be more heavily damaged by imprisonment or boredom, and subjective feelings of that sort matter to all three of our characters, or perhaps there are richer patterns of consensus that allow us to make further and finer comparisons. Still, while we are coming back to such complicating factors, such additional structure is not always available. Such complications are not generally present in such cases. At least in these respects, The Dilemma is a common and realistic situation.

While our Dilemma requires facts of consensus congruence specifying ordinal interpersonal and intrapersonal comparisons of overall well-being among normal adult human atomic agents, ordinal comparisons of that sort are often available in reality. We characteristically prefer, other things equal, to be at the races rather than on the rack, and to be rich rather than poor. And even when other things aren't equal, it is only in unusual cases that some strong preference about the future or what happens to others that may result from time on the rack or at the races or from poverty or wealth will reverse the normal ordering of these phenomena in our preferences, and even then not always in a way that will constitute a consensus congruence relevant to distributions of the sort now at issue. We all know the details all too well. Pain and suffering, injury and sickness, starvation and poverty, misery and frustration, death of children, loss of mates, loneliness, hopelessness, boredom, humiliation, fear, and real terror are worse than relatively colorless human situations, at least when they are fruitless. Mix a little more of those into somebody's life, holding all else equal, and it is worse from their perspective, indeed from any of their perspectives at different times,[5] and would be from the perspective of any normal adult human. And often that type of limited ordinality is all that is available in reality to underwrite necessary interpersonal comparisons. This does not mean of course that there will not be genuine indeterminacies about, for instance, who is worse off in some situation. But we have more consensus on these matters than we sometimes admit, since some actual disputes about who is worse off rest on lies and self-deception that do not infect preference-based good.

As I said, our test case does make sense in reality. Still, there are some comparisons required by familiar normative principles that consensus congruence among all non-decrepit adult human atomic agents, or even just those affected by most choices, will not deliver. In particular, the summable individual well-being deployed by traditional utilitarianism, *cardinal* value which allows the assessment of outcomes by regard to totals or averages of well-being of all the individuals in an outcome, does not *generally* exist in our world. The preference-based theory of the good developed in Chapter 7, in conjunction with our actual limited consensus of preference, assures this. There likely are some cases where all the preferences relevant to some distribution are so closely shared and have the right form to allow for cardinal comparisons, but the common case is not like that. In very many cases, consensus congruence cannot plausibly deliver well-being that can be added and subtracted, well-being with that level of detailed comparability across persons, or even across moments of lives. It

---

[5] But 8.6 and 8.7 discuss relevant complications.

is true that we can properly avail ourselves of any richer consensus available among all those affected by a choice. Particular individuals occasionally exhibit, for instance, the sorts of coherent preferences over risks that would deliver cardinal comparisons of individual good for them. But that is not the ordinary case.

But we need to notice not only the general case but also the important qualifications to this general skepticism. There are sometimes robust shared patterns of preference across a limited number of atomic agents, who either constitute a single life or parts of many lives, that do allow more robust sorts of comparison of their well-being than merely ordinal ones, so that it even makes at least rough sense sometimes to add and subtract amounts of their well-being, to make cardinal comparisons of their well-being. Perhaps the preferences of some limited group of people reflect cardinally measurable objective features of the world or of subjective well-being, or there are cardinally comparable times that some individuals would spend to achieve particular goods,[6] and those factors are relevant to how all those people balance tradeoffs in goods. Or perhaps there are sometimes shared preferences across various combinations of risks that meet the conditions explored in decision theory as grounds for making cardinal comparisons of goods within individual lives.[7] Sometimes factors like these, when added to the ordinal interpersonal comparisons already in play, constitute what Griffin calls "pockets of cardinality" relevant to evaluating outcomes, and we will need to return to the complexities that that qualification will introduce. But we have not the least reason to hope that there is consensus congruence among the preferences of all adult non-decrepit human atomic agents, or even most small groups of them, that will deliver cardinality by these or any other mechanisms in any reasonably wide range of cases. In general, by and large, cardinality is not available in the real world. So it will be most useful to presume that it does not govern our test case.

That is the reality we face. But we need now to determine what it implies. Consider The Dilemma again. Utilitarians propose that we add up the individual good in the two alternative outcomes and assess those wholes by reference to the sum of the good they contain. But it is very unlikely that consensus congruence can deliver in most distributional conflicts the rich arithmetical structure that requires. It seldom makes genuine sense to say that something is twice as good for Arthur as for Guinevere. It doesn't make sense in The Dilemma. We need another interpretation of equal and impartial concern for the interests of all, which can be used when only ordinal comparisons of well-being are available.

Let me jump to the punch-line. In The Dilemma, I think that the better overall outcome, from the fundamental impartial perspective of ethics, is that in which all three of our courtly characters are moderately well-off. It does not constitute equal or impartial concern to let Guinevere fall by the board. It would be better if Arthur and

---

[6] Griffin (1986: 75–124 and 98–102).   [7] Broome (1991).

Lancelot stayed at home. In the other concrete case I mentioned, a world where all three face a relatively impoverished but free period is better than a world where Guinevere is tortured and humiliated in prison while the other two do quite well.

To put it squarely, what is required is a leximin principle. There are qualifications necessary, but that is the basic core structure of LDP. If the issue is to choose among states of affairs that consist of many agents with conflicting goods, then we should maximize the individual well-being of the worst-off, as determined by consensus congruence, at least as long as they don't hence become better off than someone else involved. To be precise, we should focus on the worst-off atomic agent and hence the well-being of individuals from the perspective of moments, though we are holding that complication largely in abeyance until 8.6. In the case of indifference in the eyes of the worst-off, we should move on to a maximization of the well-being of the second worst-off, and so on, so we get a leximin rule for ordering outcomes. To put it still more exactly, the particular identity of the individuals in question doesn't matter:[8] Each state of affairs is properly characterized (modulo considerable inde-terminacy) by an ordinal value profile, that specifies for each atomic agent a certain level of ordinally comparable value. States of affairs with the same profile are equal in value, no matter what particular people are involved. And a lexical maximin rule properly orders states of affairs with different value profiles. To be yet more exact, we will need to consider how to order outcomes which involve different numbers of atomic agents. But I will suppress that complexity until 8.8.

This is the kind of impartial and properly equal treatment of moral patients that can generally be rooted in realistic consensus congruence. Still, consensus congru-ence will not always deliver even all the ordinal information this requires. There will be indeterminacies regarding the value profiles that characterize some states of affairs. But there will generally be enough determinacy of the sort now in question to make sense of commonsense ethical claims, in ways we will soon explore. There doesn't need to be a single determinately worst-off moral patient for a leximin principle to have practical application. It may still be a fact that some group of patients are all determinately worse off than those in another practically relevant group. And it is a *lexical* maximin principle that is in question.

So here's where we are: In our physical world, claims about the summation of well-being seldom if ever make sense. But facts about ordinal comparisons of levels of overall well-being do so often enough for lexical maximin to provide normative guidance and a kind of equal and impartial treatment that we can reasonably hope could support a plausible ethics and social-political philosophy.

But I have only discussed one sort of case, and ordinal information about well-being might conceivably be deployed in other ways than in leximin. However, there is work on the implications of interpersonal comparisons of merely ordinal levels of

---

[8] See Parfit (1984: 351–79 and 490–3).

preference satisfaction that supports a general leximin rule.[9] Consider Amartya Sen's summary of one key result:

Consider four utility levels a, b, c, d in decreasing order of magnitude. One can argue that in an obvious sense, the pair of extreme points (a,d) displays greater inequality than the pair of intermediate points (b,c). Note that this is a purely *ordinal* comparison based on ranking only, and the exact magnitudes of a, b, c, and d make no difference to the comparison in question. If one were *solely* concerned with equality, then it could be argued the (b,c) is superior—or at least non-inferior—to (a,d). This requirement may be seen as a strong version of preferring equality of utility distributions, and may be called 'utility equality preference.' It is possible to combine this with an axiom due to Patrick Suppes which captures the notion of *dominance* of one utility distribution over another, in the sense of each element of one distribution being at least as large as the corresponding element in the other distribution. In the two-person case this requires that state x must be regarded as at least as good as y, *either* if each person in state x has at least as much utility as himself in state y, *or* if each person in state x has at least as much utility as the *other* person in state y. If, in addition, at least one of them has strictly more, then of course x could be declared to be strictly better (and not merely at least as good). If this Suppes principle and the 'utility equality preference' are combined, then we are pushed in the direction of leximin. Indeed, leximin can be fully derived from these two principles by requiring that the approach must provide a complete ordering of all possible states no matter what the interpersonally comparable individual utilities happen to be (called 'unrestricted domain'), and that the ranking of any two states must depend on utility information concerning *those* states only (called 'independence').[10]

Unrestricted domain is required by the range of normative problems whose resolution depends on our ordering of outcomes. Independence and Suppes' dominance principle are required because the only sources of value in our physical world are the preferences of atomic agents; the orderings of outcomes properly depend on the preferences of those agents. And utility equality preference is required by impartiality. Perhaps the last point requires explaining. Utility equality preference specifies that in a case in which $a > b > c > d$, that (b,c) is better than (a,d). But remember that we are presuming only ordinal comparisons of well-being. And that means that any case of this sort must be treated as any other case of this sort. It can't be that c is relevantly close to d and a far above b in some relevant way, because there are (at least in general) no facts of that sort. And so the only sort of equality possible seems to be one in which we move towards the center and towards greater equality instead of towards the two extremes and more inequality.[11]

The general absence in reality of more than ordinal comparability of well-being is a very significant fact. Many principles for ordering outcomes are forbidden by obvious principles of coherence plus mere ordinality.[12] Still, there might seem a problem with

---

[9] Sen (1986: 1115–18).   [10] Sen (1980: 207–8).

[11] On direct maximin, see Mendola (2006: 187–270); van Roojen (2008).

[12] Majoritarian procedures can introduce intransitivity, with A better than B which is better than C which is better than A. So appeal to numbers of better and worse purely ordinal differences for individuals between outcomes cannot provide a coherent ordering of outcomes.

this form of argument, because there is one other principle for ordering outcomes plausibly consistent with ordinality. This alternative principle might seem to involve a kind of impartial treatment of likes that doesn't involve the kind of substantive equality that I have presumed. Consistent with ordinality, we could maximize the well-being of the best off, as some neo-Nietzschean might suggest.[13]

But while this ideal may have some attraction and rationale in the case of objectivist goods, when levels of highest achievement may be especially important, no one has seriously proposed such a principle for desire-based good. And in reality we lack normatively relevant intensities of desires that might conceivably underwrite the deep significance of the satisfaction for only one person of some shared but high-end preference. And there seems to be far less congruence in our preferences at the far high end than at the low end, so that there aren't likely to be facts about comparable well-being at the very high end that could legitimate redistributions upwards. Some want to be like Goethe or Napoleon in a world of Goethes and Napoleons. Some want to be the only Goethe or Napoleon in a world of weak fools. Others merely want to live in a world where academic administrators don't fancy themselves Goethe or Napoleon. So the Nietzschean mechanism is probably unworkable in reality. And the proper understanding of DC2 forbids this interpretation of impartiality anyway. You can easily imagine Nietzsche himself making that very charge as the basis of a complaint against our commonsense morality of the weak. There is no other principle than lexical maximin that depends solely on realistic ordinal comparisons of desire-based good and involves intuitively equal and hence suitably impartial treatment.

8.3 Cardinal Complications

That completes my basic argument for the leximin core of LDP. But both this core and my argument for it are subject to objections. And some require modifications and qualifications of LDP.

One natural worry is that even though lexical maximin is to be favored over standard maximizing utilitarianism in our physical world, because amounts of well-being cannot be generally added in the way that standard utilitarianism requires, still other alternatives may be even better. For one thing, there might be some realistic structure intermediate between cardinality and ordinality that can deliver something more intuitive. Maybe we can sometimes compare the size of increments to well-being. Perhaps in some cases it makes sense to say that someone prefers A to B more than they prefer C to D, and not because they prefer A to C to D to B. For instance,

---

[13] Hurka (1993: 75–9) floats this for objectivist well-being involving achievement. Perhaps if compositional achievement is an objective good, resources should be transferred to Bach. And see Hurka (1993: 79–82) on single-peak perfection.

perhaps they would risk more to move from B to A than from D to C, or the move from B to A would make a more dramatic difference to their feelings of happiness.

But remember that normatively relevant comparisons of the well-being of different individuals in our world require consensus congruence. And there is little reason to believe that such preferences among risks or effects on happiness are generally shared, congruent among enough atomic agents to deliver facts about the comparison of most humans' preferences that will generally fix sizes of increments to desire-based well-being, beyond those our rough ordinal ranking already delivers. We'd all risk more to preserve our limbs than our finger nails, but we all prefer options in which we keep limbs to those in which we keep our finger nails anyway. We all like to be happier, but different things make us happy and in different ways. Perhaps someone would smile or sigh a lot more if they moved from B to A than from D to C, but people do not smile or sigh with equal facility or under the same conditions. We considered other differences that may be relevant to intuitive desire strengths in Chapters 6 and 7, but they are normatively irrelevant, and even if they weren't, there's no particular reason to think they would allow us to refine the consensus congruence of all adult humans. So there seems to be no richer structure of comparison generally available in reality.

Still, it is plausible that there are the limited pockets of cardinality I mentioned earlier. This is most likely within the life of a single agent, given the greater likelihood of the preservation of a robust psychological basis of desire across at least parts of an individual life, and so perhaps there are cases in which such comparisons are normatively relevant to paternalistic action in which only one person is affected or to individual action that affects only oneself. Probably there are also sometimes sufficient grounds for such cardinal comparisons among some limited number of distinct individuals who are the only individuals affected by a choice, or who include the only individuals for whom some outcome is not at least as good as some relevant alternative.[14] Or perhaps cardinal comparisons in highly limited kinds of cases, say involving only particular kinds of goods, for instance subjective well-being, make sense even across large numbers of individuals. Perhaps there are also some cases where there are limited pockets of ordinal comparisons of *differences* in well-being available but without full cardinality. These real possibilities require qualifications to the basic leximin form of LDP.

The first qualification is required when cardinal comparisons of well-being are available. It specifies in the traditional way that an outcome with the greater sum of cardinal well-being is better, at least when all else is equal in respect to merely ordinal well-being and each outcome includes the same affected atomic agents. When the only (atomic) individuals for whom outcome A is ordinally worse than or indifferent

---

[14] Interpersonal comparability of cardinal utilities might be partly rooted in the interpersonal comparability of ordinal value previously discussed. Impartiality implies that we should not introduce interpersonal differences in cardinal utilities when there is no positive reason to.

to B have a good that is cardinally comparable to that of all other such individuals and (as the next clause of this sentence requires) at least one further individual, and when outcome A has a greater sum of that cardinally comparable good than B, then A is better than B.[15] It seems to me that the legitimacy of that manner of ordering these outcomes is forced by the nature of the cardinal value in question. Addable value can sum.[16] On the other hand, if the value in a local pocket of cardinality might be increased at cost to the merely ordinally comparable well-being of someone outside the pocket, then ordinal value, all that is properly available to govern the widest distribution in question, must be dominant. The cardinal value should not be maximized in that case. This emendation has an awkward and complicated sound, but that is because some of the orderings required by cardinal comparisons are already implied by the basic leximin form of LDP, and because of the dominance of more widely comparable ordinal value.

There might be other sorts of pockets of cardinality or something close to it, which require a closely analogous second emendation of LDP. The contribution of certain particular types of goods to well-being might be generally close to cardinally comparable for all. All the facts that go to make up desire strength discussed in Chapters 6, including normatively relevant preferences over risks and effects on subjective well-being, might pull in the same direction even across a general consensus congruence of actual normal human atomic agents when we are concerned merely with the distributions of certain specific goods or evils. For instance, it might make sense to say in this way of four levels of physical pain, with pain A worse than B worse than C worse than D, that A is much worse than B while C is only slightly worse than D, for all of us.[17] It might even make sense in some cases to say that A is at least approximately twice as bad as B, even according to a consensus spanning all normal adult humans at all times. This is also grounds for a qualification of LDP, which I won't attempt to formulate in any exact and general way. But in a case where cardinality is available in one of these ways, and all else is equal, LDP specifies that distributions of such particular cardinally comparable goods and evils among all individuals, regardless of their general level of well-being, are properly governed by that cardinality, in other words that the sum of cardinally comparable value should be maximized. This emendation may be important for instance when individuals' overall well-being is not even ordinally comparable.

I also think that there may be considerably less than cardinal but more than merely ordinal comparisons possible across enough cases so that additional qualifications to LDP are required. There might be consensus congruence that delivers some relative

---

[15] More precisely, what matters is not the identity of the individuals but their relative location in a value profile, as suggested earlier.

[16] Differences between total and average utilitarianism are not relevant here, because the numbers of atomic individuals are fixed.

[17] Cummiskey (2009).

sizes of increments or differences in well-being, but nothing approximating cardinality. I think it might even be fairly commonly the case that, if there are two atomic agents involved, with agent A worse off than B, and we are presented with the choice of a second outcome in which A is intuitively very slightly worse off and B is intuitively hugely better off, that the second outcome may not be worse overall in any way rooted in the proper comparison of their desire-based well-being, and is even perhaps better. At the very least, I think, the first is often not determinately better. And if we are confronted with another choice in which there are millions (of atomic agents) involved, and in which one outcome is intuitively slightly worse for the single worst-off (atomic) individual, but intuitively hugely better for all the others, then I think that that first outcome may even generally be determinately better in similar ways. Some refinement of these rough generalizations should be incorporated into LDP for cases in which there is relevant value structure that allows more than ordinal level comparisons but much less than cardinal comparisons across all the relevantly affected human atomic agents. But I believe that reality does not often provide us with analogous comparisons sufficient to favor an outcome in which a single worse off atomic agent is intuitively significantly much worse off but millions are each intuitively a little better off. That would require something approximating determinate cardinality that cannot realistically be rooted in consensus congruence over any plausibly wide range of cases. The difference is that in the first two cases deviations from ordinality can be justified by appeal to comparisons that do not involve the dominance of the sum of huge numbers of tiny benefits for many people over one large individual loss. Reality also does not generally provide us with an adequate basis of comparison to resolve many complex tradeoffs, for instance between a first baseline outcome A and a second outcome B in which many will lose and many will gain relative to A in significant ways, except by appeal to a structure no richer than ordinal comparisons between levels of well-being, and hence to leximin.

A final emendation to LDP, due in essence to Sidgwick,[18] may be appropriate for a very limited range of cases, in which there are two outcomes that are otherwise equal, but each involves a pocket of cardinality that delivers the same sum of well-being while yet one of the outcomes involves a more equal distribution of that value. In that case, a more egalitarian distribution, in particular priority for the worse off, is in the spirit of leximin, and involves more equal and hence impartial treatment of moral patients. Still, there are cases in which the intuitive equality of a situation is not primarily a matter of how well the worse off fare,[19] so this is another place where greater development of my roughly specified LDP is probably required.

We have seen that, while LDP has a basically leximin form, that form must be significantly qualified in any complete articulation of the principle. Fortunately, we

---

[18] Sidgwick (1907: 416–17).   [19] Temkin (1993: 19–90).

won't need to work out all of the details for our purposes in what follows. But in certain limited cases, LDP is equivalent to traditional maximizing utilitarianism. This means that LDP specifies one sort of intermediate point between the mere cardinal summation of traditional utilitarianism and the full ordinality of unmodified leximin, which is required by the kind of desire-based value that exists in reality. But there are also other kinds of intermediate proposals that we should consider as intuitive competitors and grounds for objection.

8.4 Egalitarian Middle Ground

Many ethicists are attracted to some intuitive middle ground, between the distribution-insensitive evaluation of outcomes by regards to sums of well-being favored by traditional utilitarianism, and the extreme distributional sensitivity to the fate of the worst-off characteristic of maximin. Reality-based qualifications to the leximin core of LDP provide one middle ground. But other forms are more popular. Still, we will see in this section that these more familiar forms of middle ground are not available in reality.

There are different ways in which equality, and hence impartiality, is conceived in different moral theories. Thomas Nagel distinguishes three forms of equality of persons in normative theory.[20] In "utilitarian conceptions" founded on the maximization of the satisfaction of interests, each person's interests are granted the same weight. In "rights-based conceptions" each person has an equal claim not to be interfered with in certain ways, but aggregation of interests plays no role. In "egalitarian conceptions," which like utilitarian conceptions focus on outcomes but like rights-based conceptions do not aggregate, the urgency of individual interests is of central concern. One way in which rights-based conceptions are reflected in my overall theory MM involves its treatment of deontic duties, which we aren't yet in position to consider, and a basic distributional right is reflected in LDP. But focus on the other two conceptions of equality, requiring the maximization of the satisfaction of interests and priority for urgent interests. They are reconciled in one way in LDP, on the basis of the kind of individual good that there is in reality. But there are other attempts to reconcile egalitarianism with maximization, alternative middle ground positions between leximin and utilitarian maximization, that should be considered.

Strictly egalitarian evaluations of outcomes face what is called the Leveling Down Objection,[21] because they favor an outcome in which the now relatively well off are made equally badly off with the rest. Here is Parfit's vivid version:

Suppose that, in some natural disaster, those who are better off lose all their extra resources, and become as badly off as everyone else. Since this change would remove the inequality, it

---

[20] Nagel (1979: 111–18).
[21] Parfit (1997: 211); Raz (1986: Chapter 9); Temkin (1993: 247–8).

must be in one way welcome, on [such a view]. Though this disaster would be worse for some people, and better for no one, it must be, in one way, a change for the better. Similarly, it would be in one way an improvement if we destroyed the eyes of the sighted, not to benefit the blind, but only to make the sighted blind. These implications can be…regarded as monstrous, or absurd.[22]

Such a strictly egalitarian view is in severe conflict with any concern to maximize the satisfaction of interests. It violates that type of Nagelian equality.

But various authors prefer instead what Parfit calls The Priority View,[23] which holds that benefiting people matters more the worse off they are. This is a way to provide some respect for egalitarian concerns, but evade the Leveling Down Objection. There are many different versions of The Priority View, and LDP is indeed one of them. But other versions may suggest preferable ways to rectify a concern with maximization and distributional equality.

There is a distinction between versions of The Priority View which rate the moral significance of a benefit on an absolute scale, so that fixed levels of lesser well-being receive a fixed distributional priority, and those which rate the moral significance of a benefit on a relative scale, so that no matter how absolutely well off the worse off are, their being relatively worse off demands some distributional priority. In the first case, for instance, it may be that only the satisfaction of certain primary needs should receive distributional priority.[24] Another distinction between forms of The Priority View involves the nature of the priority that is given to distributions to the worse off. For instance, perhaps the size of an aggregate benefit to well-off others and also the numbers of well-off others benefited may outweigh some alternative distribution that favors the badly off.[25] And some specific rate of prioritization for the badly off must be determined. These various complexities provide an opportunity to develop orderings of outcomes that may seem more intuitive than what LDP requires.

But the big problem from our perspective with these alternatives to LDP is that if legitimate they must be supported by argument rooted in the abstract considerations specified by DC2-BASIS. There must be grounds in the world for their truth; they must be provided with that sort of asymmetric rationale, independent of the consensus of normative judgment reflected in DC1-NORMS which they support. And in our physical world it is not possible to legitimate in that way any particular form of The Priority View that differs from LDP. The various complications and qualifications, the particular balance of maximization and egalitarianism, required by LDP, in which the relatively badly off receive a kind of priority no matter what their absolute level of ordinal well-being, but cardinal value is maximized wherever it exists, is required by the kind of value that there is in our world. But alternative versions of The Priority View, though potentially more intuitive in form, have no

---

[22] Parfit (1997: 210–11).   [23] Parfit (1997: 213).

[24] Crisp (2003). However, Crisp contrasts this with The Priority View and calls it a sufficiency principle.

[25] Nagel (1991: 66–74); McKerlie (1984). But see Temkin (1993: 245–82) and Crisp (2003: 747–8).

similar reality-based rationale. We cannot in the necessary asymmetric way legit-imate any particular alternative discount rate for the well-being of the better off, any particular alternative way to trade off numbers of benefits to the better off for fewer to the worse off, or any particular target level of absolute well-being at which distribution to the worse off should cease to receive priority.[26] There aren't the necessary normative facts in reality to specify these things. Proponents of such views characteristically appeal to a reflective equilibrium of moral intuition, but we are requiring a more robust and asymmetrical form of legitimation.

There is also a second problem with most familiar alternative formulations of The Priority View. They are not specified sufficiently exactly so that we can understand their implications. This masks their lack of a suitably specific rationale.

Still, this second problem is not universal. For instance, Paul Weirich has made one quite specific proposal about a way to temper utility rooted in the satisfaction of desire with equality that differs from LDP, and which it is instructive to consider. His

> basic idea... is that for a small, fixed value of r, the moral value of granting a person changes he desires to degree r depends on his present degree of desire for his present situation. In other words, the moral value of a small, fixed utility gain depends on the initial utility level. The higher the initial utility level, the lower the moral value of the gain.... It is further proposed that the moral value of a small, fixed utility gain is inversely proportional to the initial utility level. Accordingly, a gain to someone twice as well off has ½ the moral value.[27]

We should applaud Weirich's specificity. But after our previous discussions we are generally skeptical about the existence of such degrees of desire. And in any case the main problem for such proposals is finding some way to asymmetrically vindicate such a very particular tradeoff between gains and initial distributions of utility, and Weirich's specificity makes the problem manifest. Why inversely proportional in particular? Another key problem is that Weirich's proposal involves proportions of utility levels and gains, in other words cardinal comparisons. Though these are generally unavailable in our physical world, whenever cardinal utility is available, then it seems to press on towards the maximization of utility. If good can be added, then the good of an outcome seems to be the total good in the outcome, at least when the same numbers of individuals are involved in all relevant outcomes.

We are insisting on an asymmetric legitimation of ethical principles based in DC-2 and the world. It isn't appropriate for moral theories to rest merely on air. And points between leximin and traditional maximizing utilitarianism seem incapable of such a

---

[26] Section 8.8 considers whether it is better for some atomic agent not to exist. However, that cutoff would not underwrite any intuitive form of The Priority View that differs from LDP, but only requires that we make people slightly better off than dead. Crisp suggests that the compassion of an ideal observer might fix the point at which priority for the needs of the worse off can properly cease, but unless compassion is specified in a suitably non-arbitrary way this cannot deliver a specific point. He also appeals to intuition to support such details without specifying a further rationale, while we are insisting on a rationale.

[27] Weirich (1983: 431). He intends this principle as only one component of the true moral principle.

rationale. That is, except for LDP. We are stuck with a basically leximin principle qualified for cases where there are pockets of cardinality or other robust comparisons of value underwritten by consensus congruence.

8.5 Objections

There are standard intuitive objections to the direct use of leximin principles to assess outcomes in the way that the core of LDP requires. I am doubtful that such intuitions reflect any general consensus of judgment, and hence doubt that they matter very much. I doubt that common sense has very well-considered views about the details of how to assess the relative value of outcomes when tradeoffs of well-being are in question. And in the absence of a general account of outcome assessment coherently systematizing commonsense intuitions about all cases, we have little reason to believe that intuitions about a limited set of cases have much significance, since they may be in tension with intuitive treatments of other cases. And even a coherent and systematic intuitive account could easily lack a sufficient reality-based rationale. But I will be concessive, and consider these intuitive objections anyway. Whatever their probity, such conflicts of "intuition" with LDP are more apparent than real.

One standard complaint is that leximin favors a tiny benefit to the worst-off individual over an enormous total benefit distributed among everyone else in the world, which seems intuitively wrong. But, I reply, LDP is qualified for the case when such cardinal value, which can be summed into a total, is available; so LDP does not have this implication. Whenever cardinal value is available, LDP functions much like traditional utilitarianism.

However, another way to put a similar complaint can avoid the need to postulate cardinal value, and also tugs at our egalitarian intuitions, and so is perhaps a more telling objection.[28] Perhaps the world has one worst-off individual, many fairly badly off individuals, and many well off individuals, and there are two possible situations to choose between: Situation A is the status quo. But in Situation B the worst-off individual will be made slightly worse off but the many fairly badly off individuals will be made much better off, indeed as well off as the well-off group. This degree of value comparability doesn't require cardinality. And Situation B may seem intuitively better overall, while LDP may seem to specify that Situation A is better.

But, I reply, LDP does not in fact have this apparently unintuitive implication either. We saw earlier that there is another qualification built into LDP for cases when consensus congruence delivers relative sizes of increments or differences in well-being of this sort, that specifies that B is better than A.

A somewhat analogous case for which LDP does *not* have a handy qualification available is a case in which even approximately cardinal value does not exist but in

---

[28] Temkin (1993: 103–5).

which, compared to the status quo Situation A, Situation B would *dramatically* worsen the situation of the single worst-off individual but generate some intuitively tiny benefit for each of many other relatively well-off individuals. LDP favors A. I doubt that many of us have any strong intuition that such a case provides considerable objection to LDP. Still, perhaps someone does, so let me say something more about it.

Someone may claim that it would be a better world if some already badly off individual ended up working, through ruthless price competition interacting with local poverty, in a yet more frightfully horrific sweatshop than they already do, so as to absolutely minimize the price of some electronic geegaw in a way that would make millions of already well-off individuals slightly happier. Perhaps while there is nothing to underwrite legitimate cardinal comparisons in such a case, still the tiny benefit to each of millions may seem to trump more horror for only one badly off individual. But most of the friends of intuition who would field such an objection to LDP would also intuit that it is wrong to torture somebody even a little bit to bring about extra well-being for the better off. In other words, they would intuit that while Situation B is better, we shouldn't act directly to move the world from situations that are like A in regard to individual well-being, to situations like B, which would be highly immoral.[29] It is important to stare at these two intuitions at once. I think we should worry whether this is a pair of intuitions that can be given a suitable rationale. I also think that if we look carefully at such cases we can see which intuition should survive the confrontation.

There are many issues between deontological ethicists and consequentialists that we have yet to consider, and will consider in Part III. But remember that the effect of adopting consequentialism is usually to extend our sense of responsibility, not to limit it. Consequentialists characteristically think that we are equally responsible for all the consequences of our actions or inactions, not that we are equally irresponsible for the results of our action and inaction. Failing to save a starving person is about as bad as killing them yourself according to the most characteristic forms of consequentialism; it is not that killing someone is as morally trivial as some deontologists think that letting them starve by your inaction would be. It is the overall effects that count morally, whether they are due to action or inaction, according to the most characteristic forms of consequentialism. Now focus again on the current objection to LDP. If we are properly confident in our intuition that it is wrong to bring situation B about by intentional action, then the *consequentialist* should conclude that we shouldn't be confident that B is better. In fact, the consequentialist should conclude that A is better. That is what I conclude, since MM is a form of consequentialism. And notice that the cases for which LDP is already qualified do not engage the same sorts of intuitions, at least not so dramatically.[30]

---

[29] Temkin (1993: 104–5, especially n15 and n20).

[30] Perhaps it seems that pain and pleasure generate cardinally comparable value, and hence that one of our qualifications to the leximin basis of LDP allows for a case like this. But it is unlikely that the pain of a

The intuitions that tend against leximin in scenarios like the sweatshop case are intuitions that depend on our sense that we are not responsible for the outcomes in question. But that is just the sort of situation in which we can avoid a serious consideration of their real relative goodness. In actual fact, we are in the most central sense responsible for all the (non-flukey) outcomes of our actions and inactions, and so any intuitions that seem to cut against leximin in such cases are corrupted by a false sense of what is and is not our responsibility, by a false sense that the value of outcomes is not directly relevant to what we should do.[31] We understand our real valuation of such outcomes when we'd be obviously responsible for what happens, for instance if we ourselves had to torture someone who was already badly off so as to deliver slightly more well-being for millions of the better off.

Still, my use here of a torture case is subject to reasonable objection. We probably don't like to be tortured even more than we don't like suffering the equivalent horror in a sweatshop. Our reaction to being tortured is partly moralized, partly a reflection of the extreme moral disrespect shown to us when we are tortured. Someone performing the same sort of activity on us in a medical procedure, even a futile medical procedure that is yet well-intentioned, may not seem nearly as bad a thing to happen to us. And while moralized desires like all others should play into a determination of our well-being, it may be that our sense that some forms of torture are much worse than other similar procedures is often a reflection of a moral judgment, that they are strongly worse only in the sense that they cross a moral line, not because of the actual suffering involved. And so perhaps this means that I cheated when I compared the case of torture to a case where someone is squeezed more in a sweatshop. Indeed, as our discussion of Multiple-Act Consequentialism will eventually reveal, I certainly cheated some by using such case. Even the form of consequentialism I favor implies that performing a torture is morally worse than letting something comparable happen, though not quite in the way that deontologists characteristically presume. But I cheated no more than familiar formulations of the Leveling Down Objection, which is foundational in the literature on these topics, and I cheated merely to nudge our commonsense out of its tendency to overlook features of outcomes for which it feels diminished responsibility. And now I hope you have a similar intuition about a more sedate and less distorting case, in which you in the guise of a remote and detached bureaucrat deciding on some regulation must choose between a situation in which the worst off person will be, although indirectly and unintentionally, even further screwed for a generally tiny benefit distributed to each of the already well off, and another in which the better off remain as they complacently are. Unlike Ivan Karamazov's questionable God building the general happiness of the world on the suffering of a small child, I trust that you will hesitate. That

---

torture is exactly cardinally comparable to pleasure, so as to allow many tiny increases in pleasure to trump such a huge pain for an individual. In any case, another element of LEXIMAC forbids torture.

[31] Mendola (2006: 249–60) provides more discussion of Temkin's objections.

hesitation reveals, I believe, your deepest and most revealing intuition about which outcome is really better.

There are other natural objections to LDP. Sen's argument and LDP screen out facts that may seem relevant to assessing the probity of distributions. Independence requires that outcomes be assessed without reference to desert. And Suppes' dominance principle, applied directly to atomic agents, requires assessments without regard to which continuing individuals enjoy a certain historical level of well-being. LDP also has these features. But it may seem that certain individuals deserve more over time by fruit of their greater efforts. And it may seem that the well-being of the vicious should be discounted when determining the overall value of an outcome.

We will return to worries about desert at length in Chapters 10, 11, and 12. I will attempt to provide a suitably intuitive overall treatment of desert, and yet in various ways debunk its deep foundational significance in our physical world. So much of my reply to this objection comes later. But for now I can note that in its most intuitive forms, a focus on desert involves desert accrued over time. Lancelot now deserves honor because of his past accomplishments. And because the basic loci of distributional concern of LDP are atomic agents, not continuing individuals, facts about desert over time are not straightforwardly applicable to such a locus. The atomic agents who did the famous deeds of Lancelot are now, in his doddering age, long gone. This is not to deny that one person did the deeds and lives on now; it is merely to remind us that the primary distributional locus of LDP is short periods of lives and not lives.

But this may simply invite a more pressing objection. It is that people and not moments of people's lives should receive our primary distributional concern. Before we go any further, I need to address this central worry about LDP, a worry focused on its second central feature.

8.6 Moments or Lives?

The primary reason for LDP's distributional focus on atomic agents is that the only sort of good that we have discerned in physical reality is the preference-based good of Chapter 7. Since preferences of individuals can change over time, so too can their preference-based good. And basic preferences are had at times. So good accrues to us so to speak at moments, from the perspective of moments. By a moment I mean the briefest period in which coherent preferences can be had, about two seconds.

But it is very important to remember that someone's good from the perspective of this moment includes the satisfaction of their current desires focused on the future, including their own future. It doesn't merely include things that happen now.

Consider the implications of this conception a little before returning to pressing objections.[32] There can be conflicts involving the good of a single individual at

---

[32] See also Nagel (1979: 124–5 n16); Parfit (1984: 332–4 and 342–5); Parfit (1986: 837–43 and 869–72).

different times, seen from the perspective of those different times. And in reality these aren't always spanned by a very detailed sort of individual good that might help properly resolve the conflicts in some standard ways, say by the summation of cardinal value. Consensus congruence even within a life is limited. Many of the things individuals care about, say the success of their careers or their children, they care about over long periods, and it is important to notice that these occasion no distributional conflicts of the sort in question here. But there can be distributional conflicts within a life that involve more temporally localized goods—pains and pleasures, labors and enjoyments—as preferences wax and wane or the present moves on. And LDP implies that when cardinal or intermediate sorts of comparable value are not available, leximin governs these distributional conflicts. Other things equal, we must maximize the well-being of the life from the perspective of its worse-off brief period. Another important implication of this locus of distribution is that it isn't the intuitively worst-off *person* that must receive the strongest sort of distributional priority according to LDP, but the worst-off affected moment of any person's life. This puts a special premium on the avoidance of severe pain and suffering. Still, the qualifications to the basic leximin form of LDP required by the more robust comparability of some sorts of well-being also qualify these implications in important ways.

When considering this conception, it is important always to remember that we care about things outside of the moment, and that the satisfaction of those preferences may be very important to well-being from the perspective of our current selves as assessed by LDP. But still, on this conception, Lancelot's future states do not have any very deep and basic normative significance for him, different from the states of other people. They have a preference-based good comparable to his immediate well-being, like the goods of other humans. He shouldn't ignore their interests, since they are other moral patients. In fact, he has no more basic moral right to ignore his future interests than those of other people. He also cares about them deeply, as people care about their children, and this means that what happens to them is directly relevant to his current well-being, his well-being from the perspective of this moment. And there are also institutionally sanctioned compensations that span his current behavior and his later states, that engage his current motivation and are relevant to his well-being figured from the perspective of this moment. He will certainly sacrifice some of his more immediate interests to win that tournament tomorrow, and even now he is happy to do so. But it isn't really possible in any normatively deep way to make up for the good he lacks from the perspective of this moment in some future moment of his life, at least any more than Arthur's current sufferings can be compensated by treating his well-beloved children very well after his death.

These implications of LDP may seem quite objectionable. It may be insisted that Lancelot is exactly the same person tomorrow as today, so that bad things that happen to him today can be compensated tomorrow in a special and normatively fundamental way that can't be accomplished by compensating his future children.

My reply to this objection does not involve denying that there are facts about the identity over time of persons. And indeed a part of that reply requires that we care about our identity over time. But I do insist that only some understandings of personal identity over time are plausibly consistent with physicalism, and that they qualify the significance of these intuitions about compensation. Reality lacks the robust metaphysical resources required to legitimate some types of basic distributional focus on lives rather than moments. Perhaps if what is called an "endurantist" conception of personal identity over time were true, so that literally the same identical entity with hence the very same intrinsic properties, strangely lithe and also bent, hirsute and also bald, with shining teeth and toothless, spans Lancelot's life, then compensation within a life would have very fundamental significance. Identity over time would be literal identity. But such a conception of personal identity over time is highly implausible. If Lancelot is sitting that is not consistent with his standing, and yet he stood yesterday. So we should conclude that he has temporal parts, one today which stands and another yesterday that sat. Each has preferences and hence a good, which can conflict. It is implausible to think that those properties of sitting and standing, or any fundamental relation of predication that links them with Lancelot, are fundamentally relativized to times, so that one literally identical thing sitting and standing involves no contradiction;[33] no one but a philosopher has ever dreamed of such an unnatural conception. And in any case such an endurantist conception is not consistent with physicalism, since the particles that make up Lancelot in youth don't persist in constituting him across his entire life.[34] And indeed natural physical properties aren't in their deep metaphysical nature indexed to times or instantiated in a time-relative way such as a coherent endurantism requires; when a particle retains a stable charge, it doesn't exchange natural properties, or relations with that charge, simply because it has that charge at more than one moment.[35]

Lancelot has temporal parts; there is Lancelot today and Lancelot tomorrow, which differ in properties and so are not literally identical. But Lancelot of course persists over time, whatever the correct conception of so-called personal "identity" over time. His temporal parts are parts of one life. I am not relying on Parfit's arguments that personal identity of that sort shouldn't matter to us, that personal identity over time only matters to us because of metaphysical errors.[36] I'm not telling people what they ought to care about, beyond the ways morality demands, and I think many of us do care about our identity over time in a way that would survive exposure of our metaphysical errors. I am just insisting that identity over time does

---

[33] D. Lewis (1986: 202–4).

[34] A plausible physicalism is inconsistent with presentism—the view that only the present is real—because Special Relativity implies there is no absolute simultaneity, and hence no absolute present.

[35] But see Myro (1986); Johnston (1987); D. Lewis (2002).

[36] Parfit (1984: 199–347); Parfit (1986: 837–43).

not automatically allow the kind of fundamental compensation that literal identity itself would allow.

And a second point of reply is more important: The realistic value that might accrue to even an implausibly endurantist Lancelot must accrue to him at moments, and is of a nature that allows in the basic case merely ordinal comparisons, properly governed not be summation but by leximin. We generally *cannot* make up to Lancelot tomorrow with an extra bit of happiness to compensate for torturing him today, simply because of the nature of the value in question, even if he is in reality an unchanging endurantist being, just as we cannot make up to him with some sensual pleasure on his right side for a little torture on his left.

Still, it is true that there are sometimes pockets of cardinality within a life, perhaps because someone has unusually coherent and stable preferences over risks.[37] But that is not the normal case. And of course when such conditions obtain, then LDP is suitably qualified also. LDP allows for compensations involving cardinal value within one individual's life, since it also allows such compensations across different lives, just like utilitarianism.

Despite what I've said, it may seem that distributional compensation within a life is still possible in deep ways it is not possible across different lives. In particular, it may seem that we care about things in ways that provide our lives with a kind of narrative unity that determines the proper relative weight of our well-being in different parts of those lives. Maybe Arthur deeply prefers a life that is always getting better, and maybe that should be relevant to determining his overall individual good in a way relevant to assessing outcomes. But remember that the future satisfaction of Arthur's current desires for his own future counts on my proposal towards his current well-being, his well-being from the perspective of this moment. Any actual preferences we have for narrative trajectories of this sort do matter on my proposal. When they are strong and stable over time they have considerable significance. But note also that many real people lack such preferences, or grant them little weight, and that at different times a given individual may have conflicting preferences for the narrative trajectory of their life. So such notions cannot be granted a very fundamental role in determining the overall value of outcomes.

While there is a consequentially justified practice of compensation to which we will return in Chapter 12 that suitably underwrites many of our intuitions about desert and compensation within lives,[38] a fundamental normative principle like LDP that governs the distribution of well-being in outcomes must have an asymmetric rationale in the nature or locus of the well-being that exists. And there are no grounds in our physical world that can legitimate any very basic status for good figured over a

---

[37] While pleasures may provide pockets of cardinality, no pocket bridges the pleasure/pain divide.
[38] Parfit (1986: 871) calls this "quasi-compensation."

life. Perhaps certain forms of objectivism about the good could legitimate a basic focus on an individual life as a whole, but robust objectivism is unworkable in reality. And Lancelot cannot properly insist that it is more ethically appropriate in any very fundamental sense for him to favor some future interest because it is his. Normative evaluation is founded on impartial reasons, so any special appeal by Lancelot to his irreducible individuality or to normatively irrelevant features that happen to pick out him alone, in discussions of overall and fundamental valuations of outcomes, would change the subject away from ethics. Still, of course, the preferences that define Lancelot's good at a moment are his own. Since we care greatly about our continuing lives, any desire-based consequentialist moral theory like MM will cede them significant non-fundamental normative significance. And it is really because we care about our lives in this way, a weighty fact according to LDP, that they seem intuitively to have such deep normative significance to us.

So here we are: Despite the fact that there will undoubtedly sometimes be indeterminacies regarding which of two lives is best for some individual, LDP does in many cases deliver a relative evaluation of two states of a single individual's life when considered in isolation that is reasonably intuitive, especially because the good of an atomic agent from the perspective of a moment includes things that happen at other times. And that is the only relative evaluation that can be suitably legitimated in reality, that can meet the strictures of DC2-BASIS. There is no robust metaphysics that provides further guidance about the relevance of whole lives to the evaluation of overall outcomes. And while what LDP implies may sometimes conflict with an individual's own preferred narrative trajectory for their own life, that is largely because real people conflict with themselves over time about such narratives anyway, or don't care about them very much. It is conceivable that the commonsense notion of a better individual life frays under these difficult conditions. And we will return to the possibility of its virulent indeterminacy in Chapter 10. But I do not rest my reply here on that extreme possibility.

There are also further positive considerations that support my treatment of these issues. For one thing, distribution of well-being within a life intuitively matters, even by general consensus, in a way that is sometimes overlooked by philosophers. It doesn't make much sense to pile up all the well-being of a life in a single period; it rather makes more intuitive sense to be sure that each period meets at least some minimum. Athletes may want to live fast and so achieve their greatest. But while someone may always want goods like success or objective achievements piled into one period of their life, in the most intuitively pressing form of such a case desire-based good is temporally stable. Such an athlete always wants that young success at whatever earlier and later costs. So there is no relevant cross-temporal conflict. But if a former athlete, after a brief period of achievement that permanently ruins her health, is miserable and regretful, that counts against the intuitive probity of that temporal distribution.

THE LEXIMIN DESIRE PRINCIPLE   245

Distribution within a life matters, and it is hard to deliver this distribution in reality without an appeal to leximin within lives.[39] We certainly can't generally appeal to individual preferences for a certain shape of life, say ever upwards towards greater satisfactions, to vindicate a concern with temporally complicated distributions within a life, because, as I've said, such preferences are not characteristically stable over the length of our lives, because they are not characteristically strong enough to plausibly trump other desires, because many of us don't have them, and because even when they are strong and stable they constitute a significant good that accrues from the perspective of each moment in life. If distribution matters within a life even intuitively, and we have no realistic mechanism to deliver it other than by appeal to leximin within lives, there is less grounds to object on grounds of intuition to my focus on atomic agents as the basic locus of distribution than would otherwise be the case. Instead it is the relatively standard philosopher's claim that within lives it is only totals of well-being that rationally matter that more notably fails to fit the relevant intuitions, as well as requiring conditions of value comparability that don't generally make realistic sense. I think that the current tendency to focus principally on lives is also a bit of an idiosyncratic characteristic of contemporary philosophers; a focus rather on bits of lives engages many other elements of common sense. We aren't often picking between features of whole lives. Mostly we are just faced vividly with our immediate concerns. And when we distribute medical aid in emergencies, we don't stop to ask how well off people have been over their lives, but rather what their situation is now. We don't even consider such factors when we think about how people should be taxed this year for the benefit of the worse off.[40]

Perhaps you object that we should be more focused on our lives than in the moment. But remember that desire-based good does not involve just what we want for our own sakes, let alone whatever it is we might be said to want for our sake as an atomic agent, even when there are facts about such highly indeterminate things. It isn't that those who are currently stubbing their toes or suffering in the dentist chair are the relevantly worst-off atomic agents. Our desires and so our desire-based goods spread out into the larger world. Real people would much rather stub a toe or go to the dentist right now than to have their future lives collapse in a significant way. Our special concerns about our immediate trivial injuries are only dominant when all else is equal. And of course serious injuries are a concern because they will persist. People

---

[39] One complication is that leximining within lives and then over lives would yield different comparisons in some cases than direct leximining across all moments of all lives. Consider two lives with three moments each, A = (4, 8, 9) and B = (1, 11, 12), where the numbers are ordinal. Now consider the transformation to A = (4, 7, 9) and B = (1, 12, 12). Do we make the transformation because B, with the worse life, will be better off? Or do we avoid the transformation because the worse moment affected is made worse? LDP avoids it.

[40] Perhaps we always consider the context of people's lives implicitly in such cases, but I see no reason to believe so.

characteristically care more in the present about what happens to them in their future lives then what happens to them in the moment.

But this may in turn suggest another set of problems for LDP's focus on moments of lives. It may seem that our desires wax and wane with great rapidity, so that while in the dentist chair we have considerably different desires than when on the way to the dentist or on our way home again. But while this may be true of our conscious desires, it is much less true of our preferences in my sense, which are rooted in dispositional facts about what we would try to do if we believed ourselves presented with various options. And of course our real concern here is consensus congruence among relevant individual preferences, not individual peculiarities of preference of atomic agents.

Despite all I've said, LDP's focus on moments of lives may still seem problematic. So perhaps it will be helpful to consider a concrete case: Gwen's life is pretty bad but not awful throughout. Lance's is middling throughout. Art's is fantastic on the whole, but has a brief period that is worse than any period in Gwen's life. It involves imprisonment and a little torture. This situation requires more than ordinal comparisons, but less than cardinal comparisons, and is probably realistic. Now imagine that we have a choice between (A) leaving well enough alone and (B) making Lance's life as bad throughout as Gwen's while improving that bad moment of Art's life just a trifle. That too seems realistic short of cardinality. And LDP may seem, by its focus on priority for the worse off moment of a life, to require (B), which seems wrong.

But I reply in three ways: First, we do intuitively cede some ethical priority to mollifying certain sorts of immediate suffering even in the lives of the very well off. Second, this case may involve injury to Lance in a way that introduces distorting complexities that we won't be in position to treat properly until MAC is in play. Third and most important, even the pattern of realistic non-cardinal value comparisons involved in the example invokes the qualifications of the leximin form of LDP for cases in which there are less than fully cardinal but more than merely ordinal comparisons of well-being available. It involves the first qualification I introduced for that sort of case in 8.3, and it also involve the second and more significant such qualification as well, since millions of moments of Lance's life are affected.

You may still worry that leximin within a life is an implausible view, since it implies, when all else is equal, that one should seek to make the worst moments of one's own life slightly better to the cost, even, of all the better moments of one's life. So consider another concrete case: Adolescent training for important tournaments may be grueling and horrible and a low point in Lancelot's life. But he should certainly not give up his championships simply for a slightly better period of training.

There are two parts of my reply. First, as I've said before, when conditions of comparability beyond simple ordinality are available, as is suggested here, LDP is qualified in relevant ways. For instance, when cardinal comparability is available, LDP tells us, other things equal, to maximize sums of well-being within our life. Second, as I've also implied before, characteristic forms of hedonism and objectivism do not interact with leximin within a life in the same way as my desire-based proposal, and that may create confusion here. The desire-based value that accrues from the perspective of a current moment of life includes the satisfaction of present desires by the future. If adolescent Lancelot wants very much to train in a grueling way at some cost to his current pleasure, and only his own life is involved, and that training eventually achieves its goal, LDP implies that even from the perspective of that adolescent moment his well-being is better served by training.

But perhaps my proposal may not seem to give preferences about one's future life enough weight. Lance always wants someday to ask Gwen out, but each day prefers to do it tomorrow. Each of his atomic agents gets what it most wants at the moment, but not in the long run, and neither does he. But, I reply, this example is an artifact of the realistic choice situations involving such outcomes, and desire-based good rests on a wider set of preferences. If he really much prefers in the long run to ask her out, at each moment he would choose a life in which he asks Gwen out sometime later if that were provided to him as an option, say in which he become less burdened by weakness of will over the interim, and that is relevant to his good in my sense. If he wouldn't make that choice even when he believed he had that option, then he doesn't prefer asking Gwen out as much as he believes he does, in part because basic preferences do not rest on fancy distinctions between conditions that make the will weak and that constitute high-toned valuing. And my second reply is that distribution is also relevant in such cases, and tomorrow he may be very sorry that he wasn't bolder today. Consensus congruence is in play.

8.7 Time

What is relevant to an evaluation of outcomes is consensus congruence among all atomic agents (in the first place all normal adult human atomic agents) affected by a choice, as characterized in Chapter 7. Do all atomic agents whose interests are affected count, be they future, present, or past? Yes, I think, and have already implied, though there are some limits to the relevance of past and future agents. Let me explain this point, which interacts with issues about lives in ways we need to consider.

Long ago past agents seldom had deep enough or determinate enough preferences about the future to much constrain any current choice. And while it is true that real people do have some concerns about their descendants and the future success of particular projects, still these are unlikely to constitute a suitably restrictive consensus congruence when other people are involved. Our prudish religious ancestors might have been horrified by our lives, but we don't agree. However, it is likely that there is a much stronger consensus among a given individual's past preferences governing their own future life.

It is relevant to any consensus including future agents that it may depend on what alternative is taken from among some set of options which future agents will exist. Not all possible future agents have normative status, merely those possible agents which would exist if some real alternative were actualized have such status, indeed which would exist without flukes, that are incorporated in the *ex ante* objective probabilities that specify alternatives. In other words, only possible future agents that are enclosed within the real alternatives in question in a choice have normative status relevant to consensus congruence. There will undoubtedly be some indeterminacy about the future agents contained in our current options, because of the indeterminacies of Part I, even though relevant options ignore flukes. There will certainly be indeterminacy about what their preferences will be. Still, it won't often be details of these future agents' preferences that matter anyway, but rather their consensus congruence with us. Perhaps we might have reason to believe that in the future there will be a general change in preferences that will at least on some of our options affect relevant consensus congruence, and perhaps there might be *ex ante* objective probabilities about that relevant to our current options, so it is practically relevant. But human history and even contemporary life span a huge range of conditions, so it is hard to see what sorts of conditions in the future might cause an otherwise broad consensus congruence to fail.

There are possible worries about this temporally neutral way of treating atomic agents. Dennis McKerlie is a pioneer of the thought that the basic distributional locus should be not entire lives but portions of lives. As he says,

We seem to be troubled by extremely deep inequality between the temporal parts of different lives even if the inequality is reversed at other times so that people's lifetimes turn out to be equal. In a different example, suppose we must choose between helping someone who is very badly off and someone who used to be miserable but is now happy. Because of past suffering, the second person might have a worse lifetime. Nevertheless, I think that we would feel a pull towards helping the person who is experiencing misery now, even if that person could be helped less.[41]

I agree. But McKerlie distinguishes between three ways in which we might compare the well-being of certain periods with other periods: by comparing a particular person's condition at a time to the condition of every other person at every particular time their lives (which is what LDP does), by comparing simultaneous periods of different lives, or by comparing comparable periods, say youth or old age, of different lives.[42] He rejects the first proposal, which LDP adopts, on the ground that "it would object to inequality between non-corresponding and non-simultaneous parts of different lives, and this objection has no intuitive support."[43] But, I reply, we have a rationale for such a view that does not depend on this kind of intuitive support. Past, present, and future agents all have a desire-based good.

---

[41] McKerlie (2001: 275), omitting a paragraph break.
[42] McKerlie (2001: 276). See also McKerlie (1989) and Temkin (1993: 232–44). But note that by a priority view McKerlie means a view that cedes priority to absolute levels of well-being of the worse off. The relative assessment of well-being of LDP makes it analogous to what he calls "equality views."
[43] McKerlie (2001: 277).

Still, there is a type of intuitive case that may motivate McKerlie's rejection of the first proposal, and which we should consider: Perhaps atomic agents near the end of a life are very badly off relative to other atomic agents, and hence would receive too much distributional concern from LDP.

But, I reply, there are two sorts of cases of the right dramatic sort. In the first case, it is only towards the end of life that people become specially worried about dying immediately, specially concerned to prolong life at whatever cost. But then this would not be part of a relevant consensus congruence, and so would not be directly relevant to determining proper distributions.[44] Many of the very same individuals earlier in life would not want to distribute resources in such a way as to give their own late preferences significant weight, nor would the current preferences of many others in relatively early life cede those late preferences significant weight. In the second case, we are all always very concerned about not dying tomorrow, at almost whatever cost to the future, though we aren't often conscious of that. But then it seems that proper normative evaluation should respect that consensus, even though it involves one kind of discrimination against the young. I think that the real preferences of real people, who often have many interests that they prefer to some more life, are more complex than the cartoonish suggestions now in play. But I also think that there may be consensus congruence supporting *some* sacrifice of other interests to live on a while longer even in age, in a way that is distributionally significant. Real people in fairly wealthy societies do seem to prefer some redistribution of social resources towards expensive medical care that allows for the noticeable extension of at least enjoyable life, though qualified by widespread desires to die at home and not be resuscitated under various conditions. There are complications: These preferences may be more widespread in the U.S. than in the Netherlands, and sometimes such preferences may rest on cognitive errors. But I see no strong reason to presume some deep normative error here. There is no robust normative fact to be wrong about. I am not in the business of giving paternalistic advice about the propriety of such preferences, though I do insist that the preferences of the poor should go into the distributional hopper along with them.

Perhaps the worry though is something else, that when we know we will die tomorrow, then we become very badly off in my sense, so that the satisfaction of deathbed preferences would hence become too normatively important according to LDP. Perhaps your dying grandparent could then properly tell you who to marry, or what to do with your life. But notice that it is at most not very common that there is a consensus congruence among the preferences of all affected normal human adult atomic agents specifying that it is, other things equal, better to be forced to marry who you don't want to marry while you are young than to be at the end of a full and

---

[44] There may be mitigated and indirect relevance through effects on consensus goals of happiness or satisfaction.

happily successful life.[45] There isn't sufficient consensus for LDP to generally favor the satisfaction of such deathbed preferences.

There are other troublesome cases involving time. Consider Parfit's case in which you wake up in the hospital not knowing whether you will have a short painful operation tomorrow or had a long painful operation yesterday.[46] It intuitively seems appropriate to have different attitudes towards your suffering when it is tomorrow or yesterday, though that conflicts with our contrary intuition that good matters equally whenever it occurs. What does LDP say about such a case? If the preferences of atomic agents generally incorporate some sort of time preference for the distribution of personal pain that constitutes a consensus congruence, which is not unlikely, still it will be true that many atomic agents constituting different periods of your life are relevant to any distributional decision involving pain in your life, and there is a distributional conflict in this case. There is no reason to expect that your current preferences for a long operation yesterday will generally trump your preferences yesterday for a shorter one further in the future.[47]

While consensus congruence is helpful in screening out the normative significance of some of the oddities that a focus on atomic agents might otherwise introduce, other worries about LDP remain. LDP was motivated by appeal to a situation in which only the same agents were involved in a comparison and in which the same agent is relevantly worse off (or at least as badly off as anyone else) in both options. But LDP is much more general. A state of affairs is characterized by its ordinal value profile, with occasional pockets of cardinality. The individual identity of atomic agents, whatever that might be taken to mean, is not relevant to the value of a whole in any way beyond its relevance to specifying that value profile. So this is a further sense in which individuality is granted scant respect by my proposal.

But, I reply, this feature is shared by traditional utilitarianism, and is in fact required by the impartial normative evaluation we seek given the kind of simple preference-based value that is found in our world. This feature implies, for instance, that a future that consists of entirely different individuals with very good lives would be better than a world in which our own shabby lives continue, and so it might be thought morally abhorrent and a recipe for mass murder under certain circumstances. But if so then that would be an implication it shared with traditional utilitarianism.[48] And the proper way for consequentialism to reply to such an objection will be our concern when we explore the implications of the next element of LEXIMAC: Multiple-Act Consequentialism. This is a promissory note about murder, to which we will return.

---

[45] Similar things are true of other badly off potential LDP dictators, say those in pain.

[46] Parfit (1984: 165).

[47] But if our worries about deathbeds were realistic, and if periods of lives immediately preceding or during not just dying but suffering have special distributional significance by consensus congruence, then your preferences just before or during each operation would be important.

[48] Henson (1971) objects that average utilitarianism requires killing all those below average utility.

8.8 Population

Other objections to LDP involve population issues. Since infinite collections can be in one-to-one correspondence with parts of themselves, an ordinal comparison of infinite populations can be highly paradoxical. And since LDP focuses on atomic agents, and I've been loosely calling them moments of lives, it may seem that each real life involves an infinite number of atomic agents.

But, I reply, atomic agents are the briefest period of a life in which coherent basic preferences can be had, which implies that the relevant moments have finite length, about 2 seconds. Though there is some analytical arbitrariness involved in where exactly we fix the barriers of such finite "moments," there will not be infinities of atomic agents involved in each finite life. And there is no infinity of different humans at any moment. We might optimistically hope there will be an infinite number of people out into the future of the world, but realistic *ex ante* objective probabilities that govern our alternatives won't specify an infinity of differences between future possible people. So LDP can ignore issues introduced by infinity.

But a second objection in this vicinity is that LDP is under-characterized. How do we compare outcomes in which there are different numbers of atomic agents? My reply to this objection requires a refinement:

Presume that we are dealing with outcomes that involve only ordinally comparable value. Each of two outcomes is characterized by an ordinal value profile, specifying the ordinally comparable good of each of the atomic agents it includes. Consider first two outcomes with the same size populations. We can serially order the value profile representing each outcome from worst to best off atomic agent, allowing for ties. And then we can compare the two in this way: Compare the worst-off atomic agent of each, the first represented in each of our serially ordered value profiles. If one of the two is better off, it is part of the better outcome, and we're done. If both are equally well off, move on to a comparison of the second worst-off in each. And so on.

Now consider two outcomes with different size populations. To perform the same sort of pair-wise comparison between the value profiles that represent these outcomes, we need some sort of null level of value that can stand in for the absence of an atomic agent in the profile that represents the smaller population. We then can add into the value profile that represents the smaller outcome as many null levels as it has fewer atomic agents, so pair-wise comparison is possible.

But what's the null level? It might be that an atomic agent is better off existing than not existing, or would be better off not existing than existing. Although we'll need to talk more about what it means, it seems then that there might be a null point in between, at which it is indifferent whether the atomic agent exists or doesn't exist. That is the null level we need to represent the absence of an atomic agent in a smaller population. And if we are dealing with a case in which there is a consensus congruence among all the affected that determines such a null point, our problem is solved. When all else is equal, to add an atomic agent which is above this level makes the world better, and to add one below this level makes the world worse. To add or subtract one at this level makes no difference. And that is the result that will be rendered by a leximin principle applied to two value profiles that have been swelled into pair-wise comparability by use of the null level of value.[49] We don't even need to adjust LDP, since we can now apply it by deploying the null level to cases where populations differ.

Of course, all else is seldom equal. When we are considering real options, sometimes adding an atomic agent to a population will make other atomic agents worse or better off. Generally speaking, LDP applied to such cases will favor increasing the population by addition of atomic agents who are better off existing as long as already existing atomic agents that are worse off than the null level are not made thereby still worse off.

Of course this mechanism depends on there being a null level of value, resting on consensus congruence among the affected determining when it is better for atomic agents to exist or not to exist. But notice that the relevant comparison to the existence of an atomic agent is not death for the whole individual in question but rather just the absence of that particular moment from a life or the world. Arthur might be better off as an individual, according to a consensus congruence that governs his entire adult life, if some of the moments of his life were edited out of it not to be replaced, even though he wouldn't be better off dying than suffering through those moments. The absence of an atomic agent is not the absence of the whole person from all of history. We don't need to hope for a consensus about whether to suffer something is worse than dying; simply about whether it is better to have a moment of life of that sort rather than to have a momentarily shorter life. And note that we aren't here considering possibly indeterminate counterfactuals about the causal effects of the absence of some moment of one's life on reality. We are rather considering just the satisfaction of preference-based good which that moment delivers, as an object or source of preferences.

But as an object of whose preferences? We hope for a consensus of preference involving all the affected, by which I mean that from the perspective of all of them it would be better (or worse) to undergo such a moment than to lack it. But perhaps to undergo the moment in question would be good from the perspective of some affected people and bad from the perspective of the individual in question. In that case there is no sufficiently robust interpersonal fact, and it would hence seem most reasonable to leave it up to the individual whose life is in question, so that the preferences of others become irrelevant. As in the case of comparisons of the well-being of humans and other animals, when comparability is lacking we must retreat from the point of view of the universe. There can also be conflicts of this sort over time within an individual. But then, for similar reasons, it would seem that the value

---

[49]   For more on leximin see Mendola (2006: 187–225).

of a moment from the perspective of that moment itself is what should be dominant. There is another important complexity. Perhaps the ordinal value of a moment of life will depend on how many other moments we have left. But then any relevant consensus congruence will incorporate those context effects.

Here's where we are so far in understanding the implications of LDP for varying population cases: Other things equal, if there is a relevant consensus congruence that constitutes it as better to be the worst off atomic agent in some more populous option then for such an agent not to exist, then the more populous alternative is better. That is one basic drift of LDP on population issues. But these conditions don't always obtain. This is partly because of the point we recently discussed about editing Arthur's life. And it is partly because of effects on other atomic agents of increasing population sizes. Too populous a world can be worse for all of us at each actual moment in our lives than a less populous world would be. So there is contrary population pressure, whereby LDP suggests that populations of atomic agents should shrink until all of the moments of all of our lives are worth having.

This suggests another objection. One might worry that LDP implies that a world with any atomic agents in it is worse than nothing, since there is almost certain to be some agent who would prefer even the destruction of the world to what they actually suffer. Perhaps they are facing torture, and have no children or projects that they care about sufficiently to trump their self-focused concern about suffering. Or perhaps under torture their basic preferences shift in some radical way, so that they cease to care about their children or projects.

But, I reply, that will only be significant according to LDP when there is consensus congruence that specifies that their situation is worst of all those affected. And many are likely to find their own future non-existence, let alone the destruction of the world including their children and projects, worse than any torture they might realistically encounter in life. What we would generally try to do if we believed ourselves to face such a horrible alternative is relevant to our basic preferences, and to consensus congruence, but what we would do if in fact we were currently undergoing torture would often be due to perturbation of our basic preferences into a very abnormal state. The fussy and negative do not have a veto to our existence according to LDP, because they are sensitive to conditions that other people don't care about, and hence there isn't the consensus required to constitute them as in fact worse off. And even those who are currently undergoing torture have no veto, since they have unusual preferences just because they are being tortured. So while LDP may require populations to shrink, it will not imply that the world is best destroyed.

I've been focusing on population issues involving only ordinal comparisons, and sometimes there may be pockets of cardinality that span all of those relevantly affected by an outcome, whether they are intuitively distinct individuals or moments of some intuitive individual's life. And then sums are what matter. The other qualifications built into LDP for cases with more than ordinal but less than cardinal value will also govern some population cases.

These are the rudiments of how LDP handles outcomes with different populations. But this aspect of LDP may seem objectionable. Begin by considering, as background, standard worries about the interaction of population issues and utilitarianism.

If we are average utilitarians, who compare outcomes by regard to the average yielded by first summing the value in a situation and then dividing by the number of individuals in the situation, we face the intuitive difficulty called The Mere Addition Problem.[50] If the world already has just a few very well off people, adding another life that will involve no cost to the others, but while very much worth living will not be quite as good as those of the very well off people, will lower the average, and hence make the world worse according to such a principle. And that seems wrong. On the other hand, if we are total utilitarians, who evaluate outcomes by regard to total sums of utility, we face The Repugnant Conclusion:

For any possible population of at least ten billion people, all with a very high quality of life, there must be some larger imaginable population whose existence, if other things are equal, would be better, even though its members have lives that are barely worth living.[51]

In its pursuit of highest total utility, total utilitarianism seems to drive on towards ever larger populations, until every individual has a very mediocre life, and that also seems wrong. Utilitarianism seems problematic in either case.

Like total utilitarianism, LDP implies, either when cardinal value is involved or in a different way when merely ordinal value is involved and other things are equal, that bigger populations are generally better, and so may seem likewise objectionable.

But remember this key difference: Particular moments are properly edited out of individual lives according to LDP when they meet a much weaker test than being parts of lives that are barely worth living, namely when they are moments that, other things equal, the life in question would be better off without. A life can be very much worth living and still have moments that it were better did not exist. So there is contrary population pressure present in LDP, towards smaller populations of atomic agents in which each moment within a life is worth having. Clearly there are many real lives that contain moments that would be better edited from reality according to this weaker test, and which would be made even worse off by any significantly larger population of atomic agents than there already is. So in fact LDP suggests in many cases that populations should shrink, or at least not increase wildly.

So LDP is in one sense an attractive middle ground. And it is not evident what suitably asymmetric rationale there could be for some other eclectic principle that deals with population issues in some possibly more intuitive way midway between total and average utilitarianism,[52] nor do we even have any intuitively attractive candidates.[53]

---

[50] Sikora (1978); Parfit (1984: 420).   [51] Parfit (1984: 388).
[52] This is another instance of the second abstract pattern of argument found in Chapters 8 and 9.
[53] Parfit (1984: 351–443) discusses relevant complexities.

Still, it may be objected that I have proposed a highly speculative account of how to deal with population issues, without firm grounding in commonsense intuition. But it is rooted in an application of the impartial rationale supporting LDP, given apparent facts about a consensus of preference that exists and will continue to exist. If I am wrong about these facts of preference, then I am wrong about these population issues.

It may also be worrisome that it is very hard to determine what the effects of particular acts on future populations will be. But whatever our evidence about our alternatives, it is the facts that matter. And fortunately relevant alternatives involve objective *ex ante* probabilities that include no flukes, which makes the relevant facts not completely inaccessible, and also undercuts some worries about objective consequentialism that we discussed in Chapter 3.

And so we come to one last complication regarding LDP: How are probabilities of outcomes handled on this conception? They are incorporated into the alternatives to be ordered by regard to consensus congruence among preferences. The alternatives themselves incorporate risks, and preferences over those various risks are parts of the basic preferences on which individual good rests.

That completes my exposition of LDP. It is just a sketch, but sufficient for our purposes. There are indeterminacies of both our individual and social options. There are also indeterminacies regarding which option of certain sets of fixed options is best according to LDP. But these indeterminacies aren't virulent, because, as we will see, LDP can provide the minimal level of determinacy in assessing outcomes that a workable ethics and political philosophy require. But anyway, in cold reality, LDP is all we can reasonably hope for. It can be applied directly to evaluate social alternatives, in a standard consequentialist manner, so that the proper social alternative is the best of the alternatives as assessed by that principle. But appropriate application of LDP in ethics requires another important piece of mechanism, the second element of LEXIMAC, which will be our next concern.

9

MAC2

The second part of LEXIMAC is one variant of a novel form of consequentialism called Multiple-Act Consequentialism, or "MAC." Actions sometimes involve conflicts of a different sort than the conflicts of well-being resolved by LDP, the Leximin Desire Principle. And these conflicts of action are properly resolved by a different form of like and impartial treatment, a different sort of equal standing. This underwrites MAC.

9.1 Core Argument

Recall from Chapter 3 that there are group agents and acts, rooted in accepted reasons. Indeed, any human agent of a moment, any human atomic agent, is likely to be part of more than one group agent. They may be part of a group agent that is a continuing self with a long-term project or two, and also of other group agents besides. Guinevere at the moment is part of a continuing self whose temporal parts cooperatively pursue long-range projects, but also a member of two couples with other projects.

Acts often have different and conflicting goals; they aim at different outcomes. But the overlap of various group agents in a given atomic agent creates the possibility of conflicts even when there is no disagreement about the ordering of outcomes, even when their actions share a goal. These are not passive distributional conflicts, conflicts about outcomes, but rather conflicts of agency. You at this moment may have no choice but to act in such a way that, if you fulfill your role in one group act of which you are part, you will hence violate your role in another group act, and also fail to pursue overall good in a direct way. And this can be so even if all the acts in question aim at the good. The first group act may pursue that goal in a different way, and the way in which it pursues the goal may specify a role for you that conflicts with your role in the second group act and also with direct pursuit of best outcomes.

The Round Table may be highly beneficent, but Lancelot's role in that group act may require him to ignore the emergency in front of him. He could defect now and achieve a little extra well-being for someone on the side, and yet not by his defection disable The Table from successful pursuit of its goal. He hence might be a morally motivated free-rider. Or perhaps two group acts, by two scheming couples of which Guinevere is part, pursue the maximization of the good, but in conflicting ways.

What should be done? Somehow these conflicts must be resolved. Given a rough ordering of outcomes of the sort supplied by LDP, the proper way to resolve these conflicts is through the mechanism of Multiple-Act Consequentialism.[1] MAC has four key tenets:

(1) Direct consequentialist evaluation of the options of group or individual agents is appropriate. In other words, among a particular set of options for a particular agent the most choiceworthy is the best.[2]

(2) Sometimes we ought to follow our roles in a group act even at the cost of the overall good we could achieve by defection from those roles. In particular, one should only defect from a group act with good consequences if one can achieve better consequences by the defecting act alone than the entire group act achieves. This is the principle of Very Little Defection, or "VLD."

(3) When different beneficent group acts of which one is part specify roles that conflict, one ought to follow the role in the group act with more valuable consequences. This is the principle of Defect to the Dominant, or "DD."

(4) One ought to join whatever group acts it is consequentially best to join, given the constraints set by VLD and DD.

This mechanism has a ratchet effect.[3] It enjoins, when various conditions are met, participation in consequentially valuable group acts, on familiar direct consequentialist grounds. But then it requires that a stronger test be met, say VLD, if defection from those group acts is to be appropriate. You are not required to join a beneficent group act when your participation would add nothing to its goal, but you are characteristically required not to defect from a weighty beneficent group act in which you are already participating even when your participation adds nothing to its goal.[4] So the notion of defection plays a key role here.

The basic agents are atomic agents, and it might be thought that each is in its moment born anew, without any prior commitments to particular standing group acts. For genuinely atomic agents, it might seem that defection is impossible. But in real humans there is a kind of temporal inertia of the accepted reasons that crucially constitute group and continuing individual action. Each moment of your adult life you are an atomic agent that finds itself already accepting certain reasons with requisite motivational weight, so that you are a relevant participant, are relevantly inside, various group acts. And when they conflict, the question is how to act in the face of these conflicts. When you do act, when you resolve the conflict of the moment, it may be that you will hence put yourself completely outside participation in some group act, which would constitute one sort of defection. But often you will remain inside the group action in the requisite motivational sense, but simply fail at that moment to do the part enjoined to you by that group project. That is another sort of defection. We will return to other complications of defection, but those are the main points.

---

[1] Mendola (2006: 23–102).   [2] In ties, all best alternatives are choiceworthy.
[3] Hajdin (2007).   [4] This undercuts the "paradox of group beneficence" of Otsuka (1991).

MAC is required, I believe, by the impartiality towards agents specified by DC2-BASIS, the second subject-matter constraint on ethics. It is required by a proper conception of equal status for moral agents, given the truth of a good-based ranking of outcomes such as that provided by LDP. This is analogous to the way in which LDP itself is rooted in a proper conception of impartiality and hence equal status for moral patients. This section explains in an unadorned way why equal status for moral agents requires MAC, although this explanation may not be fully convincing until we consider objections in later sections.

LDP provides the basic normative information required by consequentialism. It specifies a rough ordering of the alternatives in any set of options from worst to best, and hence in that sense most choiceworthy. It is our basic moral principle. But we need more. We need some way to balance conflicting forms of agency. VLD and DD are the characteristic ways in which MAC balances conflicting forms of agency. So I need to argue that VLD and DD are the proper ways to do that on the basis of such a basic consequentialist principle. Begin with VLD.

Imagine that an atomic agent may defect as an individual from a cooperative group act with a good end, a group project that will not be undercut by that single defection. And imagine that in defecting that atomic agent can grab some extra positive consequences on the side. This might be Lancelot contemplating beneficent defection from The Round Table.

There are a variety of possible consequentialist responses to this sort of case. Traditional act consequentialists prescribe that each person act in direct accord with the proper ordering of options from worst to best, in the simplest case that each choose the best. A basic normative principle like LDP is applied directly to evaluate individual options. Indirect consequentialists assess other things than acts by reference to valuable consequences, and then assess acts indirectly, by reference to those other things, for instance as requirements of the best motives, characters, or rules. Indirect consequentialism seems to many to lack a genuine consequentialist rationale, though to promise more intuitive implications. The best social moral rules or individual character may strictly proscribe murder, even the occasional beneficent murder, while on the other hand it is hard to see, if consequences matter, why the consequences of acts don't directly matter.

But in the case we face, there is the possibility of something novel. We have the conflict of two acts which each have a direct consequentialist rationale.

One response to such a situation is that of the traditional act consequentialist, focused on the direct maximization of value by an individual: the atomic agent should defect. Another is that of a rigid group-act consequentialist: the atomic agent should not defect from the beneficent group act, which is better than the relevant alternative of no group act. The atomic agent should play its role in the beneficent group act. But neither defecting nor cooperating has a more direct consequentialist rationale, because neither the group act nor the individual act has a more direct rationale. They both have direct rationales. And each act and agent must have suitably equal status.

This suggests that in some cases of this sort an atomic agent should defect from the beneficent group act, and in others it should not. It should depend in particular on the relative normative weight of the independent individual act on the one hand and the group project on the other, as assessed by our basic normative principle. But how does it so depend? If the background of cooperative activity is preserved when figuring the options relevant to assessing defection, then defection gains a little on the side and loses nothing. If instead the action of the atomic agent is taken as fixed, with the cooperative activity of the group as the only variable item with normative weight, we get a predictably different answer. The crucial question is what to properly leave fixed and what to take as properly variable when assessing the situation.

Equal status for both sorts of agents involved in this type of case, both the individual agent and the group agent, requires that we must properly consider what happens when each factor varies, both the group act and the individual act. It is those two alternatives which the atomic agent will pursue or shun by its choice, since to pursue a group act in the relevant sense is to perform one's role in that act and to defect from a group act is to fail to perform it.[5] And it is only by letting both acts vary that we can assess their relative normative weight. That is what VLD does, in the only workable manner with a direct consequentialist rationale. According to VLD, we assess the weight of both the group and individual act in question by reference to the effects of its particular presence and absence, in the traditional direct way. Greater normative weight of that straightforward, well-motivated sort determines which act is properly dominant according to MAC. That is what it is to treat the acts and their agents as having equal status.

There is another characteristic situation for MAC. We also need to balance conflicting forms of group agency, like Guinevere inside the two couples. But in that case the considerations we have already surveyed support DD. When different beneficent group acts of which one is part specify roles that conflict, one should follow the role in the group act with more valuable consequences. That has a weightier direct rationale.

That is my basic argument for VLD and DD, and hence for MAC. I think it is sufficient, except for some qualifications to which we return. But I don't expect you to believe me until we consider a series of objections.

9.2 Structural Objections

The first class of objections to MAC are enmeshed with some of its characteristic advantages. These objections and advantages are both due to its key structural features, which we need to better explore in any case. Begin by considering one key feature.

---

[5] Both types of defection imply failing to perform it.

I have been talking as if the defecting atomic agent in a case governed by VLD is more or less an intuitive individual. That is the most natural way to think about the cases in question, as cases in which an intuitive individual defects from an intuitive group. But that may be misleading. In truth, it is more exactly characteristic of DD than of VLD. This is because temporally extended actions of individuals are group acts in my sense.

So focus squarely on whether we should countenance defection of *atomic* agents from beneficent group agents of which they are part, when they can by that defection grab a little extra good on the side. MAC says they shouldn't defect. And recall that individual acts that require a series of temporal steps are group acts in my sense. And finally remember Castañeda's classic problem for act consequentialism:[6]

Sometimes the conjunction of two acts A and B can be very good, while each of them done on their own would be very bad. And this can happen in temporal cases.[7] It may have excellent effects if Lancelot talks first to Guinevere and then to Arthur, but a disaster to do either of those things without the other. It takes a certain amount of time to perform many individual actions, perhaps especially actions aiming at overall good. And it may be that maximization of value in the moment may conflict with something you need to do as part of an individual but longer-lasting action that also aims at the good. Perhaps Arthur is in the midst of some long-term moral project of significant consequential weight, but at certain moments he has various moral temptations to do small-scale local good. Perhaps if at each moment he acts as an atomic agent that maximizes the value available from among its options as an atomic agent, then his long-term and consequentially more significant project will be disrupted and fail.[8]

The most intuitive and familiar form of commitment to direct consequentialist rationales for action does not forbid beneficent individual acts that are temporal conjunctions of acts that are not in isolation beneficent, and in fact the dominant response to Castañeda's problem has been to conclude that such conjunctive acts are the only proper locus of direct consequentialist evaluation. Likewise, I think, commitment to direct consequentialist rationales does not forbid participation in larger-scale beneficent group acts involving many people in which one's particular role is not individually beneficent. In fact, I think, the proper analysis of these two types of cases is exactly the same. They both involve dominance for weighty group acts. Any legitimate rationale for traditional act consequentialism, which focuses not on the momentary acts of atomic agents but on the temporally extended acts of intuitive individuals, is in fact a rationale for the significance of group acts generally. That is

---

[6] Castañeda (1968). This explicitly suggests, despite an endearing typo, that obligation always distributes through conjunction, while that it does not is the problem's heart. See the exchange between Castañeda (1965) and Sidorsky (1965).

[7] Westphal (1972) observes that Castañeda's cases seem temporal.

[8] We shortly consider the conditions this requires.

because the temporally extended action of an individual is in fact a group act involving some of the atomic agents who make up the history of that individual. There is a single type of direct consequentialist rationale, rooted in the value of the consequences of acts, that legitimately applies whether a group act involves many individuals or just one individual over time.

But let me go slowly at this key point. There is an important complication, which requires a little background. Consequentialists focused on the general good can be in circumstances in which if they act individually as consequentialists they will fail to achieve as much individual good as if they coordinate their activity. Gibbard gives the example of

a village of act-utilitarians threatened with destruction by a giant boulder; each villager rescues as many children and possessions as possible, each doing the best he can given what others are disposed to do. Jointly, though, they might have pushed the boulder harmlessly down the other side of the hill.[9]

But there is also a theorem that shows that if the act utilitarians together form a consequentially optimal agreement, for instance to act jointly in such a case, and it is common knowledge that they will each keep that agreement, then each will keep the agreement.[10] After all, if the agreement is optimal, there is nothing to be gained on the side by defection. But notice that no such optimal agreement may exist. And it can be foolish on utilitarian grounds to participate in a merely hypothetical optimal agreement. If one of our act utilitarians tries to push the boulder alone, they will simply waste their effort. However, they may be party to a less than optimal but actual agreement, perhaps through a momentary lapse or miscalculation, or an analogue of such an agreement, say an actual group act, which requires working vigorously together with the others to blow up the boulder. And while that group act or agreement may not be quite optimal, it may still be very beneficent, productive of much good. It would have been a little better for all to have agreed to push the boulder rather than blow it up, since that would avoid the small ruin that the explosion will create, but that's not how the agreement went. And it might also be that it wouldn't take everyone to actually blow up the boulder. Someone could defect from the agreement they made or the group act in which they are participating, and do some extra good, but not hence disable the group act or agreement from reaching its goal. So if they follow their agreement or their role in the group act, it would be a case of what Gibbard calls "surplus cooperation."[11] It is specially characteristic of MAC that it requires that one not defect in such cases of surplus cooperation.

---

[9] Gibbard (1971) and Gibbard (2008: 85).
[10] Gibbard (1971 and 1978). The theorem presumes perfect memories and complete agreement in subjective probabilities when the agreement is made. Broome (1991: 152–4) develops a problem with relaxing the second assumption. But we are focused on objective *ex ante* probabilities, facts all parties share, so this doesn't matter.
[11] Gibbard (1971: 20).

Now return to the juxtaposition of the temporally conjunctive acts of Castañeda's problem and MAC. In the key case on which VLD is based, the group act will *not* be disabled by one's individual defection. It is a case of surplus cooperation. And that is a difference from the Castañeda case we were considering. Rather, a perfect temporal analogue is a case in which you have made an agreement with yourself to act in a certain way, so that you are performing an individual group act spread over time, but it isn't strictly optimal, so that if you keep to your role, there will be surplus cooperation.

But many of our beneficent individual actions that take some time to execute are cases like that. We might have formed a slightly better plan, but we didn't, and now it is possible to defect and gain a little extra good on the side. In this case, as in a case involving a more intuitive group act of many individuals, VLD instructs us not to defect, it tells us to follow through.

One may object at this point to VLD, and to MAC generally, that there can be no direct consequentialist rationale that supports playing one's role in a group act when there is surplus cooperation. So let me repeat the genuinely direct consequentialist rationale for this general feature of MAC, which I applied in detail to the case of VLD in the last section. It will be more revealing and less repetitive if I focus this time on how it applies to the kinds of conflicts between different group acts characteristic of DD.

Presume that there are two group acts that intersect in Lancelot of the moment. He can't play his role in both. There is a conflict between the acts. DD says he ought to perform his role in the consequentially more beneficial act, because that act has a weightier direct consequential rationale. There are two acts in conflict, and DD says the conflict between the two acts should be decided by straightforward appeal to LDP.

However, it may be retorted, he should instead determine what to do in this circumstance by another sort of consequentialist calculation. He should determine whether his individual contribution to one act or the other would have better consequences according to LDP. If, for instance, one of the group acts is an individual act extending over time and the other involves many individuals and does not extend over time, this would be a way of saying that he should be an *atomic* act consequentialist, that each atomic agent should only act in direct accord with LDP.

But, I reply, *act* consequentialism is consequentialism applied to *acts*. And this proposal does not allow sufficient integrity to most intuitive acts for many real and weightily beneficent acts, of individuals as well as groups, even to exist. Let me explain this key point.

The smallest agent is surely not always the dominant locus of proper direct consequentialist evaluation. You can try to do distinct things with various limbs and fingers. Perhaps with practice you might become capable of the dexterity required so that we could literally speak of your various limbs and fingers trying to do various things. But it would not be appropriate to require that each of your limbs and fingers act individually, as much as possible, in direct accord with the basic consequentialist normative principle, so that you become incapable of unified action even in a moment. And neither does consequentialism require that the atomic agents that make you up over this day act independently in pursuit of the good, so that you cannot execute some cooperative scheme with yourself that takes all day to perform. Direct consequentialist rationales for our real actions instead apply to continuing individual acts, and hence require the sort of balancing that I have proposed, which weighs actual group acts already in progress at their true consequential weight, whether they are continuing acts of individuals or acts of more intuitive groups.

Many of our actual acts, as individuals over time or as groups of individuals, are both highly beneficent and just like the boulder explosion case. They are not strictly optimal, since they involve surplus cooperation. But yet they are highly beneficent. They do actual good of a weighty sort, though not as much as might have been done by some alternative group act that, however, does not exist. They have the very significant advantage over optimal group acts that they actually exist. To do your part alone in a merely hypothetical optimal group act may be a disaster. And the very existence of many consequentially important group acts, including temporally extended acts of persisting individual agents, requires that atomic agents not defect in cases of the sort under consideration. Ordinary commonsense individual action *is* group action of various momentary cooperating selves. So to countenance defections from consequentially dominant group actions in the cases of conflict that motivate MAC, to gain small extra positive consequences on the side, is to open the possibility of frequent defection, by component atomic agents, from actual beneficent *individual* projects, as well as from beneficent and more intuitive group acts involving many people. Act consequentialism requires actions, and actions require a certain minimal integrity of actions, and that is what MAC provides.

Still, perhaps it seems that if one defects to grab a little side good only when it is optimal to do so, there can be no disaster. Perhaps it seems that the beneficent acts are still sufficiently respected. It will be fine if only those defect who can gain a little more on the side and yet not undercut the success of the group act. But, I reply, the difference between some actual group act and an alternative but non-existent optimal group act might not involve merely one or two individuals in the actual act refraining from grabbing extra utility on the side; the actual group act in question might be very specific in the roles that it prescribes for cooperators, and those roles may forbid individual maximization of utility. For instance, it might be important to the successful functioning of the group act that everyone can trust everyone else involved to never under any circumstances lie, even when utility would be served by lying. So at least some of the cooperators might be required not to maximize utility as individuals or the beneficent group act will collapse. In such a case, if all will defect even only when it is optimal to do so, still the benefits of the actual though admittedly not strictly optimal coordination will be lost. It may be impossible for those prepared to defect whenever they can maximize utility by doing so to participate in the only actual cooperative scheme that is in fact available to them. If nothing else, the other cooperators may shun cooperation with act utilitarians. There is no theorem that shows that traditional act utilitarians will generally play their roles in less than optimal utilitarian agreements. But our most beneficent group acts are seldom optimal.

There is also another important point. I am not introducing this now as an extra positive argument for VLD or DD. I've already supplied an argument for these principles that I think is sufficient, though I will buttress it in various ways in Chapter 10. But if complaints about MAC's treatment of surplus cooperation are to be fairly considered, it is important to balance those complaints against the real advantages of that treatment. We shouldn't lose sight of traditional worries about act utilitarianism, which would if anything be magnified for the radical atomic act utilitarianism now under consideration. Act utilitarians will lie, cheat, or murder, as long as the maximization of utility requires it, as sometimes it does. Only if group acts or agreements are truly optimal, only if they build in all the little exceptions that an act utilitarian will require, say for when an opportunity to perform a secret beneficent immorality arises, can act utilitarians be trusted to keep those agreements or play their roles in group acts. And so optimal agreements have unsavory features. Of course, in many cases continued cooperation with an actual agreement or in an actual group act may be required by traditional act consequentialism even if the group act or agreement isn't optimal, and in fact many defect from consequentially beneficent moral practices that do not hence collapse. But consider these cases: Presume that some traditional act utilitarians have agreed together, through some momentary lapse, to always tell the truth, in particular to participate in a group act of telling the truth that is very beneficent. It would be very bad if many of them often lied, which would undercut the benefit gained by that group act. But given the fact that almost no one else ever lies, it may be beneficial for one of them to tell a few lies and grab a little extra utility on the side. This is a case where defection when there would otherwise be surplus cooperation generates the characteristic problems of act utilitarianism. Or consider our highly beneficent practice of not murdering one another. If that moral practice is a group act, grabbing utility on the side by defecting from such a group action to avoid surplus cooperation has a rather unpleasant implication. A truly optimal act utilitarian agreement must allow for the possibility of the occasional cold-blooded murder or lie.

Our moral practices, reflected in DC1-NORMS as a constraint on the subject-matter of ethics, aren't optimal in these ways. And many of these moral practices, as we will see in Chapter 11, are in fact beneficent group acts. As we will see, MAC forbids murder and most lying by appeal to the consequential weight of ongoing moral practices that are group acts. MAC is a new form of direct consequentialism, which retains the intuitive direct rationale of traditional act consequentialism, but yet has the suitably intuitive implications of indirect forms. That is a serious advantage for the view, not a disadvantage, and it depends squarely on MAC's treatment of surplus cooperation.

But let me repeat. The principal rationale for MAC, through which it is supported by DC2-BASIS, is that it weights conflicting acts at their consequential weight. To defect from a weightily beneficent group act that is already ongoing, even to grab a few positive consequences on the side, is to violate the direct consequentialist rationale of that act, even if the act is not strictly optimal. It is to place the small good that can be gained by defection above the large good that the group achieves. And this rationale applies both to group acts involving many individuals and to the temporally extended acts on which traditional utilitarians focus. There is no relevant difference between these cases. There is no plausible rationale for some happy medium between MAC and a truly radical form of act consequentialism that focuses not on the acts of temporally extended people but rather of mere atomic agents, lasting but a moment.

But this suggests another important class of objections, that there *are* plausible rationales for some happy medium. In particular, it may seem that there are other ways to defend the propriety of unified individual action over time, without appeal to the group act status of temporally enduring individual acts, in other words without appeal to a rationale which then generalizes in a way that leads to MAC. So it may seem that there are other responses to Castañeda's problem that are better than the one I have just developed and defended.

There are various ways to motivate this objection. Perhaps it seems that Guinevere *controls* what she does but not what is done by other members of some intuitive group of which she is part. Perhaps it seems that *she* should just do the best *she* can.[12] I don't accept these ways of motivating the objection. A part of my point is that at each moment when Guinevere participates in an intuitive group action, that group act is a part of what she can be said to be doing at that moment, just as in the case when she performs a temporally extended but intuitively individual group act. And a part of my point is that she no more now controls her future actions than she controls many acts of those who currently cooperate with her. And a focus on control may be motivated by a concern with blameworthiness, while Chapter 3 argued that an identification of consequentially relevant options with those that might be blameworthy is a confusion.

But this response to these motivations may seem idiosyncratic, and in any case the main worry in play is that there are other sorts of responses possible to Castañeda's problem, which treat it in a different way than I am proposing. Even if we insist, as I have insisted, that Guinevere's acts that are properly subject to direct consequentialist evaluation should include temporally extended acts, that may not be because they are group acts. And so the rationale for ceding those acts direct consequential

---

[12] I owe this to Tom Carson.

weight may not extend to cover the more intuitive group acts in which she participates, contrary to what I have contended.

The standard proposal in this class is Fred Feldman's.[13] There are complexities in
his formulations, but his key idea is that we should at each moment do what would be
a temporal part of our best temporally extended action. This is analogous to a focus
on optimal agreements. We should act towards the best future accessible to us given
appropriate action from this point onwards on our part. This requires that Guinevere
do her momentary part in temporally extended and properly beneficent actions, but
it does nothing to rationalize her performing her part in more intuitive group acts
involving many people.

Still, this sort of proposal, which seems natural for those who would focus in a less
idiosyncratic manner than me on what Guinevere controls or on what Guinevere can
best do, is subject to debilitating objection.[14] Guinevere may know that tomorrow,
though she *can* in the relevant sense (defined in Part I) do what is part of the long-
range plan that would lead to the greatest good, still in all probability she won't,
because of temptation that she can foresee that she will not withstand. And it can be
that if she does her part today in the best long-range plan but fails to do her part
tomorrow, a horrible result will occur. Feldman's proposal requires that she do her
current part in the optimal long-range action, even though she reliably and accurately
predicts that she won't in fact do what she should tomorrow, and so this will just lead
to disaster. But this seems obviously incorrect, and to lack any plausible consequentialist rationale. My proposal instead focuses on what in fact she will do tomorrow, at
least within the range of determinacy allowed by her relevant current options. If she
can reliably foresee that she will improperly defect tomorrow, then that should
certainly be taken into account today. Such a procedure has a proper consequentialist
rationale.

Rule consequentialism and analogous indirect forms that tell us to do *not* what
would in fact lead to best consequences but rather what would lead to best consequences under variously hypothetical and ideal conditions, say in a world where
everyone acted according to the consequentially best moral rules, can lead us in a
reality that is not in these ways ideal to consequentially harmful acts. That is a
standard and pressing objection to such indirect forms, and at least requires of such
forms a different sort of rationale than a direct appeal to the value of consequences.
And so structurally analogous but allegedly *direct* forms of act consequentialism, like
Feldman's, or those that tell you to play your role in optimal agreements that have
never been made, seem to have an incoherent rationale. Rather, a direct consequentialist rationale suggests that we should focus on what other cooperating participants
in group acts will in fact do, either other people or your future selves. And that is

---

[13] Feldman (1986), especially 36–8.
[14] H. Goldman (1976); H. Sobel (1976). Feldman (1986: 52–7) responds. The text incorporates my
counter-response.

exactly what MAC does. It provides a suitable rationale for the right treatment of cases involving individual action over time. And the surprise is that that rationale also extends to a similar treatment of cases involving other group agents.

Still, there are other sorts of proposals about how to handle such cases that are closer to my suggestion than Feldman's. Some of what I won't do tomorrow may be psychologically impossible for me (or psychologically impossible for me given constraints of rationality). And perhaps it seems that this constrains my current best option while my own less excusable but foreseeable weakness does not.[15] But, I reply, a proper direct consequentialist rationale incorporates all that can be reliably foreseen.

Still, perhaps you should defect from your ongoing but non-optimal individual long-range beneficent acts only in cases of surplus cooperation, when you can gain some positive consequences on the side, perhaps unforeseen in your original plan, without disabling the ongoing act. But the problem with this is that, although of course some of your cooperation with yourself may be also be momentarily benefi-cent and an act may not be undercut by occasional defection, still in general this pattern of response fails to allow for the integrity of individual action over time. We are back in the position of the momentary atomic agent acting alone, no more on the basis of its history than the history of the world. We are back to the very radical form of atomic act consequentialism.

But maybe for the proper assessment of each of your actions at a time, we should instead take into account not what you will do but rather the current *ex ante* objective probabilities of your future actions, up to the level of determinacy allowed by the facts about your options. In fact this is all that we can do even according to my proposal, given Part I's treatment of options. Still, there is a difference between this proposal and MAC, since MAC treats those of your future acts that are within some current group act asymmetrically with those of your future acts that are outside of it. And MAC is more plausible at this point. Let me put it this way: Moral responsibility does not plausibly spread between, on one hand, all of one's future actions that are outside one's current continuing individual group action and, on the other, that current action, as it does within that group act itself. If you do something heinous next year that undercuts the effect of your current beneficent continuing action, that will of course be relevant to an assessment of its actual consequences. But it doesn't mean that your current act incorporates that immorality, and hence has the same sort of negative moral status that it would have if that heinous future action were part of that continuing group act itself. It is relevant to the effects of what you are doing now, but it is not part of what you are intentionally doing now. But your current efforts towards a long-term evil goal are now immoral. These asymmetries of MAC are intuitively plausible.

---

[15] Portmore (2011: 166–7).

Still, it might seem that there is some other sort of rationale for the integrity of individual action over time that does not extend to intuitive group acts. I have not argued that there are no facts about personal identity, about at least such unity as continuing individual human animals or minds possess. But the facts of personal identity over time are not of basic normative significance of any sort that we have managed to discover. The basis of value is preference, and preferences change with time. The basis of value is the preferences of atomic agents. What's more, the basis of action is trying, and the basis of trying is the trying of atomic agents. What an individual tries to do can change over time. Individuals over time can try only in the same sense in which groups of distinct individuals can try, by cooperating in group action. In the deepest and most direct sense, individuals only *control* their own actions at the current moment. They "control" their own future actions only indirectly, largely by forming current intentions and plans, and they can also form cooperative intentions and make plans with others.

So neither the basic moral agents nor the basic moral patients in our physical world are continuing individuals in any deep way that is relevant irrespective of the existence of continuing group acts or the content of our preferences. There is nothing in reality to provide our continuing lives or continuing individual actions some sort of special and fundamental normative status. Being melts like snowballs in our coward hands.[16]

The real choice is between MAC and a very hard-core and radical form of act consequentialism, that focuses on direct consequentialist evaluation of the alternatives of atomic agents. Such a radical act consequentialism at least has a coherent rationale, though it neglects the proper impartial treatment of all agents. In a sense more literal than Bernard Williams probably intended,[17] radical act consequentialism would undermine familiar individual agency, which includes temporally extended projects. Traditional act consequentialists, focused on longer-scale individual actions but ignoring group acts of many people, intend a happy medium for which there can be no coherent rationale, at least in our physical world.

9.3 Other Objections

I still don't quite expect you to believe me. There are other natural objections to MAC that we need to consider. And they will require qualifications that turn it into a variant called "MAC2."

First objection: MAC deploys group acts, and there may be indeterminacies regarding the group acts in which an individual participates. I agree, but in Chapter 11 will argue that, in the case of the weighty group acts most important for ethics, this indeterminacy is at most moderate. Since group acts can stretch over

---

[16] Dryden (1678: V 131–4).   [17] Williams (1973: 117).

time, there may also be significant epistemic difficulties in figuring out what group acts we participate in. But this is merely an epistemic difficulty. And, while I am not confident that the facts of what we should do are always open to our epistemic determination, I will argue in Chapter 11 that, for the cases that most concern us, this epistemic difficulty can be overcome. Still, other forms of threatening indeterminacy remain.

Second objection: VLD and DD depend on the notion of an act having good consequences, but the viability of this notion has been questioned by Alastair Norcross.[18] Perhaps it is indeterminate whether an act has good consequences.

Reply: I prefer a more or less counterfactual understanding of what this means, that an act A is good if and only if the world would have been worse if A hadn't been performed. And while the indeterminacy of counterfactuals does suggest that there is some indeterminacy about this, I think that there is less problem with such a notion than Norcross thinks. Consider his problem case:

When we ask what the world would have been like if the action hadn't been performed, we are considering a world in which the agent simply doesn't exercise her agency. So, what is it not to exercise her agency? One obvious possibility is that it is to remain completely immobile. But this clearly won't do. Consider the following case.... Agent stumbles onto an experiment conducted by a twisted scientist named Scientist. He is seated at a desk with ten buttons, numbered "0" through "9", in front of him. He tells Agent that the buttons control the fates of ten people. If no button is pressed within the next thirty seconds, all ten will die. If the button marked "9" is pressed, only nine will die; if "8" is pressed, eight will die, and so on down to "0".... [H]e turns control of the buttons over to Agent.... Agent pushes "9", killing nine people. If she had remained immobile, all ten would have died.[19]

It looks like the counterfactual understanding of a good action that I have embraced says that pushing "9" was a good action, but it wasn't. What then do I say about Norcross' ingenious case? What I say is that there are a variety of different sorts of cases that require relevantly different treatments, that require a different understanding of the baseline of inaction relevant to counterfactual assessment. One related complication is that sometimes when you try to do something by not moving, not moving does constitute doing something. In fact, in Norcross' case it seems to me that Agent could kill all ten intentionally by not moving. The most convincing case of this sort is Heidi Malm's:[20] You are canoeing, and if you don't paddle you will run over a swimmer and kill them, but if you do paddle, you will pull your canoe out of reach of a fainting swimmer reaching out for your canoe. If you are active and paddle, then you will let someone die, but if you don't paddle, then you will kill someone. But still, it doesn't seem *generally* true that you can be said to be doing something positive intentionally by doing nothing. Cases differ. Sometimes there will be nothing in particular that you are saliently doing by just standing there immobile, other than

[18] Norcross (1997).   [19] Norcross (1997: 15).   [20] Malm (1989).

just intentionally doing nothing. So while I don't think that the relevant baseline of inaction involves not moving in all cases, I do think it involves not moving in some. Now consider the acts that specially concern us, group acts. They involve various conditions that ensure that participation in such a group act requires acceptance of reasons pointing towards some at least apparent good or goal to be achieved by the act, though it is also relevant that there can be negative group acts, involving the intentional refraining from certain sorts of positive activity, where the absence of that sort of positive activity is the goal to be achieved. For instance, we might be participants in the group act of refraining from murder. It seems to be this intentional content of the group acts in question that helps specify the correct baseline of comparison, the correct baseline of suitable inaction, relevant by the counterfactual analysis to the goodness of those actions. If the group act in question is a negative group act that involves refraining from a certain sort of positive activity, the baseline will involve the amount of individual activity of that sort by participants in the group action that would occur if the negative group act did not exist. If the group act is a positive group act, specifying certain positive roles for participants, say positive individual work towards the specific goal of the act, then the relevant baseline will involve inaction by the participants of that same sort. Norcross' problem does not undercut the proper understanding of the counterfactual analysis of the goodness of acts at least in the cases that concern us. We have a general mechanism for dealing with such cases, by appeal to the intentional content of the actions in question. This is not to say that other factors, for instance environmental factors, are never relevant. Perhaps sometimes whether the baseline involves no action turns crucially on something more than intentional content. But this mechanism delivers centrally relevant considerations that are sufficient to undercut the problem in the cases we need.

Objection Three: VLD and DD require even more than a notion of what acts are good. They require a comparison of the valuable consequences of two actions. And so more indeterminacies loom.

Fortunately, it is merely an ordinal comparison that is required. All we need to do is ordinally compare the relevant situation in which an act A occurs to the exclusion of act B and a second situation in which act B occurs to the exclusion of A. But still this comparison may involve considerable indeterminacy. There may be indeterminacy regarding the various alternatives of various agents, and there is indeterminacy of the well-being of agents, and the proper ordering of options from worst to best also suffers from indeterminacy, rooted in the indeterminacy of proper comparisons of well-being of distinct atomic individuals. But MAC introduces a fourth level of indeterminacy, again because of the indeterminate truth of certain subjunctive conditionals. That is because VLD and DD deploy counterfactual tests regarding the effects of the absence of various group agents and acts. In some cases there will be difficulties disentwining background conditions in the way required to yield determinate truth values for the conditionals in question. So MAC will introduce more normative indeterminacy, which I believe to be unavoidable in our world. We will discuss the key instances of this problem in detail in Chapter 11, which involve the particular complexities of the cases that matter most to us. We will come back to this worry, as we will to the first objection. But we will circumvent it.

But there are also some ways in which the indeterminacy of options and its implications help us to evade other natural objections to MAC. Consider Objection Four: It might be a mere fluke that would make defection from a beneficent group act more consequentially weighty than the group act, and that defection also may be intuitively immoral. But, I reply, remember that mere flukes are ruled out of consideration by the conception of alternatives that we are presuming, and so presuming as a means to circumscribe the indeterminacy of options. Objective *ex ante* probabilities are all that matter. And if there is a large objective likelihood that some hitherto unknown asteroid will crash to earth in a consequentially significant way, that is not intuitively irrelevant to what we ought to do in the same way as a mere fluke would be.

There are also other ways in which indeterminacy underwrites more intuitive implications for MAC. It is highly likely that the great expanse of many morally important group acts makes their consequential weight less relevantly indeterminate than that of individual defection. Such group acts almost certainly have excellent consequences, while it may be much more risky whether defection will, even when we ignore flukes. Risks are bundled into the alternatives that are evaluated by regard to consensus among our basic preferences, and since we do favor more likely goods to less likely goods this suggests significant discounting for the risky positive value of a defection. There are also some other revealing cases that involve merely normative risks or indeterminacies. Perhaps it is highly risky or indeterminate whether it is better to be a pig than a human. But remember that we are beginning with normal adult human interests and working outwards. This is one way in which we have abandoned the point of view of the universe. Normative speculation of the sort in question, assuming the normative risk of a positive species transformation, is not appropriate according to LEXIMAC. This is perhaps an important qualification of MAC, though I've already smuggled its aspects that immediately concern us into human-centered LDP.

Another class of objections requires amplification of MAC into MAC2. Consider Objection Five: As so far described, MAC can tell us what we ought to do, and also suggests that we ought not to defect from consequentially weighty group acts. But it lacks an account of what it is very wrong to do. It doesn't provide an account of morally heinous group action, for instance unjust wars.

Reply: MAC assesses the primary moral weight of contributing participation in group acts at the consequential weight of the entire group act. Consider for instance DD. And when some group act has horrendous consequences, a properly extended MAC2 would hence naturally weight participation in those group acts at that whole horrendous negative weight.[21] What is horrendous? Well, perhaps that notion doesn't make completely determinate sense in our world. Perhaps our principle for ranking outcomes cannot often deliver facts about how much worse one outcome is than another. But the intuitively horrendous is at least worse than nothing. A horrendous act at least makes things worse than the baseline of inaction. And different acts can be differently worse than nothing. And so horrendous group acts are at least worse than nothing and many other bad acts. But let me focus principally on the easier notion of a harmful group act. A relevantly harmful group acts makes things worse than the baseline of inaction.

So the short answer to the normative question we face is that you ought to defect from all harmful group acts. But maybe you must participate in at least one of two conflicting harmful group acts. If so, MAC2 says to defect from the more harmful. And aside from that complexity, it implies that it is wrong not to defect from consequentially harmful group acts in which you find yourself participating, where the size of that wrong is tied to the size of the harm done by the group act. What is it to defect from participation in such a group action? The motivational components of belonging to a group act are relatively weak, and often not easily outrun by conscious decision, so in realistic cases it will characteristically require defecting from your role in that group act. We will come back to some of the complexities of defection in Chapters 11 and 12, including its application to war.

The implications of this clause of MAC2 of course turn on what the facts are about our group acts, to which we will return. But the clause may invite Objection Six, even independent of its implications: Some do not accept that there is collective responsibility of any sort.

However, I reply, we have seen that there is genuine group action, so this denial is implausible. Still, even those who accept that there is collective responsibility often favor a different conception of the distribution of the basic sort of moral responsibility among the members of a group than that presumed by MAC2.[22] Call this Objection Seven. MAC2 holds all non-defecting participants in a group act fully responsible for the whole. But perhaps instead one's *contribution* to a group act, reflecting one's individual consequential contribution, or the significance of one's assigned task in the act, or one's level of authority in the group, modulates one's moral responsibility of this sort.[23]

But, I reply, your group acts are yours, although others' as well. You are engaged in the relevant trying, just as when the you of today participates in a long-range individual action. Recall our basic argument for VLD, applicable to continuing individual action and intuitive group action alike. The whole is your responsibility

---

[21] Dreaming acts and intense participation in video-gaming may involve participation in horrendous group acts.

[22] Recall from Chapter 3 that we do not focus on excuse-modified Strawsonian attitudes.

[23] Feinberg (1968: 685) is classic. May and Hoffman (1991) is an anthology. And see McKenna (2006).

in the most basic moral sense if you do not defect. Recall also our earlier discussion of how this responsibility spreads within temporally extended group action by a single individual. If you are now only performing a consequentially small part of a long-range heinous action that you fully intend and indeed know you will perform in total, the evil inhabits even your current consequentially trivial bit, as you merely sharpen the knife or check the address of your victim in the phone book or run to catch the early bus to do the deed. And consider Parfit's Harmless Torturers case: Each of a thousand torturers presses a button. The victim suffers severe pain. But none of the torturers individually makes the pain perceptibly worse.[24] Still, each torturer is intuitively evil. Each has something like full intuitive responsibility for the whole group act. I should admit that this treatment has some intuitive cost. Tom Carson suggests this hard case: Your individual contribution to the evil produced by some heinous group in which you participate is completely null, but you will be severely punished if you defect; you will be shot. MAC requires that you defect, to no good effect and at the cost of your life. But, I reply, in such a case you may be able to defect in a motivational sense while evading the punishment, in a way we will consider for realistic political cases in Chapter 12. And of course you may not be seriously blameworthy if you do what is wrong in such a fraught situation.

Objection Eight: Imagine that your choice is between defection between two beneficent group acts.[25] The first has somewhat less weighty consequences than the second. But your role in the first is more significant. The first group act will collapse if you don't play your part. But the second group can be successful even if you defect. MAC incorporates DD, and DD says to stick with the weighty second group. So you should play your unnecessary role in the second group, which role will gain nothing for the good, and abandon the first group, which will cause the loss of all the good effects of that first group act. This seems wrong.

But there is some question regarding what is involved in defection from a group action, and the correct account can be turned to MAC's advantage in dealing with this type of case. I think that you are only truly defecting from a group act if you would be criticized for that defection on grounds of violation of the reasons accepted by the group. If following your role in the less weighty group action in a case like this would not be criticized by members of the weightier act, that suggests that there is an implicit exception built into the weightier group project to cover a case of this sort. For instance, you are in a large group act of not lying, but you will unlikely be criticized by the other participants if you defect to save a life. So there are fewer actual problem cases of the type under consideration here than it may first appear. And this also helps with cases of surplus cooperation in which it is intuitively appropriate for a single atomic agent to defect. It provides a suitably motivated difference between

---

[24] Parfit (1984: 80). But see Gruzalski (1986); Parfit (1986); Otsuka (1991).
[25] These cases are due to Tom Carson and Torbjörn Tännsjö.

those cases and others in which forbidding defection is to MAC's intuitive advantage.[26]

This response may make you uncomfortable. Perhaps some of our actual group acts include a few absolutists, who brook no exceptions. Still, there will also likely be a significant consensus among most members of the group act that is not absolutist, and will hence constitute a kind of concentric group act, inside the broader act that includes the absolutists, in which you take part even when you don't act as the absolutists demand. And there is another point: Some are as absolutist about lying as Kant, but not many. And that in turn suggests something analogous to a non-absolutist consensus congruence across even the whole original group. I think that this would also be sufficient to constitute an implicit exception built into the larger group act project. We will return to this point, and to concentric group acts, in Chapter 11.

My response may also make you uncomfortable for a second reason. It depends on the actual details of the group acts in which we participate. Since some of the group acts that I will crucially deploy later involve moral practices, it even depends on the moral beliefs that are a part of our participation in those acts. And it is at least *possible* that there would have been merely groups of rigid deontologists, who brook no exceptions. It may seem that MAC should allow for exceptions even in that sort of hypothetical case. But, I reply, it is not my ambition to provide a vindication of our moral judgments that is independent in this way of our actual group acts. In our physical world, I think it cannot be done. And this very feature of my proposal is also an obvious advantage in other contexts, as for instance our discussion of optimal agreements revealed. What's more, there's a close interaction between our moral beliefs and the group acts in which we participate, some of which I will trace in the next part, and it hence seems pretty clear that if our forms of group action were different than they are in fact, we would have significantly different intuitions about such cases. In our physical world, I certainly do not think that it is possible to deliver the truth of some of our intuitions about moral cases even in most situations in which we would lack those very intuitions. It might seem that it shouldn't matter to you what the attitudes of other members in the group acts in which you participate are when you are deciding to defect. But that determines what in fact you are doing if you do not defect and what you are defecting from if you do, and so it does matter.

Objection Nine is Parfit's "First Rescue Mission Case," which unites some of our recent worries:

A hundred miners are trapped in a shaft with flood-waters rising. . . . If I and three other people go to stand on some platform, this would . . . raise the lift, and would save the lives of these hundred men. If I do not join this rescue mission, I could go elsewhere and save . . . ten other

---

[26] What if only a few participants in a large group act would criticize defection? By Chapter 3's analysis, tendencies to criticize defectors are constitutive of group act participation, so this is impossible.

people. There is a fifth potential rescuer. If I go elsewhere, this person will join the other three and . . . save the hundred miners.[27]

It may seem that MAC will require joining the mission, which would be wrong. But, I reply, it doesn't, since you are not yet inside the group act in question. MAC treats cases in which you are already inside a group act differently from cases in which you are outside and deciding to join. Still, it may seem that it will require you to continue to participate in the group act and ignore the ten if you are already on the way to the platform. It is a case of surplus cooperation. But that isn't plausibly true either, because you would not be criticized for defecting if you go to save the ten while you are replaced in the project to save the hundred. There is an implicit exception for such a case built into realistic group acts of this sort.

9.4 Intricate Objections

Objection Eight involved a case in which an individual's contribution to a group act is very significant to the overall effect of the whole. And other cases of this general sort suggest a series of objections that plausibly require considerable complication of a fully developed MAC2. On the other hand, these cases are mostly irrelevant to the applications of MM that we will consider in Part III, except in the rare and relatively unimportant situation that there is an unusual form of special obligation that is not seconded by a large institutional form, in a way I will explain in Chapter 11. All the weightily important group acts relevant to morality lack these complicating features, because individual contributions are not very significant to their overall effects. So in reality it would not be very significant normatively if we bit all the bullets suggested by these cases with an unmodified MAC2, or if MAC2 incorporated only some of the modifications I am about to suggest, or even if MAC2 was normatively indeterminate among these various possibilities. Nevertheless, these cases and objections are worth considering, and I will sketch here the emendations to MAC2 that I think they plausibly require.

Objection Ten is a counterexample to MAC due to Ben Bradley:[28]

Suppose Beth is an influential member of a group of teenagers. The teenagers are engaged in a group action that has slightly good consequences. However, the action is very fragile; the teenagers tend to get into trouble, but Beth's good influence helps keep them bringing about the small good. Like most teenagers, they are harmless when alone; it is only when acting together that they tend to be destructive (though Beth's influence helps keep the group on the

---

[27] Parfit (1984: 67–8).
[28] Bradley (2012: 239). Bradley (2012: 238–9) attempts another counterexample: "Suppose you can achieve a great good by defecting from some group act with good (but not great) consequences. But you can achieve that great good only if the group actually does its good group act. . . . MAC doesn't give us any result at all in this case." But I reply that MAC says not to defect, because what is positively relevant to defection is only what you can achieve on your own, in the absence of the original group act.

right track). Beth faces the following situation. She can do a kindness for someone, bringing about a medium amount of intrinsic goodness (greater than the amount of goodness the group would produce); but this requires her to defect from the group, which would result in the teenagers wreaking havoc. On the other hand, she could refrain from the small kindness, remain in the group, and help the group bring about the small good. In this situation, it seems clear that Beth should *not* defect from the good group action. But MAC allows her to defect, because the situation in which she brings about the benefit of defecting (the medium good), *and the teenagers do not act in concert* (and thus bring about nothing bad), is a better situation than the situation in which Beth and the teenagers act in concert to bring about the small good. The source of the problem is that MAC requires us to make the wrong comparison. In order to get the intuitively correct result, we need to somehow take into consideration what the group act would achieve *without Beth in it*.

I think this is a good case.[29] Let me first state the modification required and then its rationale: VLD as so far formulated only properly applies to cases in which any defections it enjoins would not constitute the beneficent act hence defected from to be instead worse than the baseline of inaction. Defection in cases in which those otherwise beneficent acts would be constituted as worse than nothing is only appropriate when it meets a second test, beyond VLD as so far formulated, namely when more good is gained than lost by defection, in other words when the situation in which both (i) the group act defected from exists and has its hence bad consequences and (ii) the defection occurs, is better than the situation in which no defection occurs. This modification is supported by the same type of rationale that we developed earlier in support of unmodified VLD in the range of cases then considered. One way to put it is that VLD requires a strong rationale for defection from a weighty group act, and this qualification is required to assure that a rationale for proper defection is sufficiently strong in the relevant cases. What should be compared is the weight the original group act would have if Beth participated, on one hand, and all the relevant implications of her individual defection on the other, which include in this instance not merely, as in the cases we formerly considered, the absence of the positive effects of the group act defected from, but also all the effects of her defecting act including the negative effects that are mediated by its corruption of the original group act. The basic idea of MAC is that defection from a beneficent group action requires a weightier consequentialist rationale than the current form of the group action possesses, and in the case Bradley envisions, VLD must be buttressed in the way suggested here to assure that.

Objection Eleven is due to Aaron Bronfman. It is that Bradley-style cases also afflict DD. Because DD involves conflicts between more than one group act, Bradley-style defection, which changes a good group act into a bad one, can affect such

---

[29] But there are two group acts involved in Bradley's case, constituting the group and constituting its specific project. And it is important, if this is to be a proper counterexample, that there be a single project that would in the absence of Beth create havoc and yet with her involvement create a mild good.

conflicts in more than one way, so things get a little complicated. But begin with this relatively simple case:

(1) DD enjoins you to stick with the more consequentially weighty of two conflicting group acts A and B. But assume that defecting from B, the less weighty of the two acts, will make the effects of B worse than nothing, and even much worse than nothing, so that the entire positive weight of A is over-balanced. DD says to stick with A, and that seems wrong, But in fact, I think, the basic consequentialist rationale for DD suggests a modification of DD in this type of case, analogous to the modification Bradley's original case requires of VLD: You should still stick with A unless the additional harm done by defecting from B trumps the entire weight of A. In other words, you should compare the situation in which both (i) A has its positive weight consequent on your participation and (ii) B is worse than nothing because of your defection, with a second situation in which both (iii) A does not exist and (iv) B has its positive weight consequent on your participation, and you should stick with A except when the second situation is better than the first, in which case you should stick with B.

But there is another type of case in this general class. (2) Assume that not only B but A would be disabled by one's defection in such a way that it would become worse than nothing. There are two conflicting acts that involve the Bradley phenomenon. Then I think that a similar rationale requires a more complicated emendation: *If B is dominant according to the test just noted*, one should go on to flip things around, to compare a situation in which both (i) B is disabled by one's defection but (ii) A has its positive weight consequent on one's participation, with a second situation in which both (iii) A is disabled by one's defection but (iv) B has its positive weight consequent on one's participation. And if the second situation is worse than the first, one should stick with A after all.

But we still aren't done with this general class of cases. (3) Assume there are many conflicting group acts some or all of which will be disabled by one's defection in such a way that they will become worse than nothing. Then, I think, we should make many pair-wise comparisons by the procedures already specified. (i) For instance, if all the relevant group acts would become worse than nothing if one defects, and if all the others are dominated by the most consequentially weighty group act A by the two-step procedure already noted, then one should stick with A. (ii) If A is dominated by one other, one should stick with it. (iii) If A is dominated by several others, then we compare each pair of those others by the tests just specified, and if one of those alternative group acts dominates all the others, one should stick with it. (iv) If there is no single dominant group act that wins all the relevant pair-wise comparisons, MAC2 yields a normative indeterminacy. As far as I can see, no morally relevant group actions have this highly specific character, so this normative indeterminacy is not practically relevant.

The complexity of this three-part fix is required by the complexity of possible cases, but its rationale is simple. However, it may in turn suggest another problem.

The reasoning behind this fix may also suggests a second reply to Objection Eight, which was based on a case in which your choice is between defection from two beneficent group acts C and D, and while C has more weighty consequences still your role in D is more weighty. That second reply would be a modification of DD in which we figure into the consequential weight of your choice of C in such cases the resulting cost of your defection from D, and also figure into the consequential weight of your choice of D the resulting cost of your defection from C. And remember that I earlier tried to evade such cases without modification of MAC. Here is a two-case scenario, also due to Bronfman, that brings out the intuitive cost of a differential treatment of Objections Eight and Eleven in this respect: In Case 1, you are the member of group acts that assign you conflicting roles. Group act C will produce 0 without you, and 15 with you. Group act D will produce –10 without you, and 10 with you. MAC2 as so far specified says to go with D. But now consider Case 2, in which the outcomes are the same except that Arthur will be provided with 10 units of happiness by either group act whatever you do. So group act C will produce 10 without you, and 25 with you; group act D will produce 0 without you, and 20 with you. And MAC2 without the modification presently under consideration would say to go with C. The apparent problem with forgoing the modification now under consideration is that the addition of 10 units of happiness for Arthur whatever you do may not seem to introduce a plausible difference between the cases. And while this modification would not imply a collapse into traditional act consequentialism, because the weight of the group acts in question still figures into the proper comparison, in many cases it would move MAC further in that direction. However, I reply that, despite Bronfman's case, we should stick to my first reply to Objection Eight. The modification now under consideration is not supported by the same types of rationales as the analogous modifications I have already embraced, which require only that extra conditions beyond those specified by unmodified VLD and DD be met for defection from weighty group acts to be appropriate. This modification makes defection from weighty acts easier to justify rather than harder.

Objection Twelve is a worry about defection from beneficent group acts that would better achieve their explicit goal if one were to defect. Here's my answer: The group act of refraining from lying is beneficent, but beneficence is not the explicit goal of the act. If one would be criticized by participants when one defects to pursue some local good, one should not defect. This is a case of surplus cooperation of the sort characteristic of MAC, in which the integrity of a consequentially weighty act requires that one not defect. There is no implicit exception in the project of the group act for such a case. But if a group act explicitly pursues consequential good, then it is plausible that similar defection would not be criticized, at least given full knowledge of the circumstances, and hence that the so-called defection would be allowed or even enjoined as an implicit exception. In either case, emendation of MAC2 is not required.

Objection Thirteen is also due to Bronfman: Perhaps one's participation in a harmful group act makes it less harmful than it otherwise would be. But so far MAC2 says to defect, which seems wrong. Reply: Such cases are a little tricky. There is the possibility of heroically beneficent participation in an evil act, driving the evil act into the ground at dramatic cost to one's own well-being, but that is likely to be criticized by participants in such a way as to constitute such heroism as defection. Still, perhaps your very presence in an act mitigates its negative effect without being criticizable by participants, like a kind medic or chaplain in Hitler's army. And there is also inept participation in evil group acts, which though it may be in some cases sufficiently inept to put one outside of those acts, nevertheless in some cases plausibly leaves one inside. So these cases also arguably require an emendation, analogous to that required by Objection Ten: MAC2 only requires defection[30] from a harmful act in such a case when more will be gained through the defection than will be lost in the greater harm caused by the group act under that circumstance, in other words when the situation in which both (i) the group act defected from exists and has its more harmful consequences and (ii) the defection occurs, is better than the situation in which the defection does not occur.

MAC suggests a class of views. It may well require further emendation and development.[31] But we now have more than enough mechanism for our purposes in this book. Because I believe that the significant cases we consider in Part III have none of the special features introduced in this section, I will mostly hereafter ignore the complicated amendments to MAC2 that these objections suggest.

9.5 Conclusion

This completes my sketch of and my more or less direct argument for MAC2, and indeed for LEXIMAC and MM as a whole. Do I expect you to believe me yet?

Our standing worry in this book is indeterminacy, especially due to conditional claims like those that MAC2 deploys, and I have promised to return to that topic in detail in Chapter 11, once we are in position to understand the particular group acts that are most relevant to our concerns. And if I can't deliver the consensus of normative judgment specified by DC1-NORMS from MM in Part III, then I've admitted that I think MM is false. But Chapters 8 and 9 have provided what I take to be a sufficient argument for MAC2, and LEXIMAC in general, from the weak and abstract premises of DC2-BASIS. Still, in case that doesn't seem sufficient to you,

---

[30] Ordinary consequentialist grounds will require continued participation in the group act if defection is not required.

[31] Other modifications of MAC might be rooted in alternative conceptions of the relevance of personal identity over time, for instance involving cross-temporal dominance, where DD is applied between atomic agents who constitute a given individual at different times. Or perhaps only intuitive group agents and not those who constitute continuing individuals should be governed by MAC.

Chapter 10 will show how LEXIMAC is supported by and reconciles the three traditional ethical methods of DC3-METHODS. This way of fleshing out my abstract direct arguments may seem more convincing, even if I think it isn't necessary. And in Part III we will see that MM does deliver the consensus of normative judgment specified by DC1-NORMS. I myself believe that this argument from DC1 alone would not be enough. But perhaps you disagree.

10

From the Good

The third descriptive constraint DC3-METHODS specifies traditional mechanisms for moving from individual good to normative judgments, methods which may seem distinct from and preferable to LEXIMAC, the conjunction of MAC2 and LDP. These mechanisms are developed in the utilitarian tradition, the contractarian tradition, and the golden rule tradition in both its Kantian and non-Kantian varieties.

But this chapter argues that, in our physical world, the only viable forms of these apparent alternatives in fact support LEXIMAC. This will undercut objections rooted in these methods, and deliver on promissory notes. But the main point is that the three central methods of ethics specified by DC3 are properly unified and rectified only by LEXIMAC.[1] So this is a second positive argument for its truth. We begin with an introduction to the methods.

10.1 Reason and Sentiment

Ancient philosophers held that ethics is rooted in fancy self-interest that is nonsense in reality. The just are not well-off on the rack. Medieval philosophers held that ethics is rooted in selfishness aimed at congruence with the dictates of God and salvation. More nonsense. But the first great philosopher in English was a physicalist. In Hobbes' vision, implausibly selfish people accept a minimal morality under threat from a mundane despot. Philosophical ethics in English began as reactions to this dark conception.

We inherit two main traditions of response. Cudworth, More, Cumberland, and Richard Price conceived of morality as commands of reason. Shaftesbury, Hutcheson, Hume, and Adam Smith conceived of morality as commands of sentiment.[2] Consider these two traditions in turn.

There are three complexities that attend any attempt to root morality in a specific sentiment. First, despite what some moralists say, humans are characterized by motivational complexity, variety, and contingency. Not all human psychologies are the same simple way, dominantly pursuant of just pleasure or life or lust. Even the

---

[1] This is analogous to Sidgwick (1907) and Parfit (2011a).   [2] Sidgwick (1892).

same moral judgment can be rooted in a variety of motives in different individuals, say resentment, fear, and empathy.[3]

Second, there are a variety of specific sentiments that might be basic to morality. Some utilitarians suggest that benevolence is the central moral motive. Facts about everyone's well-being are supposed to have motivational significance because of our generally benevolent or sympathetic inclinations. But the contractarian tradition suggests another central motive. If morality is a scheme of cooperation, then morality is rooted in reciprocity. And indeed, both benevolence and reciprocity are suggested as basic moral motives by ethological work.[4] Since both utilitarianism and contractarianism are part of our normative tradition, and since both deploy motives to which most of us are susceptible, we face a strain in our moral inheritance, not unlike the one between self-interest and morality that Sidgwick discerned in our practical reason.[5] In fact, Sidgwickian self-interest and ancient and medieval moralists suggest that prudence might be a third basic moral motive. And while reciprocity encompasses a variety of forms, still if it requires mutual benefit,[6] then it is reasonable to claim that there is yet a fourth basic moral motive. That is an inertial tendency to do what our local social rules require regardless of mutual benefit.[7]

A third complexity is that there are a variety of ways to deploy any basic moral motive. For instance, the golden rule tradition combines a concern with both reciprocity and benevolence. And Adam Smith developed Hume's sympathy-based conception by suggesting two kinds of sympathy, sympathy with the motives of someone who performs an act, and sympathy with someone who is the object of someone's act. The first constitutes our sense of the propriety of acts, and the second our sense of their merit relevant to punishment and reward. And Smith thought that correction of our moral sentiments is appropriate, that we properly judge our own traits by "endeavouring to view them with the eyes of other people."[8]

These three complexities give us maneuvering room. We can develop a moral theory that combines most of the candidate basic moral motives, in a way that rectifies diverse and apparently conflicting strands in our tradition. That theory is LEXIMAC. Reciprocity supports our commitment to ongoing beneficent group acts in the way required by MAC2. A reciprocal concern for all is reflected in the leximin element of LDP, by its focus on the worst-off among us. These points will be amplified by our discussion of the relationship of LEXIMAC to the contractarian tradition. And benevolence supports the commitment of LDP to the desire-based good of all, as we will see during our discussion of the utilitarian tradition. By MAC2's asymmetric treatment of group acts that we are inside, it even provides a role for inertia.

---

[3] Consider Nietzsche (1990: 54) on diverse emotions that underlie "peace of soul."
[4] de Waal, Macedo, and Ober (2006), but see 131.   [5] Sidgwick (1907: 496–509).
[6] Including absence of mutual harm.   [7] Heath (2008); Gibbard (1990: 255–69).
[8] A. Smith (1976: 110).

But let me be clear. I don't think that all of us always have these motives; I don't even claim that all moral action is rooted in these motives. But they do seem characteristic of morality, and LEXIMAC shows how they are so.

That still leaves prudence out in the snow. And there is of course another large tradition that regards the source of morality not as sentiment but as reason. Some of that tradition deploys physically unacceptable non-natural properties. But some does not.

DC2-BASIS specifies that ethics is a form of impartial reason-giving that governs moral agents in actions affecting moral patients. And the utilitarian and contractarian traditions develop two different forms of impartial treatment, respectively of moral patients and moral agents, which are also reconciled in LEXIMAC, in ways we considered in an abstract way in the last two chapters, and will consider in more detail. These traditions antedate Hobbes and English; the forms of impartiality they require are enlaced in at least rudimentary ways in the ancient golden rule tradition, in a manner we will explore. Not only the utilitarian and contractarian traditions but also the golden rule tradition find their proper form in LEXIMAC.

But prudence is still outside. And it is not only one traditional moral motive; it is also traditionally linked with reason. Many think is has an obvious default rationality. Still, I have already said why I think that prudence and prudential rationality have no fundamental role in ethics. That would violate the impartiality of ethics. And we will shortly consider other reasons they cannot fill such a role. What's more, the thought that they are central to morality is linked with other mistakes about reason and reasons, which may root mistaken objections to my overall normative proposal MM.

MM attempts to deliver truth for ethical claims. But, an objector may claim, ethics is about normative reasons for doing things, and our reasons for doing things must be available to us like our evidence, so that rational people can follow those reasons. And that suggests that evidence rather than truth in ethics is where we should focus first. What's more, any practical ethics must give us a decision procedure for what to do, and so MM's concern with actual consequences of enormous group acts and a consensus of preferences across disparate individuals, things that we don't know much about, may seem irrelevant to what we ought to do.

But, I reply, we can't isolate the proper evidence for an ethical claim without first having some sense of what might make it true. And it is sometimes easier to determine the relevant actual consequences of our acts out in the world than to determine the convoluted internal psychological details regarding our individual intentions that Kantians deploy, or to determine what would prudentially maximize our individual expected utility, depending as it does on fine details of our attitudes towards complex combinations of conceived risks. As we will see in the next part, MM is at least as easy to apply in important cases as ethical or prudential decision procedures like these. Remember from Chapter 3 that the correct conception of our objective options does not include flukes.

Other mistakes about reasons may suggest other objections to MM. Our judgments about our ethical or other normative reasons are sometimes thought not to be truth-evaluable claims, but rather mere expressions of, or prescriptions rooted in, certain of our motivational states.[9] And normative reasons for us are also sometimes thought to be reasons for our action in a sense very closely constrained by our given desires.[10] These conceptions may suggest strict limits on the ways in which the demands of morality can outrun our motivational states or prudence, which could undercut MM. But, I reply, we saw in Chapter 4 that there is a legitimate descriptive meaning for ethical claims, which makes them robustly truth-evaluable, and it supports MM. And in preceding chapters we have developed allied forms of impartiality that allow the construction of a model of suitably rational motivation, an extension of the simpler conception of impartial motivation by hedonic value sketched in Chapter 5, which, while rooted in our own desires, fits the strictures of MM. MM is supported by the proper internalism about reasons; it delivers that aspect of quasi-normativity. And to insist on any stricter link between our actual desires or emotions and morality is a mistake. Given our emotional diversity, it is unlikely that our ethical judgments generally express emotion of any very specific sort.[11] And one apparent tight connection between overall ethical reasons for Guinevere and her desires is merely a bad pun on "reason." There are *reasons* as justifications, which I have been calling "normative reasons." But there are also *reasons* as motivations. And they are different things, even though a form of internalism about normative reasons is true. Selfish King Mark had reasons as motivations to do heinous things that he had no reasons as justifications to do. He had reasons as justifications to do things that he had no motives to do. There is no weighty ground to believe there is any highly restrictive link between normative reasons and our actual motives. We should not be bewitched by a word. But we should spend some more time on the original sin in this vicinity.

10.2 Against Prudence

We should abandon the hoary philosophical tradition that conceives of morality as a form of long-term prudential self-interest.[12] First, the cold fact is that long-term prudence sometimes conflicts with morality. Absent theological silliness that links morality and self-interest by karma or the brute force of hell fire, or absurd objective conceptions that suggest that the tortured just person is well-off, it is clear that sometimes self-interest does not recommend morality. Of course, morality is supported by social sanctions, and the obvious immorality of the relatively powerless often has a cost. But society is not omniscient and often unjust. And while we have

---

[9] Gibbard (1990). [10] Falk (1948); Frankena (1958); Williams (1981); M. Smith (1994).
[11] But see Gibbard (1990: 126–50); D'Arms and Jacobson (2000a, 2000b, 2009); and (2008: 16–17).
[12] Brink (1992) summarizes options.

moral sentiments, we also have others. By all plausible standards, some of the morally evil flourish in this our only world, and some of the morally upright suffer badly because of their morality. That, unfortunately, is reality.[13]

Perhaps we can reasonably hope that in normal circumstances the moral do fairly well. Perhaps prudence requires morality in easy circumstances. But there is a second point. Even in easy circumstances, perhaps especially in easy circumstances, prudential self-interest is too indeterminate to play a serious role in specifying or constraining morality. Any reasonably specific sense of our proper self-interest must be somewhat moralized, must rest on specific normative judgments whose propriety is secured in some other way, as I will shortly explain. We have already seen why the traditional unmoralized notion of what would be most in your self-interest on balance over your life is quite indeterminate: There is an indeterminacy of your options, especially in regard to very precise details, like whether you will be slightly better off on one option than another. Chapter 6 argued that there is no very determinate distinction between your self-regarding and other-regarding desires, and in any case it is not normatively relevant. As we saw in Chapter 7, the normatively relevant matter of the satisfaction of your consensus preferences will depend on which interpersonal comparisons and hence which consensus congruence are relevant to a particular choice. And there are in ordinary circumstances no meaningful sums of well-being within a life, just very rough ordinal comparisons of lives based on leximin. There is enough determinacy of unmoralized prudential self-interest to see that some vicious people do better than some morally upright people. But there is no reason to believe that there is a determinate fact that your life would be better overall if you ceased to give, or began to give, significant sums to charity. It is easier to see what morality requires in such a case than what unmoralized prudence demands. And that is partly because there is no very determinate fact about what unmoralized prudence demands.

My third point is to repeat that there is no default rationality of long-term prudent selfishness, despite Sidgwick and our tradition. It has been grafted by the historical accidents of our tradition onto morality only through false theological assumptions and highly implausible objectivist conceptions. Morality is, as we have seen, essentially impartial, and it is only through false religious or metaphysical beliefs that prudence has seemed properly linked to impartiality.

Most people are not usually all that calculatingly prudent. Many people smoke, and even begin to smoke knowing what we all know. And we do not always take the most efficient means to our given long-term ends. We don't even always have given long-term ends. Nor is this always a bad thing. We are sometimes motivated more by our neighbor's current suffering than by our own distant self-interest. So it is a serious mistake to attempt to make us first more calculatingly selfish so that given the

---

[13] Bloomfield (2011) says happiness requires self-respect which requires justice. But an erroneous, inflated sense of one's justice seems sufficient.

properly wise selfishness we will eventually become ethical and worry about others again. That is an extremely risky gambit for the moralist.

What's more, to convince people that they must be coherent in the optional ways that prudence and clever long-term selfishness require involves a kind of normative criticism of them, which properly requires as much justification as any normative criticism. It has no default natural precedence over normative criticism that would aim at making them less selfish by a direct route. Despite tradition, there is no reason to believe that long-term selfishness is more antecedently rational in any normatively relevant sense than benevolence. To the contrary. Since it treats quite differently cases whose differences cannot be expressed except by indexicals like "my" or proper names, it is not suitably impartial. The desire to maximize one's self-interest over time, with equal weight given to the future and to the present, isn't altogether natural and inevitable for human beings. Even when this goal makes determinate sense, it is something that we need to be trained into pursuing, and that we can pursue only very imperfectly. We come to be at least somewhat prudentially self-interested partly because we accept moralistic arguments that we ought to be. More appropriate normative arguments would lead us in a better direction.

Still, it may seem that somehow long-term maximization of individual self-interest is rational by definition or default, in some way that moral concerns are not. But this is a mistake. We have already observed one bad pun on "reason," but there is another involving "rational." Long-term prudential self-interest may involve a kind of *rational* individual coherence in one sense, and the pursuit of the good of all is *rational*, rooted in reason, in another sense. And the difference between these senses of "rational" is one reason why long-term prudential interest does not provide a proper basis for ethics. If I think that it would have been long-term prudentially coherent for Hitler to have invaded England before he invaded the Soviet Union, I am not normatively endorsing his invading England in any sense.[14] I am not claiming that he had any justification for that. Rather than infer from his premises or act on his desires, I think he should have shot himself or gone back to painting, or continued being incoherent. The normativity of the right and the good has nothing fundamental to do with rationality as long-term coherence; morality does not need to be legitimated by appeal to long-term coherent prudence.

Of course, people have personally dangerous preferences that they will regret in the morning, and sometimes that is normatively relevant. Sometimes people ought to be more long-term coherent. But I am not saying that we should never try to argue someone into long-term prudence. I am just saying that that is normative criticism quite like ordinary ethical criticism, which should properly rest on MM. Our duties to ourselves tomorrow are in fact a kind of social duty. MM does not throw prudence

---

[14] On such "bootstrapping," see Broome (2000, 2007); Kolodny (2005, 2007); Setiya (2007).

to the wind, but it rather relocates prudence as one among many normative duties to others, in particular as a duty to our future selves.[15]

The proper form of prudence is the conclusion of normative arguments, not a key independent premise rooting all normative theory. Calculating selfishness must justify itself to morality, not morality to calculating selfishness. We should just drop the old mug's game about deep prudential self-interest necessitating morality. It doesn't, and it doesn't matter that it doesn't. Still, there are traditional ways in which both reason and characteristic motives do root morality, which we will now explore.

10.3 Consequentialism

The utilitarian tradition of Hutcheson,[16] Hume, Bentham, Mill, and Sidgwick favors one form of equal treatment of moral patients, and engages our motive of benevolence. MM is recognizably in this tradition. It is a form of act consequentialism that assesses outcomes by appeal to desire-based good of a sort characteristic of the utilitarian tradition. But most utilitarian accounts deploy two-part mechanisms that differ from LEXIMAC, along two axes. They deploy alternatives to LDP and to MAC2. We need to consider these more familiar candidates to determine whether they can in reality provide viable alternatives to LEXIMAC. We will begin with competitors to MAC2.

Act utilitarianism, and act consequentialism generally, assesses the propriety of acts directly, by the value of their consequences. Chapter 9 discussed act consequentialism. It isolated only two forms with a suitable rationale, MAC2 and a radical form of act consequentialism focused on the acts of atomic agents. But there are other forms of consequential assessment of acts. Rule consequentialism assesses acts indirectly, by reference to their accord with proper moral rules, where the propriety of moral rules is determined by the value of their consequences.[17] Right acts, on this conception, are those required by the best rules. We need to consider rule consequentialism.

Since murder, lying, theft, and assault would occasionally be routes to overall best consequences, the central worry about act consequentialism is that it does not deliver plausible moral implications. MAC2 is an unusual form of act consequentialism that can deliver intuitive moral implications. But still the traditional worry about traditional forms remains, and is indeed exacerbated for radically atomic act consequentialism. While intuitions alone are not enough to support a moral theory in the absence of a legitimate rationale that explains how that theory is true, and while intuitions differ, still there is enough consensus on certain common moral claims, reflected in DC1-NORMS, so that any moral theory that flouts those commitments is

---

[15] Parfit (1984: 318–20).   [16] Hutcheson (2008: 125).   [17] Brandt (1963, 1967).

incorrect. But it has seemed that indirect forms like rule consequentialism do better in this respect, that they can deliver suitable moral implications.

My primary complaint against rule consequentialism will be that in its best forms it is not as distinct from traditional act consequentialism as it has sometimes seemed, which I'll call "the collapse problem." But to understand the depth of this problem, we will need first to consider a second problem for rule consequentialism, which will help us to isolate its best forms. We should worry whether rule consequentialism has any legitimate rationale, and hence whether it can provide an adequate asymmetric explanation of its normative claims. Intuitive implications are not enough; an asymmetric argument for the truth of a moral theory is required. To understand the force of this second problem, consider prominent recent candidates for such a rationale for rule consequentialism.

First, by focusing on a code of rules, rule consequentialism expresses our basic moral motive of reciprocity, in one recognizable sense. For instance, Brad Hooker suggests that morality is "ideally a collective enterprise, a practice to be shared."[18] However, I object that it is an unusual and implausible form of reciprocity that focuses on cooperation with ideal people rather than real ones, which requires you to do your part in the best cooperative scheme of rules even if no one else does.[19] And there are other forceful objections to rule consequentialism due to this space between the ideal and the real. It doesn't seem wrong to do something that in reality will have good consequences just because in the fanciful scenario in which everyone did it that would be bad.[20] And in reality it can have disastrous consequences to do alone what it would be ideal for everyone to do.[21] There is a possible fix of rule consequentialism to evade these objections, which involves the use of conditional or analogously complicated rules, which allow us to tailor the moral demands specified by the best rules to the reality of what others do.[22] But, as we will shortly see, this fix will only serve to magnify the problem of collapse. So let's consider other possible rationales for rule consequentialism first.

In *Reasons and Persons*, Parfit motivates a focus for morality on ideal collective action in another way, by the claim that moral theories should not be directly collectively self-defeating, by the claim that a true moral theory cannot be such that it would be worse in its own terms if all successfully followed it.[23] But Parfit's constraint is inappropriate, since all moral theories that grant a suitable importance to human well-being are directly collectively self-defeating in at least hypothetical cases. Powerful Martians could make all of our individual and indeed social options vastly worse for all of us if we successfully follow such a theory than if we don't.[24]

---

[18] Hooker (2000: 1).   [19] But see Hooker (2000: 99–102).

[20] Parfit (2011a: 308–12) calls this the Threshold Objection.

[21] Parfit (2011a: 312–20) calls this the Ideal World Objection.

[22] Ridge (2006); Parfit (2011a: 308–20). Hooker (2000: 98–9) says we are not required to follow ideal rules when that will lead to disaster. But following ideal rules can be very bad even when not a disaster.

[23] Parfit (1984: 53–66 and 87–110).   [24] Mendola (1986).

Perhaps, however, it will be claimed that moral theories should not be directly collectively self-defeating at least in reality. Still, LEXIMAC is not actually self-defeating in that way, so this cannot be a sufficient rationale for rule consequentialism in particular.

Third try: Parfit's *On What Matters* attempts to reconcile three methods of ethics that are somewhat distinct from DC3's, and in a way that may provide another rationale for rule consequentialism.[25] Sidgwick's original list of methods encompassed prudential self-interest, which I have already dismissed, but also utilitarianism and commonsense morality, which by the end of Part III I hope to have reconciled in MM. But Parfit's list includes (i) the consequentialist tradition, (ii) what he holds to be the ideal form of the Kantian tradition, and (iii) what he holds to be the ideal and hence Scanlonian form of the contractarian tradition.[26] In particular, Parfit tries to show that an act is wrong if and only if such acts are disallowed by some principle that is, (i) as in the rule consequentialist tradition, one of the principles whose being universal laws would make things go best, (ii) as in the Kantian tradition, one of the only principles whose being universal laws everyone could rationally will, and (iii) as in Scanlon's formulation, a principle that no one could reasonably reject.[27] My reconciliation will also encompass Kant, Scanlon, and the utilitarian tradition in a somewhat different way. But my first complaint is that Parfit's attempt takes place in a framework that is not available in reality: It is founded on a non-natural conception of facts about reasons that we have already rejected. And it deploys an allegedly irresolvable conflict within practical reason of a quasi-Sidgwickian kind that I have already disallowed, between impartial reasons on one hand and, on the other hand, partial reasons that favor ourselves and those we love, a practical conflict due to the alleged fact that such impartial and partial reasons are only very imprecisely comparable. Parfit believes that when "one of our two possible acts would make things go in some way that would be impartially better, but the other act would make things go better either for ourselves or for those to whom we have close ties, we often have sufficient reason to act in either of these ways."[28] But we have already seen that impartial reasons are fundamental in ethics. And it is indeed doubtful that any coherent account of what reasons are could plausibly deliver this sort of conflict situation, because any coherent account will plausibly favor either impartial or partial reasons.

Still, perhaps Parfit's reconciliation can be disentwined from these questionable commitments, and in any case our immediate interest in his proposal is located at a different point. Parfit's three constraints are meant to filter our allegedly imprecisely comparable partial and impartial reasons in such a way as to deliver a suitably impartial morality. But whatever the significance of that point, we can locate within Parfit's complex construction some possible rationales for the moral theory he

---

[25] Parfit (2011a and 2011b), especially (2011a: 275–419).   [26] We return to Scanlon.
[27] Parfit (2011a: 412–13).   [28] Parfit (2011a: 137).

attempts to build on the confluence of his three traditions, and hence for its rule consequentialist aspect, rationales that can be divorced from their physicalistically unacceptable context.

One significant aspect of Parfit's overall tale is to suggest the importance to morality of what he calls "Each-We Dilemmas," in which if *each* rather than none of us does what would be in a certain way better, *we* would be doing what would be, in this same way, worse.[29] For instance, there are cases that involve public goods: "outcomes that benefit even those who do not help to produce them. Some examples are clean air, national defence, and law and order. In many of these cases, if everyone contributed to such public goods, that would be better for everyone than if no one did. But it would be better for each person if he himself did not contribute. He would avoid the costs to himself, and he would be no less likely to receive the greater benefits from others."[30] About these cases, the characteristically Kantian question "what if everyone did that?" seems to capture something essential about moral thinking and also, Parfit now presumes, some key aspects of the moral significance of direct collective self-defeat.[31] But, I complain, the problem with Each-We Dilemmas as a rationale for rule consequentialism in particular is that, as Parfit admits, act consequentialism also evades them.[32]

Parfit also holds that there are other sorts of cases that motivate the kind of moral thinking reflected in the golden rule, a kind of thinking that the characteristic Kantian question should, he thinks, be revised to respect. In particular, when "people act wrongly, they may either be doing something that cannot often be done, or be giving themselves benefits that are unusually great.... [And m]any wrong acts benefit the agent but impose much greater burdens on others."[33] These people could rationally will everyone to act like them, because of their own privileged situations, and hence the traditional Kantian question cannot capture what is wrong with what they do. But what is wrong can be revealed if we ask instead the revised question "Can everyone rationally will that everyone act so?" So our current Parfitian proposal is that rule consequentialism has a rationale in "the belief that we ought to follow principles whose being universal laws everyone could rationally will."[34] But there are two problems with this as a motivation for rule consequentialism in particular. First, the arguments of the preceding chapters of this part imply that MM provides the best in this line that is available in reality. Morality cannot quite deliver universal laws, its true and hence rationally acceptable laws are what we have descried, and internal reasons support MM in the rational in the way I have sketched. Second, the alternative and highly idealized conception of universal laws that Parfit favors is undercut by the very worries about ideality that undercut Hooker's rationale for rule consequentialism.

[29] Parfit (2011a: 301–8).   [30] Parfit (2011a: 303).   [31] Parfit (2011a: 17).
[32] Parfit (2011a: 305).   [33] Parfit (2011a: 19).   [34] Parfit (2011a: 26).

We have surveyed prominent rationales for rule consequentialism. We've noted that when significant they do not serve to properly privilege that view over act consequentialism, and in particular over my novel form of it, except when they exacerbate the next problem with rule consequentialism, which will be debilitating.

That worry is that rule consequentialism in fact collapses into traditional act consequentialism, that it is extensionally equivalent, and hence cannot have more plausible normative implications.[35] Optimal rules will have to include exceptions for all possible circumstances in which defections would generate better consequences, and in this way rule consequentialism will end up requiring exactly the same acts as traditional act consequentialism.

Still, there are a variety of ways to attempt to prevent this collapse, which we need to consider, along with their rationales. I believe that it is most natural for rule consequentialism to assess rules by considering the consequences of compliance with those rules. I think that the most natural form of rule consequentialism has what is called the "compliance form." But the archetypical rule consequentialists focus rather on the consequences of the acceptance or internalization of the rules;[36] they prefer what are called "acceptance forms," which seem to help with the collapse problem.[37] So now I need to argue that compliance forms should be preferred.

What's the difference? Differentiating conditions of mere acceptance of rules that have been proposed include the fact that certain sorts of rules when internalized will not be fully complied with because of mistakes and backsliding, that there are expectation and assurance effects on others that come from knowing that particular rules will be followed by someone, and that there are costs of inculcating and maintaining internalization of particular codes.[38] Because of such differentiating phenomena, it is said, the best rules will not always enjoin acts directly maximizing utility.

But while acceptance forms of rule consequentialism may have intuitive implications, I do not think it is possible to provide a suitable asymmetric rationale for these forms in particular, and so we return once again to that issue. Hooker claims that morality is ideally a collective enterprise, a practice to be shared; Parfit focuses in other ways on ideal collective action. But there is nothing in those ideals of cooperation that suggests a need to consider mistakes and backsliding. Mistakes and backsliding will not occur within the cooperative ideal. Nor do mistakes and backsliding seem intuitively plausible justifying rationales for features of moral rules. Perhaps it will be said that moral rules are rules for real people, and real people make mistakes and backslide. But rule consequentialism enjoins us to follow ideal rules, and we won't be doing that when we backslide and make mistakes. Indeed, Hooker himself agrees that mistakes and backsliding can't be the point.[39] There are other differentia to which those who favor acceptance forms also point. Still, expectation

---

[35] Lyons (1965).   [36] Brandt (1963, 1979, 1992, 1996); Hooker (2000: 93–9).
[37] Parfit (2011a: 406–8) attempts to leave both possibilities in play.
[38] Hooker (2000: 76–80).   [39] Hooker (2000: 77).

and assurance effects are some of the consequential effects that even act consequentialists might deploy. And the costs of inculcating and maintaining codes because of our cognitive and emotional limitations seem to be poor justifying rationales. It seems implausible to claim that an overall beneficent murder is wrong only because we aren't a little smarter or more easily brainwashed. Of course, MAC itself depends for its intuitive implications on cases of surplus cooperation, and hence on group acts that are not optimal. But these are actual ongoing beneficent acts that should engage our real reciprocity, not merely hypothetical ideal practices.

Perhaps there are other ways to provide the necessary rationale for acceptance forms of rule consequentialism in particular. While Hooker opens his book on rule consequentialism with a question suggesting the cooperative motivation for that view I have noted,[40] he moves immediately to a second and apparently different question and motivation. Let me quote both: "Shouldn't we try to live by the moral code whose communal acceptance would, as far as we can tell, have the best consequences? Isn't the code best suited for internalization by humanity the one we should try to follow?"[41] Hooker later elaborates this second motivation, suggesting that "general internalization of rule-consequentialism would produce better consequences [than act consequentialism] because of the ... inefficiency, mistakes, and negative expectation effects that would result from an act-consequentialist decision procedure, and because of act-consequentialism's prohibitive internalization costs."[42] But this mostly appeals to factors we have already dismissed. And he also himself replies to his own suggestion here by noting that many think that "to show that belief in act-consequentialism is not optimal would not invalidate act-consequentialism's criterion of rightness."[43] And so then he retreats merely to an appeal to a better "match with our convictions," to more intuitive implications.[44] But we know this is not enough to adequately support a moral theory.

Rule consequentialists are stuck with compliance forms. Such forms may conceivably have coherent asymmetric rationales in the forms of communal cooperation to which Hooker and Parfit point, even if, as I have suggested, those rationales are not highly specific to rule consequentialism in particular. But compliance forms do not avoid collapse into act consequentialism in the same ways as acceptance forms.

Still, perhaps they do so in some other way. An apparent counterexample to the extensional equivalence of act consequentialism and compliance forms of rule consequentialism is due to Allan Gibbard.[45] There can be situations in which (1) if two agents cooperate on pursuit of some outcome then that would generate considerable utility, so rule consequentialism would require them to cooperate, but (2) in which if one of them fails to act that way, then it would be bad for the second to play their part in the ideal cooperative scheme. Act consequentialism and rule consequentialism apparently tell the second party to do different things.

---

[40] Despite his technical term "acceptance."   [41] Hooker (2000: 1).   [42] Hooker (2000: 100).
[43] Hooker (2000: 100).   [44] Hooker (2000: 101).   [45] Gibbard (1965).

But there is a problem with this case.[46] Recall that some have suggested that the proper rules may be conditional, in the sense that they require one thing under one set of conditions and another thing under other conditions.[47] And the conditionals can be tailored to take into account local circumstances, to allow for the pursuit of extra utility allowed by local conditions. Perhaps there seem to be limits to the use of this mechanism set by the limited complexity of rules that humans can actually understand, and of course two individuals may have limited knowledge about what each other will do or have done. But remember that we have forsworn appeal to human cognitive limitations as an adequate ground for the immorality, say, of murder. We are talking about compliance forms of rule consequentialism. And the problem is that conditional rules undercut Gibbard's argument against extensional equivalence.[48] Conditional rules, compliance with which would have better consequences than rules that specify no conditions, would tell the second agent to defect from cooperative behavior when the second clause of Gibbard's case obtains. And so otherwise plausible compliance forms of rule consequentialism in fact collapse into act consequentialism after all. The most optimal rules, when conditional rules are allowed, require defections in all the cases that act consequentialism itself requires. Otherwise there will be surplus cooperation.

Parfit suggests another way to block collapse. He suggests that even compliance forms of rule consequentialism have some of the intuitive advantages of acceptance forms. He claims that it is incorrect to think that compliance forms of rule consequentialism support an act consequentialist decision procedure, because in that case the "good effects of everyone's acts would be outweighed...by the ways in which it would be worse for all if we all had the motives to follow [act consequentialism. As in the case of acceptance forms, it is relevant that] in losing many of our strong loves, loyalties, and personal aims, many of us would lose too much of what makes our lives worth living."[49] But, I reply, if those effects are consequentially significant, they would be taken into account by an act consequentialist decision procedure, as indeed act consequentialists have long proclaimed. So this route does not block collapse, though it may suggest that traditional act consequentialism is not as deeply counter-intuitive in implications as would otherwise be the case.

There are other forms of indirect consequentialism. Perhaps we should focus not on rules but on the stable individual characters that would have the best consequences, and actions should be assessed indirectly by regard to those characters.[50] Or perhaps we should focus on the acts required by consequentially best motives.[51] But the considerations we have just surveyed suggest a collapse into traditional act consequentialism of appropriately motivated forms of indirect consequentialisms of these sorts also. It can't be that what makes murder wrong is just that people can't

---

[46] Mendola (2006) missed this.   [47] Ridge (2006); Parfit (2011a: 310–12).
[48] A point due to Virendra Tripathi.   [49] Parfit (2011a: 406).
[50] Railton (1984) discusses but does not endorse this.   [51] R. Adams (1976).

adjust their behavioral tendencies or motives fast enough or they can't have more complicated ones.

The collapse of properly motivated indirect forms of consequentialism into act consequentialism is especially significant because of a related point. Remember Chapter 9's discussion of Casteñeda's problem and the fact that individuals might in various moments of their lives act so as to maximize the value of consequences irrespective of what they do in other moments. As we saw, if we set MAC (and its variants) aside, there is no plausible rationale for thinking that what individuals do over time has any special status. And so, if we set MAC aside, then in its proper and hence compliance form, rule consequentialism in fact collapses not merely into act consequentialism, but into radical act consequentialism applied to atomic agents. That form suffers most acutely from the traditional worries about the unintuitive implications of act consequentialism; it will require the odd beneficent murder of the innocent. Radical atomic act consequentialism violates DC1-NORMS, and so it isn't true.

Have I just argued that consequentialism is unworkable, that any specific form is either too unintuitive to be true or lacks a coherent rationale? No, but I have just argued, in conjunction with my arguments in the last chapter, that MAC and its variants, including its best variant MAC2, are the only viable forms of consequentialism, which indeed hijack any rationale that rule consequentialists can provide.

The group acts in which we participate include actual (and hence not merely ideal) forms of moral cooperation, for instance the highly beneficent group act of refraining from murder. And these group acts have direct consequentialist rationales. Each is considerably better than its absence. Impartiality requires, as we saw in Chapter 9, that it dominate less weighty attempts to grab some additional good by defection. We will return to the details of how MAC2 works to support morality in Chapter 11, but MAC2 has a suitable direct rationale, and yet provides intuitive implications like indirect forms. It evades the problem of collapse that we have just discussed by its properly motivated principles for balancing conflicting acts. Our actual group acts do not build in all the little maximizing exceptions that tend toward collapse; they involve surplus cooperation. What's more, participation in such group acts is supported by three characteristic moral motives: benevolence, a kind of reciprocity respecting real and not merely hypothetical forms of cooperative pursuit of the general good, and even inertia. On the axis we have been considering, MAC2 is our best hope.

10.4 Desert and Outcomes

There is a second axis of variation among forms of consequentialism and utilitarianism and hence among alternatives to LEXIMAC. There is a variety of ways in which the distribution of well-being might be relevant to the overall value of outcomes that are alternatives to the qualified lexical maximin structure of LDP.

But we already discussed one key aspect of this issue in Chapter 8. The most traditional forms of utilitarianism sum overall well-being, and hold that outcomes are best if they involve the greatest sum of overall well-being or the greatest average well-being per person. They involve no real distributional concern, at least beyond a focus on averages, though they do involve one recognizable form of equal treatment of moral patients. And there are also other familiar alternatives. Hooker, among others, suggests that we should give some greater weight to the well-being of the worst-off, but not such a significant weight as my leximin proposal. In particular, he proposes that some total utility be traded for some priority for the worse off.[52] But as we saw in Chapter 8, the problem is that these various alternatives to LDP have no suitable rationales in physical reality, and indeed there are not generally the robust facts about value, for instance interpersonally comparable cardinal value, that they require.

Still, we have yet to discuss some related issues. There are somewhat unusual forms of utilitarianism that import considerations of desert directly into comparisons of outcomes, into assessments of the propriety of distributions of well-being. This might involve another sort of intuitively equal or impartial treatment. And so we need to consider these alternatives to LEXIMAC. The proper understanding of desert is also important to us in other ways.

Fred Feldman has suggested that the overall valuation of states of affairs ought to reflect the deservedness of pleasures and pains,[53] and we might adapt this to our desire-based value theory. This modification would allow us to undercut certain traditional objections to desire-based conceptions of the value of overall outcomes, in particular that they treat evil satisfactions as a positive good not only for the evil individual who enjoys them but for the world, and that they ignore the intuition that it is good when the evil suffer.

I think that consequentialists in fact must adopt a different sort of response, an indirect response, to these traditional worries. A proper conception of what is deserved must emerge as a *conclusion* of normative arguments rooted in MM, in which considerations of desert play no fundamental role.

One element of the proper indirect response depends on the basically leximin form of LDP. The satisfaction of seriously sadistic desires is seriously discounted by LDP, since the victims of sadistic acts are quite likely to be among the relatively worse off. A second element is that MAC2 enjoins respect for normatively weighty group acts, and hence will forbid sadistic pleasures involving violation of standard deontic duties, for instance the duty not to torture, as we will see in Chapter 11. What about the good for the world that is alleged to accrue from the suffering of the guilty? That involves a third element of my response. Assessments of institutions of punishment should proceed on straightforward consequential grounds, as long as the strictures of MAC2 are not engaged. And standard consequentialist justifications for

---

[52] Hooker (2000: 59).
[53] Feldman (1995a). See also Kagan (1999: 298–314 and 2012). Classics include Feinberg (1970, 1974).

institutions of legal and moral punishment are available. LDP, with its focus on the worse off, does not disable these traditional arguments, because intuitive institutions of punishment protect us from severe infractions of the well-being of individuals. There are other ways in which responsibility seems to matter to questions of proper desert, and some of these can be delivered by similar indirect mechanisms. For instance, institutions of property may be consequentially legitimate, and we will see in Chapter 11 that MAC2 endorses deontic restrictions on theft built into common-sense deontic codes as long as we presume the basic justice of property arrangements. In Chapter 12, we will also consider a beneficent group act that refines our notions of individual responsibility in various other ways.

But my indirect response may not seem to take facts about individual desert seriously enough. It may seem more appropriate to incorporate considerations of desert directly into the overall evaluation of outcomes, in the normatively funda-mental way that Feldman suggests. We might call this fundamental desert "meta-physical desert." Feldman suggests a variety of ways to deploy it. Positive desert for well-being is supposed to enhance its intrinsic goodness, that is to say its contributory value relevant to assessing the value of the whole outcome of which it is part.[54] Negative desert is supposed to mitigate the intrinsic goodness of well-being.[55] Positive desert for well-being is supposed to aggravate the intrinsic badness of what is bad for someone.[56] And negative desert is supposed to mitigate the intrinsic badness of what is bad for someone.[57] Feldman presumes a sort of cardinality of well-being that is not generally available in our world, but this mechanism could be adapted to ordinal well-being.

However, there are telling objections to such a proposal. Feldman is right to say that proper metaphysical desert of this sort must not depend on a normative judgment about its good consequences. Otherwise debilitating circularities are intro-duced, because metaphysical desert is supposed to be a part of what makes conse-quences valuable. And in fact, for similar reasons, metaphysical desert must also be independent of different sorts of moral judgments, for instance those regarding whether or not someone did something morally wrong, when those judgments rest on consequences. I don't think it is plausible that any intuitive desert is independent of all those other judgments, and I certainly think it can't coherently be for a consequentialist. But the real problem is the availability of metaphysical desert in our physical world. As might be expected from Part I, there are virulent indetermin-acies of any remotely plausible metaphysical desert, any desert that has not been refined by normative judgments rooted in consequences.

For one thing, there is some ambiguity regarding what desert encompasses. Some distinguish desert from other similar factors, as for instance Nozick distinguished desert for what you work for from your entitlement to what you have inherited.[58] Or

---

[54] Feldman (1995a: 575).   [55] Feldman (1995a: 576).   [56] Feldman (1995a: 578).
[57] Feldman (1995a: 578).   [58] Nozick (1974: 159).

perhaps you are entitled to your body even though you haven't worked for it. Still, presumably Feldman intends a broad notion, to cover all relevant cases of this general sort. But that very breadth is itself problematic. It is one ground of indeterminacy. Consider the wide range of forms of desert various people hold to be relevant to the evaluation of outcomes. Some authors focus on an overall evaluation of the deservingness of an agent. For instance, Ross suggested that we all have a duty to upset any distribution of happiness not in accord with the merits of the individuals involved, which seems rather humorous in its strenuous implications.[59] Geoffrey Cupit suggests that we focus on fittingness to the status of persons.[60] Perhaps instead we could focus on moral character. But there are obvious difficulties in claiming that there is one determinate sort of status or merit or character, or one particular mixture of those factors, that should properly condition the value of someone's well-being to any particular fixed degree or in any particular way. Consider the wide variety of combinations of merits and statuses and characters that real people have. It is implausible that there is some fact about the overall evaluation of those things that is sufficiently determinate to fix what they differentially deserve, and which is independent in the necessary way of other moral judgments rooted in consequences. Remember that we are now talking about variant forms of consequentialism.

Feldman himself seems to suggest that we focus in particular on the deservingness of someone for particular goods. But on that model it may be that different sorts of deservingness for different goods pull in different directions in a way that undermines determinate overall judgment. Perhaps you deserve the pleasure that your raise would generate but not what it would buy you. And that model requires a determinate account of which goods go with what bases of desert. We have no reason to believe that such an account is possible, except perhaps on the basis of consequences. But then it could not govern metaphysical desert.

There are other axes of variation regarding proper bases of desert. Some think that whether someone deserves some extra good depends solely on matters that are up to them. But others think that excellences you are born with are such that you can deserve their fruits. Feldman suggests that you can deserve recompense for some harm done to you,[61] and that those who are innocent but about to suffer terrible harms through disease may deserve now some prior special treatment.[62] He also suggests that you can better deserve something if you haven't in the past enjoyed many goods of that kind, if you haven't stolen or destroyed things of that kind, and if it is your legally recognized property.[63] But he makes no attempt to formulate an overall account of the proper bases of desert, and it is certainly hard to see how a consequentialist could do it without appeal to consequences. For one thing, we shouldn't be quick to assume that all actual property rights are legitimate, so that some starving peasant who filches an unnoticed apple from Milord's distant tree does

---

[59] Ross (1930: 26).   [60] Cupit (1996).   [61] Feldman (1995b: 68).
[62] Feldman (1995b: 70).   [63] Feldman (1995a: 570–2).

not deserve the apple. *Legitimate* property rights depend, according to any consequentialism worthy the name, at least partly on consequential assessment.

As Sidgwick showed us long ago, any attempt to apply robust commonsense notions of desert quickly reveals confusions, conflicts, and vagueness in such notions, which must be resolved by appeal to independent normative principles, like LDP and MAC2.[64] For instance, there is no real consensus in commonsense that determines that monetary rewards should accrue on the basis of effort, actual contribution, native skill, or market forces.[65]

And these traditional difficulties are magnified by physical reality. Focus on the notion of what an individual contributes to an outcome. There is even intuitive vagueness about one's actual contributions to most outcomes, given the complex social world in which we live and act. But really our intuitions are too determinate for reality. This is closely related to the indeterminacy of options.

It may seem that someone's wealth is a result of their own labors and that someone else starves by their own fault, in some deep way that might legitimate one social practice or another, and not because of indirect consequentialist assessments. Perhaps some think that this sort of responsibility is identical to the agency responsibility discussed in Chapter 3. But agency responsibility extends no farther than alternatives that involve merely objective *ex ante* probabilities, and hence characteristically not as far as actual wealth later in life. And probably the relevant sort of desert has to involve other types of constraints, like what constitutes natural property. Still, plausibly the relevant sort of desert would rest on agency responsibility in some way. To evade resolving these complexities, call what is at issue "individual responsibility."

Now I will argue that individual responsibility involves significant indeterminacy in our physical world. My first point is that since individual options are moderately indeterminate, individual responsibility is often indeterminate to like degrees. If what we can do is indeterminate, then what we are individually responsible for is likewise indeterminate, because, whether or not individual responsibility and agency responsibility are identical, individual responsibility at least partly depends on agency responsibility. If our options are indeterminate and we in fact did something, then it may be indeterminate what would have happened if we hadn't done that thing. It may also be indeterminate, when we didn't do anything, what would have happened if we had done some particular thing. My second point is that what often matters to intuitive individual responsibility are remote effects of action, whether now you would have been happier if you'd worked a little harder when you were young. And that is one of the ways in which options are most likely to be indeterminate. Individual responsibility resting on remote effects is likely to be virulently indeterminate

---

even though options in general are only moderately indeterminate. Another way to put this is that flukes are often involved in individual responsibility, and so the only moderately indeterminate option sets on which we have focused won't deliver it at all.

Now mix in some of the intuitive worries with these analytical worries. The complex social and material circumstances in which we live make it even intuitively difficult to ascertain an individual's contribution to our collective well-being, or to their own. Individuals act into complex social and material circumstances that are in no intuitive sense due to their own action. This social background, and hence the action of others, is often a part of what makes an individual action intuitively a contribution. And of course the capacities for such actions often depend on education supported by complex social institutions. But these intuitive considerations are underscored by the indeterminacy of options and analogous conditionals. For one thing, in complex social cases where individual actions take place in an arena partly constituted by the actions of others, and indeed in which the choices of one agent are often affected by the choices of others, the indeterminacy of options ramifies. Our options can depend on others' actions, even others' future actions. And the actions of others depend partly on what their options are and are conceived by them to be. A's options would be moderately indeterminate even if later B's actions were fixed. But B has moderately indeterminate options even given what A will in fact do, and even more indeterminate options on the hypothetical assumption that A did other things, and what B will do depends partly on B's options. Intertwining indeterminacies like these reach back indefinitely into our social and individual past, as they reach forward indefinitely into our future. This deepens the already serious intuitive problems faced by the notion of what is a due to one's own action in such cases. It generates what seem to be virulent indeterminacies.

Other ways in which individual responsibility is sometimes thought to be normatively important in relatively deep ways also involve serious indeterminacies rooted in the indeterminate truth values of analogous conditional claims. For instance, in the next section we will consider contractarian conceptions that some think reflect a proper sense of individual responsibility better than consequentialism. Such conceptions sometimes rely on the notion of how well-off one would have been in a state of nature by one's own effort, or of how much social good would have been lost without one's participation. But such wild counterfactual conditionals are highly indeterminate. They rest crucially on what background conditions are relevantly important, and we have no reason to expect that the facts will resolve quite natural disputes about such importance.[66]

These metaphysical points may seem of quite limited bearing to at least some cases of intuitive desert. We have already noted other problems for notions of desert rooted

---

[66] See Murphy and Nagel (2004) on the incoherence of the notion that someone deserves their pretax income.

in character and merit, but it is intuitive to hold that one's body in some deeply natural sense belongs to one, and not to the social collective, whatever the metaphysics of action, and whatever the facts of merit- or character-based desert. Perhaps one is entitled to one's body in a way that does not depend on merit or what one has accomplished, and so evades indeterminacies.

But being entitled to one's body crucially involves being entitled to its inviolate healthy state, for instance being entitled to your organs even when they might be better used elsewhere. And there are commonsense confusions very close to the surface in such a notion, which are again magnified by the indeterminacy of options and related indeterminacies of conditionals. The health of any given individual's body and set of organs as opposed to another's is often even intuitively dependent on past conditions that are affected by social conditions, that for instance determine that someone is well-nourished and someone else badly nourished before the age of two, that someone is well-parented and someone ill-parented, that someone is surrounded by environmental toxins and someone else is not. If some differences in bodily health are due to accident or genetic endowment, then certainly some socially determined conditions increase the likelihood of that accident or the negative expression of that endowment. And indeed genetic differences and differences in the genuine accidents we suffer do not non-controversially *legitimate*, by regard to desert, differences in the distribution of well-being anyway. Exercise and healthy eating do matter. But if we consider whether someone's bodily health depends *solely* on conditions that give them an obvious intuitive right to it, for instance because they would have been healthy had no advanced medical technologies or social structures existed, the relevant conditionals are often virulently indeterminate, because they have such wildly counterfactual antecedents.

Consider another sort of case. Remember from Chapter 3 that there are grave intuitive conflicts for contemporary commonsense in determining guilt, given various sorts of childhood histories and unusual psychologies in perpetrators, in cases faced by real juries. These commonsense confusions about moral guilt are underscored by the indeterminacy of conditionals. It may simply be indeterminate whether some evildoer would have performed some act of murder or abuse if they hadn't been abused as a child.

There is also another relevant point. Most intuitive notions of desert require that one's earlier actions receive later reward. But remember that the basic moral patients are atomic agents, that exist but for a moment. This may seem just another objection to my focus on atomic agents. But stare closely at the details. Here are two identical atomic agents, with exactly the same contemporaneously determinate qualitative properties. According to some, one deeply deserves, as a fundamental matter at the deepest level of moral truth, to suffer and the other to flourish, because of differences in their histories, differences that we must presume at least one of them can no longer accurately remember so that they can be contemporaneously qualitatively identical, and hence also differences that have no bearing on their contemporary character or what they will do henceforth. This makes no strong intuitive sense. Perhaps robust individual responsibility requires a different type of picture: Assume that personal identity over time requires possession of the same immaterial soul, and it somehow gets spotted over time by past sin, so that physical duplicates at this moment are really different deep inside, a difference that perhaps has no bearing on their contemporary character or what they will do henceforth, or even perhaps that does. But of course such claims are false in reality. Certainly, if you think instead that differences in histories relevant to intuitive desert always lead to differences in contemporaneous states of character realized physically in the moment, you had better worry a little about the plausibility of that belief.

Still, it may seem that LDP has a special problem if I refuse to accept facts of responsibility or desert as basic factors in moral evaluation, just because of its other structural features. Assume that the worst-off person throughout his life is Tristram. He's in constant pain. But Tristram is also an inveterate gambler. Every time he gets some transfer of wealth that makes him momentarily somewhat better off on suitably consensual grounds, he immediately spends it all at the gaming tables, and not in an effective way. He consistently wastes his transfer. But since he's always worst-off, LDP seems to require that we give his momentary happiness priority, and keep the transfers coming, wasting all our wealth.[67] But, I reply, I do not deny that responsibility never matters to moral evaluation. In Chapter 12, I develop a considerable mechanism by which it does, a group act that is a kind of system for dealing with the responsibility of individuals. It is just that I deny that individual responsibility is directly relevant to the assessment of outcomes as better or worse, that it is fundamental in that particular way, which is the issue now under consideration. And I deny that largely because reality does not provide the resources to allow desert to be fundamentally relevant to the value of outcomes in any suitably intuitive and legitimate and yet determinate way. There is in the real world no deep metaphysical fact about what Tristram deserves because of his wasteful passion. Still, MM does not in fact require that we spend all our social wealth indulging his vice, as we will be in position to see shortly.

The metaphysics of action is normatively relevant. Even Kant—the paradigmatic philosophical source of the claim that it is a better world if the guilty suffer—struggled with the effects of character on individual action, and held that the good will on which his deontological normative claims rest required a radically free noumenal choice, outside of time, of one's individual character. I think he was right about what his false moral theory required. Determinate and forceful conceptions of normatively basic desert rest, as they historically have rested, on metaphysical presumptions that are unrealistic.

---

[67] Kagan (2012: 23–7) motivates the principle that in distributional conflicts "fault forfeits first."

We have seen in this and the preceding section that LDP and MAC (especially in its best variant, MAC2) have no viable consequentialist competitors in the real world, although the metaphysical strictures of physicalism did much of the new work only in this section. Like it or not, MM, including LEXIMAC, is the only viable inheritor of the utilitarian tradition.

10.5 Hobbes and Gauthier

The contractarian tradition of Hobbes, Locke, Rousseau, and Rawls invokes the equal status of moral *agents*, cooperating together in a way supported by the basic moral sentiment of reciprocity. This has an echo in the non-defecting cooperation in beneficent group acts required by MAC2, and also in the concern for the worst-off encompassed by the leximin features of LDP, which is modeled on Rawls' famous Difference Principle.[68] Indeed, LDP's foundation in a consensus of preference and MAC2's deference to specific goods pursued by widespread group acts capture two aspects of Rousseau's highly ambiguous notion of the general will.[69] But there are a wide variety of contractarian mechanisms for moving from desire-based well-being to normative claims, and we need to explore their range.

Hobbes held that there was an actual historical contract among a despot and citizens desperate to avoid short, nasty, brutish lives in a harsh state of nature, a contract binding on descendants and specifying certain duties.[70] But there was no such contract, it would not be morally binding on descendants, and contracts signed under such duress are not valid. To each according to their threat advantage is not a plausible moral ideal. So any plausible contractarian mechanism must be more refined. There are three traditions of refined contractarianism. But we will see that only the third is viable, and LEXIMAC is within it.

The first refined form of contractarianism focuses on the contributions of individual contractors to social good relative to a state of nature that is somewhat more palatable than Hobbes', and hence may lack duress. There is a sense in which MAC2 is also focused on the contributions of cooperators to social good. But in MAC2 each cooperating member of a group act receives the full moral credit, for good or ill, of the whole. And the first refined form of contractarianism focuses rather on the individual contributions of individual cooperators. It is alleged that a proper concern with the equal status of agents requires a concern with the contributions for which they are individually responsible.

But in 10.4 we saw that such contributions are characteristically too indeterminate to play any legitimate foundational role in normative theory. And there are also other debilitating problems for such proposals. David Gauthier's *Morals by Agreement* is

---

[68] "Social and economic inequalities are to be arranged so that they are ... to the greatest benefit of the least advantaged." Rawls (1971: 302).
[69] Rousseau (1973a: 120–4 and 1973b: 182–6).   [70] Hobbes (1955: 80–120).

the best-developed contemporary contractarianism of this type. Gauthier attempts to demonstrate the rationality for individuals of a form of morality.[71] In particular, he presumes the normative rationality of something resembling selfish prudence, and tries to show that it requires morality. This is characteristic of the first refined form, and we saw in 10.2 that such constructions are also not viable, because they assume that prudence is normatively prior to morality, while it is not. In addition, Gauthier deploys claims about utility comparisons that we have seen to be often unrealistic. But his project has three more specific features on which it will also be instructive to focus.

First, Gauthier argues that we ought to adopt a conception of individual rationality as "constrained maximization," requiring rational individuals to fulfill their roles in certain cooperative strategies.[72] Second, he argues that the particular cooperative strategies that rational cooperators would adopt and follow are those that meet the "principle of minimax relative concession" if agreed upon in a certain initial situation.[73] Third, he argues that the relevant initial situation must meet "the proviso."[74] All three claims are highly problematic, and for a revealing single reason.

Rationality as constrained maximization arises as a modification of the standard conception of rationality as individual utility maximization, which holds that a rational individual is one who acts so as to maximize his or her expected utility.[75] Individual utility maximizers who happen not to care about others or the keeping of agreements, run into trouble in Prisoner's Dilemmas, in which if all act in their self-interest, then all lose.[76] Gawain and Percival commit a sacrilege and a robbery. The penalty for sacrilege is twenty years, for robbery five years. There is only sufficient evidence to convict them of robbery, but the wily sheriff holds them separately and offers each a deal: "Rat on your partner in sacrilege and I'll overlook your part in the robbery." Each is an individual utility maximizer who cares only about himself, and can exact no revenge later. Each sees that he is better off ratting, whatever the other does. Even if they had made an agreement beforehand not to rat, they would now have no motive, barring revenge or some special desire to keep agreements, to keep it. So both will rat and get twenty years, while if they had both clammed up they would have gotten only five years. They would be better off, in even a self-interested way, if they weren't so selfish. As a general fix for such situations, Gauthier suggests we become "constrained maximizers," that we adopt a conception of rationality that does not require individuals to maximize expected individual utility in all circumstances, but rather requires them to maximize expected individual utility except when engaged in certain cooperative strategies to the benefit of all cooperators, and

---

[71] Gauthier (1986).   [72] Gauthier (1986: 167).

[73] Gauthier (1986: 145). The rational are also supposed to fulfill their roles in strategies that approximate these.

[74] Gauthier (1986: 190–232).

[75] Gauthier is an informed desire theorist. See Gauthier (1986: 32–3).

[76] Gauthier (1986: 79–80).

then to fulfill their roles in those strategies.[77] Gawain and Percival would get off with five years each if they were constrained maximizers with a cooperative strategy not to rat.

Other solutions are possible. If Percival and Gawain had an agreement not to rat and strong preferences to keep their agreements, or sufficient mutual concern, they could escape their dilemma without a change in their conception of rationality. Individual utility maximization requires that one do what one most wants, but it does not require that one have only selfish wants, that one care only for one's interests and not about agreements or compatriots. But Gauthier favors a formal solution, allowing everyone to escape Prisoner's Dilemmas regardless of the content of their desires. Still, it is quite odd for Gauthier to speak of a change in our conception of rationality, away from individual utility maximization. Barring some idealization, the conception of rationality as individual utility maximization is ordinarily supposed to do little more than capture the truism that we do what we most want. I've said that I don't believe that we exhibit the patterns of preference over risks that this conception requires, nor do I think it is normatively irrational that we do not. But individual utility maximization is ordinarily favored on the grounds that it helps define desire strengths and utilities, that it allows the assignment of utilities to individuals on the basis of their behavior. If so, it cannot be abandoned without abandoning talk of utilities. And the true oddity is that Gauthier himself holds that the conception of rationality as individual utility maximization helps to define utilities. He explicitly introduces utilities as a measure of preference defined by formal conditions equivalent to the conception of rationality as individual utility maximization.[78] And yet he holds that constrained maximizers, following a different conception of rationality than they must follow if utilities are to be defined, constrainedly maximize those very utilities. Constrained maximization is possible only when utilities exist, but when utilities exist, constrained maximization is impossible. Constrained maximization is contradictory.[79]

---

[77] Gauthier (1986: 167).   [78] Gauthier (1986: 38–46).

[79] Gauthier does not discuss this problem, but has one resource: a distinction between "parametric" and "strategic" choice situations. In the former, "the actor takes his behavior to be the sole variable in a fixed environment." In the latter, "the actor takes his behavior to be but one variable among others, so that his choice must be responsive to his expectations of others' choices, while their choices are similarly responsive to their expectations." Gauthier (1986: 21). Cooperative behavior requires a strategic situation, and individual utility maximization and constrained maximization diverge only when cooperative behavior is possible. Hence they diverge only in strategic situations. And Gauthier is only explicitly committed to the definition of utilities by principles equivalent to individual utility maximization in parametric situations, in which individual and constrained maximization do not diverge. So perhaps Gauthier thinks that utilities are defined only in parametric situations. But this is implausible. First, the features of constrained maximization that function only in strategic situations would have very different motivations than those which function in parametric situations. The former would allow the rational to escape Prisoner's Dilemmas; the latter would define their utilities. Second, we would not have utilities involving many social situations, which measure preferences that can be realized only in strategic situations. One sort of solipsism would be built into our desires.

There is a natural diagnosis for this problem. Gauthier sometimes fails to heed a crucial distinction that is closely related to puns on "reason" and "rationality" discussed earlier. Sometimes when we call someone rational we mean to attribute to them "rationality as justification," to claim that they act as reason commands or requires, that their act is supportable by proper reasons given their proper weight, that it is justified. But sometimes we mean something less. In fact sometimes we mean something considerably less, something even weaker than the coherent long-term prudence we discussed earlier. Sometimes when we say that someone is rational we mean that they possess merely "rationality as intelligibility."[80] This is a sort of rationality as *minimal* coherence that any agent must possess if they are to be an agent, if there is to be a belief–desire explanation of their actions, if they are to have preferences or a good. Those many agents who act in an unjustified way do not possess rationality as justification, even if we can explain their acts by citing their intelligible motivations for doing what they do. I think that individual utility maximization is meant by Gauthier, along with others who propose it as a basis for normative argument, to be in the first instance a theory of rationality as intelligibility. I've already said why I think they are wrong about that, but it seems to be what they presume. Otherwise they would need to provide normative argument to support such a claim. Gauthier and his friends presume individual utility maximization to characterize a relatively weak property, possessed by the justified and unjustified alike, those who escape Prisoner's Dilemmas and those who do not. It may also seem important that those who possess rationality as justification be able to escape such dilemmas. But the problem is this: We should not formulate a conception of rationality as justification as if it were an alternative to a conception of rationality as intelligibility. Gauthier appears to do just that, forgetting the difference. My diagnosis is that this is the source of the inconsistency in constrained maximization, which depends on principles of intelligibility it denies.

Other central features of Gauthier's account underwrite this diagnosis. Turn to its second key feature. Gauthier's constrained maximizers would fulfill their roles only in certain cooperative strategies, those that benefit all cooperators and are deemed rational by the principle of minimax relative concession. This principle holds that, in any cooperative interaction to the benefit of all cooperators, the rational joint strategy is determined by a bargain among the cooperators in which each first advances a claim to all the fruits he or she can glean from any cooperative strategy of at least some benefit to all and then offers a concession from that claim which is no greater in relative magnitude than "the minimax concession."[81] What is the "minimax concession"? Each cooperative strategy would require, ignoring ties, that some cooperator make the maximum concession anyone makes on that strategy. The minimax concession is the minimum maximum concession, the smallest such

---

[80] I owe this phrase to Pat Francken.   [81] Gauthier (1986: 145).

maximum concession required in any relevant strategy.[82] Gauthier proposes that we measure the size of concessions by their "relative magnitude," since he is skeptical about robust interpersonal comparisons of the absolute values of people's utilities and so concessions:

The *relative magnitude* of any concession may be expressed as the proportion its absolute magnitude bears to the absolute magnitude of a complete concession [of all the fruits of cooperation]. If the initial bargaining position [prior to bargaining] affords some person a utility u^*, and he claims an outcome affording him a utility $u\#$, then if he concedes an outcome affording him a utility u, the absolute magnitude of his concession is $(u\# - u)$, of complete concession is $(u\# - u^*)$, and so the relative magnitude of his concession is $[(u\# - u)/(u\# - u^*)]$.[83]

Though Gauthier is skeptical of robust interpersonal comparisons of utility, his unrealistic assumptions about *intrapersonal* utilities play an important role in this construction. But let me focus on two implications of the principle of minimax relative concession: (a) it requires equal relative concessions of all parties except when some can gain by a deviation from equality at no cost to others; (b) it is sensitive to what the initial bargaining position is, since this determines u^*.

There are four conditions from the conjunction of which Gauthier claims the principle follows.[84] Focus particularly on the third:

Willingness to concede: Each person must be willing to entertain a concession in relation to a feasible concession point if its relative magnitude is no greater than that of the greatest concession that he supposes some rational person is willing to entertain (in relation to a feasible concession point).[85]

Why does Gauthier suppose this to be true? He says this: "Condition (iii) expresses the equal rationality of the bargainers. Since each person, as a utility-maximizer, seeks to minimize his concession, then no one can expect any other rational person to be willing to make a concession if he would not be willing to make a similar concession."[86] In other words: (a) One cannot expect another equally rational agent, in a position symmetrical to one's own, to agree to a concession greater than one will. (b) And the size of a concession is determined by the function described. Step (a) may be problematic, but focus on (b). Is it fair here, or does it merely beg the question?

---

[82] Gauthier (1986: 137).   [83] Gauthier (1986: 136), with a typo corrected.

[84] Gauthier (1986: 145). The other three: "Each person must claim the cooperative surplus that affords him maximum utility, except that no person may claim a cooperative surplus if he would not be a participant in the interaction required to provide it.... [E]ach person must suppose that there is a feasible concession point [a point in a utility space representing an outcome that would result from a set of individual concessions by the prospective cooperators] that every rational person is willing to entertain.... No person is willing to entertain a concession in relation to a concession point if he is not required to do so by [the other] conditions." Gauthier (1986: 143).

[85] Gauthier (1986: 143).   [86] Gauthier (1986: 143–4).

Consider a situation where a person who is well off and a person who is badly off agree to some cooperative enterprise yielding a profit in some good which meets two conditions: the good can be distributed in any proportion between the two and is such that, while no interpersonal comparisons of utility are assumed, each individual would receive the same amount of utility for each unit of the good he or she receives. I don't believe this always makes realistic sense, but Gauthier disagrees, and even I think that there can be local pockets of individual cardinality of this sort. This case also presumes that we can still properly speak of people being relatively well or badly off even if Gauthier is right that there are no robust interpersonal comparisons of utility levels, but if his account implies that we cannot, then it is in direct conflict with both common sense and reality. Focus now on the key point: Gauthier's principle requires that our pair split the proceeds equally, which is an equal relative concession on the part of both parties.[87] But we might well imagine the worse-off person claiming that an equal split is really a greater concession on her part, since she needs the cooperative proceeds more. One's notion of the size of a concession depends crucially on one's notion of what a reasonable and fair expectation is. Different people have many different conceptions of what constitutes a just or fair expectation. So if rational agents will agree only to what they believe to be equal relative concessions, different agents will make different agreements depending on what their conception of a fair and reasonable expectation, and hence an equal relative concession, is.

Of course, Gauthier's point is likely to be that the truly rational have no such preconceptions of what constitutes a fair or reasonable expectation. But remember our distinction. Gauthier does not demonstrate that all cooperators who are rational as intelligible must adopt his conception of equal concession. History would prove any such demonstration wrong, and, in any case, we have seen that he seems to be developing an account of rationality as justification. But if he means his conception of the size of a concession as part of an account of rational as justified expectations, concessions, or bargains, still he makes no *normative* argument for it. Perhaps his idea is that we should begin by deploying a prudential, selfish sort of rationality as justification. But he provides no argument that it would be prudentially irrational for the worse-off bargainer to insist on their own greater need. What seems rather to happen is this: Gauthier uses a specific theoretical vocabulary for discussing the size of concessions that suggests the conception of equal concession that he adopts.[88] That theoretical vocabulary hides alternatives to the conception he adopts, which hence seems the only plausible option. Gauthier's description of a concession, in that vocabulary, abstracts away from features relevant to determining its rationality as justification, for instance the levels of well-being of the parties prior to cooperation. Gauthier's skepticism about interpersonal comparisons of utility levels does not alter

---

[87] Gauthier (1986: 153).   [88] Gauthier (1986: 134–7).

the normatively controversial nature of this exclusion. Again I offer my diagnosis: Gauthier's theoretical vocabulary may be appropriate to a discussion of the rationality as intelligibility of concessions, at least if we suspend some of our standing worries. But Gauthier imports that vocabulary into a discussion of the rationality as justification of concessions without adequate rationale. The surface plausibility of Gauthier's account of rational bargains stems from a failure to keep rationality as intelligibility and rationality as justification suitably distinct.

The third key feature of Gauthier's account is his notion that the initial bargaining position, the state of nature against which the relative gains and concessions of rational cooperation are to be measured, is a state that meets "the proviso."[89] That is to say, it is a state in which all the effects of "taking advantage" are removed, in which what Gauthier calls the "rights" of all are respected, in the sense that no one has acted in such a way as to make another worse off than he or she was prior to interaction. This idealization is perhaps some improvement on the Hobbesian principle of to each according to their actual threat advantage. But why does Gauthier suppose that rational bargains must meet the proviso? Because "without limitations that exclude the taking of advantage, a rational individual would not dispose himself to" comply with cooperative agreements.[90] The proviso is supposed to set the standard for fair and impartial agreement. Given the equal rationality of all cooperators with rational agreements, none will expect more or accept less.[91]

But does the proviso set a proper standard for fair and impartial agreements? The proviso constrains the initial bargaining situation to one in which no one has been made worse off by the forceful removal of any of the fruits of their individual labors. As Gauthier himself notes, the proviso says nothing about equalizing resources or meeting needs as a fair background to bargaining, and in fact the proviso prohibits equalization by force. But there are quite intuitively unfair bargaining advantages that accrue not only from force but from greater initial resources or lesser needs. Gauthier is well aware of this. Consider this cheeky quote: "The rich man may feast on caviar and champagne, while the poor woman starves at the gate. And she may not even take the crumbs from his table, if that would deprive him of his pleasure in feeding the birds' unless her poverty came about by a violation of the proviso or the principle of minimax relative concession."[92] Gauthier's reply to those who find this deeply unintuitive is merely an appeal to the contrary intuition that people are entitled to the fruits of their natural assets, as crystallized in an expansion of Nozick's Robinson Crusoe example.[93] We saw earlier that robust claims of individual responsibility such as those respected by the proviso are often nonsense in our world, that claims of proper responsibility must be conclusions of normative arguments and not

---

[89] Gauthier (1986: 190–232).   [90] Gauthier (1986: 225).
[91] Gauthier (1986: 225–7).   [92] Gauthier (1986: 218).
[93] Gauthier (1986: 218). At Nozick (1974: 161), many give 25 cents each to Wilt Chamberlain to see him play basketball, and he becomes rich.

first premises of such arguments. But even if we continue to suspend that piece of skepticism about Gauthier's project, bare appeals to intuition are not adequate to resolve normative disputes when intuitions conflict. And in fact Gauthier's form of argument underlines the fact that different people have different conceptions of what counts as a fair bargaining position and hence a rational-as-justified, legitimate bargain. Gauthier's appeals here are normative; he is clearly concerned to show that the proviso constrains rational-as-justified bargains. He makes no attempt to prove that the rational as intelligible would all accept his conception of the appropriate initial bargaining situation. Such a claim would be obviously false. Again, I offer my diagnosis: The boldness of Gauthier's normative presuppositions is masked by his focus on what seems sometimes to be (or at least sometimes fails to clearly not seem to be) a conception of rationality as intelligibility. This gives his construction the air of being hardheaded and realistic. If it is a truism that everyone acts to do what they most want, to maximize their own utility except when cooperating to get even more, then that may seem to legitimate one's refusal to take the suffering of others seriously when one cannot get something out of the satisfaction of those others. But we must remember that even utility maximizers are not necessarily selfish, since preferences need not be selfish. And we must recall that the intelligible but selfish are not necessarily justified, since there is more than one sense of "rationality." If it is a truism that the intelligible do what they most want, it is not a truism that it is legitimate not to care when others suffer without cost to oneself.

The first refined form of contractarianism is unworkable. It depends on the highly indeterminate notion of individual contributions to social good. And it falsely presumes the default normative rationality of something resembling selfish prudence; although the maximization of expected utility differs somewhat from the long-term maximization of individual desire-satisfaction, even under conditions of omniscience, because desires change and because stable desires can have conflicting conditions of satisfaction as time proceeds and circumstances change, still they are closely related, this egoism of a moment and of a life. What's more, in its best-developed instance, the first refined form of contractarianism confuses intelligibility and justification, in a way that seems indeed characteristic of the entire form, confusing as it generally does the minimally rational and the egoistic, the egoistic and the justified.

10.6 Harsanyi and Rawls

The second refined form of contractarianism also works forward from the presumption of the default normative rationality of something resembling prudence, and so is problematic in one of the same ways as the first. But it is not centrally concerned with individual contributions, and requires a more severe idealization of the conditions necessary for normatively binding contracts than Gauthier's proviso. These seem improvements. On this second conception, fair contracts governing social arrangements stem from a fair bargaining situation that involves or mimics something like an equality of needs and resources in the bargainers, so that none have an unfair bargaining advantage.

This class of contractarian accounts is paradigmatically represented by Harsanyi and Rawls.[94] They presume in particular that fair arrangements are those that would be chosen by individuals who are self-interested but choosing under highly hypothetical conditions of ignorance that ensure fairness.

Rawls' *A Theory of Justice* says that a just society is arranged in the manner that would be chosen by someone to govern the society in which they would live, if they were motivated to advance their own interests and their descendants', and yet situated behind a Veil of Ignorance that blocks knowledge of their place in society in regard to class or social status, their fortune in the distribution of natural assets and abilities, their conception of the good and plan of life, and their particular psychological peculiarities. In such circumstances, Rawls claims, because such a chooser has only the vaguest knowledge of the probabilities of what position they will occupy in their society, and because they can see that other alternatives won't leave them much better off and that some will leave them much worse off, they will choose a kind of maximin structure for the society in which they will live, in which the worst-off have reasonably good economic expectations, in which indeed the worst-off have the best economic expectations possible as long as equal traditional liberties are assured and economic inequalities are attached to positions open to all. Perhaps such a social-political ideal could be expanded into an ethics that governs individuals. And in fact it is from the maximin element of Rawls' proposal that the leximin core of LDP descends.

But the exact features of the psychological propensities and the Veil of Ignorance presumed in this construction are very important to what it delivers. Harsanyi's quite similar construction presumes individual utility maximization by the choosers and a Veil that prevents them from knowing who in the resulting society they will be, but allows them a general description of the society including how many people in various sorts of positions there will be. And it yields social arrangements that maximize average utility instead.[95]

So one serious difficulty is that we can torque this second contractarian tradition, by manipulating the psychological features presumed in the bargainers and the nature of the Veil, or other analogous circumstances of the contract, to yield quite variable results. Hence most of the argumentative stress is placed on the justification of some particular set of initial conditions of that sort. Rawls does suggest that in the ignorance created by his Veil, the rational would be cautious. But Harsanyi deploys alternative plausible conceptions of relevant ignorance and caution. In later work, Rawls retreats to a certain liberal normative ideal of the person as the justification for

---

[94] Rawls (1971); Harsanyi (1976); Gibbard (2008: 33–88).   [95] Harsanyi (1953).

his particular contractarian construction.[96] But we lack a consensus on such an ideal. And even in *A Theory of Justice*, he explicitly allows that it is appropriate to keep fiddling with the initial conditions of the choice on the basis of the normative implications that they yield until the package is consistent and intuitively attractive. But we are presuming that such symmetrical appeals to intuition are not sufficient. We must provide an asymmetric justification of a normative theory, working up from DC2-BASIS. We can't fiddle with the initial conditions until we get the results we like.

In any legitimate contractarian account of the second refined form, all significant argumentative stress would fall on a strong asymmetric rationale for a specific set of idealizing motivational assumptions and assumptions about relevant ignorance, or for other specific conditions that make the choice situation relevantly fair. Perhaps Harsanyi's conception of the Veil seems preferable to Rawls' in this respect, as at least allowing choosers more information. And perhaps his focus on individual utility maximization seems less arbitrary. But the very best informed choice, given Harsanyi's overall conception, would be one that merely maximized one's expected individual utility; it would be paradigmatically selfish. So it can't be claimed in general that more information for such a chooser makes their choice more fair. There must be some suitable argument that the specific kind of ignorance that Harsanyi proposes best captures fairness when allied with individual utility maximization. And we have no reason to believe that this sort of asymmetric rationale is available.

Even if this tradition could yield some properly determinate Veil of Ignorance or other suitably specific characterization of the choice situation, and do so in an asymmetrically justified way, there would remain serious problems. As we have seen, there is no default normative rationality of prudence, nor indeed of expected utility maximization. And it is not always true that if we choose something rationally under circumstances of risk, say behind a Veil of Ignorance, that the actual outcome of that risk is something of whose injustice we cannot reasonably complain. Remember flukes. Gibbard suggests that at least when we have an ongoing practice, and someone objects to one of its features, it is sufficient rebuttal to point out to them: "Before you knew how you in particular would turn out to be affected, you would have agreed to the practice—and for your own advantage."[97] But sometimes if you would have agreed to some arrangement for your own advantage not knowing who you would be in it, you yet retain the intuitive right to complain about the outcome, say because such a selfish choice in ignorance would lead you on the options available to pick a society with a few slaves, and you end up being a slave.[98] And sometimes in fact you wouldn't in fact have picked social arrangements solely on the basis of your own advantage, if you had actually been given the choice of them. And in any case

[96] Rawls (2001: 18–19).   [97] Gibbard (2008: 50).
[98] Kamm (2008: 128–35); Gibbard (2008: 155–9).

Harsanyi's and Rawls' wildly hypothetical choices do not simply underwrite ongoing practices.[99] One considerable advantage of MAC2's focus on actual cooperation over the hypothetical agreements of the second refined form of contractarianism is that it is an odd form of reciprocity that requires you to reciprocate by following agreements that have never been made.

For our purposes, namely developing an asymmetrical legitimation based in DC2 of a normative theory, the second refined tradition of contractarianism is no more useful than the first. But my complaints about these first two forms are not a denial that contractarian motives of reciprocity are a root of morality. They are not a way of denying that equal treatment of agents matters. As I've said, there are ways in which equal treatment of agents and reciprocity are incorporated into LEXIMAC. These contractarian elements of LEXIMAC make it close to the paradigmatic example of the third form of refined contractarianism.

10.7 Scanlon

The third form of refined contractarianism does not rest on the normative rationality of prudential selfishness or anything analogous, and involves a new type of idealization, and so avoids central objections to the first two forms. According to T. M. Scanlon's contractarian conception, which is the principal example of this third form, "our thinking about right and wrong is structured by... the aim of finding principles that others, insofar as they too have this aim, could not reasonably reject."[100] A basic root of morality, on this conception, is our ability to justify ourselves to others.

Unfortunately, people can be trained or duped into accepting inappropriately subservient positions and justifications, not only overly selfish ones. But I am in the process of telling a long story about what moral principles could not be rejected in reality by the truly reasonable, and why. And so MM, which incorporates LEXIMAC, is a version of this third refined form, at least when that form is specified abstractly. But Scanlon's version is more characteristic, and involves a different conception of the nature of reasonable rejection, which is intuitively closer to bargaining or making contracts. Still, there is considerable detailed normative confluence between Scanlon's proposal and my own.

Begin with Scanlon's notion of reasonable rejection. Scanlon conceives of reasonable rejection as involving something like a bargain or a contract, and yet he deploys a different sort of abstraction mechanism than Rawls to prevent unfair bargaining advantages from affecting that agreement. First of all, Scanlon focuses on what he calls the reasonable and not the rational. And he says that it can be rational to insist on your unfair bargaining advantages when it would be clearly unreasonable for you

---

[99] Actual moral practices are ongoing. So Gibbard's formulation may be relevant to their vindication.
[100] Scanlon (1982 and 1998: 191).

to do so.[101] And indeed it can be reasonable for a party to some agreement to insist on a better bargain than they can rationally expect because of their unfortunate bargaining position. What's more, what is reasonable and unreasonable are supposed to depend on the correct somewhat abstract considerations in favor of or against principles, considerations that are relevant from the perspective of morally characteristic standpoints of people, rather than considerations whose relevance depends on particular detailed facts about particular bargaining circumstances and bargainer interests.[102]

Despite its focus on bargaining, this ends up being fairly close to what might be said in argument for LEXIMAC, as we will shortly see. But there is one key feature of Scanlon's construction from which I must dissent. He allows irreducibly normative considerations into the facts that determine what is reasonable and unreasonable. But we are concerned here with a suitably asymmetric explanation, rooted in impartial treatment of moral agents and patients, of what makes normative claims true in our physical world. For us, DC2-BASIS is important. Still, if we attend to the sorts of considerations that Scanlon considers to be relevantly reasonable grounds for rejection of principles, we can see considerable confluence between Scanlon's proposal and LEXIMAC.

Reasons must be fair, Scanlon thinks. They must involve no proper names or rigged definite descriptions.[103] I concur. But they must also be generic in a stronger sense. They must be "reasons that we can see that people have in virtue of their situation, characterized in general terms, and such things as their aims and capabilities and the conditions in which they are placed."[104] We can best understand this idea by considering how generic reasons are put to work. Here is one key quote:

From the point of view of those who will be its main beneficiaries, there may be strong generic reasons to insist on [a] principle and to reject anything that offers less. From the point of view of the agents who will be constrained by it, or of those who would be beneficiaries of an alternative principle, there may be reason to reject it in favor of something different or less demanding. In order to decide whether the principle could reasonably be rejected we need to decide whether it would be reasonable to take any of these generic reasons against it to prevail, given the reasons on the other side and given the aim of finding principles that others also could not reasonably reject.[105]

But what generic reasons are appropriately strong? Scanlon argues, plausibly given the contractarian basis of his proposal, that they should be what he calls "personal"— that is to say "tied to the well-being, claims, or status of individuals."[106] And of course it is quite natural to think that effects on individual well-being, and indeed especially preference-based well-being (despite Scanlon's worries about desire-based well-being discussed in Chapter 6), are among plausible such grounds in reality. But the key

---

[101] Scanlon (1998: 192).   [102] Scanlon (1998: 203–4).   [103] Scanlon (1998: 206–13).
[104] Scanlon (1998: 204).   [105] Scanlon (1998: 213).   [106] Scanlon (1998: 218–23, 219).

point to notice is that Scanlon's mechanism does not turn centrally on some sort of prior default rationality of self-interest. We are to consider the application of generic reasons for and against principles in what are themselves generic situations too abstract for long-term prudence or individual utility maximization to play any very specific role.

So far, the fan of LEXIMAC has little reason to dissent. Still, there is more than one way in which even well-being can serve as a reason for or against a principle, and there are other reasons that Scanlon also thinks are important. We need to consider these normative details to properly understand the relationship of Scanlon's proposals about relevant generic reasons to LEXIMAC.

Scanlon grants that a maximin distributional principle like Rawls' Difference Principle, that prioritizes the well-being of individuals badly off in their lives, may make sense in determining the justice of basic social institutions.[107] And something analogous to this is what LDP requires. But he also says that "if the claims of the worst off sometimes take priority in contractualist argument, this reflects a fact about the generic reasons for rejecting certain kind of principles rather than a general structural feature of contractualism that holds in every case."[108] So we need to consider other details.

For instance, Scanlon suggests that suitable generic reasons support the Rescue Principle, which specifies that "if you are presented with a situation in which you can prevent something very bad from happening, or alleviate someone's dire plight, by making only a slight (or even moderate) sacrifice, then it would be wrong not to do so."[109] And he suggests that it is the severity of the immediate plight of an individual and not how well off they are over their life that determines relevant priority in cases where not all can be rescued.[110]

Suppose, for example, that we must choose between preventing B from losing an arm and preventing A from suffering a broken wrist. Consider a principle according to which it is at least permissible in such a case to help B, whom we can help more, whatever his level of well-being may be. Would it be reasonable to reject this principle, on the ground that a decision in such a case should take into account such things as whether A had a very happy and successful life, or, on the contrary, his main aims had been frustrated by bad luck? It does not seem to me that this would be reasonable.[111]

But LDP is quite close to this conception, since it focuses our principal concern on the worst-off moment of an individual life, not the worst-off individual over life. If A and B are realistic atomic agents and nothing else turns on the injury in question, they will have consensus congruence that it is worse to lose an arm than break a wrist. Perhaps there may be cases where such an intuitive priority is in conflict with the

---

[107] Scanlon (1998: 228).   [108] Scanlon (1998: 223).   [109] Scanlon (1998: 224).
[110] Scanlon (1998: 226–8). He suggests that for differences in level to affect the strength of someone's claim on help, the differences must be an aspect of well-being to which the help contributes.
[111] Scanlon (1998: 226–7).

overall well-being of even the atomic agents in question, as prioritized by LDP. But we all prefer many broken wrists to losing one arm. So this case probably also introduces a pocket of interpersonal cardinality or something close to it, and hence relevant qualifications to the basic leximin structure of LDP.

There are other issues about how to aggregate well-being. Scanlon's view does not allow that the aggregation of many small benefits can make up for some large individual harm.[112] But neither does LDP. However, his view does direct us to save the greater number when all face a comparable harm.[113] Still, so does LDP.

So far we have discovered a considerable normative confluence between Scanlon's proposal and LDP. But there are sorts of generic reasons that matter to Scanlon, and which bring his proposals into contrasting juxtaposition with MAC2.

He says that many "moral principles are concerned with the provision of specific forms of assurance and protection, answering to our need to be protected against intentional harm, our need to be able to rely on assurances given us, and so on."[114] These involve general deontic obligations not to kill, injure, deceive, and steal. In *What We Owe to Each Other*, these sorts of concerns are elaborated most fully by a probing treatment of promising and deception, which however is somewhat revisionary of common belief.[115] *Moral Dimensions* provides hints about cases in which factors can or cannot justify an exception to a general rule forbidding killing,[116] and also develops some complications regarding ways in which intentions play into immoral deception.[117] Scanlon's account of general deontic obligations is suggestive, but incomplete. Now the contrast. On my account, all such deontic duties are due to the functioning of MAC2 in interaction with our moral practices that are group acts. As in Scanlon, reciprocity plays a key role in underwriting these duties. It is not until Chapter 11 that we will discuss the way in which MAC2 allied with LDP can deliver our general deontic duties, and Chapter 12 will add some important details. But while the reciprocal grounds for these duties that I will cite are somewhat different from those that Scanlon proposes, and my deontic proposals are less revisionary than his, MAC2 does underwrite these general deontic duties in intuitive detail, and in a way founded, as Scanlon suggests, on reciprocity. And it also delivers a considerable normative confluence with the most intuitive and well-developed aspects of Scanlon's view of these duties. Yet it also adds details that are lacking in Scanlon's proposals, but that seem to be in the spirit of those proposals. For instance, these forms of assurance and protection can conflict. Perhaps you can deflect injury from someone only by lying to them or breaking a promise. And MAC2 provides a plausible account of how to balance these deontic duties that is rooted in reciprocity, as well as in a suitably impartial concern for well-being.

---

[112] Scanlon (1998: 235).   [113] Scanlon (1998: 233).   [114] Scanlon (1998: 223).
[115] Scanlon (1998: 295–327). One revisionary element is the implication of his Principles D and L for house bargaining: You can't deceive about your final offer.
[116] Scanlon (2008: 8–36).   [117] Scanlon (2008: 37–88).

So far we have discovered a considerable normative confluence, and no advantages rooted in the third refined contractarian tradition for Scanlon. But there is a third set of important generic reasons for Scanlon, having to do with what he calls substantive responsibility:[118] "Whether I have a morally forceful demand to be better off in a certain way will often depend, intuitively, on whether my fate is or is not my own doing."[119] And here I must be a little contrary, because some claims about what is or is not my own doing require debunking. We have seen that there are no robust sorts of individual responsibility or metaphysical desert that can be legitimate fundamental grounds for normative claims in our physical world. But, on the other hand, our consequentially weighty group actions include a beneficent practice of responsibility assignment, as we will see in Chapter 12. And other elements of intuitive substantive responsibility fall out as normative conclusions on the basis of MM. So some proper reciprocal concern with responsibility is to be found in my proposal, though at a different location than in Scanlon's proposal, supported by our beneficent group acts and legitimated by an appeal to consequences. In the real world, that is the best that can be done with such notions.

Another and somewhat surprising normative confluence between my view and Scanlon's is also worth noting. He has proposed a conception of blame for someone's action whereby it is to take "that action to indicate something about the person that impairs one's relationship with him or her, and to understand that relationship in a way that reflects this impairment."[120] This is analogous to what I will say about "normative punishment" during our discussion of special obligations in Chapter 11.

Let me summarize the main points: One important set of generic reasons for Scanlon support something like LDP. One set supports a treatment of deontic duties close to but more revisionary and less complete than that supported by MAC2, which is also grounded in a kind of reciprocity. And the concerns articulated by the third set of generic reasons are met by my proposal in a more indirect way, which is the only viable way in reality. There is considerable normative confluence between Scanlon and LEXIMAC.

There are differences, of course. The principal difference is that Scanlon deploys irreducibly normative claims as input to his contractarian mechanism. And so one can imagine someone who, for instance, intuits relevant non-natural properties and hence reasonably rejects VLD, a key part of MAC2, on the grounds that it forbids defection in cases of surplus cooperation from which they would hence have gained, or who reasonably rejects VLD on the basis of a strong normative intuition that involves no non-natural properties, or who reasonably rejects VLD simply because of a concern about actual costs to their own well-being. But in the real world there are no irreducible normative properties to intuit, and we are insisting here on asymmetric legitimation on the impartial basis of DC2 of normative intuitions, and we have

---

[118] Scanlon (1998: 248–67).   [119] Scanlon (1998: 243).   [120] Scanlon (2008: 122–214, 122–3).

seen that such a legitimation does not support any reasonable worries about surplus cooperation, and indeed that LEXIMAC's respect for surplus cooperation is closely connected with its intuitive normative implications, though we haven't considered the details yet. And in any case, I am only claiming that there is a reasonably close confluence between LEXIMAC and Scanlon's view, in its guise as the best-developed and paradigmatic form of the third and only viable sort of suitably refined contractarianism. LEXIMAC involves another understanding of reasonable rejection, which requires no input from prior normative intuitions of a sort forbidden by DC2 and reality. It is in that abstract way, not by regard to its normative confluence with Scanlon, that it is most securely within the third refined contractarian tradition.

And whatever its relation to the third refined form, LEXIMAC—in its impartial treatment of agents, and in its concern with two sorts of reciprocity, with the fulfillment of cooperative roles within beneficent group acts and distributional equality among moral patients—is certainly a version of contractarianism. In fact, by its focus on actual group acts rather than hypothetical agreements, it is in some ways closer to Hobbes and the origins of the contractarian tradition than most of the refined variants, and is supported by a more familiar and intuitive form of reciprocity. In physical reality, given constraints violated by Scanlon's proposal, we have found no other viable form of contractarianism. LEXIMAC and MM inherit the contractarian tradition.

10.8 Kant and Golden Rules

Golden rule arguments are another cluster of traditional mechanisms for moving from desire-based good or something analogous to normative judgments.[121] They weave together motives of reciprocity and benevolence, and also impartial treatment of both distinct moral agents and distinct moral patients, in a manner reminiscent of LEXIMAC.

There are differences within the golden rule tradition. In the Babylonian Talmud, Rabbi Hillel is reported to have said "What is hateful to yourself, do not do to another. That is the whole Torah. The rest is commentary."[122] Matthew reports Jesus to have said "All things whatsoever ye would that men should do to you, do ye even so to them."[123] These negative and positive formulations are not equivalent, if we accept commonsense distinctions between acting and refraining and between hating

---

[121] These arguments are associated with Confucius (*Analects* 15: 23) and the Buddha, and are present in *The Mahabarata* (bk. 13: Anusasana Parva, sec. 113). See Wattles (1996) and Gensler (2013). The six non-theological commandments of the Decalogue were traditionally subsumed under golden rules, for instance by Maimonides and Aquinas.

[122] *Shabbat of the Babylonian Talmud* 31a; Donagan (1977: 57).   [123] Matthew 7, 12.

and not happening to want, even though such distinctions may be too robust to be highly determinate in reality.[124]

But whatever the details of their coextension, these two principles are obviously closely related. And such golden rule principles capture something in our common sense. Still, there are crucial difficulties for such arguments, at least in their traditional forms and when conceived as providing a complete guide to morality.

First, the positive forms generate the possibility of conflicting duties of benevolence, without providing a means to resolve those conflicts. We may want things for ourselves that we cannot give to everyone, but which we can give to a few. If negative and positive forms are coextensive, then this worry applies to both types. If they are not, then negative forms are insufficient to ground obvious moral duties of positive benevolence.

Second, neither positive nor negative golden rule tests allow for differential roles and tastes unless the tests are augmented or modified. If I hate to be tickled that doesn't mean that I shouldn't assist in a desired tickling, and I shouldn't do dental work on everyone just because I want dental work done on me.[125] If I hate myself or am a masochist, then doing unto others as I wish to be done unto may not have pretty results. And it may be just fine that A lusts to do to B what B lusts after, though A does not lust to have that done to A by B, nor does B lust to do so.

Third, there is the classical complaint by Kant that such a principle "does not contain the ground of duties owed to others; for a criminal would argue on this ground against the judge punishing him."[126]

There are various attempts to deal with these difficulties by further development of golden rule tests. I will organize our discussion around Kant's case of the criminal, and consider three different sorts of replies, which also help with the other two clusters of complaints.[127]

The first development was proposed by Kant himself, but it is embedded in his overall theory in a way that will take a moment to explain. The core of Kant's ethical theory is the Categorical Imperative of Reason, binding on all the rational, which is the supreme principle of morality. There are several formulations of the CI, clustered in three groups in the crucial Second Section of the *Groundwork of the Metaphysics of Morals*.[128] Kant seems to say that the formulations are equivalent, which is at best not apparent. But he also suggests, as Christine Korsgaard and Allen Wood have noted, certain crucial differences and relationships between them.[129]

---

[124] The principle "Love thy neighbor as thyself," with "neighbor" traditionally interpreted broadly, is also cited by Jesus, in Luke 10, 25–37, and is sometimes claimed, for instance by Aquinas, to be roughly coextensive with a positive golden rule.

[125] Gensler (1996).

[126] Kant (1996b: 4:430, 80n.) Rousseau also makes this objection. Kant further complains that the principle cannot support duties to oneself and that a negative form cannot support the duty of benevolence.

[127] Although our second reply does not obviously help with the first cluster.

[128] Kant (1996b: 4:406–45, 61–93).

[129] Korsgaard (1996: 98–123); A. Wood (1999 and 2008: 66–105).

The central formulation of the first cluster is FUL, the Formula of Universal Law: "Act only in accordance with that maxim through which you at the same time can will that it becomes a universal law."[130] Maxims of actions are the subjective principles, the intentional descriptions, under which the actions are willed, which we know to rest on the agent's reasons. FUL requires some sort of generalization or universalization of reasons for actions, and is hence quite similar to traditional golden rules, although we also noted some key differences during our discussion of Parfit in 10.3. In demanding this universalization, it requires one sort of impartial treatment of your own case and others'.

And of course there are two ways in which LEXIMAC also involves impartial treatment: MAC2 of moral agents and LDP of moral patients. Still, there are quite important differences between FUL and LEXIMAC. LEXIMAC focuses on actual rather than merely hypothetical forms of cooperation, on actual widespread practices rather than ideal universal laws. However, in our previous discussions of rule utilitarianism and contractarianism we saw this to be a normative advantage for LEXIMAC. Another difference is that Kant thought there were rather strong constraints on what a human *can* will incorporated into FUL. For instance, he thought that a rational being necessarily wills that all their capacities be developed.[131] But these necessary constraints are fanciful. And there are analogous constraints on *relevant* human will, although they rest on contingencies, which are reflected in the consensus congruence of human desire deployed by LDP, and also in the content of our various actual beneficent group acts. So LEXIMAC incorporates one very rough interpretation of FUL, which is normatively preferable to Kant's own and also more viable in reality.

There are also other forms of confluence between LEXIMAC and Kant, which involve the relationships among the various formulations of Kant's CI. The second key formulation is FH, the Formula of Humanity: "So act that you use humanity, as much in your own person as in the person of every other, always at the same time as an end and never merely as a means."[132] This specifies that a certain sort of thing, humanity, is an unconditional end for any rational action, and so perhaps it helps delimit what we can will in Kant's sense. What does Kant mean by humanity? Something like human rational nature, our rational capacity to set ends and to consider means to them, our capacity indeed for moral and rational action. It is pretty highfalutin. And the problem is that, in physical reality, humanity in this fancy sense cannot be delivered as an end for all rational action by some independent normative fact, nor by some objective teleology residing in all our actions. When even a rational agent pursues some goal, they are not always pursuing their own rational nature, or another's. Indeed, Kant believed that humanity in this fancy sense requires a radically free choice by a noumenal self acting outside of time, while in fact we are

---

[130] Kant (1996b: 4:421, 73).   [131] Kant (1996b: 4:423, 75).   [132] Kant (1996b: 4:429, 80).

mere gabby apes. We have seen that the only plausible basis of value in our world is the rather less demanding capacity to have preferences. Kant complains that any principle enjoining us to act on the basis of such desire is not sufficiently categorical to root morality, since we differ in our desires and it is a mere empirical fact what desires we have. But all actual agents capable of fancy Kantian humanity also have a preference-based good. And so the *general* goal of desire satisfaction, whatever the details of our particular desires, is not in fact merely hypothetical in the relevant sense.[133] And of course LDP discounts idiosyncratic desires. Though FH involves humanity, humanity in any relevant realistic sense is having desire-based good comparable with that of other normal adult humans.[134] FH further specifies that we are to use humanity always as an end. But MAC2 enjoins us to special sorts of reciprocal respect for agents who cooperate with us in beneficent group acts. And the proper interpretation of being treated as an end is also plausibly reflected in the other formulations of the CI, which we are in the midst of juxtaposing with LEXIMAC. So we can conclude that LEXIMAC incorporates a rough but plausible interpretation of FH as well.

The third cluster of formulations of the CI seems to add to the form provided by the first cluster the matter of FH.[135] It is something like a conjunction of the other two clusters. This yields, for instance, FRE, the Formula of the Realm of Ends: "Act in accordance with maxims of a universally legislative member for a merely possible realm of ends."[136] It seems that we must turn to such a third cluster principle, which at least conjoins FUL and FH, for a properly full statement of Kant's supreme principle of morality. When *The Metaphysics of Morals* develops Kant's official treatment of the moral implications of his theory, both FUL and FH are deployed.[137] But we have seen that LEXIMAC incorporates a realistic understanding of FUL, and a plausible understanding of FH as well.[138] So there is a close parallel between FRE and LEXIMAC; they are very roughly equivalent. There are real differences, of course, especially because of FRE's focus on highly hypothetical cooperation and

---

[133] We have retreated to mere consensus among affected humans as the most objective good available in reality, while Kant wanted a morality binding even on rational Martians. This is not attainable. Kant might object that there are angels who will things and yet lack desire. But preference in my sense is very broad and encompasses willing angels, who are of course a fantasy.

[134] MM has several affinities with Korsgaard (2009). Pages 202–4 suggest an analogue of my treatment of continuing individual agents as group agents. But Korsgaard makes the bridge from FUL to FRE in a different and more resolutely Kantian way, which depends on the implausible assumption, at 191, 202, and 214, that reasons accepted by a group agent must be genuine reasons for all the rational.

[135] I take this from Wood and Korsgaard.

[136] Kant (1996b: 4:438–9, 87–8).

[137] Kant (1996c: 353–603). For a summary of applications of FUL and FH, see Wood's "General Introduction," xiii–xxxiii, especially xxxi–xxxii, n17. On the other hand, Kant explicitly says, in Kant (1996b) and even at Kant (1996c: 2:26), that the first formulation is privileged. Perhaps this is another reason to think the second cluster of formulations help specify what is meant by "can will."

[138] Indeed, the interpretation of FUL I have proposed stretches towards incorporation of the proper interpretation of FH. So, as Kant suggested, the three clusters of formulations may indeed be equivalent.

its focus on a fancy and highly specific end for all rational action. But we have seen that such foci are problematic.

LEXIMAC is, I think, the proper rough understanding of FRE and hence of the CI for our physical world. It is Kant for reality.[139] Nevertheless, MM cannot deploy Kant's implicit reply to his own complaint about the interaction of punishment and golden rules. While it is not entirely implausible to say with Kant that one respects the rational nature of someone who one punishes, it is far less plausible to say that one hence respects their desire-based good.[140] So we need to consider other attempts to answer the objection from criminal punishment within the golden rule tradition.

10.9 Golden Rule Consent

The second defense of golden rule arguments from the worry about punishment deploys robustly specific types of motivation of a rather different type than Kantian respect for rational nature. It has been developed by Harry Gensler and Thomas Carson.[141]

Gensler claims that:

If you are consistent and think that it would be all right for someone to do A to X, then you will think that it would be all right for someone to do A to you in similar circumstances.
If you are consistent and think that it would be all right for someone to do A to you in similar circumstances, then you will consent to the idea of someone doing A to you in similar circumstances.

Therefore,

If you are consistent and think that it would be all right to do A to X, then you will consent to the idea of someone doing A to you in similar circumstances.[142]

Notice the stress on consent, a specific motivational state. You can consent to things that you do not assent to, that you merely do not object to. You may never want to be beaten at chess, but still, if you play, you consent to being beaten. You will not object. Notice how this helps with punishment. You may not assent to being punished if various things occur, because of your desires, and yet still consent to it. And note a second point. Gensler develops a suggestion by R. M. Hare that it is not whether you would consent in fact when facing punishment that is relevant to this moral test, but rather whether you now think that it would be all right and hence consent to be punished in the case that you know to be merely hypothetical.[143] This makes the relevant consent easier, and so helps with Kant's worry.

---

[139] In 10.3, we considered the relationship of LEXIMAC to Parfit's revisionary interpretation of Kant, which focuses on FUL but also incorporates a more traditional understanding of the golden rule.
[140] But a rough analogue of Kant's conception is involved in Chapter 11's "normative punishment."
[141] Gensler (1986, 1996, 1998); Carson (2010: 129–56).
[142] Gensler (1986: 89–90, 1996: 93–5, 1998: 104–6).
[143] Hare (1963: 108). But Hare's discussion of punishment at 115–18 is more characteristic.

There are problems with this mechanism. Its second element may leave too much wiggle room. You can do whatever you like to someone as long as you can consent to it being done to you in a circumstance that you know you will not inhabit. That seems too easy a test. But perhaps we should assume that there is some condition of sincerity presupposed, that requires honestly pondering what you would in fact want in hypothetical circumstances. But that will be less constraining on the unimaginative and those who otherwise don't properly understand what they would in fact prefer in other circumstances. And these seem inappropriate grounds for moral excuse.

Perhaps these worries can be avoided by further development of Gensler's proposal, which seems required anyway because of a related problem noted by Carson. Consider a consistent and fanatical Nazi who can sincerely pronounce "Kill me if I am a Jew." Perhaps that pronouncement meets Gensler's test. As a fix, Carson proposes that Gensler-style constraints are merely necessary and not sufficient conditions on appropriate moral judgment. There are supposed to be other necessary conditions as well. He says that there might be consistent and fanatically anti-Semitic Nazis, but that such "hatred depends on numerous false beliefs about the characteristics of Jews and their responsibility for the ills of the world. Only someone who had false beliefs and/or irrational attitudes about Jews could be a consistent Nazi."[144] More generally, he suggests that correct moral judgments must be:

(1) consistent in Gensler's sense,
(2) adequately informed by knowledge of relevant facts,
(3) informed by a full and vivid understanding of relevant considerations, including an understanding of the feelings of others (which requires that one have empathy for others),
(4) made by someone who is able to reason properly and whose cognitive powers function properly.[145]

Fanatical Nazis are supposed to fail conditions 2 and 3. There are also those who are severely depressed, and who hence care nothing for their own interests or those of their children. They may consent to just about everything, out of despair. But Carson suggests that the severely depressed fail to meet conditions 3 and 4. Perhaps also conditions 2, 3, and 4 are not met by the unimaginative and those who can't understand what they would prefer in hypothetical circumstances, and hence this fix can evade the first problem that I noted.[146]

But conditions 2 through 4 cannot handle the problem cases in the way Carson suggests. One worry is that these conditions are cognitive conditions, involving knowledge, understanding, or cognitive reasoning. Empathy may sound motivational, but the fact that it is required by understanding suggests otherwise. And if instead empathy is motivationally robust, or if reasoning properly requires proper

---

[144] Carson (2010: 141).   [145] Carson (2010: 130–1).
[146] Another qualification is that Carson says his golden rule will only deliver negative duties.

practical reasoning, then the account deploys suspiciously normative claims about proper motivations for which we are owed some independent account. So it seems that Carson is relying on the problems in question, the fanaticism and depression, being cognitive problems, or at least being such as to assure false belief. But neither claim is generally correct. They are sometimes problems of motivation. My sick enjoyment of your pain may be heightened by my vivid understanding of it, while at the same time I am a masochist and like pain for myself. And we noted earlier that depressives are in some ways more accurate in assessing reality.[147] Attitudes can attach to features in non-rational ways that are not rooted or reflected in false non-normative belief or lack of information. Sometimes the problem is with our desires.

But I will focus on another cluster of problems for the class of golden rule arguments now under consideration. I think they are decisive. Remember that there are two elements that Gensler and Carson deploy against Kant's problem of punishment. First, they suggest you would if consistent consent to be punished in circumstances in which you would not want to be punished, in which you would prefer not to be. Second, they suggest that what is relevant is whether you sincerely now consent to merely hypothetical punishment, not whether in fact you would consent if in fact you faced that punishment. Both strategies serve to insulate your current judgment from the facts of what your preferences would be should you face punishment. Call them "insulating mechanisms." My point is that we need to put the punishment case in close comparison with other problem cases, in light of the insulating mechanisms.

It is important, if Gensler or Carson are to have an answer to the worries about fanatics and the depressed, that the judgments of the fanatical and depressed be corrected by vivid understanding of the situation of whoever is threatened by their madness, and also have respect for that person's desires. But the insulating mechanisms that they deploy to help with the punishment case get in the way in these other cases. And on the other hand vivid understanding and respect for the desires of the punished would increase aversion to punishment.[148] This complaint seems especially troubling if the insulating mechanisms rest heavily on cognitive distance from the desires of others, and hence on the second insulating mechanism. But certainly consent, the first insulating mechanism, cannot plausibly bear the strain alone. One problem is that the facts about consent, about what is not objected to, are soft, vague, and indeterminate in reality. But the main problem is that the notion of consent that Gensler and Carson deploy is highly moralized. It rests on moral judgments. You consent to being beaten at chess even though you don't like it, because you don't object to it, because you don't resent it. And perhaps in the same sense you must consent to your punishment if you are guilty. And that means you

---

[147] But Carson intends only catatonic depressives as relevantly irrational.
[148] Vivid awareness of the desires of all might overall support some punishment, but that is the third golden rule mechanism for avoiding Kant's objection.

don't have a tendency to get all morally worked up about these things, to be negatively judgmental in a normative way about them. If you did make such negative normative judgments about being beaten in chess, then your negative judgment would constitute lack of consent. But the problem with this is that we cannot properly root the correctness in general of moral judgments in a golden rule test that rests crucially on the existence of specific moral judgments.[149] The surface plausibility of Gensler and Carson's mechanism rests on a kind of circularity: A judgment that *X is morally okay to do* is appropriate because, even though you wouldn't like that to be done in the relevant hypothetical situation, yet you would consent to it. But you would consent to it in that way only because *you think X is morally okay to do.*[150]

In fairness, I should note that Carson doesn't deploy his golden rule mechanism to root moral judgments in the fundamental way I am contemplating here, but merely as a negative test on appropriate moral judgments, and my last criticism is not properly applicable to that deployment. But still, the Gensler–Carson development of the golden rule cannot serve the fundamental role for that rule we are currently considering. The second attempt to evade Kant's punishment criticism of golden rule tests does not succeed.

10.10 Hare

The classic development of the third golden rule strategy for dealing with punishment is embedded in R. M. Hare's non-cognitivism. I will focus on Hare's middle-period position in *Freedom and Reason*, an elaboration and clarification of the doctrine of *The Language of Morals*, which seems to me its classic and characteristic form,[151] but will also consider some important qualifications introduced later by *Moral Thinking*.[152]

Hare's metaethical position, "universal prescriptivism," has five basic tenets: First, moral terms are among the class of *evaluative* terms, which also include aesthetic terms and "good" used in non-moral contexts. Well-formed utterances involving evaluative terms possess both a determinate *descriptive meaning*—a cognitive or

---

[149] The problem is deep. The very judgment involved in your consent to be beaten at chess or punished seems to be that it isn't morally wrong to beat you or punish you. Perhaps it seems that consent is a specific emotion that can be characterized and have particular objects without regard to normative judgments. But that is unrealistic.

[150] MAC2 also rests the propriety of certain moral judgments on moral beliefs. It is wrong to lie partly because we are part of a beneficent group action that involves believing that lying is wrong; it might not be wrong if there were different sorts of beneficent group actions and hence different beliefs. But there is a crucial difference between MAC2 and these golden rule tests. MAC2 requires beneficence. Having the beliefs alone is not sufficient to legitimate them. In the golden rule tests, the presence of certain beliefs is all that is required to make those very beliefs legitimate. A fanatic Nazi arguably makes moralized judgments that meet such tests, but certainly violate MM.

[151] Hare (1952, 1963).   [152] Hare (1981).

factual content—and a *prescriptive meaning* similar to that of commands. Second, the prescriptive meaning of evaluative utterances is to commend. Like commands, such utterances *prescribe*. They guide action, tell us what to do. But unlike commands, evaluative utterance involves appeal to criteria or grounds for application. Third, the descriptive meaning of an evaluative utterance is enmeshed with these criteria or grounds. Any particular evaluative utterance will invoke certain good-making characteristics, natural and general properties that on pain of contradiction or insincerity require the speaker to make similar evaluations in other cases when the same criteria are met. Call this "universalization." Fourth, for some evaluative terms, like "tidy" and "industrious," the descriptive meaning is primary, while for some, like "right," the prescriptive meaning is so. This means that it is more invariant among different utterances of different individual speakers and over time. But, in any case, it is individual criteria of a moment which are expressed by normative words in particular utterances, and which give them their descriptive meaning in that use.[153] This is the basic difference between my metaethical proposal and Hare's. But the fifth tenet of Hare's view is another: According to Hare, it is characteristic of moral judgments, as opposed to aesthetic ones, that they cannot be overridden by other sorts of evaluative judgments, but must be altered or modified to admit of an exception.

Perhaps there is a worry about how to fit this picture onto reality, since there may not be highly determinate facts about what criteria we are sincerely invoking when we make normative judgments. But these problems seem less serious than in the case of the fine features of intentional maxims that Kant invokes. Moral judgments more plausibly contain implicit criteria than standard intentions, because they more characteristically involve linguistically mediated accepted reasons of a specific and positive sort.

To bring out central features of Hare's view, it is worth distinguishing kinds of moral judgments, judgments about actual cases and about two sorts of merely hypothetical ones, and also various sorts of stress these different cases place upon sincerity. Hare believed that the grounds one sincerely deploys for moral judgment commit one to making the same judgment in all actual relevantly similar cases, where the same natural and general criteria apply. Call this "Stage One Universalization."[154] But there is a richer pair of constraints that Hare believed are also part of the logic of moral discourse. Stage Two Universalization commits one to making the same moral judgments sincerely even about certain hypothetical cases, where one is in the actual external situation of other people, say when one is hypothetically the debtor even though in fact one never owes money and is the creditor. Stage Three Universalization commits one to making the same evaluations about hypothetical cases in which one is not only in another's actual external situation, but also has their actual inclinations and desires and not one's own.

---

[153] The descriptive meaning of such words is not *that* the individual speaker is invoking such criteria.
[154] This terminology is John Mackie's.

Hare argued (in a way I think is implausible for reasons to which we will return) that all this generates a more or less utilitarian decision procedure for ethics, except for *fanatics*.[155] Some people slip through these constraints, in a way that reason cannot address. These fanatics are people who sincerely hold *ideals*, which are conceptions of what is good (and on what grounds it is good) that cannot be overridden by the satisfaction of even their own desires and inclinations. The fanatical trumpeter next door in your building can sincerely utter: "Let the trumpet be played even in disregard of my interests, even were I to hate trumpeting and want to play the gramophone (or to sleep) instead." Reason has nothing to say against such fanatics, Hare said in *Freedom and Reason*, whether they have such (relatively) innocent ideals, or are fanatical Nazis.

Hare also said there aren't in fact many fanatics, even in the discussions that we are treating as canonical. But I think Hare was too optimistic about that. Apparently sincere normative denunciations of homosexuality, women, and some minorities have been uttered in my hearing by self-loathing individuals who seem to meet Hare's test of fanaticism, so that Hare's constraints seem to be insufficient to adjudicate some actual disputes.[156] Hare does say different things about fanatics later, in *Moral Thinking*. There we hear that if (i) one fully understands someone's situation in which they prefer with strength S that X should happen rather than not, then (ii) one knows that if one were in that situation, one would prefer it with strength S that X should happen rather than not. And (ii) is supposed to assure (iii), that one now prefers with strength S that if one were in that situation X should happen rather than not.[157] In other words, sincere moral utterance with full understanding entails that one not be a fanatic in Hare's sense.[158] But this is wrong. There is no reason to believe that (iii) is assured by (ii), or for that matter to believe that (ii) is assured by (i), unless "fully understands" and "situation" are so enriched as to make these links tautologies, which puts otherwise unsupported normative conditions on full understanding. And there are lots of intuitive reasons to doubt these links. For instance, there are fanatics, even of the special sort Hare invokes.

Because of these difficulties with fanatics, we should return to Hare's earlier formulation and work forward from it in a different way. I will attempt to develop a new moral test in the spirit of Hare but without some of his detailed difficulties. It even captures the spirit of the unsuccessful move against fanatics deployed in *Moral Thinking*.

Hare holds that moral judgments are constrained by Stage One, Stage Two, and Stage Three Universalization. One must be able to make similar judgments on similar grounds across not merely all actual but also certain hypothetical cases. Stage Three Universalization requires that we consider situations in which we have other people's

---

[155] Hare (1963). Hare (1981) differs in a way we shortly consider.
[156] Hare (1963) hints at this. Section 10.9 discussed Carson's alternative fix.
[157] Hare (1981: 94–6).   [158] Hare (1981: 169–87) discusses complications.

inclinations and desires, and that is not an obviously coherent thought. The hypotheticals are wild.[159] But at least for the most part these constraints, and in fact constraints that one make the same judgments in other wildly hypothetical and yet relevantly similar cases, are in fact entailed by the general constraint that when the same criteria for normative evaluation apply they generate the same normative status. So we should accept these constraints, or something very like them, in our new motivational test.

What gives these universalization constraints their distributional bite in Hare's system is that he holds that making moral judgments involves a prescription, something like a command, and that there are plausible psychological limits to the kinds of prescriptions one can sincerely make about even hypothetical situations. To make a moral judgment means sincerely prescribing, on his view, across not merely actual but merely hypothetical conditions, where the latter sort of sincerity turns on what one in fact wants for the hypothetical situations.

There are various difficulties regarding the moral adequacy of this sort of sincerity, related to worries we considered during our discussion of Gensler and Carson. It is clear that Hare wanted a gap, at least in his earlier formulations, between what you now sincerely prescribe for a hypothetical situation and what you would in fact want if you were in that situation. But I will suggest a distinct but related motivational test that does not deploy such a gap, and for that reason evades the relevant difficulties of the last section. It involves a different interpretation of what proper sincerity requires, that is closely connected with the notion of full information.

Focus not on a kind of sincerity that depends on your desire now for what would happen in a hypothetical situation, but rather on a kind that requires an honest and indeed truthful assessment of what one would in fact want if one occupied that hypothetical condition. And focus on Stage Three Universalization, the deepest sort, which commits one to making the same valuations about hypothetical cases in which one is not only in another's actual external situation, but also has their actual inclinations and desires and not one's own. Now put these elements together. A honest and truthful assessment of what one would in fact want if one occupied a hypothetical situation in which one has someone else's wants and not one's own reflects in fact what that someone else wants. Notice the similarity of this to MM on individual well-being.

There are two sorts of fanatics that are potentially relevant to Hare's own test. One sort somehow sincerely prefers that if they were someone else who didn't prefer something still it be done to them. The gap between reality and what is hypothetical is what allows this. But on my test, such fanatics are irrelevant. What matters is what they would in fact want if they were the other person. But a second sort of fanatic might sincerely prescribe something even for their actual current self which they

---

[159] But Hare (1963: 108) suggests, like Gensler and Carson, that it is one's actual preferences for hypothetical situations that matter.

don't in fact prefer. The gap is between two sorts of motivational state, with mere preference swamped by high ideal. But in our messy physical world there are not cleanly distinct motivational systems of that sort, and the "higher" sort is not normatively dominant in any case, for reasons we explored earlier. There is instead only one sort of basic and normatively relevant conation, which we should now take as relevant to our new golden rule test.

So how, on my proposal, should we think of fanatics who would do things that they intuitively don't prefer because they hold high ideals? Their basic preferences in my sense include a dominant preference for that ideal over more intuitive sorts of well-being for themselves, and it should help determine their own individual good in the way I proposed. But it is highly unlikely to be relevant to the consensus congruence of human good relevant to most distributional questions in reality, except in isolated cases in which a more robust consensus congruence of all the affected makes it also intuitively relevant. Similar things are true of masochists, and those with other preferences that may seem intuitively immoral. This appeal to consensus congruence is one element of MM that I have so far neglected in my variant of Hare. MM does in fact involves a little gap between the attitudes of the prescriber and of others, rooted in one kind of objectivity, and hence is a bit closer to Hare in this respect than it might so far seem. So now add this refinement to our Hare-like test.

No doubt my variant of Hare's test seems unworkable for new reasons, because it rules out almost all sincere moral judgment, even with that little gap. Almost anything one might do is likely to affect someone in a way they do not prefer, even in a way reflecting consensus congruence. This is closely related to Kant's worry about punishing criminals. But Hare's general idea in response to this class of worries is to appeal to proper distribution of the good, so that we can properly balance the criminal's interests against others.[160] And I think that this is the right strategy to defend golden rule tests.

Hare argues that universal prescriptivism yields utilitarianism as a way to properly balance interests.[161] But I will now propose another modification of Hare's view at exactly this point, at the point that bridges his universal prescriptivism and his normative theory.

Hare begins his first consideration of the normative implications of universal prescriptivism, in *Freedom and Reason*, with a two-person case. You and Guinevere are in a situation where your act will affect her, and you ask yourself in all sincerity what you would want if you were in her shoes.[162] I suggest we accept this part of Hare's bridge, under the proper understanding of what sincerity requires.

---

[160] Hare (1963: 116–17). But 108 suggests a mechanism like Gensler and Carson's.

[161] Carson (1986) exposits ways Hare's argument depends on wild counterfactuals.

[162] It is surprising that Hare initially discusses the two-person case independently of an attempt to balance the competing interests, but see Hare (1963: 113), where competing interests are a "further

Still, there is a second step. What if many people are involved? Sincere moral judgment about complex situations involving many individuals requires, according to Hare, ceding equal weight to the desires of all. At least by *Moral Thinking*, this was supposed to specifically depend either on one's preferences for a situation in which one would live all the lives *seriatem* in some random order, or in which one has an equal chance of living any of the lives.[163] But Hare's decision procedures for these second-step cases are wrong.[164] There are a variety of problems. These tests require consideration of what are not obviously coherent circumstances, and may yield radically counterintuitive implications, in which I use one of my very many lives in a rather casual way, to remove some loathsome politician. Also, we don't have very determinate preferences of this highly unusual sort. But the main problem is that the most natural extension of Hare's two-person test to the case of many people is rather different from either of those he proposed.[165]

In the two-person case, Hare suggests, your action is ruled out if you wouldn't accept it if you were in the position of the other person. Likewise, in the many-person case, your action should be ruled out if you wouldn't accept it if you were in the position of someone—anyone—who is involved. You can test whether you sincerely accept some judgment by asking yourself whether you could assent to it whoever you would be. If there is someone who is such that if you were them you would reject the judgment, then you do not sincerely assert it. Everyone has such a veto.

I think that Hare shied away from this natural extension of his treatment of two-person cases because it suggests that very few moral judgments come out as sincerely uttered. For just about everything one might do, someone will prefer that one not do it. He moves on to utilitarian summation, instead. But utilitarian summation does not make general sense in our physical world. Nor does our little gap due to consensus congruence help much. So what are we to do? We should notice the similarity of the many-person case to one key situation that we discussed in Chapter 8. Lancelot and Arthur and Guinevere are all moderately well off, but we can move to a situation where Lancelot and Arthur are yet better off but Guinevere loses something significant. Someone among Lancelot, Arthur, and Guinevere must get a veto, because there are no robust facts about summation and if everyone gets a veto nothing will be right. And this suggests another natural extension of Hare's two-person test that is workable even in our physical world. Who should get the veto?

---

question." Still, this does engage our intuitions in appropriate ways, and is in accord with Hare's Kantian roots. Hare (1963: 113), after his primary treatment of his central two-person case, does suggest that after we've gone on to argue that utilitarianism is the proper method to treat multiple-person cases, this applies backwards to two-person cases. So perhaps he accepts his initial treatment of two-person cases in a conditional and qualified way.

[163] Hare (1981: 129). This is prefigured by Hare (1963: 123).

[164] Nagel's alternative—involving what we want for a situation in which we live all lives of all people at once—is similarly problematic.

[165] And from Nagel's proposal.

Guinevere should get the veto. To be more exact, the worst-off atomic agent should get the veto. The relevantly worst-off atomic agent across the two alternatives should decide. We have come by a roundabout route back to our basically maximin distribution of desire-based well-being. And in cases where the worst-off are not affected by some choice, there is also a plausible extension of this proposal to lexical maximin. And indeed when cardinality is available Hare's own mechanism of utilitarian summation is available. We are back in the vicinity of LDP.

Nevertheless, we can preserve the abstract structure of Hare's answer to Kant's punishment case. Punishment can be fine if it serves overall value as assessed by LDP. You might worry that the punished will often hence be the worst-off. But that depends on the sorts of punishments in question and what they are punishments for. Consequentially proper punishment is that which best serves LDP and hence the interests of the worst-off. Perhaps you are worried that this means the worst-off individual will get to brutally murder whoever they want for idle entertainment without legitimate constraint. But of course institutions of punishment have very complex effects that serve the general interest. And it is highly implausible that there is a consensus congruence that supports the claim that someone who is poor and murders for enjoyment remains worse off than someone who is financially well off but brutally murdered. And the standard worry that consequentialism will some-times support a properly productive murder is also engaged by my proposal in another place. We are already assuming that MAC2 can evade the general worry about the morality of consequentially beneficial murders, although we haven't yet seen how.

What does MAC2, and its two key tenets VLD and DD, have to do with Hare? Notice that Hare's test, as well as my modification of it, along with the other golden rule arguments, provides equal respect of a sort for both moral agents and patients. It involves a role for reciprocity and benevolence. Still, there are agents other than atomic agents relevant to VLD and DD, and it may be hard to see how to extend Hare's test to encompass them, since they do not characteristically have preference-based goods that are comparable. But the consequentially weighty group acts that receive relative protection by VLD and DD are all relatively weighty by reference to LDP. It isn't the explicit content of the projects of the conflicting acts that matter in these cases, but their actual consequences as assessed by reference to what is in the relevant though often merely implicit sense a shared project of all beneficent acts. And so when such acts are relevantly weighty and ordered by VLD or DD, there are no morally relevant differences in the goods at issue between the protected and unprotected acts. It is just like a case where two people are pursuing exactly the same shareable good in the world, but the attempt of one will interfere with the attempt of another, and the attempt of the first would achieve more of that consensual good than the second. Presume you are the second. Should you act so as to pursue by some project a good that would be better achieved if you did not pursue that project but let the other party pursue their project instead? Apply a Hare-like test to that choice.

It seems possible to sincerely prescribe the other to act and yourself not to act, but it seems not possible to sincerely prescribe yourself to act and the other not to act. Of course, sometimes we want to achieve some good ourselves, but that is not the type of case in question. Our development of Hare's test in fact yields VLD and DD. It yields MAC2, and not just LDP.

10.11 Conclusion

The third and only viable answer to Kant's punishment worry about golden rule constructions leads to LEXIMAC. So too does Kant's moral theory when suitably modified for reality. And so we can conclude the argument of this chapter:

The utilitarian, the contractarian, and the golden rule tradition in both its Kantian and non-Kantian varieties, all find their only appropriate real world development in LEXIMAC. In reality, DC3-METHODS supports my overall normative theory MM. There is no viable alternative. And so we can conclude the argument of this part:

We have yet to see that MM can deliver sufficiently intuitive ethical implications, that it meets DC1-NORMS. But by appeal to the descriptive constraints DC2-BASIS and DC3-METHODS we have already seen that, in our world, if any moral theory is true, MM is true.

PART III

Applications

11

Individual Obligations

11.1 Summary of Parts I and II

We seek normative evaluation of two types of alternatives. First, a conscious human agent at a time has an option in action if and only if (i) there is something such that if they were to try to do it at that time, then they would succeed in taking that option, (ii) that thing they might try to do is coherently conceivable by humans, (iii) the conditional in (i) is such that its antecedent does not entail its consequent, and (iv) that antecedent does not involve trying to try. Second, social alternatives are at base alternative forms of reason acceptance by agents. There are moderate indeterminacies of both types of alternatives, which incorporate *ex ante* objective probabilities but not flukes.

Agents have beliefs sensitive to perception, and preferences leading to action. The primary virtue or excellence or discipline of belief is truth.[1] Because respect for truth is a precondition of proper reason-giving and evaluation, and because intentional action requires some understanding of one's options, truth may be the dominant normative property.[2] But our focus is elsewhere. Besides the truth of beliefs, there is the well-being of individuals constituted by their preference satisfaction. But the primary virtue or excellence or discipline of desire and action is prescribed by the ethical theory Material Morality. MM conjoins LDP and MAC2.

LDP orders options, whether individual or social, from worse to better, *modulo* any ties and indeterminacies. In the basic case, it holds that one alternative outcome is better than another if it is better from the perspective of the worst-off affected normal adult human atomic agent, where the worst-off is defined by consensus congruence among the preferences of all such agents. In ties, we move on to consideration of the second worst-off, and so on. But there are four complications. First, when there is consensus across all affected normal adult human atomic agents that delivers a pocket of cardinality, assessments of options that involve simply a difference within that pocket are ordered by regard to sums of value. Second, when there is such a pocket and total value is equal, then distributional equality among

---

[1] Or something epistemic in its vicinity.

[2] Don't sacrifice all humanity for one more true belief, which would be massively immoral. But if you sacrifice your intellect to the demands of morality, you will lack a real excellence. I don't know how to balance a little immorality and much cognitive excellence.

atomic agents matters. Third, when less than cardinal but more than ordinal value comparisons can be rooted in consensus among all such agents, this invokes qualifications specified in 8.3.[3] Fourth, non-human agents with a preference-based good, in particular certain non-human animals and group agents, have interests. Surely these can properly break ties in human good, and perhaps order states indeterminately ordered by human good. And when there is cross-species consensus, or human consensus spanning babies and the non-normal, that specifies relevant comparisons with normal adult human interests, which will engage other elements of LDP.

MAC2 has five central tenets, although there are complicating qualifications specified in 9.4: (1) Among a particular set of options, the most choiceworthy is the best. (2) VLD: One should only defect from a group act with good consequences if one can achieve better consequences by the defecting act alone than the entire group act achieves. (3) DD: When different beneficent group acts of which one is part specify roles that conflict, one should follow the role in the group act with more valuable consequences. (4) One should join whatever group acts it is consequentially best to join, given the constraints set by VLD and DD. (5) Defection is required from group acts with harmful consequences, and more important when those consequences are more harmful.

A natural worry is whether MM can deliver acceptably intuitive normative implications. If it cannot underwrite the consensus judgments specified by the meaning constraint DC1-NORMS, then I believe it is false. This and the following chapter consider the ethical obligations of individuals according to MM. These chapters are organized around three traditional objections to direct consequentialist theories like MM, which assess the propriety of acts by regard to the value of their consequences.

11.2 Deontic Restrictions

Commonsense morality is much concerned with general "deontic" restrictions forbidding killing, lying, causing injury, and theft. And it is often alleged that the pursuit of overall good required by direct consequentialism will require frequent violation of these strictures.

But MM incorporates MAC2, which is a very stable mechanism for delivering these commonsense duties. MAC2 can deliver commonsense deontic restrictions when it is conjoined with any reasonably plausible principle for ranking outcomes; the details of LDP don't matter very much. It will take a while to explain this fully, but the main point is that there are many forms of weightily beneficent group action that are forms of moral cooperation, and some involve the cooperative creation of spheres in which standard deontic restrictions are observed. MAC2 will seldom countenance defections from these weighty group acts.

---

[3] These qualifications are not important in this part.

There are many types of group acts to which deontic restrictions are attached. Some are informal and local, say when Jean-Paul and Simone have a special practice of not lying about certain things to each other. This may be local enough to constitute a special obligation, an obligation from particular people to particular people because of their special relations. But some group acts, though they involve specific deontic duties, are quite widespread; they enjoy almost universal participation by people spread over wide areas of space and time. These help constitute general deontic obligations, like the general obligation not to lie. It is even plausible to conceive of commonsense morality as a single widespread group act, or as involving several group acts that are relatively local but still complete commonsense moralities, though a complete commonsense morality also involves various normative components that themselves constitute group acts.

When we consider normative details in 11.4, we will focus one at a time on each widespread duty. But there are various analytical points we need to discuss first. And I will begin with the simplest analytical focus for our immediate purposes, the single group act constituting the widespread acceptance across space and time of all the commonsense general deontic restrictions. This will allow me to make my initial case in the simplest way possible, though we will eventually need to focus more finely. And I will first explain why there is such a big group act.

Group acts involve accepted reasons, and commonsense morality too involves accepted reasons, in particular the acceptance of deontic restrictions against actions of certain sorts. Still, group acts also involve a kind of entwined reciprocity and at least apparent beneficence. There is an apparent good or goal aimed at, which is characterized by the project of the act, by what the group is trying to do. And defectors from group acts will characteristically be criticized on two grounds, for failure to act for that good, and for failure of proper reciprocity with other members of the group. But that dual sort of criticism is just the kind we make of defectors from our commonsense morality of general duties, rooted as it is in enlaced benevolence and reciprocity.

There are complications. The most characteristic general deontic commitments of commonsense morality are *negative*. They require that we *not* murder. But there can be a negative group act, which involves trying together not to murder. It aims at a good, though a negative good. A second complication is that acceptance of deontic commitments seems to be a *one-off* group act. That is to say that there is no group agent that exists independent of commitment to the particular project in question, as there might be when a particular friendship or political movement is involved.[4] But still, there can be such one-off group acts.

---

[4] Those who accept the general deontic restrictions also participate in group acts that involve other elements of commonsense morality. But the two-level structure of accepted reasons present when there is a group agent independent of commitment to a particular project—the first level constituting the agent and the second its specific project—is absent here.

You and I participate in a group act involving acceptance of general deontic restrictions. It aims at least at a negative good or complex of goods, and defectors are criticized on grounds not only of failure of relevant non-maleficence but also of reciprocity. And almost everyone with whom we interact is always within the group act constituting this part of commonsense morality, at least in the sense relevant to constituting violation as defection. If Hannah at some time acts contrary to the strictures of this group act, she also accepts the reasons constituting the act, and so her violation is defection. If Martin is truly outside this portion of commonsense morality, then the fourth tenet of MAC2 requires that he join up whenever that is consequentially best and the other constraints of MAC2 allow it, and then he too will be bound inside.

The main point on which to focus is that the group act constituting the commonsense morality of general negative duties is a very consequentially weighty group act. And so VLD and DD will almost never countenance defections, except on similar enormously weighty consequential grounds. Since most moral practices, including the commonsense morality of general negative duties, are one-off group acts, the specific questions to ask to determine the normative weight of the relevant group act are how good things are in the presence of such an action, and how good things would have been had such a group act not existed. On any reasonably intuitive evaluation of outcomes, it is better that the commonsense morality of general negative duties exists than that there be the nasty and brutish state of nature in which we accept no such moral constraints. The grounds for believing this are long familiar from the history of utilitarianism and contractarianism. And almost no defecting act can be so positively weighty. Very few defecting acts can, on their own, in the absence of the commonsense morality of negative general duties, make the world better than the world would be without the defecting act but with that part of commonsense morality intact. So MAC2 will seldom countenance defections from the general deontic constraints of commonsense morality.

This is true whether we deploy a hedonist or desire-based conception of well-being, or even any intuitive objectivist conception. It is true whether we apply a maximin principle to atomic agents or lives, or sum with the utilitarians. It is true whether or not desert matters in a fundamental way to the evaluation of outcomes. All remotely plausible alternatives to LDP provide a relevantly similar ordering of the relevant outcomes.[5]

This is not to say that details about the evaluation of outcomes don't matter to morality. We will shortly turn to specific contexts in which they do matter. But there

---

[5] Because the connection between some negative goods protected by general deontic duties on one hand and pleasure and pain on the other is more indirect than the connection between those goods and the focus of desire-based and objectivist conceptions, more intermediate mechanism is required to support these claims for hedonism. See Mendola (2006: 64–9 and 279–85). Another complication is that an interaction of some deontic restrictions and the correct ordering of outcomes will gradually become significant during 11.3.

are various natural worries about my general treatment of the general deontic restrictions that we should consider first.

11.3 Analytical Worries

One cluster of worries involves the determinacy of the subjunctive conditional claims deployed here. The assessment of the effects of huge group acts, including the commonsense morality of negative duties, may seem to involve virulent indeterminacies. But let's look at the details.

What exactly are we to consider when assessing the consequential weight of the commonsense morality of negative duties? We are to consider all of the atomic agents over space and time that are participants in that morality, and we are to compare how things are in fact, with how they would be instead if those atomic agents didn't accept the reasons and meet the other tests for participating in that group act.[6] We leave all the atomic agents and everything else fixed except what constitutes their participation in that group act and what depends consequentially on that.

One worry about this is that it might not be very determinate what would be true of these people if they didn't participate in that group act. There are various necessary conditions, cognitive and conative and practical, on participation, and individuals could meet some of the conditions and not others. And even if we focus, for instance, on deontic belief as the key component of participation, still there are lots of alternative deontic beliefs.

The proper procedure is to focus on the null option, the option in which there is no alternative morality accepted, no alternative form of acceptance of general deontic restrictions, nor even another form of morality, no alternative group act. This is for two reasons. First, any act can have trivial variants, and it is not plausible to assess its consequences by considering the differences it introduces relative to trivial variants. If I can kill you in two ways that differ slightly in their effects, that doesn't mean I haven't done a great harm by choosing the only slightly worse method, or been beneficent in choosing the slightly better. Second, the deontic practice in question is a one-off group act. There is no group agent that exists independent of the particular project in question. The primary alternative to any one-off group act consists of the individuals in question not acting as a group.[7]

But what exactly is the null option? The primary component of our general deontic morality that is lacking in the null option is beneficent inaction in accord with negative deontic restrictions, so the null option includes the baseline of relevant

---

[6] This treatment of atomic agents spread over time is required by my treatment of continuing individual action as group action of cooperating atomic agents. But variants of MAC might eschew this.

[7] This feature of MAC2 aids its normative determinacy relative to rule consequentialism, which requires the consideration of the consequences of all possible alternative deontic beliefs. It might be objected here that only the alternatives a group considers are relevant. But we are focused on objective consequences.

evil acts that would occur among us if we lacked commitment to these moral restrictions. But since group acts are assessed by reference to their consequences, and since the other cognitive and affective components of group acts conceivably have independent effects, the null option lacks all of these features constitutive of the group action in question. In the relevant null option, members are not merely defecting. The group act does not exist among them, and indeed no part of it exists.

This conception still involves a measure of indeterminacy, especially because of its reliance on a baseline of wrong acts that would occur without acceptance of the restrictions. And various complications may seem to threaten further indeterminacy. Sometimes we do our external part in some group act, perhaps because of external sanctions, and yet defect within, defect from motivational conditions that we formerly accepted that are required for that individual performance to be part of the relevant group trying. I think that it is very hard for ordinary humans to defect from the group acts that are characteristic of morality in this way.[8] But the main point is that this possibility is not relevant to the null option, which includes *none* of the characteristic components of the group action, so it doesn't introduce any new indeterminacy.[9] Yet another worrisome complication is that there may be various particular ways to defect from the *content* of some specific group act. For instance, we can fail to recognize the constraints of some negative group act in only one limited arena, or alternatively in another arena. We can lie at work but not at home. Perhaps certain defections of that type are more significant than others, but if those differences are not captured by the exceptions and qualifications built into the group act itself, the direct relevance of such differences is incompatible with MAC2.[10] Still, the main point again is that this complication is not relevant to the determinacy of the null option, which involves dissent from all the conditions that constitute the group act among the atomic agents in question.

Another and more serious problem is that the conditions that must be varied to allow assessment of the relevant conditional and the background conditions that must be preserved are dangerously enmeshed. It is true that each atomic agent's participation is a relatively local phenomenon.[11] But, on the other hand, participation by *many* atomic agents involves *lots* of localized conditions, in totality spread over time and space. And the conditions that involve agents' acceptance of deontic morality are at least somewhat entwined with their other psychological features, features that would be relevant to what they would do if they didn't accept that morality. And of course the effects of our negative deontic morality are very

---

[8] Some individuals always accept morality only from the outside in this way, and hence never defect in my sense. But such cases seem rare.

[9] But if there are actual cases that is relevant to the baseline of the null option.

[10] Except if concentric acts are involved in a way shortly explained. None of this implies it is as bad to lie as to murder according to MAC2, but to see why requires a more refined analytical focus than we now engage.

[11] According to the internalism about mental content, I presume.

widespread. It may seem that virulent indeterminacy looms. Still, it is reasonable to hope that the enormous consequential weight of the practice of negative deontic morality will overwhelm any relatively small-scale and hence more plausibly indeterminate *details* of the relevant outcomes. While it may be highly indeterminate whether or not a particular agent would lie in a particular way in the absence of the acceptance of deontic morality, and also indeterminate what the effects of that particular lie would be, it can still be clear that much more lying in general would occur and would have generally bad effects. For instance, much cooperative economic activity would be impossible.

But there is another aspect of this worry.[12] The temporal spread of relevant atomic agents, out even into the future, interacts in a troubling way with intuitively relevant effects of the group act in question. We need to hold some features of the future constant when assessing the relevant conditional, not just features of the present or past, since the future includes some of the atomic agents who in fact participate in the act. And those future features of the world are among those that are intuitively relevant to the normative weight of the act, since the participants or their prepubescent parents might have been murdered if there were no moral practice of refraining from murder. If we need to hold constant the existence of all the atomic agents who accept the commonsense morality of negative duties when assessing what would be true if they did not accept that morality, then it cannot matter to the relevant normative weight of that group act that some virtuous agent would have been murdered without it and hence that some of those atomic agents wouldn't exist. But that is part of the intuitive weight of that group act.[13]

My response, which also helps with other forms of entwining, is a multiple-step test for weighing group acts that are extended in time. I believe that commonsense deontic morality can pass all of the subtests, and hence is more determinately valuable than would otherwise be the case. There are in fact two sorts of comparisons MAC2 generally requires, not only of a group act with nothing but with various possible defecting acts, so I will phrase the test to encompass both possibilities.

First, presuming that the conflict of Special Relativity with absolute simultaneity does not matter on the scale with which we are engaged, we consider at each temporal point the consequences of the current temporal slice of the group act

---

[12] Which Mendola (2006) missed.

[13] This is a problem I share with some rule consequentialists. There are other possible solutions. A Kantian constraint might stipulate that a group act cannot be properly abandoned by those who would not exist without it. But it is not immoral to use effective birth control even if your existence depends on acceptance by your parents of contrary teachings of the Pope, and even if you feel, reverberating inside you, papal teachings constituting your violation as defection. Perhaps the problem only arises for some commonsense duties, and the relevant consequential weight of the deontic prohibition on murder, for which it does arise, can ride piggyback on the weight of the whole commonsense morality of negative duty, or depend merely on collateral effects of acts aimed at murder, say the pain of poisoning. But lengthening life seems an intuitively relevant effect of many deontic duties, not just of refraining from murder.

constituting the deontic restrictions figured forward from that moment in time. If figured forward from each moment in the history of a group act there are positive consequential results—namely a greater value for the group act than either the relevant defecting act (if that is the comparison we are making) or the relevant null option[14]—or at least no determinately negative results, that is positively relevant to the consequential dominance of the group act. Remember from Chapter 3 that we ignore flukes of luck in assessing consequences, and focus on *ex ante* objective probabilities; that helps considerably in assuring there will be no determinately negative results. But a second component of our test is more important, especially when assessments relative to the null option are at issue. Another conditional that is relevant to assessing the weight of the group act relative to the null option involves a general and abstract antecedent. Details about which particular atomic agents exist or don't exist, or even which individual people exist, don't matter in a way that must be considered a fixed background condition for the assessment of that conditional. Rather, whatever general kinds of atomic agents there are should be preserved as relevant background conditions, along with suitably general conditions in which they live.[15] This abstraction will certainly introduce indeterminacies in the relevant weight of the group act. We can differ without error about what conditions are important and must be preserved when evaluating the conditional. But while there plausibly is considerable indeterminacy about what the effects of the cross-temporal absence of our commonsense morality of negative duties would be, yet it is also plausible that that morality is consequentially sufficiently weighty, despite the indeterminacy in question, to be better than the null option. And indeed, the consequential weight of the whole group act is also almost always plausibly larger, figured in this abstract way, than what someone might achieve by a relatively local defecting act.[16]

I argued earlier that there is often less determinate individual responsibility for outcomes than commonsense presumes, because of virulent indeterminacies in counterfactuals that involve fairly specific antecedents and consequents, in which given individuals refrain from certain specific actions and there are highly specific consequences. But now I am arguing that there is a close analogue of individual responsibility applied to a widespread and consequentially weighty group act that is suitably determinate. One key difference is that both the antecedents and the consequents of the conditional in question in the second and central component of our test are fairly abstract and large scale. The truth of those antecedents and consequents would be preserved over many perturbations of fine local detail. And it is the details of antecedents and especially consequents of relevant conditionals that

---

[14] Both assessed concurrently.

[15] This mechanism inches closer to Scanlon's use of generic reasons, but involves more actual contingencies.

[16] It is less evident that this mechanism will allow a determinate assessment of the consequential weight of conflicting massive group acts, such as conflicting deontic obligations involve.

in general create virulent indeterminacy problems for counterfactuals assessing consequential weight.[17] We know from Chapter 3 that consequential assessment should ignore flukes, which is very important for its determinacy. But there remain relevant worries about the determinacy of the effects of individual defections, and also of the effects of group actions and individual defections figured forward in time from a moment. Still, even a seriously indeterminate large positive effect can determinately swamp a seriously indeterminate small one, as well as be determinately better than nothing. So despite incorporating components that may be quite indeterminate, our key test for defection generally involves merely moderate indeterminacy. That is because the indeterminacies in question still allow us to make the comparisons we need to make.

Of course, some individual defections from morality are also quite dramatic. Hitler performed individual acts of defection that were quite weighty. But *beneficent* defections, which might be legitimate according to MAC2, are not very likely to be hugely weighty, and when they are, they are also unlikely to be criticized by participants in the group act itself, and so, you will recall from Chapter 9, are unlikely to be true defections. That feature of MAC2 may seem itself problematic. Perhaps criticism or failure of criticism of defectors sometimes turns on ignorance of consequences. But I presume that it is informed criticism, taking in all consequentially relevant non-normative considerations, that matters. And since flukes aren't relevant to the positive consequences of a defection, you do not properly defect from deontic morality merely because your defection will have wonderful consequences achieved through some accident. Still, there may be cases in which the effects of defection are so *ex ante* indeterminate that it is indeterminate whether defection is weightier than the deontic group act. That involves a kind of normative risk, and as I suggested earlier for analogous cases involving animal interests, it is natural to extend MM to forbid morally speculative defection, which would also plausibly occasion increased responsibility. Consider this the sixth central tenet of MAC2.

That's all about these indeterminacies. But the temporal spread of the group actions constitutive of deontic morality may also suggests other worries. It may be worrisome that tomorrow's participants in a group act get moral credit for effects of that action in olden times even when tomorrow's effects are not positive. But the multiple-part test that I have just proposed in fact requires positive effects in each moment. One may worry that sometime in the future the deontic restrictions will come to have horrific consequences, because of evil peculiarities of later cooperators or by the ministrations of some outside source, say vengeful deontological Martians. But again the multiple-part test I have proposed skirts this problem. And in any case such possibilities are fantasy. We are concerned here with the actual effects of actual group acts, not with highly hypothetical and merely possible effects. One can object

---

[17] Rule consequentialists have more difficulty at this point, because they need to make many more comparisons of the effects of different sets of rules, which turn on details.

to *any* moral theory that has a plausible commitment to human welfare by appeal to hypothetical Martians who will endlessly torture all humanity if that theory is followed.[18] That certainly doesn't suffice to show that true morality has no commitment to human welfare.

More worries: I have referred to our commonsense morality of deontic restrictions, but what are the temporal and spatial boundaries of the relevant group act? Does it include ancient Greeks and antebellum plantation owners who held slaves as property in brutal ways? Their local commonsense admitted exceptions to general deontic restrictions on brutality, and also required additional deontic restraints on interference with others' human property. And that invites a second worry. Does the enormous consequential weight of commonsense deontic morality imply that it is always wrong to attempt improvements in some brutal deontic component of one's contemporary commonsense?

My reply is this: In Chapter 9, we briefly noted concentric group acts of one type, but there is also another and more important type. Sometimes when some component norm of a moral practice that is a group action has bad effects, there is another group action that includes the same atomic agents but eschews that component norm in its project, and hence has better consequences on its own. There are two concentric group acts, such that the inner one would have better consequences on its own, and hence is dominant according to MAC2.[19] Violating the bad component norm doesn't really constitute defection from the group act that constitutes the better concentric practice, because the division is within the content of the projects of the group, and is not a matter of individual defection from a single project. Any criticism that would occasion defection is attached to the problematic norm, and not to the beneficent elements of the group project. If ancient Greeks and antebellum Americans had a commonsense morality that included in addition to the norms we share with them another norm that involved respect for another's slave property, or a qualification on a general constraint against brutality, still they also shared with us a concentric and consequentially better morality that eschewed those heinous components. And DD implies that the concentric act was dominant. This mechanism allows the relevant commonsense morality of negative duties to be shared over a very wide region of space and time, though for some participants it will be merely concentric to a norm-enriched but morally impoverished local morality. Even the slaveholders are inside our commonsense morality in the relevant sense, but it doesn't include their heinous, parochial normative errors. The few ancient Greeks and antebellum Southerners who defected and criticized local commonsense about slavery were doing what DD requires.

---

[18] Mendola (1986).
[19] Mendola (2006: 62–3). The multiple-part test proposed above can plausibly deliver the needed determinacy in these cases, even if it cannot generally resolve conflicts among deontic duties.

This mechanism implies that we must refine our analytical focus. We must focus principally not on a single widespread deontic group act incorporating all the commonsense duties, but each particular widespread deontic duty by itself, so we can test the consequential propriety of each duty. And that will be our procedure in the next section.

There are other difficulties. Some deontic norms that are quite consequentially beneficial have relevantly different forms over space and time, and there may be significant differences among even contemporaries about details. Consider one representative case. Lying seems morally problematic to almost everyone, but there are lots of differences about details even among people who are likely to read this book. First, we differ about what lying is, about what counts as lying. For instance, most prominent philosophical accounts of lying maintain that one can tell a lie that turns out inadvertently to be true,[20] while most dictionaries and my linguistic intuitions suggest that under such circumstances one would have tried but failed to tell a lie. Also, we differ about whether deception that falls short of explicit lying is seriously problematic. And while there are many implicit exceptions to prohibitions against lying found in our commonsense, which for instance allow lies to protect the innocent, we differ considerably about what sorts of exceptions are appropriate. We also differ about how in general to balance lying against other harms. And there have been communities of humans who were more absolutist about lying than we tend to be. Consider Kant and his Pietist friends.

It would be obviously wrong for me to presume universal acceptance over time of the deontic duties in exactly the form in which I accept them. But in Chapter 9 I suggested another mechanism that is somewhat helpful at this point. At least over fairly large regions of time and space, there is consensus congruence on a certain sort of relatively vague morality of deontic obligations. If we ignore some details of the commitments of a few oddballs, we can hope for more agreement. However, this mechanism is creaky. The Pietist movement doesn't count as just a few oddballs, and one might wonder what makes this appeal to mere consensus legitimate. Still, there is a way to properly underwrite this particular mechanism and also to extend it in various helpful ways. That is to embed it in a larger point, a point that is, I should admit, not just helpful but also dangerous for us. It involves various layers of a new sort of indeterminacy.

First, it is unlikely to be highly determinate even what deontic restrictions any particular individual accepts at a time. We may be averse to lying, but uncertain whether certain acts count as lies.[21] While each of us has a concept of lying, it is

---

[20] Chisholm and Feehan (1977). Carson (2010: 15–45) sketches this literature.

[21] This is obvious given internalism about mental content, but would also be true if externalism were true. There are no natural kinds in the vicinity of lying, and in any case they would be normatively irrelevant. Nor are there genuine experts on the identification of normatively relevant lying; philosophical debates rooted in linguistic intuitions about lying carry little normative weight.

somewhat vague. And, more important, most of us are more than a little vague about what exceptions to general prohibitions on lying are appropriate, and about how to balance lying against other harms and duties. There are also other layers of indeterminacy introduced by shared deontic group acts. There are certainly detailed differences among even those in the contemporary English-speaking world about what lying is, and about what exceptions are appropriate and how to balance lying against other things. It can be rather indeterminate whether two contemporary English-speaking individuals who agree in some detailed ways and disagree in others are part of one very particular group act. And it can be indeterminate what the shared project of any group act they do share is. And such indeterminacies ramify considerably for larger group acts spread across time and wider social space.

I think that there is often real indeterminacy about what group acts there are, about what their projects are and about who is inside of them at what times. And I think there is in particular considerable indeterminacy of the group acts that constitute recognition of commonsense deontic obligations. The edges of those group acts are vague, and so too are their projects. Hence so too is what constitutes defection from those acts. There will be many different detailed acts of this sort in which you and I might admissibly be considered to participate, with different detailed projects, inside of and overlapping with others in time and space and content. And even these detailed candidates are somewhat vague. If we ask whether Jean-Paul should lie in a particular tough case, there will likely be no single and highly determinate summary group act in which he participates that can deliver a highly refined single answer to that question. It is possible that other moral considerations can properly refine the correct answer to a tough question of that sort, in ways we will consider later on. And the indeterminacy in question even suggests yet another normative directive for dealing with normative indeterminacy, which might plausibly be a seventh tenet of MAC2: When the choice is between violating the determinate core of a deontic duty and its indeterminate periphery, steer for the periphery. But any true deontic duties that rest on our group acts are rather rough and ready, as will be reflected in my rough and ready treatment of particular duties in the next section.

This helps with the worry in front of us, since it allows us to abstract away from some of what might appear to be detailed differences among us. But it is also dangerous. However, despite the sorts of indeterminacy in play, I believe that there is enough determinacy for MAC2 and LDP to deliver adequate respect for our somewhat indeterminate commonsense deontic restrictions on action. The deontic restrictions that MM will underwrite are only moderately indeterminate; more so than we would like, but not so much that ethics is bankrupt. The edges and color of a cloud may be quite indeterminate, but yet clouds have different shapes, and one cloud is sometimes darker than another.

11.4 The Duties

We turn now from analytical points to details of normative content. There are various elements of our widespread commonsense morality of general deontic restrictions, various different duties. Because of the considerations involving concentric agents introduced in the last section, we need to focus on one duty at a time, according to a natural conception of how duties are individuated. We need to make sure that each duty is properly beneficent.

Begin with lying and its analogues. Lying is forbidden to one degree or another by almost all moralists. Defectors are criticized for failures of reciprocity and nonmaleficence in ways that we would expect if there is a negative group act involved. But, even if we ignore differences about what lying is, there are lots of differences in detail about when lying is forbidden, and about what analogues are also forbidden. For instance, the duty not to lie is much less defeasible according to Kant than according to Sidgwick.[22] Ross claims that the duty not to lie is a species of promise, and that there is no duty not to deceive or to provide information,[23] while Confucian *hsin* incorporates the duty not to lie in a very general virtue that extends as far as the duty to make only accurate predictions.[24] Scanlon thinks that we often have a positive duty to provide the truth,[25] and some think that actively misleading true speech or other forms of deception are as bad as lying. At least some of these controversies suggest differences or indeterminacies within relevant group acts in which you and I participate, and within any very broad commonsense morality.

Lying and deception have more than one place in my overall normative proposal, because I think that truth of belief is a dominant epistemic virtue. But I will focus here on the way such things are forbidden by moral reasons. MAC2 will deliver the propriety of our vague widespread group act of not lying when conjoined with any reasonably plausible principle for assessing the value of outcomes. But I will focus specifically on its interaction with LDP.

True belief is generally instrumentally important to the success of action within groups or outside them, and hence to the satisfaction of desires when acts are beneficent.[26] And we also care considerably about knowing the truth and being able to trust others about it. We have consensus about that. Of course there are evil actions and the interests of different individuals conflict. But true belief is weightily instrumentally important, as assessed by LDP, in service of the interests of the worse off, and also sometimes intrinsically important to those interests as a matter of consensus congruence, and so it is sometimes very significant to the relative value of overall outcomes. Because of the instrumental and intrinsic value of true

---

[22] Carson (2010: 77–88) traces the temporal evolution of Kant's view.
[23] W. D. Ross (1930: 21).   [24] Confucius (1979: 25).   [25] Scanlon (1998: 295–327).
[26] Chapter 6 suggested skepticism about the difference between instrumental and intrinsic desires, but not about the difference between goals and instrumental means.

belief, the following four relatively concrete tenets are quite general directives of MM, even independent of our actual group practices:

(1) Do not lie, and more generally do not create false belief or withhold relevant information[27] or deceive, within a beneficent group agent with a goal that is other than that cooperative practice itself,[28] unless a violation of that duty is sanctioned by VLD or DD,[29] or the violation serves the project of the group, or the failure is acceptable in the practice. (2) If other things are equal, do not lie to, and more generally do not create false expectations in or withhold relevant information from or deceive, a beneficent agent. (3) Do not lie to, and more generally do not create false expectations in, withhold relevant information from, or deceive, another agent, whenever within a beneficent group action creating a sphere of truth-telling, unless a violation of that duty is sanctioned by VLD or DD, or the failure is acceptable in the practice. (4) Join group acts of the sort mentioned in (3) whenever that is required on direct consequentialist grounds, as long as it involves no violations of VLD or DD.

In fact you and I—and Simone, Nelson, and Jean-Paul's romance Dolores for that matter—are within a quite widespread group act of the sort mentioned in directive (3), which, because of the instrumental value of truth and the intrinsic importance of truth due to consensus congruence, is quite weighty according to LDP. As I said, I believe that its directives are moderately indeterminate, but it seems relatively conservative, focused primarily on explicit lies. It doesn't require the extended truth-telling in support of beneficent actions that MM itself suggests. But still the existence of this group act means we can summarize the truth-telling directives of MM for our actual circumstances inside commonsense morality in a fairly economical way: *Do not lie, and do not create false expectations or deceive or withhold relevant information, unless a violation of that duty is sanctioned by VLD or DD, or such a failure is acceptable according to our common moral practice. And provide information whenever required by LDP, except when otherwise forbidden by MAC2.*

I think that it is doubtful that VLD and DD can always successfully balance the duty not to lie against other general deontic restrictions, because of indeterminacy. All the component deontic group acts of commonsense morality are vastly beneficent, but it may well be indeterminate which of two is more vastly beneficent.

---

[27] I have no analysis of relevant information. Clearly you shouldn't babble on about matters of no interest to anyone but yourself, but you have a general obligation to provide truths that would be practically relevant to the success of your hearer's beneficent action, requested or not. Perhaps this allows you to withhold information to make their action more beneficent, and probably also to allow a conflicting but more beneficent action to succeed. This obligation to truth is magnified by our general epistemic obligations, but also relevantly minimized within morality itself by exceptions allowed by our group acts, as I will explain. Another complication involves commercial transactions, like buying a house, which involve different local conventions about information appropriately withheld or provided, or even about what intentionally false things are properly said during the negotiating game. Local conventions of this sort if generally known constitute local exceptions to general restrictions against deception.

[28] This phrase distinguishes this obligation from that expressed by (3).

[29] The qualifications specified in 9.4 are largely irrelevant in this part, except for cases discussed in 11.54 involving only small-scale groups.

However, I do think that the group act that forbids murder that we will shortly discuss, and also that which forbids the more serious injuries, are more consequentially weighty than that which constitutes this duty. And there is also a second mechanism for reconciling possible conflicts in duties. Notice my invocation of what is acceptable according to our practice. The relevant deontic group act, despite its indeterminacy, specifies some appropriate exceptions from rigorous truth-telling. It does not even forbid some lies, and it surely allows a certain amount of misleading speech and a good deal of deception and withholding. It allows for exceptions when some important good or duty is at stake. We can surely lie to save someone's life. Still, beneficent truth-telling is almost certainly required in more cases by LDP than by commonsense morality, especially in cases where commonsense morality itself neither forbids nor requires it. That is one refinement of commonsense morality delivered by MM, although I believe that its concentration on *beneficent* truth-telling makes it less revisionary than Scanlon's proposal.[30] And there may be another refinement. Individual acts of defection from the commonsense practice in question are at least conceivably underwritten by VLD or DD. Roughly speaking, you should lie in a defecting way only when the outcome you would have achieved by your defection alone in the absence of the general group act is better than what would be achieved by the group act if you do not defect. However, that will require highly unusual circumstances. Maybe it never happens in reality.[31] One possible case is this: Kant and the Pietists may have had a morality that allowed no lies under any conditions, and it may not have involved component norms that would allow the concentric group mechanism to revise that harmful detail of an overall beneficent practice. This opens up the possibility that they had stricter duties not to lie than we do. But, on the other hand, there are not terribly many who are such absolutists, which qualifies the consequential weight of their practice. So perhaps VLD or DD would sometimes support defection in their case.

To summarize: MM sometimes requires more truth-telling than commonsense deontic restrictions regarding lying and deception. But it underwrites the commonsense restrictions. And it also allows exceptions. The content of our actual group act allows for some exceptions, when defectors will not be criticized by participants in the group action. And VLD and DD may cede dominance to some other group act constituting another deontic obligation, or to some consequentially weighty individual defection. That is my main story about the morality of truth-telling, though other elements of commonsense morality and MM that we have yet to discuss provide further refinement of this duty.

There are some new analytical worries. I framed the general precepts in the preceding paragraphs to encompass implicit and explicit promises as well as lies, while I might have separated the cases. And indeed, the deontic restriction against

---

[30] Scanlon (1998: 295–327).
[31] Carson (2010: 125–6) objects that my view is too strict here.

lying is embedded in a more general group act that involves still other deontic duties. So there are at least three group acts relevant to lying. Which is it whose consequential weight must be trumped by properly legitimate defection according to VLD or DD? The narrowest concentric act, because of the points about balancing concentric group acts that we considered earlier. We need to see that each cluster of deontic duties is legitimate according to MM. It is partly for this reason that this section has a more refined analytical focus than the preceding one. Still, a yet finer grained analysis is also possible. But too specific an analysis would be criticized as casuistry by those who participate in our moral practices, and that criticism constitutes the boundaries of our group act. Such casuistry would make distinctions not noted in the content of the reasons we actually and generally accept, and this suggests that we are now almost at the basic level of analysis that is appropriate. Still, it is true that our common practice does recognize a difference between promising and truth-telling. And it also recognizes a difference among different forms of failing to tell the truth. If these differences were consequentially significant to the workings of MM, that would be an argument for a somewhat finer level of analysis. But I have adopted the moderately abstract level of analysis of this section because I believe these differences are not consequentially significant, at least given realistic indeterminacies, and because this level of analysis is reasonably economical. Still, there may seem to be other grounds that require a finer analysis. Recall Roman and antebellum brutality against slaves, an illicit exception, and respect for others' property in slaves, an illicit expansion. I said that these involved component norms and hence concentric group acts. But if exceptions and expansions might be a proper basis for a more refined analysis, that may seem to threaten a collapse of our deontic group acts such as that which undercuts compliance forms of rule consequentialism. However, notice that the illicit components are more or less explicit in the Roman and antebellum practice. That is why they can be properly treated as component norms specifying concentric group actions. But our own more abstract norms do not include the exceptions in question, or indeed any that in fact threaten collapse, as such explicit components. And of course expansions of commonsense morality that are consequentially beneficial are appropriate according to MM, though they will not invoke the strictures of MAC2 that require deontic respect unless there is an actual group act of the relevant sort in play. So these analytical complexities do not in fact undercut my procedure here.

Let's move on to the other deontic restrictions. A precept forbidding killing is accepted by almost all of us, but we have detailed differences that matter. First, some are pacifists, and there are others differences about proper exceptions, in self-defense, in punishment, and in medical situations. Second, we have differences about the acceptability of suicide. Note that by its distributional focus on moments of lives, MM is in principle open to moral restrictions on suicide. Third, there are differences about non-human animals, and about developing or very decrepit humans.

According to LDP, the interests of non-human animals are normatively significant, but of secondary importance. So too perhaps the interests of developing humans at some stages or quite decrepit humans, when such interests exist with reasonable determinacy. But the content of any very broad commonsense morality only straightforwardly extends deontic respect of the sort in question to other cooperating humans, and to some young or somewhat decrepit humans who are currently incapable of participation in the group act in question. Call the latter "faultless human near-normal non-cooperators," or FHNCs.[32] FHNCs are cared about by other humans as a matter of consensus congruence, and have a good more comparable to that of normal adult humans than many animals do, so their interests not only receive a greater weight in our deontic practice than non-human animals, but a weight that matters more to the good consequences of that practice according to LDP.

Whatever the details, there is clearly a widespread group agent constituting commonsense acceptance that killing humans is largely forbidden, though involving complicated exceptions and also disputes about some exceptions and hence a certain vagueness. And there is more than one way in which the killing of humans may violate proper reciprocity required by MM. Killing is often contrary to LDP, but MAC2 is also relevant in more than one way. Killing others with whom one is engaged in group activity of course eliminates the possibility of cooperative activity. Even in the unlikely event that the project of the group is favored by the murder of a member, still this involves a violation of cooperative activity in pursuit of that goal, unless perhaps that possibility is endorsed by the group including the member murdered. But of course the main point is that the general cooperative practice among normal adult humans of not murdering one another, and perhaps especially fellow cooperators, as well as FHNCs, though with some exceptions, is a group agent with a very weighty project given any plausible way of evaluating outcomes. It is highly unlikely to be something from which one can properly defect according to MAC2. And it is also relevant that participation in this general form of cooperation is a likely precondition for admission into most forms of other cooperative activity, and that killing others will undercut their individual projects and those of the group agents of which they are part. MM will certainly support commonsense moral prohibitions against killing, with rare and generally unrealistic exceptions, and also possibly extend them in certain ways.

There are other complications. Some traditional moral codes allow or even require husbands to kill adulterous wives, or fathers to kill daughters fleeing forced marriages.[33] But even though this constitutes exceptions within such codes, it involves explicit component norms, and so those who follow such a code share a concentric and better morality with us. On the other hand, Mennonites have a stricter code than most of us, which forbids joining the army or killing a tyrant. I think it involves acceptance of a separate component norm, which can be assessed for propriety by

---

[32] Pronounced FINKS.   [33] Wikan (2008); Husseini (2009).

our concentric mechanism, and fails the necessary test. But it is possible that it isn't a component norm, in other words that people with such a code just focus on not killing humans without even considering exceptions, or that in fact it passes the concentric test. If it passes, we should join that group practice if allowed by other strictures of MAC2. If it isn't a component norm, then Mennonites have some stricter deontic duties than some of us.

Despite these complexities, analogues of our earlier four precepts governing truth-telling would be found among the moral directives of MM. And given the existence of the general group act forbidding killing in which we participate we can again summarize: *Do not kill humans within the cooperative sphere of non-murder or FHNCs, unless a violation of that duty is sanctioned by VLD or DD, or is sanctioned by the practice as an appropriate exception. And also do not kill if it is contrary to LDP.*

I think this largely forbids murder of innocent humans outright. You may murder an innocent to save the entire world from destruction, but you cannot murder an innocent even to stop an ordinary war, because a generally brutish state of nature is worse than the consequences of a specific war. Perhaps you have contrary intuitions. Perhaps you think that it would be morally acceptable to murder an innocent to stop a war. Perhaps you simply have a different conception of what our commonsense deontic duties require than my best guess, and whoever is right about that is correct according to MAC2. But our commonsense practice may also be indeterminate, and provide another opportunity for MM to refine our deontic duties. Or the issue may turn on another feature of commonsense morality and MM, the proper overall treatment of the distribution of risks, benefits, and harms, to which we will return in Chapter 12.

Relatively recent moralists have extended ancient concerns about killing and lying towards more general prohibitions against injuring, disabling, depriving of freedom, causing pain or depriving of pleasure, manipulating, and even causing emotional upset such as that inflicted by calumny, mockery, ridicule, disparagement, and impoliteness.[34] The gradual historical development within commonsense of prohib-itions of injury, imprisonment, and even emotional shock seems to track an historical development in the forms of important group acts, and also in what we value. We don't like to be pummeled, pained, injured, hobbled, imprisoned, or even disparaged, as a matter of consensus congruence, though maybe we are somewhat more sensitive about some of these things than some of our ancestors were. These things also interfere with other things we want. And if Nelson pummels Jean-Paul each time they meet, then they cannot function effectively together as a group agent, which is not to say that oppressive group arrangements are not stable or capable of providing opportunities for effective group action, say in war. Still, if Simone's feet are hobbled, she can't run to your assistance or to perform a task in a group project. If Dolores is

---

[34] While honor has long been significant, inflicting dishonor has not always been held immoral.

imprisoned, there are similar difficulties. Even manipulation or ridicule may undercut some cooperative abilities, as well as being distasteful to us.

Let me begin with the most traditional cases. Abstention from physical injuries and inappropriate imprisonment quite clearly preserves the conditions necessary for the existence of certain forms of group agent, in which the various atomic agents involved are able to act effectively in their individual roles. These can be effective forms of group agent in pursuit of weighty projects. And mutual abstentions from injury and imprisonment themselves constitute important group actions, which have developed historically in a way that tracks the development of these elements in commonsense moral codes. It also matters, according to LDP, that we care significantly about protection from injuries and imprisonment, and that they have always been harms in a sense captured by consensus congruence.

Causing pain even independent of lasting physical injury is also capable of undercutting agency, at least in severe cases. And any significant pain and even the significant absence of pleasure are consequentially weighty according to LDP, and also the subject of deontic restrictions plausibly resting on a widespread group act.

There are also the more recently recognized and still somewhat controversial moral evils of manipulation and causing emotional upset through calumny, mockery, ridicule, disparagement, and even impoliteness. Except perhaps for manipulation, these are less likely to disable beneficent group action. Since many of these more ethereal evils have only a tenuous connection with physical pain, but we really don't like some of them, an extension of deontic restrictions to cover at least some of these cases is easier to justify according to MM than for the conjunction of hedonism and LEXIMAC that I explore in *Goodness and Justice*. But, going in the other direction, hedonism may support a more severe restriction on the causing of pain and elimination of pleasure. Different forms of objectivism seem to span these divides. So it is worth saying both something general about the interaction of MAC2 and all these types of cases, traditional and recent, and also something more specifically suited to LDP.

Begin with analogues of our four initial tenets against lying. Whatever the roughly intuitive ordering of outcomes with which it is allied, and even independent of the existence of a group act constituting commonsense morality, MAC2 will generally enjoin the following precepts: (1) Do not injure, disable, deprive of freedom, manipulate, or cause serious pain to, other cooperating members of a beneficent group agent, in any manner that undercuts its effectiveness, when that group agent has a project that lies outside of that cooperative practice, unless a violation of that duty is sanctioned by VLD or DD, the violation serves the project of the group, or the failure is acceptable in the practice.[35] (2) If other things are equal, do not do these things to other beneficent agents. (3) Do not do these things or cause significant pain

---

[35] The qualifications of 9.4 seem irrelevant here.

or the serious absence of pleasure whenever within a beneficent group agent creating such a cooperative sphere, unless a violation of that duty is sanctioned by VLD or DD, or unless an exception is allowed by that practice. (4) Join groups of the type noted in (3) whenever that is required on direct consequentialist grounds, unless it is forbidden by VLD or DD. Of course, LDP also cedes significant weight to individual pains and emotional upsets outside of the strictures of MAC2.

I think we are within a very widespread group act that invokes clause (3). Its constraints apparently generally apply only to the treatment of humans, but do cover FHNCs. Still, there are concentric group acts that extend such restrictions at least against gratuitous pain and injury inflicted on non-humans, and this extension would be supported by most plausible principles for evaluating outcomes, including LDP. Recall that animal pleasure is likely to be the sort of animal good most comparable to human good, and it certainly can break ties in human good. What's more, LDP and some forms of objectivism probably underwrite another amendment to these widespread tenets, whereby severe mockery and ridicule, and even significant disparagement, of humans are forbidden, except when they are overall consequentially helpful. Perhaps there are even forms of group action towards beneficent goals that would be undercut by the presence of such disrespect within the group. And it is likely that there are relatively recent or local group acts that involve a commitment to the creation of deontic spheres forbidding these somewhat ethereal harms that have at least some weight. Some forms of hedonism may also underwrite an extension forbidding the causing of mild pains and the less serious remission of pleasures except when they are consequentially helpful. But it seems to me that, at least when they are constrained by proper truth-telling and various special obligations, for instance to children, any very widespread commonsense morality does not determinately rule infliction of the more ethereal harms noted in these extensions to be immoral in any very specific way even when other humans are involved.[36] Manipulation is the most likely case for the relevance of an ethereal harm to commonsense morality, but I've already incorporated it in clauses 1 and 2 as more likely to undercut beneficent group action, and also hypothetically in clause 3. Still, widespread commonsense does determinately rule out, against humans, the more traditional injuries mentioned in clause 3, though hedged around by various qualifications, in a group act that MAC2 would support, probably whatever plausible principle for ordering outcomes it is allied with, but certainly given LDP. And that group act is quite weighty, probably weightier than that which forbids lying.

All this suggests a summary based principally on the content of that centrally relevant deontic group act: *Do not injure, disable, deprive of freedom, or cause significant pain or serious deprivation of pleasure to humans, unless a violation of that duty is sanctioned by VLD or DD, or unless an exception is allowed by our deontic*

---

[36] Thomson (1990: Chapter 10) plausibly discounts the significance of "belief-mediated distress," such as offense or indignation. But Buss (1999a) argues that even impoliteness is immoral.

practice. Also, do not engage in consequentially harmful mockery, manipulation, impoliteness, ridicule, disparagement, causing of mild pains, and less serious remission of pleasures, and if you are inside cooperative group acts protecting us from such things, defect only as VLD or DD allow.

Stealing is also a very central negative concern of traditional morality. But there are relevant questions about the justice of property arrangements. They are quite complex. For instance, even if a practice of recognizing property includes the recognition of slaves as owned, that does not imply that the rest of the property arrangements supported by the practice are illegitimate, nor is it intuitively plausible to claim that the overall beneficence of a practice of property-holding legitimates ownership of the occasional slave. I think that the legitimacy of our actual property arrangements is a real question, and we will return to some elements of the issue of legitimate property in Chapter 12, though only in a rudimentary and abstract way.[37] Still, in general, we can say that stealing will be forbidden by MAC2 under now familiar conditions. It will be forbidden when it is defection from beneficent group agents of which one is part, when those agents and projects are sufficiently weighty and no exceptions are relevant. It will also be forbidden when other agents' projects of sufficient normative weight would be undercut, or when it directly violates LDP. This mechanism will provide greater normative protection for property that is deployed in support of beneficent projects or that itself constitutes part of such a project. But if an institution of property itself constitutes a beneficent group act, then members of that group agent will be forbidden to steal except when that is sanctioned by VLD or DD, or by exception clauses internal to the practice itself, or when the concentric mechanism allows it.[38] Those on the outside of that group agent, who may not necessarily include all those without property recognized in that practice, would have no very special obligation to respect that property, though they will have relevant direct obligations under LDP and also obligations to respect beneficent group acts of which they are not part.

That completes my summary of the general deontic restrictions required by commonsense morality, and properly protected by MAC2 especially when it is conjoined with LDP. There is the possibility of conflicts in these duties. Simone may have no choice but to lie to Jean-Paul or to significantly hurt his feelings. But there are several methods for resolving these conflicts. First, they may be resolved by exceptions in the contents of the group acts themselves; the participants in the relevant group act may not be inclined to criticize apparent defection in some cases, at least not on the usual grounds of failure of entwined benevolence and reciprocity.[39] Second, DD suggests defection to the consequentially dominant group act, though as I said there are sometimes debilitating indeterminacies that

---

[37] If desert mattered in a fundamental way to the evaluation of outcomes, that would matter here.

[38] This allows stealthy freeing of others' slaves.

[39] Defection may be legitimate even when they are inclined to criticize, when that criticism is attached to a bad component norm and hence there is a better concentric act.

hobble this mechanism. And there are indeed other mechanisms for refining and balancing the deontic restrictions, related to special obligations and to issues that we will consider in Chapter 12.

Still, it is already clear that MM adequately respects the general deontic restrictions. They provide no legitimate grounds for objection to MM, even though it is a type of direct consequentialism.

11.5 Special Obligations

A second standard objection to direct consequentialist theories like MM is that they cannot properly account for our intuitive special obligations to those to whom we have special personal relations, for instance with whom we are intimate or to whom we owe gratitude or reparation.[40] But the mechanisms of MM help considerably in this regard.

There is some arbitrariness in how to draw the line between special obligations and general obligations. For instance, promise-keeping is a kind of special obligation that was encompassed by our discussion of lying. And many moralists recognize a general commonsense duty not to break laws and also related positive obligations of citizenship that are recognizably special obligations, but that are naturally treated by MM in the same manner as stealing, and to which we will come back in roughly that guise in Chapter 12. But we need to give some special attention at least to duties of gratitude and reparation, to obligations among friends, and to family obligations, which constitute important features of many traditional moral codes.

Begin with obligations to friends and family. As I just suggested, it is possible to treat these as beneficent elements of general group acts, much as we recently treated the general deontic restrictions.

But there are some reasons to worry about this treatment. For instance, Parfit has argued that we often face "many-person parent's dilemmas," in which if we all favor our own children, then all our children shall lose.[41] If we all pursue bigger weddings for our own children, we may bankrupt us all. So perhaps these are not properly beneficent component norms of commonsense morality. Perhaps a dominant concentric general group act embedded in commonsense morality eschews them. But I think that not all the general practices supporting our target special obligations are questionable in this way. I think that it is only when we favor our children in extreme and unnecessary ways, reflecting a vice analogous to greed that is not determinately required by any widespread commonsense morality, that we really face many-person parent's dilemmas. In fact, I think that, by the tenets of MM, the moderate special obligations to children generally recognized by widespread commonsense morality even conceivably dominate some of the general deontic restrictions. A part of this has

---

[40] Except by recourse to relative valuations of outcomes.   [41] Parfit (1984: 98).

to do with the details of LDP. I believe that there is a consensus congruence of preference according to which each favors their own children in a quite robust and emotional way, though not to the utmost limits that extreme graspingness for our children might demand, and also according to which each cares about being cared for by their parents in that way.[42] And remember that there is no firm distinction between one's own well-being and other things one deeply cares about. So deep caring within special relationships, when it exists and is quite general among humans, has a quite fundamental role in my proposal. It would be very harmful to most of us in the most basic way recognized by LDP and hence MM if our children were harmed, or even merely removed from our own special care and favor, indeed even if we were merely required to treat them no better than other children. It also harms us in a deep way if we aren't cared for by our parents in an intimate and resolute way. Similar though less robust things might be said about attachments between friends, lovers, partners, and spouses, and between other family members. Deep attachments among family and friends are a strong component of our own good,[43] and reflected in general group acts protected by MAC2.

Of course, some are parentless or friendless, and there is certainly danger that they will be relatively badly off by the tenets of LDP. This means that MM will not likely support specific forms of partiality for our children or friends that harm the parent-less or friendless. We will come back to that issue, which is also relevant to many-person parent's dilemmas, in a moment. First there is another point about the interaction of special obligations and MM that we need to discuss, and which is perhaps more important than the two key points—the respect of LDP for personal relations and the importance of general group acts fixing special obligations—already in play.

MAC2 also treats special obligations in another way, as arising within relatively small-scaled group agents, at least when those particular group agents are themselves properly beneficent. Specific families and friendships, when beneficent, are themselves often group agents that invoke the protections provided by VLD and DD. Perhaps they require forms of cooperative behavior and the acceptance of norms beyond anything required by generally recognized duties. Perhaps it is of the essence of a certain kind of cooperative friendship to take the interest of your friend to heart in an unusual way.

This element of MM implies that unusual forms of beneficent small-scale group action can be morally weighty, even though they are not seconded by a large general form of social cooperation in which they are embedded. The family is a well-known institution. But if Simone and Jean-Paul think up some new but beneficent form of group action for themselves, a new kind of intimacy, then it too has status in MM. There are of course likely to be considerable indeterminacies about what special

---

[42] There is a similar preference requiring care for parents.
[43] Hooker (2000: 136–41).

group agents of this sort exist, about the details of their projects, and about what constitutes defection.

There are many relevant complications. First, friendships and families with negative consequences receive no special status from MM, unless it is folded into general beneficent group practices in the way suggested above or is required by consensus congruence. Second, there may be significant indeterminacies regarding whether a bad family is worse for one of its members than no family, because of indeterminacies regarding what sort of adoption, foster care, orphanage, or abandonment such a person would face if they lacked that family. Third, conflicts between small-scale beneficent group agents of the type just noted can be resolved by recourse to DD, at least when there is enough determinacy in the relative value of their consequences. Fourth, the complicating qualifications to MAC2 specified in 9.4 are realistically applicable to small-scale group agents that are not seconded by a large-scale group practice. Fifth, seldom will even a beneficent small-scale group agent have sufficient consequential weight to trump the general deontic restrictions on action according to MAC2.[44] Sixth, a key limitation on special obligations reflects limitations in the kind of conditions that deep caring really requires. That is the point about many-person parent's dilemmas I promised to come back to.

We all share a general and weighty deontic duty to educate our children well. And we no doubt wouldn't care enough about them, probably even for our own well-being, if, rather than send them to Harvard instead of Nebraska, we'd spend the money on expanding our model train set. But this does not itself legitimate wasteful greed and extravagance even for our children, or our friends. Generally speaking, if you'd need to pay the full tab, MM forbids sending your child to Harvard rather than to Nebraska, as opposed to spending the difference on your positive obligations to feed the starving. Perhaps the only way it could allow the extravagant education would be if the differences hence purchased were consequentially beneficial, as assessed by LDP, in some sufficiently compensating way.

That may seem an objectionable consequence of MM, implying that it is too morally demanding or even immoral. But we will come back to this worry about all forms of direct consequentialism in Chapter 12. There is another sort of special obligation that we need to consider first.

Gratitude and reparation have, along with punishment, a natural and intuitive place in MM. Practices of punishment may be consequentially appropriate according to MM. But there is another and more characteristic point. If I defect from a weighty deontic group act, that may put me outside of its protection. The murderer may conceivably leap outside the customary deontic restrictions on murder. And that change in normative status can itself be one kind of normative punishment, that may allow in turn a more concrete form, say rooted in purely consequential assessment.

---

[44] The only real chance for a trump involves a general group act supporting certain special obligations.

Depending on the nature of our group acts, the murderer may by their own act lose a status that otherwise would protect them from the normative propriety of certain sorts of direct maximization of the good.[45] In fact, there are two kinds of defection from a group act that may constitute two levels of normative punishment. Someone may murder through some temptation but still accept norms that leave them inside the group action in question. Or they may leap entirely outside. And of course they may have never been inside. These three different cases may conceivably allow for the legitimacy of three different sorts of concrete punishment.[46]

Now think of gratitude and reparation on something like the same model. We should reflect on the consequential propriety of our general practices, our shared group acts, of gratitude and reparation. And some of these practices are properly inflected by the correct treatment of risks, benefits, and harms that we are coming back to in Chapter 12. But obligations of gratitude or reparation also can arise within smaller group acts in a way suggested directly by MAC2. Duties of reparation are sometimes duties to restore forms of group action that one has violated, or, better put, to make it be that in fact one hasn't in the end really violated a reciprocal obligation in the way suggested by one's past activity. And duties of gratitude are sometimes duties to avoid the failures that occasion duties of reparation.[47]

Guilt and gratitude and our relations with our children may suggest another objection to MM. It is primarily focused on telling us what to do, not what to feel, while quite particular feelings or emotions are sometimes thought absolutely central to morality.[48]

But this worry is more apparent than real, since MM invokes our feelings in several ways: Reciprocity and benevolence are basic moral sentiments, feelings seem sometimes crucial to reason acceptance, your emotions are among the factors that determine what you would try to do if you believed yourself presented with certain options and hence help determine your basic preferences, emotions are also relevant to whether you can successfully execute certain attempts and hence to your options, some emotions are in part actions, and some are significant to humans by consensus congruence either directly or as instrumental means, as our discussion of special obligations has already implied.

Still, beyond all that, I do not aspire to give you robust advice on what to feel. There is no one emotional way people should be. To understand why not, we will need to turn now to matters intertwined with a third classical worry about direct consequentialist theories like MM.

---

[45] This is analogous to Scanlon (2008: 122–214).

[46] For practical attempts, see S. Schwartz (2009).

[47] I am sliding between different atomic agents in one life, but in Chapter 12 we will engage the interaction of that commonsense practice and MM. This phenomenon may be further complicated by the two sorts of defection mentioned above as relevant to punishment. Notice also that only beneficent group acts are protected by MAC2.

[48] One source is Gibbard (1990: 126–50). Another is Brentano.

But here's where we are now: While there are many complications, and we have left some worries hanging, we have already seen in a general way how MM, partly because of MAC2 and partly because of LDP, supports intuitive special obligations, as well as intuitive general deontic restrictions. To that degree at least, it meets the constraints set by DC1-NORMS.

12

What Morality Demands

The third standard objection to direct consequentialist theories like MM is that they are too demanding, perhaps so demanding as to violate DC1-NORMS. They require that we spend our resources to produce the best possible outcome whatever the cost to ourselves. In a world where 15 000 to 35 000 children under five die each day from starvation and poverty-related diseases,[1] they demand that we divert most of our income and time to poverty relief. And that seems too much.

My reply to this objection has several components. Some involve the higher-order structure of the moral code implied for our situation by MM, which also helps refine our general deontic duties and special obligations. Discussion of these components of my reply will serve multiple roles. But some parts of that reply are implicit in what has come before.

12.1 Duties and Demandingness

First, individual action even towards poverty relief can seldom have better conse-quences on its own than the huge group acts constituting general deontic restrictions. So MAC2 will rarely allow the violation of these deontic restrictions in pursuit of the good of the starving, although the restrictions may themselves incorporate relevant exceptions. You cannot murder to pursue famine relief.

Perhaps it seems that LDP, because of its basically leximin form, sometimes tells us, even when conjoined with MAC2, to do almost anything in service of the interests of the very worst-off individual at whatever cost to slightly better-off individuals. Perhaps it tells us to defect from deontic morality to feed a particular starving child. But LDP focuses on worst-off atomic agents, not worst-off individuals. Also, we are bound by a deontic group act whose positive weight includes the absence of many murders, and it is fantasy to think there is enough determinacy of options to allow cases in which the entire negative group act of not murdering is less consequentially weighty when assessed by LDP than food for a particular starving child. We are never able to compare pair-wise the death of that child with specifically and merely the

---

[1] USDA (1999: p. III); www.worldhunger.org/articles/Learn/world%20hunger%20facts%202002.htm

worst death that would occur if murder were morally acceptable, as a leximin principle may seem to threaten. There are no determinate facts about that second thing. All we can do is compare one horrible death with many.

The widespread general duties that support some special obligations also place significant restrictions on charity. You should not abandon your children to pursue the relief of extreme poverty, nor even act in a way that would undercut your deep and preferential care for them. But remember that there are limits on how much this can shield you from demands of the starving. Expensive schools, big houses, fancy vacations, and large trust funds are not a deontic commitment of our general practice of caring for our children, and if they were it would not be in that respect consequentially beneficial, and so would not be endorsed by MM.

There will also be cases in which small-scale group acts constituting particular families or friendships are themselves more consequentially significant than some particular defection to aid the starving would be. But it seems to be seldom the case that significant aid to the starving requires defection from such group acts, at least when they are beneficent. And counting defections in an artificially narrow way will not suffice to evade morality's demands. While the dollar you give to charity on any particular day may not in itself be more consequentially weighty than some small-scale group act in which you participate, still the act of giving many dollars over many days may be so, and hence required by MAC2.[2]

We have reviewed some ways in which MM somewhat mitigates our duties to the starving. They may not seem sufficient. But there are others.

12.2 The Virtues

It is customary to distinguish virtues from duties, and they are a key focus of much traditional morality and hence DC1. One form of the demandingness objection against direct consequentialism is that it is so demanding as to undercut even the traditional virtues.

But MM underwrites a conception of the traditional virtues that answers this worry. Attention to this conception can also help flesh out the moral directives of MM in other ways, especially by specifying their relatively high-order structure. I will begin with some analytical issues about moral virtues, and then discuss particular virtues, working towards a positive proposal.

I believe that there is considerable analytical variety in states that can properly be called moral virtues. To the contrary, Aristotle, in the paradigmatic philosophical treatment of virtue, said that a moral virtue is in particular a state of character, at least characteristically rooted in habit.[3] He also said that virtue is a mean of feeling and

---

[2] When backsliding is anticipated, give the whole now.
[3] Aristotle, *Nicomachean Ethics*, II, 1 and 5.

action between two vices, one of excess and one of deficiency.[4] Consider these two specific analytical claims.

Aristotle conceived virtues to be stable dispositions. But John Doris stresses the empirical credentials of situationism, the view that there are no stable dispositions of any familiar sort, that situational determinants of, for instance, helping behavior are dominant over individual differences.[5] On the other hand, even if situational determinants are dominant in explaining certain sorts of behaviors, that doesn't imply that we don't have stable and individually distinctive characters of some sort, as Doris himself admits.[6] It simply means that they must be individuated in a somewhat unfamiliar narrow way;[7] someone may be truthful in personal life but lie at work. What's more, it is not really evident that intuitive moral virtues have to be *very* stable.[8] It is intuitively plausible to say that someone was charitable for a while, after a Scrooge-like dream, but then backslid. It is also true that a moral ideal need not be reflected very well in reality.[9] Even if particular individuals are only courageous in particular sorts of circumstances, perhaps they *should* be courageous in all. But, in any case, intuitive virtues are structurally heterogeneous in the ways just noted.

Now consider Aristotle's second analytical point. Some ethicists see moral virtues as essentially dispositions to types of action.[10] And indeed some traditional virtues do dominantly involve a relationship to action. Proper charity is not primarily a state of mind. But some see virtues as more centrally involving states of mind, for instance a motivational focus on goodness[11] or practical wisdom.[12] And some traditional virtues do involve a close relationship to states of mind. The vice of irascibility is not centrally a tendency to action. So Aristotle's ecumenical focus on feeling and action seems correct. On the other hand, his specific focus on excess and deficiency as constituting two vices of deviation from a golden mean does not comport well with the commonsense view that there is no such thing as too much of the traits characteristic of some virtues.

These two clusters of considerations support eclecticism about the analytical structure of the virtues. Traditional virtues are of many structural types. And perhaps there might be virtues of a structural type that tradition fails to recognize.

Another important type of virtue variety is normative variety.[13] Our central concern is with a temporally and socially broad consensus morality, relevant to the meaning constraint DC1, so we should consider some of the revered authorities on virtue across that wide range.

Despite the attention of contemporary virtue ethicists to Aristotle, it is worth remembering the somewhat foreign sound of Aristotle's detailed list of moral

---

[4] Aristotle, *Nicomachean Ethics*, II, 6.

[5] Mischel (1968); Ross and Nisbett (1991); Doris (1998 and 2002); Harman (1999); Vranas (2005).

[6] Doris (1998: 507–8 and 2002: 25).

[7] R. Adams (2006).   [8] Hurka (2001: 43–4).

[9] Blum (1994: 94–6). See also Doris (1998); Kamtekar (2004).   [10] Driver (2001).

[11] Hurka (2001).   [12] Hursthouse (1999).   [13] But see Nussbaum (1980).

virtues.[14] It encompasses courage, temperance, liberality in giving small sums of money and magnificence in giving large sums, proper pride, proper ambition, good temper, friendliness, truthfulness about oneself, ready wit, and justice.[15] Notice the absence of the important contemporary and ancient religious virtue of general benevolence. Notice wit, and the strange-sounding restriction of truthfulness.

It is also worth considering some contrasting authorities. Confucius was a virtue ethicist before Aristotle, though *The Analects* are also leavened with deontological elements.[16] The gentleman has various moral virtues:[17] First and foremost is benevolence (*jen*). One way to analyze benevolence is as a conjunction of *shu* and *chung*.[18] *Chung* is doing one's best (for instance in pursuit of *shu*). It is a kind of executive virtue. And *shu* is captured by a negative golden rule.[19] But there are also other virtues that accompany *jen* in a gentleman. Courage and wisdom are two. Fan Ch'ih asked about the nature of wisdom. "The Master said, 'Know your fellow men.' "[20] Courage can apparently exist without benevolence, but then is not a virtue, or at least doesn't suffice to make a man virtuous.[21] There is also the virtue of *hsin*, or reliability in word, which extends beyond promise-keeping and truth-telling to carrying out resolutions and even to making accurate predictions about the future.[22] And there are reverence (*ching*) and respectfulness (*kung*), especially in performing rites, where the first is a state of mind and the second a visible manner. And there is another virtue connected by Confucius with benevolence. "The Master said, 'To return to the observance of the rites through overcoming the self constitutes benevolence.' "[23] But the rites (*li*) "were a body of rules governing action in every aspect of life."[24] When correct, the rites express *yi*, or rightness.[25] This is a deontological element in *The Analects*.[26]

---

[14]   *Nicomachean Ethics* 1103a15 through 1115a7 is a general account, followed by particular virtues until 1145a11.

[15]   Justice includes law-abidingness and fairness. Fairness includes distributive and rectificatory justice.

[16]   Confucius (1979). Confucius (1979: 9–55) and H. Smith (1958: 179–91) provide summary. I focus on the moral ideal of the gentleman (*chun tzu*), but Confucius (1979: VI, 30) specifies the more excellent sage, who gives extensive charity.

[17]   The gentleman also has substantial natural capacities and acquired "beautiful qualities," including skills in music and literature. See Confucius (1979: 37–9). But moral virtues seem central.

[18]   Confucius (1979: IV, 14).

[19]   "Do not impose on others what you yourself do not desire." (Confucius (1979: XV, 24)). Confucius (1979: XII, 22) gives a second formulation for benevolence which parallels what Aquinas claims a positive golden rule: "Love your fellow men."

[20]   Confucius (1979: XII, 22).   [21]   Confucius (1979: XIV, 4).   [22]   Confucius (1979: 25).

[23]   Confucius (1979: XII, 1).   [24]   Confucius (1979: 20).   [25]   Confucius (1979: 26–7).

[26]   *Li* encompasses more than rites. "Its first meaning is propriety, the way things should be done.... [This encompasses] teachings on ... the Mean, [and] the Five Key Relationships.... The Mean ... is the way that is 'constantly in the middle' between life's extremes. With 'nothing in excess' its guiding principle, its closest Western equivalent is the Golden Mean of Aristotle.... The Five Relationships ... are ... those between father and son, elder brother and junior brother, husband and wife, elder friend and junior friend, and ruler and subject.... A father should be loving, a son reverential; an elder brother gentle, a younger brother respectful; a husband good, a wife 'listening'; an elder friend considerate, a younger friend deferential; a ruler benevolent, a subject loyal." H. Smith (1958: 181–3).

Confucius is in many ways closer to our contemporary commonsense than Aristotle. But reverence and respectfulness in performing rites are an exception, and there is the surprising extension of *hsin* beyond truth-telling or even promise-keeping to correct prediction. There is also an expanded sense of special obligations. They arise primarily from the family, and are asymmetrical and hierarchical. There are also special obligations to friends, but even friendship enjoins different roles on elder and younger friends.

The Buddhist tradition incorporates a more positive and demanding form of benevolence, and even utilitarian tendencies. Both Theravada and Mahayana Buddhists recognize not only five deontological precepts forbidding killing, stealing, sexual misconduct, lying, and drunkenness, but also four exceptional virtues: concern for the happiness of all the sentient, concern that all the sentient be free of suffering, empathetic joy in the success and good fortune of others, and indeed equal care and concern for all the sentient.[27]

The Stoics developed a familiar conception of four primary or "cardinal" virtues that is nascent in Plato,[28] and also influential on later writers and hence our common sense, although once again benevolence receives little explicit emphasis:

The primary virtues are four: prudence, moderation, courage, justice.... To prudence are subordinated good sense, good calculation, quick-wittedness, discretion, resourcefulness; to moderation, good discipline, seemliness, modesty, self-control; to courage, endurance, confidence, high-mindedness, cheerfulness, industriousness; to justice, piety, honesty, equity, fair dealing.[29]

The Qur'an includes ethical formulations that seem to me evenly deontological and virtue-based. But perhaps centrally relevant to our concerns are Surāh LXX (Ascensions), 19–34, and Surāh XIII (Thunder), 19–24.[30] The former articulates an ideal which incorporates non-religious elements, of *patient* individuals "in whose wealth is a rightful allotment, to the beggar and the indigent;... who guard their chastity, save with their spouses and slaves,... who respect their trusts and their contracts, who render true witness."[31] The latter suggests that "patient men... expend of that... provided them, secretly and in public, and... avert evil with good."[32] This is also in some ways more familiar than Aristotle's proposal, and it is relatively close, along with the Stoic conception, to our final authoritative treatment:

Thomas Aquinas' account in *Summa Theologica*[33] is rooted in Aristotle, but also in theological tradition. Its dominant structure combines the three traditional Christian

---

[27] C. Goodman (2009); Flanagan (2011: 93–114).   [28] *Protagorus*.

[29] Stobaeus, in Long and Sedley (1987: 380).

[30] But see also Surāh II (The Cow), Surāh IV (Women), Surāh XVII (The Night Journey), Surāh XXV (Salvation), and Surāh XLIX (Apartments).

[31] Khalidi (2008: 478–9), capitalization suppressed. Arberry (1996) is beautiful but less literal. In Arberry, Surāh LXX is "The Stairways."

[32] Arberry (1996: Volume One, 270). Khalidi (2008) is similar.

[33] Aquinas (1920: especially Second Part of the Second Part).

theological virtues—faith, hope, and charity—and the four traditional classical cardinal virtues of prudence, justice, fortitude, and temperance. Aquinas' overall
account does incorporate a deontological element. He develops the traditional
derivation of the final six commandments of the Decalogue from the Golden Rule
and the general duty (or virtue) to love others as oneself.[34] And more specific
principles of morality, it is alleged, can be inferred from the precepts of the Decalogue
by diligent inquiry. But the virtues are even more central to his proposal. Three of the
primary virtues are deeply theological, despite the promisingly non-theological
names of two. Hope is above all hope for eternal life; charity is above all love for
God. And faith is what it is. This creates some structural awkwardness in Aquinas.
Certain elements of the four classical moral virtues seem to duplicate in a non-
theological realm certain elements of the theological virtues, as for instance despair
features as a vice that undercuts fortitude as well as hope. But we cannot simply cut
away the theological virtues from Aquinas' account and end up with a remotely
plausible secular torso. Charity in Aquinas is above all love for God, and is in some
sense a completion of justice, though the natural expression of this charity involves
significant mundane benevolence.

So there is some variety in commonsense over space and time about the virtues,
reflected in these local authorities. And it is also worth noting that even within
relatively narrow traditions there may be a good deal of diversity. For instance, there
is a second traditional medieval Christian list of seven virtues, distinct from the now
familiar three theological plus four cardinal virtues. They were ordinarily conceived in
ascending order and as virtues to which specific contrary vices were attached. That list
is humility, benignity, temperance, fortitude, mercy, understanding, and wisdom.[35]

Despite this variation, there is also a degree of consensus among Aquinas, the
second medieval tradition, *The Qu'ran, The Analects*, the Buddhist tradition, our
current commonsense, and even Aristotle and the Stoics if we overlook their relative
inattention to the vice of selfishness. And other traditions share that core, though
they require other extensions of morality out beyond any current consensus that
includes most readers of this book.[36] Thad Metz suggests that sub-Saharan Bantu-
speaking Africans favor a summary virtue *ubuntu* or humanness that *pro tanto*
forbids making policy decisions in the face of dissent as opposed to seeking consensus, making retribution as opposed to reconciliation the aim of punishment, the
creation of wealth on a competitive as opposed to cooperative basis, the distribution
of wealth on the basis of individual rights as opposed to need, and ignoring others

---

[34] Aquinas (1920: First Part of the Second Part, Questions 98–108).

[35] Tuve (1966: 85–102). Aquinas hints at this structure.

[36] The Hindu tradition is too complex to summarize. See Sen (2005 and 2009), but also Anderson (2012: 30). Perhaps the *Bhagavad Gita* stages a confrontation between consequentialism and deontology, and the *Mahabharata* underlines negative consequences of defection from deontic morality.

and violating traditional ritual.[37] This contrasts with the intuitions of some contemporary ethicists.

This quick survey of the normative content of various important traditional accounts of virtue reveals many similarities and a certain vague, shared, normative core, but also suggests that any very broad commonsense morality will harbor considerable normative differences about details. And there is also a third type of relevant variety to note, beyond the types of structural variety and content variety we have reviewed.

The conception of virtues that a moralist inherits is often modulated by their various other commitments. Much is kept, but something is changed. This flexibility is a key feature of virtue terminology. Remember how Aristotle squeezes traditional virtues into his virtues-between-two-vices schema. Recall Aquinas' reconciliation of Aristotle and one theological tradition. Other esteemed cultural artifacts involve other systematizations of traditional virtues, which deploy other refinements in organizational architectonics, sometimes because of local aesthetic considerations or an attempt to unite diverse traditional accounts. Giotto in the Arena Chapel illustrates seven virtues reminiscent of Aquinas' familiar list, but accompanied by corresponding vices that help explain and refine them and are also in other ways reminiscent of the alternative medieval seven: There is wisdom (contrasted with foolishness), fortitude (contrasted with inconstancy), temperance (contrasted with ire), justice (contrasted with injustice), faith (contrasted with unfaithfulness), charity (contrasted with envy), and hope (contrasted with despair).[38] Dante also bent a structure somewhat like Aquinas' to his own purposes. He incorporated a hierarchical structure reminiscent of the alternative list of seven, and doubled corresponding vices in purgatory and hell. The capital of the morally central pillar of the Ducal Palace in Venice includes the eight virtues faith, hope, charity, prudence, temperance, fortitude, justice, and humility, perhaps so there can be one virtue for each of the eight sides of the capital.[39] Spenser organized the virtues treated in the *Faerie Queene* around the central or summative virtue of magnificence, embodied in King Arthur, though on a deeply non-Aristotelian understanding of what that virtue involves.[40]

We have noted various sorts of variety regarding the virtues within any very broad commonsense morality, but also a shared normative core.[41] I will now exploit this variety to develop a conception of the virtues within the wide commonsense range, that respects its consensual normative core, and yet that fits well with MM. This

---

[37] Metz (2007a and 2007b). Metz (2007a) is particularly concerned with right action that follows from this ideal: an action is right when it promotes shared identity among people grounded on good will. But see Ramose (2003). Perhaps some of these differences from our commonsense are required by localized beneficent group acts, and perhaps some revision of our commonsense is necessary.

[38] Formenton and Poletti (1999).

[39] Ruskin (1886: 312–39) summarizes important accounts of virtue as background to discussion of the pillar capitals of the Venetian Ducal Palace.

[40] Despite mentioning Aristotle in a famous letter. Tuve (1966: 57–143) discusses Spenser's influences.

[41] "Variety" rather than "indeterminacy" because it clusters in certain ways within sub-traditions.

particular modulation of commonsense specifies some of the higher-order structure of the code of morality that MM supports, and also helps with the demandingness objection.[42]

The account of virtues supported by MM has three elements. First of all, intuitive individual agents are made up of a series of atomic agents. So intuitive duties to self, say to preserve one's future capacities or not to mutilate oneself, may be duties of one agent to another. Some duties to future selves are duties to other moral patients, and are directly supported by LDP. But others are duties constituted by participation in a cooperating group agent, a continuing self acting over time. They are a kind of special obligation to your cooperating future selves, and hence supported by MAC2. These various duties are closely related to some of the traditional virtues. Indeed, they might be summarized as proper prudence, temperance, and courage.

Of course, there are complications. Proper prudence has various sides. One is a kind of benevolence focused on your future selves, required by LDP, though as we will see later this form of benevolence does not properly stretch as far as some presume. But prudence also modulates action in a different way, analogous to ways in which temperance and courage are closely related to proper reciprocity and group action. Even if at the moment you feel like drinking heavily or running away or not doing what will best serve your dominant long-term goal, the fact is that your future and past selves may sometimes be owed the same kinds of respect that other individuals with whom you are cooperating in beneficent group actions are owed, as a precondition of any group action, as a matter of a localized but weighty group act, as a matter of a general deontic obligation, or as a matter of a general beneficent group act supporting certain special obligations. These mechanisms require certain sorts of prudence, courage, and temperance.[43] Because courage, temperance, and prudence are commitments of certain beneficent group acts, they have a significant stature within MM. And so the proper consequentialism does not constitute, as Bernard Williams charged, an attack on one's literal integrity as a continuing agent.[44] You have various forms of protected cooperation with yourself.

As in any systematic account of the virtues, there is spin on the traditional virtues incorporated in this conception. Prudence has one form rooted merely in benevolence to your future selves. And courage and temperance are only virtues when supported by consequentially beneficent group acts. But even that bit of spin is prefigured in ancient debates about the unity of the virtues. There are also other

---

[42] Elstein and Hurka (2009) develop metaethical proposals for wide moral concepts that support such modulations.

[43] Because prudence, temperance, and courage are summary virtues, they may be interpreted to encompass various traditional virtues: good temper, moderate ambition and pride, Confucian *chung*, and a lack of servility. Intellectual virtues, despite their independent value rooted in truth, are also useful related virtues. Traditional examples include intelligence, practical wisdom, and the Confucian wisdom of knowing others' hearts.

[44] Williams (1973: 116–17).

complications. Perhaps some particular instance of virtuous courage conflicts with some instance of temperance. But we already know that such conflicts are to be resolved by various now familiar mechanisms, including the higher-order structure already incorporated into MM: MAC2 and LDP.

That higher-order structure is also reflected in one plausible interpretation of other traditional virtues. This is the second element of the account of virtues supported by MM. Benevolence and justice are two very traditional virtues. But notice that they are already enlaced in two different ways in MM. LDP incorporates in its benevolent pursuit of the good of all a concern with equitable and hence just distribution. Proper benevolence is hence tempered by distributional justice. And VLD and DD enjoin just cooperation, but only in beneficent cooperatives schemes, whose relative weight is assessed consequentially. So the proper justice of doing one's part is tempered by overall beneficence.

So we already have a very traditional list of summary virtues. Temperance, courage, prudence, benevolence or charity, and justice, understood in the modulated way I have proposed, are primary moral virtues. It may seem that MM, because of its focus on actions, cannot support the proper moral constraints on motives that virtues involve. But remember that not all of the traditional virtues intuitively involve constraints on more than action. And remember that group acts have crucial motivational conditions, and that benevolence and reciprocity are basic moral motives according to MM. It may seem that MM cannot require the stability of character needed for virtue. But remember that not all intuitive traditional virtues are very stable, and that a degree of stability is required by my treatment of selves with continuing projects as group agents.

It is already clear that MM is not so demanding as to undercut the traditional virtues. It respects their consensual normative core. It involves a certain modulation of commonsense, but so too do all traditional accounts. But there is also a third element of my proposal about the virtues.

Beyond the level of detail already incorporated into MM, many ethicists aspire to a determinate single conception of ideal humanity. Aristotle thinks that there is a hierarchy of lives with the contemplative on top. Jesus says the meek shall inherit the earth. Confucius favors another hierarchy. But I do not aspire to such advice, save for *one* hierarchy I do embrace. I have admitted priority for true beliefs over even the discipline of desire and action enjoined by MM, and there are allied cognitive virtues. Faith is not the road to truth; reason and evidence are the road to truth. Maybe they are what Aristotle meant by the contemplative life, but in any case let me call this summary cognitive virtue "respect for truth." Still, that's it for any hierarchy of virtues I endorse beyond that already incorporated into MM.

This moral modesty of MM is required by reality. MM does not aspire to any detailed direction on how we should all be, since there are no facts about that. Indeed, it encourages the individual variety that is required by differing local conditions in pursuit of proper consequences, sometimes by group action. Some write best if they oscillate between less and more critical states. There is your enthusiastic and positive colleague, and your reflective and negative one, and maybe the result that the group ends up with is better because both are involved. Soldiers and judges can be engaged in a group act, and it may be best if they differ in character. And different sorts of individual characters require different sorts of correction. In some, patience would be a great virtue, but in others it would just slow them down even more, because some are too quick to jump to conclusions, while others never get there, fussing about every conceivable objection. And conditions differ. If somebody wants to drink, and there are no beneficent projects at stake, then drunkenness may not be a vice, though it will no doubt interfere with excellence in acrobatics. Robust physical courage and aggressiveness may be virtuous when many forts must be stormed, and harmful in city life.[45] And different individual virtues may be the reflection of different ideals of music, etiquette, food, literature, or even refined moral character. These different things we care about may prescribe different corresponding virtues.

I think we should welcome these sorts of variety. They are grounds for another reinterpretation, of the traditional virtue of humility. Proper humility involves respect for the singular nature of things other than yourself, and for the peculiar excellences they enshrine in the peculiar conditions they inhabit. Humility in the face of that range of excellences, sometimes in service of morality or truth, but sometimes beyond (or maybe within) truth and morality, in service of the various incommensurable ideals of music and art and etiquette that we care about, befits a view like MM that accepts that there is no robust good, beyond our consensus of preference.

I have proposed a modulation of traditional virtues in accord with MM. MM involves a list of virtues closely related to Aquinas' traditional seven, and indeed Dante's and Giotto's: temperance, courage, prudence, benevolence, justice, humility, and respect for truth. And MM also provides a mechanism for resolving the conflicts of moral virtues with each other and with other commitments of morality. By providing such an intuitive account of the virtues, MM hence evades one form of the demandingness objection. It is certainly consistent with any wide commonsense consensus about the virtues.

12.3 The Responsibility System

The next step of my reply to the demandingness objection involves two large group acts that further circumscribe our duties to the very poor. The second constitutes further refinement of the higher-order structure of the moral code supported by MM and hence our virtues, and indeed of our general deontic duties and special obligations. It captures more features of DC1. But the first merely suggests a certain minimum level of charity that is morally required.

---

[45] On changing attitudes to curiosity, see Kenny (2004) and Daston (2005). On social changes relevant to lying and hypocrisy, see Runciman (2008).

I argue in *Goodness and Justice* that there is a very large group act, involving many members of traditional religions and also some atheists spread over millennia, that requires the contribution by the reasonably well-off like you and me of at least 2.5 percent of annual income to support the starving and malnourished.[46] That number represents the rough overlap among various traditional practices. I should also have noted that this traditional group act includes a concern with poverty-related diseases and other serious poverty-related problems. Since LDP requires a concern for the worst-off, and consensus congruence of our preferences places the extremely poor among the worst-off at least at many moments of their lives, this group act is quite weighty. If you are inside—and I think almost all of us feel the traditional sting of morality that constitutes acceptance of the relevant reasons to at least some degree— then, by the tenets of MAC2, you are bound inside with virtually deontic force. What if our deeply narcissistic friend Martin is so corrupt that he is not inside even to that degree? Then, while it is possible that traditional forms of utilitarianism or a view that deploys natural desert in a fundamental way will evaluate outcomes differently, LDP almost certainly implies that the marginal contribution of his joining up yields a better overall outcome than he could otherwise achieve. So he is required to join, and then he too will be bound inside by the strictures of MAC2.

We have considered what it is to defect from a group act, but what is minimally required to join up, in the sense required for someone's subsequently failing to perform their role to be defection? It is not enough, nor even strictly required, to merely act in certain external ways. To join the group act, the group trying, requires taking on the characteristic motivational commitments of the action, and that involves acceptance of reasons and also tendencies to criticize defectors for failures of entwined beneficence and reciprocity. But these tendencies and motives need not be stronger, say, than contrary tendencies to politeness. They may not lead you to actually fulfill your role in the group act, and hence leave you a defector. This is why very many of us are already inside the group act, even when we fail to give. And if almost all of us managed to get to the mailbox with a check for UNICEF, we would at that time have the tendencies and motives in question. And indeed developing those tendencies and motives would tend to be consequentially beneficial even beyond the effects of that immediate check, since they increase *ex ante* probabilities of future giving. So if Martin is fully outside this group act, he is likely required on consequential grounds not only to send a check but to join the group act in question, to develop the necessary motivations.[47]

Despite the popularity of the demandingness objection in quite extreme forms, a contribution of 2.5 percent of annual income cannot plausibly be said to be too

---

[46] Mendola (2006: 99–102).

[47] While the tendencies to criticism that partly constitute group action sometimes underwrite training of others, or at least one's future selves, there are forms of training that do not constitute participation. Teaching is not enough.

demanding, at least on the basis of any widespread commonsense moral consensus reflected in DC1.[48] Very many in our tradition have given at least this much, and thought that we all were morally required to do so. Nor is this a trivial drop in the bucket. One reasonable recent estimate suggests that shifting approximately 1.25 percent of the aggregate income enjoyed by the billion people who live in high-income economies would plausibly eradicate serious poverty worldwide.[49] If the well-off did their moral duty, there would be no serious chronic poverty in the world.[50]

Still, it may seem that MM is much more demanding than this decent minimum. Given that many in high-income economies do not contribute to the relief of starvation, and given that MM requires that we focus as individual atomic agents on the good of the worst-off when we are not bound by the demands of weightier group acts, it may seem that MM requires much higher levels of sacrifice on our part to make up for those who don't do their part, even when we figure in the moral constraints required by our deontic duties, special obligations, and virtues, especially because on the correct understanding prudence is not ravenously selfish. We face an extreme moral emergency. It may seem MM implies that a starving child abroad is as much our moral concern as a drowning child in a pond in front of us. And MM's implying serious charitable duties to the child abroad may seem an objection to it.

Still, there is another very large group act that delimits our duties of charity in another relevant way, and is also important in other ways to the structure of morality supported by MM. I call it the Responsibility System, or RS.

In Part II, I debunked claims that continuing individual lives, desert, and responsibility are relevant in a fundamental way to moral theory. But there is a very widespread commonsense practice of assigning risks, benefits, harms, blame, rewards, responsibilities, and opportunities that takes continuing individual people seriously. And it is, or more exactly includes, two weightily beneficent component group acts, whose conjunction is RS.

While this practice has many components even beyond RS, its first and most fundamental component is its focus on continuing individuals over time. It assigns to continuing individuals, by name, a broad category of things we might call with a considerable stretch "entitlements": positions, property, legal status, personal and other social relations, punishments, rewards, gratitude, and reparations. And it specifies such distributions sometimes from more than one direction. A particular named individual owes gratitude to another particular named individual, Simone to Nelson. These entitlements are underwritten in various ways. Some have legal status, but they are also supported by commonsense morality, and by very natural cognitive

---

[48] But see Wein (2002).

[49] Pogge (2002: 2 and 96–100). Hooker (1991) and Brandt (1996: Chapter 8) provide other calculations. Means to effective international charity are controversial: Levine et al. (2004); Sachs (2005); Calderisi (2006); Easterly (2006 and 2010); Collier (2007).

[50] Sen (1994) dismantles the canard that saving some poor now will mean that more poor die later. Birth rates fall when poverty is alleviated and women have better situations.

and emotional tendencies of humans. Focus particularly on their support by commonsense morality. I will call it Lifetime Entitlements, or LE.

LE, even on its own, is a weightily beneficent group act. Other social arrangements are possible than those positively sanctioned by LE. It is possible that your organs be open to harvesting by those in greater need.[51] It is possible that you wake up each morning and learn what your assigned family, job, wealth, and punishments for the day are to be. But such alternative social arrangements certainly cut against the natural grain for humans, and while that does not automatically mean they are impossible or immoral, it is consequentially relevant to their value. And many other factors point towards the positive consequential significance of LE according to LDP, or any remotely plausible principle for ranking outcomes. Certainly there is considerable stability of individual differences that are consequentially relevant to the various social roles we play, which even situationists cannot plausibly deny. It won't be good to assign me the role of performing heart surgery tomorrow. Certainly we care considerably about our own future selves in a way that makes rewards and punishments meted out to them very effective in controlling us today. And certainly our sentiments are specially engaged with other specific continuing individuals in a deep way. LE is weightily beneficent according to LDP. But is it a group act? We accept reasons that support this practice. Do we also criticize defectors on grounds of failure of enlaced reciprocity and beneficence in the way characteristic of group acts? This practice is so natural to us that we can barely imagine defectors of any serious sort, so defection may initially seem to be beyond a failure of beneficence or reciprocity. Defectors would seem mad, to be failing to respect obvious important facts. But we have seen that there are no very deep, practice-independent facts about these things, about desert and responsibility. And if some tyrant attempted to enforce a contrary scheme, or some individual resolutely acted against it, we would criticize them as extremely hurtful and unjust, indeed so much so as to be almost outside of the bare minimum of reciprocity and beneficence required to be fully human. LE is a weightily beneficent group act.

LE refines other elements of the moral code underwritten by MM. It is for instance relevant to our special obligations. But RS also has a second and even more complex second component, which I will call Deontological Entitlements or DE. And this adds other very significant refinements, for instance to the virtues and to the sorts of exceptions implicit in many of the general deontic duties.

The deontological tradition in ethical theory provides significant illumination regarding DE. I include in that tradition not only general deontological theorists like Kant, Ross, and Gert,[52] but also case-based intuitionists like Frances Kamm and Judith Thomson who work on the trolley problem.[53] I think that even in the absence

---

[51] Harris (1975).   [52] W. D. Ross (1930); Kant (1996b); Gert (1998).
[53] Kamm (1993, 1996, and 2007). For Philippa Foot's and Thomson's classic discussions, see Fischer and Ravizza (1992). See also Mendola (2006: 70–81).

in reality of the non-natural moral properties that some of these deontologists claim to access, MM can provide a suitable rationale for the moral significance of some their intuitive moral distinctions between cases, distinctions that consequentialists have traditionally ignored. And MM can also provide a mechanism to adjudicate some differences among these deontologists.

I believe that there is a widespread and weightily beneficent group act, which I am calling DE, that recognizes the normative significance of many of the moral distinctions in question, though of course it has somewhat indeterminate details, and we cannot ascertain its exact form by consulting merely the fine peculiarities of our own individual intuition about cases or even about general principles.[54] Much about DE is epistemically unclear; the deontologists have not charted all of its intricacies. Still, I do not believe it underwrites any highly indefeasible duties beyond those we have already noted, though it surely provides significant further refinement of our deontic duties and virtues by introducing many morally relevant differences between cases. However, it may also have some component norms that must be modified according to MM.

While the details are unclear, I will list several factors that I believe are components of DE that plausibly introduce morally relevant distinctions between cases. And then I will say something about why I think this practice is a group act and also about its rationale according to MM. Some components of DE:

First, when other things are equal, it is characteristically worse to harm someone than to fail to aid them. We earlier noted a case where this distinction does not correspond to the commission/omission distinction, so it is perhaps also worth saying that, when other things are equal, it is worse to cause a harm (or the absence of a benefit) by commission than by omission.

This does not at all imply that it is always wrong to harm some to benefit others. As most deontologists admit, in a case in which a trolley is rolling along and will otherwise run over five people tied to the tracks, it is appropriate to turn the trolley onto a side track on which one person is tied, killing the one to save the five.[55] Still, it is often wrong to kill one to save five. It is wrong to push a fat man into the course of a trolley and to his death, using his bulk to stop the trolley before it decapitates five others.[56] It is wrong to kill a healthy person and harvest their organs to save five deathly ill people.[57] And these cases suggest the next component of DE:[58]

Second, when other things are equal, it is characteristically worse to do a harm so that a greater good will come of it (like pushing the fat man in front of the trolley or harvesting the organs) rather than to do a good that will cause a lesser harm (like

---

[54] Kamm's methodology (Kamm 2007: 5) problematically relies on admittedly idiosyncratic intuitions. And intuitions about cases are subject to order of presentation effects and other distortions. See Unger (1996); Mendola (2006: 74–5); but also Kamm (2007: 190–224).

[55] This version of Foot's trolley problem is due to Thomson.   [56] This is Thomson's case.

[57] This is Foot's case.

[58] Mendola (2006: 70–81) provides other possible explanations of these differences.

turning the trolley). This is a weak form of the traditional Pauline Principle: Do no evil for the good that will come of it. But there are many relevant details. First, while LDP as so far specified does not obviously deliver a contrastive account of individual goods and evils, it is very likely that early death and loss of limbs can be delivered as evils and continued life as a good by consensus congruence. For instance, if we mix some more of the first pair into any life, it will characteristically be worse from the perspective of all the atomic agents who make up the life, and that is indeed a matter of consensus congruence spanning normal adult human atomic agents generally. Second, the most intuitive good that can be achieved by turning the trolley away from the five occurs after the other one is run over, and so we must conceive the relevant good as something like the turning itself or the loss of the threat, if it is to be the greater good that causes the lesser evil in this case.[59] But third, sometimes it seems that similarly conceived goods have side effects that occur afterwards that yet constitute the act in question as quite wrong. If you can only drive to the hospital to save five by splashing through a puddle of acid that will hence kill a bystander, that seems wrong.[60] Fourth, it is also sometimes wrong even to omit to do something that will lead to an evil that will in turn lead to a greater good. It would be wrong to fail to give someone penicillin so that they will die so one can harvest their organs to save five.[61] Fifth, sometimes it isn't any morally better that the evil results from the good. It is wrong to save five by an operation knowing that it will release a poison gas into the hospital that will kill another patient.[62] But despite these complications, something in the general area of the Pauline Principle seems to be a commitment of commonsense morality, and we may hope that the intricate explorations of the deontologists will eventually provide us with greater clarity about it.[63]

Harming is generally worse than not aiding, and something like the Pauline Principle is true. But further illumination is also available from trolley cases and analogous observations of deontologists. The third major component of DE permits self-defense even in cases in which, like the turned trolley, one might be properly sacrificed by someone else. It seems also to permit such defense of others who happen to be in one's near vicinity.[64]

Fourth, it also seems intuitively relevant that the turning of the trolley merely involves redirecting a threat, rather than starting one up or forcing someone into its

---

[59] This worry may explain the questionable claims about event identity of Kamm (2007: 140–1).

[60] Kamm (2007: 132).   [61] Kamm (2007: 131).

[62] This case is Foot's. One relevant difference here involves the special institutional roles of doctors and hospitals. See Mendola (2006: 70–81).

[63] For recent developments, see Kamm (2007: 130–89); Persson (2008). There is disagreement whether subjective factors like intentions (as in the Doctrine of Double Effect) or objective features of situations are more relevant. I phrased the constraints objectively, but MM is middle of the road, since what acts one does or defects from is relevant to MAC2, and those involve subjective factors. And since intentions are crucial to act identity, these disagreements are overblown.

[64] It probably allows for such defense of those to whom one owes special obligations, but that is not an element of DE.

path. In general, other things equal, those other things are worse.[65] This is relevant to permissible forms of self-defense, which in turn suggest some expansions of that element of DE. It seems better to duck and hence cause someone else to be hit by a bullet than to pull them in front of you as a human shield.[66]

Fifth, when a harm can be directed away from an innocent towards the culpable originator of that harm, it should be that "fault forfeits first."[67]

Sixth, distance intuitively matters.[68] Other things equal, we do intuitively seem to have extra responsibility to rescue those quite near to us rather than off somewhere in another land, and even to rescue those whom we have been recently near. We further seem to have special responsibility when threats to individuals emanate from our vicinity, or when we control means to their rescue which are near to them or to the threats. These emergencies seem our moral business in the way that others often do not.[69]

Most of us have, I think, commonsense moral intuitions of these sorts, at least if we haven't spent many hours drilling ourselves into accepting implications of familiar forms of utilitarianism. And we engage in corresponding practices governing action and criticism of action. You will notice that I have phrased these components of DE in a very weak, other-things-equal and for-the-most-part way. But that is mostly because we await the details of commonsense that I hope the deontologists eventually deliver. I think that something in this vicinity, but indeed stronger and more restrictive in certain ways that we do not yet fully understand, is correct.

Still, if you've been with me so far, you now may be aghast. To most consequentialists, DE may seem a tangle of absurdities.[70] But MM does underwrite it, at least in general outline, and also provides for rational grounds to evaluate and refine its details.

First of all, DE is a group act. When someone fails to act in the way that it requires, most of us criticize them on grounds of intertwined reciprocity and at least non-maleficence. Such a person does not extend the respect to others that we expect of each other.

Still, it may seem that this conception of the good of the practice is a fantasy on our part. It may seem that this group act is not weightily beneficent according to LDP. It may seem that it fails to pursue the greatest good, and rather gets lost in irrational distinctions between actions that have nothing to do with production of the good.

---

[65] Unger (1996: 101–3) considers factors like these, which he thinks are "silly ideas."

[66] Bourse and Sorensen (1988).   [67] Kagan (2012: 23–7).

[68] These components do not exhaust DE. Another implies that other agents in causal chains leading to outcomes complicate moral responsibility. But the complexities are daunting.

[69] Kamm (2007: 345–97) provides argument. These factors unattractively imply that you can diminish moral responsibility by avoiding emergencies, but if pursued intentionally that policy involves avoiding emergencies that you foresee to be your business, and hence are your business in a second way.

[70] Singer (1972); Unger (1996).

But notice that all of the component factors of DE I noted—the precedence of the good required by the Pauline Principle, the priority of not harming over helping, turning threats rather than starting them up or shoving people in the way of them, deflection of harms from the innocent towards those responsible, self-defense against even proper redirection of threats, analogous support for those who are in our area, and even distance sensitivity—involve a kind of greater responsibility for what is close to us in causal chains, what is closer to basic action. And remember the indeterminacy of options, and the conception of options as involving *ex ante* objective probabilities it required.[71]

There will never be *ex ante* objective certainty that throwing a fat man in front of a trolley will stop the trolley. But there can be something approximating *ex ante* objective certainty that throwing the fat man in front of the trolley will kill the fat man. If you take someone's organs to save five others, it will be quite *ex ante* uncertain that all five transplants will succeed, but quite certain that someone will die. And indeed in some cases like this there is not just objective uncertainty but full-blown indeterminacy. If you don't push the fat man off the bridge, there may be no fact of the matter about whether he would have stopped the trolley. And there are not only these uncertainties and indeterminacies of objective fact. No real agent is ever in position to know the fine details of even such objective facts that do obtain. In fact, DE has a seventh important tenet in this vicinity, which implies that, other things equal, we bear more responsibility for features of outcomes about which we know or ought to know. This is a complex aspect whose details are too convoluted to probe in any short space, relevant to Jackson-style cases introduced in 3.10.

Because of these factors, most plausible rankings of outcomes would support DE. But it is also relevant that LDP is a leximin principle, which is more sensitive to certain fine details of outcomes than standard utilitarianism, details which are specially prone to indeterminacy when outcomes are indeterminate. LDP suggests that, here in the real world, we should make it our special business to consider goods and harms that are under our greater and more immediate consequential control and understanding. Otherwise we will engage in often consequentially harmful and usually very risky moral speculation, and LDP is quite sensitive to what happens when we lose these bets. On balance, as assessed by LDP, more would be lost by a general practice of such speculation than gained by it. And indeed there won't characteristically be *ex ante* objective determinacy of the sort that constitutes a particular speculative option as relevantly better according to MM. So to take that option, given our general deontic obligations not to harm, involves a specific kind of moral speculation that the sixth tenet of MAC2, you will recall, forbids.

---

[71] The cases which introduce the deontological distinctions are often oddly irrelevant to their vindication. They make us think they have less consequentialist rationale than they do. Trolleys have rails, but most acts have causal effects that are not narrowly constrained that way. And some classic cases are very determinately specified, while there is indeterminacy of options.

There are other consequential factors that support DE. DE allows greater certainty about our own condition and that of those we care about than alternative practices, say involving the harvesting of needed organs, would allow. It provides a kind of status for us and those we care about that we value by consensus congruence, which we might call being deserving of Kantian respect. And there are consequential advantages to having a pre-assigned division of moral labor, with those most immediately confronted with an emergency assigned to deal with it. But among these factors I think the points resting on option indeterminacy are central. DE is a very widespread group act, and in the real world of indeterminate options, it is properly weighty according to MM.[72]

RS is the conjunction of LE and DE. It is, I believe, reflected in DC1-NORMS. It refines our duties, special obligations, and virtues. And it specifically refines our duties to the starving. Some refinements involve interactions between LE and DE. Perhaps you have less obligation to sacrifice yourself in an emergency today because you have engaged in similar sacrifices every day for the last two years, or perhaps you have finally done enough for the one needy stranger in your vicinity. But the main point is that because of RS you have a greater moral responsibility to save someone in an emergency here in front of you than to make a financial contribution that will have a remote effect on a starving person elsewhere.

Most of us accept that we have an obligation, even at serious cost, to rescue someone here in front of us from death. Some consequentialists, like Singer and Unger, argue that such cases are not relevantly different from cases in which we can save a starving someone far away by contributing to UNICEF. But what seems to them a true implication of consequentialism, seems to many a significant objection from demandingness. Still, MM is a form of consequentialism, indeed a direct form of consequentialism, that does not have this unintuitive implication. There is a relevant difference between these cases. When there is a choice between two actions, to save somebody drowning in front of you and to attend to some far away starving person, the first is required by the strictures of RS.

But still, that is not a very common situation. Most often, many starving people can be saved by our contributions, and that will not require violation of the strictures of RS, or indeed of any plausible but stronger refinement that the deontologists may eventually deliver.[73] It is clear that the demands of charity are still quite strong. So another way to put what I am arguing here is that is inappropriate to dismiss direct consequentialist theories like MM on the grounds that they are demanding in the face

---

[72] Perhaps this group act has traditionally been beneficent, and only our current technological situation and extreme wealth disparities make it not now so. Hence by the multiple-part test of Chapter 11, it would not be determinately beneficent. Under such conditions, for it to provide moral cover, we must ensure that it isn't harmful figured from now.

[73] If commonsense did include a stricture violated by charity here, it would not be endorsed by LDP.

of worldwide poverty when plausible deontological views are also very demanding in such circumstances.

There are other weightily beneficent group actions that may provide some of us with further moral cover. Some of us support practices of education or community development, or artistic or intellectual endeavor, or even industrial discovery and creation, that are group acts that are weightily beneficent and also require money or time that might otherwise be spent to save starving children. Perhaps you are even Gauguin. And in our world of indeterminate options, some of these group acts dominate individual defection to support a far away starving child, even according to LDP. Those who aren't so covered, and who wish not to have the moral obligation to divert most of their surplus cash (that is to say their cash and cash-convertible property that is not protected by other moral obligations) to famine relief, should look around for some weightily beneficent group act that requires that surplus cash, and join it when it is more consequentially weighty to do so than to spend the money on famine relief.[74] Then they will be nearly bound inside by the ratchet effect of MAC2.[75] There is also another type of protection mechanism built into MM. Remember that it merely characterizes the primary excellence of desire and action. There is also truth, the primary excellence of belief. So I am not telling you to believe any falsehood, or to sacrifice your intellect to famine relief.

Still, there is no doubt that most of us in wealthy societies will have considerable surplus cash and time that is not protected by any of these mechanisms, that peeks out around the corners of our weightily beneficent group actions and is not defended by MM in other ways. LDP tells us, when direct assessment of individual action is in question, to focus on benefiting the worst-off. In reality there is considerable indeterminacy about what our options are and about who is worst-off. And the relevantly worst-off are atomic agents. We will not need to be resolutely maximizing the well-being of the poorest with every morally unprotected dollar and in every moment of our time, because there aren't always facts about how to do that, and because LDP doesn't always require that. But it is unrealistic to believe that the mechanisms we have surveyed so far will provide enough of us who are very well-off enough moral cover so that the moral demands of the extremely poor on us will not be significant.

So there is another important moral virtue for us, which we might call austerity, which demands the deflection of considerable money and time to the service of those who are badly off, including the very poor. I have yet to say what it really requires. And perhaps the commitment of MM to this virtue in itself seems quite objectionable, contrary to the commonsense consensus of DC1. So we need to come at the demandingness objection in one more way.

---

[74] But your relevant alternative contributions to relief are not properly assessed one dollar at a time.

[75] This has a sleazy aspect, like machinations allowed by the relevance of distance to DE.

12.4 Austerity

The main task of this section is to make you accept austerity. It has two steps.

The first step is simple. It is to point out that austerity won't be too bad. You would be better off with more free cash than it will allow you. Other things equal, more money is better for everyone as a matter of consensus congruence, it seems. But more important is the subjective experience of happiness. And the surprising empirical fact is that the already moderately financially well-off are wrong to think that further wealth will make much difference to their subjective happiness.[76] As Diener and Seligman summarize, "income, a good surrogate historically [for happiness] when basic needs went unmet, is now a weak surrogate ... in wealthy nations."[77] Austerity, at least in what we will soon see to be its relevant middling forms, would make trivial differences to your happiness. The contrary belief is an illusion. You don't need to spend all your time on poverty relief, just write some checks.[78] If your happiness matters to you, exercise and eat well and avoid unhealthy habits, and concentrate most of your time on close stable relationships and meaningful pursuits.[79] You'll be just fine with less luxury.

Still, it may seem that this depends on how demanding austerity is, on how much luxury we must forgo. I am coming back to that point. But the second step of my main task here is to increase your motivation to do something demanding about extreme poverty, by making you feel guilty about it.

It is sometimes claimed that widespread commonsense morality does not involve a demanding duty of charity. I believe that is false, because of the prominence of charity in many traditional and religious-based codes, and because modernity puts us in touch with a wider arena for our charitable action. I believe I am not being revisionary about this matter. But, in any case, the commitments of many traditional codes certainly imply that no wide consensus reflected in DC1 is violated by a significant demand of charity. Still, my primary attempt to make you accept austerity will turn on other commitments of commonsense morality and DC1. Thomas Pogge has had a troubling but plausible idea. It is that extreme poverty is due to harm we have caused, and so is in a robust sense our responsibility. We owe reparation to the very poor, whatever our duties of charity. And MM is one way to develop Pogge's idea.[80]

---

[76] Kahneman, Diener, and Schwarz (2003); Diener and Seligman (2004); Offner (2006). However, Kahneman and Deaton (2010) report that, while subjective well-being stops rising in the U.S. above an income of approximately $75,000, judgments about how well life is going continue rising. And when someone is accustomed to wealth, taking some can make them quite unhappy.

[77] Diener and Seligman (2004: 1). They call happiness "well-being."

[78] You might also relevantly volunteer, mentor, or engage in political action. But most of us can most effectively deal with *world* poverty by writing checks, if we want to keep our jobs.

[79] Diener and Seligman (2004). There are no experts on what well-being is, but there are experts on how to get things that are part of it.

[80] Pogge (2002). May (1992) and Kutz (2000) develop the stricter view that we have attenuated responsibility for acts in which we do not participate by groups in which we do participate. May (1992) furthermore suggests responsibility for group inaction.

Some issues that we have recently discussed are directly relevant. DE counts harming as worse than not aiding. Probably when the deontologists get done probing it, we will see that it counts harming as significantly worse, and yet remains a weighty group act. And MAC2 endorses special obligations of reparation, which are modulated by LE. But it will take a moment to introduce the most important points relevant to this new application of MM. Begin with key analytical considerations:

The fifth tenet of MAC2 weights participation in heinous group acts at the full negative consequential weight of the whole, just as it weights participation in beneficent group acts at the full consequential weight of the whole. And so, according to MAC2, if group action in which we participate has very negative consequences, we are in very serious violation of morality.

MAC2 strictly requires that we defect from all harmful group actions.[81] But defection from more harmful acts is more important, because they are more negatively weighty. When you are a member of two heinous group acts and can only defect from one, MAC2 tells you to defect from the most consequentially harmful, the one that leaves things most worst than the relevant null option, barring complications mentioned in 9.4 which are not relevant in the current context.

There are some quirks of this mechanism related to worries about DD that we discussed earlier. What if you can defect from a very bad group act and a bad group act, but not both, and your evil contribution to the very bad act is less than your evil contribution to the bad group act? Then it may seem that you should defect from the lesser bad act, since it will be consequentially better to do so. But in this case I cannot plausibly appeal to your not being criticized for the trivial defection from the weightier act to deliver that result. So MAC2 requires that you defect from the worst group act instead, with the possible exception of special circumstances discussed in 9.4 that do not obtain in this context. That is where the arguments lead us; that is what a direct consequentialist rationale requires. What if you cannot defect from all the component norms of some very bad act? Then you should give priority to defection from consequentially worse component norms, as suggested by a generalization of our earlier discussions of concentric group acts.

Another analytical complexity involves the nature of defection: Remember that there are different but relevant sorts of participation in group acts. You can be inside a group act in the sense relevant to defection when you accept the relevant reasons, but at the same time act contrary to your role in the group act in question.[82] In one sense you do not participate, but in another sense you do. Or you can be outside of the conditions required for any sort of participation in the group act. You not only fail to act, you fail even to accept the reasons in question. Just as your positive moral credit for a beneficent group action requires performing your role, since otherwise

---

[81] Barring here irrelevant complications discussed in Chapter 9.

[82] You can act in accord with the strictures of a group act without meeting the act's motivational conditions, but then you are outside the group trying.

you are defecting, the full heinous normative weight of a heinous group action is only inherited by you when you act in accord with your role in that group act, when you do not defect. But notice this important wrinkle: You are participating in the group acts in question when you accept the relevant reasons but no opportunity to act your role is available to you.[83] At least in moments when defecting action or inaction is unavailable to you, when you cannot act out your defection, even acceptance of the reasons still places you relevantly inside the act, even if it is heinous. You still suffer the full negative moral accounting. What then can you do to escape that responsibility? Perhaps you can dig down deep enough in yourself to root out acceptance of the relevant reasons. But more likely you will need to join a suitably countervailing group act, which will involve contrary motivation even when you cannot act on it or otherwise act out your defection from the original act, so that the conflict in your motivation leaves it not determinately true that you are still inside the first act at such an inactive moment. You accept conflicting reasons and do not dominantly accept the immoral ones.

We will return to the relevance of these analytical niceties about defection. But the central theoretical point to focus on is that we each have normative responsibility for the entire negative weight of bad group acts in which we participate. Now I'm going to put this component of MM to work. I am going to argue that we participate in group acts that are responsible for extreme poverty, that we have harmed the very poor in something like the way that Pogge suggests.

My case will have two elements. The first element will be the observation that those of us who are well off engage in practices (whether or not they are group acts) that are extremely harmful to the very poor and in other ways that it is important to recognize, and also that those who represent us and our interests even *act* in ways extremely harmful to the very poor and in these other ways. The second element of my case will involve uncovering relationships between these acts of others and practices on the one hand, and group acts in which we participate on the other.

There are various ways in which our practices and the acts of our representatives are very harmful as assessed by LDP. First of all, most of us, the well-off, consume goods, including food, that are produced by a massively complex capitalist economic and industrial system, based largely on petroleum, that is ravaging the earth. There is consequent global warming, loss of forests, loss of land, loss of freshwater, loss of marine fisheries, toxic pollution, loss of biodiversity, over-fertilization with nitrogen, acid deposition, and ozone depletion.[84] This worldwide disaster is bad for all of us and our descendants. It is also harmful for many animals, which is of some secondary importance according to MM. But the key point for our current purposes is that it is also extremely harmful to the very poor, whose status is weighty according to LDP.

---

[83] Varying MAC at this point would have many implications.

[84] Speth (2008: 17–45); Working Group II (2008); Rockström et al. (2009). For solutions, see MacKay (2009); McKibben (2010); Foley et al. (2011); Hertsgaard (2011).

They are often those least well-placed to deal with environmental disasters that face them, and many are located where the environmental disasters will be most dramatic.[85] Indeed, much of the harm occasioned by our industrial juggernaut is deflected onto those with least power to resist it, especially the very poor.[86] For instance, firms negatively affected by the phase-out of leaded gas in the U.S. expanded overseas markets, so that by 1990 80 percent of the nations using leaded gas were very poor.[87]

Second, extreme poverty is itself a great harm rooted in our practices and the acts of our representatives. Over a billion people are undernourished every day.[88] And the "main reason hunger and nutritional deficiencies persist is poverty; many millions of households simply cannot afford to buy nutritious food or the farming supplies they need to grow enough of their own."[89] The majority of the chronically malnourished live in rural areas of developing countries.[90] But an overlapping billion of extremely impoverished people live in urban shantytowns also in developing countries.[91] Still what, you may ask, does this have to do with *us*, with our practices or the acts of our representatives? Many things: The poor of Europe once fled slums in the Old World for a better life in the New, but the borders of many nations are now more or less closed. Our governments engage in strong-arm bargaining when trade deals are made, that are to our benefit overall or at least to the benefit of powerful agricultural interests in our nations, but to the cost of less powerful and wealthy nations and the poorest people in them.[92] For instance, European and American negotiators insist on retaining agricultural subsidies for their own farmers but also the elimination of agricultural subsidies and trade barriers in poor nations. What's more, our banks make loans to poor nations whose dictators slip the money into accounts abroad and leave the bill to their nation; our industries grab the natural resources of poor nations at a good price even if the dictators take the cash.[93] The IMF and the World Bank, often at U.S. and British prodding, have enforced SAPs, structural adjustment programs, that have decimated agriculture in the third world and helped drive the poor into urban slums.[94] Our nations arm many of the dictators, and we are not shy about using our military power to prop them up when it seems expedient.

Still, you might say, what do these things have to do with *me*? I don't negotiate trade pacts or police the borders or buy resources or run the IMF or the Pentagon. And while I may buy a gas-guzzling, pollution-belching SUV to cruise to the grocery store for some cigarettes and to the mall for window shopping, still that is not a consequentially significant harm.

---

[85] Warner (2009). See also http://www.each-for.eu   [86] Dauvergne (2008).
[87] Dauvergne (2008: 86–7). But things have improved. See Dauvergne (2008: 89–96).
[88] http://www.fao.org The estimate is based on USDA figures.
[89] Pinstrup-Andersen and Cheng (2007).   [90] Pinstrup-Andersen and Cheng (2007: 97).
[91] M. Davis (2006). But Perlman (2010) notes recent improvements.
[92] Pogge (2002).   [93] Pogge (2002). Shaxson (2007) has hair-raising details.
[94] M. Davis (2006: 150–73).

So now my job is to find some group acts in which you and I participate that underlie some of the obvious huge horrendous effects of the world of the well-off—including our practices and the acts of our representatives—on the world of the extremely poor. And we don't have far to look.

The first is a bad old friend. I have already argued that the long-term maximization of individual self-interest has no default rationality, and that it frequently makes no determinate sense, at least when unrefined by moral considerations. But now I am going to argue that such a pursuit and the normative support of such a conception is highly immoral.

Someone who pursues the resolute maximization of long-term self-interest in a moralistic way, in a way supported by the acceptance of reasons, is part of a large group act that is analogous to a large deontic group act. They criticize others and not just themselves (or their past and future selves) for relevant failures, though perhaps they occasionally suppress the external expression of that criticism when talking with those whom they hope to sucker in a deal. They teach the ideal to their children and their students. They judge defectors to be irrationally imprudent, as failing to uphold the proper ideal of universal rationality. Indeed, we philosophers have ourselves been engaged for millennia in support of the default rationality of this beast. Prudence of some minimal and traditional sort is one thing. I am talking now about ravenous and relentless long-term selfishness, squeezing out over life every last dollar when we care about dollars, aiming always at maximum individual desire-satisfaction figured over one's life. Of course, sometimes our desires are for the intuitive good of others, and so our interests encompass those of others. But very often they do not.

It is a striking fact that many *ethicists* criticize those who are not ravenously and ruthlessly self-interested over time as irrational. Mostly, of course, such a goal is a fantasy. We have already seen that the maximization of self-interest over time often makes no determinate sense in reality, though the goal of maximizing satisfaction sometimes makes a little more determinate sense under capitalism, when we care so much about wealth, competitive markets force efficiencies of production, and most everything is for sale in cash.[95] But it can be consequentially harmful to pursue even a fantasy.

There is no default rationality of this selfishness. To the contrary. This group act must be assessed by the value of its consequences according to LDP. No doubt humans have a certain selfishness and instinctive prudence more or less by nature, relevant to the baseline of assessment for the group act in question. And we have seen that some sorts of prudence are a virtue. But the negative consequences of the inflated, artificial selfishness that we are now discussing are our responsibility. We train ourselves to be more greedy and grabbing and craftily resolute about trivial

---

[95] E. Wood (2002) reviews debates on capitalism's historical origins. But selfishness is not special to capitalism. We have long been buying low and selling high, and some traditional religious doctrines provide a high-end selfish goal.

details of our future interest than we are by any plausible nature, and certainly more than virtuous prudence requires. While the notion of maximizing one's self-interest over time really doesn't often make coherent sense, still there is no mistaking the fact that its pursuit encourages us to be more selfish and greedy and grabbing than we otherwise would be.

It is not an accident that people are reluctant to give to charity or restrain even obscene and unimportant consumption. It is not an accident that our politicians know that they will prosper if they make sure our trivial interests are served by trade policies even at severe cost to the world's most vulnerable. It is not an accident that our banks and industries close their eyes to corruption in third world markets, since they face their stockholders. It is not an accident that our economic and industrial system inflicts enormous harm for trivial reasons, that terrible world-wide damage is done in pursuit of cheap, unhealthy hamburgers for the wealthy. But it isn't inevitable or natural in some deep way either. Nor is it virtuous or rationally required. There is no reason that we need to be so grasping. We are somewhat grasping by nature, but we have been trained into its hideous contemporary refinements. And we have already seen that this doesn't make any of us as individuals appreciably happier. Perhaps historically it had some good effects. Perhaps it helped us leave feudalism behind for the greater abundance allowed by industrial capitalism. But there is no question that it is now ravaging the earth and making the poor off even worse off. MM cannot countenance these injuries. Even if our ancestors' artificial selfishness was suitably beneficent, those days are gone.

The moralized conception of rationality as maximization of long-term self-interest is now a genuinely evil group act when assessed by MM, a major cause of environmental disaster and extreme poverty in the world, because it undergirds the harmful practices and acts of our representatives that we recently surveyed. I think that most of us are to one degree or another inside it. We are morally obligated to defect. When we fail to do so, we are in the central sense normatively responsible for all of its heinous effects.[96]

A key question, of course, is how to defect, and we will return to that key point in a moment. But other elements of MM introduce another of Pogge's ideas. Pogge suggests that we owe *reparation* to the very poor. And MM respects our special obligations of reparation, as ways of making it be that we haven't defected from deontic group acts in a way that otherwise would be the case. But still it is possible that our deontic group acts forbidding injury do not stretch to cover the sorts of remote harms in question here, and even that LE does not firmly project moral responsibility from our individual past participation in harmful group acts to our current selves. In fact, LE may more plausibly somewhat limit the demands of giving

---

[96] If the act was formerly beneficent but is now harmful, we are responsible for its current harmful effects, which are huge.

on individuals over time, even in cases of reparation. So I will focus here just on our need to defect from harmful group acts.

I think that moralized selfishness is our principal relevantly sinful group act, but there are others. I bet you would have some tendency to criticize someone on grounds of their failure of proper respect and reciprocity who stole your chrome hubcaps, even before you stopped to ask how poor they were and whether they needed the money. This suggests that you bear responsibility for a very vast group act of respect for property that includes the bank account of the deposed dictator living down the road who bled his nation dry. Or consider your responsibility for the actions of the corporations whose stock you buy on grounds that require that they maximize profits, and would criticize if they went resolutely green. You seem relevantly inside the corporation.

Or consider this case: Margaret Gilbert has argued that group action constitutes a solution to the "problem of political obligation,"[97] in other words to the question of whether membership in a political society obligates one to uphold the political institutions of that country. She thinks that membership constitutes a kind of group action, and that such a group action constitutes an other-things-equal obligation to, for instance, obey the law. This is because of her particular conception of group action, whereby there is only genuine group action when there are genuine normative reasons to participate. My model of group action is based on hers, but modified at exactly this point. I don't think that actual normative reasons are required for there to be group action, merely that there must be the acceptance that there are reasons. Just as beliefs may be false, so too reasons may be accepted that are not genuine. This allows for the existence of heinous group acts, which there is not even an other-things-equal obligation to maintain. They aim at a merely apparent good. But if Gilbert is right in her contention that membership in a political society constitutes group action, which I think she is, that in turn suggests another model of political obligation.

Genuine political obligation will require positive consequences of the political society in question. The strength of the obligation versus conflicting demands will turn on the size of those positive consequences, as assessed by LDP. Group action occurs at many levels. There may be forms of polity beyond national boundaries, say the European Union, that are constituted by relevant group action, and this may involve various conflicts resolved by the structure of MM, and also indeterminacies. But in our present situation some national state agents are consequentially quite significant. Wars matter, of course,[98] but I am now thinking principally of trade policy and pressure on the IMF, though we shouldn't forget support for the despotic governments of the world. What if the state agent of which you are part has overall negative consequences? Then you must defect, with the strength of that obligation dependent on how negative the consequences are.

---

[97] Gilbert (2006).   [98] Pfaff (2010).

A focus on the case of political obligation can help us better understand some of the analytical complexities of defection. Whether you are a citizen or not, when you are resident in a country, it is hard to prevent elements of the law from running around in your head as accepted reasons supporting criticism of defectors on grounds of failure of reciprocity and beneficence. It is hard to avoid being in one sense inside the group act in question. If you act in accord with those laws, you are not in that respect even defecting from the polity. And it will certainly not be possible to constantly act out your defection, at least if one is to meet other weighty moral strictures of MM. So probably most Americans and even resident aliens have something like full moral responsibility for what the U.S. does, not only internally but in the world, figured over the entire history of a very large group act. That should be a sobering thought.[99] And even if we as a whole are for the good, particular sub-actions of our group are very harmful. There can be a concentric group act within our general citizenship that is quite harmful on its own, even if the whole is for the best. As a citizen, you are a participant in all the bad component acts, even if you voted against the bums, unless you somehow defect from those components. And oppor-tunities to act out your defection will not always be available. What should you do? Perhaps, if you can, you should try to get the relevant reasons out of your head.[100] And perhaps you should act out defection at every morally acceptable opportunity. But another mechanism I've noted is quite helpful at this point. If you could somehow participate in a countervailing group act, whose reasons you would accept in some sufficiently strong way even when you are not physically active, that might make it sometimes true that you are in fact at a given inactive moment in a complex motivational state that leaves you not determinately inside the state actor or some bad component act of that state actor. So maybe you can make contrary reasons active inside your head, and only obey as any partisan would be forced to obey an occupying power, at least in respect of the bad components of the state actor. Of course, one route is to emigrate, but it would be better to stay inside as you might an occupying power and change the damn thing. Paying taxes and obeying the law isn't quite enough to constitute participation in a group act, when you pay and obey as you would pay and obey alien occupiers, though sometimes not paying them may be a way of acting out defection. If you cannot defect in any of these ways from harmful state actors and the harmful component acts of beneficent state actors, or the costs are too great, then you must discover some way to better the consequences of the group action in question, for which you have something like full normative respon-sibility. You will be as guilty as if you did it all on your own. And remember that mere flukes won't get you off the hook.

---

[99] But counterfactuals relevant to the overall consequences of some states, for instance those with significant colonial pasts but which have made technological contributions, are wild, and ripe for complicated indeterminacies.

[100] Macdonald (1957).

Certainly many Americans bear heavy responsibility for the effects of U.S. trade policy, even if they know nothing about our trade policies through ordinary but still culpable inattention and ignorance. And now you know. Moreover, there are related evils to which group acts are also relevant in a similar way. Traditional just war doctrine suggests that individual patriotic participation in even an unjust war is morally acceptable. But Jeff McMahan has argued that it is morally wrong to participate in a war without a just cause.[101] And MAC2 also suggests that participation in such a war, at least when it is consequentially quite harmful as assessed by LDP, is highly immoral. MM also underwrites McMahan's unargued suggestion that participating in unnecessary or disproportionate wars with just causes is immoral.[102]

We have noted some key harmful group acts. But there are others. In between moralized selfishness and participation in particular national actors, there is also an intermediate case, a moralized group commitment to patriotism in general of a sort that supports havoc in the outside world for benefit at home, death for the out-group to favor the in-group, whatever our in-group. And there are allied forms of cultural, ethnic, religious, and gender enthusiasm. There are moralized group acts that support sexual, gender, orientation, religious, ethnic, economic, and racial oppression of many kinds, along with various forms of slavery and abuse of power. Many members of the relevant oppressing groups, and even some members of the oppressed groups, accept reasons and criticize defectors in the ways characteristic of group action. What's more, non-human animals, even outside the depredations of industrial capitalism, are abused in ways that violate LDP, despite its central focus on human interests, and our artificial selfishness is surely reflected in the tendencies to ravenous consumption and indulgence of unhealthy appetites that have much to do with this abuse.

Unless we defect from these various very harmful group acts, we are steeped in secular sin, frequently towards the very poor. Whether or not we owe reparations, we must defect. But how can we do that?

First, of course, we must not play our roles in these harmful group acts. MM forbids most externally aggressive patriotic action, or activity in support of the wilder and more harmful shores of our property and corporate arrangements, or participation in oppression. It is not consistent with morality to be an aggressive and competent corporate lawyer, trade negotiator, volunteer soldier in an unjust war, slave trader, or religious or sexual bigot. Nor is it morally appropriate for citizens or stock-holders or politicians to vote or agitate in support of such harmful actions. But the second key point is that defection also requires participation in countervailing group acts for those moments when we can't act out our defection, at least if we aren't

---

[101] McMahan (2009).

[102] McMahan (2009: 6). Contributing required taxes and accepting a draft may not constitute group act participation, depending on one's motivations. It may seem that to participate in a war in bad conscience shouldn't be morally preferable to participating in good conscience. But MAC2 implies it sometimes is.

psychological prodigies who can get the relevant reasons out of our heads. You had better be a lawyer for the poor, or politically active in support of the downtrodden, or a pacifist, or in some way engage in long-range individual or group action of suitably countervailing sorts.

Let me focus on the key group act of moralized selfishness. How can you defect from that? A minimal start would be to participate in the group act of charity sketched in 12.3, to give 2.5 percent. But that is so easy to do and so undemanding, so clearly consistent with traditional selfishness even absent traditional fairy tales about the requirements of salvation, that something more is plausibly required. Perhaps at the very moment you are writing a check to UNICEF that minimal charity will be enough to constitute defection, but you will need more moral cover for moments when you aren't acting out your defection and selfishness may rampage inside. Perhaps various other unrelated beneficent group acts of the sort mentioned in 12.3 sometimes provide you sufficient cover for these moments. Perhaps even the philosopher's project of enlightenment is sometimes one of these, or perhaps various more obviously helping professions are another route. But for most of us, I think, something more generous with our time or money or effort or mental space is required. To stick to the minimums is itself evidence of a failure to defect.

Still, we can hear old Martin demanding: "How much is morally required? What exactly does austerity demand? Tell me what I need to do to be not immoral according to MM, so that after I meet that minimum constraint I can do what I want with the rest of my time and money and effort, and so I can see at last whether MM is too demanding to be true."

But I don't think there are highly determinate minimums that are sufficient to place you and me and especially Martin firmly and at all moments of our lives outside of the group act of moralized selfishness. I certainly don't think that there is some dollar or percentage figure that will do it for all of us. We are too diverse. And in any case, I think that none of us will ever in fact be wholly and determinately morally innocent in this way. Even at best, very few of the likes of us will succeed in being wholly and determinately beyond the secular sin of artificial selfishness at every moment of our lives, which is not to say that many of us are not more determinately beyond it than many others, at least at many moments, and not to say we couldn't do a little better with our children if this became an educational priority for most of us. And, of course, even if we get beyond artificial selfishness, we will not be morally perfect, just not highly immoral.

To be determinately and wholly morally perfect in our world would be very demanding indeed. I think no one is. All the moral demands of the many starving on us in reality will never be met by any real human being, which is not to say that none of us could meet them. But my main job now is only to make you feel guilty, and hence motivated to accept demands somewhat beyond the bare minimum, not to tell you some higher minimum that will project you wholly, determinately, and always beyond our basic form of guilt. And I'm certainly not trying to find an easy formula to make you into a moral paragon in our demanding world.

Austerity comes in degrees. Still, if you want some concrete directions to the middle regions of austerity, which I think may suffice to often make it at least not determinately true that you are seriously immoral, then give *more* than 2.5 percent of your annual income to organizations that fight global hunger like:

Action Against Hunger-USA, http://www.actionagainsthunger.org
The Hunger Project, http://www.thp.org
Oxfam America, http://www.oxfamamerica.org
Stop Hunger Now, http://www.stophungernow.org
Global Partners for Development, http://www.gpf.org

And give *another* 2.5 percent for cost-effective relief of severe poverty-related diseases to:

Village Reach, http://www.villagereach.org
Stop TB Partnership, http://www.stoptb.org
Against Malaria, http://www.againstmalaria.com

In general, give enough, and pay enough attention, so that the relief of extreme poverty becomes a significant project of your life. This cannot plausibly be said to be too demanding in the eyes of any very widespread commonsense morality reflected in DC1, since members of traditional religions tithe or practice *zakāt* in a way that is *more* financially demanding, and also lead lives steeped in further moral observance, and yet do not pretend to moral perfection even in charity. And yet I think it can suffice to ensure that even when you are not acting out your defection from artificial selfishness you are not determinately highly immoral. Of course, if you want to be morally pristine, much more is required.

All the secular sins we have recently surveyed imply corresponding virtues. There are other people out there, on the other side, in all these cases. They are not moral paragons. They do not meet the full demands of complete austerity and proper charity. But they are moderately austere, and work to alleviate extreme poverty. And they are virtuous in other ways. They generally avoid harmful and wasteful consumption. For instance, they avoid eating meat when things that grow efficiently in the local ground will do.[103] And they strive to minimize other forms of environmental damage and other harms to animals.[104] They also defect from and work against social forms that are harmful to humans in other ways, and strive to create forms that are just and beneficent. For instance, they invest their wealth where it does good

---

[103] For practical suggestions, see Pollan (2006); Bittner (2008); Safran Foer (2009).
[104] Speth (2008) and Dauvergne (2008) have concrete suggestions. Or consult http://www.footprint calculator.org and www.peta.org

rather than harm.[105] These individuals have, despite the fact that they are not perfectly austere, at least a middling degree of a summary virtue that I will call, with very little irony, political correctness.

This too is a group act. These people accept relevant reasons, and they certainly criticize those who defect on grounds of failure of reciprocity and benevolence. Perhaps they also criticize in a similar way those who never join, but still they meet the conditions required for group action. If few people are out there in the past and present and future cooperating in this act, it may not have such a weighty effect. But if there are many, and so there seem to be, then it is likely to be quite weighty as assessed by LDP. If on your way to pick up your new SUV, you have a weak moment and feel the sting, you are inside and almost deontically bound by the strictures of MAC2. And even if you are completely outside such an act, LDP will require you to join when that is otherwise allowed by MAC2, which is very often, and then you will be bound inside. You must not merely desist from the horrendous group acts we have been discussing, but cooperate on a group project that includes desisting and fixing these horrors. And I think you are probably already inside it to one degree or another.[106] I think we both feel the sting. We are morally required to be politically correct. Fortunately, as we have seen, because of the complexities of defection, participation in such a countervailing act is also one way to aid our defection from participation in various morally heinous group acts, including that of artificial selfishness.

We have no right to complain about political correctness or austerity. But they come in degrees, and it's a good thing for us that at least their middling regions won't be too unpleasant. There is no denying that MM is a little demanding. It doesn't require violation of general and special deontic obligations. It is consistent with traditional virtues. It admits RS. But it demands austerity and political correctness of at least some degree. It requires abandoning the fantastical rigors of long-term maximizing selfishness and other evil group acts. It demands more than minimum charity. Still, it is highly implausible to claim that in our world, in which we participate in actions with huge heinous effects, that we *know* that we do not face moral demands that interfere with trivial self-indulgent details of our highly privileged lives, but leave plenty of room for our happiness. We should be embarrassed even to make the objection.[107] We must change our lives, at least a little bit, to avoid serious immorality, though of course even then we will not be moral saints.

---

[105] Possibilities include http://moveyourmoney.info www.agorapartnerships.org www.microplace.com www.swwb.org
[106] There are various concentric group acts here, some which involve desisting from only some of the things that others involve. If you start cooperating with the good guys on cars but not on air conditioning, which act you have joined depends on the reasons you accept.
[107] Wilson (1993) argues that the demandingness objection can be self-serving ideology.

12.5 Conclusion

Good politics are a virtue and a moral duty. Greedy politics in the well-off are immoral. And we have seen that the group act of political correctness has various aspects; austerity is only one. They are unified by a commitment to proper social and political arrangements.

We already know the true general theory of that. We saw in Chapter 3 that social and political philosophy should evaluate the way groups justify, the reasons they accept. And they are properly evaluated by MM. Many social forms constitute group actions, because they involve criticism of defectors on grounds of entwined reciprocity and apparent beneficence, and hence invoke MAC2. But many involve no group action, and so require only straightforward consequentialist assessment by LDP.

But that is vast topic for another day. Here, in summary, is my normative advice for individuals:

Aim at truth, and accept MM, which includes LDP and MAC2, the proper understanding of benevolence and justice. So seek truth; be benevolent; be just. And we have seen in this part what benevolence and justice more specifically require: Be truthful to others and keep your promises. Don't murder. Don't injure. Don't steal morally legitimate property. Be grateful and attentive to your children and friends. Be temperate, courageous, suitably humble towards the wide range of excellence, and reasonably prudent. Be austere, charitable, and politically correct. Defect from all harmful group acts.

I have given a long argument for familiar conclusions. But there are a few surprises. We overlook indeterminacies in options, and hence make normative mistakes. We are too focused on individuals, not enough on distribution within lives and across lives and on group actions. We are too absurdly selfish. And we overlook many social options, real alternatives to our current forms of life, current forms for which we have considerable collective responsibility.

Whether or not there is any robust human nature, there are robust human potentials, which we do not begin to understand. Whether we admit it or our nerve has failed, we have it in our power to begin again. We can feel the air of another planet, a new and better world.

Bibliography

Adams, Ernest (1970), "Subjunctive and Indicative Conditionals," *Foundations of Language* 6, 39–94.

Adams, Ernest (1975), *The Logic of Conditionals* (Dordrecht: Reidel).

Adams, Robert Merrihew (1976), "Motive Utilitarianism," *Journal of Philosophy* 73, 467–81.

Adams, Robert Merrihew (1977), "Middle Knowledge and the Problem of Evil," *American Philosophical Quarterly* 14, 109–17.

Adams, Robert Merrihew (2006), *A Theory of Virtue* (New York: Oxford University Press).

Alloy, Lauren and Lyn Abramson (1979), "Judgment of Contingency in Depressed and Nondepressed Students," *Journal of Experimental Psychology, General* 108, 441–85.

Anderson, Perry (2012), "After Nehru," *London Review of Books*, Aug. 2, 21–36.

Anscombe, G. E. M. (1981), *Collected Philosophical Papers*, Volume III (Minneapolis: University of Minnesota Press).

Anscombe, G. E. M. (2000), *Intention*, 2nd edn. reprint (Cambridge, Mass.: Harvard University Press).

Aquinas, Thomas (1920), *Summa Theologica*, 2nd edn., Fathers of the English Dominican Province (trans.) (London: Burns, Oates, and Washbourne).

Arberry, A. J. (1996), *The Koran Interpreted* (New York: Simon & Schuster).

Aristotle (1984), *Complete Works*, Jonathan Barnes (ed.) (Princeton: Princeton University Press).

Armstrong, David (1989), *A Combinatorial Theory of Possibility* (New York: Cambridge University Press).

Arneson, Richard (1999), "Egalitarianism and Responsibility," *Journal of Ethics* 3, 225–47.

Austin, J. L. (1961), "Ifs and Cans," in *Philosophical Papers* (Oxford: Clarendon Press), 153–80.

Bach, Kent (1999), "The Myth of Conventional Implicature," *Linguistics and Philosophy* 22, 367–421.

Barker, Stephen (2000), "Is Value Content a Component of Conventional Implicature?," *Analysis* 60, 268–79.

Barry, Brian (1965), *Political Argument* (London: Routledge & Kegan Paul).

Beardsley, Monroe (1975), "Actions and Events: The Problem of Individuation," *American Philosophical Quarterly* 12, 263–76.

Bennett, Jonathan (1984), "Counterfactuals and Temporal Direction," *Philosophical Review* 93, 57–91.

Bennett, Jonathan (2003), *A Philosophical Guide to Conditionals* (New York: Oxford University Press).

Bergstrom, Lars (1966), *The Alternatives and Consequences of Actions* (Stockholm: Almqvist and Wiksell).

Bergstrom, Lars (1976), "On the Formulation and Application of Utilitarianism," *Nous* 10, 121–44.

Bittner, Michael (2008), *Food Matters* (New York: Simon & Schuster).

Bloomfield, Paul (2011), "Justice as a Self-Regarding Virtue," *Philosophy and Phenomenological Research* 32, 46–64.

Blum, L. A. (1994), *Moral Perception and Particularity* (Cambridge: Cambridge University Press).

Boisvert, Daniel (2008), "Expressivism-Assertivism," *Pacific Philosophical Quarterly* 89, 169–203.

Bourse, Christopher and Roy Sorensen (1988), "Ducking Harm," *Journal of Philosophy* 85, 115–34.

Boyd, Richard (1988), "How to Be a Moral Realist," in Geoffrey Sayre-McCord (ed.), *Essays on Moral Realism* (Ithaca: Cornell University Press), 181–228.

Bradley, Ben (2009), *Well-Being and Death* (New York: Oxford University Press).

Bradley, Ben (2012), "Goodness and Justice," *Philosophy and Phenomenological Research* 84, 233–43.

Brandt, Richard (1963), "Toward a Credible Form of Utilitarianism," in Hector-Neri Casta-ñeda and George Nakhnikian (eds.), *Morality and the Language of Conduct* (Detroit: Wayne State University Press), 104–43.

Brandt, Richard (1967), "Some Merits of One Form of Rule Utilitarianism," *University of Colorado Studies in Philosophy* 3, 39–65.

Brandt, Richard (1979), *A Theory of the Good and the Right* (Oxford: Oxford University Press).

Brandt, Richard (1992), *Morality, Utilitarianism, and Rights* (New York: Cambridge University Press).

Brandt, Richard (1996), *Facts, Values, and Morality* (New York: Cambridge University Press).

Bratman, Michael (2008), "Normative Thinking and Planning, Individual and Shared," in Stroud (2008), 91–101.

Brink, David (1989), *Moral Realism and the Foundations of Ethics* (Cambridge: Cambridge University Press).

Brink, David (1992), "A Puzzle About the Rational Authority of Morality," *Philosophical Perspectives* 6, 1–26.

Brink, David (1997), "Realism, Naturalism, and Moral Semantics," *Social Philosophy and Policy* 4, 154–76.

Broome, John (1991), *Weighing Goods* (Oxford: Blackwell).

Broome, John (2000), "Normative Requirements," in J. Dancy (ed.), *Normativity* (Oxford: Blackwell), 79–99.

Broome, John (2007), "Wide or Narrow Scope?," *Mind* 116, 359–70.

Broome, John (2008), "Comments on Allan Gibbard's Tanner Lectures," in Stroud (2008), 102–19.

Buckareff, Andrei (2005), "How (Not) To Think About Mental Action," *Philosophical Explorations* 8, 83–9.

Buss, Sarah (1999a), "Appearing Respectful: The Moral Significance of Manners," *Ethics* 109, 798–826.

Buss, Sarah (1999b), "What Practical Reasoning Must Be If We Act for Our Own Reasons," *Australasian Journal of Philosophy* 77, 399–421.

Calderisi, Robert (2006), *The Trouble with Africa* (New Haven: Yale University Press).

Carlson, Erik (1999), "The Oughts and Cans of Objective Consequentialism," *Utilitas* 11, 91–6.

Carson, Thomas (1986), "Hare's Defense of Utilitarianism," *Philosophical Studies* 50, 97–115.

Carson, Thomas (2000), *Value and the Good Life* (South Bend: Notre Dame University Press).

Carson, Thomas (2010), *Lying and Deception* (Oxford: Oxford University Press).

Castañeda, Hector-Neri (1965), "The Logic of Change, Action, and Norms," *Journal of Philosophy* 62, 333–44.

Castañeda, Hector-Neri (1968), "A Problem for Utilitarianism," *Analysis* 28, 141–2.

Chalmers, David (1996), *The Conscious Mind* (New York: Oxford University Press).

Chalmers, David (2010), *The Character of Consciousness* (New York: Oxford University Press).

Chan, David (2004), "Are There Extrinsic Desires?," *Nous* 38, 326–50.

Chisholm, Roderick (1946), "The Contrary-to-Fact Conditional," *Mind* 55, 289–307.

Chisholm, Roderick (1964), "J. L. Austin's Philosophical Papers," *Mind* 73, 1–26.

Chisholm, Roderick and Thomas Feehan (1977), "The Intent to Deceive," *Journal of Philosophy* 74, 143–59.

Clark, Randolph (2003), *Libertarian Accounts of Free Will* (New York: Oxford University Press).

Collier, Paul (2007), *The Bottom Billion* (New York: Oxford University Press).

Confucius (1979), *The Analects*, D. C. Lau (trans.) (Harmondsworth: Penguin).

Copp, David (2001), "Realist-Expressivism: A Neglected Option for Moral Realism," *Social Philosophy and Policy* 18, 1–43, reprinted with corrections in Copp (2007), 153–202.

Copp, David (2007), *Morality in a Natural World* (Cambridge: Cambridge University Press).

Copp, David (2009), "Realist-Expressivism and Conventional Implicature," *Oxford Studies in Metaethics* 4, 167–202.

Coyne, Jerry and H. Allen Orr (2004), *Speciation* (Sunderland, Mass.: Sinauer Associates).

Crisp, Roger (2003), "Equality, Priority, and Compassion," *Ethics* 113, 745–63.

Crisp, Roger (2006), *Reason and the Good* (Oxford: Oxford University Press).

Crowther, Thomas (2009), "Perceptual Activity and the Will," in Lucy O'Brien and Matthew Soteriou (eds.), *Mental Actions* (Oxford: Oxford University Press), 173–91.

Cummiskey, David (2009), "Review of *Goodness and Justice*," *Utilitas* 21, 521–5.

Cupit, Geoffrey (1996), *Justice as Fittingness* (Oxford: Clarendon Press).

D'Arms, Justin and Daniel Jacobson (2000a), "Sentiment and Value," *Ethics* 110, 722–48.

D'Arms, Justin and Daniel Jacobson (2000b), "The Moralistic Fallacy: On the 'Appropriateness' of Emotions," *Philosophy and Phenomenological Research* 61, 65–90.

D'Arms, Justin and Daniel Jacobson (2009), "Regret and Irrational Action," in David Sobel and Steven Wall (eds.), *Reasons for Action* (Cambridge: Cambridge University Press), 179–99.

Darwall, Stephen (1983), *Impartial Reason* (Ithaca: Cornell University Press).

Darwall, Stephen (2002), *Welfare and Rational Care* (Princeton: Princeton University Press).

Daston, Lorraine (2005), "All Curls and Pearls," *London Review of Books*, June 23, 37–8.

Dauvergne, Peter (2008), *The Shadows of Consumption* (Cambridge, Mass.: MIT Press).

Davidson, Donald (1980a), "Actions, Reasons, and Causes," in Davidson (1980b), 3–20.

Davidson, Donald (1980b), *Essays on Actions & Events* (Oxford: Clarendon Press).

Davidson, Donald (1980c), "Mental Events," in Davidson (1980b), 207–25.

Davis, Lawrence (1970), "Individuation of Actions," *Journal of Philosophy* 67, 520–30.

Davis, Mike (2006), *Planet of Slums* (London: Verso).

Davis, Wayne (1986), "The Two Senses of Desire," in Joel Marks (ed.), *The Ways of Desire* (Chicago: Precedent), 63–82.

de Waal, Frans, Stephen Macedo, and Josiah Ober (eds.) (2006), *Primates and Philosophers* (Princeton: Princeton University Press).

Diener, Ed and Martin Seligman (2004), "Beyond Money: Towards an Economy of Well-Being," *Psychological Science in the Public Interest* 5, 1–31.

Dobson, K. and R. L. Franche (1989), "A Conceptual and Empirical Review of the Depressive Realism Hypothesis," *Canadian Journal of Behavioral Science* 21, 419–33.

Donagan, Alan (1977), *The Theory of Morality* (Chicago: University of Chicago Press).

Doris, John (1998), "Persons, Situations, and Virtue Ethics," *Nous* 32, 504–30.

Doris, John (2002), *Lack of Character* (Cambridge: Cambridge University Press).

Doris, John and Alexandra Plakias (2008), "How to Argue about Disagreement: Evaluative Diversity and Moral Realism," in Walter Sinnott-Armstrong (ed.), *Moral Psychology*, Volume 2 (Cambridge, Mass.: MIT Press), 303–31.

Dreier, James (1990), "Internalism and Speaker Relativism," *Ethics* 101, 6–26.

Dretske, Fred (1988), *Explaining Behavior* (Cambridge, Mass.: MIT Press).

Driver, Julia (2001), *Uneasy Virtue* (Cambridge: Cambridge University Press).

Dryden, John (1678), *All for Love, or, The World Well Lost*.

Dupré, John (1993), *The Disorder of Things* (Cambridge, Mass.: Harvard University Press).

Dworkin, Ronald (1981), "What is Equality? I. Equality of Welfare," *Philosophy and Public Affairs* 10, 185–246.

Earman, John (1986), *A Primer on Determinism* (Dordrecht: Reidel).

Easterly, William (2006), *The White Man's Burden* (Oxford: Oxford University Press).

Easterly, William (2010), "Foreign Aid for Scoundrels," *New York Review of Books*, Nov. 25, 37–8.

Elliott, Carl (2007), *Better than Well* (New York: Norton).

Elstein, Daniel and Thomas Hurka (2009), "From Thick to Thin: Two Moral Reduction Plans," *Canadian Journal of Philosophy* 39, 515–36.

Falk, W. D. (1948), " 'Ought' and Motivation," *Proceedings of the Aristotelian Society*, 111–38.

Feinberg, Joel (1968), "Collective Responsibility," *Journal of Philosophy* 65, 674–88.

Feinberg, Joel (1970), *Doing and Deserving* (Princeton: Princeton University Press).

Feinberg, Joel (1974), "Non-Comparative Justice," *Philosophical Review* 83, 297–338.

Feldman, Fred (1975), "World Utilitarianism," in K. Lehrer (ed.), *Analysis and Metaphysics* (Dordrecht: Reidel), 255–71.

Feldman, Fred (1986), *Doing the Best We Can* (Dordrecht: Reidel).

Feldman, Fred (1995a), "Adjusting Utility for Justice: A Consequentialist Reply to the Objection from Justice," *Philosophy and Phenomenological Research* 55, 567–85.

Feldman, Fred (1995b), "Desert: Reconsideration of Some Received Wisdom," *Mind* 104, 63–77.

Feldman, Fred (2004), *Pleasure and the Good Life* (Oxford: Clarendon Press).

Fine, Terrence (2007), *Theories of Probability* (New York: Academic Press).

Firth, R. (1952), "Ethical Absolutism and the Ideal Observer Theory," *Philosophy and Phenomenological Research* 12, 317–45.

Fischer, John Martin (ed.) (1986), *Moral Responsibility* (Ithaca: Cornell University Press).

Fischer, John Martin (1994), *The Metaphysics of Free Will* (Oxford: Blackwell).

Fischer, John Martin (2002), "Frankfurt-type Examples and Semi-Compatibilism," in Kane (2002), 281–307.

Fischer, John Martin and Mark Ravizza (eds.) (1992), *Ethics: Problems and Principles* (Fort Worth: Holt, Rinehart and Winston).

Fischer, John Martin and Mark Ravizza (1998), *Responsibility and Control* (Cambridge: Cambridge University Press).

Flanagan, Owen (2011), *The Bodhisattva's Brain* (Cambridge, Mass.: MIT Press).

Foley, Jonathan et al. (2011), "Solutions for a Cultivated Planet," *Nature* 478, Oct. 20, 337–42.

Foot, Philippa (2001), *Natural Goodness* (Oxford: Clarendon Press).

Formenton, G. and S. Poletti (1999), *Giotto in the Chapel of the Scrovegni* (Oriago: Medoacus).

Frankena, William (1958), "Obligation and Motivation in Recent Philosophy," in A. I. Melden (ed.), *Essays on Moral Philosophy* (Seattle: University of Washington Press), 40–81.

Frankfurt, Harry (1969), "Alternative Possibilities and Moral Responsibility," *Journal of Philosophy* 66, 828–39.

Frankfurt, Harry (1971), "Freedom of the Will and the Concept of a Person," *Journal of Philosophy* 68, 5–20.

Gärdenfors, Peter (1988), *Knowledge in Flux* (Cambridge, Mass.: MIT Press).

Gauthier, David (1986), *Morals by Agreement* (Oxford: Oxford University Press).

Geirsson, Heimir (2003), "Moral Twin-Earth: The Intuitive Argument," *Southwest Philosophy Review* 19, 115–24.

Gensler, Harry (1986), "A Kantian Argument Against Abortion," *Philosophical Studies* 49, 83–98.

Gensler, Harry (1996), *Formal Ethics* (London: Routledge).

Gensler, Harry (1998), *Ethics* (London: Routledge).

Gensler, Harry (2013), *Ethics and the Golden Rule* (New York: Routledge).

Gert, Bernard (1998), *Morality* (Oxford: Oxford University Press).

Gibbard, Allan (1965), "Rule-Utilitarianism: Merely an Illusory Alternative?," *Australasian Journal of Philosophy* 43, 211–20.

Gibbard, Allan (1971), *Utilitarianism and Coordination*, Harvard dissertation; reprinted (New York: Garland, 1990).

Gibbard, Allan (1978), "Act-Utilitarian Agreements," in A. Goldman and J. Kim (eds.), *Values and Morals* (Dordrecht: Reidel), 91–119.

Gibbard, Allan (1990), *Wise Choices, Apt Feelings* (Cambridge, Mass.: Harvard University Press).

Gibbard, Allan (2003), *Thinking How to Live* (Cambridge, Mass.: Harvard University Press).

Gibbard, Allan (2008), "Reconciling Our Aims" and "Reply to Commentators" in Stroud (2008), 33–88 and 147–88.

Gibbons, John (2013), *The Norm of Belief* (Oxford: Oxford University Press).

Gilbert, Margaret (2006), *A Theory of Political Obligation* (Oxford: Clarendon Press).

Ginet, Carl (1990), *On Action* (Cambridge: Cambridge University Press).

Goldman, Alvin (1970), *A Theory of Human Action* (Englewood Cliffs: Prentice Hall).

Goldman, Alvin (1971), "The Individuation of Actions," *Journal of Philosophy* 68, 761–4.

Goldman, Holly (1976), "Dated Rightness and Moral Imperfection," *Philosophical Review* 85, 449–87.

Goldman, Holly (1978), "Doing the Best One Can," in J. Kim and A. Goldman (eds.), *Values and Morals* (Dordrecht: Reidel), 185–214.

Goldstein, Irwin (1989), "Pleasure and Pain: Unconditional, Intrinsic Values," *Philosophy and Phenomenological Research* 50, 255–76.

Goldstein, Irwin (2003), "Malicious Pleasure Evaluated," *Pacific Philosophical Quarterly* 84, 24–31.

Goodman, Charles (2009), *Consequences of Compassion: An Interpretation and Defense of Buddhist Ethics* (Oxford: Oxford University Press).

Goodman, Nelson (1947), "The Problem of Counterfactual Conditionals," *Journal of Philosophy* 44, 113–28.

Gosling. J. C. B. (1969), *Pleasure and Desire* (Oxford: Clarendon Press).

Grice, Paul (1989), *Studies in the Way of Words* (Cambridge, Mass.: Harvard University Press).

Griffin, James (1986), *Well-Being* (Oxford: Clarendon Press).

Gruzalski, Bart (1986), "Parfit's Impact on Utilitarianism," *Ethics* 96, 760–83.

Haidt, Jonathan (2012), *The Righteous Mind* (New York: Pantheon).

Hajdin, M. (2007), "Review of *Goodness and Justice*," *Philosophy in Review* 27, 204–6.

Hájek, Alan (2007), "The Reference Class Problem is Your Problem Too," *Synthese* 156, 563–85.

Hare, R. M. (1952), *The Language of Morals* (Oxford: Oxford University Press).

Hare, R. M. (1963), *Freedom and Reason* (Oxford: Oxford University Press).

Hare, R. M. (1981), *Moral Thinking* (Oxford: Oxford University Press).

Harman, Gilbert (1999), "Moral Philosophy Meets Social Psychology: Virtue Ethics and the Fundamental Attribution Error," *Proceedings of the Aristotelian Society* 99, 315–31.

Harman, Gilbert (2000), *Explaining Value* (New York: Oxford University Press).

Harper, W. L., R. Stalnaker, and G. Pearce (eds.) (1981), *IFS* (Dordrecht: Reidel).

Harre, R. and E. Madden (1975), *Causal Powers* (Totowa: Rowman and Littlefield).

Harris, John (1975), "The Survival Lottery," *Philosophy* 50, 81–7.

Harsanyi, John (1953), "Cardinal Utility in Welfare Economics and in the Theory of Risk-Taking," *Journal of Political Economy* 61, 434–5, reprinted in Harsanyi (1976), 3–5.

Harsanyi, John (1976), *Essays on Ethics, Social Behavior, and Scientific Explanation* (Dordrecht: Reidel).

Hay, Ryan (2013), "Hybrid Expressivism and the Analogy between Perjoratives and Moral Language," *European Journal of Philosophy* 21, 450–74.

Haybron, Daniel (2009), *The Pursuit of Happiness* (Oxford: Oxford University Press).

Heath, Joseph (2008), *Following the Rules: Practical Reasoning and Deontic Constraint* (New York: Oxford University Press).

Heathwood, Chris (2005), "The Problem of Defective Desires," *Australasian Journal of Philosophy* 83, 487–504.

Heller, Mark (1985), "Non-Backtracking Counterfactuals and the Conditional Analysis," *Canadian Journal of Philosophy* 15, 75–86.

Henson, Richard (1971), "Utilitarianism and the Wrongness of Killing," *Philosophical Review* 80, 320–37.

Hertsgaard, Mark (2011), *Hot: Living Through the Next Fifty Years on Earth* (Boston: Houghton Mifflin Harcourt).

Hobbes, Thomas (1955), *Leviathan* (Oxford: Basil Blackwell).

Hooker, Brad (1991), "Rule-Consequentialism and Demandingness: Reply to Carson," *Mind* 100, 269–76.

Hooker, Brad (2000), *Ideal Code, Real World* (Oxford: Clarendon Press).

Horgan, Terence (1984), "Supervenience and Cosmic Hermeneutics," *Southern Journal of Philosophy Supplement* 22, 19–38.

Horgan, Terence and Mark Timmons (1991), "New Wave Moral Realism Meets Moral Twin Earth," *Journal of Philosophical Research* 16, 447–65.

Horgan, Terence and Mark Timmons (2009), "Analytical Functionalism Meets Moral Twin Earth," in I. Ravenscroft (ed.), *Minds, Ethics, and Conditionals* (Oxford: Clarendon Press).

Hornsby, Jennifer (1980), *Actions* (London: Routledge & Kegan Paul).

Howard-Snyder, Frances (1997), "The Rejection of Objective Consequentialism," *Utilitas* 9, 241–8.

Howard-Snyder, Frances (1999), "Response to Carlson and Qizilbash," *Utilitas* 11, 106–11.

Hubin, Donald (1991), "Irrational Desires," *Philosophical Studies* 62, 23–44.

Hubin, Donald (1996), "Hypothetical Motivation," *Nous* 30, 31–54.

Hume, David (2000), *A Treatise of Human Nature*, David Fate Norton and Mary Norton (eds.) (Oxford: Oxford University Press).

Hurka, Thomas (1993), *Perfectionism* (New York: Oxford University Press).

Hurka, Thomas (2001), *Virtue, Vice, and Value* (New York: Oxford University Press).

Hursthouse, Rosalind (1999), *On Virtue Ethics* (Oxford: Oxford University Press).

Husseini, Rana (2009), *Murder in the Name of Honour* (Oxford: One World).

Hutcheson, Francis (2008), *An Inquiry into the Original of Our Ideas of Beauty and Virtue* (Indianapolis: Liberty Fund).

Irwin, Terence (1988), *Aristotle's First Principles* (Oxford: Oxford University Press).

Irwin, Terence and Gail Fine (trans.) (1995), *Aristotle: Selections* (Indianapolis: Hackett).

Jackson, Frank (1991), "Decision-theoretic Consequentialism and the Nearest and Dearest Objection," *Ethics* 101, 461–82.

Jackson, Frank (1998), *From Metaphysics to Ethics* (Oxford: Clarendon Press).

Jackson, Frank and Philip Pettit (1995), "Moral Functionalism and Moral Motivation," *Philosophical Quarterly* 45, 20–40.

Johnston, Mark (1987), "Is There a Problem about Persistence?," *Proceedings of the Aristotelian Society Supplement* 61, 107–35.

Jones, O. R. (1983), "Trying," *Mind* 92, 368–85.

Kagan, Shelly (1999), "Equality and Desert," in Louis Pojman and Owen McLeod (eds.), *What Do We Deserve?* (New York: Oxford University Press), 298–314.

Kagan, Shelly (2012), *The Geometry of Desert* (New York: Oxford University Press).

Kahneman, Daniel and Angus Deaton (2010), "High Income Improves Evaluation of Life but not Emotional Well-Being," *Proceedings of the National Academy of Sciences* 107, Sept. 21, 16489–93.

Kahneman, Daniel, Ed Diener, and Norbert Schwarz (eds.) (2003), *Well-Being: The Foundations of Hedonic Psychology* (New York: Russell Sage Foundation).

Kail, P. J. E. (2007), *Projectivism and Realism in Hume's Philosophy* (Oxford: Oxford University Press).

Kaiser, P. K. and R. M. Boynton (1996), *Human Color Vision* (Washington: Optical Society of America).

Kamm, Frances (1993), *Morality, Mortality*, Volume 1 (Oxford: Oxford University Press).

Kamm, Frances (1996), *Morality, Mortality*, Volume 2 (Oxford: Oxford University Press).

Kamm, Frances (2007), *Intricate Ethics* (New York: Oxford University Press).

Kamm, Frances (2008), "Intuitions, Contractualism, and Strains," in Stroud (2008), 120–44.

Kamtekar, Rachana (2004), "Situationism and Virtue Ethics on the Content of Our Character," *Ethics* 114, 458–91.

Kane, Robert (1996), *The Significance of Free Will* (New York: Oxford University Press).

Kane, Robert (ed.) (2002), *The Oxford Handbook of Free Will* (New York: Oxford University Press).

Kant, Immanuel (1996a), *Critique of Practical Reason*, in Mary J. Gregor (trans.), *Practical Philosophy* (Cambridge: Cambridge University Press), 133–271.

Kant, Immanuel (1996b), *Groundwork of The Metaphysics of Morals*, in Mary J. Gregor (trans.), *Practical Philosophy* (Cambridge: Cambridge University Press), 37–108.

Kant, Immanuel (1996c), *The Metaphysics of Morals*, in Mary J. Gregor (trans.), *Practical Philosophy* (Cambridge: Cambridge University Press), 363–603.

Kant, Immanuel (1998), *Religion Within the Boundaries of Mere Reason*, Allen Wood and George di Giovanni (trans.) (Cambridge: Cambridge University Press).

Kenny, Neil (2004), *The Uses of Curiosity in the Early Modern Period* (Oxford: Oxford University Press).

Khalidi, Tarif (2008), *The Qur'an* (London: Penguin).

Kim, Jaegwon (1979), "Supervenience and Nomological Commensurables," *American Philosophical Quarterly* 15, 149–56.

Kim, Jaegwon (1984), "Concepts of Supervenience," *Philosophy and Phenomenological Research* 45, 153–76.

Kim, Jaegwon (1993), *Supervenience and Mind* (Cambridge: Cambridge University Press).

Kim, Jaegwon (1998), *Mind in a Physical World* (Cambridge, Mass.: MIT Press).

Knobe, Joshua (2003a), "Intentional Action and Side Effects in Ordinary Language," *Analysis* 63, 190–3.

Knobe, Joshua (2003b), "Intentional Action in Folk Psychology: An Experimental Investigation," *Philosophical Psychology* 16, 309–24.

Knobe, Joshua (2006), "The Concept of Intentional Action: A Case Study in the Uses of Folk Psychology," *Philosophical Studies* 130, 203–31.

Kolnai, Aurel (1977), "Deliberation is of Ends," in *Ethics, Value, and Reality* (London: Athlone Press), 44–62.

Kolodny, Niko (2005), "Why Be Rational?," *Mind* 114, 509–63.

Kolodny, Niko (2007), "State or Process Requirements?," *Mind* 116, 371–85.

Korsgaard, Christine (1983), "Two Distinctions in Goodness," *Philosophical Review* 92, 169–95.

Korsgaard, Christine (1986), "Skepticism About Practical Reason," *Journal of Philosophy* 83, 5–25.

Korsgaard, Christine (1996), *The Sources of Normativity* (Cambridge: Cambridge University Press).

Korsgaard, Christine (2009), *Self-Constitution* (Oxford: Oxford University Press).

Kraut, Richard (1994), "Desire and the Human Good," *Proceedings and Addresses of the American Philosophical Association* 68, 39–54.

Kraut, Richard (2007), *What Is Good and Why* (Cambridge, Mass.: Harvard University Press).

Kripke, Saul (1980), *Naming and Necessity* (Cambridge, Mass.: Harvard University Press).

Kutz, Christopher (2000), *Complicity* (Cambridge: Cambridge University Press).

Kyburg, Henry (1974), *The Logical Foundations of Statistical Inference* (Dordrecht: Reidel).

Kyburg, Henry (1977), "Randomness and the Right Reference Class," *Journal of Philosophy* 74, 501–22.

Lehrer, Keith (1968), "Cans Without Ifs," *Analysis* 29, 29–32.

Lehrer, Keith (1975), "'Can' in Theory and Practice: A Possible Worlds Analysis," in Myles Brand and Douglas Walton (eds.), *Action Theory* (Dordrecht: Reidel), 241–70.

Lehrer, Keith and Richard Taylor (1968), "Time, Truth, and Modalities," *Mind* 74, 390–8.

Lenman, James (1999), "The Externalist and the Amoralist," *Philosophia* 27, 441–57.

Levi, Isaac (1977), "Direct Inference," *Journal of Philosophy* 74, 5–28.

Levine, Ruth et al. (2004), *Millions Saved* (Washington: Center for Global Development).

Lewis, C. I. (1946), *An Analysis of Knowledge and Valuation* (LaSalle, Ill.: Open Court).

Lewis, David (1970), "How to Define Theoretical Terms," *Journal of Philosophy* 67, 427–46.

Lewis, David (1973a), "Causation," *Journal of Philosophy* 70, 556–67.

Lewis, David (1973b), *Counterfactuals* (Cambridge, Mass.: Harvard University Press).

Lewis, David (1979), "Counterfactual Dependence and Time's Arrow," *Nous* 13, 455–76.

Lewis, David (1981), "Causal Decision Theory," *Australasian Journal of Philosophy* 59, 5–30.

Lewis, David (1986), *On the Plurality of Worlds* (Oxford: Blackwell).

Lewis, David (1989), "Dispositional Theories of Value," *Proceedings of the Aristotelian Society Supplement* 63, 113–37.

Lewis, David (2002), "Tensing the Copula," *Mind* 111, 1–13.

Locke, Don (1976), "The 'Can' of Being Able," *Philosophia* 6, 1–20.

Locke, John (1975), *An Essay Concerning Human Understanding*, Peter Nidditch (ed.) (Oxford: Oxford University Press).

Loeb, Don (1995), "Full-Information Theories of the Good," *Social Theory and Practice* 21, 1–30.

Long, A. A. and D. N. Sedley (1987), *The Hellenistic Philosophers*, Volume 1 (Cambridge: Cambridge University Press).

Lycan, William (2001), *Real Conditionals* (New York: Oxford University Press).

Lyons, David (1965), *Forms and Limits of Utilitarianism* (Oxford: Clarendon Press).

McDaniel, Kris and Ben Bradley (2008), "Desires," *Mind* 117, 267–302.

Macdonald, Dwight (1957), *The Responsibility of Peoples, and Other Essays in Political Criticism* (London: Gollancz).

McDowell, John (1998), "Two Sorts of Naturalism," in *Mind, Reality, and Value* (Cambridge, Mass.: Harvard University Press), 167–97.

MacKay, David (2009), *Sustainable Energy—Without the Hot Air* (Cambridge: UIT Cambridge Ltd.).

McKenna, Michael (1997), "Alternative Possibilities and the Failure of the Counterexample Strategy," *Journal of Social Philosophy* 28, 71–85.

McKenna, Michael (2006), "Collective Responsibility and an Agent Meaning Theory," *Midwest Studies in Philosophy* 30, 16–34.

McKerlie, Dennis (1984), "Egalitarianism," *Dialogue* 23, 223–37.

McKerlie, Dennis (1989), "Equality and Time," *Ethics* 99, 475–91.

McKerlie, Dennis (2001), "Dimensions of Equality," *Utilitas* 13, 263–88.

McKibben, Bill (2010), *Eaarth: Making a Life on a Tough New Planet* (New York: Henry Holt).

Mackie, J. L. (1965), "Causes and Conditions," *American Philosophical Quarterly* 2, 245–64.

Mackie, J. L. (1973), *Truth, Probability, and Paradox* (Oxford: Clarendon Press).

Mackie, J. L. (1977), *Ethics: Inventing Right and Wrong* (New York: Penguin).

McMahan, Jeff (2009), *Killing in War* (Oxford: Oxford University Press).

Malm, H. M. (1989), "Killing, Letting Die and Simple Conflicts," *Philosophy and Public Affairs* 18, 238–58.

Mason, Elinor (2007), "Review of *Goodness and Justice*," *Notre Dame Philosophical Review* 2007.08.04, <http://ndpr.nd.edu/review.cfm?id=10583>.

May, Larry (1992), *Sharing Responsibility* (Chicago: University of Chicago Press).

May, Larry and Stacey Hoffman (eds.) (1991), *Collective Responsibility* (Savage, Md.: Rowman and Littlefield).

Mele, Alfred (1995), *Autonomous Agents* (New York: Oxford University Press).

Mele, Alfred (2003a), "Agents' Abilities," *Nous* 37, 447–70.

Mele, Alfred (2003b), *Motivation and Agency* (New York: Oxford University Press).

Mele, Alfred and David Robb (1998), "Rescuing Frankfurt-Style Cases," *Philosophical Review* 107, 97–112.

Mendola, Joseph (1986), "Parfit on Directly Collectively Self-Defeating Moral Theories," *Philosophical Studies* 50, 153–66.

Mendola, Joseph (1988), "On Rawls's Basic Structure: Forms of Justification and the Subject Matter of Social Philosophy," *The Monist* 71, 437–54.

Mendola, Joseph (1997), *Human Thought* (Dordrecht: Kluwer).

Mendola, Joseph (2006), *Goodness and Justice* (Cambridge: Cambridge University Press).

Mendola, Joseph (2008), *Anti-Externalism* (Oxford: Oxford University Press).

Metz, Thaddeus (2007a), "Toward an African Moral Theory," *The Journal of Political Philosophy* 15, 321–41.

Metz, Thaddeus (2007b), "Ubuntu as a Moral Theory: Reply to Four Critics," *South African Journal of Philosophy* 26, 369–87.

Mill, John Stuart (1972), *Utilitarianism*, in H. B. Acton (ed.), *Utilitarianism, Liberty, Representative Government* (London: Dent), 1–61.

Mischel, W. (1968), *Personality and Assessment* (New York: Wiley).

Moody-Adams, Michelle (1997), *Fieldwork in Familiar Places* (Cambridge, Mass.: Harvard University Press).

Moore, G. E. (1903), *Principia Ethica* (Cambridge: Cambridge University Press).

Moore, G. E. (1912), *Ethics* (New York: Henry Holt).

Moore, G. E. (1923), "Are the Characteristics of Particular Things Universal or Particular?," *Proceedings of the Aristotelian Society Supplement* 3, 95–113.

Moore, G. E. (1968), "A Reply to My Critics," in Paul Arthur Schilpp (ed.), *The Philosophy of G. E. Moore*, 3rd edn. (LaSalle, Ill.: Open Court), 535–677.

Murphy, Liam and Thomas Nagel (2004), *The Myth of Ownership* (New York: Oxford University Press).

Myro, George (1986), "Identity and Time," in R. Grandy and R. Warner (eds.), *Philosophical Grounds of Rationality* (Oxford: Oxford University Press), 383–410.

Nagel, Thomas (1970), *The Possibility of Altruism* (Princeton: Princeton University Press).

Nagel, Thomas (1979), "Equality," in *Mortal Questions* (Cambridge: Cambridge University Press), 106–27.

Nagel, Thomas (1986), *The View from Nowhere* (Oxford: Oxford University Press).

Nagel, Thomas (1991), *Equality and Partiality* (New York: Oxford University Press).

Nietzsche, Friedrich (1990), *Twilight of the Idols and the Anti-Christ*, R. J. Hollingdale (trans.) (London: Penguin).

Norcross, Alastair (1997), "Good and Bad Actions," *Philosophical Review* 106, 1–34.

Nowell-Smith, H. (1960), "Ifs and Cans," *Theoria* 26, 85–101.

Nozick, Robert (1974), *Anarchy, State, and Utopia* (New York: Basic Books).

Nussbaum, Martha (1980), "Non-Relative Virtues: An Aristotelian Approach," *Midwest Studies in Philosophy* XIII, 32–53.

Nussbaum, Martha (2000), *Women and Human Development* (New York: Cambridge University Press).

Nussbaum, Martha (2001), *Upheavals of Thought* (Cambridge: Cambridge University Press).

Offner, Avner (2006), *The Challenge of Affluence* (Oxford: Oxford University Press).

Orbach, Susie (2009), *Bodies* (New York: Picador).

O'Shaughnessy, Brian (1974), "Trying (as the Mental 'Pineal Gland')," *Journal of Philosophy* 71, 365–86.

O'Shaughnessy, Brian (2000), *Consciousness and the World* (Oxford: Oxford University Press).

Otsuka, Michael (1991), "The Paradox of Group Beneficence," *Philosophy and Public Affairs* 20, 132–49.

Otsuka, Michael (1998), "Incompatibilism and the Avoidability of Blame," *Ethics* 108, 685–701.

Overvold, Mark (1980), "Self-Interest and the Concept of Self-Sacrifice," *Canadian Journal of Philosophy* 10, 105–18.

Parfit, Derek (1984), *Reasons and Persons* (Oxford: Oxford University Press).

Parfit, Derek (1986), "Comments," *Ethics* 96, 832–72.

Parfit, Derek (1997), "Equality and Priority," *Ratio* 10, 202–21.

Parfit, Derek (2011a), *On What Matters*, Volume One (Oxford: Oxford University Press).

Parfit, Derek (2011b), *On What Matters*, Volume Two (Oxford: Oxford University Press).

Peacocke, Christopher (2007), "Mental Action and Self-Awareness," in J. Cohen and B. McLaughlin (eds.), *Contemporary Debates in Philosophy of Mind* (Oxford: Blackwell), 358–76.

Pereboom, Derk (2000), "Alternative Possibilities and Causal Histories," *Philosophical Perspectives* 14, 119–37.

Perlman, Janice (2010), *Favela* (New York: Oxford University Press).

Perry, Ralph Barton (1967), *General Theory of Value* (Cambridge, Mass.: Harvard University Press).

Persson, Ingmar (2008), "When We Have to Kill Vic," *TLS*, Feb. 22, 31.

Pfaff, William (2010), *The Irony of Manifest Destiny: The Tragedy of America's Foreign Policy* (New York: Walker).

Pietroski, Paul (2000), *Causing Actions* (Oxford: Oxford University Press).

Pinstrup-Andersen, Per and Fuzhi Cheng (2007), "Still Hungry," *Scientific American* 297(3), 96–103.

Plantinga, Alvin (2007), "Two Dozen (or so) Theistic Arguments," in Deane-Peter Baker (ed.), *Alvin Plantinga* (New York: Cambridge University Press), 203–38.

Plato (1997), *Philebus*, Dorothea Frede (trans.), in John Cooper (ed.), *Plato, Complete Works* (Indianapolis: Hackett), 398–456.

Pogge, Thomas (2002), *World Poverty and Human Rights* (Cambridge: Polity Press).

Pollan, Michael (2006), *The Omnivore's Dilemma* (New York: Penguin).

Portmore, Douglas (2011), *Commonsense Consequentialism* (New York: Oxford University Press).

Potts, Christopher (2007), "Into the Conventional-Implicature Dimension," *Philosophy Compass* 2, 665–79.

Prinz, Jesse (2004), *Gut Reactions* (New York: Oxford University Press).

Prinz, Jesse (2007), *The Emotional Construction of Morals* (Oxford: Oxford University Press).

Putnam, Hilary (1975), "The Meaning of 'Meaning'," in *Philosophical Papers*, Volume II (Cambridge: Cambridge University Press), 215–71.

Quine, W. V. O. (1960), *Word and Object* (Cambridge, Mass.: MIT Press).

Quinn, Warren (1993), "Putting Rationality in Its Place," in *Morality and Moral Action* (Cambridge: Cambridge University Press), 228–55.

Railton, Peter (1984), "Alienation, Consequentialism, and the Demands of Morality," *Philosophy and Public Affairs* 13, 134–71.

Railton, Peter (2003a), "Facts and Values," in Railton (2003b), 43–68.

Railton, Peter (2003b), *Facts, Values, and Norms* (Cambridge: Cambridge University Press).

Railton, Peter (2003c), "Moral Realism," in Railton (2003b), 3–42.

Railton, Peter (2003d), "On the Hypothetical and Non-Hypothetical in Reasoning about Belief and Action," in Railton (2003b), 293–321.

Ramose, Mogobe (2003), "The Ethics of Ubuntu," in P. H. Coetzee and A. P. J. Roux (eds.), *Philosophy from Africa*, 2nd edn. (Oxford: Oxford University Press), 324–30.

Rawls, John (1971), *A Theory of Justice* (Cambridge, Mass.: Harvard University Press).

Rawls, John (2001), *Justice as Fairness* (Cambridge, Mass.: Harvard University Press).

Raz, Joseph (1986), *The Morality of Freedom* (Oxford: Oxford University Press).

Regan, Donald (1980), *Utilitarianism and Cooperation* (Oxford: Oxford University Press).

Ridge, Michael (2006), "How to Be a Rule-Utilitarian: Introducing Variable-Rate Rule-Utilitarianism," *Philosophical Quarterly* 56, 242–53.

Rockström, Johan et al. (2009), "A Safe Operating Space for Humanity," *Nature* 461, Sept. 24, 472–5.

Rodzinski, W. (1979), *A History of China* (Oxford: Pergamon Press).

Rosati, Connie (1995), "Persons, Perspectives, and Full-Information Accounts of the Good," *Ethics* 105, 296–325.

Ross, L. and R. E. Nisbett (1991), *The Person and the Situation* (Philadelphia: Temple University Press).

Ross, W. D. (1930), *The Right and the Good* (Oxford: Clarendon Press).

Rousseau, Jean-Jacques (1973a), "A Discourse on Political Economy," in G. D. H. Cole, J. H. Brumfitt, and John Hall (trans.), *The Social Contract and Discourses* (London: Dent), 115–53.

Rousseau, Jean-Jacques (1973b), "The Social Contract," in G. D. H. Cole, J. H. Brumfitt, and John Hall (trans.), *The Social Contract and Discourses* (London: Dent), 163–278.

Runciman, David (2008), *Political Hypocrisy* (Princeton: Princeton University Press).

Ruskin, John (1886), *The Stones of Venice*, 4th edn. (Kent: George Allen).

Ryle, Gilbert (1949), *The Concept of Mind* (London: Hutchinson).

Sachs, Jeffrey (2005), *The End of Poverty* (New York: Penguin).

Safran Foer, Jonathan (2009), *Eating Animals* (New York: Little, Brown).

Scanlon, T. M. (1975), "Preference and Urgency," *Journal of Philosophy* 72, 655–69.

Scanlon, T. M. (1982), "Contractualism and Utilitarianism," in Amartya Sen and Bernard Williams (eds.), *Utilitarianism and Beyond* (Cambridge: Cambridge University Press), 103–28.

Scanlon, T. M. (1998), *What We Owe to Each Other* (Cambridge, Mass.: Harvard University Press).

Scanlon, T. M. (2008), *Moral Dimensions* (Cambridge, Mass.: Harvard University Press).

Schroeder, Mark (2009), "Hybrid Expressivism: Virtues and Vices," *Ethics* 119, 257–309.

Schroeder, Severin (2001), "The Concept of Trying," *Philosophical Investigations* 24, 213–27.

Schroeder, Timothy (2004), *Three Faces of Desire* (New York: Oxford University Press).

Schueler, G. F. (1995), *Desire* (Cambridge, Mass.: MIT Press).

Schwartz, Sunny with David Boodell (2009), *Dreams from the Monster Factory* (New York: Scribner).

Schwartz, Thomas (1982), "Human Welfare: What It Is Not," in Harlan Miller and William Williams (eds.), *The Limits of Utilitarianism* (Minneapolis: University of Minnesota Press), 195–206.

Sen, Amartya (1980), "Equality of What?," in S. M. McMurrin (ed.), *The Tanner Lectures on Human Values*, Volume 1 (Salt Lake City: University of Utah Press), 195–220.

Sen, Amartya (1986), "Social Choice Theory," in K. J. Arrow and M. D. Intriligator (eds.), *Handbook of Mathematical Economics*, Volume III (North-Holland: Elsevier), 1073–160.

Sen, Amartya (1994), "Population: Delusion or Reality," *New York Review of Books*, Sept. 29, 62–71.

Sen, Amartya (2005), *The Argumentative Indian* (London: Penguin).

Sen, Amartya (2009), *The Idea of Justice* (Cambridge, Mass.: Harvard University Press).

Setiya, Kieran (2003), "Explaining Action," *Philosophical Review* 112, 339–93.

Setiya, Kieran (2007), "Cognitivism about Instrumental Reason," *Ethics* 117, 649–73.

Shafer-Landau, Russ (2003), *Moral Realism* (Oxford: Oxford University Press).

Shaxson, Nicholas (2007), *Poisoned Wells: The Dirty Politics of African Oil* (New York: Palgrave Macmillan).

Shoemaker, Sydney (1984), "Causality and Properties," in *Identity, Cause, and Mind* (Cambridge: Cambridge University Press), 206–33.

Sidelle, Alan (1989), *Necessity, Essence, and Individuation* (Ithaca: Cornell University Press).

Sidgwick, Henry (1892), *Outlines of the History of Ethics* (London: Macmillan).

Sidgwick, Henry (1907), *The Methods of Ethics*, 7th edn. (London: Macmillan).

Sidorsky, David (1965), "A Note on Three Criticisms of Von Wright," *Journal of Philosophy* 62, 739–42.

Sikora, R. I. (1978), "Is It Wrong to Prevent the Existence of Future Generations?," in R. I. Sikora and Brian Barry (eds.), *Obligations to Future Generations* (Philadelphia: Temple University Press), 112–66.

Singer, Peter (1972), "Famine, Affluence, and Morality," *Philosophy and Public Affairs* 1, 229–43.

Smith, Adam (1976), *The Theory of Moral Sentiments* (Oxford: Oxford University Press).

Smith, Huston (1958), *The Religions of Man* (New York: Harper & Row).

Smith, Michael (1994), *The Moral Problem* (Oxford: Blackwell).

Smith, Michael (2003), "Rational Capacities, or: How to Distinguish Recklessness, Weakness, and Compulsion," in Sarah Stroud and Christine Tappolet (eds.), *Weakness of Will and Practical Irrationality* (Oxford: Clarendon Press), 17–38.

Smith, Michael (2004), "Instrumental Desires, Instrumental Rationality I," *Proceedings of the Aristotelian Society Supplement* 78, 95–109.

Sobel, David (1994), "Full Information Accounts of Well-Being," *Ethics* 104, 784–810.

Sobel, David (2001), "Explanation, Internalism, and Reasons for Action," *Social Philosophy and Policy* 18, 218–35.

Sobel, Howard (1976), "Utilitarianism and Past and Future Mistakes," *Nous* 10, 195–219.

Speth, James Gustave (2008), *The Bridge at the Edge of the World* (New Haven: Yale University Press).

Spinoza, Benedict de (1994), *The Ethics*, Edwin Curley (trans.), in *A Spinoza Reader* (Princeton: Princeton University Press), 85–265.

Sprigge, Timothy (1985), "Utilitarianism and Idealism: A Rapprochement," *Philosophy* 60, 447–63.

Sprigge, Timothy (2000), "Is the Esse of Intrinsic Value Percipi? Pleasure, Pain, and Value," in Anthony O'Hear (ed.), *Philosophy, the Good, the True, and the Beautiful* (Cambridge: Cambridge University Press), 119–40.

Sripada, Chandra Sekhar (2010), "Philosophical Questions About the Nature of Willpower," *Philosophy Compass* 5, 793–803.

Stalnaker, Robert (1975), "A Theory of Conditionals," in E. Sosa (ed.), *Causation and Conditionals* (Oxford: Oxford University Press), 41–55.

Stalnaker, Robert (1984), *Inquiry* (Cambridge, Mass.: MIT Press).

Stampe, Dennis (1986), "Defining Desire," in Joel Marks (ed.), *The Ways of Desire* (Chicago: Precedent), 149–73.

Stampe, Dennis (1987), "The Authority of Desire," *Philosophical Review* 96, 335–81.

Stampe, Dennis (1988), "Needs," *Australasian Journal of Philosophy* 66, 129–60.

Stevenson, Charles (1944), *Ethics and Language* (New Haven: Yale University Press).

Stocker, Michael (1979), "Desiring the Bad: An Essay in Moral Psychology," *Journal of Philosophy* 76, 738–53.

Strawson, Galen (1994), *Mental Reality* (Cambridge, Mass.: MIT Press).

Strawson, Galen (2003), "Mental Ballistics or the Involuntariness of Spontaneity," *Proceedings of the Aristotelian Society* 103, 227–56.

Strawson, Peter (1962), "Freedom and Resentment," *Proceedings of the British Academy* 48, 187–211.

Streumer, Bart (2008), "Are There Irreducibly Normative Properties," *Australasian Journal of Philosophy* 86, 537–61.

Stroud, Barry (ed.) (2008), *Reconciling Our Aims* (Oxford: Oxford University Press).

Sturgeon, Nicholas (2003), "Moore on Ethical Naturalism," *Ethics* 113, 528–56.

Svavarsdóttir, Sigrún (1999), "Moral Cognitivism and Motivation," *Philosophical Review* 108, 161–219.

Swanton, Christine (2003), *Virtue Ethics: A Pluralist View* (Oxford: Oxford University Press).

Tännsjö, Torbjörn (2008), *Understanding Ethics*, 2nd edn. (Edinburgh: University of Edinburgh Press).

Temkin, Larry (1993), *Inequality* (New York: Oxford University Press).

Tenenbaum, Sergio (2007), *Appearances of the Good* (New York: Cambridge University Press).

Thomas, Keith (2008), *The Ends of Life* (Oxford: Oxford University Press).

Thompson, Michael (2008), *Life and Action* (Cambridge, Mass.: Harvard University Press).

Thomson, Judith Jarvis (1971), "The Time of a Killing," *Journal of Philosophy* 68, 115–32.

Thomson, Judith Jarvis (1977), *Acts and Other Events* (Ithaca: Cornell University Press).

Thomson, Judith Jarvis (1990), *The Realm of Rights* (Cambridge, Mass.: Harvard University Press).

Thomson, Judith Jarvis (2001), *Goodness & Advice* (Princeton: Princeton University Press).

Tomberlin, James (1979), "Some Recent Work in Action Theory," *Philosophy and Phenomenological Research* 40, 576–93.

Tuve, Rosemond (1966), *Allegorical Imagery* (Princeton: Princeton University Press).

Tyldesley, Joyce (2008), *Cleopatra; Last Queen of Egypt* (New York: Basic Books).

Unger, Peter (1996), *Living High and Letting Die* (New York: Oxford University Press).

USDA (1999), *U.S. Action Plan on Food Security*, <http://www.fas.usda/gov/icd/summit/pressdoc.html>.

van Inwagen, Peter (1983), *An Essay on Free Will* (Oxford: Clarendon Press).

van Inwagen, Peter (2002), "Free Will Remains a Mystery," in Kane (2002), 158–80.

van Roojen, Mark (2005), "Expressivism, Supervenience and Logic," *Ratio* 18, 190–205.

van Roojen, Mark (2006), "Knowing Enough to Disagree," *Oxford Studies in Metaethics* 1, 161–93.

van Roojen, Mark (2008), "Some Advantages of One Form of Argument for the Maximin Principle," *Acta Analytica* 23, 319–35.

van Roojen, Mark (2010), "Moral Rationalism and Rational Amoralism," *Ethics* 120, 499–525.

Velleman, David (1988), "Brandt's Definition of 'Good'," *Philosophical Review* 97, 353–72.

Velleman, David (1991), "Well-Being and Time," *Pacific Philosophical Quarterly* 72, 48–77.

Vihvelin, Kadri (2000), "Libertarian Compatibilism," *Philosophical Perspectives* 14, 139–66.

von Neumann, J. and O. Morgenstern (1944), *Theory of Games and Economic Behavior* (Princeton: Princeton University Press).

Vranas, Peter (2005), "The Indeterminacy Paradox: Character Evaluations and Human Psychology," *Nous* 39, 1–42.

Wallace, Jay (1994), *Responsibility and the Moral Sentiments* (Cambridge, Mass.: Harvard University Press).

Walton, Douglas (1980), "Cans and Counterfactuals," *Canadian Journal of Philosophy* 10, 489–96.

Warner, Koko et al. (2009), *In Search of Shelter: Mapping the Effects of Climate Change on Human Migration and Displacement*, <http://www.ciesin.columbia.edu/clim-migr-report-june09_media.pdf>.

Watson, Gary (ed.) (1982), *Free Will* (Oxford: Oxford University Press).

Wattles, Jeffrey (1996), *The Golden Rule* (New York: Oxford University Press).

Wein, Sheldon (2002), "Rescuing Charitable Duties," *International Journal of Social Economics* 29, 45–53.

Weirich, Paul (1983), "Utility Tempered with Equality," *Nous* 17, 423–39.

Westphal, Fred (1972), "Utilitarianism and 'Conjunctive Acts': A Reply to Professor Castañeda," *Analysis* 32, 82–5.

Widerker, David (1995), "Libertarianism and Frankfurt's Attack on the Principle of Alternative Possibilities," *Philosophical Review* 104, 247–61.

Wikan, Unni (2008), *In Honor of Fadime: Murder and Shame*, Anna Paterson (trans.) (Chicago: University of Chicago Press).

Williams, Bernard (1973), "A Critique of Utilitarianism," in J. J. C. Smart and Bernard Williams (eds.), *Utilitarianism, For and Against* (Cambridge: Cambridge University Press), 75–150.

Williams, Bernard (1981), "Internal and External Reasons," in *Moral Luck* (Cambridge: Cambridge University Press), 101–13.

Williams, Bernard (1985), *Ethics and the Limits of Philosophy* (Cambridge, Mass.: Harvard University Press).

Williams, Bernard (1995), "Internal Reasons and the Obscurity of Blame," in *Making Sense of Humanity* (Cambridge: Cambridge University Press), 35–45.

Williams, Bernard (2006), "Values, Reasons, and the Theory of Persuasion," in *Philosophy as a Humanistic Discipline* (Princeton: Princeton University Press), 109–18.

Wilson, Catherine (1993), "On Some Alleged Limitations to Moral Endeavor," *Journal of Philosophy* 90, 275–89.

Wittgenstein, Ludwig (1961), *Tractatus Logico-Philosophicus*, D. F. Pears and B. F. McGuinness (trans.) (London: Routledge & Kegan Paul).

Wittgenstein, Ludwig (1968), *Philosophical Investigations*, 3rd edn., G. E. M. Anscombe (trans.) (New York: Macmillan).

Wood, Allen (1999), *Kant's Ethical Thought* (New York: Cambridge University Press).

Wood, Allen (2008), *Kantian Ethics* (New York: Cambridge University Press).

Wood, Ellen Meiksins (2002), *The Origins of Capitalism*, 2nd edn. (London: Verso).

Working Group II Contribution to the Fourth Assessment Report of the Intergovernmental Panel on Climate Change (2008), *Climate Change 2007: Impacts, Adaptation and Vulnerability* (Cambridge: Cambridge University Press).

Yablo, Stephen (2000), "Red, Bitter, Best," *Philosophical Books* 41, 13–23.

Zimmer, Carl (2008), "What is a Species?," *Scientific American* 298(6), 72–9.

Zimmerman, Michael (2008), *Living with Uncertainty* (Cambridge: Cambridge University Press).

Index

ability 16–19, 42–3
accepting reasons 6, 68–74, 81–2, 337
  moderate acceptance 81–2
  strong acceptance 71, 91–2, 103
  weak acceptance 69–71
act consequentialism 256–80, 291–4
act-individuation 15, 75–6
Adams, E. 20
agency responsibility 51–8
alternatives 15–16, 40, 74–80, 83–5, 335
animal interests 215–18
Anscombe, G. E. M. 69, 147, 172
Aquinas, T. 365–6, 370
Aristotle 2, 143–58, 192, 362–4, 369
atomic agents 220–1, 240–7, 257–9, 335–6, 368
Austin, J. L. 17
Ayer, A. J. 69

baby counting cases 47–9, 68
background conditions for
        counterfactuals 22–3, 25, 35–8, 76–7
Barker, S. 114
basic actions 75–6
basic preferences 186–90
Bentham, J. 287
Berkeley, G. 124
Boyd, R. 146–7
Bradley, B. 275–6
Brink, D. 96, 158
Bronfman, A. 276–9
Burge, T. 108

Carson, T. 161, 163, 166, 184–5, 321–4, 327
Castañeda, H.-N. 260–2, 265, 294
Chisholm, R. 17, 19, 43–5
Clark, R. 47
compatibilism, see conditional analysis of ability
concentric group acts 274, 344–5
conditional analysis of ability 6, 40–77
Confucius 364–5, 369
consensus congruence 191–201, 224–8, 231–3
consequentialism 1, 8–9, 40–2, 106, 256–80,
        282, 287–302, 326, 331, 336
constitution 95–6
contractarianism 1, 106, 282, 302–17, 331
conventional imputation 114
Copp, D. 114–15
counterfactuals 6, 13–39, 72–4
  Type One 24, 47, 67–8
  Type Two 24–5

Type Three 25–8
  Failed Type Three 26–32
Crisp, R. 131, 235 n24, 235 n25, 236 n26
Cummiskey, D. 232 n17
Cupit, G. 297

Dante 367, 370
Darwall, S. 136, 213 n34
Davis, W. 167–8, 177
DD, see Defect to the Dominant
DE, see Responsibility System
Defect to the Dominant 9, 257, 259, 262,
        276–8, 338
defection 9, 273–5, 343, 381–2, 387–9
demandingness of morality 9, 361–91
deontology 1, 336–60, 370–9
descriptive constraints 91
  DC1-NORMS 91, 100–2, 279–80, 331, 335–91
  DC2-BASIS 91, 102–5, 219–80, 258, 265,
        279–80, 331
  DC3-METHODS 91, 105–7, 280, 281–331
descriptive meaning, see descriptive constraints
desert 240, 294–302
desire 166–77
  intensity 182–5
  intrinsic vs. instrumental 177–82
  nature of 166–77
desire-based good 119, 160–218
  informed desire accounts 160–4
  simple desire accounts 165–6, 186–218
    sophisticated 165–6
    unsophisticated 186–201
determinism 25, 30, 33, 40–1, 58–60, 74
Diener, E. 199–200, 380
distribution 219–80, 294–301
distribution within a life, see intrapersonal
        distribution
Doris, J. 363
Dretske, F. 172, 175–6, 180
duties 9, 336–9, 347–56, 360–2
Dworkin, R. 206

evaluative discourse 91–3, 103
evolutionary functions 145–6
external reasons 99–100

Feldman, F. 132–7, 148, 266–7, 295–301
flukes 41, 77–80, 85, 271, 343
Foot, P. 147, 154–5
Frankfurt, H. 52–8, 69

Frege, G. 117
full normativity 93–4, 95–9, 119–21, 125

Gärdenfors, P. 20, 22
Gauthier, D. 302–9
Geach, P. 117, 147
Gensler, H. 321–4, 327
Gert, B. 373
Gibbard, A. 69, 115–16, 162, 261,
    292–3, 311
Gilbert, M. 386
Ginet, C. 59, 64–6, 67
Giotto 367, 370
global trying 190
golden rule 107, 282, 317–31
Goodman, N. 19
Grice, P. 61–2, 114–15
Griffin, J. 161, 162–3, 166, 184
group acts, 80–3, 216–18, 256–80
group agents, see group acts

Haidt, J. 103
Hajdin, M. 257 n3
hard determinism 13 n2, 58–60
Hare, R. M. 114, 117, 321, 324–31
Harsanyi, J. 310–12
Haybron, D. 212–13
Heathwood, C. 165, 182, 184–5, 205, 209
hedonism 119, 122–39
    attitudinal 132–7
    sensory 122–32
Hillel 317
Hobbes, T. 6, 281, 302, 308, 317
Hooker, B. 288, 291–2, 295
Hornsby, J. 61–2
Hubin, D. 165, 177, 179, 205, 209
Hume, D. 6, 124, 125–6, 282, 287
Hurka, T. 144–5, 155–6
Hursthouse, R. 147, 149, 153–4
Hutcheson, F. 124, 287

Ide, H. 59 n41, 93 n6
idling 60–1
immediate trying 62–3
indeterminacy 4, 14, 15, 34
    moderate 4, 7, 35–9, 85, 187–90, 270–1,
        339–46
    of options 7, 13–39, 77–80, 85
    virulent 4, 7, 162–4, 181–2, 185, 296
injury 9, 352–5
inqcus condition 56–7
internal reasons 99–100, 125–6, 193, 203
internalism in philosophy of mind 31,
    72–3, 188
interpersonal good 198–201
intrapersonal distribution 240–7

Jackson, F. 78–80, 110
Jesus 317, 369
Johnson, D. 59
justificatory regresses 93–4, 119, 125, 203–4

Kail, P. J. E. 124
Kamm, F. 70, 373–7
Kant, I. 1, 113, 136–7, 289–90, 301, 318–21,
    323, 328, 330, 331, 373
Kim, J. 2 n5
Knobe, J. 70
Kolnai, A. 180–1
Korsgaard, C. 126, 180–1, 318
Kraut, R. 147, 155, 156–8, 211
Kripke, S. 108, 144–5

LDP, see Leximin Desire Principle
LE, see Responsibility System
Lehrer, K. 18, 43–5, 48, 60
Leveling Down Objection 234–5
Lewis, C. I. 130–1
Lewis, D. 19–23, 25, 31
LEXIMAC 219–80; see also Leximin Desire
    Principle; MAC2
Leximin Desire Principle 8, 219–55, 258, 282,
    335–6, 369
libertarianism 58–60
Locke, J. 6, 54–6, 124
Loeb, D. 162
Lycan, W. 20, 22, 72–4
lying 9, 287, 345–6, 347–50

McKay, T. 59
McKerlie, D. 235 n25, 248–9
MAC2 8–9, 256–80, 282, 336–9, 357
Mackie, J. 19, 56
Malebranche, N. 124
Malm, H. 269
Mason, E. 127 n21
Material Morality 89, 186–280, 335–6, 392;
    see also Leximin Desire Principle; MAC2
maximin 8, 221, 222–30; see also Leximin
    Desire Principle
Mele, A. 46
mental actions 66–8
Mere Addition Problem 254
metaethics 3, 7, 89–118
Metz, T. 366–7
Mill, J. S. 215
MM, see Material Morality
modal stability 77–80
momentary individual good 194–8
Moore, G. E. 1, 93–4, 96, 98, 111–12, 119, 123,
    124, 125, 127–9, 136, 139, 143
moral agents 8, 220
moral patients 8, 220

Morgenstern, O. 184
multiple-act consequentialism 8, 222; *see also* MAC2
murder 9, 287, 350–2

Nagel, T. 126, 219, 221, 234
natural normative property 94, 119–20, 122–30
Nietzsche, F. 229–30, 282 n3
non-cognitivism 111–16, 324–5
non-naturalism 1, 93–4, 98–100, 119, 143
Norcross, A. 269–70
normative ethics 2–3
Nozick, R. 308
null level 251–3
null option 339–40
Nussbaum, M. 199

objectivism 119, 139–58
obligations, *see* duties
one-off group acts 83
options
    individual 6, 13–39, 40–80, 335
    social 80–5, 335
O'Shaughnessy, B. 61–2

Parfit, D. 80, 98–9, 139–40, 210–11, 219, 221, 234–5, 242, 250, 273, 274–5, 288–91, 293, 356
Pettit, P. 110
physicalism 2–5, 23, 40–1, 94, 95–9, 124, 129–30, 143
Plantinga, A. 21
Plato 2, 125, 140, 365
pockets of cardinality 8, 231, 243
Pogge, T. 380, 385
Portmore, D. 267 n15
precision problems 25, 29, 190
primary actions 74–5
Priority View 235–6
probability 22–3, 76–7, 255
    ex ante objective 41, 77–80, 85, 377
promising 348–50
prudence
    improper, *see* self-interest
    proper 368
Putnam, H. 108, 144–5

quasi-normativity 95, 119–21, 125–7, 193, 203–4
Quinn, W. 170

Railton, P. 161, 163–4, 166
Rawls, J. 2 n6, 109, 219, 221, 310–12
reflective equilibrium 2 n6, 109
Regan, D. 80
relativism 90–1, 143
Repugnant Conclusion 254

responsibility 49–52, 55, 265, 267, 272–3, 294–302, 370–9, 380–91
Responsibility System 370–9
    Deontological Entitlements (DE) 373–8
    Lifetime Entitlements (LE) 372–3
robust accounts of well-being 121
Rosati, C. 162
Ross, W. D. 1, 94, 136, 139, 143, 297, 373
RS, *see* Responsibility System
rule consequentialism 287–94
Ryle, G. 67–8

Scanlon, T. M. 169–71, 206, 289, 312–17
Schroeder, S. 62
Schroeder, T. 172–3, 176–7, 180, 183
Schueler, G. F. 168–9
self-apparent agency responsibility 52–3
self-interest 105–6, 221, 281, 283, 284–7, 303, 384–6
Seligman, M. 199–200, 380
Sen, A. 229, 240
Shafer-Landau, R. 96
Sidgwick, H. 1, 94, 113, 138, 233, 282, 285, 287, 289, 298
Singer, P. 378
Smith, A. 282
Smith, M. 69, 71, 162, 172, 181
soft determinism, *see* hard determinism
special obligations 356–60, 362
Special Relativity 32, 33, 341
species 147–58
Spenser, E. 367
Stalnaker, R. 19, 172
Stampe, D. 171
Strawson, G. 172, 173–5
Strawson, P. 49–52
Streumer, B. 97
subjunctive conditionals, *see* counterfactuals
supervenience 23, 95, 129
Suppes, P. 229, 240

Temkin, L. 235 n25, 237–40
theft 9, 355
Thompson, M. 147
Thomson, J. J. 140, 142, 373–4
Tripathi, V. 293 n48
trying 6, 17, 18, 29, 35, 44, 60–72, 74–5, 81, 189–90, 220

Unger, P. 378
utilitarianism, *see* consequentialism

van Inwagen, P. 59
van Roojen, M. 147
Velleman, D. 162
Very Little Defection 9, 257–9, 276, 338
virtue 362–70, 379–91

VLD, *see* Very Little Defection
von Neumann, J. 184

Weirich, P. 236
well-being 7, 102, 119–218; *see also* desire-
        based good; hedonism; objectivism

Wiggins, D. 59
Williams, B. 89–90, 99–100, 125–6, 368
Wittgenstein, L. 61–2
Wood, A. 318

Yaffe, G. 54 n33